P9-DCR-061

3 7

American Public Policy

Documents and Essays

American Public Policy

Documents and Essays

Edited by

Thomas R. Dye
The Florida State University

Charles E. Merrill Publishing Company
A Bell & Howell Company
Columbus, Ohio

Copyright © 1969 by Charles E. Merrill Publishing
Company, Columbus, Ohio. All rights reserved. No
part of this book may be reproduced in any form,
electronic or mechanical, including photocopy, recording, or any information storage and retrieval system
without permission in writing from the publisher.

Standard Book Number 675-09502-6

Library of Congress Catalog Card Number: 71-76883

1 2 3 4 5 6 7 8 9 10 — 73 72 71 70 69

Printed in the United States of America

X-4667

Preface

American Public Policy is a documentary reader of source materials which focus on the *content* of public policy. This volume provides students an opportunity to deal first-hand with documentary materials on public policy — legislative acts, court decisions, statements and reports from the executive branch of government, and clear statements of alternative policy positions by national figures. Students are encouraged to read for themselves from the Civil Rights Act of 1964, the Economic Opportunity Act of 1964, the Report of the President's Commission on Civil Disorder, *Engle* v. *Vitale,* the Geneva Agreements of 1954, the Report of the U.S. Civil Rights Commission, the Testimony of Secretary of State Dean Rusk before the Senate Foreign Relations Committee, and other primary sources and materials for public policy. In addition, students are provided with clear and forceful statements of alternative policies — for example, the Black Power alternative from Stokely Carmichael, the negative income tax proposal by Milton Friedman, a plan for federal-state revenue sharing by Walter Heller, and the "Arrogance of Power" critique of U.S. foreign policy by Senator J. William Fulbright.

This documentary reader is distinguished from the many books of readings currently on the market by: (1) its focus on public policy rather than the structure and organization of American government; and (2) its focus on documentary source materials rather than argumentative writing.

Clear, succinct essays on the separate policy areas — segregation, civil rights, protest and public order, health, welfare, poverty, housing and urban affairs, business and labor, foreign policy, military affairs, and government finance — provide a context for reading the source materials.

MAY 22 1969

343020

These essays are straightforward narratives of policy developments in each area under study.

American Public Policy provides the student with source materials, but it is the responsibility of the instructor to provide the student with an analytic framework for understanding public policy. This volume does not pretend to provide a comprehensive analysis or interpretation of the policy-making process, but it can be a very useful tool in achieving that objective. More importantly, this volume helps to insure that students will not come away from American Government courses with a surplus of analytical models and conceptual approaches, but with an embarrassing shortage of information about the content of public policy.

Thomas R. Dye

Contents

3   Protest and Public Order   121

4   Educational Policy   191

5   Health, Welfare, and Poverty   249

6   Housing and Urban Affairs   331

American Public Policy

Documents and Essays

1

Segregation in Public Schools

The 14th Amendment of the United States Constitution contains a fundamental policy statement on racial affairs in America:

> All persons born or naturalized in the United States, and subject to the jurisdiction thereof, are citizens of the United States and of the state wherein they reside. No state shall make or enforce any law which shall abridge the privileges or immunities of citizens in United States; nor shall any state deprive any person of life, liberty, or property, without due process of law; nor deny to any person within its jurisdiction the equal protections of the laws.

The language of the 14th Amendment and its historical context leave little doubt that its original purpose was to insure a full measure of citizenship and equality for the American Negro. The 14th Amendment was passed in 1867 by a Republican Congress which intended to reconstruct southern society after the Civil War. The 13th Amendment had abolished slavery anywhere in the United States in 1865; the 14th Amendment made "equal protection of the laws" a command for every state to obey; and the 15th Amendment passed in 1869 provided the right to vote could not be abridged by either federal or state governments "on account of race, color, or previous condition of servitude." In addition, Congress passed a series of civil rights statutes in the 1860's and the 1870's guaranteeing the new Negro freedman protection in the exercise of his constitutional rights. The Civil Rights Act of 1875 specifically outlawed segregation by owners of public accommodation facilities. Between 1865 and the early 1880's the success of the civil rights movement was reflected in widespread Negro voting throughout

1

the South, the presence of many Negroes in federal and state offices, and almost equal treatment afforded Negroes in theaters, restaurants, hotels and public transportation.

But by 1877, support for reconstruction policies began to crumble. In what has been described as the Compromise of 1877, the national government agreed to end military occupation of the South, give up its efforts to rearrange southern society, and lend tacit approval to white supremacy in that region. In return, the southern states pledged their support for the Union, accepted national supremacy, and agreed to permit the Republican candidate, Rutherford B. Hayes, to assume the presidency after the disputed election of 1876 in which the Democrat, Samuel Tilden, had received a majority of the popular vote. The Supreme Court adhered to the terms of this compromise. In the famous Civil Rights Cases of 1883 the Supreme Court declared unconstitutional those federal civil rights laws preventing discrimination by private individuals. By denying Congress the power to protect Negroes from discrimination, the Court paved the way for the imposition of segregation as the prevailing social system of the South. In the 1880's and 1890's segregation was imposed in public accommodations, housing, education, employment, and almost every other sector of private and public life. By 1895 most southern states had passed laws *requiring* segregation of the races in education and in public accommodations.

In 1896 in the famous case of *Plessy* v. *Ferguson* the Supreme Court upheld state laws requiring segregation of the races. Even though segregation laws involved state action, the court held that segregating the races did not violate the equal protection clause of the 14th Amendment so long as the persons in each of the separated races were treated equally. Schools and other public facilities which were "separate but equal" won constitutional approval. *Plessy* v. *Ferguson* was the constitutional bulwark of segregation.

While the *Plessy* v. *Ferguson* doctrine of "separate but equal" remained prevailing public policy until 1954, as early as 1944 it was clear that the United States Supreme Court had begun to alter its approach to segregation. While failing to overrule Plessy, the Court outlawed racial discrimination in primary elections on the grounds that these were an intregral part of the official election process; struck down segregation of passengers on interstate travel as a "burden on interstate commerce"; held that enforcement of racially discriminatory contracts in housing in federal or state courts would violate the 14th Amendment; and ruled that federal courts must demand genuine equality in the separate schools provided for Negroes. In the case of *Sweatt* v. *Painter* the court ruled that Texas must provide a law school for Negroes which was not only comparable to the white University of Texas Law School with respect to physical plant, library, and faculty, but also comparable in terms of the influence of its alumni and the reputation of the two schools in the community. But leaders of the newly emerging civil rights movement in the 1940's and 1950's were not satisfied with court decisions which examined the circumstances in each case to determine if separate school facilities were equal. Led by Roy Wilkins, executive director of the National Association for the Advancement of Colored People, and Thurgood Marshall, Chief Consul for the NAACP, the civil rights movement pressed for a court decision that segregation itself meant inequality within the meaning of the 14th Amendment, whether or not facilities were equal in all tangible respects. In short, they wanted a complete reversal of the "separate but equal" interpretation of the 14th Amendment, and a holding that laws separating the races were unconstitutional.

The civil rights groups chose to bring suit for desegregation in Topeka, Kansas, where segregated Negro and white schools were equal with respect to buildings, curricula, qualifications and salaries of teachers, and other tangible factors. The object was to prevent the Court from ordering the admission of a Negro because tangible facilities were not equal, and to force the court to review the doctrine of segregation itself. On May 17, 1954, the Supreme Court rendered its historic decision in *Brown* v. *Board of Education of Topeka, Kansas.*

While the Supreme Court had spoken forcefully in the Brown case in 1954, the real battle over segregation was just beginning. Segregation would remain a part of American life, regardless of its constitutionality, until effective political power was brought to bear to end it. The practice of segregation was widespread and deeply engrained in American life. Seventeen states required segregation of the races in public schools. The seventeen states were: Alabama, Arkansas, Florida, Georgia, Louisiana, Mississippi, North Carolina, South Carolina, Tennessee, Texas, Virginia, West Virginia, Delaware, Kentucky, Maryland, Missouri, and Oklahoma. Four other states — Arizona, Kansas, New Mexico, and Wyoming — authorized segregation on the option of local school boards. Even the Congress of the United States required the segregation of the races in the public schools in the District of Columbia. Moreover, Congress, the President, state Governors, and legislatures, and even mobs have more force at their disposal than the federal judiciary. The Supreme Court must rely largely on other branches of the federal government, on the states, and on private individuals and organizations to enforce the law of the land.

The question of enforcement was such a troublesome one that the Supreme Court asked attorneys for the civil rights groups and attorneys for the southern states to come before the court again in 1955 to determine how the court should go about enforcing its 1954 decision. Civil rights groups argued for immediate court-ordered nationwide desegregation in the prompt elimination of dual school systems. But in *Brown* v. *the Board of Education of Topeka, Kansas, (1955)* the court chose to recognize "varied and local school problems" and declined to order immediate nationwide desegregation. Instead it turned over the responsibility for desegregation to state and local authorities under the supervision of federal district courts. Local courts need only require "a prompt and reasonable start toward full compliance" of the 1954 ruling. School authorities were ordered to proceed "with all deliberate speed" in desegregation.

On the whole, those states which chose to resist desegregation were quite successful in doing so during the ten year period from 1954 to 1964. Figures from the *Southern Education Reporting Service* indicate that in late 1964 only about 2 per cent of the Negro school children in the 11 southern states were attending integrated schools. Only 604 of the South's 2,220 school districts which encompass Negro students were officially desegregated; and most of these 604 districts experienced only token desegregation. The effectiveness of states in resisting the policy of the federal courts up to 1964 is an important, even if regrettable, comment on the powers of the judiciary in our federal system. In the Civil Rights Act of 1964 Congress finally entered the civil rights field in support of court efforts to achieve desegregation. Among other things, the Civil Rights Act of 1964 (see Chapter 3) provided that all federal departments and agencies must take action to end segregation in all programs or activities receiving federal financial assistance. It was specified that this action was to include termination of financial assistance if states and school districts receiving federal funds refused to comply with federal desegregation orders. Thus, in addition to court orders requiring desegregation, states and school districts after 1964 faced administrative orders, or "guidelines," from the U. S. Office of Education threatening loss of federal funds for schools by non-compliance. Acting under the authority of Title VI of the Civil Rights Act the U. S. Office of Education required all school districts in the 17 formerly segregated states to submit desegregation plans as a condition of further federal assistance.

School desegregation figures clearly indicate that the U. S. Office of Education has been a great deal more successful than federal courts in ending segregation. In two years of administering federal funds according to Title VI of the Civil Rights Act, the percentage of Negro pupils in southern states attending schools with whites increased from 2 to 16, an eight-fold increase in only two years.

In the Brown case the Supreme Court stated that segregation had "a tendency to retard the education and mental development of Negro children and to deprive them of some of the benefits they would receive in a racially integrated school." The U. S. Civil Rights Commission in a report entitled *Racial Isolation in Public Schools* stated that even when the segregation was *de facto,* that is, a product of segregated housing patterns in neighborhood schools rather than direct discrimination in law, the adverse effects on Negro students were still significant. The Commission reported that in all of America's central cities, 75 per cent of all Negro students in elementary schools were attending schools with nearly all-Negro enrollments. In other words, the vast majority of white and Negro school children attend segregated schools in both the North and South. The Commission's report documents segregation in major cities and also summarizes research showing the adverse effects this segregation has upon Negro children. Negro students attending predominantly Negro schools had lower achievement scores and lower aspiration levels than Negroes from similar economic backgrounds attending predominantly white schools. When a group of Negro students in class with a majority of advantaged whites was compared with a control group of Negroes attending school with a majority of disadvantaged Negroes, the difference in achievement amounted to more than two grade levels. On the other hand, the Commission contended that the achievement of white students in classes which were roughly half white was no different than that of a control group of white students in all-white schools. Therein lies the essential argument for ending *de facto* segregation in northern urban school systems.

Moreover, the Commission suggests a number of remedies for *de facto* segregation. These remedies included the "pairing" or merging of attendance areas of two or more schools; the establishment of central "educational parks" integrating students throughout the school district and the closing of predominantly Negro schools and the dispersal of their students among other schools in the community. These policies are commonly referred to as "bussing."

While the Supreme Court has shown its distaste for color or racial classification under the Constitution, those classifications which have been declared unconstitutional under the 14th Amendment have all been harmful to the minority race. (See U. S. Civil Rights Commission, *De Facto Segregation and the Law*) It is very unlikely the Supreme Court will hold that racial classification and "bussing" for the purpose of achieving integration are unconstitutional, since the racial classification is aimed at helping rather than harming the minority race. Thus, there is no constitutional barrier to "bussing." To date, federal courts have not held that there is any affirmative duty to correct *de facto* racial imbalance in the schools. In other words, as yet there is no constitutional duty to eliminate *de facto* segregation, so long as school attendence lines were drawn with no real intention to segregating the races.

While the U.S. Civil Rights Commission recommended "bussing" to end *de facto* segregation and improve educational opportunities for Negroes, Stewart Alsop presents an alternative approach to equalizing educational opportunities for Negroes. (See Stewart Alsop, *Ghetto Education*) Alsop believes that the political obstacles to "bussing" are so great that *de facto* segregation may not be ended in a generation or more. Alsop does not oppose bussing but instead feels that it would be ineffective in improving education in the ghettoes as rapidly as needed. He suggests a heavy investment in compensatory education programs in ghetto schools, providing Negro ghetto schools with special remedial instruction, cultural enrichment activities, programs to improve self-esteem and aspiration levels, intensive pre-school education, and so on. In other words, rather than close ghetto schools, Alsop argues that they should be made into the nation's best educational facilities. A heavy investment in Negro schools, he contends, can equalize educational opportunities for Negro pupils without the necessity of bussing Negroes and whites around the city.

Plessy v. Ferguson*

United States Supreme Court

Mr. Justice Brown. . . . delivered the opinion of the court. . . .

The constitutionality of this act[1] is attacked upon the ground that it conflicts both with the Thirteenth Amendment of the Constitution, abolishing slavery, and the Fourteenth Amendment, which prohibits certain restrictive legislation on the part of the states.

1. That it does not conflict with the Thirteenth Amendment, which abolished slavery and involuntary servitude, except as punishment for crime, is too clear for argument. . . .

2. By the Fourteenth Amendment. . . . the states are forbidden from making or enforcing any law which shall abridge the privileges or immunities of citizens of the United States, or shall deprive any person of life, liberty or property without due process of law, or deny to any person within their jurisdiction the equal protection of the laws. . . .

The object of the amendment was undoubtedly to enforce the absolute equality of the two races before the law, but in the nature of things it could not have been intended to abolish distinction based upon color, or to enforce social, as distinguished from political, equality, or a commingling of the two races upon terms unsatisfactory to either. Laws permitting, and even requiring, their separation in places where

---

*163 U.S. 537 (1896).
[1]A Louisiana statute of 1890 requiring railroad companies carrying passengers within the state to provide "equal but separate" accommodations for white and colored persons.

7

they are liable to be brought into contact do not necessarily imply the inferiority of either race to the other, and have been generally, if not universally, recognized as within the competency of the state legislatures in the exercise of their police power. The most common instance of this is connected with the establishment of separate schools for white and colored children, which has been held to be a valid exercise of the legislative power even by courts of states where the political rights of the colored race have been longest and most earnestly enforced. . . .

The distinction between laws interfering with the political equality of the Negro and those requiring the separation of the two races in schools, theaters, and railway carriages has been frequently drawn by this court. Thus in *Strauder v. West Virginia,* 100 U. S. 303, it was held that a law of West Virginia limiting to white male persons, 21 years of age and citizens of the State, the right to sit upon juries, was a discrimination which implied a legal inferiority in civil society, which lessened the security of the right of the colored race, and was a step toward reducng them to a condition of servility. . . .

(I)t is also suggested by the learned counsel for the plaintiff in error that the same argument that will justify the State legislature in requiring railways to provide separate accommodations for the two races will also authorize them to require separate cars to be provided for people whose hair is of a certain color, or who are aliens, or who belong to certain nationalities, or to enact laws requiring colored people to walk upon one side of the street, and white people upon the other, or requiring white men's houses to be painted white, and colored man's black, or their vehicles or business signs to be of different colors, upon the theory that one side of the street is as good as the other, or that a house or vehicle of one color is as good as one of another color. The reply to all this is that every exercise of the police power must be reasonable, and extend only to such laws as are enacted in good faith for the promotion of the public good, and not for the annoyance or oppression of a particular class. . . .

So far, then, as a conflict with the Fourteenth Amendment is concerned, the case reduces itself to the question whether the statute of Louisiana is a reasonable regulation, and with respect to this there must necessarily be a large discretion on the part of the legislature. In determining the question of reasonableness it is at liberty to act with reference to the established usages, customs and traditions of the people, and with a view to the promotion of their comfort, and the preservation of the public peace and good order. Gauged by this standard, we cannot say that a law which authorizes or even requires the separation of the two races in public conveyances is unreasonable or more obnoxious to the Fourteenth Amendment than the acts of Congress requiring separate schools for colored children in the District of Columbia, the constitutionality of which does not seem to have been questioned, or the corresponding acts of state legislatures.

We consider the underlying fallacy of the plaintiff's argument to consist in the assumption that the enforced separation of the two races stamps the colored race with a badge of inferiority. If this be so, it is not by reason of anything found in the act, but solely because the colored race chooses to put that construction upon it. The argument necessarily assumes that if, as has been more than once the case, and is not unlikely to be so again, the colored race should become the dominant power in the state legislature, and should enact a law in precisely similar terms, it would thereby relegate the white race to an inferior position. We imagine that the white race, at least, would not acquiesce in this assumption. The argument also assumes that social prejudices may be overcome by legislation and that equal rights cannot be secured to the Negro except by an enforced commingling of the two races. We cannot accept this proposition. If the two races are to meet upon terms of social equality, it must be the result of natural affinities, a mutual appreciation of each other's merits, and a voluntary consent of individuals. . . .

Legislation is powerless to eradicate racial instincts or to abolish distinctions based upon physical differences, and the attempt to do so can only result in accentuating the difficulties of the present situation. If the civil and political rights of both races be equal, one cannot be inferior to the other civilly or politically. If one race be inferior to the other socially, the Constitution of the United States cannot put them upon the same plane. . . .

The judgment of the court below is, therefore, affirmed.

Brown v.
Board of Education of Topeka*

United States Supreme Court

Mr. Chief Justice Warren delivered the opinion of the Court, saying in part:

These cases come to us from the States of Kansas, South Carolina, Virginia, and Delaware. They are premised on different facts and different local conditions, but a common legal question justifies their consideration together in this consolidated opinion.

In each of the cases, minors of the Negro race, through their legal representatives, seek the aid of the courts in obtaining admission to the public schools of their community on a nonsegregated basis. In each instance, they had been denied admission to schools attended by white children under laws requiring or permitting segregation according to race. This segregation was alleged to deprive the plaintiffs of the equal protection of the laws under the Fourteenth Amendment. In each of the cases other than the Delaware case, a three-judge federal district court denied relief to the plaintiffs on the so-called "separate but equal" doctrine announced by this Court in *Plessy* v. *Ferguson.* . . .

The plaintiffs contend that segregated public schools are not "equal" and cannot be made "equal," and that hence they are deprived of the equal protection of the laws. Because of the obvious importance of the question presented, the Court took jurisdiction. . . .

In the first cases in this Court construing the Fourteenth Amendment, decided shortly after its adoption, the Court interpreted it as proscribing all state-imposed discriminations against the Negro race. The doctrine of "separate but equal" did not make its appearance in this Court until

---

*347 U.S. 483 (1954).

1896 in the case of *Plessy* v. *Ferguson, supra,* involving not education but transportation. American courts have since labored with the doctrine for over half a century. In this Court, there have been six cases involving the "separate but equal" doctrine in the field of public education. . . . In more recent cases, all on the graduate school level, inequality was found in that specific benefits enjoyed by white students were denied to Negro students of the same educational qualifications. . . . In none of these cases was it necessary to re-examine the doctrine to grant relief to the Negro plaintiff. And in *Sweatt* v. *Painter* [339 U.S. 629 (1950)], the Court expressly reserved decision on the question whether *Plessy* v. *Ferguson* should be held inapplicable to public education.

In the instant cases, that question is directly presented. Here, unlike *Sweatt* v. *Painter,* there are findings below that the Negro and white schools involved have been equalized, or are being equalized, with respect to buildings, curricula, qualifications and salaries of teachers, and other "tangible" factors. Our decision, therefore, cannot turn on merely a comparison of these tangible factors in the Negro and white schools involved in each of the cases. We must look instead to the effect of segregation itself on public education.

In approaching this problem, we cannot turn the clock back to 1868 when the Amendment was adopted, or even to 1896 when *Plessy* v. *Ferguson* was written. We must consider public education in the light of its full development and its present place in American life throughout the Nation. Only in this way can it be determined if segregation in public schools deprives these plaintiffs of the equal protection of the laws.

Today, education is perhaps the most important function of state and local governments. Compulsory school attendance laws and the great expenditures for education both demonstrate our recognition of the importance of education to our democratic society. It is required in the performance of our most basic public responsibilities, even service in the armed forces. It is the very foundation of good citizenship. Today it is a principal instrument in awakening the child to cultural values, in preparing him for later professional training, and in helping him to adjust normally to his environment. In these days, it is doubtful that any child may reasonably be expected to succeed in life if he is denied the opportunity of an education. Such an opportunity, where the state has undertaken to provide it, is a right which must be made available to all on equal terms.

We come then to the question presented: Does segregation of children in public schools solely on the basis of race, even though the physical facilities and other "tangible" factors may be equal, deprive the children of the minority group of equal educational opportunities? We believe that it does.

In *Sweatt* v. *Painter, supra,* in finding that a segregated law school for Negroes could not provide them equal educational opportunities, this Court relied in large part on "those qualities which are incapable of objective measurement but which make for greatness in a law school." In *McLaurin* v. *Oklahoma State Regents, supra* [339 U.S. 637 (1950)], the Court, in requiring that a Negro admitted to a white graduate school be treated like all other students, again resorted to intangible considerations: ". . . his ability to study, to engage in discussions and exchange views with other students and, in general, to learn his profession." Such considerations apply with added force to children in grade and high schools. To separate them from others of similar age and qualifications solely because of their race generates a feeling of inferiority as to their status in the community that may affect their hearts and minds in a way unlikely ever to be undone. The effect of this separation of their educational opportunities was well stated by a finding in the Kansas case by a court which nevertheless felt compelled to rule against the Negro plaintiffs:

"Segregation of white and colored children in public schools has a detrimental effect upon the colored children. The impact is greater when it has the sanction of the law; for the policy of separating the races is usually interpreted as denoting the inferiority of the Negro group. A sense of inferiority affects the motivation of a child to learn. Segregation with the sanction of law, therefore, has a tendency to retard the educational and mental development of Negro children and to deprive them of some of the benefits they would receive in a racially integrated school system." Whatever may have been the extent of psychological knowledge at the time of *Plessy* v. *Ferguson,* this finding is amply supported by modern authority. Any language in *Plessy v. Ferguson* contrary to this finding is rejected.

We conclude that in the field of public education the doctrine of "separate but equal" has no place. Separate educational facilities are inherently unequal. Therefore, we hold that the plaintiffs and others similarly situated for whom the actions have been brought are, by reason of the segregation complained of, deprived of the equal protection of the laws guaranteed by the Fourteenth Amendment. This disposition makes unnecessary any discussion whether such segregation also violates the Due Process Clause of the Fourteenth Amendment.

Because these are class actions, because of the wide applicability of this decision, and because of the great variety of local conditions, the formulation of decrees in these cases presents problems of considerable complexity. On re-argument, the consideration of appropriate relief was necessarily subordinated to the primary question—the constitutionality of segregation in public education. We have now announced that such segregation is a denial of the equal protection of the laws. In order that we may have the full assistance of the parties in formulating decrees, the cases will be restored to the docket, and the parties are requested to present further argument on Questions 4 and 5 previously propounded by the Court for the re-argument this Term [which deal with the implementation of desegregation]. The Attorney General of the United States is again invited to participate. The Attorneys General of the states requiring or permitting segregation in public education will also be permitted to appear as *amici curiae* upon request to do so by September 15, 1954, and submission of briefs by October 1, 1954.

It is so ordered.

With All Deliberate Speed*

United States Supreme Court

Mr. Chief Justice Warren delivered the opinion of the Court, saying in part:

These cases were decided on May 17, 1954. The opinions of that date, declaring the fundamental principle that racial discrimination in public education is unconstitutional, are incorporated herein by reference. All provisions of federal, state, or local law requiring or permitting such discrimination must yield to this principle. There remains for consideration the manner in which relief is to be accorded.

Because these cases arose under different local conditions and their disposition will involve a variety of local problems, we requested further argument on the question of relief. . . . The parties, the United States, and the States of Florida, North Carolina, Arkansas, Oklahoma, Maryland, and Texas filed briefs and participated in the oral argument.

These presentations were informative and helpful to the Court in its consideration of the complexities arising from the transition to a system of public education freed of racial discrimination. The presentations also demonstrated that substantial steps to eliminate racial discrimination in public schools have already been taken, not only in some of the communities in which these cases arose, but in some of the states appearing as *amici curiae,* and in other states as well. Substantial progress has been made in the District of Columbia and in the communities in Kansas and Delaware involved in this litigation. The defendants in the cases coming to us from South Carolina and Virginia are awaiting the decision of this Court concerning relief.

---

*Brown v. Board of Education of Topeka 349 U.S. 294 (1955).

Full implementation of these constitutional principles may require solution of varied local school problems. School authorities have the primary responsibility for elucidating, assessing, and solving these problems; courts will have to consider whether the action of school authorities constitutes good faith implementation of the governing constitutional principles. Because of their proximity to local conditions and the possible need for further hearings, the courts which originally heard these cases can best perform this judicial appraisal. Accordingly, we believe it appropriate to remand the cases to those courts.

In fashioning and effectuating the decrees, the courts will be guided by equitable principles. Traditionally, equity has been characterized by a practical flexibility in shaping its remedies and by a facility for adjusting and reconciling public and private needs. These cases call for the exercise of these traditional attributes of equity power. At stake is the personal interest of the plaintiffs in admission to public schools as soon as practicable on a nondiscriminatory basis. To effectuate this interest may call for elimination of a variety of obstacles in making the transition to school systems operated in accordance with the constitutional principles set forth in our May 17, 1954, decision. Courts of equity may properly take into account the public interest in the elimination of such obstacles in a systematic and effective manner. But it should go without saying that the vitality of these constitutional principles cannot be allowed to yield simply because of disagreement with them.

While giving weight to these public and private considerations, the courts will require that the defendants make a prompt and reasonable start toward full compliance with our May 17, 1954, ruling. Once such a start has been made, the courts may find that additional time is necessary to carry out the ruling in an effective manner. The burden rests upon the defendants to establish that such time is necessary in the public interest and is consistent with good faith compliance at the earliest practicable date. To that end, the courts may consider problems related to administration, arising from the physical condition of the school plant, the school transportation system, personnel, revision of school districts and attendance areas into compact units to achieve a system of determining admission to the public schools on a nonracial basis, and revision of local laws and regulations which may be necessary in solving the foregoing problems. They will also consider the adequacy of any plans the defendants may propose to meet these problems and to effectuate a transition to a racially nondiscriminatory school system. During this period of transition, the courts will retain jurisdiction of these cases.

The judgments below, except that in the Delaware case, are accordingly reversed and the cases are remanded to the District Courts to take such proceedings and enter such orders and decrees consistent with this opinion as are necessary and proper to admit to public schools on a racially nondiscriminatory basis with all deliberate speed the parties to these cases. The judgment in the Delaware case—ordering the immediate admission of the plaintiffs to schools previously attended only by white children—is affirmed on the basis of the principles stated in our May 17, 1954, opinion, but the case is remanded to the Supreme Court of Delaware for such further proceedings as that Court may deem necessary in the light of this opinion.

It is so ordered.

Progress In School Desegregation*

Southern Education Reporting Service

Percent of Negro School Children in Public School with Whites 1955-1967

	1955	1956	1957	1958	1959	1960	1961	1962	1963	1964	1965	1966	1967
SOUTH													
Alabama	00.0	00.0	00.0	00.0	00.0	00.0	00.0	00.0	00.0	00.0	00.0	00.4	04.4
Arkansas	00.0	00.0	00.0	00.1	00.1	00.1	00.1	00.1	00.2	00.3	00.8	06.0	15.1
Florida	00.0	00.0	00.0	00.0	00.0	00.3	00.0	00.3	00.7	01.5	02.7	09.8	22.3

Georgia	00.0	00.0	00.0	00.0	00.0	00.0	00.0	00.0	00.0	00.1	00.4	02.7	08.8
Louisiana	00.0	00.0	00.0	00.0	00.0	00.0	00.0	00.0	00.0	00.1	01.1	00.9	03.4
Mississippi	00.0	00.0	00.0	00.0	00.0	00.0	00.0	00.0	00.0	00.0	00.0	00.6	02.5
North Carolina	00.0	00.0	00.0	00.0	00.0	00.0	00.0	00.1	00.3	00.5	01.4	05.2	15.4
South Carolina	00.0	00.0	00.0	00.0	00.0	00.0	00.0	00.0	00.0	00.0	00.1	01.7	05.6
Tennessee	00.0	00.1	00.1	00.1	00.1	00.1	00.2	00.8	01.1	02.7	05.4	16.3	28.6
Texas	00.0	01.1	01.4	01.4	01.2	01.2	01.2	01.3	02.3	05.5	07.8	17.4	44.9
Virginia	00.0	00.0	00.0	00.0	00.0	00.1	00.1	00.2	00.5	01.6	05.2	11.0	25.3
BORDER													
Delaware	01.9	11.0	28.5	36.2	43.7	44.1	45.0	53.7	55.9	56.5	62.2	83.3	100.0
Kentucky	00.0	00.8	20.9	28.4	27.5	38.9	47.2	51.2	54.1	54.4	68.1	78.1	90.1
Maryland	05.1	13.9	19.1	22.1	32.4	29.3	33.6	41.5	45.1	47.8	50.9	55.6	65.3
Missouri	*	*	*	*	*	42.7	41.7	41.4	38.9	42.1	42.3	75.1	77.7
Oklahoma	00.0	*	08.7	18.2	21.2	26.0	24.0	25.6	23.6	28.0	31.7	38.3	50.8
West Virginia	04.3	*	*	38.7	39.8	50.0	66.6	62.0	61.4	58.2	63.4	79.9	93.4

*Indicates that no data is available.

*Figures compiled from various editions of Southern Education Reporting Service, *Southern School News.*

Racial Isolation in Public Schools*

United States Commission on Civil Rights

Extent of Racial Isolation in the Public Schools

Twelve years after the Supreme Court's decision, the U.S. Office of Education in its national survey, *Equality of Educational Opportunity,* found that:

> . . . when measured by that yardstick [segregation], American public education remains largely unequal in most regions of the country, including all those where Negroes form any significant proportion of the population.
>
> . . . the great majority of American children attend schools that are largely segregated — that is, almost all of their fellow students are of the same racial background as they are.[1]

Sixty-five percent of all first grade Negro pupils surveyed attend schools that have an enrollment 90 percent or more Negro, while almost 80 percent of all first grade white students surveyed attend schools that are 90 percent or more white. A substantially greater proportion of Negro students attend schools that are 50 percent or more Negro. Approximately 87 percent of all Negro first graders are in such schools — 72 percent in the urban North; 97 percent in the urban South.

National or regional averages such as these, however, do not reflect the full dimensions of school segregation. The Commission's investiga-

---

*U.S. Commission on Civil Rights, *Racial Isolation in Public Schools* (Washington, D.C.: U.S. Government Printing Office, 1967).

[1] Coleman *et al., Equality of Educational Opportunity* 3 (1966). The study, which was required in title IV of the Civil Rights Act of 1964, was carried out by the National Center for Educational Statistics of the U.S, Office of Education. Dr. James Coleman of The Johns Hopkins University had major responsibility for the design, administration, and analysis of the study. Hereinafter cited as the *OE Survey.*

tions found that in the Nation's metropolitan areas — where two-thirds of both the Nation's Negro and white populations now live — school segregation is more severe than the national figures suggest. And it is growing.

In 15 large metropolitan areas in 1960, 79 percent of the nonwhite public school enrollment was in central city schools, while 68 percent of the white enrollment was suburban. In Cleveland, 98 percent of the nonwhite metropolitan public school children were in the central city schools in 1960, and 69 percent of the whites were in suburban public schools. The Cleveland city schools were 47 percent nonwhite in 1960. By 1965, they were more than 50 percent nonwhite. In Philadelphia, 77 percent of the nonwhite metropolitan public school children were in the ctiy schools in 1960, and 73 percent of the white children were in suburban public schools. In 1960, the Philadelphia city schools were 48 percent Negro. By 1965, they were almost 60 percent Negro. This pattern of racial concentration is typical of major metropolitan areas.

Racial concentration also is severe within the central cities. Table 1 shows the extent of elementary school segregation in 75 cities. In these cities 75 percent of the Negro students are in elementary schools with enrollments that are nearly all-Negro (90 percent or more Negro), while 83 percent of the white students are in nearly all-white schools. Nearly 9 of every 10 Negro elementary school students attend majority-Negro schools.[2]

The high degree of racial separation in the schools shown by these national figures is found in the North as well as in Southern and border States. In Buffalo, N.Y., for example, 77 percent of the Negro elementary schoolchildren attend schools that are more than 90 percent Negro, while 81 percent of the whites are in nearly all-white schools (90 percent or more white). In Gary, Ind., the figures are 90 percent and 76 percent, respectively. Again, in the North, the proportion of Negro children in majority-Negro schools often equals or exceeds the national average. In Flint, Mich., 86 percent of the Negro elementary schoolchildren are in majority-Negro schools; in Milwaukee, 87 percent; in Chicago, 97 percent.

A high degree of racial separation of Negro students frequently prevails regardless of the size of the school system. Examples from

---

[2]The total elementary school enrollment for these 75 cities is 1.6 million Negro and 2.4 million white. Of the Negro school children, 1.2 million (75 percent) are in 90-100 percent Negro schools and 1.4 million (88 percent) are in majority-Negro schools. Of the white school children, 2.0 million (83 percent) are in 90-100 percent white schools. In describing the extent of segregation the Commission has used three basic terms throughout this report. The term "nearly all-Negro" means 90.5-100 percent Negro. "Majority-Negro" means 50.5-100 percent Negro. The term "nearly all-white" means 0-10.5 percent Negro.

Table 1.   Extent of elementary school segregation in 75 school systems[3]

City	Percentage of Negroes in 90 to 100 percent Negro schools	Percentage of Negroes in majority-Negro schools	Percentage of whites in 90 to 100 percent white schools
Mobile, Ala	99.9	99.9	100.0
Tuscaloosa, Ala	99.6	99.6	100.0
Little Rock, Ark	95.6	95.6	97.1
Pine Bluff, Ark	98.2	98.2	100.0
Los Angeles, Calif	39.5	87.5	94.7
Oakland, Calif	48.7	83.2	50.2
Pasadena, Calif	None	71.4	82.1
Richmond, Calif	39.2	82.9	90.2
San Diego, Calif	13.9	73.3	88.7
San Francisco, Calif	21.1	72.3	65.1
Denver, Colo	29.4	75.2	95.5
Hartford, Conn	9.4	73.8	66.2
New Haven, Conn	36.8	73.4	47.1
Wilmington, Del	49.7	92.5	27.3
Miami, Fla	91.4	94.4	95.3
Tallahassee, Fla	99.7	99.7	100.0
Americus, Ga	99.3	99.3	100.0
Atlanta, Ga	97.4	98.8	95.4
Augusta, Ga	99.2	99.2	100.0
Marietta, Ga	94.2	94.2	100.0
Chicago, Ill	89.2	96.9	88.8
East St. Louis, Ill	80.4	92.4	68.6
Peoria, Ill	21.0	86.9	89.6
Fort Wayne, Ind	60.8	82.9	87.7
Gary, Ind	89.9	94.8	75.9
Indianapolis, Ind	70.5	84.2	80.7
Wichita, Kans	63.5	89.1	94.8
Louisville, Ky	69.5	84.5	61.3

[3]These percentages make no reference to the large Puerto Rican enrollment in New York City elementary schools. The data provided to the Commission by the New York City public school system are based on classroom counts by teachers. According to Mr. Leonard Moriber, research associate, New York City Board of Education, students with Spanish surnames are counted as Puerto Ricans, regardless of their race. Thus it is likely that the actual number and proportion of Negro elementary school students is somewhat higher than the data show. According to the school system's data, of the total of 592,000 elementary school students in the New York City school system, 183,000 are Negroes and 130,000 are Puerto Ricans. Of the total of 313,000 Negro and Puerto Rican students, 177,000 (56 percent) are in schools whose student bodies are 90-100 percent Negro and Puerto Rican. 267,000 (85 percent) are in schools whose student bodies are majority-Negro and Puerto Rican.

Table 1. Extent of elementary school segregation in 75 school systems — Continued

City	Percentage of Negroes in 90 to 100 percent Negro schools	Percentage of Negroes in majority-Negro schools	Percentage of whites in 90 to 100 percent white schools
New Orleans, La	95.9	96.7	83.8
Baltimore, Md	84.2	92.3	67.0
Boston, Mass	35.4	79.5	76.5
Springfield, Mass	15.4	71.9	82.8
Detroit, Mich	72.3	91.5	65.0
Flint, Mich	67.9	85.9	80.0
Minneapolis, Minn	None	39.2	84.9
Hattiesburg, Miss	98.7	98.7	100.0
Vicksburg, Miss	97.1	97.1	100.0
Kansas City, Mo	69.1	85.5	65.2
St. Joseph, Mo	39.3	39.3	91.3
St. Louis, Mo	90.9	93.7	66.0
Omaha, Nebr	47.7	81.1	89.0
Newark, N.J	51.3	90.3	37.1
Camden, N.J	37.0	90.4	62.4
Albany, N.Y	None	74.0	66.5
Buffalo, N.Y	77.0	88.7	81.1
New York City, N.Y	20.7	55.5	56.8
Charlotte, N.C	95.7	95.7	94.7
Raleigh, N.C	98.5	98.5	100.0
Winston-Salem, N.C	88.7	95.1	95.6
Cincinnati, Ohio	49.4	88.0	63.3
Cleveland, Ohio	82.3	94.6	80.2
Columbus, Ohio	34.3	80.8	77.0
Oklahoma City, Okla	90.5	96.8	96.1
Tulsa, Okla	90.7	98.7	98.8
Portland, Oreg	46.5	59.2	92.0
Chester, Pa	77.9	89.1	37.9
Harrisburg, Pa	54.0	81.3	56.2
Philadelphia, Pa	72.0	90.2	57.7
Pittsburgh, Pa	49.5	82.8	62.3
Providence, R.I	14.6	55.5	63.3
Columbia, S.C	99.1	99.1	100.0
Florence, S.C	99.1	99.1	100.0
Sumter, S.C	99.0	99.0	100.0
Knoxville, Tenn	79.3	79.3	94.9
Memphis, Tenn	95.1	98.8	93.6
Nashville, Tenn	82.2	86.4	90.7
Amarillo, Tex	89.6	89.6	98.3

Table 1.   Extent of elementary school segregation in 75 school systems — Continued

City	Percentage of Negroes in 90 to 100 percent Negro schools	Percentage of Negroes in majority-Negro schools	Percentage of whites in 90 to 100 percent white schools
Austin, Tex	86.1	86.1	93.1
Dallas, Tex	82.6	90.3	90.1
Houston, Tex	93.0	97.6	97.3
San Antonio, Tex	65.9	77.2	89.4
Richmond, Va	98.5	98.5	95.3
Seattle, Wash	9.9	60.4	89.8
Milwaukee, Wis	72.4	86.8	86.3
Washington, D.C	90.4	99.3	34.3

NOTE — Percentages shown in this table are for 1965-66 school year, except for Seattle, Wash. (1964-65), Los Angeles, Calif. (1963-64), and Cleveland, Ohio (1962-63).

Northern and border State school systems are illustrative. Kansas City, Mo., has an elementary school enrollment twice as large as Fort Wayne, Ind., yet in each city more than 60 percent of the Negro children are in nearly all-Negro schools. Detroit, Mich., has an elementary school enrollment almost four times as large as Newark, N.J., yet in each city more than 90 percent of the Negro children are in majority-Negro schools.

Nor does the pattern necessarily vary according to the proportion of Negroes enrolled in the school system. For example, Negroes are 26 percent of the elementary school enrollment in Milwaukee, Wis., and almost 60 percent of the enrollment in Philadelphia, Pa., yet in both cities almost three of every four Negro children attend nearly all-Negro schools. Negroes are only 19 percent of the elementary school enrollment in Omaha, Nebra., and almost 70 percent of the enrollment in Chester, Pa., yet in both cities at least 80 percent of the Negro children are enrolled in majority-Negro schools.

Although levels of segregation are discernibly higher in the South than in the North, the two regions do not fall into discrete categories. Table 2, p. 27 shows the extent of Negro elementary school segregation in 20 Southern and Northern cities. The extent of racial isolation in Northern school systems does not differ markedly from that in the South.

Racial isolation in the schools, then, is intense whether the cities are large or small, whether the proportion of Negro enrollment is large or small, whether they are located North or South.

Racial Isolation and the Outcomes of Education

Since 1954, when the Supreme Court ruled that segregation in public schools sanctioned by law violated the Constitution, increasing attention has been given to the effects of school segregation not based on law. Does such segregation have a negative effect upon the performance and attitudes of Negro students?

The question is difficult to answer, for it requires that the influence of one aspect of a child's education—the racial composition of his school—be determined apart from all other relevant factors. The question is further complicated by the fact that the intellectual and emotional development of children is related not only to their schools but to a much broader social and educational context. Apart from the possible effects of a school's racial composition, the results of schooling also are affected by the social and economic circumstances in which children grow up, the quality of education provided in their schools, and the achievement and aspirations of their classmates. It is not a simple matter to separate elements which in reality are so closely interwoven. And the outcomes of education cannot be measured solely by children's grades in school—they extend also to their attitudes and experiences as adults.

There are a number of tested standards by which the effects of education can be assessed. Although none is absolutely accurate, each is a useful indicator of the outcomes of education. Most familiar is students' performance on achievement tests. Since achievement in other subjects depends strongly upon reading, tests of reading or verbal achievement are the usual measure of academic progress. The effects of education also include children's attitudes and aspirations. Thus measures have been devised to assess the schools' influence upon these factors.

The main purpose of education in America is to prepare students for future careers and lives as citizens. Occupational success now requires highly developed knowledge and technical skills, and public schools increasingly are expected to provide preparation for later education. One measure of their long-range effect, therefore, is a student's success in further education. Another is his relative occupational and economic attainment as an adult.

Marked differences exist between Negro and white Americans when measured by each of these standards. The disparities appear early in school. The verbal achievement of the average third grade Negro student in the Northeastern United States is about a year behind the average white in the same region. Differences of the same magnitude exist in all other regions of the Nation.

This disparity typically is greater in higher grades. The average third grade Negro student in the Midwest has a verbal achievement level approximately one year behind the average white student, but in the 12th grade the difference is nearly 3 years. Commission studies in individual cities revealed that this pattern is general.[4]

Differences in achievement also are apparent on other standard tests. The U.S. Army administers tests to all inductees, the results of which depend upon ". . . the level of . . . educational attainment [and] . . . the quality of . . . education . . ." The most recent test was given in 1965; it shows that while 18 percent of all whites failed, more than half of all Negroes failed.

In spite of these differences in academic performance, Negro students generally express a desire for academic success. Nevertheless they are less likely to have definite plans to attend college. Moreover, Negro students more often feel that they will be unsuccessful later in life.

There also are dissimilarities when further education is considered. Negroes less often are enrolled in college than whites and they are much more likely to be enrolled in high schools which send a relatively small proportion of their graduates to college. Indeed, Negro students finish

---

[4]In Boston, predominantly Negro schools made consistently lower median scores in reading achievement at every grade level tested than the predominantly white schools. In the higher levels, the difference in the achievement increased steadily. *Boston Study,* Section F-1, tables 2 and 3.

In Philadelphia differences in average reading achievement (expressed in grade level equivalents) between predominantly Negro and white schools increased from 0.8 in the second grade to 3.3 in the tenth grade. Scores from the School and College Aptitude Test for the eleventh grade, 1965-66, revealed a similar disparity: All schools over 90 percent Negro obtained school percentiles in the lowest quarter. Generally, the scores for predominantly white schools were consistently higher than those for the predominantly Negro schools; the highest Negro school ranked considerably below the white schools. (Test scores from Department of Research and Development, School District of Philadelphia.)

In Cleveland, a similar pattern was found. Nearly all-Negro schools start off at approximately one half of a grade level below white schools according to scores made in kindergarten on the Lee Clark Reading Readiness Test; at the ninth grade level medians for Negro schools typically were nearly two years behind white schools; grade equivalents for Negro schools ranged from 7.7 to 8.3, while for white schools the range was 8.3 to 10.1. By the twelfth grade, Negro schools were *all* below the city median, the white schools were all above the city median, and the lowest white school scored substantially higher than the highest score for the nearly all-Negro schools. (Scores obtained from Bureau of Educational Research, Cleveland Board of Education.)

In Atlanta, in 1965, in the Negro schools the median grade equivalent of the eighth grade in reading achievement was 3.9; in predominantly white schools it was almost 5 grades higher, 8.7 (Scores obtained from the Department of Research, Atlanta Public Schools). Similar disparities were noticed in test scores received from the public schools in Oakland, Milwaukee, and St. Louis.

Table 2. Extent of elementary school segregation in 20 selected Northern and Southern cities — based on proportion of Negro students in 90-100 percent Negro and majority-Negro elementary schools

Southern cities	Percent in 90-100% Negro schools	Percent in majority-Negro schools	Northern cities	Percent in 90-100% Negro schools	Percent in majority-Negro schools
Richmond, Va............	99	99	Gary, Ind....................	90	95
Atlanta, Ga.................	97	99	Chicago, Ill.................	89	97
Little Rock, Ark..........	96	96	Cleveland, Ohio..........	82	95
Memphis, Tenn..........	95	99	Chester, Pa.................	78	89
Marietta, Ga...............	94	94	Buffalo, N.Y..............	77	89
Houston, Tex..............	93	98	Detroit, Mich.............	72	92
Miama, Fla.................	91	94	Milwaukee, Wis..........	72	87
Winston-Salem, N.C....	89	95	Indianapolis, Ind.......	71	84
Dallas, Tex.................	83	90	Flint, Mich.................	68	86
Nashville, Tenn..........	82	86	Newark, N.J...............	51	90

public school less often than whites and they are much more likely to attend schools with high dropout rates.

Differentials also exist in the distribution of income and occupations in later life. Negroes with college education earn less on the average than high school-educated whites. Negroes with some college education are less likely than similarly educated whites to be employed in white collar trades.

These disparities arise from a variety of sources. In many respects they are related to factors which do not affect all children, such as racial discrimination in employment. Yet the outcomes of education for all students are shaped by a number of common factors.

One, the importance of which long has been recognized, is the educational and economic circumstances of a child's family. Students from differing circumstances, i.e., different social class backgrounds, bring to school differently developed attitudes and verbal skills. Both have a strong influence upon their performance in school and later in life.

Similarly, the social class level of a given student's classmates usually has a strong bearing upon his performance and aspirations. A student who attends school with other youngsters who intend to go to college is more likely to desire this himself than if most of his schoolmates do not plan to attend college or even finish public school.

Students also are influenced by the quality of education they receive in school. The elements of school quality generally thought to be important can be gauged in part by those factors which educators typically emphasize when they seek to improve the schools. One is reduced class size, permitting more attention to individual students. Another is the recruitment of more highly qualified teachers, which often requires improved salaries and teaching conditions. It also has been recognized that an important aspect of a teacher's qualifications is his attitudes and the level of performance he expects of his students. A fourth is the development of more advanced educational curricula and facilities, particularly in such areas as language and science.

Finally, increasing numbers of educators believe that the racial composition of schools can affect the performance and attitudes of students. There is some evidence that the academic achievement of Negro students is lower in majority-Negro than in majority-white schools, and many educators have said that attending school almost exclusively with children of the same race has a negative effect upon the attitudes of both Negro and white students.

•   •   •

The Racially Isolated School

What is it, then, about the racially isolated school which seems to result in the poorer achievement of many Negro students? And conversely, what factors in the majority-white school account for the more positive attitudes and higher achievement of Negro students?

Negro students often come to school with attitudes and experiences which bear upon their performance in school. Like all children they become aware of racial differences at an early age. Young Negro children, however, often tend to reject their own skin color, and to have problems of self-esteem. Kenneth Morland, Chairman of the Department of Sociology and Anthropology at Randolph-Macon College, has written:

> In a sense, American society educates for prejudice. Studies in both Northern and Southern communities . . . show that Negro as well as white children develop a bias for the white race at an early age. This bias is indicated by both a preference for and an identification with whites rather than with Negroes.[5]

---

[5]Morland, "The Development of Racial Bias in Young Children," 2 *Theory Into Practice* 120 (1963). In another study, Morland found that Negro nursery school children attending segregated schools in Lynchburg, Virginia, tended to identify themselves as white rather than Negro. "Racial Self-Identification: A Study of Nursery School Children," 24 *The American Catholic Sociological Review* 231 (Fall, 1963). In a later study, Morland compared two groups of children, one from Lynchburg, Virginia, and the other from Boston, Massachusetts. He found that both groups of Negroes manifested a bias for whites. Morland, "A Comparison of Race Awareness in Northern and Southern Children," 36 *American Journal of Orthopsychiatry* 22 (January, 1966). This bias toward whites does not appear to be a regional phenomenon.

There is reason to believe that the racial composition of schools can serve either to overcome or to compound these problems of low self-esteem. For example, Calvin Brooks, during his testimony at the Cleveland hearing, described the environment at his school and its effects upon the students:

> . . . it had an effect because they were there and all they saw were Negroes and they were raised in an environment of poverty and the building was old and it had an effect I don't know of — of hopelessness. They didn't think that they could do anything because their fathers had common labor jobs and they didn't think they could ever get any higher and they didn't work, some of them.

In part, the relationship between racially isolated schools and poor performance and low self-esteem is based upon the fact that predominantly Negro schools are generally regarded as inferior by the community. James Allen, Commissioner of Education for the State of New York, pointed out at the Commission hearing in Rochester that:

> . . . the all-Negro schools . . . are looked upon by the community as being poor schools. . . . No matter what you do to try to make them better, in the minds of most white people in these communities, they are poor schools.

At other Commission hearings parents and teachers often testified that predominantly Negro schools are stigmatized institutions. Dr. Charles Pinderhughes, a psychiatrist who testified at the Boston hearing, said that "the Negro school carries with it a stigma that influences the attitudes both on the part of outsiders and on the part of parents, students, and teachers . . ." Dr. John Fischer, President of Teachers College at Columbia University, has written of the

> . . . unfortunate psychological effect upon a child of membership in a school where every pupil knows that, regardless of his personal attainments, the group with which he is identified is viewed as less able, less successful, and less acceptable than the majority of the community.

The impact of negative community attitudes upon children was illustrated at the Commission hearing in Cleveland where a teacher at an all-Negro high school was asked about a student exchange between his school and an all-white suburban high school. He explained how his students felt about themselves and the school after the exchange:

> . . . I think the reaction is somewhat illuminating as one of my students in one of my classes said last year, "Well, it was nice of them to come down to the zoo to see us."

Community attitudes toward schools which identify them as inferior also are recognized by their teaching and administrative staff. Testimony

at Commission hearings tended to confirm the conclusions of some
researchers that teachers in racially isolated schools recognize the stigma
of inferiority which is attached to their schools. At the Cleveland hearing, one teacher, asked how he felt when he was informed that he had
been assigned to a school that was 95 percent Negro, replied:

> Well, I think I was a little bit disappointed personally. I knew . . . that
> any time a school is predominantly Negro . . . that there is a stigma that
> goes with it, that it just can't be first class. I not only feel that this is true
> in the minds of Negroes, but also in the minds of most whites.

There is evidence that this affects the attitudes and performance of
many teachers in majority-Negro schools. At the Commission hearing
in Rochester, Franklyn Barry, Superintendent of Schools in Syracuse,
N.Y., testified that in such schools teachers often "average down" their
expectations of the students. A study of schools in Harlem discussed
the low teacher expectations there, and concluded that:

> The atmosphere stemming from such expectations cannot be conducive
> to good teaching, and is manifest in friction between teachers, abdication
> of teaching responsibilities . . . [and] a concern with discipline rather
> than learning . . .

This is consistent with data from the *Equality of Educational Opportunity* survey which noted that Negro students were more likely to have
teachers who did not want to remain in their present school. Their
teachers also were more likely to feel that other teachers regarded their
school as a poor one.

Conversely the student environment in desegregated schools can offer
substantial support for high achievement and aspirations. The majority
of the children in such schools do not have problems of self-confidence
due to race and the schools are not stigmatized as inferior. The students
are likely to assume that they will succeed in school and in their future
careers, for the school reflects the mainstream of American society. The
environment in such schools is well endowed with models of academic
and occupational success. For Negro children, desegregated schools
may pose problems of racial identification. But they also offer association
with other students who see a clear connection between their education
and later careers with no contradictions or serious doubts. High aspirations held by Negro students in such schools are more likely to be
supported by the similar aspirations of their schoolmates.

School personnel in predominantly white schools more often feel that
their students have the potential and the desire for high attainment. The
Equality of Educational Opportunity survey found that white students

are more likely to have teachers with high morale, who want to remain in their present school, and who regard their students as capable.

The environment of schools with a substantial majority of Negro students, then, offers serious obstacles to learning. The schools are stigmatized as inferior in the community. The students often doubt their own worth, and their teachers frequently corroborate these doubts. The academic performance of their classmates is usually characterized in continuing difficulty. The children often have doubts about their chances of succeeding in a predominantly white society and they typically are in school with other students who have similar doubts. They are in schools which, by virtue both of their racial and social class composition are isolated from models of success in school.

* * *

Recommendations

This report describes conditions that result in injustices to children and require immediate attention and action. The responsibility for corrective action rests with government at all levels and with citizens and organizations throughout the Nation. We must commit ourselves as a Nation to the establishment of equal educational opportunity of high quality for all children. *As an important means of fulfilling this national goal, the Commission recommends that the President and the Congress give immediate and urgent consideration to new legislation for the purpose of removing present racial imbalances from our public schools, thus to eliminate the dire effects of racial isolation which this report describes, and at long last, providing real equality of educational opportunity by integrating presently deprived American children of all races into a totally improved public educational system.*

Without attempting to outline needed legislation in great detail, our study of the problem convinces the Commission that new legislation must embody the following essential principles:

1. *Congress should establish a uniform standard providing for the elimination of racial isolation in the schools.*

Since large numbers of Negro children suffer harmful effects that are attributable in part to the racial composition of schools they attend, legislation should provide for the elimination of schools in which such harm generally occurs. No standard of general applicability will fit every case precisely; some schools with a large proportion of Negro students may not in fact produce harmful effects while others with a smaller proportion may be schools in which students are disadvantaged because of their race. But the alternative to establishing such a standard is to require a time-consuming and ineffective effort to determine on a case-by-case basis the schools in which harm occurs. As it has in analogous situations, Congress should deal with this problem by establishing reasonable and practical standards which will correct the injustice without intruding unnecessarily into areas where no corrective action is needed.

In prescribing a reasonable standard, there is much to commend the criterion already adopted by the legislature in Massachusetts and the Commissioner of Education of New York, defining as racially imbalanced, schools in which Negro pupils constitute more than 50 percent of the total enrollment. It was found in this report that when Negro students in schools with more than 50 percent Negro enrollment were compared with similarly situated Negro students in schools with a majority-white enrollment, there were significant differences in attitude and performance. It is the schools that have a majority-Negro enrollment that tend to be regarded and treated by the community as segregated and inferior schools. Although there are many factors involved, the racial composition of schools that are majority-Negro in enrollment tends to be less stable that that of majority-white schools and to be subject to more rapid change.

Similar arguments might be advanced for a standard which would deviate slightly from a 50-percent criterion, but a standard set significantly higher would not be adequate to deal with the problem and probably would not result in lasting solutions.

2. *Congress should vest in each of the 50 States responsibility for meeting the standard it establishes and should allow the States maximum flexibility in devising appropriate remedies. It also should provide financial and technical assistance to the States in planning such remedies.*

It would be unwise for the Federal Government to attempt to prescribe any single solution or set of solutions for the entire Nation. There is a broad range of techniques which are capable of achieving education of high quality in integrated public schools. Each State should be free to adopt solutions best suited to the particular needs of its individual communities.

At the same time it is clear that the responsibility should be placed upon the States rather than the individual school districts. The States, and not individual communities alone, have the capacity to develop and implement plans adequate to the objective. The States have assumed the responsibility for providing public education for all of their citizens and for establishing the basic conditions under which it is offered. Responsibility for achieving the goal of high-quality integrated education can and should be placed upon the States under terms which afford broad scope for local initiative. But in many jurisdictions, particularly the major cities, solutions are not possible without the cooperation of neighboring communities. The States possess the authority and the means for securing cooperation, by consolidating or reorganizing school districts or by providing for appropriate joint arrangements between school districts.

To help the States in devising appropriate remedies, the Federal Government should provide technical and financial assistance.

3. *The legislation should include programs of substantial financial assistance to provide for construction of new facilities and improvement in the quality of education in all schools.*

In many cases, particularly in the major cities, integrating the public schools will require the construction of new facilities designed both to serve a larger student population and to be accessible to all children in the area to be served. Substantial Federal assistance is needed to supplement the resources of States and localities in building new schools of this kind and providing higher quality education for all children. Federal assistance also can be helpful in encouraging cooperative arrangements between States which provide education services to the same metropolitan area and between separate school districts in a metropolitan area. In addition, Federal financial assistance now available under programs such as aid for mass transportation and community facilities should be utilized in ways which will advance the goal of integration.

Regardless of whether the achievement of integration requires new facilities, Federal financial assistance is needed for programs to improve the quality of education. States and localities should have broad discretion to develop programs best suited to their needs. Programs that are among the most promising involve steps—such as the reduction of pupil-teacher ratios, the establishment of ungraded classes and team teaching, and the introduction of specialized remedial instruction—which enable teachers to give more attention to the individual needs of children. Funds also could be used for purposes such as assisting the training of teachers, developing new educational techniques, and improving curriculum.

4. *Congress should provide for adequate time in which to accomplish the objectives of the legislation.*

It is clear that equal opportunity in education cannot be achieved overnight. Particularly in the large cities where problems of providing equal educational opportunity have seemed so intractable, time will be necessary for such matters as educational and physical planning, assembling and acquiring land, and building new facilities. However, since the problem is urgent a prompt start must be made toward finding solutions, progress must be continuous and substantial, and there must be some assurance that the job will be completed as quickly as possible. The time has come to put less emphasis on "deliberate" and more on "speed."

•   •   •

The goals of equal educational opportunity and equal housing opportunity are inseparable. Progress toward the achievement of one goal necessarily will facilitate achievement of the other. Failure to make progress toward the achievement of either goal will handicap efforts to achieve the other. *The Commission recommends, therefore, that the President and Congress give consideration to legislation which will:*

5. *Prohibit discrimination in the sale or rental of housing, and*

6. *Expand programs of Federal assistance designed to increase the supply of housing throughout metropolitan areas within the means of low- and moderate-income families.*

Additional funds should be provided for programs such as the rent supplement program and FHA 221 (d) (3), and these two programs should be amended to permit private enterprise to participate in them free from the special veto power now held by local governments under present Federal statutes.

In addition, *the Commission recommends that the Department of Housing and Urban Development:*

7. *Require as a condition for approval of applications for low- and moderate-income housing projects that the sites will be selected and the projects planned in a nondiscriminatory manner that will contribute to reducing residential racial concentrations and eliminating racial isolation in the schools.*

8. *Require as a condition for approval of urban renewal projects that relocation will be planned in a nondiscriminatory manner that will contribute to reducing residential racial concentrations and eliminating racial isolation in the schools.*

De Facto Segregation and the Law*

United States Commission On Civil Rights

Actions by States To Eliminate Racial Isolation

The courts have ruled that purposeful segregation of Negro and white pupils, whether the result of action or inaction by school authorities, is unconstitutional even where such segregation is not formally imposed or expressly permitted by law and even where it is less than complete. The courts have been less prepared to hold that there is a constitutional duty to eliminate adventitious school segregation. Beyond the matter of constitutional obligation, however, lies the area of State and local legislative and administrative action to relieve racial isolation in the schools. We now turn to what the States have done to require local school authorities to correct or reduce racial isolation.

A. States Which Have Taken The Position That Racial Isolation In The Public Schools Is Harmful

California, Massachusetts, New York, New Jersey, Wisconsin, and Connecticut have taken the position, in executive or judicial statements, that racial isolation in the schools has a damaging effect on the educational opportunities of Negro pupils. The Supreme Court of California so stated in the *Jackson* case.[1] Three years earlier, in 1960, the Board of Regents of the State of New York stated that:

> Modern psychological knowledge indicates that schools enrolling students largely of homogeneous ethnic origin, may damage the personality of minority group children. Such schools decrease their motivation and thus

---

*U.S. Commission on Civil Rights, *Racial Isolation in the Public Schools,* Appendix (Washington: U.S. Government Printing Office, 1967).

[1] *Jackson v. Pasadena City School District,* 31 Cal. Rptr. at 609, 610, 382 P. 2d at 881, 882.

impair the ability to learn. Public education in such a setting is socially unrealistic, blocks the attainment of the goals of democratic education, and is wasteful of manpower and talent, whether this situation occurs by law or by fact.

In the same year, the New Jersey Commissioner of Education concluded that "in the minds of Negro pupils and parents a stigma is attached to attending a school whose enrollment is completely or almost exclusively Negro, and that this sense of stigma and resulting feeling of inferiority have an undesirable effect upon attitudes related to successful learning."[2] In 1965, a report adopted by the Massachusetts State Board of Education concluded that a racially imbalanced school was detrimental to sound education.

On December 7, 1966, the Connecticut Board of Education adopted a policy statement which recognized that "the high concentration of minority group children in urban schools produces special problems in providing quality education. Isolation and lack of exposure to the mainstream of American society make it difficult for these children to achieve their full education potential."

B. Standards

A small number of States have required some type of action to correct or alleviate racial imbalance in the public schools. These States have established guidelines on the degree of imbalance which should trigger relief.

The Massachusetts legislature has defined a racially imbalanced school as one where the percentage of nonwhites exceeds 50 percent of the total enrollment. The New York Commissioner of Education has defined a racially imbalanced school as one having 50 percent or more Negro pupils enrolled. The Supreme Court of California and the Supreme Court of New Jersey have indicated that "substantial" imbalance would call for relief.[3] Illinois, which by statute requires consideration of ethnic factors in drawing school attendance areas and in selecting school sites, imposes no statutory requirement upon local school authorities to take corrective action which is dependent upon the proportion of Negroes to

---

[2]*Fischer* v. *Board of Education* (Orange), 8 *Race. Rel. L. Rep.* 730, 733-734 (N.J. Comm. of Ed. 1963). See also *Booker* v. *Board of Education* (Plainfield), 8 *Race Rel. L. Rep.* 1228 (1963); *Spruill* v. *Board of Education,* 8 *Race Rel. L. Rep.* 1234 (1963).

[3]*Jackson* v. *Pasadena City School District,* 31 Cal. Rptr. at 609, 382 P. 2d at 881; *Booker* v. *Board of Education* (Plainfield), 45 N.J. 161, 178, 212 A. 2d 1, 10 (1965).

whites in a particular school, but an Illinois court has construed the statute to require corrective action where a school was 76 percent Negro.[4] On November 30, 1966, the Maryland State Board of Education, in a formal opinion, announced that "as long as the neighborhood school concept is not violated, efforts ought to be made to avoid lopsided racial imbalance in the composition of the student bodies.

C. Extent of Duty

Massachusetts and New York purport to require the elimination of racial imbalance in all schools. The Supreme Court of California has cautioned that "consideration must be given to the various factors in each case, including the practical necessities of governmental operation," including the "difficulty and effectiveness of revising school boundaries so as to eliminate segregation and the availability of other facilities to which students can be transferred."[5] The Supreme Court of New Jersey requires "a reasonable plan achieving the greatest dispersal consistent with sound educational values and procedures." Many factors must be "conscientiously weighed by the school authorities," including "considerations of safety, convenience, time economy, and the other acknowledged virtues of the neighborhood policy."[6] The Illinois law requires local school authorities to consider the effects of racial imbalance, along with other relevant educational factors, in selecting school sites and drawing attendance zones. In Maryland, the State Board of Education requires school districts to eliminate "lopsided" racial imbalance, but only when consistent with the neighborhood school concept.

D. Implementation

The Massachusetts policy is supported by the strongest enforcement powers. In August 1965, the Massachusetts Legislature enacted a Racial Imbalance Act, which provides that upon notification by the State Board that a school within its system is racially imbalanced, a school committee must prepare and file with the board a plan to eliminate the imbalance. If the committee fails to show progress within a reasonable time in eliminating racial imbalance in its school system, the Commissioner of Education must refuse to certify all State school aid for that system.

Massachusetts is the only State which requires, either by law or administrative regulation, that State educational funds be withheld from school systems operating racially imbalanced schools.

---

[4]*Tometz* v. *Board of Education, Waukegan City School, School District No. 61,* Civil No. 65-3917, Cir. Ct. of the 19th Jud. Cir., Lake County, Ill., July 20, 1966.
[5]*Jackson* v. *Pasadena City School District,* 31 Cal. Rptr. at 610, 382 P. 2d at 882.
[6]*Booker* v. *Board of Education,* 45 N.J. 161, 180, 212 A. 2d 1, 11 (1965).

Like Massachusetts, Illinois has passed legislation designed to alleviate racial imbalance. In June 1963, in the Armstrong Act, Illinois amended its school code by adding the following sentence to the sections dealing with the erection and acquisition of school buildings:

> In erecting, purchasing, or otherwise acquiring buildings for school purposes, the board shall not do so in such a manner as to promote segregation and separation of children in public schools because of color, race or nationality.

To the sections dealing with attendance units and subdistricts the following provision was added:

> As soon as practicable, and from time to time thereafter, the board shall change or revise existing units [subdistricts] or create new units [subdistricts] in a manner which will take into consideration the prevention of segregation and the elimination of separation of children in public schools because of color, race or nationality.

Enforcement of these provisions appears to be left to the courts upon the complaints of aggrieved individuals.

New Jersey, New York, and California have taken action against racial imbalance either through administrative regulations, quasi-judicial rulings of the State Commissioner of Education, judicial decisions of State courts, or a combination of these means. In New Jersey and New York, reliance has been placed on general provisions of State law guaranteeing equal educational opportunity. The sanctions available to enforce these regulations and rulings vary. In New York, where the Commissioner of Education has required local school authorities to eliminate racial imbalance the Commissioner has authority under State law to withhold funds or to remove school board members for failure to comply with his determinations. The New Jersey Commissioner of Education has the power to withhold funds if a school district fails to "comply with the regulations and standards for the equalization of opportunity which have been or . . . may be prescribed by law or formulated by the Commissioner of Education or the State Board pursuant to law."

The sanctions available to the New York and New Jersey commissioners are lacking in California, where the State Board of Education, pursuant to its statutory rule-making authority, has issued regulations— approved by the Supreme Court of California—requiring school boards to take certain action to avoid racial imbalance. It is not clear what sanctions, if any, the State Board may impose in the event of failure to comply.

In Maryland the State Board, which is charged with the power of determining the educational policies of the State and has "the last word on any matter concerning educational policy or the administration of its system of public education," has the power to specify school district boundaries.

In Massachusetts, the State Board is required to provide technical assistance to school committees in formulating plans to relieve racial imbalance. The school building assistance commission, moreover, is required to increase the amount of grants for school construction to 65 percent of the approved cost whenever the board of education is satisfied that the construction or enlargement of a school is for the purpose of reducing or eliminating racial imbalance in the school system. In 1966, the New York State Legislature appropriated a million dollars partly to assist school districts in the State to develop plans and programs for correcting racial isolation in the schools.

E.   Judicial Challenges to Remedial Action

The courts consistently have upheld actions at the State or local level designed to eliminate or alleviate racial imbalance in the public schools against the charge by white parents that it is unconstitutional or unlawful to take race into consideration.

In *Fuller* v. *Volk*,[7] the Englewood School Board, under a plan to reduce racial imbalance in the elementary schools, assigned all sixth-grade pupils to one city-wide school (Lincoln) and gave all the students in grades one through five at Lincoln the option to attend other specified elementary schools. The plaintiffs, parents of white sixth-grade children, argued that the plan had been adopted solely because of racial consider-ations, that their children were being discriminated against on the basis of race because they could not attend their neighborhood school, and that therefore the plan was unconstitutional. Disagreeing, the court held that "a local board of education is not constitutionally prohibited from taking race into account in drawing or redrawing school attendance lines for the purpose of reducing or eliminating de facto segregation in its public schools."

Action taken to implement the New York policy on racial imbalance has been challenged frequently in the courts as repugnant to the due process and equal protection clauses of the 14th amendment and to New York State law. But except in one case where the results were held to be arbitrary and capricious, the lawsuits have been uniformly unsuccessful. Although the State courts at first looked to see whether the school board plan was justified by educational factors other than a

---

[7] 230 F. Supp. 25 (D. N.J. 1964), vacated and remanded for determination of jurisdiction, 351 F. 2d 323 (3d Cir. 1965), on remand 250 F. Supp. 81 (D. N.J. 1966).

desire to overcome racial imbalance, more recently a New York court indicated that a plan designed solely to correct racial imbalance would not for that reason be unconstitutional.[8] In Buffalo, after the commissioner of education had ordered the school board to remedy racial imbalance in the schools, suit was brought in Federal court attacking the order as a violation of the 14th amendment. Rejecting this argument, the court held that ". . . the 14th amendment, while prohibiting any form of invidious discrimination, does not bar cognizance of race in a proper effort to eliminate racial imbalance in a school system."[9]

The rationale of these decisions has been articulated by the Court of Appeals for the First Circuit. Commenting on a plan to relieve racial imbalance, the court stated in dictum:

> It has been suggested that classification by race is unlawful regardless of the worthiness of the objective. We do not agree. The defendants' proposed action does not concern race except insofar as race correlates with proved deprivation of educational opportunity. This evil satisfies whatever "heavier burden of justification" there might be. Cf. *McLaughlin* v. *State of Florida,* 1964, 379 U.S. 184, 194. . . . It would seem no more unconstitutional to take into account plaintiffs' special characteristics and circumstances that have been found to be occasioned by their color than it would be to give special attention to physiological, psychological, or sociological variances from the norm occasioned by other factors. That these differences happen to be associated with a particular race is no reason for ignoring them. [Citations omitted.][10]

Ironically, those who maintain the position that school boards may not take race into account in formulating student assignment plans have relied on Mr. Justice Harlan's statement, dissenting in *Plessy* v. *Ferguson,* that "our Constitution is colorblind, and neither knows nor tolerates classes among citizens." On August 15, 1963, the Attorney General of California, ruling in an official opinion that a school board may adopt a plan to relieve imbalance which utilizes race as a factor ". . . if the purpose of considering the racial factor is to effect desegregation in the schools, and the plan is reasonably related to the accomplishment of that purpose," gave the following response to this argument:

> "Our Constitution is colorblind" was Justice Harlan's admonition against the "separate but equal" doctrine. To decide that the combined thinking and efforts of persons of all races may not recognize a present inequality as the starting point in a program designed to help achieve that equality

---

[8]*Katalinic* v. *City of Syracuse,* supra, at 736, 254 N.Y.S. 2d at 962.
[9]*Offermann* v. *Nitkowski,* 248 F. Supp. 129 (W.D. N.Y. 1965).
[10]*Springfield School Committee* v. *Barksdale,* 348 F. 2d 261, 266 (1st Cir. 1965)

which Justice Harlan sought would be to conclude not merely that the Constitution is colorblind, but that it is totally blind.[11]

Summary: The courts have held purposeful school segregation to be unconstitutional—including segregation that is less than total. They have indicated that purposeful segregation which is the product of inaction is as repugnant to the 14th amendment as purposeful segregation which is the result of affirmative conduct. The courts have not been so ready to say that adventitious segregation is unconstitutional. That result has been reached only in a few cases involving smaller cities and suburban jurisdictions in which the Negro population did not constitute a large portion of the population and where the problem seemed susceptible of a judicial remedy. In these cases the courts have reached the question of whether adventitious segregation is harmful to Negro children and unanimously have concluded that it is. In suits against school systems of large cities, on the other hand, where the Negro school age population is a much larger proportion of the total school age enrollment, and where judges often have been troubled by the difficulty of devising a remedy which the school system could implement, the courts have ruled that adventitious segregation is not unconstitutional, without reaching the factual question of whether Negro students are harmed by such segregation. The courts have rejected claims by white parents that where the State or the school authorities take corrective action, the Constitution is violated.

Thus, the result of most judicial decisions to date has been to leave the question of remedying racial imbalance to the legislative and executive branches of the Federal and State governments. A small number of States have enumerated policies directed at correcting racial imbalance, and fewer still have provided machinery for implementing these policies.

---

[11]42 Ops. Cal. Atty. Gen. 33, 34-35 (1963), 8 *Race Rel L. Rep.* 1303, 1305 (1963).

Ghetto Education:
An Alternative View*

Joseph Alsop

It is time to stop talking nonsense about Negro education. It is time to start dealing with the hard, cruel facts of the problem of the ghetto schools, which is in turn the very core of the race problem in the United States. Above all it is time to cease repeating, "End *de facto* segregation!" as though this virtuous incantation were a magical spell. For school desegregation must always be a central and essential goal; but sad experience has proved that desegregation is very far from being an instant remedy.

Indeed, this kind of forcible homogenization would quite certainly result in even greater segregation; for the predictable consequence would be an increase in the Negro percentage in the primary and elementary schools from 93 percent to 98 or 99 percent.

Unprepared desegregation in a grossly underfinanced school system has in fact been one of the two main causes of this city's [Washington, D.C.] transformation into an urban super-ghetto—a kind of near-Watts on a metropolitan scale. Since the war, every one of the great urban centers above the Mason-Dixon line has received countless thousands of Negro immigrants from the South. From this cause alone, Washington's Negro population has grown very greatly; but Negro immigration has been only one aspect of the two-sided demographic movement that has now produced a city two-thirds Negro and one-third white. The other aspect, equally important, has been white emigration to the affluent suburbs. And the crucial role of the schools in this white emigration can in turn be clearly seen, if you merely look at those who have fled and

---

*Reprinted by permission of Joseph Alsop. Copyright © 1967 by Joseph Alsop.

those who have stayed behind. Those who have stayed behind number close to 250,000; yet this white population of about a quarter of a million includes only 13,000 children of school age! Of the District's 13,000 white children of school age, furthermore, rather more than 5,000 attend parochial or other private schools. The conclusion is inescapable that Washington's remaining white population is almost exclusively composed of (a) old people, (b) single people, (c) couples without children of school age, and (d) couples who can afford to send their children to parochial or private schools or who live in the few neighborhoods where the schools are still mainly white. No such demographic result as that shown above could conceivably have been produced in the normal course of events. It means, beyond question, that just about every white couple outside the above-listed categories has moved to the suburbs, at least as soon as it came time to send the children to school.

The available statistics are grossly inadequate, but enough is known to show that precisely the same kind of two-sided demographic movement is tending to produce much the same sort of result in a good many other American urban centers. Washington, which has been treated as an exceptional case, is merely an *advanced* case. The best figures I have got thus far are for last year. Taking the percentage of Negro children in the primary and elementary schools as the gauge, one can then show how far six other major cities have traveled to date, along the road that has made the nation's capital into a concealed super-ghetto. Here is the picture:

Baltimore, schools 64 percent Negro, equals Washington in 1954-55.
Chicago, schools 56 percent Negro, equals Washington in 1952-53.
Cleveland, schools 53 percent Negro, equals Washington in 1951-52.
Detroit, schools 57 percent Negro, equals Washington in 1953-54.
Philadelphia, schools 60 percent Negro, nearly equals Washington in 1954-55.
St. Louis, schools 64 percent Negro, equals Washington in 1954-55.

Two fundamental problems are revealed by these figures. The first is what may be called the progressive ghettoization of a whole series of America's great urban conglomerations. In the fairly near future, this phenomenon can too easily produce social and economic consequences that hardly bear thinking about. Ghetto city centers, from which even commerce, banking and industry will have fled to the flatly affluent white suburbs, are not an attractive prospect, either for the wretched ghetto-denizens, or for anyone else. But this is not the problem to which I have been trying to address myself. I have been trying to show, rather, that in almost all cases, the practical result of *unprepared* desegregation is *an enlarged ghetto with a greater number of segregated schools than there were in the first instance.* This has in truth been the experience in every major Northern city known to me. Furthermore, it has been the experience in a good many cases in which the ugly influence of racial prejudice can be effectively ruled out. In the first flush of civil rights enthusiasm, for example, the parents of a liberal-Jewish neighborhood in Brooklyn voted all but unanimously to pair their school with a nearby ghetto school. The New York Board of Education promised special support (which took the ludicrously inadequate form of a general patch-up of the school buildings). PS 7 and PS 8 were then merged, wholly on the motion of the white parents. But within a very short time, two segregated schools had come into being where there had been one before. The pairing caused school quality to go to Hell in a hack; and the white parents, seeing their children's education in jeopardy, either sent them to private schools or moved to the suburbs. And these were the very same parents, mind you, who had sponsored the pairing.

As an example of the scandal, consider the recent Civil Rights Commission report on "Racial Isolation in the Public Schools." It shows that America's schools are just about as segregated as they ever were, despite all the court orders that have been issued since 1954, and all the attempts, more or less sincere, to comply with those court orders. It says nothing of the white emigration that has played such a huge role in making a nonsense of the court orders. Using evidence chosen with suspicious selectivity (and misusing it gravely at that, if the Philadelphia data are any guide), the report further seeks to discredit school improvement inside the ghettos. By implication, it takes the shocking though fashionable liberal educators' view once so bitterly but accurately summarized by Floyd McKissick in this journal's pages, that if you "put Negro with Negro, you get stupidity." And having established school desegregation as the unique remedy, the report finally proposes busing on a massive scale as the best means to secure desegregation. Yet the report is datelined Washington, where no amount of busing would make the school system anything but segregated — short of a constitutional amendment permitting forcible imposition of wholly different living and schooling patterns in the District, Maryland and Virginia. Are we then to conclude that more than 90,000 Negro schoolchildren in Washington are to be forever condemned to defeat and despair? Or are we to conclude that this report, like so many other very similar documents, is the product of the kind of self-serving reasoning that must too often be expected, alas, from virtuous academics with a personal vested interest in a badly researched theory?

The answer is, of course, that it is not only viciously heartless and socially disastrous, but also wholly needless, to accept the viewpoint of the Civil Rights Commission and Judge Wright. There is something arrogant, there is even something disgusting, in this strange view that ghetto children can never be rescued, can never be educated, unless they are subjected to the benign classroom influence of white middle-class children. Ghetto children have all the potential of any other children; but in their background of poverty and deprivation, they have a heavy handicap. What is needed, therefore, is to overcome the handicap, by those special measures I have already mentioned as useful and needful to prepare for school desegregation, wherever desegregation is feasible. This means taking a series of steps of the most ABC simplicity. First, the children's school experience must begin early, at least in pre-kindergarten. For the inability to speak common English, which afflicts so many children of the ghettos, can only be overcome by catching them very young. Second, they must be taught in small classes — not more than 15 in pre-kindergarten and kindergarten, and not more than 22 or so in grades one through six. Otherwise, *teaching* will cease and keeping order will become the sole aim. For ghetto children mainly come from homes wholly unoriented to learning and to books. Gaining and holding their learning-attention (which is the right way to maintain sound discipline) is therefore the most difficult feat for every teacher in every ghetto school. And only reduced classes permit good, average teachers to accomplish this feat. Third, a certain number of backup teachers are needed — one extra for each three or four classes — so that when Billy and Sally, Victor and Jane begin to fall behind, these laggards can be promptly gathered into still smaller classes, for more concentrated work until they catch up again. Fourth, all the obvious extras in the way of remedial reading, health care, psychiatric care, etc., also have to be provided. These are, in fact, the principal features of the More Effective Schools program, that has been under way in New York City for three years. One wonders why this program was not chosen for study by the authors of the Civil Rights Commission's report. Perhaps the answer is that in the More Effective Schools, all children have shown a very great average improvement, and those children who have begun in pre-kindergarten and continued on from there are actually performing, on average, *at grade level or above*. If this program had been chosen for analysis, it would have sadly undermined the thesis of the authors of the Civil Rights Commission report; but it is nonetheless quite wonderful news, which should be published in Mao-style Big Character Posters in the corridors of every university where educational theorists flourish.

That it should be news at all, is a considerable show up of the ways of thinking and working and dealing with facts of all too many American white liberal intellectuals. In this instance, it goes without saying that properly prepared school desegregation is the ideal solution of the educational problem of America's Negro minority. It goes without saying, too, that wherever desegregation can be successfully accomplished, the moral and social duty to accomplish it must never be dodged or ducked, even if the needed preparations for successful desegregation are difficult, time-consuming and costly. But a good many of our liberal intellectuals never appear to have heard the rule, *"Le mieux est l'annemi du bien"*; it never appears to occur to them, in fact, that exclusive pursuit of the ideal solution can prevent the practical solution; and few of them seem to have bothered to do the tedious homework, on urban demographic patterns, for instance, that would have shown them how far the ideal solution is out of reach for most ghetto children at present. Their performance would be less unadmirable, I must add, if they had been content to urge their ideal solution, despite its unreality for all but a small minority of ghetto children. But they have not been content. A good many of the liberal educators and sociologists have done everything possible to discredit and to block the practical solution of the educational problem of our Negro minority, which is radical school improvement inside the ghetto. These people seem to have taken the attitude, in fact, that if they could not get desegregation, nothing else would do — and to hell with the millions of Negro children who have little hope of entering integrated schools!

The truth is that in our approach to almost every aspect of the race problem — whether segregation, or discrimination, or Negro poverty, or whatever it may be — we have persistently been placing the moral cart before the practical horse. Education is the key to the whole problem, because education leads to jobs; jobs lead to achievement; and achievement reduces discrimination. That is the common-sense formula, which puts the horse ahead of the cart. And if we do not get the moral cart moving at long last — if we cannot provide good education and decent jobs for our Negro fellow citizens, and if these first steps do not begin to erode discrimination and open ever wider doors of opportunity — then this country can too soon become a place in which none will wish to live, who still care much about the things that America is supposed to stand for.

2

The Negro in American Society

The initial objective of the civil rights movement in America was to prevent discrimination and segregation which was practiced by *governments,* particularly public school districts. But even while important victories for the civil rights movement were being recorded in the prevention of discrimination by governments, the movement began to broaden its objectives to include the elimination of discrimination in *all segments of American life,* private as well as public. Civil rights was redefined to mean not merely a legal but an actual possibility of developing human capacities and sharing in the goods which a society has produced and the way of life which it has built. This was a more positive concept of civil rights. It involved not merely restrictions on government, but a positive obligation of government to act forcefully to end discrimination in public accommodations, employment, housing, and all other sectors of private life.

When the civil rights movement turned to combatting private discrimination, it had to carry its fight into the legislative branch of government. The federal courts could employ constitutional guarantees to help prevent discrimination of state and local governments and school authorities, but only Congress and the legislative branches of state and local governments could restrict discriminatory practice by private owners, hotels and motels, private employers, other individuals who were not government officials. In 1957 and 1960 Congress passed weak civil rights bills which made it illegal for any person to interfere with the exercise of rights under a federal court order, or to use interstate commerce for the purpose of burning or bombing any building. So strong was the early reluctance of Congress to enter the field of civil rights that even these bills were extensively debated and compromised before final passage. Yet by 1964 the demand for strong civil rights legislation was so great that Congress could no longer ignore the nation's most pressing domestic issue. The Civil Rights Act of 1964 passed both houses of Congress by better than a two-thirds favorable vote; it won the overwhelming support of both Republican and Democratic Congressmen. It ranks with the Emancipation Proclamation, the 14th Amendment, and *Brown* v. *Topeka,* as one of the most important steps toward full equality for the Negro in America.

Opponents of the Civil Rights Act of 1964 argued that Congress unconstitutionally exceeded its delegated powers when it prohibited discrimination and segregation in practice by *privately owned* public accommodations and *private* employers. Nowhere among the delegated powers of Congress in Article One of the Constitution, or even in the 14th or 15th amendments is Congress specifically given the power to prohibit discrimination practiced by *private* individuals. In reply, supporters of the Act said that Congress has the power to regulate interstate commerce. Instead of relying upon only the 14th Amendment which prohibits only *state supported* discrimination, Congress was relying upon its powers over interstate commerce. In unanimous opinions in *Heart of Atlanta Motel* v. *the United States* and *Katzenbach* v. *McClung* in December of 1964, the Supreme Court upheld the constitutionality of the Civil Rights Act.

The 15th Amendment directly states that "the right of citizens . . . to vote shall not be denied or abridged . . . by any state on account of race, color or previous condition of servitude." It is a tribute to the ingenuity of southern statesmen that such a direct constitutional demand could be evaded for nearly a century. Negroes were kept from the polls primarily by the threat of social, economic, and physical sanctions at the hands of private individuals and groups (the Constitution forbade only *state* interference with voting, not interference from private individuals). At least three additional legal devices were also employed in the disenfranchisement of southern Negroes — the white primary, the poll tax, and the literacy test. Negroes were barred from voting in Democratic primaries in some southern states until 1944 on the grounds that political parties were *private* associations and elections *within* the parties were purely private affairs involving no state action. Of course, in the one-party South, the Democratic Party's primaries were the only important political contests, since all white men tacitly agreed to support the winner of the Democratic primary in the general election. But in 1944 in the case of *Smith* v. *Alwright,* the Supreme Court declared that primary elections were an integral part of state government. As such the 15th Amendment prevented the exclusion of Negro voters from primary elections. Poll taxes, generally one or two dollar fees for voting, also disenfranchised a large number of Negroes. Of course, the tax was applicable to Negroes and whites alike, but in view of the greater poverty among Negroes, it cut most heavily against that race. The 24th Amendment to the Constitution banned the use of poll taxes in federal elections and in 1966 the Supreme Court struck down the use of poll taxes in any public election, on the grounds that it was inherently discriminatory.

Literacy tests and complicated registration procedures were the last bastion against Negro voting in the South. In principle the literacy test prevented both the Negro and white illiterates from voting, but in practice whites were rarely given literacy tests while Negroes were given very difficult tests. Title I of the Civil Rights Act of 1964 stipulated that literacy tests must be uniformly administered, but they must be given in writing, and that a person with a sixth grade education must be presumed illiterate unless proven otherwise. But even after Title I had become law, southern registrars found innumerable ways of keeping Negroes off of voter roles. For example, registration boards would remain closed for all but a few hours a month, or they would process only one or two new registrants (Negro) per month, or they would make registration procedures so cumbersome and difficult that few Negroes could succeed in becoming voters. By 1965 it became apparent that only federal registrars standing in place of local officials could insure non-discrimination in voting. The Voting Rights Act authorized direct federal intervention in voter registration in counties where less than 50 per cent of voting age residents were registered to vote on November 1, 1964, or actually voted in the 1964 Presidential elections and literacy tests or similiar qualifying devices were in effect. Upon evidence of voter discrimination in such counties, the attorney general was authorized to replace the local voting registrars with federal voting examiners and to suspend literacy tests and similar qualifying devices. The constitutionality of the Voting Rights Act of 1965 was challenged before the Supreme Court in *South Carolina* v. *Katzenbach,* but the Court found that this legislation was a reasonable exercise of Congressional power in preventing voter discrimination pursuant to the 15th Amendment.

While Negroes constitute only 11 per cent of the total population of the United States, they are rapidly approaching a numerical majority in many of the nation's largest of cities. (See U.S. Bureau of the Census, *Negro Population Trends in Large Cities*) Negroes constitute a majority of the population of Washington, D.C., and by 1970 they will make up more than 40 per cent of the population of Detroit, Baltimore, New Orleans, Atlanta, St. Louis, Newark, Oakland, Birmingham, and Gary. This concentration of Negroes in large central cities is a product of the availability of low price rental units in older run-down sections of central cities and of discriminatory housing practices of private owners and developers. Of course, underlying the concentration of Negroes in run-down sectors of central cities is often a lack of sufficient income to purchase housing in suburbs or in better city neighborhoods. This poverty and unemployment which contributes to the concentration of Negroes in ghettoes is in turn a product of inadequate training and education, low aspiration levels, and a lack of incentive and motivation. And problems in education and motivation are themselves related to a breakdown in family life, delinquency and crime. Thus, urban Negroes face a whole series of interrelated problems in addition to discrimination: poverty, slum housing, undereducation, lack of job skills, family problems, lack of motivation, delinquency and crime. It is difficult to talk about any one of these problems without reference to them all.

Politically, these population trends mean that there will be an increase in organized Negro participation in urban politics and increasing Negro power in city administrations. The election of Negro mayors in Cleveland and Gary provide evidence that there will be a rise in the number of Negro office holders. However, increasing Negro percentages in central cities are not likely to lead to Negro "takeovers" in the sense that Negro office holders can afford to ignore or override the interests of white city dwellers. Negro candidates are more likely to find that there is more political mileage in appealing to white votes by pledging impartiality and promising to be "mayor to *all* the people." There is little incentive in a strict racist appeal by Negro candidates as long as whites remain a substantial proportion of the city voting population.

It is not easy for white middle class Americans to understand what ghetto life is all about. Figures can only reveal the bare outline of the Negro's position in American society. Yet figures make it very clear that, on the whole, Negroes do not enjoy the same affluence as white Americans. The average income of the Negro family is only half that of the average white family's. Nearly half of all Negro families are below the recognized poverty line of $3000 annual income. Twice as many Negroes live in substandard housing as white. Negro unemployment rate is twice as high as white. The average Negro does not acquire as much education as the average white. Negroes are less likely to hold prestigious white collar jobs in professional, managerial, clerical or sales work. They do not hold many skilled craft jobs in industry, but are concentrated in operative service and laboring positions. Negro women not only have more children but have them earlier, and too many children too early make it difficult for parents to finish school.

Daniel P. Moynihan has argued effectively that one of the worst effects of slavery and segregation has been the impact on Negro family life. (See Daniel P. Moynihan, *The Negro Family*) It was the Negro male who was most humiliated by segregation. The submissiveness which segregation implies is surely more destructive to the male than the female personality. Keeping the Negro "in his place" usually meant keeping the Negro *male* in his place; the female was not a threat to anyone. The female-headed Negro family emerges as one of the striking features of life in the ghetto. Almost 25 per cent of all Negro families are headed by women. For the male offspring of a matriarchal ghetto family, the future is often depressing, with defeat and frustration repeating itself throughout his life.

America's Negro ghettoes not only reflect economically-imposed *de facto* housing segregation but also a great deal of direct discrimination in the sale and renting of housing. Until recently a large proportion of housing in America carried racially restrictive covenants in deeds: "No part of the land hereby conveyed shall ever be used, or be occupied by or sold, demised, transferred, conveyed unto, or in trust for leased, rented, or given to Negroes, or to any other person or persons of Negro blood or extraction, or to any person of the Semitic race, blood, or origin which racial description shall be deemed to include Armenians, Jews, Hebrews, Persians, and Syrians." Not until 1948 was the judicial enforcement of such covenants held unconstitutional, and not until 1953 was enforcement by way of money damages held unlawful. Although racially restrictive convenants are no longer judicially enforceable, they are still used in that the pattern they helped to create still exists.

The separation of racial groups between cities and suburbs, and within cities, is enforced by the practices of the housing industry — builders, mortgage lenders, landlords and real estate brokers. While the housing industry contends that it is merely reflecting the preferences and financial resources of its customers, in 1958 the Commission on Race and Housing concluded that "it is real estate brokers, builders, and mortgage finance institutions which translate prejudice into discriminatory action." The Civil Rights Act of 1964 made no mention of discrimination in the sale or renting of housing, but after 1964 pressure mounted rapidly for a national fair housing law which would forbid discrimination in the sale or rental of private housing. Nicholas de B. Katzenbach, Attorney General of the United States, made a persuasive argument in testimony before

Congress on behalf of a national fair housing law. (See Nicholas de B. Katzenbach, *Testimony on Open Housing*) After the assassination of Dr. Martin Luther King in Memphis, Tennessee, in the spring of 1968, Congress enacted a National Fair Housing Law in the *Civil Rights Act of 1968*. The *Property Owners Bill of Rights* by the National Association of Real Estate Boards summarizes the opposition to fair housing legislation.

Civil Rights Act of 1964

Congress and the President

AN ACT

To enforce the constitutional right to vote, to confer jurisdiction upon the district courts of the United States to provide injunctive relief against discrimination in public accommodations, to authorize the Attorney General to institute suits to protect constitutional rights in public facilities and public education, to extend the Commission on Civil Rights, to prevent discrimination in federally assisted programs, to establish a Commission on Equal Employment Opportunity, and for other purposes.

Be it enacted by the Senate and House of Representatives of the United States of America in Congress assembled, That this Act may be cited as the "Civil Rights Act of 1964".

TITLE I — VOTING RIGHTS

Sec. 101. Section 2004 of the Revised Statutes (42 U.S.C. 1971), as amended by section 131 of the Civil Rights Act of 1957 (71 Stat. 637), and as further amended by section 601 of the Civil Rights Act of 1960 (74 Stat. 90), is further amended as follows:

No person acting under color of law shall —

"(A) in determining whether any individual is qualified under State law or laws to vote in any Federal election, apply any standard, practice, or procedure different from the standards, practices, or procedures applied under such law or laws to other individuals within the same county, parish, or similar political subdivision who have been found by State officials to be qualified to vote;

"(B) deny the right of any individual to vote in any Federal election because of an error or omission on any record or paper relating to any application, registration, or other act requisite to voting, if such error or omission is not material in determining whether such individual is qualified under State law to vote in such election; or

"(C) employ any literacy test as a qualification for voting in any Federal election unless (i) such test is administered to each individual and is conducted wholly in writing, and (ii) a certified copy of the test and of the answers given by the individual is furnished to him within twenty-five days of the submission of his request made within the period of time during which records and papers are required to be retained and preserved pursuant to title III of the Civil Rights Act of 1960 (42 U.S.C. 1974-74e; 74 Stat. 88): *Provided, however,* That the Attorney General may enter into agreements with appropriate State or local authorities that preparation, conduct, and maintenance of such tests in accordance with the provisions of applicable State or local law, including such special provisions as are necessary in the preparation, conduct, and maintenance of such tests for persons who are blind or otherwise physically handicapped, meet the purposes of this subparagraph and constitute compliance therewith.

For purposes of this subsection — "If in any such proceeding literacy is a relevant fact there shall be a rebuttable presumption that any person who has not been adjudged an incompetent and who has completed the sixth grade in a public school in, or a private school accredited by, any State or territory, the District of Columbia, or the Commonwealth of Puerto Rico where instruction is carried on predominantly in the English language, possesses sufficient literacy, comprehension, and intelligence to vote in any Federal election."

. . .

"(f) When used in subsection (a) or (c) of this section, the words 'Federal election' shall mean any general, special, or primary election held solely or in part for the purpose of electing or selecting any candidate for the office of President, Vice President, presidential elector, Member of the Senate, or Member of the House of Representatives."

TITLE II — INJUNCTIVE RELIEF AGAINST DISCRIMINATION IN PLACES OF PUBLIC ACCOMMODATION

Sec. 201. (a) All persons shall be entitled to the full and equal enjoyment of the goods, services, facilities, privileges, advantages, and accommodations of any place of public accommodation, as defined in this section, without discrimination or segregation on the ground of race, color, religion, or national origin.

(b) Each of the following establishments which serves the public is a place of public accommodation within the meaning of this title if its operations affect commerce, or if discrimination or segregation by it is supported by State action:

(1) any inn, hotel, motel, or other establishment which provides lodging to transient guests, other than an establishment located within a building which contains not more than five rooms for rent or hire and which is actually occupied by the proprietor of such establishment as his residence;

(2) any restaurant, cafeteria, lunchroom, lunch counter, soda fountain, or other facility principally engaged in selling food for consumption on the premises, including, but not limited to, any such facility located on the premises of any retail establishment; or any gasoline station;

(3) any motion picture house, theater, concert hall, sports arena, stadium or other place of exhibition or entertainment; and

(4) any establishment (A) (i) which is physically located within the premises of any establishment otherwise covered by this subsection, or (ii) within the premises of which is physically located any such covered establishment, and (B) which holds itself out as serving patrons of such covered establishment.

(c) The operations of an establishment affect commerce within the meaning of this title if (1) it is one of the establishments described in paragraph (1) of subsection (b); (2) in the case of an establishment described in paragraph (2) of subsection (b), it serves or offers to serve interstate travelers or a substantial portion of the food which it serves, or gasoline or other products which it sells, has moved in commerce; (3) in the case of an establishment described in paragraph (3) of subsection (b), it customarily presents films, performances, athletic teams, exhibitions, or other sources of entertainment which move in commerce; and (4) in the case of an establishment described in paragraph (4) of subsection (b), it is physically located within the premises of, or there is physically located within its premises, an establishment the operations of which affect commerce within the meaning of this subsection. For purposes of this section, "commerce" means travel, trade, traffic, commerce, transportation, or communication among the several States, or between the District of Columbia and any State, or between any foreign country or any territory or possession and any State or the District of Columbia, or between points in the same State but through any other State or the District of Columbia or a foreign country.

(d) Discrimination or segregation by an establishment is supported by State action within the meaning of this title if such discrimination or segregation (1) is carried on under color of any law, statute, ordinance, or regulation; or (2) is carried on under color of any custom or usage required or enforced by officials of the State or political subdivision thereof; or (3) is required by action of the State or political subdivision thereof.

(e) The provisions of this title shall not apply to a private club or other establishment not in fact open to the public, except to the extent that the facilities of such establishment are made available to the customers or patrons of an establishment within the scope of subsection (b).

Sec. 202. All persons shall be entitled to be free, at any establishment or place, from discrimination or segregation of any kind on the ground of race, color, religion, or national origin, if such discrimination or segregation is or purports to be required by any law, statute, ordinance, regulation, rule, or order of a State or any agency or political subdivision thereof.

Sec. 203. No person shall (a) withhold, deny, or attempt to withhold or deny, or deprive or attempt to deprive any person of any right or privilege secured by section 201 or 202 or (b) intimidate, threaten, or coerce, or attempt to intimidate, threaten, or coerce any person with the purpose of interfering with any right or privilege secured by section 201 or 202, or (c) punish or attempt to punish any person for exercising or attempting to exercise any right or privilege secured by section 201 or 202.

Sec. 204. (a) Whenever any person has engaged or there are reasonable grounds to believe that any person is about to engage in any act or practice prohibited by section 203, a civil action for preventive relief, including an application for a permanent or temporary injunction, restraining order, or other order, may be instituted by the person aggrieved and, upon timely application, the court may, in its discretion, permit the Attorney General to intervene in such civil action if he certifies that the case is of general public importance. . . .

TITLE III—DESEGREGATION OF PUBLIC FACILITIES

Sec. 301. (a) Whenever the Attorney General receives a complaint in writing signed by an individual to the effect that he is being deprived of or threatened with the loss of his right to the equal protection of the laws, on account of his race, color, religion, or national origin, by being denied equal utilization of any public facility which is owned, operated, or managed by or on behalf of any State or subdivision thereof, other than a public school or public college as defined in section 401 of title IV hereof, and the Attorney General believes the complaint is meritorious and certifies that the signer or signers of such complaint are unable, in his judgment, to initiate and maintain appropriate legal proceedings for relief and that the institution of an action will materially further the orderly progress of desegregation in public facilities, the Attorney General is authorized to institute for or in the name of the United States a civil action in any appropriate district court of the United States against such parties and for such relief as may be appropriate, and such court shall have and shall exercise jurisdiction of proceedings instituted pursuant to this section. The Attorney General may implead as defendants such additional parties as are or become necessary to the grant of effective relief hereunder.

(b) The Attorney General may deem a person or persons unable to initiate and maintain appropriate legal proceedings within the meaning of subsection (a) of this section when such person or persons are unable, either directly or through other interested persons or organizations, to bear the expense of the litigation or to obtain effective legal representation; or whenever he is satisfied that the institution of such litigation would jeopardize the personal safety, employment, or economic standing of such person or persons, their families, or their property.

TITLE IV—DESEGREGATION OF PUBLIC EDUCATION

DEFINITIONS

Sec. 401. As used in this title—

(a) "Commissioner" means the Commissioner of Education.

(b) "Desegregation" means the assignment of students to public schools and within such schools without regard to their race, color, religion, or national origin, but "desegregation" shall not mean the assignment of students to public schools in order to overcome racial imbalance.

(c) "Public school" means any elementary or secondary educational institution, and "public college" means any institution or higher education or any technical or vocational school above the secondary school level, provided that such public school or public college is operated by a State, subdivision of a State, or governmental agency within a State, or operated wholly or predominantly from or through the use of governmental funds or property, or funds or property derived from a governmental source.

(d) "School board" means any agency or agencies which administer a system of one or more public schools and any other agency which is responsible for the assignment of students to or within such system. . . .

GRANTS

Sec. 405. (a) The Commissioner is authorized, upon application of a school board, to make grants to such board to pay, in whole or in part, the cost of—

> (1) giving to teachers and other school personnel inservice training in dealing with problems incident to desegregation, and
>
> (2) employing specialists to advise in problems incident to desegregation.

(b) In determining whether to make a grant, and in fixing the amount thereof and the terms and conditions on which it will be made, the Commissioner shall take into consideration the amount available for grants under this section and the other applications which are pending before him; the financial condition of the applicant and the other resources available to it; the nature, extent, and gravity of its problems incident to desegregation; and such other factors as he finds relevant. . . .

SUITS BY THE ATTORNEY GENERAL

Sec. 407. (a) Whenever the Attorney General receives a complaint in writing—

> (1) signed by a parent or group of parents to the effect that his or their minor children, as members of a class of persons similarly situated, are being deprived by a school board of the equal protection of the laws, or
>
> (2) signed by an individual, or his parent, to the effect that he has been denied admission to or not permitted to continue in attendance at a public college by reason of race, color, religion, or national origin,

and the Attorney General believes the complaint is meritorious and certifies that the signer or signers of such complaint are unable, in his judgment, to initiate and maintain appropriate legal proceedings for relief and that the institution of an action will materially further the orderly achievement of desegregation in public education, the Attorney General is authorized, after giving notice of such complaint to the appropriate school board or college authority and after certifying that he is satisfied that such board or authority has had a reasonable time to adjust the conditions alleged in such complaint, to institute for or in the name of the United States a civil action in any appropriate district court of the United States against such parties and for such relief as may be appropriate, and such court shall have and shall exercise jurisdiction of proceedings instituted pursuant to this section, provided that nothing herein shall empower any official or court of the United States to issue any order seeking to achieve a racial balance in any school by requiring the transportation of pupils or students from one school to another or one school district to another in order to achieve such racial balance, or otherwise enlarge the existing power of the court to insure compliance with constitutional standards. The Attorney General may implead as defendants such additional parties as are or become necessary to the grant of effective relief hereunder.

TITLE V—COMMISSION ON CIVIL RIGHTS

DUTIES OF THE COMMISSION

"Sec. 104. (a) The Commission shall—

"(1) investigate allegations in writing under oath or affirmation that certain citizens of the United States are being deprived of their right to vote and have that vote counted by reason of their color, race, religion, or national origin; which writing, under oath or affirmation, shall set forth the facts upon which such belief or beliefs are based;

"(2) study and collect information concerning legal developments constituting a denial of equal protection of the laws under the Constitution because of race, color, religion or national origin or in the administration of justice;

"(3) appraise the laws and policies of the Federal Government with respect to denials of equal protection of the laws under the Constitution because of race, color, religion or national origin or in the administration of justice;

"(4) serve as a national clearinghouse for information in respect to denials of equal protection of the laws because of race, color, religion or national origin, including but not limited to the fields of voting, education, housing, employment, the use of public facilities, and transportation, or in the administration of justice;

"(5) investigate allegations, made in writing and under oath or affirmation, that citizens of the United States are unlawfully being accorded or denied the right to vote, or to have their votes properly counted, in any election of presidential electors, Members of the United States Senate, or of the House of Representatives, as a result of any patterns or practice of fraud or discrimination in the conduct of such election; and

"(6) Nothing in this or any other Act shall be construed as authorizing the Commission, its Advisory Committees, or any person under its supervision or control to inquire into or investigate any membership practices or internal operations of any fraternal organization, any college or university fraternity or sorority, any private club or any religious organization."

TITLE VI—NONDISCRIMINATION IN FEDERALLY ASSISTED PROGRAMS

Sec. 601. No person in the United States shall, on the ground of race, color, or national origin, be excluded from participation in, be denied the benefits of, or be subjected to discrimination under any program or activity receiving Federal financial assistance.

Sec. 602. Each Federal department and agency which is empowered to extend Federal financial assistance to any program or activity, by way of grant, loan, or contract other than a contract of insurance or guaranty, is authorized and directed to effectuate the provisions of section 601 with respect to such program or activity by issuing rules, regulations, or orders of general applicability which shall be consistent with achievement of the objectives of the statute authorizing the financial assistance in connection with which the action is taken. No such rule, regulation, or order shall become effective unless and until approved by the President. Compliance with any requirement adopted pursuant to this section may be effected (1) by the termination of or refusal to grant or to continue assistance under such program or activity to any recipient as to whom there has been an express finding on the record, after opportunity for hearing, of a failure to comply with such requirement, but such termination or refusal shall be limited to the particular political entity, or part thereof, or other recipient as to whom such a finding has been made and, shall be limited in its effect to the particular program, or part thereof, in which such non-compliance has been so found, or (2) by any other means authorized by law: *Provided, however,* That no such action shall be taken until the department or agency concerned has advised the appropriate person or persons of the failure to comply with the requirement and has determined that compliance cannot be secured by voluntary means. In the case of any action terminating, or refusing to grant or continue, assistance because of failure to comply with a requirement imposed pursuant to this section, the head of the Federal department or agency shall file with the committees of the House and Senate having legislative jurisdiction over the program or activity involved a full written report of the circumstances and the grounds of such action. No such action shall become effective until thirty days have elapsed after the filing of such report. . . .

TITLE VII—EQUAL EMPLOYMENT OPPORTUNITY

DEFINITIONS

Sec. 701. For the purposes of this title—

(a) The term "person" includes one or more individuals, labor unions, partnerships, associations, corporations, legal representatives, mutual companies, joint-stock companies, trusts, unincorporated organizations, trustees, trustees in bankruptcy, or receivers.

(b) The term "employer" means a person engaged in an industry affecting commerce who has twenty-five or more employees for each working day in each of twenty or more calendar weeks in the current or preceding calendar year, and any agent of such a person, but such term does not include (1) the United States, a corporation wholly owned by the Government of the United States, an Indian tribe, or a State or political subdivision thereof, (2) a bona fide private membership club (other than a labor organization) which is exempt from taxation under section 501 (c) of the Internal Revenue Code of 1954: *Provided,* That during the first year after the effective date prescribed in subsection (a) of section 716, persons having fewer than one hundred employees (and their agents) shall not be considered employers, and, during the second year after such date, persons having fewer than seventy-five employees (and their agents) shall not be considered employers, and during the third year after such date, persons having fewer than fifty employees (and their agents) shall not be considered employers: *Provided further,* That it shall be the policy of the United States to insure equal employment opportunities for Federal employees without discrimination because of race, color, religion, sex or national origin and the President shall utilize his existing authority to effectuate this policy.

DISCRIMINATION BECAUSE OF RACE, COLOR, RELIGION, SEX, OR NATIONAL ORIGIN

Sec. 703. (a) It shall be an unlawful employment practice for an employer—

(1) to fail or refuse to hire or to discharge any individual, or otherwise to discriminate against any individual with respect to his compensation, terms, conditions; or privileges of employment, because of such individual's race, color, religion, sex, or national origin; or

(2) to limit, segregate, or classify his employees in any way which would deprive or tend to deprive any individual of employment opportunities or otherwise adversely affect his status as an employee, because of such individual's race, color, religion, sex, or national origin.

(b) It shall be an unlawful employment practice for an employment agency to fail or refuse to refer for employment, or otherwise to discriminate against, any individual because of his race, color, religion, sex, or national origin, or to classify or refer for employment any individual on the basis of his race, color, religion, sex, or national origin

(c) It shall be an unlawful employment practice for a labor organization—

(1) to exclude or to expel from its membership, or otherwise to discriminate against, any individual because of his race, color, religion, sex, or national origin;

(2) to limit, segregate, or classify its membership, or to classify or fail or refuse to refer for employment any individual, in any way which would deprive or tend to deprive any individual of employment opportunities, or would limit such employment opportunities or otherwise adversely affect his status as an employee or as an applicant for employment, because of such individual's race, color, religion, sex, or national origin; or

(3) to cause or attempt to cause an employer to discriminate against an individual in violation of this section.

(d) It shall be an unlawful employment practice for any employer, labor organization, or joint labor-management committee controlling apprenticeship or other training or retraining, including on-the-job training programs to discriminate against any individual because of his race, color, religion, sex, or national origin in admission to, or employment in, any program established to provide apprenticeship or other training.

(e) Notwithstanding any other provision of this title, (1) it shall not be an unlawful employment practice for an employer to hire and employ employees, for an employment agency to classify, or refer for employment any individual, for a labor organization to classify its membership or to classify or refer for employment any individual, or for an employer, labor organization, or joint labor-management committee controlling apprenticeship or other training or retraining programs to admit or employ any individual in any such program, on the basis of his religion, sex, or national origin in those certain instances where religion, sex or national origin is a bona fide occupational qualification reasonably necessary to the normal operation of that particular business or enterprise, and (2) it shall not be an unlawful employment practice for a school, college, university, or other educational institution or institution of learning to hire and employ employees of a particular religion if such school, college, university, or other educational institution or institution of learning is, in whole or in substantial part, owned, supported, controlled, or managed by a particular religion or by a particular religious corporation, association, or society, or if the curriculum of such school, college, university, or other educational institution or institution of learning is directed toward the propagation of a particular religion . . . .

(j) Nothing contained in this title shall be interpreted to require any employer, employment agency, labor organization, or joint labor-management committee subject to this title to grant preferential treatment to any individual or to any group because of the race, color, religion, sex, or national origin of such individual or group on account of an imbalance which may exist with respect to the total number or percentage of persons of any race, color, religion, sex, or national origin employed by any employer, referred or classified for employment by any employment agency or labor organization, admitted to membership or classified by any labor organization, or admitted to, or employed in, any apprenticeship or other training program, in comparison with the total number or percentage of persons of such race, color, religion, sex, or national origin in any community, State, section, or other area, or in the available work force in any community, State, section, or other area . . . .

EQUAL EMPLOYMENT OPPORTUNITY COMMISSION

Sec. 705. (a) There is hereby created a Commission to be known as the Equal Employment Opportunity Commission, which shall be composed of five members, not more than three of whom shall be members of the same political party, who shall be appointed by the President by and with the advice and consent of the Senate . . . .

(g) The Commission shall have power—

(1) to cooperate with and, with consent, utilize regional, State, local, and other agencies, both public and private, and individuals;

(2) to pay to witnesses whose depositions are taken or who are summoned before the Commission or any of its agents the same witness and mileage fees as are paid to witnesses in the courts of the United States;

(3) to furnish to persons subject to this title such technical assistance as they may request to further their compliance with this title or an order issued thereunder;

(4) upon the request of (i) any employer, whose employees or some of them, or (ii) any labor organization, whose members or some of them, refuse or threaten to refuse to cooperate in effectuating the provisions of this title, to assist in such effectuation by conciliation or such other remedial action as is provided by this title;

(5) to make such technical studies as are appropriate to effectuate the purposes and policies of this title and to make the results of such studies available to the public;

(6) to refer matters to the Attorney General with recommendations for intervention in a civil action brought by an aggrieved party under section 706, or for the institution of a civil action by the Attorney General under section 707, and to advise, consult, and assist the Attorney General on such matters.

PREVENTION OF UNLAWFUL EMPLOYMENT PRACTICES

Sec. 706. (a) Whenever it is charged in writing under oath by a person claiming to be aggrieved, or a written charge has been filed by a member of the Commission where he has reasonable cause to believe a violation of this title has occurred (and such charge sets forth the facts upon which it is based) that an employer, employment agency, or labor organization has engaged in an unlawful employment practice, the Commission shall furnish such employer, employment agency, or labor organization (hereinafter referred to as the "respondent") with a copy of such charge and shall make an investigation of such charge, provided that such charge shall not be made public by the Commission. If the Commission shall determine, after such investigation, that there is reasonable cause to believe that the charge is true, the Commission shall endeavor to eliminate any such alleged unlawful employment practice by informal methods of conference, conciliation, and persuasion. . . .

(e) If within thirty days after a charge is filed with the Commission or within thirty days after expiration of any period of reference under subsection (c) (except that in either case such period may be extended to not more than sixty days upon a determination by the Commission that further efforts to secure voluntary compliance are warranted), the Commission has been unable to obtain voluntary compliance with this title, the Commission shall so notify the person aggrieved and a civil action may, within thirty days thereafter, be brought against the respondent named in the charge (1) by the person claiming to be aggrieved, or (2) if such charge was filed by a member of the Commission, by any person whom the charge alleges was aggrieved by the alleged unlawful employment practice. . . .

(g) If the court finds that the respondent has intentionally engaged in or is intentionally engaging in an unlawful employment practice charged in the complaint, the court may enjoin the respondent from engaging in such unlawful employment practice, and order such affirmative action as may be appropriate, which may include reinstatement or hiring of employees, with or without back pay (payable by the employer, employment agency, or labor organization, as the case may be, responsible for the unlawful employment practice).

Heart of Atlanta Motel v. United States*

United States Supreme Court

Mr. Justice Clark delivered the opinion of the Court in the Heart of Atlanta Motel case, saying in part:

This is a declaratory judgment action attacking the constitutionality of Title II of the Civil Rights Act of 1964. . . . Appellees counterclaimed for enforcement under § 206 (a) of the Act and asked for a three-judge district court under § 206 (b). A three-judge court . . . sustained the validity of the Act and issued a permanent injunction on appellees' counterclaim restraining appellant from continuing to violate the Act. . . . We affirm the judgment.

1. The Factual Background and Contentions of the Parties

The case comes here on admissions and stipulated facts. Appellant owns and operates the Heart of Atlanta Motel which has 216 rooms available to transient guests. The motel is located on Courtland Street two blocks from downtown Peachtree Street. It is readily accessible to interstate highways 75 and 85 and state highways 23 and 41. Appellant solicits patronage from outside the State of Georgia through various national advertising media, including magazines of national circulation; it maintains over 50 billboards and highway signs within the State, soliciting patronage for the motel; it accepts convention trade from outside Georgia and approximately 75% of its registered guests are from out of State. Prior to passage of the Act the motel had followed a practice of

*379 U.S. 241 (1964).

refusing to rent rooms to Negroes, and it alleged that it intended to continue to do so. In an effort to perpetuate that policy this suit was filed.

The appellant contends that Congress in passing this Act exceeded its power to regulate commerce under Art I, §, cl 3, of the Constitution of the United States; that the Act violates the Fifth Amendment because appellant is deprived of the right to choose its customers and operate its business as it wishes, resulting in a taking of its liberty and property without due process of law and a taking of its property without just compensation; and finally, that by requiring appellant to rent available rooms to Negroes against its will, Congress is subjecting it to involuntary servitude in contravention of the Thirteenth Amendment. . . .

2. The History of the Act

[The Court notes the passage by Congress of earlier civil rights acts, and reviews briefly the struggle to enact the present statute.]

The Act as finally adopted was most comprehensive, undertaking to prevent through peaceful and voluntary settlement discrimination in voting, as well as in places of accommodation and public facilities, federally secured programs and employment. Since Title II is the only portion under attack here, we confine our consideration to those public accommodation provisions.

3. Title II of the Act

This Title is divided into seven sections beginning with § 201 (a) which provides that:

"All persons shall be entitled to the full and equal enjoyment of the goods, services, facilities, privileges, advantages, and accommodations of any place of public accommodation, as defined in this section, without discrimination or segregation on the ground of race, color, religion, or national origin."

There are listed in § 201 (b) four classes of business establishments, each of which "serves the public" and "is a place of public accommodation" within the meaning of § 201 (a) "if its operations affect commerce, or if discrimination or segregation by it is supported by State action." The covered establishments are:

"(1) any inn, hotel, motel, or other establishment which provides lodging to transient guests, other than an establishment located within a building which contains not more than five rooms for rent or hire and which is actually occupied by the proprietor of such establishment as his residence; (2) any restaurant, cafeteria . . . [not here involved]; (3)

any motion picture house . . . [not here involved]; (4) any establishment . . . which is physically located within the premises of any establishment otherwise covered by this subsection, or . . . within the premises of which is physically located any such covered establishment . . . [not here involved]."

Section 201 (c) defines the phrase "affect commerce" as applied to the above establishments. It first declares that "any inn, hotel, motel, or other establishment which provides lodging to transient guests" affects commerce per se. . . .

Finally, § 203 prohibits the withholding or denial, etc., of any right or privilege secured by § 201 . . . or the intimidation, threatening or coercion of any person with the purpose of interfering with any such right or the punishing, etc., of any person for exercising or attempting to exercise any such right.

The remaining sections of the Title are remedial ones for violations of any of the previous sections. Remedies are limited to civil actions for preventive relief. The Attorney General may bring suit where he has "reasonable cause to believe that any person or group of persons is engaged in a pattern or practice of resistance to the full enjoyment of any of the rights secured by this title, and that the pattern or practice is of such a nature and is intended to deny the full exercise of the rights herein described. . . ."

4. Application of Title II to Heart of Atlanta Motel

It is admitted that the operation of the motel brings it within the provisions of § 201 (a) of the Act and that appellant refused to provide lodging for transient Negroes because of their race or color and that it intends to continue that policy unless restrained.

The sole question posed is, therefore, the constitutionality of the Civil Rights Act of 1964 as applied to these facts. The legislative history of the Act indicates that Congress based the Act on § 5 and the Equal Protection Clause of the Fourteenth Amendment as well as its power to regulate interstate commerce under Art I, § 8, cl 3 of the Constitution.

The Senate Commerce Committee made it quite clear that the fundamental object of Title II was to vindicate "the deprivation of personal dignity that surely accompanies denials of equal access to public establishments." At the same time, however, it noted that such an objective has been and could be readily achieved "by congressional action based on the commerce power of the Constitution." . . . Our study of the legislative record, made in the light of prior cases, has brought us to the conclusion that Congress possessed ample power in this regard, and we have therefore not considered the other grounds relied upon. This is not to say that the remaining authority upon which it acted was not adequate, a question upon which we do not pass, but merely that since the commerce power is sufficient for our decision here we have considered it alone. . . .

5. The Civil Rights Cases, 109 U.S. 3 (1883), and their Application

In light of our ground for decision, it might be well at the outset to discuss the Civil Rights Cases, supra, which declared provisions of the Civil Rights Act of 1875 unconstitutional. We think that decision inapposite, and without precedential value in determining the constitutionality of the present Act. Unlike Title II of the present legislation, the 1875 Act broadly proscribed discrimination in "inns, public conveyances on land or water, theaters, and other public places of amusement," without limiting the categories of affected businesses to those impinging upon interstate commerce. In contrast, the applicability of Title II is carefully limited to enterprises having a direct and substantial relation to the interstate flow of goods and people, except where state action is involved. Further, the fact that certain kinds of businesses may not in 1875 have been sufficiently involved in interstate commerce to warrant bringing them within the ambit of the commerce power is not necessarily dispositive of the same question today. Our populace had not reached its present mobility, nor were facilities, goods and services circulating as readily in interstate commerce as they are today. Although the principles which we apply today are those first formulated by Chief Justice Marshall in Gibbons v. Ogden, the conditions of transportation and commerce have changed dramatically, and we must apply those principles to the present state of commerce. The sheer increase in volume of interstate traffic alone would give discriminatory practices which inhibit travel a far larger impact upon the Nation's commerce than such practices had in the economy of another day. . . .

6. The Basis of Congressional Action

While the Act as adopted carried no congressional findings the record of its passage through each house is replete with evidence of the burdens that discrimination by race or color places upon interstate commerce. . . . This testimony included the fact that our people have become increasingly mobile with millions of people of all races traveling from State to

State; that Negroes in particular have been the subject of discrimination in transient accommodations, having to travel great distances to secure the same; that often they have been unable to obtain accommodations and have had to call upon friends to put them up overnight . . . ; and that these conditions have become so acute as to require the listing of available lodging for Negroes in a special guidebook which was itself "dramatic testimony to the difficulties" Negroes encounter in travel. . . . These exclusionary practices were found to be nationwide, the Under Secretary of Commerce testifying that there is "no question that this discrimination in the North still exists to a large degree" and in the West and Midwest as well. . . . This testimony indicated a qualitative as well as quantitive effect on interstate travel by Negroes. The former was the obvious impairment of the Negro traveler's pleasure and convenience that resulted when he continually was uncertain of finding lodging. As for the latter, there was evidence that this uncertainty stemming from racial discrimination had the effect of discouraging travel on the part of a substantial portion of the Negro community. . . . This was the conclusion not only of the Under Secretary of Commerce but also of the Administrator of the Federal Aviation Agency who wrote the Chairman of the Senate Commerce Committee that it was his "belief that air commerce is adversely affected by the denial to a substantial segment of the traveling public of adequate and desegregated public accommodations." . . . We shall not burden this opinion with further details since the voluminous testimony presents overwhelming evidence that discrimination by hotels and motels impedes interstate travel.

7. The Power of Congress Over Interstate Travel

The power of Congress to deal with these obstructions depends on the meaning of the Commerce Clause. Its meaning was first enunciated 140 years ago by the great Chief Justice John Marshall in Gibbons v. Ogden, in these words:

[The Court here quotes at length from the opinion concerning the nature of interstate commerce and congressional power over it.]

In short, the determinative test of the exercise of power by the Congress under the Commerce Clause is simply whether the activity sought to be regulated is "commerce which concerns more States than one" and has a real and substantial relation to the national interest. Let us now turn to this facet of the problem.

That the "intercourse" of which the Chief Justice spoke included the movement of persons through more States than one was settled as early as 1849, in the Passenger Cases, 7 How. 283, where Mr. Justice McLean stated: "That the transportation of passengers is a part of commerce is not now an open question." Again in 1913 Mr. Justice McKenna, speaking for the Court, said: "Commerce among the States, we have said, consists of intercourse and traffic between their citizens, and includes the transportation of persons and property." Hoke v. United States, 227 U. S. 308. And only four years later in 1917 in Caminetti v. United States, 242 U. S. 470, Mr. Justice Day held for the Court:

"The transportation of passengers in interstate commerce, it has long been settled, is within the regulatory power of Congress, under the commerce clause of the Constitution, and the authority of Congress to keep the channels of interstate commerce free from immoral and injurious uses has been frequently sustained, and is no longer open to question."

Nor does it make any difference whether the transportation is commercial in character. In Morgan v. Virginia, 328 U. S. 373 (1946), Mr. Justice Reed observed as to the modern movement of persons among the States:

"The recent changes in transportation brought about by the coming of automobiles [do] not seem of great significance in the problem. People of all races travel today more extensively than in 1878 when this Court first passed upon state regulation of racial segregation in commerce. [It but] emphasizes the soundness of this Court's early conclusion in Hall v. DeCuir, 95 U. S. 485."

The same interest in protecting interstate commerce which led Congress to deal with segregation in interstate carriers and the white slave traffic has prompted it to extend the exercise of its power to gambling . . . ; to criminal enterprises . . . ; to deceptive practices in the sale of products . . . ; to fraudulent security transactions . . . ; to misbranding of drugs . . . ; to wages and hours . . . ; to members of labor unions . . . ; to crop control . . . ; to discrimination against shippers . . . ; to the protection of small business from injurious price cutting . . . ; to resale price maintenance . . . ; to professional football . . . ; and to racial discrimination by owners and managers of terminal restaurants. . . .

That Congress was legislating against moral wrongs in many of these areas rendered its enactments no less valid. In framing Title II of this Act Congress was also dealing with what it considered a moral problem. But that fact does not detract from the overwhelming evidence of the disruptive effect that racial discrimination has had on commercial intercourse. It was this burden which empowered Congress to enact appropriate legislation, and, given this basis for the exercise of its power, Congress was not restricted by the fact that the particular obstruction to interstate commerce with which it was dealing was also deemed a moral and social wrong.

It is said that the operation of the motel here is of a purely local character. But, assuming this to be true, "[i]f it is interstate commerce that feels the pinch, it does not matter how local the operation which applies the squeeze." . . . As Chief Justice Stone put it in United States v. Darby [312 U. S. 100 (1941)]:

"The power of Congress over interstate commerce is not confined to the regulation of commerce among the states. It extends to those activities intrastate which so affect interstate commerce or the exercise of the power of Congress over it as to make regulation of them appropriate means to the attainment of a legitimate end, the exercise of the granted power of Congress to regulate interstate commerce. . . ."

Thus the power of Congress to promote interstate commerce also includes the power to regulate the local incidents thereof, including local activities in both the States of origin and destination, which might have a substantial and harmful effect upon that commerce. One need only examine the evidence which we have discussed above to see that Congress may—as it has—prohibit racial discrimination by motels serving travelers, however "local" their operations may appear.

Nor does the Act deprive appellant of liberty or property under the Fifth Amendment. The commerce power invoked here by the Congress is a specific and plenary one authorized by the Constitution itself. The only questions are: (1) whether Congress had a rational basis for finding that racial discrimination by motels affected commerce, and (2) if it had such a basis, whether the means it selected to eliminate that evil are reasonable and appropriate. If they are, appellant has no "right" to select its guests as it sees fit, free from governmental regulation.

There is nothing novel about such legislation. Thirty-two States now have it on their books either by statute or executive order and many cities provide such regulation. Some of these Acts go back four-score years. It has been repeatedly held by this Court that such laws do not violate the Due Process Clause of the Fourteenth Amendment.

. . . As a result the constitutionality of such state statutes stands unquestioned. "The authority of the Federal Government over interstate commerce does not differ . . . in extent or character from that retained by the states over intrastate commerce." . . .

It is doubtful if in the long run appellant will suffer economic loss as a result of the Act. Experience is to the contrary where discrimination is completely obliterated as to all public accommodations. But whether this be true or not is of no consequence since this Court has specifically held that the fact that a "member of the class which is regulated may suffer economic losses not shared by others . . . has never been a barrier" to such legislation. . . . Likewise in a long line of cases this Court has rejected the claim that the prohibition of racial discrimination in public accommodations interferes with personal liberty. . . .

We find no merit in the remainder of appellant's contentions, including that of "involuntary servitude." . . .

We, therefore, conclude that the action of the Congress in the adoption of the Act as applied here to a motel which concededly serves interstate travelers is within the power granted it by the Commerce Clause of the Constitution, as interpreted by this Court for 140 years. It may be argued that Congress could have pursued other methods to eliminate the obstructions it found in interstate commerce caused by racial discrimination. But this is a matter of policy that rests entirely with the Congress not with the courts. How obstructions in commerce may be removed — what means are to be employed — is within the sound and exclusive discretion of the Congress. It is subject only to one caveat— that the means chosen by it must be reasonably adapted to the end permitted by the Constitution. We cannot say that its choice here was not so adapted. The Constitution requires no more.

Affirmed.

Mr. Justice Black, concurring, said in part:

Long ago this Court, again speaking through Mr. Chief Justice Marshall, said:

"Let the end be legitimate, let it be within the scope of the constitution, and all means which are appropriate, which are plainly adapted to that end, which are not prohibited, but consist with the letter and spirit of the constitution, are constitutional." M'Culloch v. Maryland.

By this standard Congress acted within its power here. In view of the Commerce Clause it is not possible to deny that the aim of protecting interstate commerce from undue burdens is a legitimate end. In view of the Thirteenth, Fourteenth and Fifteenth Amendments, it is not possible to deny that the aim of protecting Negroes from discrimination is also a legitimate end. The means adopted to achieve these ends are also appropriate, plainly adopted to achieve them and not prohibited by the Constitution but consistent with both its letter and spirit.

Mr. Justice Douglas, concurring, said in part:

Though I join the Court's opinion, I am somewhat reluctant here, as I was in Edwards v. California, 314 U. S. 160, to rest solely on the Commerce Clause. My reluctance is not due to any conviction that Congress lacks power to regulate commerce in the interests of human rights. It is rather my belief that the right of people to be free of state action that discriminates against them because of race, like the "right of persons to move freely from State to State" . . . "occupies a more protected position in our constitutional system than does the movement of cattle, fruit, steel and coal across state lines." Moreover, when we come to the problem of abatement in Hamm v. City of Rock Hill, 379 U. S. 306, the result reached by the Court is for me much more obvious as a protective measure under the Fourteenth Amendment than under the Commerce Clause. For the former deals with the constitutional status of the individual not with the impact on commerce of local activities or vice versa.

Hence I would prefer to rest on the assertion of legislative power contained in § 5 of the Fourteenth Amendment which states: "The Congress shall have power to enforce, by appropriate legislation, the provisions of this article"—a power which the Court concedes was exercised at least in part in this Act.

A decision based on the Fourteenth Amendment would have a more settling effect, making unnecessary litigation over whether a particular restaurant or inn is within the commerce definitions of the Act or whether a particular customer is an interstate traveler. Under my construction, the Act would apply to all customers in all the enumerated places of public accommodation. And that construction would put an end to all obstructionist strategies and finally close one door on a bitter chapter in American history.

Mr. Justice Goldberg, concurring, said in part:

I join in the opinions and judgements of the Court, since I agree "that the action of the Congress in the adoption of the Act as applied here . . . is within the power granted it by the Commerce Clause of the Constitution, as interpreted by this Court for 140 years. . . ."

In my concurring opinion in Bell v. Maryland, 378 U. S. 226, . . . I expressed my conviction that § 1 of the Fourteenth Amendment guarantees to all Americans the constitutional right "to be treated as equal members of the community with respect to public accommodations," and that "Congress [has] authority under § 5 of the Fourteenth Amendment, or under the Commerce Clause, Art I, § 8, to implement the rights protected by § 1 of the Fourteenth Amendment. In the give-and-take of the legislative process, Congress can fashion a law drawing the guidelines necessary and appropriate to facilitate practical administration and to distinguish between genuinely public and private accommodations." The challenged Act is just such a law and, in my view, Congress clearly had authority under both § 5 of the Fourteenth Amendment and the Commerce Clause to enact the Civil Rights Act of 1964.

Katzenbach v. McClung*

United States Supreme Court

Mr. Justice Clark delivered the opinion of the Court in the McClung case, saying in part:

This case was argued with Heart of Atlanta Motel v. United States in which we upheld the constitutional validity of Title II of the Civil Rights Act of 1964 against an attack by hotels, motels, and like establishments. This complaint for injunctive relief against appellants attacks the constitutionality of the Act as applied to a restaurant. . . .

2. The Facts

Ollie's Barbecue is a family-owned restaurant in Birmingham, Alabama, specializing in barbecued meats and homemade pies, with a seating capacity of 220 customers. It is located on a state highway 11 blocks from an interstate one and a somewhat greater distance from railroad and bus stations. The restaurant caters to a family and white-collar trade with a take-out service for Negroes. It employs 36 persons, two-thirds of whom are Negroes.

In the 12 months preceding the passage of the Act, the restaurant purchased locally approximately $150,000 worth of food, $69,683 or 46% of which was meat that it bought from a local supplier who had procured it from outside the State. The District Court expressly found that a substantial portion of the food served in the restaurant had moved in interstate commerce. The restaurant has refused to serve

---

*379 U.S. 294 (1964).

Negroes in its dining accommodations since its original opening in 1927, and since July 2, 1964, it has been operating in violation of the Act. The court below concluded that if it were required to serve Negroes it would lose a substantial amount of business.

On the merits, the District Court held that the Act could not be applied under the Fourteenth Amendment because it was conceded that the State of Alabama was not involved in the refusal of the restaurant to serve Negroes. . . . As to the Commerce Clause, the court found . . . that the clause was . . . a grant of power "to regulate intrastate activities, but only to the extent that action on its part is necessary or appropriate to the effective execution of its expressly granted power to regulate interstate commerce." There must be, it said, a close and substantial relation between local activities and interstate commerce which requires control of the former in the protection of the latter. The court concluded, however, that the Congress, rather than finding facts sufficient to meet this rule, had legislated a conclusive presumption that a restaurant affects interstate commerce if it serves or offers to serve interstate travelers or if a substantial portion of the food which it serves has moved in commerce. This, the court held, it could not do because there was no demonstrable connection between food purchased in interstate commerce and sold in a restaurant and the conclusion of Congress that discrimination in the restaurant would affect that commerce. . . .

3. The Act As Applied

Section 201 (a) of Title II commands that all persons shall be entitled to the full and equal enjoyment of the goods and services of any place of public accommodation without discrimination or segregation on the ground of race, color, religion, or national origin; and § 201 (b) defines establishments as places of public accommodation if their operations affect commerce or segregation by them as supported by state action. Sections 201 (b) (2) and (c) place any "restaurant . . . principally engaged in selling food for consumption on the premises" under the Act "if . . . it serves or offers to serve interstate travelers or a substantial portion of the food which it serves . . . has moved in commerce."

Ollie's Barbecue admits that it is covered by these provisions of the Act. The Government makes no contention that the discrimination at the restaurant was supported by the State of Alabama. There is no claim that interstate travelers frequented the restaurant. The sole question, therefore, narrows down to whether Title II, as applied to a restaurant annually receiving about $70,000 worth of food which has moved in commerce, is a valid exercise of the power of Congress. The Government has contended that Congress had ample basis upon which to find that racial discrimination at restaurants which receive from out of state a substantial portion of the food served does, in fact, impose commercial burdens of national magnitude upon interstate commerce. The appellees' major argument is directed to this premise. They urge that no such basis existed. It is to that question that we now turn.

4. The Congressional Hearings

As we noted in Heart of Atlanta Motel both houses of Congress conducted prolonged hearings on the Act. And, as we said there, while no formal findings were made, which of course are not necessary, it is well that we make mention of the testimony at these hearings the better to understand the problem before Congress and determine whether the Act is a reasonable and appropriate means toward its solution. The record is replete with testimony of the burdens placed on interstate commerce by racial discrimination in restaurants. A comparison of per capita spending by Negroes in restaurants, theaters, and like establishments indicated less spending, after discounting income differences, in areas where discrimination is widely practiced. This condition, which was especially aggravated in the South, was attributed in the testimony of the Under Secretary of Commerce to racial segregation. . . . This diminutive spending springing from a refusal to serve Negroes and their total loss as customers has, regardless of the absence of direct evidence, a close connection to interstate commerce. The fewer customers a restaurant enjoys the less food it sells and consequently the less it buys. . . . In addition, the Attorney General testified that this type of discrimination imposed "an artificial restriction on the market" and interfered with the flow of merchandise. . . . In addition, there were many references to discriminatory situations causing wide unrest and having a depressant effect on general business conditions in the respective communities. . . .

Moreover there was an impressive array of testimony that discrimination in restaurants had a direct and highly restrictive effect upon interstate travel by Negroes. This resulted, it was said, because discriminatory practices prevent Negroes from buying prepared food served on the premises while on a trip, except in isolated and unkempt restaurants and under most unsatisfactory and often unpleasant conditions. This obviously discourages travel and obstructs interstate commerce for one can hardly travel without eating. Likewise, it was said, that discrimination deterred professional, as well as skilled, people from moving into areas where such practices occurred and thereby caused industry to be reluctant to establish there. . . .

We believe that this testimony afforded ample basis for the conclusion that established restaurants in such areas sold less interstate goods because of the discrimination, that interstate travel was obstructed directly by it, that business in general suffered and that many new businesses refrained from establishing there as a result of it. Hence the District Court was in error in concluding that there was no connection between discrimination and the movement of interstate commerce. The court's conclusion that such a connection is outside "common experience" flies in the face of stubborn fact.

It goes without saying that, viewed in isolation, the volume of food purchased by Ollie's Barbecue from sources supplied from out of state was insignificant when compared with the total foodstuffs moving in commerce. But, as our late Brother Jackson said for the Court in Wickard v. Filburn, 317 U. S. 111 (1942):

"That appellee's own contribution to the demand for wheat may be trivial by itself is not enough to remove him from the scope of federal regulation where, as here, his contribution, taken together with that of many others similarly situated, is far from trivial."

We noted in Heart of Atlanta Motel that a number of witnesses attested the fact that racial discrimination was not merely a state or regional problem but was one of nationwide scope. Against this background, we must conclude that while the focus of the legislation was on the individual restaurant's relation to interstate commerce, Congress appropriately considered the importance of that connection with the knowledge that the discrimination was but "representative of many others throughout the country, the total incidence of which if left unchecked may well become far-reaching in its harm to commerce." . . .

With this situation spreading as the record shows, Congress was not required to await the total dislocation of commerce. . . .

5. The Power of Congress to Regulate Local Activities

Article I, § 8, cl 3, confers upon Congress the power "[t]o regulate Commerce . . . among the several States" and Clause 18 of the same Article grants it the power "[t]o make all Laws which shall be necessary and proper for carrying into Execution the foregoing Powers. . . ." This grant, as we have pointed out in Heart of Atlanta Motel "extends to those activities intrastate which so affect interstate commerce, or the exertion of the power of Congress over it, as to make regulation of them appropriate means to the attainment of a legitimate end, the effective execution of the granted power to regulate interstate commerce." . . . Much is said about a restaurant business being local but "even if appellee's activity be local and though it may not be regarded as commerce, it may still, whatever its nature, be reached by Congress if it exerts a substantial economic effect on interstate commerce. . . ." . . . The activities that are beyond the reach of Congress are "those which are completely within a particular State, which do not affect other States, and with which it is not necessary to interfere, for the purpose of executing some of the general powers of the government." . . . This rule is as good today as it was when Chief Justice Marshall laid it down almost a century and a half ago. . . .

Nor are the cases holding that interstate commerce ends when goods come to rest in the State of destination apposite here. That line of cases has been applied with reference to state taxation or regulation but not in the field of federal regulation.

The appellees contend that Congress has arbitrarily created a conclusive presumption that all restaurants meeting the criteria set out in the Act "affect commerce." Stated another way, they object to the omission of a provision for a case-by-case determination—judicial or administrative—that racial discrimination in a particular restaurant affects commerce.

But Congress' action in framing this Act was not unprecedented. In United States v. Darby, this Court held constitutional the Fair Labor Standards Act of 1938. There Congress determined that the payment of substandard wages to employees engaged in the production of goods for commerce, while not itself commerce, so inhibited it as to be subject to federal regulation. The appellees in that case argued, as do the appellees here, that the Act was invalid because it included no provision for an independent inquiry regarding the effect on commerce of substandard wages in a particular business. . . . But the Court rejected the argument, observing that:

[S]ometimes Congress itself has said that a particular activity affects the commerce, as it did in the present Act, the Safety Appliance Act and the Railway Labor Act. In passing on the validity of legislation of the class last mentioned the only function of courts is to determine whether the particular activity regulated or prohibited is within the reach of the federal power.

Here, as there, Congress has determined for itself that refusals of service to Negroes have imposed burdens both upon the interstate flow of food and upon the movement of products generally. Of course, the mere fact that Congress has said when particular activity shall be deemed to affect commerce does not preclude further examination by this Court. But where we find that the legislators, in light of the facts and testimony before them, have a rational basis for finding a chosen regulatory scheme necessary to the protection of commerce, our investigation is at an end. The only remaining question—one answered in the affirmative by the court below—is whether the particular restaurant either serves or offers to serve interstate travelers or serves food a substantial portion of which has moved in interstate commerce. . . .

Confronted as we are with the facts laid before Congress, we must conclude that it had a rational basis for finding that racial discrimination in restaurants had a direct and adverse effect on the free flow of interstate commerce. Insofar as the sections of the Act here relevant is concerned, § § 201(b) (2) and (c), Congress prohibited discrimination only in those establishments having a close tie to interstate commerce, i.e., those, like the McClungs', serving food that has come from out of the State. We think in so doing that Congress acted well within its power to protect and foster commerce in extending the coverage of Title II only to those restaurants offering to serve interstate travelers or serving food, a substantial portion of which has moved in interstate commerce.

The absence of direct evidence connecting discriminatory restaurant service with the flow of interstate food, a factor on which the appellees place much reliance, is not, given the evidence as to the effect of such practices on other aspects of commerce, a crucial matter.

The power of Congress in this field is broad and sweeping; where it keeps within its sphere and violates no express constitutional limitation it has been the rule of this Court, going back almost to the founding days of the Republic, not to interfere. The Civil Rights Act of 1964, as here applied, we find to be plainly appropriate in the resolution of what the Congress found to be a national commercial problem of the first magnitude. We find it in no violation of any express limitations of the Constitution and we therefore declare it valid.

Justices Black, Douglas, and Goldberg concur.

Voting Rights Act of 1965

Congress and the President

AN ACT

To enforce the fifteenth amendment to the Constitution of the United States, and for other purposes.

Be it enacted by the Senate and House of Representatives of the United States of America in Congress assembled, That this Act shall be known as the "Voting Rights Act of 1965".

Sec. 2. No voting qualification or prerequisite to voting, or standard, practice, or procedure shall be imposed or applied by any State or political subdivision to deny or abridge the right of any citizen of the United States to vote on account of race or color.

Sec. 3. (a) Whenever the Attorney General institutes a proceeding under any statute to enforce the guarantees of the fifteenth amendment in any State or political subdivision the court shall authorize the appointment of Federal examiners by the United States Civil Service Commission in accordance with section 6 to serve for such period of time and for such political subdivisions as the court shall determine is appropriate to enforce the guarantees of the fifteenth amendment (1) as part of any interlocutory order if the court determines that the appointment of such examiners is necessary to enforce such guarantees or (2) as part of any final judgment if the court finds that violations of the fifteenth amendment justifying equitable relief have occurred in such State or subdivision: *Provided,* That the court need not authorize the appointment of examiners if any incidents of denial or abridgement of the right to vote on account of race or color (1) have been few in number and have been promptly and effectively corrected by State or local action, (2) the continuing effect of such incidents has been eliminated, and (3) there is no reasonable probability of their recurrence in the future.

(b) If in a proceeding instituted by the Attorney General under any statute to enforce the guarantees of the fifteenth amendment in any State or political subdivision the court finds that a test or device has been used for the purpose or with the effect of denying or abridging the right of any citizen of the United States to vote on account of race or color, it shall suspend the use of tests and devices in such State or political subdivisions as the court shall determine is appropriate and for such period as it deems necessary. . . .

Sec. 4. (a) To assure that the right of citizens of the United States to vote is not denied or abridged on account of race or color, no citizen shall be denied the right to vote in any Federal, State, or local election because of his failure to comply with any test or device in any State with respect to which the determinations have been made under subsection (b) or in any political subdivision with respect to which such determinations have been made as a separate unit, unless the United States District Court for the District of Columbia in an action for a declaratory judgment brought by such State or subdivision against the United States has determined that no such test or device has been used during the five years preceding the filing of the action for the purpose or with the effect of denying or abridging the right to vote on account of race or color.

(b) The provisions of subsection (a) shall apply in any State or in any political subdivision of a state which (1) the Attorney General determines maintained on November 1, 1964, any test or device, and with respect to which (2) the Director of the Census determines that less than 50 per centum of the persons of voting age residing therein were registered on November 1, 1964, or that less than 50 per centum of such persons voted in the presidential election of November 1964.

(c) The phrase "test or device" shall mean any requirement that a person as a prerequisite for voting or registration for voting (1) demonstrate the ability to read, write, understand, or interpret any matter, (2) demonstrate any educational achievement or his knowledge of any particular subject, (3) possess good moral character, or (4) prove his qualifications by the voucher of registered voters or members of any other class.

(d) For purposes of this section no State or political subdivision shall be determined to have engaged in the use of tests or devices for the purpose or with the effect of denying or abridging the right to vote on account of race or color if (1) incidents of such use have been few in number and have been promptly and effectively corrected by State or local action, (2) the continuing effect of such incidents has been eliminated, and (3) there is no reasonable probability of their recurrence in the future.

(e) (1) Congress hereby declares that to secure the rights under the fourteenth amendment of persons educated in American-flag schools in which the predominant classroom language was other than English, it is necessary to prohibit the States from conditioning the right to vote of such persons on ability to read, write, understand, or interpret any matter in the English language.

(2) No person who demonstrates that he has successfully completed the sixth primary grade in a public school in, or a private school accredited by, any State or territory, the District of Columbia, or the Commonwealth of Puerto Rico in which the predominant classroom language was other than English, shall be denied the right to vote in any Federal, State, or local election because of his inability to read, write, understand, or interpret any matter in the English language, except that in States in which State law provides that a different level of education is presumptive of literacy, he shall demonstrate that he has successfully completed an equivalent level of education in a public school in, or a private school accredited by, any State or territory, the District of Columbia, or the Commonwealth of Puerto Rico in which the predominant classroom language was other than English. . . .

Sec. 7. (a) The examiners for each political subdivision shall, at such places as the Civil Service Commission shall by regulation designate, examine applicants concerning their qualifications for voting. An application to an examiner shall be in such form as the Commission may require and shall contain allegations that the applicant is not otherwise registered to vote.

(b) Any person whom the examiner finds, in accordance with instructions received under section 9(b), to have the qualifications prescribed by State law not inconsistent with the Constitution and laws of the United States shall promptly be placed on a list of eligible voters.

South Carolina v. Katzenbach*

United States Supreme Court

Mr. Chief Justice Warren delivered the opinion of the court, saying in part:

By leave of the Court, South Carolina has filed a bill of complaint, seeking a declaration that selected provisions of the Voting Rights Act of 1965 violate the Federal Constitution, and asking for an injunction against enforcement of these provisions by the Attorney General. Original jurisdiction is founded on the presence of a controversy between a State and a citizen of another State under Art. III, § 2, of the Constitution. . . .

The Voting Rights Act was designed by Congress to banish the blight of racial discrimination in voting, which has infected the electoral process in parts of our country for nearly a century. The Act creates stringent new remedies for voting discrimination where it persists on a pervasive scale, and in addition the statute strengthens existing remedies for pockets of voting discrimination elsewhere in the country. Congress assumed the power to prescribe these remedies from § 2 of the Fifteenth Amendment, which authorizes the national legislature to effectuate by "appropriate" measures the constitutional prohibition against racial discrimination in voting. We hold that the sections of the Act which are properly before us are an appropriate means for carrying out Congress' constitutional responsibilities and are consonant with all other provisions of the Constitution. We therefore deny South Carolina's request that enforcement of these sections of the Act be enjoined.

---

*383 U.S. 301 (1966).

I.

The constitutional propriety of the Voting Rights Act of 1965 must be judged with reference to the historical experience which it reflects. Before enacting the measure, Congress explored with great care the problem of racial discrimination in voting. The House and Senate Committees on the Judiciary each held hearings for nine days and received testimony from a total of 67 witnesses. More than three full days were consumed discussing the bill on the floor of the House while the debate in the Senate covered 26 days in all. At the close of these deliberations, the verdict of both chambers was overwhelming. The House approved the Act by a vote of 328-74, and the measure passed the Senate by a margin of 79-18.

Two points emerge vividly from the voluminous legislative history of the Act contained in the committee hearings and floor debates. First: Congress felt itself confronted by an insidious and pervasive evil which had been perpetuated in certain parts of our country through unremitting and ingenious defiance of the Constitution. Second: Congress concluded that the unsuccessful remedies which it had prescribed in the past would have to be replaced by sterner and more elaborate measures in order to satisfy the clear commands of the Fifteenth Amendment. We pause here to summarize the majority reports of the House and Senate Committees, which document in considerable detail the factual basis for these reactions by Congress. . . . [The Court here summarizes the systematic efforts of southern states to disfranchise the Negro.]

According to the results of recent Justice Department voting suits, . . . [discriminatory application of voting tests is now the principal] method used to bar Negroes from the polls. Discriminatory administration of voting qualifications has been found in all eight Alabama cases, in all nine Louisiana cases, and in all nine Mississippi cases which have gone to final judgment. Moreover, in almost all of these cases, the courts have held that the discrimination was pursuant to a widespread "pattern or practice." White applicants for registration have often been excused altogether from the literacy and understanding tests or have been given easy versions, have received extensive help from voting officials, and have been registered despite serious errors in their answers. Negroes, on the other hand, have typically been required to pass difficult versions of all the tests, without any outside assistance and without the slightest error. The good morals requirement is so vague and subjective that it has constituted an open invitation to abuse at the hands of voting officials. Negroes obliged to obtain vouchers from registered voters have found it virtually impossible to comply in areas where almost no Negroes are on the rolls.

In recent years, Congress has repeatedly tried to cope with the problem by facilitating case-by-case litigation against voting discrimination. The Civil Rights Act of 1957 authorized the Attorney General to seek injunctions against public and private interference with the right to vote on racial grounds. Perfecting amendments in the Civil Rights Act of 1960 permitted the joinder of States as party defendants, gave the Attorney General access to local voting records, and authorized courts to register voters in areas of systematic discrimination. Title I of the Civil Rights Act of 1964 expedited the hearing of voting cases before three-judge courts and outlawed some of the tactics used to disqualify Negroes from voting in federal elections.

Despite the earnest efforts of the Justice Department and of many federal judges, these new laws have done little to cure the problem of voting discrimination. According to estimates by the Attorney General during hearings on the Act, registration of voting age Negroes in Alabama rose only from 10.2% to 19.4% between 1958 and 1964; in Louisiana it barely inched ahead from 31.7% to 31.8% between 1956 and 1965; and in Mississippi it increased only from 4.4% to 6.4% between 1954 and 1964. In each instance, registration of voting age whites ran roughly 50 percentage points or more ahead of Negro registration.

The previous legislation has proved ineffective for a number of reasons. Voting suits are unusually onerous to prepare, sometimes requiring as many as 6,000 man-hours spent combing through registration records in preparation for trial. Litigation has been exceedingly slow, in part because of the ample opportunities for delay afforded voting officials and others involved in the proceedings. Even when favorable decisions have finally been obtained, some of the States affected have merely switched to discriminatory devices not covered by the federal decrees or have enacted difficult new tests designed to prolong the existing disparity between white and Negro registration. Alternatively, certain local officials have defied and evaded court orders or have simply closed their registration offices to freeze the voting rolls. The provision of the 1960 law authorizing registration by federal officers has had little impact on local maladministration because of its procedural complexities.

During the hearings and debates on the Act, Selma, Alabama, was repeatedly referred to as the pre-eminent example of the ineffectiveness of existing legislation. In Dallas County, of which Selma is the seat, there were four years of litigation by the Justice Department and two findings by the federal courts of widespread voting discrimination. Yet in those four years, Negro registration rose only from 156 to 383, although there are approximately 15,000 Negroes of voting age in the county. Any possibility that these figures were attributable to political apathy was dispelled by the protest demonstrations in Selma in the early months of 1965. . . .

II.

The Voting Rights Act of 1965 reflects Congress' firm intention to rid the country of racial discrimination in voting. The heart of the Act is a complex scheme of stringent remedies aimed at areas where voting discrimination has been most flagrant. . . .

At the outset, we emphasize that only some of the many portions of the Act are properly before us. . . .

Coverage Formula

The remedial sections of the Act assailed by South Carolina automatically apply to any State, or to any separate political subdivision such as a county or parish, for which two findings have been made: (1) the Attorney General has determined that on November 1, 1964, it maintained a "test or device," and (2) the Director of the Census has determined that less than 50% of its voting age residents were registered on November 1, 1964, or voted in the presidential election of November 1964. . . . As used throughout the Act, the phrase "test or device" means any requirement that a registrant or voter must "(1) demonstrate the ability to read, write, understand, or interpret any matter, (2) demonstrate any educational achievement or his knowledge of any particular subject, (3) possess good moral character, or (4) prove his qualifications by the voucher of registered voters or members of any class." § 4 (c).

Statutory coverage of a State or political subdivision under § 4 (b) is terminated if the area obtains a declaratory judgment from the District Court for the District of Columbia, determining that tests and devices have not been used during the preceding five years to abridge the franchise on racial grounds. The Attorney General shall consent to entry of the judgment if he has no reason to believe that the facts are otherwise. . . .

South Carolina was brought within the coverage formula of the Act on August 7, 1965, pursuant to appropriate administrative determinations which have not been challenged in this proceeding. On the same day, coverage was also extended to Alabama, Alaska, Georgia, Louisiana, Mississippi, Virginia, 26 counties in North Carolina, and one county in Arizona. Two more counties in Arizona, one county in Hawaii, and one county in Idaho were added to the list on November 19, 1965. Thus far Alaska, the three Arizona counties, and the single county in Idaho have asked the District Court for the District of Columbia to grant a declaratory judgment terminating statutory coverage.

Suspension of Tests

In a State or political subdivision covered by § 4 (b) of the Act, no person may be denied the right to vote in any election because of his failure to comply with a "test or device." § 4 (a).

On account of this provision, South Carolina is temporarily barred from enforcing the portion of its voting laws which requires every applicant for registration to show that he:

"Can both read and write any section of [the State] Constitution submitted to [him] by the registration officer or can show that he owns, and has paid all taxes collectable during the previous year on, property in this State assessed at three hundred dollars or more." . . .

Similar tests and devices have been temporarily suspended in the other sections of the country listed above.

Review of New Rules

In a State or political subdivision covered by § 4 (b) of the Act, no person may be denied the right to vote in any election because of his failure to comply with a voting qualification or procedure different from those in force on November 1, 1964. This suspension of new rules is terminated, however, under either of the following circumstances: (1) if the area has submitted the rules to the Attorney General, and he has not interposed an objection within 60 days, or (2) if the area has obtained a declaratory judgment from the District Court for the District of Columbia, determining that the rules will not abridge the franchise on racial grounds. These declaratory judgment actions are to be heard by a three-judge panel, with direct appeal to this Court. § 5.

South Carolina altered its voting laws in 1965 to extend the closing hour at polling places from 6 p.m. to 7 p.m. The State has not sought judicial review of this change in the District Court for the District of Columbia, nor has it submitted the new rule to the Attorney General for his scrutiny, although at our hearing the Attorney General announced that he does not challenge the amendment. There are indications in the record that other sections of the country listed above have also altered their voting laws since November 1, 1964.

Federal Examiners

In any political subdivision covered by § 4 (b) of the Act, the Civil Service Commission shall appoint voting examiners whenever the Attorney General certifies either of the following facts: (1) that he has received meritorious written complaints from at least 20 residents alleging that they have been disenfranchised under color of law because of their race, or (2) that the appointment of examiners is otherwise necessary to effectuate the guarantees of the Fifteenth Amendment. In making the latter determination, the Attorney General must consider, among other factors, whether the registration ratio of non-whites to whites seems reasonably attributable to racial discrimination, or whether there is substantial evidence of good-faith efforts to comply with the Fifteenth Amendment. § 6 (b). . . .

The examiners who have been appointed are to test the voting qualifications of applicants according to regulations of the Civil Service Commission prescribing times, places, procedures, and forms. §§ 7 (a) and 9 (b). Any person who meets the voting requirements of state law, insofar as these have not been suspended by the Act, must promptly be placed on a list of eligible voters. . . . Any person listed by an examiner is entitled to vote in all elections held more than 45 days after his name has been transmitted. § 7 (b). . . .

On October 30, 1965, the Attorney General certified the need for federal examiners in two South Carolina counties, and examiners appointed by the Civil Service Commission have been serving there since November 8, 1965. Examiners have also been assigned to 11 counties in Alabama, five parishes in Louisiana, and 19 counties in Mississippi.

III.

These provisions of the Voting Rights Act of 1965 are challenged on the fundamental ground that they exceed the powers of Congress and encroach on an area reserved to the States by the Constitution. . . .

Has Congress exercised its powers under the Fifteenth Amendment in an appropriate manner with relation to the States?

The ground rules for resolving this question are clear. The language and purpose of the Fifteenth Amendment, the prior decisions construing its several provisions, and the general doctrines of constitutional interpretation, all point to one fundamental principle. As against the reserved powers of the States, Congress may use any rational means to effectuate the constitutional prohibition of racial discrimination in voting. Cf. our rulings last Term, sustaining Title II of the Civil Rights Act of 1964, in Heart of Atlanta Motel v. United States, and Katzenbach v. McClung. We turn now to a more detailed description of the standards which govern our review of the Act.

Section 1 of the Fifteenth Amendment declares that "the right of citizens of the United States to vote shall not be denied or abridged by the United States or by any State on account of race, color, or previous condition of servitude." This declaration has always been treated as self-executing and has repeatedly been construed, without further legislative specification, to invalidate state voting qualifications or procedures which are discriminatory on their face or in practice. . . . Guinn v. United States, . . . Smith v. Allwright. The gist of the matter is that the Fifteenth Amendment supersedes contrary exertions of state power. . . .

South Carolina contends that the cases cited above are precedents only for the authority of the judiciary to strike down state statutes and procedures—that to allow an exercise of this authority by Congress would be to rob the courts of their rightful constitutional role. On the contrary, § 2 of the Fifteenth Amendment expressly declares that "Congress shall have the power to enforce this article by appropriate legislation." By adding this authorization, the Framers indicated that Congress was to be chiefly responsible for implementing the rights created in § 1. . . .

Congress has repeatedly exercised these powers in the past, and its enactments have repeatedly been upheld. For recent examples, see the Civil Rights Act of 1957, which was sustained in United States v. Raines, 362 U. S. 17. . . .

The basic test to be applied in a case involving § 2 of the Fifteenth Amendment is the same as in all cases concerning the express powers of Congress with relation to the reserved powers of the States. Chief Justice Marshall laid down the classic formulation, 50 years before the Fifteenth Amendment was ratified:

"Let the end be legitimate, let it be within the scope of the constitution, and all means which are appropriate, which are plainly adapted to that end, which are not prohibited, but consist with the letter and spirit of the constitution, are constitutional." McCulloch v. Maryland.

The Court has subsequently echoed his language in describing each of the Civil War Amendments:

"Whatever legislation is appropriate, that is, adapted to carry out the objects the amendments have in view, whatever tends to enforce submission to the prohibitions they contain, and to secure to all persons the enjoyment of perfect equality of civil rights and the equal protection of the laws against State denial or invasion, if not prohibited, is brought within the domain of congressional power." Ex parté Virginia, 100 U. S., at 345-346. . . .

We therefore reject South Carolina's argument that Congress may appropriately do no more than to forbid violations of the Fifteenth Amendment in general terms—that the task of fashioning specific remedies or of applying them to particular localities must necessarily be left entirely to the courts. Congress is not circumscribed by any such artificial rules under § 2 of the Fifteenth Amendment. In the oft-repeated words of Chief Justice Marshall, referring to another specific legislative authorization in the Constitution, "This power, like all others vested in Congress, is complete in itself, may be exercised to its utmost extent, and acknowledges no limitations, other than are prescribed in the constitution." Gibbons v. Ogden.

IV.

Congress exercised its authority under the Fifteenth Amendment in an inventive manner when it enacted the Voting Rights Act of 1965. First: The measure prescribes remedies for voting discrimination which go into effect without any need for prior adjudication. This was clearly a legitimate response to the problem, for which there is ample precedent under other constitutional provisions. . . . Congress had found that case-by-case litigation was inadequate to combat widespread and persistent discrimination in voting, because of the inordinate amount of time and energy required to overcome the obstructionist tactics invariably encountered in these lawsuits. After enduring nearly a century of systematic resistance to the Fifteenth Amendment, Congress might well decide to shift the advantage of time and inertia from the perpetrators of the evil to its victims. The question remains, of course, whether the specific remedies prescribed in the Act were an appropriate means of combatting the evil, and to this question we shall presently address ourselves.

Second: The Act intentionally confines these remedies to a small number of States and political subdivisions which in most instances were familiar to Congress by name. This, too, was a permissible method of dealing with the problem. Congress had learned that substantial voting discrimination presently occurs in certain sections of the country, and it knew no way of accurately forecasting whether the evil might spread elsewhere in the future. In acceptable legislative fashion, Congress chose to limit its attention to the geographic areas where immediate action seemed necessary. . . . The doctrine of the equality of States, invoked by South Carolina, does not bar this approach, for that doctrine applies only to the terms upon which States are admitted to the Union, and not to the remedies for local evils which have subsequently appeared. See Coyle v. Smith. . . .

Coverage Formula

We now consider the related question of whether the specific States and political subdivisions within § 4 (b) of the Act were an appropriate target for the new remedies. Congress began work with reliable evidence of actual voting discrimination in a great majority of the States and political subdivisions affected by the new remedies of the Act. The formula eventually evolved to describe these areas was relevant to the problem of voting discrimination. . . .

To be specific, the new remedies of the Act are imposed on three States—Alabama, Louisiana, and Mississippi—in which federal courts have repeatedly found substantial voting discrimination. Section 4 (b) of the Act also embraces two other States—Georgia and South Carolina— plus large portions of a third State—North Carolina—for which there was more fragmentary evidence of recent voting discrimination mainly adduced by the Justice Department and the Civil Rights Commission. All of these areas were appropriately subjected to the new remedies. In identifying past evils, Congress obviously may avail itself of information from any probative source. . . .

The areas listed above, for which there was evidence of actual voting discrimination, share two characteristics incorporated by Congress into the coverage formula: the use of tests and devices for voter registration, and a voting rate in the 1964 presidential election at least 12 points below the national average. Tests and devices are relevant to voting discrimination because of their long history as a tool for perpetrating the evil; a low voting rate is pertinent for the obvious reason that widespread disenfranchisement must inevitably affect the number of actual voters. Accordingly, the coverage formula is rational in both practice and theory. It was therefore permissible to impose the new remedies on the few remaining States and political subdivisions covered by the formula, at least in the absence of proof that they have been free of substantial voting discrimination in recent years. . . .

It is irrelevant that the coverage formula excludes certain localities which do not employ voting tests and devices but for which there is evidence of voting discrimination by other means. Congress had learned that widespread and persistent discrimination in voting during recent years has typically entailed the misuse of tests and devices, and this was the evil for which the new remedies were specifically designed. . . . Legislation need not deal with all phases of a problem in the same way, so long as the distinctions drawn have some basis in practical experience. . . . There are no States or political subdivisions exempted from coverage under § 4 (b) in which the record reveals recent racial discrimination involving tests and devices. This fact confirms the rationality of the formula.

Acknowledging the possibility of overbreadth, the Act provides for termination of special statutory coverage at the behest of States and political subdivisions in which the danger of substantial voting discrimination has not materialized during the preceding five years. . . .

South Carolina contends that these termination procedures are a nullity because they impose an impossible burden of proof upon States and political subdivisions entitled to relief. As the Attorney General pointed out during hearings on the Act, however, an area need do no more than to submit affidavits from voting officials, asserting that they have not been guilty of racial discrimination through the use of tests and devices during the past five years, and then to refute whatever evidence to the contrary may be adduced by the Federal Government. Section 4 (d) further assures that an area need not disprove each isolated instance of voting discrimination in order to obtain relief in the termination proceedings. The burden of proof is therefore quite bearable, particularly since the relevant facts relating to the conduct of voting officials are peculiarly within the knowledge of the States and political subdivisions themselves. . . .

Suspension of Tests

We now arrive at consideration of the specific remedies prescribed by the Act for areas included within the coverage formula. South Carolina assails the temporary suspension of existing voting qualifications. . . . The record shows that in most of the States covered by the Act, including South Carolina, various tests and devices have been instituted with the purpose of disenfranchising Negroes, have been framed in such a way as to facilitate this aim, and have been administered in a discriminatory fashion for many years. Under these circumstances, the Fifteenth Amendment has clearly been violated. . . .

The Act suspends literacy tests and similar devices for a period of five years from the last occurrence of substantial voting discrimination.

This was a legitimate response to the problem, for which there is ample precedent in Fifteenth Amendment cases. *Ibid.* Underlying the response was the feeling that States and political subdivisions which had been allowing white illiterates to vote for years could not sincerely complain about "dilution" of their electorates through the registration of Negro illiterates. Congress knew that continuance of the tests and devices in use at the present time, no matter how fairly administered in the future, would freeze the effect of past discrimination in favor of unqualified white registrants. Congress permissibly rejected the alternative of requiring a complete re-registration of all voters, believing that this would be too harsh on many whites who had enjoyed the franchise for their entire adult lives.

Review of New Rules

The Act suspends new voting regulations pending scrutiny by federal authorities to determine whether their use would violate the Fifteenth Amendment. This may have been an uncommon exercise of congressional power, as South Carolina contends, but the Court has recognized that exceptional conditions can justify legislative measures not otherwise appropriate. . . . Congress knew that some of the States covered by § 4 (b) of the Act had resorted to the extraordinary stratagem of contriving new rules of various kinds for the sole purpose of perpetuating voting discrimination in the face of adverse federal decrees. Congress had reason to suppose that these States might try similar maneuvers in the future, in order to evade the remedies for voting discrimination contained in the Act itself. Under the compulsion of these unique circumstances, Congress responded in a permissibly decisive manner. . . .

Federal Examiners

The Act authorizes the appointment of federal examiners to list qualified applicants who are thereafter entitled to vote, subject to an expeditious challenge procedure. This was clearly an appropriate response to the problem, closely related to remedies authorized in prior cases. . . . In many of the political subdivisions covered by § 4 (b) of the Act, voting officials have persistently employed a variety of procedural tactics to deny Negroes the franchise, often in direct defiance or evasion of federal decrees. Congress realized that merely to suspend voting rules which have been misused or are subject to misuse might leave this localized evil undisturbed. As for the briskness of the challenge procedure, Congress knew that in some of the areas affected, challenges had been persistently employed to harass registered Negroes. It chose to forestall this abuse, at the same time providing alternative ways for removing persons listed through error or fraud. In addition to the judicial challenge procedure, § 7 (d) allows for the removal of names by the examiner himself, and § 11 (c) makes it a crime to obtain a listing through fraud. . . .

After enduring nearly a century of widespread resistance to the Fifteenth Amendment, Congress has marshalled an array of potent weapons against the evil, with authority in the Attorney General to employ them effectively. Many of the areas directly affected by this development have indicated their willingness to abide by any restraints legitimately imposed upon them. We here hold that the portions of the Voting Rights Act properly before us are a valid means for carrying out the commands of the Fifteenth Amendment. Hopefully, millions of non-white Americans will now be able to participate for the first time on an equal basis in the government under which they live. We may finally look forward to the day when truly "the right of citizens of the United States to vote shall not be denied or abridged by the United States or by any State on account of race, color, or previous condition of servitude."

The bill of complaint is dismissed.

Mr. Justice Black concurred except as to the validity of § 5.

Negro Population Trends in Large Cities

U.S. Bureau of the Census

Negro Population of Nation's Largest Cities

The figures [on pages 96-97] show the percentage of Negroes in the total population of the nation's largest cities for selected years. Percentages for 1940, 1950 and 1960 are based on census data. Population and percentage figures for 1965 and 1970 were developed by the Center for Research in Marketing, a market research firm. Cities are ranked according to total population in 1965.

City	Percent Negro			Estimates for 1965			Projections for 1970		
	1940	1950	1960	Total Population	Negro Population	Negro %	Total Population	Negro Population	Negro %
New York	6%	9%	14%	8,282,000	1,300,000	16%	8,100,000	1,500,000	19%
Chicago	8	14	23	3,600,000	960,000	27	3,610,000	1,150,000	32
Los Angeles	4	9	14	2,750,000	500,000	18	3,000,000	700,000	23
Philadelphia	13	14	26	2,070,000	610,000	29	2,200,000	700,000	32
Detroit	9	16	29	1,650,000	650,000	39	1,700,000	800,000	47
Houston	22	21	23	1,040,000	260,000	25	1,140,000	310,000	27
Baltimore	19	24	35	930,000	378,000	41	920,000	432,000	47
Cleveland	10	16	29	811,000	277,000	34	805,000	305,000	38
Wash., D.C.	28	38	54	801,000	506,000	63	840,000	574,000	68
Milwaukee	2	3	9	780,000	102,000	13	800,000	146,000	18
Dallas	17	13	19	740,000	165,000	22	800,000	200,000	25
San Francisco	1	6	10	740,000	100,000	14	750,000	126,000	17
St. Louis	13	18	29	705,000	260,000	37	700,000	320,000	46
Boston	3	5	9	685,000	75,000	11	675,000	85,000	13
New Orleans	30	32	37	656,000	269,000	41	680,000	303,000	45
San Antonio	7	7	7	655,000	57,000	9	720,000	72,000	10
San Diego	2	4	6	648,000	53,000	8	723,000	72,000	10
Pittsburgh	9	12	17	607,000	115,000	19	610,000	126,000	21
Seattle	1	3	5	602,000	40,000	7	647,000	56,000	9
Memphis	41	37	37	539,000	205,000	38	580,000	226,000	39
Buffalo	3	6	13	520,000	96,000	18	510,000	114,000	22
Phoenix	6	5	5	520,000	40,000	8	600,000	60,000	10
Atlanta	38	37	38	515,000	198,000	38	540,000	212,000	39
Denver	2	4	6	502,000	40,000	8	510,000	51,000	10
Columbus, Ohio	12	13	16	500,000	117,000	23	525,000	167,000	32
Indianapolis	13	15	21	490,000	120,000	24	500,000	145,000	29
K.C., Mo.	11	12	17	488,000	100,000	20	500,000	120,000	24
Cincinnati	12	15	22	470,000	130,000	28	470,000	150,000	31

Fort Worth	14	13	16	389,000	18	69,000	18	422,000	83,000	20
Louisville	15	16	18	387,000	21	80,000	21	385,000	91,000	24
Long Beach	1	2	3	372,000	5	17,000	5	410,000	28,000	7
Portland, Ore.	1	3	4	370,000	5	20,000	5	370,000	25,000	7
Oklahoma City	9	9	12	364,000	15	55,000	15	404,000	72,000	18
Oakland, Calif.	3	12	23	360,000	31	112,000	31	360,000	140,000	39
Birmingham	41	40	40	348,000	40	138,000	40	354,000	141,000	40
Norfolk, Va.	32	29	26	343,000	24	84,000	24	380,000	89,000	23
Miami, Fla.	22	16	22	330,000	26	85,000	26	370,000	105,000	28
Omaha	5	6	8	330,000	10	34,000	10	360,000	44,000	12
Toledo	5	8	13	325,000	18	58,000	18	330,000	77,000	23
Tampa	21	22	17	315,000	17	54,000	17	350,000	61,000	17
Rochester	1	2	8	303,000	11	33,000	11	305,000	42,000	14
Tulsa	11	9	8	302,000	8	25,000	8	342,000	28,000	8
Akron	5	9	13	300,000	18	54,000	18	305,000	68,000	22
St. Paul	1	2	3	296,000	3	10,000	3	280,000	12,000	4
Wichita	5	5	8	282,000	12	33,000	12	310,000	44,000	14
Dayton	9	14	22	271,000	26	71,000	26	280,000	85,000	30
Jersey City	4	7	13	270,000	17	45,000	17	265,000	52,000	20
Sacramento	1	4	6	245,000	16	40,000	16	290,000	64,000	22
Mobile	37	36	33	233,000	33	76,000	33	263,000	86,000	33
Charlotte	31	28	28	225,000	27	61,000	27	248,000	67,000	27
Des Moines	4	4	5	225,000	5	12,000	5	250,000	14,000	6
St. Petersburg	20	14	13	219,000	13	29,000	13	259,000	34,000	13
Richmond	32	32	42	215,000	47	101,000	47	215,000	110,000	51
Austin	17	14	13	212,000	13	28,000	13	237,000	32,000	14
Syracuse	1	2	5	210,000	7	15,000	7	205,000	20,000	10
Flint	4	9	18	200,000	22	44,000	22	200,000	52,000	26
Jacksonville	36	35	41	200,000	44	88,000	44	202,000	94,000	47
Providence	1	3	5	200,000	7	14,000	7	200,000	18,000	9

The Negro Family: The Case for National Action*

Daniel P. Moynihan

Slavery

The most perplexing question about American slavery, which has never been altogether explained, and which indeed most Americans hardly know exists, has been stated by Nathan Glazer as follows: "Why was American slavery the most awful the world has ever known?" The only thing that can be said with certainty is that this is true: it was.

American slavery was profoundly different from, and in its lasting effects on individuals and their children, indescribably worse than, any recorded servitude, ancient or modern. The peculiar nature of American slavery was noted by Alexis de Tocqueville and others, but it was not until 1948 that Frank Tannenbaum, a South American specialist, pointed to the striking differences between Brazilian and American slavery. The feudal, Catholic society of Brazil had a legal and religious tradition which accorded the slave a place as a human being in the hierarchy of society — a luckless, miserable place, to be sure, but a place withal. In contrast, there was nothing in the tradition of English law or Protestant theology which could accommodate to the fact of human bondage — the slaves were therefore reduced to the status of chattels — often, no doubt, well cared for, even privileged chattels, but chattels nevertheless.

Glazer, also focusing on the Brazil-United States comparison, continues.

*Reprinted from Daniel P. Moynihan, *The Negro Family: The Case for National Action* (Washington: Government Printing Office, 1965), pp. 15-23. Footnotes in original text omitted.

In Brazil, the slave had many more rights than in the United States: he could legally marry, he could, indeed had to, be baptized and become a member of the Catholic Church, his family could not be broken up for sale, and he had many days on which he could either rest or earn money to buy his freedom. The Government encouraged manumission, and the freedom of infants could often be purchased for a small sum at the baptismal font. In short: the Brazilian slave knew he was a man, and that he differed in degree, not in kind, from his master.

[In the United States,] the slave was totally removed from the protection of organized society (compare the elaborate provisions for the protection of slaves in the Bible), his existence as a human being was given no recognition by any religious or secular agency, he was totally ignorant of and completely cut off from his past, and he was offered absolutely no hope for the future. His children could be sold, his marriage was not recognized, his wife could be violated or sold (there was something comic about calling the woman with whom the master permitted him to live a "wife"), and he could also be subject, without redress, to frightful barbarities—there were presumably as many sadists among slaveowners, men and women, as there are in other groups. The slave could not, by law, be taught to read or write; he could not practice any religion without the permission of his master, and could never meet with his fellows, for religious or any other purposes, except in the presence of a white; and finally, if a master wished to free him, every legal obstacle was used to thwart such action. This was not what slavery meant in the ancient world, in medieval and early modern Europe, or in Brazil and the West Indies.

More important, American slavery was also awful in its effects. If we compared the present situation of the American Negro with that of, let us say, Brazilian Negroes (who were slaves 20 years longer), we begin to suspect that the differences are the result of very different patterns of slavery. Today the Brazilian Negroes are Brazilians; though most are poor and do the hard and dirty work of the country, as Negroes do in the United States, they are not cut off from society. They reach into its highest strata, merging there—in smaller and smaller numbers, it is true, but with complete acceptance—with other Brazilians of all kinds. The relations between Negroes and whites in Brazil show nothing of the mass irrationality that prevails in this country.

Stanley M. Elkins, drawing on the aberrant behavior of the prisoners in Nazi concentration camps, drew an elaborate parallel between the two institutions. This thesis has been summarized as follows by Thomas F. Pettigrew:

Both were closed systems, with little chance of manumission, emphasis on survival and a single, omnipresent authority. The profound personality change created by Nazi internment, as independently reported by a number of psychologists and psychiatrists who survived, was toward childishness and total acceptance of the SS guards as father-figures—a syndrome strikingly similar to the "Sambo" caricature of the Southern slave. Nineteenth-century racists readily believed that the "Sambo" personality was simply an inborn racial type. Yet no African anthropological data have ever shown any personality type resembling Sambo; and the concentration camps molded the equivalent personality pattern in a wide variety of Caucasian prisoners. Nor was Sambo merely a product of "slavery" in the abstract, for the less devastating Latin American system never developed such a type.

Extending this line of reasoning, psychologists point out that slavery in all its forms sharply lowered the need for achievement in slaves . . . Negroes in bondage, stripped of their African heritage, were placed in a completely dependent role. All of their rewards came, not from individual initiative and enterprise, but from absolute obedience—a situation that severely depresses the need for achievement among all peoples. Most important of all, slavery vitiated family life. . . . Since many slaveowners neither fostered Christian marriage among their slave couples nor hesitated to separate them on the auction block, the slave household often developed a fatherless matrifocal (mother-centered) pattern.

The Reconstruction

With the emancipation of the slaves, the Negro American family began to form in the United States on a widespread scale. But it did so in an atmosphere markedly different from that which has produced the white American family.

The Negro was given liberty, but not equality. Life remained hazardous and marginal. Of the greatest importance, the Negro male, particularly in the South, became an object of intense hostility, an attitude unquestionably based in some measure on fear.

When Jim Crow made its appearance towards the end of the 19th century, it may be speculated that it was the Negro male who was most humiliated thereby; the male was more likely to use public facilities, which rapidly became segregated once the process began, and just as important, segregation, and the submissiveness it exacts, is surely more destructive to the male than to the female personality. Keeping the Negro "in his place" can be translated as keeping the Negro male in his place: the female was not a threat to anyone.

Unquestionably, these events worked against the emergence of a strong father figure. The very essence of the male animal, from the bantam rooster to the four-star general, is to strut. Indeed, in 19th century

America, a particular type of exaggerated male boastfulness became almost a national style. Not for the Negro male. The "sassy nigger" was lynched.

In this situation, the Negro family made but little progress toward the middle-class pattern of the present time. Margaret Mead has pointed out that while "In every known human society, everywhere in the world, the young male learns that when he grows up one of the things which he must do in order to be a full member of society is to provide food for some female and her young." This pattern is not immutable, however: it can be broken, even though it has always eventually reasserted itself.

> Within the family, each new generation of young males learn the appropriate nurturing behavior and superimpose upon their biologically given maleness this learned parental role. When the family breaks down —as it does under slavery, under certain forms of indentured labor and serfdom, in periods of extreme social unrest during wars, revolutions, famines, and epidemics, or in periods of abrupt transition from one type of economy to another—this delicate line of transmission is broken. Men may flounder badly in these periods, during which the primary unit may again become mother and child, the biologically given, and the special conditions under which man has held his social traditions in trust are violated and distorted.

E. Franklin Frazier makes clear that at the time of emancipation Negro women were already "accustomed to playing the dominant role in family and marriage relations" and that this role persisted in the decades of rural life that followed.

Urbanization

Country life and city life are profoundly different. The gradual shift of American society from a rural to an urban basis over the past century and a half has caused abundant strains, many of which are still much in evidence. When this shift occurs suddenly, drastically, in one or two generations, the effect is immensely disruptive of traditional social patterns.

It was this abrupt transition that produced the wild Irish slums of the 19th Century Northeast. Drunkenness, crime, corruption, discrimination, family disorganization, juvenile delinquency were the routine of that era. In our own time, the same sudden transition has produced the Negro slum — different from, but hardly better than its predecessors, and fundamentally the result of the same process.

Negroes are now more urbanized than whites.

Negro families in the cities are more frequently headed by a woman than those in the country. The difference between the white and Negro proportions of families headed by a woman is greater in the city than in the country.

The promise of the city has so far been denied the majority of the Negro migrants, and most particularly the Negro family.

In 1939, E. Franklin Frazier described its plight movingly in that part of *The Negro Family* entitled "In the City of Destruction:"

> The impact of hundreds of thousands of rural southern Negroes upon northern metropolitan communities presents a bewildering spectacle. Striking contrasts in levels of civilization and economic well-being among these newcomers to modern civilization seem to baffle any attempt to discover order and direction in their mode of life.
>
> In many cases, of course, the dissolution of the simple family organization has begun before the family reaches the northern city. But, if these families have managed to preserve their integrity until they reach the northern city, poverty, ignorance, and color forces them to seek homes in deteriorated slum areas from which practically all institutional life has disappeared. Hence, at the same time that these simple rural families are losing their internal cohesions, they are being freed from the controlling force of public opinion and communal institutions. Family desertion among Negroes in cities appears, then, to be one of the inevitable consequences of the impact of urban life on the simple family organization and folk culture which the Negro has evolved in the rural South. The distribution of desertions in relation to the general economic and cultural organization of Negro communities that have grown up in our American cities shows in a striking manner the influence of selective factors in the process of adjustment to the urban environment.

In every index of family pathology — divorce, separation, and desertion, female family head, children in broken homes, and illegitimacy — the contrast between the urban and rural environment for Negro families is unmistakable.

Harlem, into which Negroes began to move early in this century, is the center and symbol of the urban life of the Negro American. Conditions in Harlem are not worse, they are probably better than in most Negro ghettos. The social disorganization of central Harlem, comprising ten health areas, was thoroughly documented by the HARYOU report, save for the illegitimacy rates. These have now been made available to the Labor Department by the New York City Department of Health. There could hardly be a more dramatic demonstration of the crumbling — the breaking — of the family structure on the urban frontier.

Unemployment and Poverty

The impact of unemployment on the Negro family, and particularly on the Negro male, is the least understood of all the developments that have contributed to the present crisis. There is little analysis because there has been almost no inquiry. Unemployment, for whites and non-whites alike, has on the whole been treated as an economic phenomenon, with almost no attention paid for at least a quarter-century to social and personal consequences.

In 1940, Edward Wight Bakke described the effects of unemployment on family structure in terms of six stages of adjustment. Although the families studied were white, the pattern would clearly seem to be a general one, and apply to Negro families as well.

The first two stages end with the exhaustion of credit and the entry of the wife into the labor force. The father is no longer the provider and the elder children become resentful.

The third stage is the critical one of commencing a new day-to-day existence. At this point two women are in charge:

> Consider the fact that relief investigators or case workers are normally women and deal with the housewife. Already suffering a loss in prestige and authority in the family because of his failure to be the chief bread winner, the male head of the family feels deeply this obvious transfer of planning for the family's well-being to two women, one of them an outsider. His role is reduced to that of errand boy to and from the relief office.

If the family makes it through this stage Bakke finds that it is likely to survive, and the rest of the process is one of adjustment. *The critical element of adjustment was not welfare payments, but work.*

> Having observed our families under conditions of unemployment with no public help, or with that help coming from direct [sic] and from work relief, we are convinced that after the exhaustion of self-produced resources, work relief is the only type of assistance which can restore the strained bonds of family relationship in a way which promises the continued functioning of that family in meeting the responsibilities imposed upon it by our culture.

Work is precisely the one thing the Negro family head in such circumstances has not received over the past generation.

The fundamental, overwhelming fact is that *Negro unemployment,* with the exception of a few years during World War II and the Korean War, *has continued at disaster levels for 35 years.*

Once again, this is particularly the case in the northern urban areas to which the Negro population has been moving.

The 1930 Census (taken in the spring, before the depression was in full swing) showed Negro unemployment at 6.1 percent, as against 6.6 percent for whites. But taking out the South reversed the relationship: white 7.4 percent, nonwhite 11.5 percent.

By 1940, the 2 to 1 white-Negro unemployment relationship that persists to this day had clearly emerged. Taking out the South again, whites were 14.8 percent, nonwhites 29.7 percent.

Since 1929, the Negro worker has been tremendously affected by the movements of the business cycle and of employment. He has been hit worse by declines than whites, and proportionately helped more by recoveries.

From 1951 to 1963, the level of Negro male unemployment was on a long-run rising trend, while at the same time following the short-run ups and downs of the business cycle. During the same period, the number of broken families in the Negro world was also on a long-run rise, with intermediate ups and downs.

Divorce is expensive: those without money resort to separation or desertion. While divorce is not a desirable goal for a society, it recognizes the importance of marriage and family, and for children some family continuity and support is more likely when the institution of the family has been so recognized.

The conclusion from these and similar data is difficult to avoid: During times when jobs were reasonably plentiful (although at no time during this period, save perhaps the first 2 years, did the unemployment rate for Negro males drop to anything like a reasonable level) the Negro family became stronger and more stable. As jobs became more and more difficult to find, the stability of the family became more and more difficult to maintain.

This relation is clearly seen in terms of the illegitimacy rates of census tracts in the District of Columbia compared with male unemployment rates in the same neighborhoods.

In 1963, a prosperous year, 29.2 percent of all Negro men in the labor force were unemployed at some time during the year. Almost half of these men were out of work 15 weeks or more.

The impact of poverty on Negro family structure is no less obvious, although again it may not be widely acknowledged. There would seem to be an American tradition, agrarian in its origins but reinforced by attitudes of urban immigrant groups, to the effect that family morality and stability decline as income and social position rise. Over the years this may have provided some consolation to the poor, but there is little evidence that it is true. On the contrary, higher family incomes are unmistakably associated with greater family stability — which comes first may be a matter for conjecture, but the conjunction of the two characteristics is unmistakable.

The Negro family is no exception. In the District of Columbia, for example, census tracts with median incomes over $8,000 had an illegitimacy rate one-third that of tracts in the category under $4,000.

The Wage System

The American wage system is conspicuous in the degree to which it provides high incomes for individuals, but is rarely adjusted to insure that family, as well as individual needs are met. Almost without exception, the social welfare and social insurance system of other industrial democracies provide for some adjustment or supplement of a worker's income to provide for the extra expenses of those with families. American arrangements do not, save for income tax deductions.

The Federal minimum wage of $1.25 per hour provides a basic income for an individual, but an income well below the poverty line for a couple, much less a family with children.

The 1965 Economic Report of the President revised the data on the number of persons living in poverty in the United States to take account of the varying needs of families of different sizes, rather than using a flat cut off at the $3,000 income level. The resulting revision illustrates the significance of family size. Using these criteria, the number of poor families is smaller, but the number of large families who are poor increases, and the number of children in poverty rises by more than one-third — from 11 million to 15 million. This means that one-fourth of the Nation's children live in families that are poor.

A third of these children belong to families in which the father was not only present, but was employed the year round. In overall terms, median family income is lower for large families than for small families. Families of six or more children have median incomes 24 percent below families with three. (It may be added that 47 percent of young men who fail the Selective Service education test come from families of six or more.)

During the 1950-60 decade of heavy Negro migration to the cities of the North and West, the ratio of nonwhite to white family income in cities increased from 57 to 63 percent. Corresponding declines in the ratio in the rural nonfarm and farm areas kept the national ratio virtually unchanged. But between 1960 and 1963, median nonwhite family income slipped from 55 percent to 53 percent of white income. The drop occurred in three regions, with only the South, where a larger proportion of Negro families have more than one earner, showing a slight improvement.

Ratio of Nonwhite to White Family Median Income,
United States and Regions, 1960-63

Region	1960	1961	1962	1963
United States	55	53	53	53
Northeast	68	67	66	65
North Central	74	72	68	73
South	43	43	47	45
West	81	87	73	76

Because in general terms Negro families have the largest number of children and the lowest incomes, many Negro fathers literally cannot support their families. Because the father is either not present, is unemployed, or makes such a low wage, the Negro woman goes to work. Fifty-six per cent of Negro women, age 25 to 64, are in the work force, against 42 percent of white women. This dependence on the mother's income undermines the position of the father and deprives the children of the kind of attention, particularly in school matters, which is now a standard feature of middle-class upbringing.

The Dimensions Grow

The dimensions of the problems of Negro Americans are compounded by the present extraordinary growth in Negro population. At the founding of the nation, and into the first decade of the 19th century, 1 American in 5 was a Negro. The proportion declined steadily until it was only 1 in 10 by 1920, where it held until the 1950's, when it began to rise. Since 1950, the Negro population has grown at a rate of 2.4 percent per year compared with 1.7 percent for the total population. If this rate continues, in seven years 1 American in 8 will be nonwhite.

These changes are the result of a declining Negro death rate, now approaching that of the nation generally, and a fertility rate that grew steadily during the postwar period. By 1959, the ratio of white to nonwhite fertility rates reached 1:1.42. Both the white and nonwhite fertility rates have declined since 1959, but the differential has not narrowed.

Family size increased among nonwhite families between 1950 and 1960 — as much for those without father as for those with fathers. Average family size changed little among white families, with a slight increase in the size of husband-wife families balanced by a decline in the size of families without fathers.

Negro women not only have more children, but have them earlier. Thus in 1960, there were 1,247 children ever born per thousand ever-married nonwhite women 15 to 19 years of age, as against only 725 among white women, a ratio of 1.7:1. The Negro fertility rate overall is now 1.4 times the white, but what might be called the generation rate is 1.7 times the white.

This population growth must inevitably lead to an unconcealable crisis in Negro unemployment. The most conspicuous failure of the American social system in the past 10 years has been its inadequacy in providing jobs for Negro youth. Thus, in January 1965 the unemployment rate for Negro teenagers stood at 29 percent. This problem will now become steadily more serious.

During the rest of the 1960's the nonwhite civilian population 14 years of age and over will increase by 20 percent — more than double the white rate. The nonwhite labor force will correspondingly increase 20 percent in the next 6 years, double the rate of increase in nonwhite labor force of the past decade.

As with the population as a whole, there is much evidence that children are being born most rapidly in those Negro families with the least financial resources. This is an ancient pattern, but because the needs of children are greater today it is very possible that the education and opportunity gap between the offspring of these families and those of stable middle-class unions is not closing, but is growing wider.

A cycle is at work; too many children too early make it most difficult for the parents to finish school. (In February, 1963, 38 percent of the white girls who dropped out of school did so because of marriage or pregnancy, as against 49 percent of nonwhite girls.) An Urban League study in New York reported that 44 percent of girl dropouts left school because of pregnancy.

Low education levels in turn produce low income levels, which deprive children of many opportunities, and so the cycle repeats itself.

Testimony on Open Housing*

Nicholas deB. Katzenbach †

TITLE IV—HOUSING

In the Civil Rights Act of 1866, Congress declared:

> All citizens of the United States shall have the same right, in every state and territory, as is enjoyed by white citizens thereof to inherit, purchase, lease, sell, hold, and convey real and personal property.

Again, in the National Housing Act of 1949, Congress made an even broader commitment by pledging the nation to the goal of a decent home and a suitable living environment for every American family.

Yet today, 100 years after the Civil Rights Act and 17 years after the Housing Act, we find, in the words of the U.S. Commission on Civil Rights, that

> housing . . . seems to be the one commodity in the American market that is not freely available on equal terms to everyone who can afford to pay.

Title IV of the President's bill is designed to help achieve equality in the marketplace.

The past 20 years have provided the country with millions upon millions of new dwelling units and have vastly changed the character of our urban residential areas. Suburbia has come into being around the boundaries of our cities and continues to spread.

---

*Committee on the Judiciary, *Hearings,* May, 1966.
†Former Attorney General of the United States.

Except for our Negro citizens, virtually all Americans have had an equal opportunity to share in these developments in our national life. The Negro's choice in housing, unlike that of his fellow citizens, is not limited merely by this means.

It is limited by his color. By and large, desirable new housing in our cities and suburbs is foreclosed to him, and, ironically, because of its scarcity, what housing is left available to him frequently costs him more, judged by any fair standard, than comparable housing open to whites.

The result is apparent to all: impacted Negro ghettos that are surrounded and contained by white suburbia. The problem has arisen in metropolitan communities everywhere in the country.

Segregated housing is deeply corrosive both for the individual and for his community. It isolates racial minorities from the public life of the community. It means inferior public education, recreation, health, sanitation, and transportation services and facilities.

It means denial of access to training and employment and business opportunities. It prevents the inhabitants of the ghettos from liberating themselves, and it prevents the federal, state, and local governments and private groups and institutions from fulfilling their responsibility and desire to help in this liberation.

Through the years, there has been considerable state and private response to discrimination in housing. Seventeen states, the District of Columbia, Puerto Rico, the Virgin Islands, and a large number of municipalities have enacted a variety of fair housing laws.

Volunteer efforts by private citizens also have been organized in many communities, such as Neighbors, Inc., here in the District of Columbia.

In addition, there has been a series of actions by the federal government.

In the judicial branch, the Supreme Court acted decisively as early as 1948 when it held racially restrictive covenants to be unenforceable in either the state or federal Courts.

In the executive branch, President Kennedy's Executive Order 11063 of November 20, 1962, established the President's Committee on Equal Housing Opportunity and forbade discrimination in new FHA- or VA-insured housing.

By now it should be plain that a patchwork of state and local laws is not enough. The work of private volunteer groups is not enough. Court decisions are not enough. The limited authority now available to the executive branch is not enough.

The time has now surely come for decisive action by the legislative branch of the federal government. Durable remedies for so endemic and deep-seated a condition as housing segregation should be based on the prescription and sanction of Congress. This is all the more so as the issue is national in scope and as it penetrates into so many other sectors of public policy such as the rebuilding and physical improvement of our cities.

The extent to which the decisions of individual homeowners reduce the availability of housing to racial minorities is hard to estimate. But I believe it is accurate to say that individual homeowners do not control the pattern of housing in communities of any size. The main components of the housing industry are builders, landlords, real estate brokers, and those who provide mortgage money. These are the groups which maintain housing patterns based on race.

I do not mean to suggest that the enforcement of segregation in housing is necessarily motivated by racial bias. More often the conduct of those in the housing business reflects the misconception that neighborhoods must remain racially separate to maintain real estate values.

While there exist studies which indicate that desegregated housing does not depress real estate values, many in the real estate business fear to take the chance. I have no doubt that they simply feel trapped by custom and the possibility of competitive loss. The fact is, however, that their policies and practices are what perpetuate segregated housing.

At present a particular builder or landlord who resists selling or renting to a Negro most often does so not out of personal bigotry but out of fear that his prospective white tenants or purchasers will move to housing limited to whites and that, because similar housing is unavailable to Negroes, what he has to offer will attract only Negroes. If all those in the housing industry are bound by a universal law against discrimination, there will be no economic peril to any one of them. All would be in a position to sell without discrimination. Indeed, experienced developers have stated that they would welcome such a law.

Therefore, I think it would be a mistake to regard the most significant aspect of a federal fair housing measure as its sanctions against builders, landlords, lenders, or brokers. What is more significant, rather, is that they can utilize this law as a shield to protect them when they do what is right.

The same protection would be given an individual homeowner who privately has no reservation about selling his home to a Negro but who may be inhibited by the fears he could generate among the neighbors he is leaving. A uniform statute would outlaw segregation in all neighborhoods.

There is a close parallel here with the impact of the public accommodations title of the Civil Rights Act of 1964. Restaurant or motel owners, willing to desegregate, failed to do so because of economic fears. Once the act was passed—and all of their competitors had to serve Negroes—many quickly complied. . . .

As one of the justices of the Supreme Court said in the very recent Guest case—to which I shall return shortly—the Fourteenth Amendment includes a "positive grant of legislative power, authorizing Congress to exercise its discretion in fashioning remedies to achieve civil and political equality for all citizens."

I have pointed out already how segregated living is both a source and an enforcer of involuntary second-class citizenship. To the extent that this blight on our democracy impedes states and localities from carrying out their obligations under the Fourteenth Amendment to promote equal access and equal opportunity in all public aspects of community life, the Fourteenth Amendment authorizes removal of this impediment.

That there is official and governmental involvement in the real estate and construction industries needs little demonstration. Apart from zoning and building codes, there are the obvious facts of regulations covering credit, mortgages, interest rates, and banking practices, and there is the universal licensing of real estate agents.

But there are more basic considerations.

Are we to tell our Negro citizens that the Congress which has guaranteed them access to desegregated public schools and to swimming pools and to golf courses is powerless to guarantee them the basic right to choose a place to live? I would find this hard to explain, for I would not be able to understand it myself.

To me it is clear that the Fourteenth Amendment gives Congress the power to address itself to the vindication of what is, in substance, the freedom to live.

Congress can and must make the legislative judgment that without equal housing opportunity there cannot be full equality under law. Congress can and must determine that the enforcement of involuntary segregation through discriminatory housing practices is inconsistent with the words, spirit, and purpose of the Fourteenth Amendment.

These are the human terms in which the Constitution speaks and cries out for quick response. There are also economic terms. The Congress is charged with the protection and promotion of interstate commerce in all its forms.

I cannot doubt that housing is embraced under this congressional power. The construction of homes and apartment buildings, the production and sale of building materials and home furnishings, the financing of construction and purchases all take place in or through the channels of interstate commerce.

When the total problem is considered, it requires no great leap of the imagination to conclude that interstate commerce is significantly affected by the sale even of single dwellings, multiplied many times in each community.

It was almost 30 years ago that the Supreme Court faced and resolved this problem in *Wickard* v. *Filburn*. In that case the court held that the Agricultural Adjustment Act could validly apply to a farmer who sowed only 23 acres of wheat, almost all of which was consumed on his farm.

The housing industry last year represented $27.6 billion of new private investment. This expenditure on residential housing is considerably more than the $22.9 billion which all American agriculture contributed to the gross national product in 1965.

Simply consider in practical terms how housing is financed, built, and sold.

Take the case of a real estate developer in California who wants to construct a subdivision on land in Arizona. He and a group of associates raise money from banks in New York, from insurance companies in Connecticut, from pension funds in Chicago. They go to Arizona to purchase the land; hire a contractor from Texas to build the homes; he leases construction equipment in Colorado, orders lumber from Oregon, millwork from Michigan, steel products from Pennsylvania, appliances from Ohio, furnishings from North Carolina. Meanwhile the developer is advertising for buyers from all over the nation in national magazines and in newspapers from coast to coast. Buyers are found; they in turn secure mortgages from banks and insurance companies throughout the country. One might almost say that everything in each of those homes—from the land to the homeowner—"moved" in interstate commerce; but certainly the "housing" as a marketable commodity, was created, financed, and sold in and through the channels of interstate commerce.

Of course, like Mr. Filburn's wheat, not every home has all of these connections with interstate commerce. But most housing has some of these. For example, of the total of almost 15 million single-family occupant-owned dwellings that carried mortgages in 1960, two and one-half million were mortgaged to out-of-state lenders. More than half the home mortgages held by insurance companies were held by companies outside the homeowner's state. What is more, in many of our largest cities with the most serious housing problems, the local real estate markets are themselves in interstate commerce, seeking owners and tenants from multistate metropolitan areas or through national listings. Such cities as Kansas City, New York, Chicago, St. Louis, Cincinnati, Omaha, Philadelphia, have "bedroom areas" crossing into other states.

There thus can be no doubt that anything which significantly affects the housing industry also affects interstate commerce. Discriminatory housing practices produce such an effect. They restrict the amount and type of new housing; discourage the repair and rehabilitation of existing housing; remove incentives to the purchase of new furniture and appliances; and frustrate the efforts of people to move from job to job and from state to state.

Clearly the people, the money, the materials, the entrepreneurial talent which move in and to the housing market are not confined within single states. Rather they are well within the range of congressional regulation, and within this range Congress' judgment as to what problems need solving and how they should be solved is necessarily broad.

Civil Rights Act of 1968

Congress and the President

TITLE VIII — FAIR HOUSING

POLICY

Sec. 801. It is the policy of the United States to provide, within constitutional limitations, for fair housing throughout the United States.

EFFECTIVE DATES OF CERTAIN PROHIBITIONS

Sec. 803. (a) Subject to the provisions of subsection (b) and section 807, the prohibitions against discrimination in the sale or rental of housing set forth in section 804 shall apply:

(1) Upon enactment of this title, to—

(A) dwellings owned or operated by the Federal Government;

(B) dwellings provided in whole or in part with the aid of loans, advances, grants, or contributions made by the Federal Government, under agreements entered into after November 20, 1962, unless payment due thereon has been made in full prior to the date of enactment of this title;

(C) dwellings provided in whole or in part by loans insured, guaranteed, or otherwise secured by the credit of the Federal Government, under agreements entered into after November 20, 1962, unless payment thereon has been made in full prior to the date of enactment of this title: *Provided,* That nothing contained in sub-paragraphs (B) and (C) of this subsection shall be applicable to dwellings solely by virtue of the fact that they are subject to mortgages held by an FDIC or FSLIC institution; and

(D) dwellings provided by the development or the redevelopment of real property purchased, rented, or otherwise obtained from a State or local public agency receiving Federal financial assistance for slum clearance or urban renewal with respect to such real property under loan or grant contracts entered into after November 20, 1962.

(2) After December 31, 1968, to all dwellings covered by paragraph (1) and to all other dwellings except as exempted by subsection (b).

(b) Nothing in section 804 shall apply to—

(1) any single-family house sold or rented by an owner: *Provided,* That such private individual owner does not own more than three such single-family houses at any one time:

Provided further, That after December 31, 1969, the sale or rental of any such single-family house shall be excepted from the application of this title only if such house is sold or rented (A) without the use in any manner of the sales or rental facilities or the sales or rental services of any real estate broker, agent, or salesman, or of such facilities or services of any person in the business of selling or renting dwellings, or of any employee or agent of any such broker, agent, salesman, or person and (B) without the publication, posting or mailing, after notice, of any advertisement or written notice in violation of section 804 (c) of this title; but nothing in this proviso shall prohibit the use of attorneys, escrow agents, abstractors, title companies, and other such professional assistance as necessary to perfect or transfer the title,

(2) rooms or units in dwellings containing living quarters occupied or intended to be occupied by no more than four families living independently of each other, if the owner actually maintains and occupies one of such living quarters as his residence.

DISCRIMINATION IN THE SALE OR RENTAL OF HOUSING

Sec. 804. As made applicable by section 803 and except as exempted by sections 803 (b) and 807, it shall be unlawful—

(a) To refuse to sell or rent after the making of a bona fide offer, or to refuse to negotiate for the sale or rental of, or otherwise make unavailable or deny, a dwelling to any person because of race, color, religion, or national origin.

(b) To discriminate against any person in the terms, conditions, or privileges of sale or rental of a dwelling, or in the provision of services or facilities in connection therewith, because of race, color, religion, or national origin.

(c) To make, print, or publish, or cause to be made, printed, or published any notice, statement, or advertisement, with respect to the sale or rental of a dwelling that indicates any preference, limitation, or discrimination based on race, color, religion, or national origin, or an intention to make any such preference, limitation, or discrimination.

(d) To represent to any person because of race, color, religion, or national origin that any dwelling is not available for inspection, sale, or rental when such dwelling is in fact so available.

(e) For profit, to induce or attempt to induce any person to sell or rent any dwelling by representations regarding the entry or prospective entry into the neighborhood of a person or persons of a particular race, color, religion, or national origin.

DISCRIMINATION IN THE FINANCING OF HOUSING

Sec. 805. After December 31, 1968, it shall be unlawful for any bank, building and loan association, insurance company or other corporation, association, firm or enterprise whose business consists in whole or in part in the making of commercial real estate loans, to deny a loan or other financial assistance to a person applying therefor for the purpose of purchasing, constructing, improving, repairing, or maintaining a dwelling, or to discriminate against him in the fixing of the amount, interest rate, duration, or other terms or conditions of such loan or other financial assistance, because of the race, color, religion, or national origin of such person or of any person associated with him in connection with such loan or other financial assistance or the purposes of such loan or other financial assistance, or of the present or prospective owners, lessees, tenants, or occupants of the dwelling or dwellings in relation to which such loan or other financial assistance is to be made or given: *Provided,* That nothing contained in this section shall impair the scope or effectiveness of the exception contained in section 803 (b).

DISCRIMINATION IN THE PROVISION OF BROKERAGE SERVICES

Sec. 806. After December 31, 1968, it shall be unlawful to deny any person access to or membership or participation in any multiple-listing service, real estate brokers organization or other service, organization, or facility relating to the business of selling or renting dwellings, or to discriminate against him in the terms or conditions of such access, membership, or participation, on account of race, color, religion, or national origin.

ADMINISTRATION

Sec. 808. (a) The authority and responsibility for administering this Act shall be in the Secretary of Housing and Urban Development.

ENFORCEMENT

Sec. 810. (a) Any person who claims to have been injured by a discriminatory housing practice or who believes that he will be irrevocably injured by a discriminatory housing practice that is about to occur (hereafter "person aggrieved") may file a complaint with the Secretary. Complaints shall be in writing and shall contain such information and be in such form as the Secretary requires. Upon receipt of such a complaint the Secretary shall furnish a copy of the same to the person or persons who allegedly committed or are about to commit the alleged discriminatory housing practice. Within thirty days after receiving a complaint, or within thirty days after the expiration of any period of reference under subsection (c), the Secretary shall investigate the complaint and give notice in writing to the person aggrieved whether he intends to resolve it. If the Secretary decides to resolve the complaint, he shall proceed to try to eliminate or correct the alleged discriminatory housing practice by informal methods of conference, conciliation, and persuasion.

. . .

(d) If within thirty days after a complaint is filed with the Secretary or within thirty days after expiration of any period of reference under subsection (c), the Secretary has been unable to obtain voluntary compliance with this title, the person aggrieved may, within thirty days thereafter, commence a civil action in any appropriate United States district court, against the respondent named in the complaint, to enforce the rights granted or protected by this title, insofar as such rights relate to the subject of the complaint: *Provided,* That no such civil action may be brought in any United States district court if the person aggrieved has a judicial remedy under a State or local fair housing law which provides rights and remedies for alleged discriminatory housing practices which are substantially equivalent to the rights and remedies provided in this title. Such actions may be brought without regard to the amount in controversy in any United States district court for the district in which the discriminatory housing practice is alleged to have occurred or be about to occur or in which the respondent resides or transacts business. If the court finds that a discriminatory housing practice has occurred or is about to occur, the court may, subject to the provisions of section 812, enjoin the respondent from engaging in such practice or order such affirmative action as may be appropriate.

Property Owners' Bill of Rights*

National Association of Real Estate Boards

In 1789, the people of America were fearful that Government might restrict their freedom. The first Congress of the United States, in that year, proposed a Bill of Rights.

The Bill of Rights, essentially, tells the Government what it cannot do. The statements comprise the first ten amendments to the United States Constitution.

The Bill of Rights has had a profound impact upon the history of the World.

Forty million immigrants gave up much to come to this land, seeking something promised here — and only here. Many countries have abundant natural resources, vast vacant lands and climate as good as America.

They came here for the promise of security—the promise of freedom—for the precious right to live as free men with equal opportunity for all.

In July of 1868, a new guarantee of freedom was ratified. Its purpose was to guard against human slavery. Its guarantees were for the equal protection of all.

This new guarantee of freedom is the 14th Amendment. It reads, in part, as follows:

"No state shall make or enforce any law which shall abridge the privileges or immunities of citizens of the United States; nor shall any state deprive any person of life, liberty or property, without due process of law; nor deny to any person within its jurisdiction, the equal protection of the laws."

---

*Reprinted from National Association of Real Estate Boards, "Property Owners Bill of Rights," June 4, 1963.

The vital importance of these federal laws was reemphasized in a recent statement of the Chief Justice of the United States in which he urged the retention of "Government of laws in preference to a Government of men."

Today, the rights and freedoms of the individual American property owner are being eroded. This endangers the rights and freedoms of all Americans. Therefore, a Bill of Rights to protect the American property owner is needed.

It is self-evident that the erosion of these freedoms will destroy the free enterprising individual American.

It is our solemn belief that the individual American property owner, regardless of race, color or creed, must be allowed, under law, to retain:

1. The right of privacy.

2. The right to choose his own friends.

3. The right to own and enjoy property according to his own dictates.

4. The right to occupy and dispose of property without governmental interference in accordance with the dictates of his conscience.

5. The right of all equally to enjoy property without interference by laws giving special privilege to any group or groups.

6. The right to maintain what, in his opinion, are congenial surroundings for tenants.

7. The right to contract with a real estate broker or other representative of his choice and to authorize him to act for him according to his instructions.

8. The right to determine the acceptability and desirability of any prospective buyer or tenant of his property.

9. The right of every American to choose who, in his opinion, are congenial tenants in any property he owns — to maintain the stability and security of his income.

10. The right to enjoy the freedom to accept, reject, negotiate or not negotiate with, others.

Loss of these rights diminishes personal Freedom and creates a springboard for further erosion of Liberty.

3

Protest and Public Order

Public protest was essential to progress in civil rights in America. The civil rights movement first had to attract the attention of the nation's apathetic and disinterested white majority to the injustices of segregation and discrimination before progress in legislation could be expected. Only open dramatic appeals to the conscience of America could move men to action in eliminating inequality. Until 1954, Negro protests were primarily in the form of legal cases brought by the National Association for the Advancement of Colored People (NAACP) to federal courts; negotiation and bargaining with white businessmen and government officials by the National Urban League; and local lobbying on behalf of Negro constituents by Negro political leaders. But in 1955 the Negro community of Montgomery, Alabama, began a year-long boycott with frequent demonstrations against the Montgomery city buses over segregated seating practices. This dramatic appeal and the eventual success of the boycott in Montgomery brought nation-wide attention to a local Negro minister, Martin Luther King Jr., and led to the creation in 1956 of the Southern Christian Leadership Conference. In 1960 Negro students from the North Carolina Agricultural and Technical College began a "sit-in" demonstration at the segregated Woolworth lunch counter in Greensboro, North Carolina. Soon, "sit-ins" in restaurants, "read-ins" in libraries, "pray-ins" in white churches spread throughout the South, generally under the direction of the Southern Christian Leadership Conference which followed a philosophy of non-violent direct action in its protests. The Congress of Racial Equality (CORE), which at this time was also committed to the philosophy of non-violence, initiated a series of "freedom-rides" in the South, in which

121

groups of white-Negro bus travellers attempted to desegregate bus travel and terminal facilities. These freedom-riders underwent arrest and mob-violence in many southern cities. Often police looked on while freedom-riders were attacked by white segregationists. In 1961 President Kennedy was obliged to send 400 federal marshals to Montgomery, Alabama to protect the freedom-riders.

Perhaps the most dramatic protest against segregation occurred in Birmingham, Alabama, in the spring of 1963. In support of a request for desegregation of downtown eating places and the formation of a bi-racial committee to work out integration in public schools, Dr. Martin Luther King Jr. led several thousand Birmingham Negroes in a series of orderly street marches. The demonstrators met with strong police action including fire hoses, police dogs and electric cattle prods. News-paper pictures of Negroes being attacked by the police and bitten by dogs were flashed all over the world. More than 25,000 demonstrators including Dr. King were jailed. A group of Alabama clergymen in a *Letter to Martin Luther King Jr.,* petitioned Dr. King to call off protests and demonstrations which they believed incited people to hatred and violence. They urged Dr. King to drop his public protest and to press his case instead in the courts and established political channels. Dr. King's *Letter from a Birmingham City Jail* written in reply to the Alabama clergymen quickly became the most widely read defense of non-violent protest in American political literature.

The most important year for non-violent direct action was probably 1963. The Birmingham incident set off demonstrations in many parts of the country; the scene remained one of non-violence, and it was usually whites rather than Negroes who resorted to violence in these demonstrations. Responsible Negro leadership remained in control of the movement and won widespread support from the white community. The culmination of the non-violent philosophy was a giant yet orderly march on Washington on August 28, 1963. More than 200,000 Negroes and whites participated in the march which was endorsed by many labor leaders, religious groups and political figures. It was in response to this march that President Kennedy sent a strong civil rights bill to Congress, which was later passed after his death as the famous Civil Rights Act of 1964.

Again in 1965 Martin Luther King Jr. led a successful non-violent voting rights march from Selma to Montgomery, Alabama. This march was a protest against the refusal of local southern registrars to register Negro voters. The hostility of southern segregationists and the failure of state and local authorities to protect the marchers led President Johnson to federalize the national guard and order them to protect the demonstrators. After the march President Johnson sent another historic Civil Rights measure to the Congress — the Voting Rights Act of 1965.

It is very doubtful that in the absence of public protest and demonstrations Congress ever would have passed the Civil Rights Act of 1964 or the Voting Rights Act of 1965. Yet mass demonstrations, sit-ins, and other militant tactics often involve the violation of state and local laws. For example, remaining at a segregated lunch counter after the owner orders one to leave may violate trespass laws. Marching in the street may involve the obstruction of traffic, "disorderly conduct," or "parading without a permit." Demonstrations may involve "disturbing the peace," or "disobeying the orders of a police officer." Even though these tactics are non-violent, they involve disobedience to civil law.

Civil disobedience is not new in American life. Patriots staged the Boston Tea Party, abolitionists hid run-away slaves, suffragettes paraded and demonstrated for women's rights, labor organizers picketted to form the nation's major industrial unions, and all of the nation's wars have been protested. Civil disobedience is a tactic of minorities, since majorities can more easily change laws, and seldom have to disobey them.

Charles Frankel directs himself to the perplexing question: *Is It Ever Right to Break the Law?* Frankel notes that the political purpose of disobedience is to call attention, or "bear witness," to the existence of injustice. The object is to stir the consciousness of an apathetic majority. Punishment inflicted for an unjust law can shame a majority and make it ask itself how far it is willing to go to protect the status quo. But civil disobedience cannot be lightly undertaken. It can arouse extreme passions on either side, excite and provoke the masses, and make disrespect for law commonplace and a popular attitude.

The philosophy of non-violent direct action expressed by Martin Luther King Jr. reflected a belief in the underlying goodness of America. Non-violence appealed to the conscience of white America, and by so doing implied that white America does have a conscience capable of responding to the plight of black America. Martin Luther King expressed confidence and optimism about America: "I have no despair about the future . . . we will reach the goal of freedom in Birmingham and all over the nation because the goal of America is freedom."

But there are other black leaders in the land who have much less confidence in white America than Dr. King. Stokely Carmichael expressed deep distrust and bitterness toward the white society: "We cannot be expected any longer to march and have our heads broken in order to say to whites: 'Come on, you're nice guys.' For you are not nice guys. We have found you out." Carmichael talks of an alternate course for American Negroes, *Black Power* — and defines this course in a policy statement issued by the Student Non-Violent Coordinating Committee.

Civil disorder and violence are not new on the American scene. The nation itself was founded in armed revolution. In 1786 farmers who were in debt forceably stopped the trial of debtors and laid seige to the courthouse in Springfield, Massachusetts. The state militia was required to put down "Shays' Rebellion." Nat Turner's Slave Insurrection in 1831 resulted in the death of 51 white persons and later the execution of Turner and his followers. On July 13, 1863, New York City was the seat of the nation's first major draft riot. Negroes were the objects of much of the rioters wrath, since many attributed conscription to Lincoln's attempt to free the slaves. Violence was a constant companion of the early labor movement in America. The famous Homestead strike of 1892 turned Homestead, Pennsylvania into an open battlefield. The Pullman Strike of 1893 required federal troops to restore order in Chicago. In 1914 over 100 persons were killed in the Ludlow Colorado Massacre where company guards attacked a tent city of striking miners. In 1943 racial violence erupted in Detroit resulting in 35 deaths.

Yet even though domestic violence has played a prominent role in America's history, the urban riots of the 1960's were the most massive and widespread civil disorders ever to face the nation. In city after city, Negro ghettoes were wracked with burning, sniping and rioting. All of these riots involve Negro attacks on established authority — policemen, firemen, national guardsmen, whites in general and property owned by whites.

The President's *National Advisory Committee on Civil Disorders,* perhaps in an attempt to shock the nation's white majority to action on urban problems, asserted that "white racism" was responsible for urban rioting. According to the Commission, the "bitter fruits of white racial attitudes" are "pervasive discrimination and segregation," "black migration and white exodus," and "black ghettos." The Commission added that "powerful ingredients" helped to "catalyze the mixture" and bring about the disorders: "frustrated hopes," "legitimation of violence," and "powerlessness."

The Commission directed itself to three basic questions: What happened? Why did it happen? What can be done to prevent it from happening again?

President Johnson appointed his Commission on Civil Disorders on July 27, 1967, during a summer in which the nation experienced its most disastrous riots. Governor Otto Kerner of Illinois was designated as Chairman, and the Commission is sometimes referred to as the

"Kerner Commission." John Lindsay, Republican Mayor of New York, was Vice Chairman. The Commission included, Senator Fred Harris, Democrat of Oklahoma; Representative James Corman, Democrat of California; Representative William M. McCulloch, Republican of Ohio; Miss Kathryn G. Peden, Commissioner of Commerce of Kentucky; I. W. Abel, President of the Steel Workers of America; Herbert Jenkins, Chief of Police, Atlanta, Georgia; Charles B. Thornton, Chairman of Litton Industries; Senator Edward Brooke, Republican of Massachusetts; and Roy Wilkins, Executive Director of the NAACP. The composition of the Commission was obviously moderate; there was no Stokely Carmichael, Floyd McKissick of CORE, or even Martin Luther King, Jr. Yet the Commission's report startled many Americans.

Mass violence and disorder of a different nature occurred in view of a national television audience during the Democratic National Convention in August, 1968. Unlike earlier city riots, there was no looting or burning, and the civilian participants were primarily white, student youths, rather than black ghetto residents. The youths were engaged in mass protest activity; the violence was perpetrated for the most part by the police.

In a careful report to the President's Commission on the Causes and Prevention of Violence, entitled "Rights in Conflict," Chicago attorney Daniel Walker describes and documents *The Police Riot in Chicago*. While there was provocation by word and act on the part of the demonstrators, "the nature of the response was unrestrained and indiscriminate police violence." The demonstrators in Chicago tested the commitment of our society to the right of dissent, and, by and large, society failed the test. Not only was dissent met with overwhelming police violence, but public officials and public opinion throughout the nation generally approved of police violence directed against demonstrators.

Letter to Martin Luther King

A Group of Alabama Clergymen

Following is the text of the public statement on Negro demonstrations directed to Dr. Martin Luther King Jr. by eight Alabama clergymen.

April 12, 1963

We clergymen are among those who, in January, issued "An Appeal for Law and Order and Common Sense," in dealing with racial problems in Alabama. We expressed understanding that honest convictions in racial matters could properly be pursued in the courts, but urged that decisions of those courts should in the meantime be peacefully obeyed.

Since that time there has been some evidence of increased forbearance and a willingness to face facts. Responsible citizens have undertaken to work on various problems which cause racial friction and unrest. In Birmingham, recent public events have given indication that we all have opportunity for a new constructive and realistic approach to racial problems.

However, we are now confronted by a series of demonstrations by some of our Negro citizens, directed and led in part by outsiders. We recognize the natural impatience of people who feel that their hopes are slow in being realized. But we are convinced that these demonstrations are unwise and untimely.

We agree rather with certain local Negro leadership which has called for honest and open negotiation of racial issues in our area. And we believe this kind of facing of issues can best be accomplished by citizens of our own metropolitan area, white and Negro, meeting with their knowledge and experience of the local situation. All of us need to face that responsibility and find proper channels for its accomplishment.

Just as we formerly pointed out that "hatred and violence have no sanction in our religious and political traditions," we also point out that such actions as incite to hatred and violence, however technically peaceful those actions may be, have not contributed to the resolution of our local problems. We do not believe that these days of new hope are days when extreme measures are justified in Birmingham.

We commend the community as a whole, and the local news media and law enforcement officials in particular, on the calm manner in which these demonstrations have been handled. We urge the public to continue to show restraint should the demonstrations continue, and the law enforcement officials to remain calm and continue to protect our city from violence.

We further strongly urge our own Negro community to withdraw support from these demonstrations, and to unite locally in working peacefully for a better Birmingham. When rights are consistently denied, a cause should be pressed in the courts and in negotiations among local leaders, and not in the streets. We appeal to both our white and Negro citizenry to observe the principles of law and order and common sense.

Signed by:

C. C. J. Carpenter, D.D., LL.D., *Bishop of Alabama*

Joseph A. Durick, D.D., *Auxiliary Bishop, Diocese of Mobile-Birmingham*

Rabbi Milton L. Grafman, *Temple Emanu-El, Birmingham, Alabama*

Bishop Paul Hardin, *Bishop of the Alabama-West Florida Conference of the Methodist Church*

Bishop Nolan B. Harmon, *Bishop of the North Alabama Conference of the Methodist Church*

George M. Murray, D.D., LL.D., *Bishop Coadjutor, Episcopal Diocese of Alabama*

Edward V. Ramage, *Moderator, Synod of the Alabama Presbyterian Church in the United States*

Earl Stallings, *Pastor, First Baptist Church, Birmingham, Alabama*

Letter From Birmingham City Jail

Martin Luther King

April 16, 1963

My Dear Fellow Clergymen,

While confined here in the Birmingham City Jail, I came across your recent statement calling our present activities "unwise and untimely." Seldom, if ever, do I pause to answer criticism of my work and ideas. . . . But since I feel that you are men of genuine good will and your criticisms are sincerely set forth, I would like to answer your statement in what I hope will be patient and reasonable terms. . . .

I am in Birmingham because injustice is here. Just as the 8th century prophets left their little villages and carried their "thus saith the Lord" far beyond the boundaries of their home town, and just as the Apostle Paul left his little village of Tarsus and carried the gospel of Jesus Christ to practically every hamlet and city of the Graeco-Roman world, I too am compelled to carry the gospel of freedom beyond my particular home town. Like Paul, I must constantly respond to the Macedonian call for aid.

Moreover, I am cognizant of the interrelatedness of all communities and states. I cannot sit idly by in Atlanta and not be concerned about what happens in Birmingham. Injustice anywhere is a threat to justice everywhere. We are caught in an inescapable network of mutuality tied in a single garment of destiny. Whatever affects one directly affects all indirectly. Never again can we afford to live with the narrow, provincial "outside agitator" idea. Anyone who lives inside the United States can never be considered an outsider anywhere in this country.

128

You deplore the demonstrations that are presently taking place in Birmingham. But I am sorry that your statement did not express a similar concern for the conditions that brought the demonstrations into being. I am sure that each of you would want to go far beyond the superficial social analyst who looks merely at effects, and does not grapple with underlying causes. I would not hesitate to say that it is unfortunate that so-called demonstrations are taking place in Birmingham at this time, but I would say in more emphatic terms that it is even more unfortunate that the white power structure of this city left the Negro community with no other alternative.

In any nonviolent campaign there are four basic steps: 1) collection of the facts to determine whether injustices are alive; 2) negotiation; 3) self-purification; and 4) direct action. We have gone through all of these steps in Birmingham. There can be no gain-saying of the fact that racial injustice engulfs this community. Birmingham is probably the most thoroughly segregated city in the United States. Its ugly record of police brutality is known in every section of this country. Its unjust treatment of Negroes in the courts is a notorious reality. There have been more unsolved bombings of Negro homes and churches in Birmingham than any city in this nation. These are the hard, brutal, and unbelievable facts. On the basis of these conditions Negro leaders sought to negotiate with the city fathers. But the political leaders consistently refused to engage in good faith negotiation. . . .

As in so many experiences of the past, we were confronted with blasted hopes, and the dark shadow of a deep disappointment settled upon us. So we had no alternative except that of preparing for direct action, whereby we would present our very bodies as a means of laying our case before the conscience of the local and national community. We were not unmindful of the difficulties involved. So we decided to go through a process of self-purification. We started having workshops on nonviolence and repeatedly asked ourselves the questions, "Are you able to accept blows without retaliating?" "Are you able to endure the ordeals of jail?" . . .

You may well ask, "Why direct action? Why sit-ins, marches, etc.? Isn't negotiation a better path?" You are exactly right in your call for negotiation. Indeed, this is the purpose of direct action. Nonviolent direct action seeks to create such a crisis and establish such creative tension that a community that has constantly refused to negotiate is forced to confront the issue. It seeks so to dramatize the issue that it can no longer be ignored.

I just referred to the creation of tension as a part of the work of the nonviolent resister. This may sound rather shocking. But I must confess that I am not afraid of the word tension. I have earnestly worked and preached against violent tension, but there is a type of constructive nonviolent tension that is necessary for growth. Just as Socrates felt that it was necessary to create a tension in the mind so that individuals could rise from the bondage of myths and half-truths to the unfettered realm of creative analysis and objective appraisal, we must see the need of having nonviolent gadflies to create the kind of tension in society that will help men rise from the dark depths of prejudice and racism to the majestic heights of understanding and brotherhood. So the purpose of the direct action is to create a situation so crisis-packed that it will inevitably open the door to negotiation. We, therefore, concur with you in your call for negotiation. Too long has our beloved Southland been bogged down in the tragic attempt to live in monologue rather than dialogue. . . .

My friends, I must say to you that we have not made a single gain in civil rights without determined legal and nonviolent pressure. History is the long and tragic story of the fact that privileged groups seldom give up their privileges voluntarily. Individuals may see the moral light and voluntarily give up their unjust posture; but as Reinhold Niebuhr has reminded us, groups are more immoral than individuals.

We know through painful experience that freedom is never voluntarily given by the oppressor; it must be demanded by the oppressed. Frankly I have never yet engaged in a direct action movement that was "well timed," according to the timetable of those who have not suffered unduly from the disease of segregation. For years now I have heard the word "Wait!" It rings in the ear of every Negro with a piercing familiarity. This "wait" has almost always meant "never." It has been a tranquilizing Thalidomide, relieving the emotional stress for a moment, only to give birth to an ill-formed infant of frustration. We must come to see with the distinguished jurist of yesterday that "justice too long delayed is justice denied." We have waited for more than 340 years for our constitutional and God-given rights. The nations of Asia and Africa are moving with jet-like speed toward the goal of political independence, and we still creep at horse and buggy pace toward the gaining of a cup of coffee at a lunch counter.

I guess it is easy for those who have never felt the stinging darts of segregation to say wait. But when you have seen vicious mobs lynch your mothers and fathers at will and drown your sisters and brothers at whim; when you have seen hate-filled policemen curse, kick, brutalize, and even kill your black brothers and sisters with impunity; when you see the vast majority of your 20 million Negro brothers smothering in an air-tight cage of poverty in the midst of an affluent society; when you suddenly find your tongue twisted and your speech stammering as you seek to explain to your six-year-old daughter why she can't go to the public amusement park that has just been advertised on television, and see tears welling up in her little eyes when she is told that Funtown is closed to colored children, and see the depressing clouds of inferiority begin to form in her little mental sky, and see her begin to distort her little personality by unconsciously developing a bitterness toward white people; when you have to concoct an answer for a five-year-old son asking in agonizing pathos: "Daddy, why do white people treat colored people so mean?"; when you take a cross country drive and find it necessary to sleep night after night in the uncomfortable corners of your automobile because no motel will accept you; when you are humiliated day in and day out by nagging signs reading "white" men and "colored"; when your first name becomes "nigger" and your middle name becomes "boy" (however old you are) and your last name becomes "John," and when your wife and mother are never given the respected title "Mrs."; when you are harried by day and haunted by night by the fact that you are a Negro, living constantly at tip-toe stance never quite knowing what to expect next, and plagued with inner fears and outer resentments; when you are forever fighting a degenerating sense of "nobodiness" — then you will understand why we find it difficult to wait. There comes a time when the cup of endurance runs over, and men are no longer willing to be plunged into an abyss of injustice where they experience the bleakness of corroding despair. I hope, sirs, you can understand our legitimate and unavoidable impatience.

You express a great deal of anxiety over our willingness to break laws. This is certainly a legitimate concern. Since we so diligently urge people to obey the Supreme Court's decision of 1954 outlawing segregation in the public schools, it is rather strange and paradoxical to find us consciously breaking laws. One may well ask, "How can you advocate breaking some laws and obeying others?" The answer is found in the fact that there are two types of laws: There are *just* laws and there are *unjust* laws. I would be the first to advocate obeying just laws. One has not only a legal but a moral responsibility to obey just laws. Conversely, one has a moral responsibility to disobey unjust laws. I would agree with Saint Augustine that "An unjust law is no law at all."

Now what is the difference between the two? How does one determine when a law is just or unjust? A just law is a man-made code that squares with the moral law or the law of God. An unjust law is a mode that is out of harmony with the moral law. To put it in the terms of Saint

Thomas Aquinas, an unjust law is a human law that is not rooted in eternal and natural law. Any law that uplifts human personality is just. Any law that degrades human personality is unjust.

All segregation statutes are unjust because segregation distorts the soul and damages the personality. It gives the segregator a false sense of superiority and the segregated a false sense of inferiority. To use the words of Martin Buber, the great Jewish philosopher, segregation substitutes an "I-it" relationship for the "I-thou" relationship, and ends up relegating persons to the status of things. So segregation is not only politically, economically, and sociologically unsound, but it is morally wrong and sinful. Paul Tillich has said that sin is separation. Isn't segregation an existential expression of man's tragic separation, an expression of his awful estrangement, his terrible sinfulness? So I can urge men to obey the 1954 decision of the Supreme Court because it is morally right, and I can urge them to disobey segregation ordinances because they are morally wrong.

Let me give another example of just and unjust laws. An unjust law is a code that a majority inflicts on a minority that is not binding on itself. This is *difference* made legal. On the other hand a just law is a code that a majority compels a minority to follow that it is willing to follow itself. This is *sameness* made legal.

Let me give another explanation. An unjust law is a code inflicted upon a minority which that minority had no part in enacting or creating because they did not have the unhampered right to vote. Who can say the legislature of Alabama which set up the segregation laws was democratically elected? Throughout the state of Alabama all types of conniving methods are used to prevent Negroes from becoming registered voters and there are some counties without a single Negro registered to vote despite the fact that the Negro constitutes a majority of the population. Can any law set up in such a state be considered democratically structured?

These are just a few examples of unjust and just laws. There are some instances when a law is just on its face but unjust in its application. For instance, I was arrested Friday on a charge of parading without a permit. Now there is nothing wrong with an ordinance which requires a permit for a parade, but when the ordinance is used to preserve segregation and to deny citizens the First Amendment privilege of peaceful assembly and peaceful protest, then it becomes unjust.

I hope you can see the distinction I am trying to point out. In no sense do I advocate evading or defying the law as the rabid segregationist would do. This would lead to anarchy. One who breaks an unjust law must do it *openly, lovingly* (not hatefully as the white

mothers did in New Orleans when they were seen on television screaming "nigger, nigger, nigger") and with a willingness to accept the penalty.
I submit that an individual who breaks a law that conscience tells him
is unjust, and willingly accepts the penalty by staying in jail to arouse
the conscience of the community over its injustice, is in reality expressing
the very highest respect for law.

Of course there is nothing new about this kind of civil disobedience.
It was seen sublimely in the refusal of Shadrach, Meshach, and Abednego
to obey the laws of Nebuchadnezzar because a higher moral law was
involved. It was practiced superbly by the early Christians who were
willing to face hungry lions and the excruciating pain of chopping blocks
before submitting to certain unjust laws of the Roman Empire. To a
degree academic freedom is a reality today because Socrates practiced
civil disobedience.

We can never forget that everything Hitler did in Germany was
"legal" and everything the Hungarian freedom fighters did in Hungary
was "illegal." It was "illegal" to aid and comfort a Jew in Hitler's
Germany. But I am sure that, if I had lived in Germany during that
time, I would have aided and comforted my Jewish brothers even though
it was illegal. If I lived in a Communist country today where certain
principles dear to the Christian faith are suppressed, I believe I would
openly advocate disobeying these anti-religious laws. . . .

In your statement you asserted that our actions, even though peaceful, must be condemned because they precipitate violence. But can this
assertion be logically made? Isn't this like condemning the robbed man
because his possession of money precipitated the evil act of robbery?
Isn't this like condemning Socrates because his unswerving commitment
to truth and his philosophical delvings precipitated the misguided popular
mind to make him drink the hemlock? Isn't this like condemning Jesus
because His unique God consciousness and never-ceasing devotion to His
will precipitated the evil act of crucifixon? We must come to see, as Federal courts have consistently affirmed, that it is immoral to urge an individual to withdraw his efforts to gain his basic constitutional rights
because the quest precipitates violence. Society must protect the robbed
and punish the robber.

I had also hoped that the white moderate would reject the myth of
time. I received a letter this morning from a white brother in Texas which
said: "All Christians know that the colored people will receive equal
rights eventually, but is it possible that you are in too great of a religious
hurry? It has taken Christianity almost 2,000 years to accomplish what
it has. The teachings of Christ take time to come to earth." All that is
said here grows out of a tragic misconception of time. It is the strangely

irrational notion that there is something in the very flow of time that will inevitably cure all ills. Actually time is neutral. It can be used either destructively or constructively. I am coming to feel that the people of ill will have used time much more effectively than the people of good will.

We will have to repent in this generation not merely for the vitriolic words and actions of the bad people, but for the appalling silence of the good people. We must come to see that human progress never rolls in on wheels of inevitability. It comes through the tireless efforts and persistent work of men willing to be co-workers with God, and without this hard work time itself becomes an ally of the forces of social stagnation.

We must use time creatively, and forever realize that the time is always ripe to do right. Now is the time to make real the promise of democracy, and transform our pending national elegy into a creative psalm of brotherhood. Now is the time to lift our national policy from the quicksand of racial injustice to the solid rock of human dignity.

You spoke of our activity in Birmingham as extreme. At first I was rather disappointed that fellow clergymen would see my non-violent efforts as those of the extremist. I started thinking about the fact that I stand in the middle of two opposing forces in the Negro community. One is a force of complacency made up of Negroes who, as a result of long years of oppression, have been so completely drained of self-respect and a sense of "somebodiness" that they have adjusted to segregation, and of a few Negroes in the middle class who, because of a degree of academic and economic security, and because at points they profit by segregation, have unconsciously become insensitive to the problems of the masses. The other force is one of bitterness and hatred and comes perilously close to advocating violence. It is expressed in the various black nationalist groups that are springing up over the nation, the largest and best known being Elijah Muhammad's Muslim movement. This movement is nourished by the contemporary frustration over the continued existence of racial discrimination. It is made up of people who have lost faith in America, who have absolutely repudiated Christianity, and who have concluded that the white man is an incurable "devil."

I have tried to stand between these two forces saying that we need not follow the "do-nothingism" of the complacent or the hatred and despair of the black nationalist. There is the more excellent way of love and nonviolent protest. I'm grateful to God that, through the Negro church, the dimension of nonviolence entered our struggle. If this philosophy had not emerged I am convinced that by now many streets of the South would be flowing with floods of blood. And I am further convinced that if our white brothers dismiss us as "rabble rousers" and "outside agitators" — those of us who are working through the channels of nonviolent direct action — and refuse to support our nonviolent efforts, millions of Negroes, out of frustration and despair, will seek solace and security in black nationalist ideologies, a development that will lead inevitably to a frightening racial nightmare.

Oppressed people cannot remain oppressed forever. The urge for freedom will eventually come. This is what has happened to the American Negro. Something within has reminded him of his birthright of freedom; something without has reminded him that he can gain it. Consciously and unconsciously, he has been swept in by what the Germans call the *Zeitgeist,* and with his black brothers of Africa, and his brown and yellow brothers of Asia, South America, and the Caribbean, he is moving with a sense of cosmic urgency toward the promised land of racial justice. Recognizing this vital urge that has engulfed the Negro community, one should readily understand public demonstrations.

The Negro has many pent-up resentments and latent frustrations. He has to get them out. So let him march sometime; let him have his prayer pilgrimages to the city hall; understand why he must have sit-ins and freedom rides. If his repressed emotions do not come out in these non-violent ways, they will come out in ominous expressions of violence. This is not a threat; it is a fact of history. So I have not said to my people, "Get rid of your discontent." But I have tried to say that this normal and healthy discontent can be channeled through the creative outlet of non-violent direct action. Now this approach is being dismissed as extremist. I must admit that I was initially disappointed in being so categorized.

But as I continued to think about the matter I gradually gained a bit of satisfaction from being considered an extremist. Was not Jesus an extremist in love? "Love your enemies, bless them that curse you, pray for them that despitefully use you." Was not Amos an extremist for justice — "Let justice roll down like waters and righteousness like a mighty stream." Was not Paul an extremist for the gospel of Jesus Christ — "I bear in my body the marks of the Lord Jesus." Was not Martin Luther an extremist — "Here I stand; I can do none other so help me God." Was not John Bunyan an extremist — "I will stay in jail to the end of my days before I make a butchery of my conscience." Was not Abraham Lincoln an extremist — "This nation cannot survive half slave and half free." Was not Thomas Jefferson an extremist — "We hold these truths to be self evident that all men are created equal."

So the question is not whether we will be extremist but what kind of extremist will we be. Will we be extremists for hate or will we be extremists for love? Will we be extremists for the preservation of injustice — or will we be extremists for the cause of justice? In that dramatic scene on Calvary's hill three men were crucified. We must never forget that all three were crucified for the same crime — the crime of extremism. Two were extremists for immorality, and thus fell below their environment. The other, Jesus Christ, was an extremist for love, truth, and goodness, and thereby rose above His environment. So, after all, maybe the South, the nation, and the world are in dire need of creative extremists. . . .

I hope the Church as a whole will meet the challenge of this decisive hour. But even if the Church does not come to the aid of justice, I have no despair about the future. I have no fear about the outcome of our struggle in Birmingham, even if our motives are presently misunderstood. We will reach the goal of freedom in Birmingham and all over the nation, because the goal of America is freedom. Abused and scorned though we may be, our destiny is tied up with the destiny of America.

Before the pilgrims landed at Plymouth, we were here. Before the pen of Jefferson etched across the pages of history the majestic words of the Declaration of Independence, we were here. For more than two centuries our foreparents labored in this country without wages; they made cotton "king"; and they built the homes of their masters in the midst of brutal injustice and shameful humiliation — and yet out of a bottomless vitality they continued to thrive and develop. If the inexpressible cruelties of slavery could not stop us, the opposition we now face will surely fail. We will win our freedom because the sacred heritage of our nation and the eternal will of God are embodied in our echoing demands.

I must close now. But before closing I am impelled to mention one other point in your statement that troubled me profoundly. You warmly commended the Birmingham police force for keeping "order" and "preventing violence." I don't believe you would have so warmly commended the police force if you had seen its angry violent dogs literally biting six unarmed, nonviolent Negroes. I don't believe you would so quickly commend the policemen if you would observe their ugly and inhuman treatment of Negroes here in the city jail; if you would watch them push and curse old Negro women and young Negro girls; if you would see them slap and kick old Negro men and young Negro boys; if you will observe them, as they did on two occasions, refuse to give us food because we wanted to sing our grace together. I'm sorry that I can't join you in your praise for the police department. . . .

It is true that they have been rather disciplined in their public handling of the demonstrators. In this sense they have been rather publicly "nonviolent." But for what purpose? To preserve the evil system of segregation. Over the last few years I have consistently preached that nonviolence demands that the means we use must be as pure as the ends we seek. So I have tried to make it clear that it is wrong to use immoral means to attain moral ends. But now I must affirm that it is just as wrong, or even more so, to use moral means to preserve immoral ends. . . . T. S. Eliot has said that there is no greater treason than to do the right deed for the wrong reason.

I wish you had commended the Negro sit-inners and demonstrators of Birmingham for their sublime courage, their willingness to suffer, and their amazing discipline in the midst of the most inhuman provocation. One day the South will recognize its real heroes. They will be the James Merediths, courageously and with a majestic sense of purpose, facing jeering and hostile mobs and the agonizing loneliness that characterizes the life of the pioneer. They will be old, oppressed, battered Negro women, symbolized in a 72-year-old woman of Montgomery, Alabama, who rose up with a sense of dignity and with her people decided not to ride the segregated buses, and responded to one who inquired about her tiredness with ungrammatical profundity: "My feets is tired, but my soul is rested." They will be young high school and college students, young ministers of the gospel and a host of the elders, courageously and non-violently sitting in at lunch counters and willingly going to jail for conscience sake. One day the South will know that when these disinherited children of God sat down at lunch counters they were in reality standing up for the best in the American dream and the most sacred values in our Judeo-Christian heritage, and thus carrying our whole nation back to great wells of democracy which were dug deep by the founding fathers in the formulation of the Constitution and the Declaration of Independence.

Yours for the cause of Peace and Brotherhood
M. L. King Jr.

Is It Ever Right
to Break the Law?*

Charles Frankel

During recent months, public events have repeatedly dramatized an old and troublesome problem. A group of students defies the State Department's ban on travel to Cuba; a teachers' union threatens a strike even though a state law prohibits strikes by public employees; advocates of civil rights employ mass demonstrations of disobedience to the law to advance their cause; the Governor of a Southern state deliberately obstructs the enforcement of Federal laws, and declares himself thoroughly within his rights in doing so. . . .

When is it justified for the citizen to act as his own legislator, and to decide that he will or will not obey a given law?

An answer that covers all the issues this question raises cannot be given here, nor can a set of principles be proposed that will allow anyone to make automatic and infallible judgments concerning the legitimacy or illegitimacy of specific acts of civil disobedience. Such judgments require detailed knowledge of the facts of specific cases, and such knowledge is often unavailable to the outsider. Nevertheless, it is possible to indicate some of the principal issues that are raised by civil disobedience, some of the more common mistakes that are made in thinking about these issues, and, at least in outline, the approach that one man would take toward such issues.

We can begin, it seems to me, by rejecting one extreme position. This is the view that disobedience to the law can never be justified in any circumstances. To take this position is to say one of two things: either

---

*©1964 by The New York Times Company. Reprinted by permission.

every law that exists is a just law, or a greater wrong is always done by breaking the law. The first statement is plainly false. The second is highly doubtful. If it is true, then the signers of the Declaration of Independence, and those Germans who refused to carry out Hitler's orders, committed acts of injustice.

It is possible, however, to take a much more moderate and plausible version of this position, and many quite reasonable people do. Such people concede that disobedience to the law can sometimes be legitimate and necessary under a despotic regime. They argue, however, that civil disobedience can never be justified in a democratic society, because such a society provides its members with legal instruments for the redress of their grievances.

This is one of the standard arguments that is made, often quite sincerely, against the activities of people like supporters of the Congress of Racial Equality, who set about changing laws they find objectionable by dramatically breaking them. Such groups are often condemned for risking disorder and for spreading disrespect for the law when, so it is maintained, they could accomplish their goals a great deal more fairly and patriotically by staying within the law, and confining themselves to the courts and to methods of peaceful persuasion.

Now it is perfectly true, I believe, that there is a stronger case for obedience to the law, including bad law, in a democracy than in a dictatorship. The people who must abide by the law have presumably been consulted, and they have legal channels through which to express their protests and to work for reform. One way to define democracy is to say that it is a system whose aim is to provide alternatives to civil disobedience. Nevertheless, when applied to the kind of situation faced, say, by CORE, these generalizations, it seems to me, become cruelly abstract.

The basic fallacy in the proposition that, in a democracy, civil disobedience can never be justified, is that it confuses the *ideals* or *aims* of democracy with the inevitably less than perfect accomplishments of democracy at any given moment. In accordance with democratic ideals, the laws of a democracy may give rights and powers to individuals which, in theory, enable them to work legally for the elimination of injustices.

In actual fact, however, these rights and powers may be empty. The police may be hostile, the courts biased, the elections rigged — and the legal remedies available to the individual may be unavailing against these evils.

Worse still, the majority may have demonstrated, in a series of free and honest elections, that it is unwavering in its support of what the minority regards as an unspeakable evil. This is obviously the case today in many parts of the South, where the white majority is either opposed to desegregation or not so impatient to get on with it as is the Negro minority. Are we prepared to say that majorities never err? If not, there is no absolutely conclusive reason why we must invariably give the results of an election greater weight than considerations of elementary justice.

It is true, of course, that one swallow does not make a summer, and that the test of legal democratic processes is not this or that particular success or failure, but rather the general direction in which these processes move over the long run. Still, the position that violation of the law is never justifiable so long as there are legal alternatives overstates this important truth. It fails to face at least three important exceptions to it.

In the first place, dramatic disobedience to the law by a minority may be the only effective way of catching the attention or winning the support of the majority. Most classic cases of civil disobedience, from the early Christians to Gandhi and his supporters, exemplify this truth. Civil disobedience, like almost no other technique, can shame a majority and make it ask itself just how far it is willing to go, just how seriously it really is committed to defending the status quo.

Second, there is the simple but painful factor of time. If a man is holding you down on a bed of nails, it is all very well for a bystander to say that you live in a great country in which there are legal remedies for your condition, and that you ought, therefore, to be patient and wait for these remedies to take effect. But your willingness to listen to this counsel will depend, quite properly, on the nature of the injury you are suffering.

Third, it is baseless prejudice to assume that observance of the laws is *always* conducive to strengthening a democratic system while disobedience to the law can never have a salutary effect. A majority's complacent acquiescence in bad laws can undermine the faith of a minority in the power of democratic methods to rectify manifest evils; yet a vigorous democracy depends on the existence of minorities holding just such a faith.

Disobedience to bad laws can sometimes jolt democratic processes into motion. Which strengthens one's hope for democracy more — the behavior of the Negroes in Birmingham who broke municipal ordinances when they staged their protest marches, or the behavior of the police, using dogs and fire hoses to assert their legal authority?

Another factor should also be taken into account. In our Federal system, there are often legitimate doubts concerning the legal validity, under our Constitution, of various state or local ordinances. Disobedience to these laws is in many cases simply a practical, though painful, way of testing their legality. But even where no thought of such a test is involved, there is often present a moral issue which no one can easily dodge —

least of all the man whose personal dignity and self-respect are caught up in the issue.

A citizen caught in a conflict between local laws and what he thinks will be upheld as the superior Federal law can sometimes afford to wait until the courts have determined the issue for him. But often he cannot afford to wait, or must take a stand in order to force a decision. This is the situation of many Negro citizens in Southern states as they confront the conflict between local and Federal laws.

Yet there is another side to the story. It would be a mistake to conclude from what has been said that civil disobedience is justified, provided only that it is disobedience in the name of higher principles. Strong moral conviction is not all that is required to turn breaking the law into service to society.

Civil disobedience is not simply like other acts in which men stand up courageously for their principles. It involves violation of the law. And the law can make no provision for its violation except to hold the offender liable to punishment. This is why President Kennedy was in such a delicate position last spring at the time of the Negro demonstrations in Birmingham. He gave many signs that, as an individual, he was in sympathy with the goals of the demonstrators. As a political leader, he probably realized that these goals could not be attained without dramatic actions that crossed the line into illegality. But as Chief Executive he could not give permission or approval to such actions.

We may admire a man like Martin Luther King, who is prepared to defy the authorities in the name of a principle, and we may think that he is entirely in the right; just the same, his right to break the law cannot be officially recognized. No society, whether free or tyrannical, can give its citizens the right to break its laws: To ask it to do so is to ask it to proclaim, as a matter of law, that its laws are not laws.

In short, if anybody ever has a right to break the law, this cannot be a legal right under the law. It has to be a moral right against the law. And this moral right is not an unlimited right to disobey any law which one regards as unjust. It is a right that is hedged about, it seems to me, with important restrictions.

First of all, the exercise of this right is subject to standards of just and fair behavior. I may be correct, for example, in thinking that an ordinance against jaywalking is an unnecessary infringement of my rights. This does not make it reasonable, however, for me to organize a giant sit-down strike in the streets which holds up traffic for a week. Conformity to the concept of justice requires that there be some *proportion* between the importance of the end one desires to attain and the power of the means one employs to attain it.

When applied to civil disobedience, this principle constitutes a very large restriction. Civil disobedience is an effort to change the law by making it impossible to enforce the law, or by making the price of such enforcement extremely high. It is a case, as it were, of holding the legal system to ransom. It can arouse extreme passions on one side or the other, excite and provoke the unbalanced, and make disrespect for the law a commonplace and popular attitude.

Although violence may be no part of the intention of those who practice civil disobedience, the risks of violence are present, and are part of what must be taken into account when a program of civil disobedience is being contemplated.

In short, civil disobedience is a grave enterprise. It may sometimes be justified, but the provocation for it has to be equally grave. Basic principles have to be at issue. The evils being combated have to be serious evils that are likely to endure unless they are fought. There should be reasonable grounds to believe that legal methods of fighting them are likely to be insufficient by themselves.

Nor is this the only limitation on the individual's moral right to disobey the law. The most important limitation is that his cause must be a just one. It was right for General de Gaulle to disobey Marshal Pétain; it was wrong for the commanders of the French Army in Algeria, 20 years later, to disobey General de Gaulle.

Similarly, if it is absolutely necessary, and if the consequences have been properly weighed, then it is right to break the law in order to eliminate inequalities based on race. But it can never be necessary, and no weighing of consequences can ever make it right, to break the law in the name of Nazi principles.

In sum, the goals of those who disobey the law have to lie at the very heart of what we regard as morality before we can say that they have a moral right to do what they are doing.

But who is to make these difficult decisions? Who is to say that one man's moral principles are right and another man's wrong? We come here to the special function that civil disobedience serves in a society. The man who breaks the law on the ground that the law is immoral asks the rest of us, in effect, to trust him, or to trust those he trusts, in preference to the established conventions and authorities of our society.

He has taken a large and visible chance, and implicitly asked us to join him in taking that chance, on the probity of his personal moral judgment. In doing so, he has put it to us whether we are willing to take a similar chance on the probity of our own judgment.

Thomas Hobbes, who knew the trouble that rebels and dissenters convinced of their rectitude can cause, once remarked that a man may be convinced that God has commanded him to act as he has, but that God, after all, does not command other men to believe that this is so. The man who chooses to disobey the law on grounds of principle may be a saint, but he may also be a madman. He may be a courageous and lonely individualist, but he may also merely be taking orders and following his own crowd. Whatever he may be, however, his existence tends to make us painfully aware that we too are implicitly making choices, and must bear responsibility for the ones we make.

This, indeed, may be the most important function of those who practice civil disobedience. They remind us that the man who obeys the law has as much of an obligation to look into the morality of his acts and the rationality of his society as does the man who breaks the law. The occurrence of civil disobedience can never be a happy phenomenon; when it is justified, something is seriously wrong with the society in which it takes place.

But the man who puts his conscience above the law, though he may be right or he may be wrong, does take personal moral responsibility for the social arrangements under which he lives. And so he dramatizes the fascinating and fearful possibility that those who obey the law might do the same. They might obey the law and support what exists, not out of habit or fear, but because they have freely chosen to do so, and are prepared to live with their consciences after having made that choice.

Black Power*

Stokely Carmichael

One of the tragedies of the struggle against racism is that up to now there has been no national organization which could speak to the growing militancy of young black people in the urban ghetto. There has been only a civil rights movement, whose tone of voice was adapted to an audience of liberal whites. It served as a sort of buffer zone between them and angry young blacks. None of its so-called leaders could go into a rioting community and be listened to. In a sense, I blame ourselves—together with the mass media—for what has happened in Watts, Harlem, Chicago, Cleveland, Omaha. Each time the people in those cities saw Martin Luther King get slapped, they became angry; when they saw four little black girls bombed to death, they were angrier; and when nothing happened, they were steaming. We had nothing to offer that they could see, except to go out and be beaten again. We helped to build their frustration.

For too many years, black Americans marched and had their heads broken and got shot. They were saying to the country, "Look, you guys are supposed to be nice guys and we are only going to do what we are supposed to do — why do you beat us up, why don't you give us what we ask, why don't you straighten yourselves out?" After years of this, we are at almost the same point — because we demonstrated from a position of weakness. We cannot be expected any longer to march and have our heads broken in order to say to whites: Come on, you're nice guys. For you are not nice guys. We have found you out.

*A public statement by Stokely Carmichael, Executive Director, Student Nonviolent Coordinating Committee, 1966.

An organization which claims to speak for the needs of a community
— as does the Student Nonviolent Coordinating Committee — must
speak in the tone of that community, not as somebody else's buffer zone.
This is the significance of black power as a slogan. For once, black
people are going to use the words they want to use — not just the words
whites want to hear. And they will do this no matter how often the press
tries to stop the use of the slogan by equating it with racism and
separatism.

An organization which claims to be working for the needs of a community — as SNCC does — must work to provide that community with
a position of strength from which to make its voice heard. This is the significance of black power beyond the slogan.

Black power can be clearly defined for those who do not attach the
fears of white America to their questions about it. We should begin with
the basic fact that black Americans have two problems: they are poor
and they are black. All other problems arise from this two-sided reality:
lack of education, the so-called apathy of black men. Any program to
end racism must address itself to that double reality.

Almost from its beginning, SNCC sought to address itself to both conditions with a program aimed at winning political power for impoverished
southern blacks. We had to begin with politics because black Americans
are a propertyless people in a country where property is valued above all.
We had to work for power, because this country does not function by
morality, love, and nonviolence, but by power. Thus we determined to
win political power, with the idea of moving on from there into activity
that would have economic effects. With power, the masses could *make or
participate in making* the decisions which govern their destinies, and
thus create basic change in their day-to-day lives.

But if political power seemed to be the key to self-determination, it
was also obvious that the key had been thrown down a deep well many
years earlier. Disenfranchisement, maintained by racist terror, made it
impossible to talk about organizing for political power in 1960. The right
to vote had to be won, and SNCC workers devoted their energies to this
from 1961 to 1965. They set up voter registration drives in the Deep
South. They created pressure for the vote by holding mock elections in
Mississippi in 1963 and by helping to establish the Mississippi Freedom
Democratic Party (MFDP) in 1964. That struggle was eased, though not
won, with the passage of the 1965 Voting Rights Act. SNCC workers
could then address themselves to the question: "Who can we vote for, to
have our needs met — how do we make our vote meaningful?"

SNCC had already gone to Atlantic City for recognition of the Mississippi Freedom Democratic Party by the Democratic convention and been

rejected; it had gone with the MFDP to Washington for recognition by Congress and been rejected. In Arkansas, SNCC helped thirty Negroes to run for school board elections; all but one were defeated, and there was evidence of fraud and intimidation sufficient to cause their defeat. In Atlanta, Julian Bond ran for the state legislature and was elected — twice — and unseated — twice. In several states, black farmers ran in elections for agricultural committees which make crucial decisions concerning land use, loans, etc. Although they won places on a number of committees, they never gained the majorities needed to control them.

All of the efforts were attempts to win black power. Then, in Alabama, the opportunity came to see how blacks could be organized on an independent party basis. An unusual Alabama law provides that any group of citizens can nominate candidates for county office and, if they win 20 per cent of the vote, may be recognized as a county political party. The same then applies on a state level. SNCC went to organize in several counties such as Lowndes, where black people — who form 80 per cent of the population and have an average annual income of $943 — felt they could accomplish nothing within the framework of the Alabama Democratic party because of its racism and because the qualifying fee for this year's elections was raised from $50 to $500 in order to prevent most Negroes from becoming candidates. On May 3, five new county "freedom organizations" convened and nominated candidates for the offices of sheriff, tax assessor, members of the school boards. These men and women are up for election in November — if they live until then. Their ballot symbol is the black panther: a bold, beautiful animal, representing the strength and dignity of black demands today. A man needs a black panther on his side when he and his family must endure — as hundreds of Alabamians have endured — loss of job, eviction, starvation, and sometimes death, for political activity. He may also need a gun and SNCC reaffirms the right of black men everywhere to defend themselves when threatened or attacked. As for initiating the use of violence, we hope that such programs as ours will make that unnecessary; but it is not for us to tell black communities whether they can or cannot use any particular form of action to resolve their problems. Responsibility for the use of violence by black men, whether in self-defense or initiated by them, lies with the white community.

This is the specific historical experience from which SNCC's call for "black power" emerged on the Mississippi march last July. But the concept of "black power" is not a recent or isolated phenomenon: It has grown out of the ferment of agitation and activity by different people and organizations in many black communities over the years. Our last year of work in Alabama added a new concrete possibility. In Lowndes county, for example, black power will mean that if a Negro is elected sheriff, he can end police brutality. If a black man is elected tax assessor, he can collect and channel funds for the building of better roads and schools serving black people — thus advancing the move from political power into the economic arena. In such areas as Lowndes, where black men have a majority, they will attempt to use it to exercise control. This is what they seek: control. Where Negroes lack a majority, black power means proper representation and sharing of control. It means the creation of power bases from which black people can work to change statewide or nationwide patterns of oppression through pressure from strength — instead of weakness. Politically, black power means what it has always meant to SNCC: the coming together of black people to elect representatives and *to force those representatives to speak to their needs.* It does not mean merely putting black faces into office. A man or woman who is black and from the slums cannot be automatically expected to speak to the needs of black people. Most of the black politicians we see around the country today are not what SNCC means by black power. The power must be that of a community, and emanate from there.

SNCC today is working in both North and South on programs of voter registration and independent political organizing. In some places, such as Alabama, Los Angeles, New York, Philadelphia, and New Jersey, independent organizing under the black panther symbol is in progress. The creation of a national "black panther party" must come about: It will take time to build, and it is much too early to predict its success. We have no infallible master plan and we make no claim to exclusive knowledge of how to end racism; different groups will work in their own different ways. SNCC cannot spell out the full logistics of self-determination but it can address itself to the problem by helping black communities define their needs, realize their strength, and go into action along a variety of lines which they must choose for themselves. Without knowing all the answers, it can address itself to the basic problem of poverty — to the fact that in Lowndes county, 86 white families own 90 per cent of the land. What are black people in that county going to do for jobs, where are they going to get money? There must be reallocation of land, of money.

Ultimately, the economic foundations of this country must be shaken if black people are to control their lives. The colonies of the United States—and this includes the black ghettoes within its borders, north and south—must be liberated. For a century, this nation has been like an octopus of exploitation, its tentacles stretching from Mississippi and Harlem to South America, the Middle East, southern Africa, and Vietnam; the form of exploitation varies from area to area but the essential result has been the same — a powerful few have been maintained and enriched at the expense of the poor and voiceless colored masses. This pattern must be broken. As its grip loosens here and there around the world, the hopes of black Americans become more realistic. For racism to die, a totally different America must be born.

This is what the white society does not wish to face; this is why that society prefers to talk about integration. But integration speaks not at all to the problem of poverty, only to the problem of blackness. Integration today means the man who "makes it," leaves his black brothers behind in the ghetto as fast as his new sports car will take him. It has no relevance to the Harlem wino or to the cottonpicker making three dollars a day. As a lady I know in Alabama once said, "the food that Ralph Bunche eats doesn't fill my stomach."

Integration, moreover, speaks to the problem of blackness in a despicable way. As a goal, it has been based on complete acceptance of the fact that *in order to have* a decent house or education, blacks must move into a white neighborhood or send their children to a white school. This reinforces, among both black and white, the idea that "white" is automatically better and "black" is by definition inferior. This is why integration is a subterfuge for the maintenance of white supremacy. It allows the nation to focus on a handful of southern children who get into white schools, at great price, and to ignore the 94 per cent who are left behind in unimproved all-black schools. Such situations will not change until black people have power—to control their own school boards, in this case. Then Negroes become equal in a way that means something, and integration ceases to be a one-way street. Then integration doesn't mean draining skills and energies from the ghetto into white neighborhoods; then it can mean white people moving from Beverly Hills into Watts, white people joining the Lowndes County Freedom Organization. Then integration becomes relevant.

Last April, before the furor over black power, Christopher Jencks wrote in a *New Republic* article on white Mississippi's manipulation of the antipoverty program:

> The War on Poverty has been predicated on the notion that there is such a thing as *a community* which can be defined geographically and mobilized for a collective effort to help the poor. This theory has no relationship to reality in the Deep South. In every Mississippi county there are *two* communities. Despite all the pious platitudes of the moderates on both sides, these two communities habitually see their interests in terms of conflict rather than cooperation. Only when the Negro community can muster enough political, economic, and professional strength to compete on somewhat equal terms, will Negroes

believe in the possibility of true cooperation and whites accept its necessity. En route to integration, the Negro community needs to develop greater independence—a chance to run its own affairs and not cave in whenever "the man" barks. . . . Or so it seems to me, and to most of the knowledgeable people with whom I talked in Mississippi. To OEO, this judgment may sound like black nationalism. . . .

Mr. Jencks, a white reporter, perceived the reason why America's anti-poverty program has been a sick farce in both North and South. In the South, it is clearly racism which prevents the poor from running their own programs; in the North, it more often seems to be politicking and bureaucracy. But the results are not so different: In the North, nonwhites make up 42 per cent of all families in metropolitan "poverty areas" and only 6 per cent of families in areas classified as not poor. SNCC has been working with local residents in Arkansas, Alabama, and Mississippi to achieve control by the poor of the program and its funds; it has also been working with groups in the North, and the struggle is no less difficult. Behind it all is a federal government which cares far more about winning the war on the Vietnamese than the War on Poverty; which has put the poverty program in the hands of self-serving politicians and bureaucrats rather than [in the hands of] the poor themselves; which is unwilling to curb the misuse of white power but quick to condemn black power.

To most whites, black power seems to mean that the Mau Mau are coming to the suburbs at night. The Mau Mau are coming, and whites must stop them. Articles appear about plots to "get Whitey," creating an atmosphere in which "law and order must be maintained." Once again, responsibility is shifted from the oppressor to the oppressed. Other whites chide, "Don't forget—you're only 10 per cent of the population; if you get too smart, we'll wipe you out." If they are liberals, they complain, "What about me?—don't you want my help any more?" These are people supposedly concerned about black Americans, but today they think first of themselves, or their feelings of rejection. Or they admonish, "You can't get anywhere without coalitions," without considering the problems of coalition with whom, on what terms (coalition from weakness can mean absorption, betrayal), when? Or they accuse us of "polarizing the races" by our calls for black unity, when the true responsibility for polarization lies with whites who will not accept their responsibility as the majority power for making the democratic process work.

White America will not face the problem of color, the reality of it. The well-intended say: "We're all human, everybody is really decent, we must forget color." But color cannot be "forgotten" until its weight is recognized and dealt with. White America will not acknowledge that the ways in which this country sees itself are contradicted by being black—and always have been. Whereas most of the people who settled this country came here for freedom or for economic opportunity, blacks were brought here to be slaves. When the Lowndes County Freedom Organization chose the black panther as its symbol, it was christened by the press "the Black Panther party"—but the Alabama Democratic party, whose symbol is a rooster, has never been called the White Cock party. No one ever talked about "white power" because power in this country *is* white. All this adds up to more than merely identifying a group phenomenon by some catchy name or adjective. The furor over that black panther reveals the problems that white America has with color and sex; the furor over "black power" reveals how deep racism runs and the great fear which is attached to it.

Whites will not see that I, for example, as a person oppressed because of my blackness, have common cause with other blacks who are oppressed because of blackness. This is not to say that there are no white people who see things as I do, but that it is black people I must speak to first. It must be the oppressed to whom SNCC addresses itself primarily, not to friends from the oppressing group.

From birth, black people are told a set of lies about themselves. We are told that we are lazy—yet I drive through the Delta area of Mississippi and watch black people picking cotton in the hot sun for fourteen hours. We are told, "If you work hard, you'll succeed"—but if that were true, black people would own this country. We are oppressed because we are black—not because we are ignorant, not because we are lazy, not because we're stupid (and got good rhythm), but because we're black.

I remember that when I was a boy, I used to go to see Tarzan movies on Saturday. White Tarzan used to beat up the black natives. I would sit there yelling, "Kill the beasts, kill the savages, kill 'em!" I was saying: Kill *me*. It was as if a Jewish boy watched Nazis taking Jews off to concentration camps and cheered them on. Today, I want the chief to beat hell out of Tarzan and send him back to Europe. But it takes time to become free of the lies and their shaming effect on black minds. It takes time to reject the most important lie: that black people inherently can't do the same things white people can do, unless white people help them.

The need for psychological equality is the reason why SNCC today believes that blacks must organize in the black community. Only black people can convey the revolutionary idea that black people are able to do things themselves. Only they can create in the community an aroused and continuing black consciousness that will provide the basis for political strength. In the past, white allies have furthered white supremacy without the whites involved realizing it—or wanting it, I think. Black people must do things for themselves; they must get poverty money they will control and spend themselves, they must conduct tutorial programs themselves so that black children can identify with black people. This is one reason Africa has such importance: The reality of black men ruling their own nations gives blacks elsewhere a sense of possibility, of power, which they do not now have.

This does not mean we don't welcome help, or friends. But we want the right to decide whether anyone is, in fact, our friend. In the past, black Americans have been almost the only people whom everybody and his momma could jump up and call their friends. We have been tokens, symbols, objects—as I was in high school to many young whites, who like having "a Negro friend." We want to decide who is our friend, and we will not accept someone who comes to us and says: "If you do X, Y, and Z, then I'll help you." We will not be told whom we should choose as allies. We will not be isolated from any group or nation except by our own choice. We cannot have the oppressors telling the oppressed how to rid themselves of the oppressor.

I have said that most liberal whites react to "black power" with the question, What about me?, rather than saying: Tell me what you want me to do and I'll see if I can do it. There are answers to the right question. One of the most disturbing things about almost all white supporters of the movement has been that they are afraid to go into their own communities—which is where the racism exists—and work to get rid of it. They want to run from Berkeley to tell us what to do in Mississippi; let them look instead at Berkeley. They admonish blacks to be nonviolent; let them preach nonviolence in the white community. They come to teach me Negro history; let them go to the suburbs and open up freedom schools for whites. Let them work to stop America's racist foreign policy; let them press this government to cease supporting the economy of South Africa.

There is a vital job to be done among poor whites. We hope to see, eventually, a coalition between poor blacks and poor whites. That is the only coalition which seems acceptable to us, and we see such a coalition as the major internal instrument of change in American society. SNCC has tried several times to organize poor whites; we are trying again now, with an initial training program in Tennessee. It is purely academic today to talk about bringing poor blacks and whites together, but the job of creating a poor-white power bloc must be attempted. The main responsibility for it falls upon whites. Black and white can work together in the white community where possible; it is not possible, however, to go into a poor southern town and talk about integration. Poor whites everywhere are becoming more hostile—not less—partly because they see the nation's attention focused on black poverty and nobody coming to them. Too many young middle-class Americans, like some sort of Pepsi generation, have wanted to come alive through the black community; they've wanted to be where the action is—and the action has been in the black community.

Black people do not want to "take over" this country. They don't want to "get whitey"; they just want to get him off their backs, as the saying goes. It was for example the exploitation by Jewish landlords and merchants which first created black resentment toward Jews—not Judaism. The white man is irrelevant to blacks, except as an oppressive force. Blacks want to be in his place, yes, but not in order to terrorize and lynch and starve him. They want to be in his place because that is where a decent life can be had.

But our vision is not merely of a society in which all black men have enough to buy the good things of life. When we urge that black money go into black pockets, we mean the communal pocket. We want to see money go back into the community and used to benefit it. We want to see the cooperative concept applied in business and banking. We want to see black ghetto residents demand that an exploiting landlord or storekeeper sell them, at minimal cost, a building or a shop that they will own and improve cooperatively; they can back their demand with a rent strike, or a boycott, and a community so unified behind them that no one else will move into the building or buy at the store. The society we seek to build among black people, then, is not a capitalist one. It is a society in which the spirit of community and humanistic love prevail. The word love is suspect; black expectations of what it might produce have been betrayed too often. But those were expectations of a response from the white community, which failed us. The love we seek to encourage is within the black community, the only American community where men call each other "brother" when they meet. We can build a community of love only where we have the ability and power to do so: among blacks.

As for white America, perhaps it can stop crying out against "black supremacy," "black nationalism," racism in reverse," and begin facing reality. The reality is that this nation, from top to bottom, is racist; that racism is not primarily a problem of "human relations" but of an exploitation maintained—either actively or through silence—by the society as a whole. Camus and Sartre have asked, can a man condemn himself? Can whites, particularly liberal whites, condemn themselves?

Can they stop blaming us, and blame their own system? Are they capable of the shame which might become a revolutionary emotion?

We have found that they usually cannot condemn themselves, and so we have done it. But the rebuilding of this society, if at all possible, is basically the responsibility of whites—not blacks. We won't fight to save the present society, in Vietnam or anywhere else. We are just going to work, in the way *we* see fit, and on goals *we* define, not for civil rights but for all our human rights.

Violence and Disorder in American Cities*

President's Commission on Civil Disorder

Summary of Report

Introduction

The summer of 1967 again brought racial disorders to American cities, and with them shock, fear and bewilderment to the nation.

The worst came during a two-week period in July, first in Newark and then in Detroit. Each set off a chain reaction in neighboring communities.

On July 28, 1967, the President of the United States established this Commission and directed us to answer three basic questions:

What happened?
Why did it happen?
What can be done to prevent it from happening again?

To respond to these questions, we have undertaken a broad range of studies and investigations. We have visited the riot cities; we have heard many witnesses; we have sought the counsel of experts across the country.

This is our basic conclusion: Our nation is moving toward two societies, one black, one white—separate and unequal.

---

*From President's Commission on Civil Disorder, *Report* (Washington, D.C.: U.S. Government Printing Office, 1968).

Reaction to last summer's disorders has quickened the movement and deepened the division. Discrimination and segregation have long permeated much of American life; they now threaten the future of every American.

This deepening racial division is not inevitable. The movement apart can be reversed. Choice is still possible. Our principal task is to define that choice and to press for a national resolution.

To pursue our present course will involve the continuing polarization of the American community and, ultimately, the destruction of basic democratic values.

The alternative is not blind repression or capitulation to lawlessness. It is the realization of common opportunities for all within a single society.

This alternative will require a commitment to national action—compassionate, massive and sustained, backed by the resources of the most powerful and the richest nation on this earth. From every American it will require new attitudes, new understanding, and above all, new will.

The vital needs of the nation must be met; hard choices must be made, and, if necessary, new taxes enacted.

Violence cannot build a better society. Disruption and disorder nourish repression, not justice. They strike at the freedom of every citizen. The community cannot—it will not—tolerate coercion and mob rule.

Violence and destruction must be ended—in the streets of the ghetto and in the lives of people.

Segregation and poverty have created in the racial ghetto a destructive environment totally unknown to most white Americans.

What white Americans have never fully understood—but what the Negro can never forget—is that white society is deeply implicated in the ghetto. White institutions created it, white institutions maintain it, and white society condones it.

It is time now to turn with all the purpose at our command to the major unfinished business of this nation. It is time to adopt strategies for action that will produce quick and visible progress. It is time to make good the promises of American democracy to all citizens—urban and rural, white and black, Spanish-surname, American Indian, and every minority group.

Our recommendations embrace three basic principles:

To mount programs on a scale equal to the dimension of the problems:
To aim these programs for high impact in the immediate future in order to close the gap between promise and performance;

To undertake new initiatives and experiments that can change the system of failure and frustration that now dominates the ghetto and weakens our society.

These programs will require unprecedented levels of funding and performance, but they neither probe deeper nor demand more than the problems which called them forth. There can be no higher priority for national action and no higher claim on the nation's conscience.

We issue this Report now, four months before the date called for by the President. Much remains that can be learned. Continued study is essential.

As Commissioners we have worked together with a sense of the greatest urgency and have sought to compose whatever differences exist among us. Some differences remain. But the gravity of the problem and the pressing need for action are too clear to allow further delay in the issuance of this Report.

Part I — What Happened?

Chapter 1—Profiles of Disorder

The report contains profiles of a selection of the disorders that took place during the summer of 1967. These profiles are designed to indicate how the disorders happened, who participated in them, and how local officials, police forces, and the National Guard responded. Illustrative excerpts follow:

NEWARK

. . . It was decided to attempt to channel the energies of the people into a nonviolent protest. While Lofton promised the crowd that a full investigation would be made of the Smith incident, the other Negro leaders began urging those on the scene to form a line of march toward the city hall.

Some persons joined the line of march. Others milled about in the narrow street. From the dark grounds of the housing project came a barrage of rocks. Some of them fell among the crowd. Others hit persons in the line of march. Many smashed the windows of the police station. The rock throwing, it was believed, was the work of youngsters; approximately 2,500 children lived in the housing project.

Almost at the same time, an old car was set afire in a parking lot. The line of march began to disintegrate. The police, their heads protected by World War I-type helmets, sallied forth to disperse the crowd.

A fire engine, arriving on the scene, was pelted with rocks. As police drove people away from the station, they scattered in all directions.

A few minutes later a nearby liquor store was broken into. Some persons, seeing a caravan of cabs appear at city hall to protest Smith's arrest, interpreted this as evidence that the disturbance had been organized, and generated rumors to that effect.

However, only a few stores were looted. Within a short period of time, the disorder appeared to have run its course.

*   *   *

. . . On Saturday, July 15, [Director of Police Dominick] Spina received a report of snipers in a housing project. When he arrived he saw approximately 100 National Guardsmen and police officers crouching behind vehicles, hiding in corners and lying on the ground around the edge of the courtyard.

Since everything appeared quiet and it was broad daylight, Spina walked directly down the middle of the street. Nothing happened. As he came to the last building of the complex, he heard a shot. All around him the troopers jumped, believing themselves to be under sniper fire. A moment later a young Guardsman ran from behind a building.

The Director of Police went over and asked him if he had fired the shot. The soldier said yes, he had fired to scare a man away from a window; that his orders were to keep everyone away from windows.

Spina said he told the soldier: "Do you know what you just did? You have now created a state of hysteria. Every Guardsman up and down this street and every state policeman and every city policeman that is present thinks that somebody just fired a shot and that it is probably a sniper."

A short time later more "gunshots" were heard. Investigating, Spina came upon a Puerto Rican sitting on a wall. In reply to a question as to whether he knew "where the firing is coming from?" the man said:

"That's no firing. That's fireworks. If you look up to the fourth floor, you will see the people who are throwing down these cherry bombs."

By this time four truckloads of National Guardsmen had arrived and troopers and policemen were again crouched everywhere looking for a sniper. The Director of Police remained at the scene for three hours, and the only shot fired was the one by the Guardsman.

Nevertheless, at six o'clock that evening two columns of National Guardsmen and state troopers were directing mass fire at the Hayes Housing Project in response to what they believed were snipers. . . .

DETROIT

. . . A spirit of carefree nihilism was taking hold. To riot and destroy appeared more and more to become ends in themselves. Late Sunday afternoon it appeared to one observer that the young people were "dancing amidst the flames."

A Negro plainclothes officer was standing at an intersection when a man threw a Molotov cocktail into a business establishment at the corner. In the heat of the afternoon, fanned by the 20 to 25 m.p.h. winds of both Sunday and Monday, the fire reached the home next door within minutes. As residents uselessly sprayed the flames with garden hoses, the fire jumped from roof to roof of adjacent two- and three-story buildings. Within the hour the entire block was in flames. The ninth house in the burning row belonged to the arsonist who had thrown the Molotov cocktail. . . .

* * *

. . . Employed as a private guard, 55-year-old Julius L. Dorsey, a Negro, was standing in front of a market when accosted by two Negro men and a woman. They demanded he permit them to loot the market. He ignored their demands. They began to berate him. He asked a neighbor to call the police. As the argument grew more heated, Dorsey fired three shots from his pistol into the air.

The police radio reported: "Looters, they have rifles." A patrol car driven by a police officer and carrying three National Guardsmen arrived. As the looters fled, the law enforcement personnel opened fire. When the firing ceased, one person lay dead.

He was Julius L. Dorsey . . .

. . . As the riot alternately waxed and waned, one area of the ghetto remained insulated. On the northeast side the residents of some 150 square blocks inhabited by 21,000 persons had, in 1966, banded together in the Positive Neighborhood Action Committee (PNAC). With professional help from the Institute of Urban Dynamics, they had organized block clubs and made plans for the improvement of the neighborhood. . . .

When the riot broke out, the residents, through the block clubs, were able to organize quickly. Youngsters, agreeing to stay in the neighborhood, participated in detouring traffic. While many persons reportedly sympathized with the idea of a rebellion against the "system," only two small fires were set—one in an empty building.

* * *

. . . According to Lt. Gen. Throckmorton and Col. Bolling, the city, at this time, was saturated with fear. The National Guardsmen were afraid, the residents were afraid, and the police were afraid. Numerous persons, the majority of them Negroes, were being injured by gunshots of undetermined origin. The general and his staff felt that the major task of the troops was to reduce the fear and restore an air of normalcy.

In order to accomplish this, every effort was made to establish contact and rapport between the troops and the residents. The soldiers—20 percent of whom were Negro—began helping to clean up the streets, collect garbage, and trace persons who had disappeared in the confusion. Residents in the neighborhoods responded with soup and sandwiches for the troops. In areas where the National Guard tried to establish rapport with the citizens, there was a smaller response.

NEW BRUNSWICK

. . . A short time later, elements of the crowd — an older and rougher one than the night before—appeared in front of the police station. The participants wanted to see the mayor.

Mayor [Patricia] Sheehan went out onto the steps of the station. Using a bullhorn, she talked to the people and asked that she be given an opportunity to correct conditions. The crowd was boisterous. Some persons challenged the mayor. But, finally, the opinion, "She's new! Give her a chance!" prevailed.

A demand was issued by people in the crowd that all persons arrested the previous night be released. Told that this already had been done, the people were suspicious. They asked to be allowed to inspect the jail cells.

It was agreed to permit representatives of the people to look in the cells to satisfy themselves that everyone had been released.

The crowd dispersed. The New Brunswick riot had failed to materialize.

Chapter 2—Patterns of Disorder

The "typical" riot did not take place. The disorders of 1967 were unusual, irregular, complex and unpredictable social processes. Like most human events, they did not unfold in an orderly sequence. However, an analysis of our survey information leads to some conclusions about the riot process.

In general:

The civil disorders of 1967 involved Negroes acting against local symbols of white American society, authority and property in Negro neighborhoods—rather than against white persons.

Of 164 disorders reported during the first nine months of 1967, eight (5 percent) were major in terms of violence and damage; 33 (20 percent) were serious but not major; 123 (75 percent) were minor and undoubtedly would not have received national attention as "riots" had the nation not been sensitized by the more serious outbreaks.

In the 75 disorders studied by a Senate subcommittee, 83 deaths were reported. Eighty-two percent of the deaths and more than half the injuries occurred in Newark and Detroit. About 10 percent of the dead and 38 percent of the injured were public employees, primarily law officers and firemen. The overwhelming majority of the persons killed or injured in all the disorders were Negro civilians.

Initial damage estimates were greatly exaggerated. In Detroit, newspaper damage estimates at first ranged from $200 million to $500 million; the highest recent estimate is $45 million. In Newark, early estimates ranged from $15 to $25 million. A month later damage was estimated at $10.2 million, over 80 percent in inventory losses.

In the 24 disorders in 23 cities which we surveyed:

The final incident before the outbreak of disorder, and the initial violence itself, generally took place in the evening or at night at a place in which it was normal for many people to be on the streets.

Violence usually occurred almost immediately following the occurrence of the final precipitating incident, and then escalated rapidly. With but few exceptions, violence subsided during the day, and flared rapidly again at night. The night-day cycles continued through the early period of the major disorders.

Disorder generally began with rock and bottle throwing and window breaking. Once store windows were broken, looting usually followed. Disorder did not erupt as a result of a single "triggering" or "precipitating" incident. Instead, it was generated out of an increasingly disturbed social atmosphere, in which typically a series of tension-heightening incidents over a period of weeks or months became linked in the minds of many in the Negro community with a reservoir of underlying grievances. At some point in the mounting tension, a further incident—in itself often routine or trivial—became the breaking point and the tension spilled over into violence.

"Prior" incidents, which increased tensions and ultimately led to violence, were police actions in almost half the cases; police actions were "final" incidents before the outbreak of violence in 12 of the 24 surveyed disorders.

No particular control tactic was successful in every situation. The varied effectiveness of control techniques emphasizes the need for advance training, planning, adequate intelligence systems, and knowledge of the ghetto community.

Negotiations between Negroes—including your militants as well as older Negro leaders—and white officials concerning "terms of peace" occurred during virtually all the disorders surveyed. In many cases, these negotiations involved discussion of underlying grievances as well as the handling of the disorder by control authorities.

The typical rioter was a teenager or young adult, a lifelong resident of the city in which he rioted, a high school dropout; he was, nevertheless, somewhat better educated than his nonrioting Negro neighbor, and was usually underemployed or employed in a menial job. He was proud of his race, extremely hostile to both whites and middle-class Negroes and, although informed about politics, highly distrustful of the political system. A Detroit survey revealed that approximately 11 percent of the total residents of two riot areas admitted participation in the rioting, 20 to 25 percent identified themselves as "bystanders," over 16 percent identified themselves as "counter-rioters" who urged rioters to "cool it," and the remaining 48 to 53 percent said they were at home or elsewhere and did not participate. In a survey of Negro males between the ages of 15 and 35 residing in the disturbance area in Newark, about 45 percent identified themselves as rioters, and about 55 percent as "noninvolved." Most rioters were young Negro males. Nearly 53 percent of arrestees were between 15 and 24 years of age; nearly 81 percent between 15 and 35.

In Detroit and Newark about 74 percent of the rioters were brought up in the North. In contrast, of the noninvolved, 36 percent in Detroit and 52 percent in Newark were brought up in the North.

What the rioters appeared to be seeking was fuller participation in the social order and the material benefits enjoyed by the majority of American citizens. Rather than rejecting the American system, they were anxious to obtain a place for themselves in it.

Numerous Negro counter-rioters walked the streets urging rioters to "cool it." The typical counter-rioter was better educated and had higher income than either the rioter or the noninvolved.

The proportion of Negroes in local government was substantially smaller than the Negro proportion of population. Only three of the 20 cities studied had more than one Negro legislator; none had ever had a Negro mayor or city manager. In only four cities did Negroes hold other important policy-making positions or serve as heads of municipal departments.

Although almost all cities had some sort of formal grievance mechanism for handling citizen complaints, this typically was regarded by Negroes as ineffective and was generally ignored.

Although specific grievances varied from city to city, at least 12 deeply held grievances can be identified and ranked into three levels of relative intensity:

First Level of Intensity
1. Police practices
2. Unemployment and underemployment
3. Inadequate housing

Second Level of Intensity
4. Inadequate education
5. Poor recreation facilities and programs
6. Ineffectiveness of the political structure and grievance mechanisms

Third Level of Intensity
 7. Disrespectful white attitudes
 8. Discriminatory administration of justice
 9. Inadequacy of federal programs
10. Inadequacy of municipal services
11. Discriminatory consumer and credit practices
12. Inadequate welfare programs

The results of a three-city survey of various federal programs—manpower, education, housing, welfare and community action—indicate that, despite substantial expenditures, the number of persons assisted constituted only a fraction of those in need.

The background of disorder is often as complex and difficult to analyze as the disorder itself. But we find that certain general conclusions can be drawn:

Social and economic conditions in the riot cities constituted a clear pattern of severe disadvantage for Negroes compared with whites, whether the Negroes lived in the area where the riot took place or outside it. Negroes had completed fewer years of education and fewer had attended high school. Negroes were twice as likely to be unemployed and three times as likely to be in unskilled and service jobs. Negroes averaged 70 percent of the income earned by whites and were more than twice as likely to be living in poverty. Although housing cost Negroes relatively more, they had worse housing—three times as likely to be overcrowded and substandard. When compared to white suburbs, the relative disadvantage is even more pronounced.

A study of the aftermath of disorder leads to disturbing conclusions. We find that, despite the institution of some post-riot programs:

Little basic change in the conditions underlying the outbreak of disorder has taken place. Actions to ameliorate Negro grievances have been limited and sporadic; with but few exceptions, they have not significantly reduced tensions.
In several cities, the principal official response has been to train and equip the police with more sophisticated weapons.
In several cities, increasing polarization is evident, with continuing breakdown of inter-racial communication, and growth of white segregationist or black separatist groups.

Chapter 3—Organized Activity

The President directed the Commission to investigate "to what extent, if any, there has been planning or organization in any of the riots."

To carry out this part of the President's charge, the Commission established a special investigative staff supplementing the field teams that made the general examination of the riots in 23 cities. The unit examined data collected by federal agencies and congressional committees, including thousands of documents supplied by the Federal Bureau of Investigation, gathered and evaluated information from local and state law enforcement agencies and officials, and conducted its own field investigation in selected cities.

On the basis of all the information collected, the Commission concludes that:

The urban disorders of the summer of 1967 were not caused by, nor were they the consequence of, any organized plan or "conspiracy."

Specifically, the Commission has found no evidence that all or any of the disorders or the incidents that led to them were planned or directed by any organization or group, international, national or local.

Militant organizations, local and national, and individual agitators, who repeatedly forecast and called for violence, were active in the spring and summer of 1967. We believe that they sought to encourage violence, and that they helped to create an atmosphere that contributed to the outbreak of disorder.

We recognize that the continuation of disorders and the polarization of the races would provide fertile ground for organized exploitation in the future.

Investigations of organized activity are continuing at all levels of government, including committees of Congress. These investigations relate not only to the disorders of 1967 but also to the actions of groups and individuals, particularly in schools and colleges, during this last fall and winter. The Commission has cooperated in these investigations. They should continue.

Part II — Why Did It Happen?

Chapter 4—The Basic Causes

In addressing the question "Why did it happen?" we shift our focus from the local to the national scene, from the particular events of the summer of 1967 to the factors within the society at large that created a mood of violence among many urban Negroes.

These factors are complex and interacting; they vary significantly in their effect from city to city and from year to year; and the consequences of one disorder, generating new grievances and new demands, become the causes of the next. Thus was created the "thicket of tension, conflicting evidence and extreme opinions" cited by the President.

Despite these complexities, certain fundamental matters are clear. Of these, the most fundamental is the racial attitude and behavior of white Americans toward black Americans.

Race prejudice has shaped our history decisively; it now threatens to affect our future.

White racism is essentially responsible for the explosive mixture which has been accumulating in our cities since the end of World War II. Among the ingredients of this mixture are:

> *Pervasive discrimination and segregation* in employment, education and housing, which have resulted in the continuing exclusion of great numbers of Negroes from the benefits of economic progress.
> *Black in-migration and white exodus,* which have produced the massive and growing concentrations of impoverished Negroes in our major cities, creating a growing crisis of deteriorating facilities and services and unmet human needs.
> *The black ghettos* where segregation and poverty converge on the young to destroy opportunity and enforce failure. Crime, drug addiction, dependency on welfare, and bitterness and resentment against society in general and white society in particular are the result.

At the same time, most whites and some Negroes outside the ghetto have prospered to a degree unparalleled in the history of civilization. Through television and other media, this affluence has been flaunted before the eyes of the Negro poor and the jobless ghetto youth.

Yet these facts alone cannot be said to have caused the disorders. Recently, other powerful ingredients have begun to catalyze the mixture:

> *Frustrated hopes* are the residue of the unfulfilled expectations aroused by the great judicial and legislative victories of the Civil Rights Movement and the dramatic struggle for equal rights in the South.
> *A climate that tends toward approval and encouragement of violence* as a form of protest has been created by white terrorism directed against nonviolent protest; by the open defiance of law and federal authority by state and local officials resisting desegregation; and by some protest groups engaging in civil disobedience who turn their backs on nonviolence, go beyond the constitutionally protected rights of petition and free assembly, and resort to violence to attempt to compel alteration of laws and policies with which they disagree.
> *The frustrations of powerlessness* have led some Negroes to the conviction that there is no effective alternative to violence as a means of achieving redress of grievances, and of "moving the system." These

frustrations are reflected in alienation and hostility toward the institutions of law and government and the white society which controls them, and in the reach toward racial consciousness and solidarity reflected in the slogan "Black Power."

A new mood has sprung up among Negroes, particularly among the young, in which self-esteem and enhanced racial pride are replacing apathy and submission to "the system."

The police are not merely a "spark" factor. To some Negroes police have come to symbolize white power, white racism and white repression. And the fact is that many police do reflect and express these white attitudes. The atmosphere of hostility and cynicism is reinforced by a widespread belief among Negroes in the existence of police brutality and in a "double standard" of justice and protection—one for Negroes and one for whites.

*   *   *

To this point, we have attempted to identify the prime components of the "explosive mixture." In the chapters that follow we seek to analyze them in the perspective of history. Their meaning, however, is clear:

In the summer of 1967, we have seen in our cities a chain reaction of racial violence. If we are heedless, none of us shall escape the consequences.

.   .   .

Part III — What Can Be Done?

Chapter 10—The Community Response

Our investigation of the 1967 riot cities establishes that virtually every major episode of violence was foreshadowed by an accumulation of unresolved grievances and by widespread dissatisfaction among Negroes with the unwillingness or inability of local government to respond.

Overcoming these conditions is essential for community support of law enforcement and civil order. City governments need new and more vital channels of communication to the residents of the ghetto; they need to improve their capacity to respond effectively to community needs before they become community grievances; and they need to provide opportunity for meaningful involvement of ghetto residents in shaping policies and programs which affect the community.

The Commission recommends that local governments:

Develop Neighborhood Action Task Forces as joint community-government efforts through which more effective communication can be achieved, and the delivery of city services to ghetto residents improved.

Establish comprehensive grievance-response mechanisms in order to bring all public agencies under public scrutiny.

Bring the institutions of local government closer to the people they serve by establishing neighborhood outlets for local, state and federal administrative and public service agencies.

Expand opportunities for ghetto residents to participate in the formulation of public policy and the implementation of programs affecting them through improved political representation, creation of institutional channels for community action, expansion of legal services, and legislative hearings on ghetto problems.

In this effort, city governments will require state and federal support. The Commission recommends:

State and federal financial assistance for mayors and city councils to support the research, consultants, staff and other resources needed to respond effectively to federal program initiatives.

State cooperation in providing municipalities with the jurisdictional tools needed to deal with their problems; a fuller measure of financial aid to urban areas; and the focusing of the interests of suburban communities on the physical, social and cultural environment of the central city.

Chapter 11—Police and the Community

The abrasive relationship between the police and the minority communities has been a major—and explosive—source of grievance, tension and disorder. The blame must be shared by the total society.

The police are faced with demands for increased protection and service in the ghetto. Yet the aggressive patrol practices thought necessary to meet these demands themselves create tension and hostility. The resulting grievances have been further aggravated by the lack of effective mechanisms for handling complaints against the police. Special programs for bettering police-community relations have been instituted, but these alone are not enough. Police administrators, with the guidance of public officials, and the support of the entire community, must take vigorous action to improve law enforcement and to decrease the potential for disorder.

The Commission recommends that city government and police authorities:

Review police operations in the ghetto to ensure proper conduct by police officers, and eliminate abrasive practices.

Provide more adequate police protection to ghetto residents to eliminate their high sense of insecurity, and the belief of many Negro citizens in the existence of a dual standard of law enforcement.

Establish fair and effective mechanisms for the redress of grievances against the police, and other municipal employees.

Develop and adopt policy guidelines to assist officers in making critical decisions in areas where police conduct can create tension.

Develop and use innovative programs to ensure widespread community support for law enforcement.

Recruit more Negroes into the regular police force, and review promotion policies to ensure fair promotion for Negro officers.

Establish a "Community Service Officer" program to attract ghetto youths between the ages of 17 and 21 to police work. These junior officers would perform duties in ghetto neighborhoods, but would not have full police authority. The federal government should provide support equal to 90 percent of the costs of employing CSOs on the basis of one for every ten regular officers.

Chapter 12—Control of Disorder

Preserving civil peace is the first responsibility of government. Unless the rule of law prevails, our society will lack not only order but also the environment essential to social and economic progress.

The maintenance of civil order cannot be left to the police alone. The police need guidance, as well as support, from mayors and other public officials. It is the responsibility of public officials to determine proper police policies, support adequate police standards for personnel and performance, and participate in planning for the control of disorders.

To maintain control of incidents which could lead to disorders, the Commission recommends that local officials:

Assign seasoned, well-trained policemen and supervisory officers to patrol ghetto areas, and to respond to disturbances.

Develop plans which will quickly muster maximum police manpower and highly qualified senior commanders at the outbreak of disorders.

Provide special training in the prevention of disorders, and prepare police for riot control and for operation in units, with adequate command and control and field communication for proper discipline and effectiveness.

Develop guidelines governing the use of control equipment and provide alternatives to the use of lethal weapons. Federal support for research in this area is needed.

Establish an intelligence system to provide police and other public officials with reliable information that may help to prevent the outbreak of a disorder and to institute effective control measures in the event a riot erupts.

Develop continuing contacts with ghetto residents to make use of the forces for order which exist within the community.

Establish machinery for neutralizing rumors, and enabling Negro leaders and residents to obtain the facts. Create special rumor details to collect, evaluate, and dispel rumors that may lead to a civil disorder.

The Commission believes there is a grave danger that some communities may resort to the indiscriminate and excessive use of force. The harmful effects of overreaction are incalculable. The Commission condemns moves to equip police departments with mass destruction weapons, such as automatic rifles, machine guns and tanks. Weapons which are designed to destroy, not to control, have no place in densely populated urban communities.

The Commission recognizes the sound principle of local authority and responsibility in law enforcement, but recommends that the federal government share in the financing of programs for improvement of police forces, both in their normal law enforcement activities as well as in their response to civil disorders.

To assist government authorities in planning their response to civil disorder, this report contains a Supplement on Control of Disorder. It deals with specific problems encountered during riot-control operations, and includes:

Assessment of the present capabilities of police, National Guard and Army forces to control major riots, and recommendations for improvement;

Recommended means by which the control operations of those forces may be coordinated with the response of other agencies, such as fire departments, and with the community at large;

Recommendations for review and revision of federal, state and local laws needed to provide the framework for control efforts and for the call-up and interrelated action of public safety forces.

Chapter 13—The Administration of Justice Under Emergency Conditions

In many of the cities which experienced disorders last summer, there were recurring breakdowns in the mechanisms for processing, prosecuting and protecting arrested persons. These resulted mainly from long-standing structural deficiencies in criminal court systems, and from the failure of communities to anticipate and plan for the emergency demands of civil disorders.

In part, because of this, there were few successful prosecutions for serious crimes committed during the riots. In those cities where mass arrests occurred many arrestees were deprived of basic legal rights.

The Commission recommends that the cities and states:

Undertake reform of the lower courts so as to improve the quality of justice rendered under normal conditions.

Plan comprehensive measures by which the criminal justice system may be supplemented during civil disorders so that its deliberative functions are protected, and the quality of justice is maintained.

Such emergency plans require broad community participation and dedicated leadership by the bench and bar. They should include:

Laws sufficient to deter and punish riot conduct.

Additional judges, bail and probation officers, and clerical staff.

Arrangements for volunteer lawyers to help prosecutors and to represent riot defendants at every stage of proceedings.

Policies to ensure proper and individual bail, arraignment, pretrial, trial and sentencing proceedings.

Procedures for processing arrested persons, such as summons and release, and release on personal recognizance, which permit separation of minor offenders from those dangerous to the community, in order that serious offenders may be detained and prosecuted effectively.

Adequate emergency processing and detention facilities.

Chapter 14—Damages: Repair and Compensation

The Commission recommends that the federal government:

Amend the Federal Disaster Act—which now applies only to natural disasters—to permit federal emergency food and medical assistance to cities during major civil disorders, and provide long-term economic assistance afterwards.

With the cooperation of the states, create incentives for the private insurance industry to provide more adequate property-insurance coverage in inner-city areas.

The Commission endorses the report of the National Advisory Panel on Insurance in Riot-Affected Areas: "Meeting the Insurance Crisis of our Cities."

Chapter 15—The News Media and the Disorders

In his charge to the Commission, the President asked: "What effect do the mass media have on the riots?"

The Commission determined that the answer to the President's question did not lie solely in the performance of the press and broadcasters in reporting the riots. Our analysis had to consider also the overall treatment by the media of the Negro ghettos, community relations, racial attitudes, and poverty—day by day and month by month, year in and year out.

A wide range of interviews with government officials, law enforcement authorities, media personnel and other citizens, including ghetto residents, as well as a quantitative analysis of riot coverage and a special conference with industry representatives, leads us to conclude that:

> Despite instances of sensationalism, inaccuracy and distortion, newspapers, radio and television tried on the whole to give a balanced, factual account of the 1967 disorders.
>
> Elements of the news media failed to portray accurately the scale and character of the violence that occurred last summer. The overall effect was, we believe, an exaggeration of both mood and event.
>
> Important segments of the media failed to report adequately on the causes and consequences of civil disorders and on the underlying problems of race relations. They have not communicated to the majority of their audience—which is white—a sense of the degradation, misery and hopelessness of life in the ghetto.

These failings must be corrected, and the improvement must come from within the industry. Freedom of the press is not the issue. Any effort to impose governmental restrictions would be inconsistent with fundamental constitutional precepts.

We have seen evidence that the news media are becoming aware of and concerned about their performance in this field. As that concern grows, coverage will improve. But much more must be done, and it must be done soon.

The Commission recommends that the media:

> Expand coverage of the Negro community and of race problems through permanent assignment of reporters familiar with urban and racial affairs, and through establishment of more and better links with the Negro community.
>
> Integrate Negroes and Negro activities into all aspects of coverage and content, including newspaper articles and television programming. The news media must publish newspapers and produce programs that recognize the existence and activities of Negroes as a group within the community and as a part of the larger community.
>
> Recruit more Negroes into journalism and broadcasting and promote those who are qualified to positions of significant responsibility. Recruitment should begin in high schools and continue through college; where necessary, aid for training should be provided.
>
> Improve coordination with police in reporting riot news through advance planning, and cooperate with the police in the designation of police information officers, establishment of information centers, and development of mutually acceptable guidelines for riot reporting and the conduct of media personnel.

Accelerate efforts to ensure accurate and responsible reporting of riot and racial news, through adoption by all news gathering organizations of stringent internal staff guidelines.

Cooperate in the establishment of a privately organized and funded Institute of Urban Communications to train and educate journalists in urban affairs, recruit and train more Negro journalists, develop methods for improving police-press relations, review coverage of riots and racial issues, and support continuing research in the urban field.

Chapter 16—The Future of the Cities

By 1985, the Negro population in central cities is expected to increase by 72 percent to approximately 20.8 million. Coupled with the continued exodus of white families to the suburbs, this growth will produce majority Negro populations in many of the nation's largest cities.

The future of these cities, and of their burgeoning Negro populations, is grim. Most new employment opportunities are being created in suburbs and outlying areas. This trend will continue unless important changes in public policy are made.

In prospect, therefore, is further deterioration of already inadequate municipal tax bases in the face of increasing demands for public services, and continuing unemployment and poverty among the urban Negro population:

Three choices are open to the nation:

We can maintain present policies, continuing both the proportion of the nation's resources now allocated to programs for the unemployed and the disadvantaged, and the inadequate and failing effort to achieve an integrated society.

We can adopt a policy of "enrichment" aimed at improving dramatically the quality of ghetto life while abandoning integration as a goal.

We can pursue integration by combining ghetto "enrichment" with policies which will encourage Negro movement out of central city areas.

The first choice, continuance of present policies, has ominous consequences for our society. The share of the nation's resources now allocated to programs for the disadvantaged is insufficient to arrest the deterioration of life in central city ghettos. Under such conditions, a rising proportion of Negroes may come to see in the deprivation and segregation they experience, a justification for violent protest, or for extending support to now isolated extremists who advocate civil disruption. Large-scale and continuing violence could result, followed by white retaliation, and ultimately, the separation of the two communities in a garrison state.

Even if violence does not occur, the consequences are unacceptable. Development of a racially integrated society, extraordinarily difficult today, will be virtually impossible when the present black ghetto population of 12.5 million has grown to almost 21 million.

To continue present policies is to make permanent the division of our country into two societies; one, largely Negro and poor, located in the central cities; the other predominantly white and affluent, located in the suburbs and in outlying areas.

The second choice, ghetto enrichment coupled with abandonment of integration, is also unacceptable. It is another way of choosing a permanently divided country. Moreover, equality cannot be achieved under conditions of nearly complete separation. In a country where the economy, and particularly the resources of employment, are predominantly white, a policy of separation can only relegate Negroes to a permanently inferior economic status.

We believe that the only possible choice for America is the third— a policy which combines ghetto enrichment with programs designed to encourage integration of substantial numbers of Negroes into the society outside the ghetto.

Enrichment must be an important adjunct to integration, for no matter how ambitious or energetic the program, few Negroes now living in central cities can be quickly integrated. In the meantime, large-scale improvement in the quality of ghetto life is essential.

But this can be no more than an interim strategy. Programs must be developed which will permit substantial Negro movement out of the ghettos. The primary goal must be a single society, in which every citizen will be free to live and work according to his capabilities and desires, not his color.

Chapter 17—Recommendations For National Action

INTRODUCTION

No American—white or black—can escape the consequences of the continuing social and economic decay of our major cities.

Only a commitment to national action on an unprecedented scale can shape a future compatible with the historic ideals of American society.

The great productivity of our economy, and a federal revenue system which is highly responsive to economic growth, can provide the resources.

The major need is to generate new will—the will to tax ourselves to the extent necessary to meet the vital needs of the nation.

We have set forth goals and proposed strategies to reach those goals. We discuss and recommend programs not to commit each of us to specific parts of such programs but to illustrate the type and dimension of action needed.

The major goal is the creation of a true union—a single society and a single American identity. Toward that goal, we propose the following objectives for national action:

Opening up opportunities to those who are restricted by racial segregation and discrimination, and eliminating all barriers to their choice of jobs, education and housing.

Removing the frustration of powerlessness among the disadvantaged by providing the means for them to deal with the problems that affect their own lives and by increasing the capacity of our public and private institutions to respond to these problems.

Increasing communication across racial lines to destroy stereotypes, to halt polarization, end distrust and hostility, and create common ground for efforts toward public order and social justice.

We propose these aims to fulfill our pledge of equality and to meet the fundamental needs of a democratic and civilized society—domestic peace and social justice.

EMPLOYMENT

Pervasive unemployment and underemployment are the most persistent and serious grievances in minority areas. They are inextricably linked to the problem of civil disorder.

Despite growing federal expenditures for manpower development and training programs, and sustained general economic prosperity and increasing demands for skilled workers, about two million—white and nonwhite—are permanently unemployed. About ten million are underemployed, of whom 6.5 million work full time for wages below the poverty line.

The 500,000 "hard-core" unemployed in the central cities who lack a basic education and are unable to hold a steady job are made up in large part of Negro males between the ages of 18 and 25. In the riot cities which we surveyed, Negroes were three times as likely as whites to hold unskilled jobs, which are often part time, seasonable, low-paying and "dead end."

Negro males between the ages of 15 and 25 predominated among the rioters. More than 20 percent of the rioters were unemployed, and many who were employed held intermittent, low status, unskilled jobs which they regarded as below their education and ability.

The Commission recommends that the federal government:

Undertake joint efforts with cities and states to consolidate existing manpower programs to avoid fragmentation and duplication.

Take immediate action to create 2,000,000 new jobs over the next three years—one million in the public sector and one million in the private sector—to absorb the hard-core unemployed and materially reduce the level of underemployment for all workers, black and white. We propose 250,000 public sector and 300,000 private sector jobs in the first year.

Provide on-the-job training by both public and private employers with reimbursement to private employers for the extra costs of training the hard-core unemployed, by contract or by tax credits.

Provide tax and other incentives to investment in rural as well as urban poverty areas in order to offer to the rural poor an alternative to migration to urban centers.

Take new and vigorous action to remove artificial barriers to employment and promotion, including not only racial discrimination but, in certain cases, arrest records or lack of a high school diploma. Strengthen those agencies such as the Equal Employment Opportunity Commission, charged with eliminating discriminatory practices, and provide full support for Title VI of the 1964 Civil Rights Act allowing federal grant-in-aid funds to be withheld from activities which discriminate on grounds of color or race.

The Commission commends the recent public commitment of the National Council of the Building and Construction Trades Unions, AFL-CIO, to encourage and recruit Negro membership in apprenticeship programs. This commitment should be intensified and implemented.

EDUCATION

Education in a democratic society must equip children to develop their potential and to participate fully in American life. For the community at large, the schools have discharged this responsibility well. But for many minorities, and particularly for the children of the ghetto, the schools have failed to provide the educational experience which could overcome the effects of discrimination and deprivation.

This failure is one of the persistent sources of grievance and resentment within the Negro community. The hostility of Negro parents and students toward the school system is generating increasing conflict and causing disruption within many city school districts. But the most dramatic evidence of the relationship between educational practices and civil disorders lies in the high incidence of riot participation by ghetto youth who have not completed high school.

The bleak record of public education for ghetto children is growing worse. In the critical skills—verbal and reading ability—Negro students are falling further behind whites with each year of school completed. The high unemployment and underemployment rate for Negro youth is evidence, in part, of the growing educational crisis.

We support integration as the priority education strategy; it is essential to the future of American society. In this last summer's disorders we have seen the consequences of racial isolation at all levels, and of attitudes toward race, on both sides, produced by three centuries of myth, ignorance and bias. It is indispensable that opportunities for interaction between the races be expanded.

We recognize that the growing dominance of pupils from disadvantaged minorities in city school populations will not soon be reversed. No matter how great the effort toward desegregation, many children of the ghetto will not, within their school careers, attend integrated schools.

If existing disadvantages are not to be perpetuated, we must drastically improve the quality of ghetto education. Equality of results with all-white schools must be the goal.

To implement these strategies, the Commission recommends:

Sharply increased efforts to eliminate de facto segregation in our schools through substantial federal aid to school systems seeking to desegregate either within the system or in cooperation with neighboring school systems.

Elimination of racial discrimination in Northern as well as Southern schools by vigorous application of Title VI of the Civil Rights Act of 1964.

Extension of quality early childhood education to every disadvantaged child in the country.

Efforts to improve dramatically schools serving disadvantaged children through substantial federal funding of year-round compensatory education programs, improved teaching, and expanded experimentation and research.

Elimination of illiteracy through greater federal support for adult basic education.

Enlarged opportunities for parent and community participation in the public schools.

Reoriented vocational education emphasizing work-experience training and the involvement of business and industry.

Expanded opportunities for higher education through increased federal assistance to disadvantaged students.

Revision of state aid formulas to assure more per student aid to districts having a high proportion of disadvantaged school-age children.

THE WELFARE SYSTEM

Our present system of public welfare is designed to save money instead of people, and tragically ends up doing neither. This system has two critical deficiencies:

First, it excludes large numbers of persons who are in great need, and who, if provided a decent level of support, might be able to become more productive and self-sufficient. No federal funds are available for millions of men and women who are needy but neither aged, handicapped nor the parents of minor children.

Second, for those included, the system provides assistance well below the minimum necessary for a decent level of existence, and imposes restrictions that encourage continued dependency on welfare and undermine self-respect.

A welter of statutory requirements and administrative practices and regulations operate to remind recipients that they are considered untrustworthy, promiscuous and lazy. Residence requirements prevent assistance to people in need who are newly arrived in the state. Regular searches of recipients' homes violate privacy. Inadequate social services compound the problems.

The Commission recommends that the federal government, acting with state and local governments where necessary, reform the existing welfare system to:

> Establish uniform national standards of assistance at least as high as the annual "poverty level" of income, now set by the Social Security Administration at $3,335 per year for an urban family of four.
>
> Require that all states receiving federal welfare contributions participate in the Aid to Families with Dependent Children—Unemployed Parents program (AFDC-UP) that permits assistance to families with both father and mother in the home, thus aiding the family while it is still intact.
>
> Bear a substantially greater portion of all welfare costs—at least 90 percent of total payments.
>
> Increase incentives for seeking employment and job training, but remove restrictions recently enacted by the Congress that would compel mothers of young children to work.
>
> Provide more adequate social services through neighborhood centers and family-planning programs.
>
> Remove the freeze placed by the 1967 welfare amendments on the percentage of children in a state that can be covered by federal assistance.
>
> Eliminate residence requirements.

As a long-range goal, the Commission recommends that the federal government seek to develop a national system of income supplementation based strictly on need with two broad and basic purposes:

> To provide, for those who can work or who do work, any necessary supplements in such a way as to develop incentives for fuller employment;

To provide, for those who cannot work and for mothers who decide to remain with their children, a minimum standard of decent living, and to aid in the saving of children from the prison of poverty that has held their parents.

A broad system of supplementation would involve substantially greater federal expenditures than anything now contemplated. The cost will range widely depending on the standard of need accepted as the "basic allowance" to individuals and families, and on the rate at which additional income above this level is taxed. Yet if the deepening cycle of poverty and dependence on welfare can be broken, if the children of the poor can be given the opportunity to scale the wall that now separates them from the rest of society, the return on this investment will be great indeed.

HOUSING

After more than three decades of fragmented and grossly underfunded federal housing programs, nearly six million substandard housing units remain occupied in the United States.
To reach this goal we recommend:

Expansion and modification of the rent supplement program to permit use of supplements for existing housing, thus greatly increasing the reach of the program.
Expansion and modification of the below-market interest rate program to enlarge the interest subsidy to all sponsors and provide interest-free loans to nonprofit sponsors to cover pre-construction costs, and permit sale of projects to nonprofit corporations, cooperatives, or condominiums.
Creation of an ownership supplement program similar to present rent supplements, to make home ownership possible for low-income families.
Federal writedown of interest rates on loans to private builders constructing moderate-rent housing.
Expansion of the public housing program, with emphasis on small units on scattered sites, and leasing and "turnkey" programs.
Expansion of the Model Cities program.
Expansion and reorientation of the urban renewal program to give priority to projects directly assisting low-income households to obtain adequate housing.

CONCLUSION

One of the first witnesses to be invited to appear before this Commission was Dr. Kenneth B. Clark, a distinguished and perceptive scholar. Referring to the reports of earlier riot commissions, he said:

I read that report . . . of the 1919 riot in Chicago, and it is as if I were reading the report of the investigating committee on the Harlem riot of '35, the report of the investigating committee on the Harlem riot of '43, the report of the McCone Commission on the Watts riot.

I must again in candor say to you members of this Commission—it is a kind of Alice in Wonderland—with the same moving picture re-shown over and over again, the same analysis, the same recommendations, and the same inaction.

These words come to our minds as we conclude this report.

We have provided an honest beginning. We have learned much. But we have uncovered no startling truths, no unique insights, no simple solutions. The destruction and the bitterness of racial disorder, the harsh polemics of black revolt and white repression have been seen and heard before in this country.

It is time now to end the destruction and the violence, not only in the streets of the ghetto but in the lives of people.

The housing problem is particularly acute in the minority ghettos. Nearly two-thirds of all non-white families living in the central cities today live in neighborhoods marked with substandard housing and general urban blight. Two major factors are responsible.

First: Many ghetto residents simply cannot pay the rent necessary to support decent housing. In Detroit, for example, over 40 percent of the non-white occupied units in 1960 required rent of over 35 percent of the tenants' income.

Second: Discrimination prevents access to many non-slum areas, particularly the suburbs, where good housing exists. In addition, by creating a "back pressure" in the racial ghettos, it makes it possible for landlords to break up apartments for denser occupancy, and keeps prices and rents of deteriorated ghetto housing higher than they would be in a truly free market.

To date, federal programs have been able to do comparatively little to provide housing for the disadvantaged. In the 31-year history of subsidized federal housing, only about 800,000 units have been constructed, with recent production averaging about 50,000 units a year. By comparison, over a period only three years longer, FHA insurance guarantees have made possible the construction of over ten million middle and upper-income units.

Two points are fundamental to the Commission's recommendations:

First: Federal housing programs must be given a new thrust aimed at overcoming the prevailing patterns of racial segregation. If this is not done, those programs will continue to concentrate the most impoverished and dependent segments of the population into the central-city ghettos where there is already a critical gap between the needs of the population and the public resources to deal with them.

Second: The private sector must be brought into the production and financing of low and moderate rental housing to supply the capabilities and capital necessary to meet the housing needs of the nation.

The Commission recommends that the federal government:

Enact a comprehensive and enforceable federal open housing law to cover the sale or rental of all housing, including single family homes.

Reorient federal housing programs to place more low and moderate income housing outside of ghetto areas.

Bring within the reach of low and moderate income families within the next five years six million new and existing units of decent housing, beginning with 600,000 units in the next year.

The Police Riot in Chicago*

A Report for the President's Commission on the Causes and Prevention of Violence

Foreword

The right to dissent is fundamental to democracy. But the expression of that right has become one of the most serious problems in contemporary democratic government. That dilemma was dramatized in Chicago during the Democratic National Convention of 1968 — the dilemma of a city coping with the expression of dissent.

Unlike other recent big city riots, including those in Chicago itself, the events of convention week did not consist of looting and burning, followed by mass arrests. To a shocking extent they consisted of crowd-police battles in the parks as well as the streets. And the shock was intensified by the presence in the crowds (which included some anarchists and revolutionaries) of large numbers of innocent dissenting citizens.

The initial response, precipitated by dramatic television coverage, was a horrified condemnation of city and police. When demonstrators compared the Chicago police to the Soviet troops then occupying Prague, news commentators sympathetically relayed that comparison to the world. Not since Birmingham and Selma had there been so heated a mood of public outrage.

An immediate counterresponse, however, expressed the feeling that the demonstrators got what they deserved, and the thinking that the city

---

*Excerpts from Daniel Walker, "Rights in Conflict," A Report to the President's Commission on the Causes and Prevention of Violence, December 1, 1968.

had no alternative. Many observers thought that, in view of the provocation and the circumstances, police had performed admirably and with restraint.

The commentary far outlasted the convention. Major writers in some of the world's most respected periodicals denounced the city, the police, and the Democratic leaders. For its part, the City of Chicago issued "The Strategy of Confrontation," a paper detailing the threat to the city, itemizing provocations, describing a battery of bizarre weapons allegedly intended for use against law enforcement officers, and charging the American news media with biased coverage. The city also prepared a one-hour film shown nationally on television.

These conflicting responses, and the nature of the dilemma imposed upon Chicago, make this study necessary. Our purpose is to present the facts so that thoughtful readers can decide what lessons come out of them; for it is urgent that any such lessons be speedily incorporated into American public life. The Chicago Tribune began its special report on convention week with the line, "Not everyone wins." They might have added that there are circumstances in which no one wins, in which everyone loses. Such circumstances make up this report.

The Question

We have addressed ourselves to questions like the following. What were the objectives of the planned demonstrations, and who planned them? How did the city prepare itself? What types of people made up the crowds in the parks? Were physical and verbal attacks typical of demonstrator behavior? And did they precipitate police violence or follow it? Was the clubbing done by a few tired policemen goaded into "overreacting," or was there large-scale police brutality? Is there evidence that newsmen were singled out for assault? Was Chicago itself conducive to violence, or was it merely where the convention, and the cameras, happened to be?

We believe we have laid a factual foundation for meaningful answers to those questions.

Our charge was not to decide what ought to have been done, or to balance the rights and wrongs, or to recommend a course of action for the future. Having sought out the facts, we intend to let them speak for themselves. But we urge the reader, in assessing these facts, to bear in mind that the physical confrontations in Chicago will be repeated elsewhere until we learn to deal with the dilemma they represent.

In principle, at least, most Americans acknowledge the right to dissent. And, in principle at least, most dissenters acknowledge the right of a city to protect its citizens and its property. But what happens when these undeniable rights are brought — deliberately by some — into conflict?

Convention week in Chicago is what happens, and the challenge it brings is plain: to keep peaceful assembly from becoming a contradiction in terms.

A Summary

During the week of the Democratic National Convention, the Chicago police were targets of mounting provocation by both word and act. It took the form of obscene epithets, and of rocks, sticks, bathroom tiles and even human feces hurled at police by demonstrators. Some of these acts had been planned; others were spontaneous or were themselves provoked by police action. Furthermore, the police had been put on edge by widely published threats of attempts to disrupt both the city and the Convention.

That was the nature of the provocation. The nature of the response was unrestrained and indiscriminate police violence on many occasions, particularly at night.

That violence was made all the more shocking by the fact that it was often inflicted upon persons who had broken no law, disobeyed no order, made no threat. These included peaceful demonstrators, onlookers, and large numbers of residents who were simply passing through, or happened to live in, the areas where confrontations were occurring.

Newsmen and photographers were singled out for assault, and their equipment deliberately damaged. Fundamental police training was ignored; and officers, when on the scene, were often unable to control their men. As one police officer put it: "What happened didn't have anything to do with police work."

The violence reached its culmination on Wednesday night.

An Observer's Report

A report prepared by an inspector from the Los Angeles Police Department, present as an official observer, while generally praising the police restraint he had observed in the parks during the week, said this about the events that night:

"There is no question but that many officers acted without restraint and exerted force beyond that necessary under the circumstances. The leadership at the point of conflict did little to prevent such conduct and the direct control of officers by first line supervisors was virtually nonexistent."

He is referring to the police-crowd confrontation in front of the Conrad Hilton Hotel. Most Americans know about it, having seen the 17-minute sequence played and replayed on their television screens.

But most Americans do not know that the confrontation was followed by even more brutal incidents in the Loop side streets. Or that it had been preceded by comparable instances of indiscriminate police attacks on the North Side a few nights earlier when demonstrators were cleared from Lincoln Park and pushed into the streets and alleys of Old Town.

How did it start? With the emergence long before convention week of three factors which figured significantly in the outbreak of violence. These were: threats to the city; the city's response; and the conditioning of Chicago police to expect that violence against demonstrators, as against rioters, would be condoned by city officials.

The threats to the City were varied. Provocative and inflammatory statements, made in connection with activities planned for convention week, were published and widely disseminated. There were also intelligence reports from informants.

Some of this information was absurd, like the reported plan to contaminate the city's water supply with LSD. But some were serious; and both were strengthened by the authorities' lack of any mechanism for distinguishing one from the other.

The second factor — the city's response — matched, in numbers and logistics at least, the demonstrators' threats.

The city, fearful that the "leaders" would not be able to control their followers, attempted to discourage an inundation of demonstrators by not granting permits for marches and rallies and by making it quite clear that the "law" would be enforced.

Government — Federal, state and local — moved to defend itself from the threats, both imaginary and real. The preparations were detailed and far ranging: from stationing firemen at each alarm box within a six block radius of the Amphitheatre to staging U.S. Army armored personnel carriers in Soldier Field under Secret Service control. Six thousand Regular Army troops in full field gear, equipped with rifles, flame throwers, and bazookas were airlifted to Chicago on Monday, Aug. 26. About 6000 Illinois National Guard troops had already been activated to assist the 12,000 member Chicago Police Force.

Of course, the Secret Service could never afford to ignore threats of assassination of Presidential candidates. Neither could the city, against the background of riots in 1967 and 1968, ignore the ever-present threat of ghetto riots, possibly sparked by large number of demonstrators, during convention week.

The third factor emerged in the city's position regarding the riots following the death of Dr. Martin Luther King and the April 27 peace march to the Civic Center in Chicago.

The police were generally credited with restraint in handling the first riots — but Mayor Daley rebuked the Superintendent of Police. While it was later modified, his widely disseminated "shoot to kill arsonists and shoot to maim looters" order undoubtedly had an effect.

The effect on police became apparent several weeks later, when they attacked demonstrators, bystanders and media representatives at a Civic Center peace march. There were published criticisms — but the city's response was to ignore the police violence.

Advance Contingent

That was the background. On Aug. 18, 1968, the advance contingent of demonstrators arrived in Chicago and established their base, as planned, in Lincoln Park on the city's Near North Side. Throughout the week, they were joined by others — some from the Chicago area, some from states as far away as New York and California. On the weekend before the convention began, there were about 2000 demonstrators in Lincoln Park; the crowd grew to about 10,000 by Wednesday.

There were, of course, the hippies—the long hair and love beads, the calculated unwashedness, the flagrant banners, the open lovemaking and disdain for the constraints of conventional society. In dramatic effect, both visual and vocal, these dominated a crowd whose members actually differed widely in physical appearance, in motivation, in political affiliation, in philosophy. The crowd included Yippies come to "do their thing," youngsters working for a political candidate, professional people with dissenting political views, anarchists and determined revolutionaries, motorcycle gangs, black activists, young thugs, police and Secret Service undercover agents. There were demonstrators waving the Viet Cong flag and the red flag of revolution and there were the simply curious who came to watch and, in many cases, became willing or unwilling participants.

To characterize the crowd, then as entirely hippy-Yippie, entirely "New Left," entirely anarchist, or entirely youthful political dissenters, is both wrong and dangerous. The stereotyping that did occur helps to explain the emotional reaction of both police and public during and after the violence that occurred.

Despite the presence of some revolutionaries, the vast majority of the demonstrators were intent on expressing by peaceful means their dissent either from society generally or from the Administration's policies in Vietnam.

Most of those intending to join the major protest demonstrations scheduled during convention week did not plan to enter the Amphitheatre and disrupt the proceedings of the Democratic Convention, did not plan aggressive acts of physical provocation against the authorities, and did not plan to use rallies of demonstrators to stage an assault against any person, institution, or place of business. But while it is clear that most of the protesters in Chicago had no intention of initiating violence, this is not to say that they did not expect it to develop.

It was the clearing of the demonstrators from Lincoln Park that led directly to the violence: symbolically, it expressed the city's opposition to the protesters; literally, it forced the protester into confrontation with police in Old Town and the adjacent residential neighborhoods.

The Old Town area near Lincoln Park was a scene of police ferocity exceeding that shown on television on Wednesday night. From Sunday night through Tuesday night, incidents of intense and indiscriminate violence occurred in the streets after police had swept the park clear of demonstrators.

A Police Riot

Demonstrators attacked too. And they posed difficult problems for police as they persisted in marching through the streets, blocking traffic and intersections. But it was the police who forced them out of the park and into the neighborhood. And on the part of the police there was enough wild club swinging, enough cries of hatred, enough gratuitous beating to make the conclusion inescapable that individual policemen, and lots of them, committed violent acts far in excess of the requisite force for crowd dispersal or arrest. To read dispassionately the hundreds of statements describing at firsthand the events of Sunday and Monday nights is to become convinced of the presence of what can only be called a police riot.

Here is an eyewitness talking about Monday night:

"The demonstrators were forced out onto Clark Street and once again a traffic jam developed. Cars were stopped, the horns began to honk, people couldn't move, people got gassed inside their cars, people got stoned inside their cars, police were the objects of stones, and taunts, mostly taunts. As you must understand, most of the taunting of the police was verbal. There were stones thrown of course, but for the most part it was verbal. But there were stones being thrown and of course the police were responding with tear gas and clubs and every time they could get near enough to a demonstrator they hit him.

"But again you had this police problem within—this really turned into a police problem. They pushed everybody out of the park, but this night there were a lot more people in the park than there had been during the previous night and Clark Street was just full of people and in addition now was full of gas because the police were using gas on a much larger scale this night. So the police were faced with the task, which took them about an hour or so, of hitting people over the head and gassing them enough to get them out of Clark Street, which they did."

But police action was not confined to the necessary force, even in clearing the park:

Mindless Violence

A young man and his girl friend were both grabbed by officers. He screamed, "We're going, we're going," but they threw him into the pond. The officers grabbed the girl, knocked her to the ground, dragged her along the embankment and hit her with their batons on her head, arms, back and legs. The boy tried to scramble up the embankment to her, but police shoved him back in the water at least twice. He finally got to her and tried to pull her in the water, away from the police. He was clubbed on the head five or six times. An officer shouted, "Let's get the bastards!" But the boy pulled her in the water and the police left.

Like the incident described above, much of the violence witnessed in Old Town that night seems malicious or mindless:

There were pedestrians. People who were not part of the demonstration were coming out of a tavern to see what the demonstration was . . . and the officers indiscriminately started beating everybody on the street who was not a policeman.

Another scene:

There was a group of about six police officers that moved in and started beating two youths. When one of the officers pulled back his nightstick to swing, one of the youths grabbed it from behind and started beating on the officer. At this point about ten officers left everybody else and ran after the youth, who turned down Wells and ran to the left.

But the officers went to the right, picked up another youth assuming he was the one they were chasing, and took him into an empty lot and beat him. And when they got him to the ground, they just kicked him ten times—the wrong youth, the innocent youth who had been standing there.

A Federal legal official relates an experience of Tuesday evening.

"I then walked one block north where I met a group of 12-15 policemen. I showed them my identification and they permitted me to walk with them. The police walked one block west. Numerous people were watching us from their windows and balconies. The police yelled profanities at them, taunting them to come down where the police would beat them up. The police stopped a number of people on the street demanding identification. They verbally abused each pedestrian and pushed one or two without hurting them. We walked back to Clark Street and began to walk north where the police stopped a number of people who appeared to be protesters, and ordered them out of the area in a very abusive way. One protester who was walking in the opposite direction was kneed in the groin by a policeman who was walking towards him. The boy fell to the ground and swore at the policeman who picked him up and threw him to the ground. We continued to walk toward the command post. A derelict who appeared to be very intoxicated, walked up to the policeman and mumbled something that was incoherent. The policeman pulled from his belt a tin container and sprayed its contents into the eyes of the derelict, who stumbled around and fell on his face."

It was on these nights that the police violence against media representatives reached its peak. Much of it was plainly deliberate. A newsman was pulled aside on Monday by a detective acquaintance of his who said: "The word is being passed to get newsmen." Individual newsmen were warned, "You take my picture tonight and I'm going to get you." Cries of "get the camera" preceded individual attacks on photographers.

A newspaper photographer describes Old Town on Monday at about 9 p.m.:

"When the people arrived at the intersection of Wells and Division, they were not standing in the streets. Suddenly a column of policemen ran out from the alley. They were reinforcements. They were under control but there seemed to be no direction. One man was yelling, 'Get them up on the sidewalks, turn them around.' Very suddenly the police charged the people on the sidewalks and began beating their heads. A line of cameramen was 'trapped' along with the crowd along the sidewalks, and the police went down the line chopping away at the cameras."

A network cameraman reports that on the same night:

"I just saw this guy coming at me with his nightstick and I had the camera up. The tip of his stick hit me right in the mouth, then I put my tongue up there and I noticed that my tooth was gone. I turned around then to try to leave and then this cop came up behind me with his stick and he jabbed me in the back.

"All of a sudden these cops jumped out of the police cars and started just beating the hell out of people. And before anything else happened to me, I saw a man holding a Bell & Howell camera with big wide letters on it, saying, 'CBS.' He apparently had been hit by a

cop. And cops were standing around and there was blood streaming
down his face. Another policeman was running after me and saying,
'Get the — out of here.' And I heard another guy scream, 'Get their
— cameras.' And the next thing I know I was being hit on the head,
and I think on the back, and I was just forced down on the ground
at the corner of Division and Wells."

If the intent was to discourage coverage, it was successful in at least
one case. A photographer from a news magazine says that finally,
"I just stopped shooting, because every time you push the flash, they
look at you and they are screaming about, 'Get the — photographers
and get the film.' "

Some Action Staged

There is some explanation for the media-directed violence. Camera
crews on at least two occasions did stage violence and fake injuries.
Demonstrators did sometimes step up their activities for the benefit of
TV cameras. Newsmen and photographers' blinding lights did get in the
way of police clearing streets, sweeping the park and dispersing demonstrators. Newsmen did, on occasion, disobey legitimate police orders to
"move" or "clear the streets." News reporting of events did seem to
the police to be anti-Chicago and anti-police.

But was the response appropriate to the provocation?

Out of 300 newsmen assigned to cover the parks and streets of
Chicago during convention week, more than 60 (about 20%) were
involved in incidents resulting in injury to themselves, damage to their
equipment, or their arrest. Sixty-three newsmen were physically attacked
by police; in 13 of these instances, photographic or recording equipment
was intentionally damaged.

The violence did not end with either demonstrators or newsmen on
the North Side on Sunday, Monday and Tuesday. It continued in Grant
Park on Wednesday. It occurred on Michigan Avenue in front of the
Conrad Hilton Hotel, as already described. A high-ranking Chicago
police commander admits that on that occasion the police "got out of
control." This same commander appears in one of the most vivid scenes
of the entire week, trying desperately to keep individual policemen from
beating demonstrators as he screams, "For Christ's sake, stop it!"

Thereafter, the violence continued on Michigan Avenue and on the
side streets running into Chicago's Loop. A Federal official describes
how it began:

"I heard a 10-1 call (policeman in trouble) on either my radio or
one of the other hand sets carried by men with me and then heard
'Car 100—sweep.' With a roar of motors, squads, vans and three-

wheelers came from east, west and north into the block north of Jackson. The crowd scattered. A big group ran west on Jackson, with a group of blue shirted policemen in pursuit, beating at them with clubs. Some of the crowd would jump into doorways and the police would rout them out. The action was very tough. In my judgment, unnecessarily so. The police were hitting with a vengeance and quite obviously with relish. . . ."

What followed was a club-swinging melee. Police ranged the streets striking anyone they could catch. To be sure, demonstrators threw things at policemen and at police cars; but the weight of violence was overwhelmingly on the side of the police. A few examples will give the flavor of that night in Chicago:

"At the corner of Congress Plaza and Michigan," states a doctor, "was gathered a group of people, numbering between 30 and 40. They were trapped against a railing (along a ramp leading down from Michigan Avenue to an underground parking garage) by several policemen on motorcycles. The police charged the people on motorcycles and struck about a dozen of them, knocking several of them down. About twenty standing there jumped over the railing. On the other side of the railing was a three-to-four-foot drop. None of the people who were struck by the motorcycles appeared to be seriously injured. However, several of them were limping as if they had been run over on their feet."

'A Fanatical Look'

A UPI reporter witnessed these attacks, too. He relates in his statement that one officer, "with a smile on his face and a fanatical look in his eyes, was standing on a three-wheel cycle, shouting, 'Wahoo, wahoo,' and trying to run down people on the sidewalk." The reporter says he was chased 30 feet by the cycle.

A priest who was in the crowd says he saw a "boy, about fourteen or fifteen, white, standing on top of an automobile yelling something which was unidentifiable. Suddenly a policeman pulled him down from the car and beat him to the ground by striking him three or four times with a nightstick. Other police joined in . . . and they eventually shoved him to a police van.

"A well-dressed woman saw this incident and spoke angrily to a nearby police captain. As she spoke, another policeman came up from behind her and sprayed something in her face with an aerosol can. He then clubbed her to the ground. He and two other policemen then dragged her along the ground to the same paddy wagon and threw her in."

"I ran west on Jackson," a witness states. "West of Wabash, a line of police stretching across both sidewalks and the street charged after the small group I was in. Many people were clubbed and maced as they ran. Some weren't demonstrators at all, but were just pedestrians who didn't know how to react to the charging officers yelling, 'Police!' "

"A wave of police charged down Jackson," another witness relates. "Fleeing demonstrators were beaten indiscriminately and a temporary, makeshift first aid station was set up on the corner of State and Jackson. Two men lay in pools of blood, their heads severely cut by clubs. A minister moved amongst the crowd, quieting them, brushing aside curious onlookers, and finally asked a policeman to call an ambulance, which he agreed to do . . ."

An Assistant U.S. Attorney later reported that "the demonstrators were running as fast as they could but were unable to get out of the way because of the crowds in front of them. I observed the police striking numerous individuals, perhaps 20 to 30. I saw three fall down and then overrun by the police. I observed two demonstrators who had multiple cuts on their heads. We assisted one who was in shock into a passerby's car."

Police violence was a fact of convention week. Were the policemen who committed it a minority? It appears certain that they were — but one which has imposed some of the consequences of its actions on the majority, and certainly on their commanders. There has been no public condemnation of these violators of sound police procedures and common decency by either their commending officers or city officials. Nor (at the time this Report is being completed — almost three months after the convention) has any disciplinary action been taken against most of them. That some policemen lost control of themselves under exceedingly provocative circumstances can perhaps be understood; but not condoned. If no action is taken against them, the effect can only be to discourage the majority of policemen who acted responsibly, and further weaken the bond between police and community.

Although the crowds were finally dispelled on the nights of violence in Chicago, the problems they represent have not been. Surely this is not the last time that a violent dissenting group will clash head-on with those whose duty it is to enforce the law. And the next time, the whole world will still be watching.

4

Educational Policy

In the famous Northwest Ordinance of 1787, Congress offered land grants for public schools in the new territories and gave succeeding generations words to be forever etched on grammar school cornerstones: "Religion, morality and knowledge, being necessary to good government and the happiness of mankind, schools and the means for education should ever be encouraged." Education has been a public responsibility in America since 1647, when the Massachusetts colonial legislature first required their towns to provide for the education of their children out of tax funds. The earliest democrats believed that the safest repository of the ultimate powers of society was the people themselves. If the people make mistakes, the remedy was not to remove power from their hands but to help them in forming their judgment through education. If the common man was to be granted the right to vote, he must be educated to his task. This meant that public education had to be universal, free, and compulsory. Compulsory education began in Massachusetts in 1852 and was eventually adopted by Mississippi in 1918.

Today education is second only to national defense in government expenditures. Governments spend more on education than on highways, welfare, police or fire protection, agricultural subsidies, public health, space research or any other governmental function outside of the national military establishment. The primary responsibility for public education in America rests with the 50 state governments and their subdivisions. It is the largest and most costly of state functions.

Prior to 1965 the total financial contribution of the federal government in public elementary and secondary education was quite small. (See U.S. Office of Education, *Summary of Federal Programs in Education*) Federal funds amounted to only about 4 per cent of total public school revenues. In 1862 the Morrill Land Grant Act provided grants of federal land to each state for the establishment of colleges specializing in agricultural and mechanical arts. These became known as "Land Grant Colleges." In 1867 Congress established a U.S. Office of Education which is now a part of the Department of Health, Education, and Welfare. The Smith-Hughes Act of 1917 set up the first program of federal grants-in-aid promoting vocational education which enabled schools to provide training in agriculture, home economics, trades and industries. In the Federal Impacted Areas Aid Program begun in 1950, federal aid is authorized for "federally-impacted" areas of the nation. These are areas where federal activities create a substantial increase in school enrollments or a reduction in taxable resources because of a federally-owned property. Federal funds can be used for construction, operation and maintenance of schools in these public school districts. This program is an outgrowth of the defense impacted area aid legislation in World War II.

In response to the Soviet Union's success in launching the first satellite into space, Congress became concerned that the American educational system might not be keeping abreast of advances being made in other nations, particularly in science and technology. The Russian space shot created an intensive debate over education in America and prompted Congress to re-examine the responsibilities of the national government in public education. "Sputnik" made everyone realize that education was closely related to national defense. In the National Defense Education Act of 1958 Congress provided financial aid to states and public school districts to improve instruction in science, mathematics and foreign languages; to strengthen guidance counseling and testing; to improve statistical services; and also to establish a system of loans to undergraduates, fellowships to graduate students and funds to colleges, all in an effort to improve the training of teachers in America. In the National School Lunch and Milk Programs, begun in 1946, federal grants and commodity donations are made for non-profit lunches and milk served in public and private schools.

The total financial contributions of the federal government to education through all of these early programs was quite small. Prior to 1965 large scale federal aid to education plans consistently floundered in Congress. General federal aid to education bills, authorizing federal grants for school construction and the paying of teachers salaries were lost in a series of controversies over education which plagued Congress and prevented positive action on federal aid to education. First of all, there was the fear that federal funds would expand the powers of the federal government and invade another area of public policy traditionally reserved to the states. Secondly, there was the concern of southern Congressmen that northern liberals would use federal aid as a lever to achieve more rapid school desegregation. Southerners feared a requirement that only desegregated schools would receive federal funds. Of course, after the Civil Rights Act in 1964 no federal program in education or any other field could receive federal funds if it were operated on a segregated basis.

Finally, the greatest controversy surrounding federal aid to education centered on the question of federal aid to parochial schools. Federal aid to parochial schools would greatly benefit the Roman Catholic Church, which accounts for 90 per cent of all private school enrollment in America. Many education bills floundered in Congress over the question of whether federal aid should be given to Catholic schools. President John F. Kennedy rejected aid to parochial schools saying that such aid would violate the no establishment of religion clause under the 1st Amendment to the Constitution. Catholic spokesmen argued that a denial of federal aid to parochial schools represented discrimination against Catholic children whose parents pay taxes like anyone else. They argued that federal aid to parochial schools would be an aid to the child and not an establishment of religion. This religious controversy was directly responsible for the defeat of federal aid to education bills during the Kennedy administration. Thus, three important issues in American politics — federalism, race, and religion — vitally influence educational policy-making.

With the passage of the *Elementary and Secondary Education Act of 1965* the role of the federal aid to education was greatly expanded. The Johnson administration was very skillful in writing this Act and avoiding the political pitfalls which had defeated earlier proposals to federal aid to education. First of all, the President tied the ESEA aid to the problem of poverty and to the concept of "poverty impacted areas." In Title I the federal government pledges to pay up to one half of the average state-wide per pupil expenditure for every enrolled child whose family earns less than $2000 per year. The EASA Act channels money through "state educational agencies" rather than sending federal money directly to school districts; this helped to alleviate the fears about a loss of state control over education. And Johnson avoided the religious issue by authorizing grants to "local educational agencies" which left it to the states to decide the extent to which aid would be used to benefit private school children. Title II grants for library resources, textbooks, and other instructional materials and specifically authorizes aid for private schools.

The passage of the ESEA Act brought about a doubling of federal funds for public schools in a single year; federal school funds jumped from about 4 per cent of total school revenues to about 8 per cent. For the time being, of course, over 90 per cent of the total cost of public education is still born by the states and their local subdivisions; and this means that there are marked disparities among state and local educational systems. But if federal aid to education continues to increase, the disparities among school systems may disappear. Centralization in school finance at the national level will doubtlessly bring about greater uniformity in school policy in the states and equalization of educational opportunity throughout the nation.

Despite increasing federal aid, states and communities in America carry the major burden of cost of public education and make most of the decisions in educational policy. This decentralization in educational policy results in variations in policy outcomes from state to state. The National Education Association, and its *Ranking of the States* shows the range of policy variations in educational outcomes in American states.

The 1st Amendment to the Constitution of the United States contains two important guarantees of religious freedom: 1) "Congress shall make no law respecting the establishment with religion . . ." and 2) "nor prohibiting the free exercise thereof . . ." The Due Process Clause of the 14th Amendment made these guarantees of religious liberty applicable to the states and their subdivisions as well as to the Congress. Most of the debate over religion and the public schools has centered around the "no establishment" clause of the 1st Amendment rather than the "free exercise" clause. However, it was respect for the "free exercise" clause which caused the Supreme Court in 1925 to declare unconstitutional an attempt on the part of a state to prohibit private and parochial schools and to force all children to attend public schools. In the words of the Supreme Court in *Pierce* v. *Society of Sisters* (1925): "The fundamental theory of liberty upon which all governments in this union repose excludes any general power of the state to standardize its children by forcing them to accept instruction from public teachers only. The child is not a mere creature of the state." It is this decision which protects the entire structure of parochial schools in this nation. Proponents of government aid to parochial schools frequently refer to the language found in several cases sited by the United States Supreme Court which appeared to support the idea that government can in a limited fashion support certain activities in church related activities. In *Cochran* v. *The Board of Education* (1930), the court upheld a state law providing free textbooks for children attending both public and parochial schools on the grounds that this aid benefited the children rather than the Catholic Church and hence did not constitute an "establishment" of a religion within the meaning of the 1st Amendment. In the case of *Everson* v. *the Board of Education* (1947), the Supreme Court upheld the bussing of parochial school children to and from school at public expense on the grounds that the "wall of separation between church and state" does not prevent the state from adopting a general program which helps all children regardless of religion to proceed safely to and from schools. This case suggests that the Supreme Court is willing to permit some forms of aid to parochial school children which indirectly aid religion, so long as such aid is not directly used for religious purposes. It is the Everson Case which leads many observers to believe that the Supreme Court will permit federal aid to go to parochial schools so long as it is earmarked for non-religious educational materials or facilities.

Religious conflict in the public schools also centers around prayer and Bible-reading ceremonies conducted by public schools. The practice of opening the school day with prayer and Bible-reading ceremonies was widespread in American public schools. Usually the prayer is a Protestant rendition of the Lord's Prayer and the Bible reading is from the King James version. In order to avoid denominational aspects of these ceremonies, the New York State Board of Regents substituted a non-denominational prayer which it required to be said aloud in each class in the presence of a teacher at the beginning of each school day. New York argued that this prayer ceremony did not violate the no-establishment clause because the prayer was denominationally neutral and because student participation in the prayer was voluntary. But in *Engle* v. *Vitale* (1962), the court pointed out that making prayer voluntary did not free it from the prohibitions of the no-establishment clause. The court said this clause prevented the establishment of a religious ceremony by a government agency, regardless of whether the ceremony was voluntary or not, and regardless of whether it was denominationally neutral or not.

Summary of
Federal Programs in Education*

U.S. Office of Education

Equal Education Opportunities

Background

To speed up desegregation, as well as to insure certain other rights, Congress passed the Civil Rights Act of 1964 which included two titles relating to the public schools which are administered by the Office of Education. The two titles constitute the Equal Educational Opportunities Program (EEOP).

Title IV gives public schools assistance in handling problems resulting from desegregation, which it defines as the assignment of students to and within public schools without regard "to their race, color, religion, or national origin . . ."

Title VI of the Civil Rights Act bans the disbursement of Federal funds to any program or activity that discriminates "on the grounds of race, color, or national origin . . ."

What the Program Does

Under Title VI, the EEOP staff concentrates on obtaining voluntary compliance with the Act and regulations, including the filing of acceptable desegregation plans. The EEOP also develops Guidelines for school desegregation.

The Guidelines for the 1966-67 school year emphasize performance.

---

*From U.S. Department of Health, Education, and Welfare, *Programs and Services* (Washington, D.C.: U.S. Government Printing Office, 1967).

196

Each school system is responsible for removing the effects of all past or present discriminatory practices in the assignment of teachers and professional staff beyond what was accomplished the year before.

The new Guidelines make clear that the intent of Freedom of Choice plans, in use by about 1,800 school districts, is to combine dual systems into a single system free of discrimination.

Aid to Schools in Low-Income Areas

Background

Title I of the Elementary and Secondary Education Act of 1965 provides financial assistance for special educational programs in areas with high concentrations of children from low-income families, making it possible for schools to identify the special educational needs of the poor child and to design new ways to meet them.

What the Program Does

Title I authorizes approximately $1 billion annually to help school districts strengthen programs for educationally disadvantaged children. The Office of Education allocates money to State educational agencies to carry out the purposes of the Act.

Local School Districts must develop their own plans and submit them to their State education agency for approval. Local agencies may use the money for such purposes as hiring additional staff, acquiring equipment, establishing special programs for dropouts and preschoolers, or for any other imaginative approach to remedying educational deprivation.

Supplementary Centers and Services for Elementary and Secondary Schools

Supplemental services—special instruction in science, language, music, and the arts, counseling and guidance, and health and social work— often make the difference between an excellent school and a poor one.

Title III of the Elementary and Secondary Education Act of 1965 enables schools to provide services presently unavailable to their children, to raise the quality of educational services already offered, and to stimulate the development and evaluation of experimental elementary and secondary educational programs to serve as models for regular school programs.

School Library Resources and Textbooks

Title II of the Elementary and Secondary Education Act of 1965 makes direct grants to the States, based on their school population, to give children and teachers in our schools greater access to a larger quantity of instructional materials of high quality. These Federal grants supplement, not replace, State and local spending for school library and related resources.

Aid to Schools in Federally Affected Areas

The expansion of Federal activities has created problems for States and communities since the early days of our Nation, especially during periods of national emergency.

In World War II, Congress adopted the Lanham Act, which provided for the construction, maintenance, and operation of school facilities in overburdened areas through 1946.

Congress concluded that the Federal Government had a responsibility to meet this increasingly critical situation by providing financial aid for construction as well as maintenance and operation of schools in the impacted areas.

Public Law 815, enacted in the fall of 1950, authorizes financial aid to local educational agencies in federally affected areas for construction of school facilities. Its companion bill P.L. 874, authorizes aid for current operating expenses. The program created on a temporary basis has since been made permanent and modified several times, generally in the direction of liberalizing its provisions.

Equipment and State Services for Instructional Improvement

Background

Congress makes matching grants to public schools and loans to private schools to strengthen elementary and secondary school instruction under Title III of the National Defense Education Act. The subjects included in Title III are science, mathematics, history, civics, geography, economics, modern foreign languages, English, and reading.

How the Program Works

(1) Public schools may make application to their State educational agency for approval of projects to improve instruction in one or more of the critical subjects through acquisition of special equipment, including

audiovisual materials and equipment and printed and published materials other than textbooks, and for minor remodeling of laboratory or other space used for such materials or equipment. The State furnishes application forms and guidelines in conformity with the State plan approved by the U.S. Commissioner of Education. The State also makes available to the schools supervisory services, such as inservice teacher education programs, curriculum guides, equipment standards, and consultative assistance.

(2) Private nonprofit elementary and secondary schools may obtain low interest loans from the U.S. Office of Education to purchase equipment and materials and do minor remodeling for the improvement of instruction in the same nine subject fields.

Land-Grant Colleges

Background

A "land-grant" college or university is an institution of higher learning designated by a State legislature as eligible for the benefits of the First Morrill Act of 1862 or the Second Morrill Act of 1890. The purpose of the original Act was to insure the development in each State of at least one college "to teach such branches of learning as are related to agriculture and the mechanic arts." The goal was "to promote the liberal and practical education of the industrial classes in the several pursuits and professions in life."

The First Morrill Act authorized grants to the States of 30,000 acres of land, or the equivalent in scrip, for each Senator and Representative of the State in Congress in 1860. Proceeds from the sale of land in each State were to constitute a perpetual fund, with the income going to support the land-grant institution. The State was expected to contribute to the maintenance of the institution as well as to provide the buildings.

How the Program Works

The Second Morrill Act provided for permanent annual appropriations—fixed now at $25,000—to each State and Territory. Another $25,000 uniform grant was provided by the Nelson amendment of 1907. The Bankhead-Jones Act of 1935 (Section 22), as amended June 1952 and July 1960, authorized an additional $150,000 per year for each State and Puerto Rico, plus variable amounts from $4,300,000 distributed on the basis of population.

The funds authorized under the Morrill-Nelson Act and the Bankhead-Jones Act are limited to instruction in, and facilities for, agriculture, mechanical arts, English, mathematics, natural and physical science, economics, and specialized teacher training for agriculture, mechanical arts, and home economics. In addition, the Hatch Act of 1887 authorized the establishment of a system of agricultural experiment stations in the land-grant institutions. The Smith-Lever Act of 1914 established a system of cooperative extension services for adults.

The 68 land-grant institutions represented slightly more than 3 percent of all institutions of higher learning in the U.S. as of June 30, 1963. Yet they had 21 percent of the Nation's four-year college enrollment, awarded 20 percent of all baccalaureate degrees, granted 25 percent of all master's degrees, and conferred 40 percent of all doctorate degrees.

Higher Education Facilities Construction

Background

To help the Nation's colleges and universities cope with mounting registrations, Congress enacted the Higher Education Facilities Act of 1963, which provided matching grants and loans for the construction, rehabilitation, and improvement of classrooms, laboratories, libraries, and other academic facilities. The Higher Education Act of 1965 included amendments to the 1963 Act.

What the Program Does

Under Title I, HEFA of 1963, grants of up to 40 percent of project development cost may be awarded to public community colleges and public technical institutes; and grants of up to one-third of the development cost to all other undergraduate institutions. Twenty-two percent of the funds appropriated for this Title are allotted to the States for the use of public community colleges and technical institutes, and the balance of the appropriation is allotted to the States for the use of other institutions. A State Commission determines the priority of projects within a State and recommends the Federal share according to standards in the State plan.

Under Title II, facilities grants of up to one-third of cost may be awarded for graduate school facilities or for cooperative graduate centers.

Title III authorizes loans for the construction of academic facilities, both undergraduate and graduate. The amount of a loan, plus any other Federal funds, may not exceed 75 percent of the eligible development cost of a project.

Strengthening Developing Institutions

Background

On November 8, 1965, President Johnson signed Public Law 89-329, The Higher Education Act of 1965. Title III of this law is designed to encourage and assist "developing institutions" which for financial or other reasons are struggling for survival.

What the Program Does

Grants under Title III will be used for activities such as:
—exchange of faculty or students, or bringing visiting scholars;
—faculty improvement programs using training, education, internships, research participation, and other means;
—introduction of new curriculums and teaching materials;
—development programs involving alternate periods of academic study and business or public employment;
—joint use of facilities such as libraries or laboratories, books, materials, and equipment.

Higher Education Equipment Grants

By 1973 there will be eight million college students in the United States, more than triple the 1955 total. This college population explosion has spread educational equipment so thin that in many institutions the quality of instruction has deteriorated. For example, special instructional equipment now seen in most high schools—slides, tapes, programmed materials—is still uncommon in many colleges. The National Defense Education Act has financed such equipment for secondary schools since 1958. Title VI of the Higher Education Act of 1965 finances modern instructional equipment for colleges and universities.

Language and Area Centers and Fellowships

Title VI of the National Defense Education Act of 1958 provides for Federal matching grants to support new or expanded programs in modern languages and foreign area studies at U.S. colleges and universities. It also provides for fellowships at the undergraduate, graduate, and post-doctoral level to help meet the critical national need for individuals equipped with knowledge and skills in modern foreign languages and related studies.

Libraries for Higher Education

Libraries need librarians, books, and other materials. Supplementing assistance under the Higher Education Facilities Act of 1963 which provides for library construction at colleges and universities, Congress passed the Higher Education Act of 1965 which makes Federal funds available for library materials and the training of librarians under Title II.

University Leadership for Urban Progress

University talent has long been used to solve community problems in rural America. More than 50 years ago Congress under the Smith-Lever Act of 1914 asked universities to help improve farm production and rural family living. Title I of the Higher Education Act of 1965 provided funds to spur university emphasis on urban and suburban problems—inadequate housing, inferior recreation facilities, unemployment, inadequate health services, lack of youth opportunities, local government, land use, and so on.

Educational Opportunity Grants Program

Background

In January 1965, President Johnson told Congress that each year about 100,000 high school graduates academically qualified to enter college fail to do so for lack of money. This loss of talent to the Nation, he said, cannot simply be shrugged off as another harsh fact of economic life; it is a waste that the United States cannot afford.

The Educational Opportunity Grants Program, established under Title IV, Part A, of the Higher Education Act of 1965, is the newest of three Student Financial Aid programs (The National Defense Student Loan Program and The College Work-Study Program are the other two) designed to halt this drain of talent and promise.

What the Program Does

The Educational Opportunity Grants Program provides financial assistance to students of exceptional financial need in order to enable them to receive the benefits of higher education.

College Work-Study Program

The Economic Opportunity Act of 1964 authorized the College Work-Study Program. It was extended by the Economic Opportunity Amendments of 1965 and the Higher Education Act of 1965. The Office of Education administers the program.

Under the program, students in need, and particularly those from low-income families, can pay for part or all of their educational expenses at institutions of higher education by working at part-time jobs, either for the institutions themselves or for public or nonprofit organizations.

Whether the work is for the institution itself or for an agency, the Federal Government pays 90 percent of the wages of the student employees. The remainder of the cost must be borne by the institution, the agency, or some other donor.

Loans to Students in Institutions of Higher Education

To help needy students continue their educational careers, Congress established the National Defense Student Loan Program. From funds made up of Federal and institutional contributions, the program provides long-term, low interest loans for tuition, books, supplies, and living expenses. Academically able students in a college, university, business school, or technical institution are eligible.

An additional feature of the program is the cancellation of loans of NDSL borrowers who become teachers. The "teacher forgiveness" cancellation is at the rate of 10 percent for each year of teaching up to a maximum of 50 percent. Under certain circumstances, the entire loan may be cancelled for student borrowers who teach in designated schools that have a high concentration of students from low-income families.

Vocational and Technical Education

Background

The Smith-Hughes Act of 1917 provided Federal assistance for vocational training in industry, agriculture, and home economics. A series of laws expanded the vocational training program to include distributive education, the health occupations, and the fishery industries. In 1958, the National Defense Education Act added training for technicians. The expansion of vocational and technical training has reflected a shift in emphasis from rural to urban job market demands.

What the Program Does

The Vocational Education Act of 1963 provides for vocational and technical training in high schools, postsecondary schools, vocational-technical area schools, junior and community colleges, technical institutes, and four-year colleges and universities. It increases Federal matching grants to the States to expand training programs and to build area vocational and technical schools.

Manpower Development and Training

The Manpower Development and Training Act of 1962 provides for training of unemployed people with funds appropriated to the Department of Labor. All manpower training in classrooms—as distinguished from on-the-job training—is delegated to the Office of Education in the Department of Health, Education, and Welfare.

Adult Basic Education Programs

Congress included in the Economic Opportunity Act of 1964 a major program to provide elementary-level education for adults administered by the Office of Education, under a delegation of authority from the Director of the Office of Economic Opportunity.

The program represents an effort to teach illiterate people to read and write English; improve their ability to participate in occupational training programs and, in general, make them more capable of meeting their adult responsibilities.

National Teacher Corps

Background

The National Teacher Corps was created by Congress under Title V-B of the Higher Education Act of 1965 to strengthen the educational opportunities available to children in areas having concentrations of low-income families and to encourage colleges and universities to broaden their program of teacher preparation.

What the Program Does

The Teacher Corps legislation first aims at producing more teachers specially trained to work in the slums by setting up a two-year program which turns volunteers with bachelor's degrees into teachers with master's degrees and special academic and practical training in the character of poverty. Second, by involving colleges and universities throughout the country, it expects to perpetuate interest in special training for slum teachers long after the Teacher Corps itself is ended.

NDEA Graduate Fellowships

To improve and encourage graduate study, the National Defense Education Act of 1958 included a fellowship program for graduate students to prepare for college teaching careers. It also made available grants for institutions to aid them in developing new and expanded programs of graduate study.

Modern Teaching Equipment

Growth in technology has greatly increased the variety of educational equipment available to colleges and universities. Federal grants have helped colleges buy such things as electronic learning laboratories, equipment for programmed instruction, computer-assisted instruction, films, and closed-circuit television. By the end of fiscal year 1966 nearly $30 million had been provided for this by the National Defense Education Act of 1958 and the amended version of the Communications Act of 1934. The Higher Education Facilities Act of 1963 and the Higher Education Act of 1965 also contain provisions for buying such equipment.

Research and Development Centers

Background

To meet such needs the Research and Development Center Program was created as part of the Cooperative Research Program. The Centers bring together scholars from several disciplines to work on the same educational problem from different angles. Each Center works with local schools and State departments of education.

What the Program Does

Nine Centers have been set up on five-year contracts but funded annually. At the University of Wisconsin researchers are working on central problems of learning—how much, how quickly, how early, and how well children can learn. Harvard has started a long-term study of how psychological, social, and cultural differences affect how children learn. Educational problems of socially and economically deprived children are getting special attention. The Center at the University of Georgia is concerned with how to teach children as early as possible, taking them as far as they can go as fast as they can go. The University of California (Berkeley) is focusing on the college student and the various influences of higher education on him.

Language Research and Studies

Background

Congress recognized the need for large-scale language programs in the National Defense Education Act of 1958. Title VI of the Act authorizes research into improved language teaching.

What the Program Does

In the eight years since NDEA was passed, 421 language research and study contracts have been awarded. One such project showed how small colleges could teach uncommon languages by using foreign students as instructors in the absence of a professional teacher on the faculty.

Educational Media Research

Background

The National Defense Education Act of 1958 encourages investigation of educational media under Title VII: "Research and Experimentation in More Effective Utilization of Television, Radio, Motion Pictures, and Related Media for Educational Purposes." Related media are tape recordings, teaching machines, and some published materials that represent a departure from traditional modes of using the printed word.

What the Program Does

Under Title VII, the Office of Education supports research into educational uses of these communications media. Experimental projects must promise to benefit State education agencies in the operation of their elementary and secondary schools or institutions of higher education. Title VII also directs the Office to disseminate information about new educational media to educators across the country.

Strengthening State Departments of Education

Background

Congress recognized the need for strengthening State resources in Title V of the Elementary and Secondary Education Act of 1965 (Public Law 89-10).

What the Program Does

Funds provided by Title V may be used to improve educational planning; identify educational problems and needs; evaluate educational programs; process educational data; publish and distribute curriculum materials; conduct educational research; improve teacher preparation; train personnel to serve State and local educational agencies; and provide consultative and technical assistance in special areas of educational need.

Improvement of State Statistical Services

Section 1009 of the NDEA provides for grants to State education agencies to help them improve the adequacy and reliability of educational statistics provided by State and local reports, as well as the methods for collecting, processing, and disseminating information about education in the States.

Library Services and Construction

The Library Services Act of 1956 was passed to improve and expand library service for 40.7 million rural Americans. It made more than 14 million books and other library materials available to rural libraries and purchased about 400 bookmobiles which brought library services to farm homes.

However the benefits of the 1956 Act were limited to communities of less than 10,000. The Library Services and Construction Act of 1964 increased Federal financial assistance, extended benefits to urban and suburban as well as rural areas, and provided for construction of public libraries.

Elementary and Secondary Education Act of 1965

Congress and the President

AN ACT

To strengthen and improve educational quality and educational opportunities in the Nation's elementary and secondary schools.

Be it enacted by the Senate and House of Representatives of the United States of America in Congress assembled, That this Act may be cited as the "Elementary and Secondary Education Act of 1965".

• • •

"TITLE II—FINANCIAL ASSISTANCE TO LOCAL EDUCATIONAL AGENCIES FOR THE EDUCATION OF CHILDREN OF LOW-INCOME FAMILIES

"DECLARATION OF POLICY

"SEC. 201. In recognition of the special educational needs of children of low-income families and the impact that concentrations of low-income families have on the ability of local educational agencies to support adequate educational programs, the Congress hereby declares it to be the policy of the United States to provide financial assistance (as set forth in this title) to local educational agencies serving areas with concentrations of children from low-income families to expand and improve their educational programs by various means (including preschool programs) which contribute particularly to meeting the special educational needs of educationally deprived children.

"KINDS AND DURATION OF GRANTS

"SEC. 202. The Commissioner shall, in accordance with the provisions of this title, make payments to State educational agencies for basic grants to local educational agencies for the period beginning July 1, 1965, and ending June 30, 1968, and he shall make payments to State educational agencies for special incentive grants to local educational agencies for the period beginning July 1, 1966, and ending June 30, 1968.

• • •

"BASIC GRANTS—AMOUNT AND ELIGIBILITY

"(2) In any case in which the Commissioner determines that satisfactory data for that purpose are available, the maximum basic grant which a local educational agency in a State shall be eligible to receive under this title for any fiscal year shall be (except as provided in paragraph (3) an amount equal to the Federal percentage (established pursuant to subsection (c)) of the average per pupil expenditure in that State multiplied by the sum of (A) the number of children aged five to seventeen, inclusive, in the school district of such agency, of families having an annual income of less than the low-income factor (established pursuant to subsection (c)), and (B) the number of children of such ages in such school district of families receiving an annual income in excess of the low-income factor (as established pursuant to subsection (c)) from payments under the program of aid to families with dependent children under a State plan approved under title IV of the Social Security Act.

• • •

For purposes of this subsection the 'average per pupil expenditure' in a State shall be the aggregate current expenditures during the second fiscal year preceding the fiscal year for which the computation is made, of all local educational agencies in the State (without regard to the sources of funds from which such expenditures are made), divided by the aggregate number of children in average daily attendance to whom such agencies provided free public education during such preceding year.

"(3) If the maximum amount of the basic grant determined pursuant to paragraph (1) or (2) for any local educational agency for the fiscal year ending June 30, 1966, is greater than 30 per centum of the sum budgeted by that agency for current expenditures for that year (as determined pursuant to regulations of the Commissioner), such maximum amount shall be reduced to 30 per centum of such budgeted sum.

• • •

"(c) For the purposes of this section, the 'Federal percentage' and the 'low-income factor' for the fiscal year ending June 30, 1966, shall be 50 per centum and $2,000, respectively. For each of the two succeeding fiscal years the Federal percentage and the low-income factor shall be established by the Congress by law.

"(d) For the purposes of this section, the Commissioner shall determine the number of children aged five to seventeen, inclusive, of families having an annual income of less than the low-income factor (as established pursuant to subsection (c)) on the basis of the most recent satisfactory data available from the Department of Commerce.

• • •

"APPLICATION

"Sec. 205. (a) A local educational agency may receive a basic grant or a special incentive grant under this title for any fiscal year only upon application therefor approved by the appropriate State educational agency, upon its determination (consistent with such basic criteria as the Commissioner may establish)—

"(1) that payments under this title will be used for programs and projects (including the acquisition of equipment and where necessary the construction of school facilities) (A) which are designed to meet the special educational needs of educationally deprived children in school attendance areas having high concentrations of children from low-income families and (B) which are of sufficient size, scope, and quality to give reasonable promise of substantial progress toward meeting those needs, and nothing herein shall be deemed to preclude two or more local educational agencies from entering into agreements, at their option, for carrying out jointly operated programs and projects under this title;

"(2) that, to the extent consistent with the number of educationally deprived children in the school district of the local educational agency who are enrolled in private elementary and secondary schools, such agency has made provision for including special educational services and arrangements (such as dual enrollment, educational radio and television, and mobile educational services and equipment) in which such children can participate;

"(3) that the local educational agency has provided satisfactory assurance that the control of funds provided under this title, and title to property derived therefrom, shall be in a public agency for the uses and purposes provided in this title, and that a public agency will administer such funds and property;

"(4) in the case of any project for construction of school facilities, that the project is not inconsistent with overall State plans for the construction of school facilities and that the requirements of section 209 will be complied with on all such construction projects;

"(5) that effective procedures, including provision for appropriate objective measurements of educational achievement, will be adopted for evaluating at least annually the effectiveness of the programs in meeting the special educational needs of educationally deprived children;

"(6) that the local educational agency will make an annual report and such other reports to the State educational agency in such form and containing such information, as may be reasonably necessary to enable the State educational agency to perform its duties under this title, including information relating to the educational achievement of students participating in programs carried out under this title, and will keep such records and afford such access thereto as the State educational agency may find necessary to assure the correctness and verification of such reports;

"(7) that wherever there is, in the area served by the local educational agency, a community action program approved pursuant to title II of the Economic Opportunity Act of 1964 (Public Law 88-452), the programs and projects have been developed in cooperation with the public or private nonprofit agency responsible for the community action program; and

"(8) that effective procedures will be adopted for acquiring and disseminating to teachers and administrators significant information derived from educational research, demonstration, and similar projects, and for adopting, where appropriate, promising educational practices developed through such projects.

"(b) The State educational agency shall not finally disapprove in whole or in part any application for funds under this title without first affording the local educational agency submitting the application reasonable notice and opportunity for a hearing.

• • •

TITLE II—SCHOOL LIBRARY RESOURCES, TEXTBOOKS, AND OTHER INSTRUCTIONAL MATERIALS

APPROPRIATIONS AUTHORIZED

SEC. 201. (a) The Commissioner shall carry out during the fiscal year ending June 30, 1966, and each of the four succeeding fiscal years, a program for making grants for the acquisition of school library resources, textbooks, and other printed and published instructional materials for the use of children and teachers in public and private elementary and secondary schools.

ALLOTMENT TO STATES

SEC. 202 (a) From the sums appropriated for carrying out this title for any fiscal year, the Commissioner shall reserve such amount, but not in excess of 2 per centum thereof, as he may determine and shall allot such amount among the Commonwealth of Puerto Rico,

Guam, American Samoa, the Virgin Islands, and the Trust Territory of the Pacific Islands according to their respective needs for assistance under this title. From the remainder of such sums, the Commissioner shall allot to each State an amount which bears the same ratio to such remainder as the number of children enrolled in the public and private elementary and secondary schools of that State bears to the total number of children enrolled in such schools in all of the States. The number of children so enrolled shall be determined by the Commissioner on the basis of the most recent satisfactory data available to him.

• • •

TITLE III—SUPPLEMENTARY EDUCATIONAL CENTERS AND SERVICES

APPROPRIATIONS AUTHORIZED

SEC. 301. (a) The Commissioner shall carry out during the fiscal year ending June 30, 1966, and each of the four succeeding fiscal years, a program for making grants for supplementary educational centers and services, to stimulate and assist in the provision of vitally needed educational services not available in sufficient quantity or quality, and to stimulate and assist in the development and establishment of exemplary elementary and secondary school educational programs to serve as models for regular school programs.

APPORTIONMENT AMONG STATES

SEC. 302. (a) From the sums appropriated for carrying out this title for each fiscal year, the Commissioner shall reserve such amount, but not in excess of 2 per centum thereof, as he may determine and shall apportion such amount among the Commonwealth of Puerto Rico, Guam, American Samoa, the Virgin Islands, and the Trust Territory of the Pacific Islands, according to their respective needs for assistance under this title. From the remainder of such sums the Commissioner shall apportion $200,000 to each State and shall apportion the remainder of such sums among the States as follows:

(1) he shall apportion to each State an amount which bears the same ratio to 50 per centum of such remainder as the number of children aged five to seventeen, inclusive, in the State bears to the number of such children in all the States, and

(2) he shall apportion to each State an amount which bears the same ratio to 50 per centum of such remainder as the population of the State bears to the population of all the States.

For purposes of this subsection, the term "State" does not include the Commonwealth of Puerto Rico, Guam, American Samoa, the Virgin Islands, and the Trust Territory of the Pacific Islands.

(b) The number of children aged five to seventeen, inclusive, and the total population of a State and of all the States shall be determined by the Commissioner on the basis of the most recent satisfactory data available to him.

USES OF FEDERAL FUNDS

SEC. 303. Grants under this title may be used, in accordance with applications approved under section 304(b), for—

(a) planning for and taking other steps leading to the develop ment of programs designed to provide supplementary educational activities and services described in paragraph (b), including pilot projects designed to test the effectiveness of plans so developed; and

(b) the establishment, maintenance, and operation of programs, including the lease or construction of necessary facilities and the acquisition of necessary equipment, designed to enrich the programs of local elementary and secondary schools and to offer a diverse range of educational experience to persons of varying talents and needs by providing supplementary educational services and activities such as—

(1) comprehensive guidance and counseling, remedial instruction, and school health, physical education, recreation, psychological, and social work services designed to enable and encourage persons to enter, remain in, or reenter educational programs, including the provision of special educational programs and study areas during periods when schools are not regularly in session;

(2) comprehensive academic services and, where appropriate, vocational guidance and counseling, for continuing adult education;

(3) developing and conducting exemplary educational programs, including dual-enrollment programs, for the purpose of stimulating the adoption of improved or new educational programs (including those programs described in section 503(a) (4)), in the schools of the State;

(4) specialized instruction and equipment for students interested in studying advanced scientific subjects, foreign languages, and other academic subjects which are not taught in the local schools or which can be provided more effectively on a centralized basis, or for persons who are handicapped or of preschool age;

(5) making available modern educational equipment and specially qualified personnel, including artists and musicians, on a temporary basis to public and other nonprofit schools, organizations, and institutions;

(6) developing, producing, and transmitting radio and television programs for classroom and other educational use;

(7) providing special educational and related services for persons who are in or from rural areas or who are or have been otherwise isolated from normal educational opportunities, including, where appropriate, the provision of mobile educational services and equipment, special home study courses, radio, television, and related forms of instruction, and visiting teachers' programs; and

(8) other specially designed educational programs which meet the purposes of this title.

•   •   •

Rankings of the States in Education, 1967*

National Education Association

Percent of Public Elementary- and Secondary- School Teachers Who Are Men, 1967-68

1.	California	40.3%	23.	Montana	34.0
2.	Wyoming	39.9	24.	Illinois	33.9
3.	Utah	39.7	25.	Maine	33.6
4.	Delaware	39.5	26.	Iowa	32.9
5.	Minnesota	39.2	27.	Kansas	32.2
6.	Oregon	38.2	28.	New Hampshire	32.0
7.	Pennsylvania	36.9	29.	Ohio	31.9
8.	Wisconsin	36.7			
9.	Arizona	36.2		UNITED STATES	31.7
10.	Indiana	36.1	30.	New York	31.6
11.	New Jersey	36.0	31.	Vermont	31.1
12.	New Mexico	35.9	32.	Maryland	30.5
	Rhode Island	35.9	33.	Florida	28.8
14.	Nevada	35.8	34.	Washington	28.7
15.	Michigan	35.5	35.	Texas	28.2
16.	Idaho	35.4	36.	South Dakota	27.5
17.	Oklahoma	35.3	37.	Missouri	27.3
18.	Colorado	35.2	38.	Nebraska	26.3
19.	Alaska	34.7	39.	Kentucky	26.2
	Connecticut	34.1	40.	Arkansas	25.4
20.	Massachusetts	34.1		Louisiana	25.4
	North Dakota	34.1	42.	Mississippi	23.3

*Reprinted with permission from National Education Association, *Rankings of the States 1967* (Washington. N.E.A., 1968).

Percent of Public Elementary- and Secondary- School Teachers Who Are Men, 1967-68 Cont.

43.	Tennessee	22.5	48.	Georgia	21.0
44.	West Virginia	22.2	49.	Virginia	20.3
45.	North Carolina	22.1	50.	South Carolina	18.6
46.	Alabama	21.6			
47.	Hawaii	21.4	Ref. 7:29.		

Pupils per Teacher in Public Elementary and Secondary Schools, Fall 1966

1.	South Dakota	18.6	31.	Oklahoma	24.2
2.	Wyoming	19.7		Texas	24.2
3.	North Dakota	20.0	33.	Indiana	24.5
4.	Nebraska	20.1	34.	Florida	24.9
5.	Kansas	20.4		Louisiana	24.9
6.	Maine	20.5	36.	North Carolina	25.0
7.	New York	20.6	37.	Kentucky	25.3
8.	Iowa	20.8		Missouri	25.3
9.	Vermont	21.1	39.	Hawaii	25.8
10.	Montana	21.3		West Virginia	25.8
11.	Alaska	21.8	41.	Ohio	25.9
	Oregon	21.8	42.	Washington	26.0
13.	Wisconsin	22.3	43.	Georgia	26.2
14.	Colorado	22.7	44.	California	26.4
	Delaware	22.7		Michigan	26.4
	Minnesota	22.7		South Carolina	26.4
17.	New Hampshire	22.8		Utah	26.4
18.	New Jersey	22.9	48.	Tennessee	27.3
19.	Connecticut	23.0	49.	Mississippi	28.0
	Illinois	23.0	50.	Alabama	28.1
21.	Rhode Island	23.1			
22.	Arkansas	23.3		American Samoa	28.2
	Idaho	23.3		Canal Zone	26.8§
24.	Arizona	23.4		Guam	26.0
	Massachusetts	23.4		Puerto Rico	34.9
	New Mexico	23.4		Virgin Islands	18.5
27.	Pennsylvania	23.6			
28.	Maryland	23.7	§Revised after publication of
29.	Nevada	24.0	*Estimates.*	
30.	Virginia	24.1			
	UNITED STATES	24.1	Ref. 23:19		

Estimated Average Salaries of All Teachers in Public Schools, 1967-68

1.	Alaska (24-$7,083)	$9,444	30.	Virginia	6,600
2.	California	8,900	31.	Georgia	6,595
3.	New York	8,300	32.	Kansas	6,507
4.	Hawaii	7,914§	33.	Texas	6,500
5.	Illinois	7,903	34.	Montana	6,375
6.	Connecticut	7,900	35.	New Hampshire	6,325
7.	Maryland	7,857	36.	North Carolina	6,219
8.	New Jersey	7,845	37.	Maine	6,150
9.	{Indiana	7,825	38.	Kentucky	6,100
	Nevada	7,825	39.	Oklahoma	6,095§
11.	{Michigan	7,750	40.	Nebraska	6,068
	Washington	7,750	41.	Idaho	6,045
13.	Delaware	7,625	42.	Tennessee	6,000
14.	Arizona	7,610	43.	Vermont	5,950
15.	{Massachusetts	7,550	44.	West Virginia	5,800
	Oregon	7,550	45.	Alabama	5,725
17.	Minnesota	7,465	46.	South Carolina	5,630
18.	Rhode Island	7,400	47.	Arkansas	5,596
19.	Ohio	7,300	48.	North Dakota	5,580
			49.	South Dakota	5,100
	UNITED STATES	7,296	50.	Mississippi	4,611
20.	Wisconsin	7,274			
21.	Louisiana	7,238		American Samoa	2,110
22.	Pennsylvania	7,225		Canal Zone	8,900
23.	Iowa	7,208		Guam	6,200
24.	Florida	7,200		Puerto Rico	4,150
25.	Wyoming	7,052		Virgin Islands	6,300
26.	New Mexico	6,981			
27.	Colorado	6,900			
28.	Utah	6,640			
29.	Missouri	6,623			

§Revised after publication of *Estimates.*

Ref. 7:31, 36.

Percent Increase in Instructional Staff Salaries, 1957-58 to 1967-68

1.	Kentucky	95.5%	8.	Mississippi	75.6
2.	Georgia	88.2	9.	West Virginia	74.1
3.	Iowa	86.9	10.	Alabama	73.5
4.	Virginia	81.9	11.	Maine	72.8
5.	Nebraska	79.9	12.	{Hawaii	72.2
6.	Tennessee	78.8		South Carolina	72.2
7.	Arkansas	77.2	14.	Vermont	69.3

Percent Increase in Instructional Staff Salaries, 1957-58 to 1967-68 Cont.

15.	North Dakota	69.1	34. Alaska	55.8
16.	Indiana	67.3	35. Washington	55.7
17.	North Carolina	67.0	36. Montana	54.5
18.	Kansas	66.8	37. Michigan	53.8
19.	Wyoming	66.6	38. Rhode Island	53.6
20.	Wisconsin	66.5	39. New Jersey	53.1
21.	Maryland	64.9	40. Pennsylvania	52.8
22.	Missouri	64.8	41. Oregon	52.5
23.	New Hampshire	63.0	42. Arizona	51.8
24.	Ohio	62.8	43. Florida	50.9
			44. Idaho	49.7
	UNITED STATES	61.0	45. Texas	48.4
25.	Louisiana	60.9	46. Utah	48.3
26.	Nevada	60.0	47. Oklahoma	47.3
27.	{Connecticut	59.8	48. New York	44.3
	{Massachusetts	59.8	49. New Mexico	41.1
29.	California	59.5	50. Delaware	40.9
30.	Colorado	58.8		
31.	Minnesota	57.9	Puerto Rico	109.8
32.	Illinois	57.0		
33.	South Dakota	55.9	Ref. 5:23, 30; 7:31, 36.	

Median School Years Completed by Persons 25 Years Old and Older, 1960

		All	White	Nonwhite
1.	Utah	12.2	12.2	10.1
	Alaska	12.1	12.4	6.6
	California	12.1	12.1	10.5
2.	Colorado	12.1	12.1	11.2
	Nevada	12.1	12.2	8.8
	Washington	12.1	12.2	10.5
	Wyoming	12.1	12.1	9.3
8.	{Idaho	11.8	11.8	9.6
	{Oregon	11.8	11.8	9.9
10.	Kansas	11.7	11.8	9.6
	Massachusetts	11.6	11.6	10.3
11.	{Montana	11.6	11.7	8.7
	Nebraska	11.6	11.7	9.6

Median School Years Completed by Persons 25 Years Old and Older, 1960
Cont.

14. Arizona	11.3	11.7	7.0
Hawaii	11.3	12.4	9.9
Iowa	11.3	11.3	9.5
17. New Mexico	11.2	11.5	7.1
18. Delaware	11.1	11.6	8.4
19. Connecticut	11.0	11.1	9.1
Maine	11.0	11.0	10.7
Florida	10.9	11.6	7.0
New Hampshire	10.9	10.9	11.7
21. Ohio	10.9	11.0	9.1
Vermont	10.9	10.9	10.5
Indiana	10.8	10.9	9.0
25. Michigan	10.8	11.0	9.1
Minnesota	10.8	10.8	9.9
28. New York	10.7	10.8	9.4
29. New Jersey	10.6	10.8	8.8
UNITED STATES	10.6	10.9	8.2
30. Illinois	10.5	10.7	9.0
Maryland	10.4	11.0	8.1
Oklahoma	10.4	10.7	8.6
31. South Dakota	10.4	10.5	8.6
Texas	10.4	10.8	8.1
Wisconsin	10.4	10.4	9.0
36. Pennsylvania	10.2	10.3	8.9
37. Rhode Island	10.0	10.0	9.5
38. Virginia	9.9	10.8	7.2
39. Missouri	9.6	9.8	8.7
40. North Dakota	9.3	9.3	8.4
41. Alabama	9.1	10.2	6.5
42. Georgia	9.0	10.3	6.1
Arkansas	8.9	9.5	6.5
43. Mississippi	8.9	11.0	6.0
North Carolina	8.9	9.8	7.0
Louisiana	8.8	10.5	6.0
46. Tennessee	8.8	9.0	7.5
West Virginia	8.8	8.8	8.4
49. Kentucky	8.7	8.7	8.2
South Carolina	8.7	10.3	5.9

Ref. 23.

Public High-School Graduates in 1966-67 as Percent of Ninth-Graders in Fall 1963

1.	Minnesota	92.0%		Alaska	76.9
2.	California	89.5	28.	Maryland	76.9
3.	Iowa	89.4		New York	76.9
4.	Wisconsin	89.1	31.	Missouri	76.8
5.	South Dakota	88.4	32.	Illinois	75.9
6.	Hawaii	88.1	33.	Wyoming	75.7
7.	North Dakota	86.4	34.	Kansas	75.5
8.	Washington	86.1	35.	Virginia	73.6
9.	Nebraska	85.6	36.	New Mexico	73.2
10.	Utah	85.2	37.	Oklahoma	73.0
11.	Massachusetts	84.4	38.	Arizona	72.8
12.	Montana	83.8	39.	South Carolina	72.2
	New Jersey	83.8	40.	Florida	71.9
14.	Rhode Island	82.6	41.	West Virginia	71.0
15.	Oregon	82.0	42.	Texas	70.2
16.	Ohio	81.6	43.	Tennessee	70.0
17.	Idaho	81.4	44.	Arkansas	69.4
	Pennsylvania	81.4	45.	Louisiana	67.5
19.	Delaware	80.8	46.	North Carolina	66.6
20.	Colorado	80.5	47.	Alabama	66.0
21.	Vermont	80.1		Mississippi	66.0
22.	Connecticut	79.9	49.	Kentucky	65.8
23.	Michigan	79.2	50.	Georgia	64.9
24.	New Hampshire	79.0		American Samoa	84.6
25.	Maine	78.6		Canal Zone	75.3
				Guam	74.7
	UNITED STATES	77.8		Puerto Rico	64.5
				Virgin Islands	53.2
26.	Nevada	77.6			
27.	Indiana	77.2	Ref. 3:17; 7:26, 36.		

Percent of Selective Service Draftees Failing Preinduction and Induction Mental Tests, 1966

1.	Washington	3.2%	10.	New Hampshire	5.4
2.	Montana	3.5		Vermont	5.4
3.	Iowa	3.7	12.	North Dakota	5.6
4.	Utah	3.9		South Dakota	5.6
5.	Oregon	4.2	14.	Kansas	6.0
6.	Minnesota	4.4	15.	Michigan	6.4
	Wisconsin	4.4	16.	Idaho	6.6
8.	Nebraska	4.5	17.	Oklahoma	7.2
	Wyoming	4.5		Rhode Island	7.2

Percent of Selective Service Draftees Failing Preinduction and Induction Mental Tests, 1966 Cont.

19.	California	7.5	35.	New Jersey	13.2
20.	Massachusetts	7.6	36.	Connecticut	13.9
21.	Ohio	8.0	37.	New York	14.8
22.	Colorado	8.5	38.	West Virginia	16.1
	Indiana	8.5	39.	Virginia	16.2
24.	Nevada	8.8	40.	Delaware	17.0
25.	Pennsylvania	9.1	41.	Arkansas	17.3
26.	Missouri	9.3	42.	Florida	17.9
27.	New Mexico	9.7	43.	Kentucky	18.7
28.	Maine	10.0	44.	Tennessee	18.8
29.	Alaska	10.3	45.	Alabama	24.1
30.	Hawaii	10.4	46.	North Carolina	24.8
31.	Arizona	10.9	47.	Louisiana	25.6
32.	Texas	11.1	48.	Georgia	28.0
33.	Illinois	12.2	49.	Mississippi	32.0
	UNITED STATES	12.4	50.	South Carolina	34.5
34.	Maryland	12.6	Ref. 9:46.		

Percent of 18-Year-Old Youths Disqualified for Military Service for Mental Reasons, July 1964 Through December 1965

1.	Washington	5.8%	22.	Vermont	15.1
2.	Minnesota	6.9	23.	New Hampshire	16.1
3.	Oregon	7.4	24.	Massachusetts	17.0
4.	Wyoming	7.5	25.	Illinois	17.8
5.	Iowa	7.7	26.	Michigan	18.2
6.	Utah	8.2	27.	California	19.5
7.	Montana	8.3	28.	Delaware	20.8
8.	Wisconsin	9.4	29.	Maine	20.9
9.	Idaho	11.4	30.	Colorado	21.2
10.	Nebraska	12.1	31.	Missouri	21.6
11.	Rhode Island	12.4	32.	Oklahoma	23.3
12.	South Dakota	12.6	33.	New York	24.9
13.	Alaska	13.1	34.	Arizona	25.9
14.	Kansas	13.5	35.	Maryland	27.8
15.	Pennsylvania	13.7		UNITED STATES	28.0
16.	Connecticut	13.8			
17.	Ohio	13.9	36.	Hawaii	28.3
18.	North Dakota	14.1	37.	New Mexico	29.4
19.	Indiana	14.2	38.	Florida	32.9
20.	New Jersey	14.4	39.	Arkansas	33.7
21.	Nevada	14.9	40.	West Virginia	35.5

Percent of 18-Year-Old Youths Disqualified for Military Service for Mental Reasons, July 1964 Through December 1965 Cont.

41.	Texas	38.6	50.	South Carolina	54.6
42.	Kentucky	39.1			
43.	Georgia	43.2		Guam ⎫	
44.	Alabama	44.5		Mariana Islands ⎬	58.9
45.	Virginia	45.3		Canal Zone ⎫	
46.	Louisiana	46.0		Puerto Rico ⎬	
47.	Tennessee	49.0		Virgin Islands ⎭	72.9
48.	North Carolina	53.0			
49.	Mississippi	53.8	Ref. 8:37.		

Per-Capita Personal Income, 1966

1.	Connecticut	$3,690	26.	New Hampshire	2,808
2.	Illinois	3,532	27.	Wyoming	2,739
3.	Delaware	3,529	28.	Montana	2,623
4.	Nevada	3.497	29.	Florida	2,614
	New York	3,497	30.	Virginia	2,605
6.	California	3,457	31.	Vermont	2,595
7.	New Jersey	3,445	32.	Arizona	2,544
8.	Alaska (31-$2,566)	3,421	33.	Texas	2,542
9.	Massachusetts	3,271	34.	Utah	2,485
10.	Michigan	3,269	35.	Maine	2,477
11.	Washington	3,222	36.	Oklahoma	2,462
12.	Maryland	3,204	37.	Idaho	2,445
13.	Hawaii	3,124	38.	South Dakota	2,420
14.	Indiana	3,076	39.	New Mexico	2,385
15.	Ohio	3,056	40.	North Dakota	2,384
16.	Rhode Island	3,047	41.	Georgia	2,379
17.	Iowa	2,992	42.	Louisiana	2,277
18.	Wisconsin	2,973		North Carolina	2,277
19.	Pennsylvania	2,968	44.	Kentucky	2,246
	UNITED STATES	2,963	45.	Tennessee	2,227
			46.	West Virginia	2,176
20.	Colorado	2,916	47.	Alabama	2,066
21.	Oregon	2,908	48.	South Carolina	2,052
22.	Nebraska	2,905	49.	Arkansas	2,010
23.	Minnesota	2,904	50.	Mississippi	1,777
24.	Kansas	2,862			
25.	Missouri	2,817	Ref. 1:31.		

Per-Capita General Revenue of State and Local Governments from Own Sources, 1965-66

1.	New York	$482.75	26.	Maryland	349.88
2.	California	476.28	27.	Vermont	345.19
3.	Alaska (25-$350.67)	467.56	28.	South Dakota	344.03
4.	Hawaii	456.13	29.	New Jersey	342.88
5.	Nevada	447.02	30.	Louisiana	334.77
6.	Wyoming	445.89	31.	Florida	329.52
7.	Delaware	441.27	32.	Rhode Island	327.58
8.	Washington	438.19	33.	Oklahoma	322.65
9.	Colorado	419.15	34.	Nebraska	321.35
10.	Minnesota	418.17	35.	Pennsylvania	311.13
11.	Wisconsin	405.58	36.	Ohio	305.25
12.	North Dakota	390.21	37.	Missouri	298.91
13.	Oregon	388.99	38.	Maine	295.92
14.	Michigan	388.41	39.	Texas	288.47
15.	Iowa	387.55	40.	New Hampshire	287.54
16.	Massachusetts	384.05	41.	Georgia	270.95
17.	New Mexico	380.14	42.	Virginia	267.07
18.	Montana	372.89	43.	West Virginia	261.37
19.	Connecticut	370.88	44.	North Carolina	256.38
20.	Kansas	370.15	45.	Kentucky	249.93
21.	Arizona	369.18	46.	Alabama	245.75
22.	Idaho	357.50	47.	Mississippi	244.84
	UNITED STATES	356.97	48.	Tennessee	243.93
23.	Indiana	352.85	49.	Arkansas	233.50
24.	Utah	352.04	50.	South Carolina	227.70
25.	Illinois	351.39	Ref. 15:45.		

Current Expenditure per Pupil in Average Daily Membership, 1966-67

1.	New York	$840	10.	California	567
2.	Alaska (4-$621)	828	11.	Nevada	564
3.	New Jersey	686	12.	Pennsylvania	562
4.	Wyoming	633	13.	Rhode Island	561
5.	Connecticut	611	14.	Illinois	560
6.	Oregon	609	15.	Maryland	559
7.	Delaware	591	16.	Hawaii	554
8.	Wisconsin	582	17.	Montana	550
9.	Minnesota	571	18.	New Mexico	543

Current Expenditure per Pupil in Average Daily Membership, 1966-67 Cont.

19.	Massachusetts	538	38.	West Virginia		391
20.	Colorado	536	39.	North Carolina		390
21.	Indiana	534	40.	Tennessee		378
	UNITED STATES	529	41.	Alabama		374
22.	Arizona	521	42.	Arkansas		371
			43.	South Carolina		348
23.	{Louisiana	516	44.	Mississippi		291
	{Virginia	516		Idaho		
25.	Vermont	501		Iowa		
26.	New Hampshire	495		Kansas	Data not	
27.	Utah	476		Michigan	available	
28.	North Dakota	469		Missouri		
29.	South Dakota	462		Washington		
30.	Florida	451				
31.	Oklahoma	444				
32.	{Nebraska	443		Canal Zone		796
	{Ohio	443		Guam		371
34.	Texas	425		Puerto Rico		257
35.	Maine	417		Virgin Islands		538
36.	{Georgia	398				
	{Kentucky	398	Ref. 5:34, 35.			

General Revenue of State and Local Governments from Own Sources, 1965-66, as Percent of Personal Income in 1966

1.	Wyoming	16.8%	18.	Nevada		13.5
2.	North Dakota	16.5	19.	{Oregon		13.3
3.	New Mexico	16.3		{Washington		13.3
4.	Hawaii	14.7	21.	Vermont		13.1
5.	{Arizona	14.6	22.	Oklahoma		13.0
	{Idaho	14.6	23.	Iowa		12.9
	{Louisiana	14.6	24.	Kansas		12.8
8.	Colorado	14.5	25.	Florida		12.7
9.	Minnesota	14.4	26.	Delaware		12.5
10.	South Dakota	14.3	27.	Maine		12.0
11.	{Montana	14.2				
	{Utah	14.2		UNITED STATES		12.0
13.	Alaska	14.0	28.	{Alabama		11.9
14.	California	13.9		{West Virginia		11.9
15.	New York	13.8	30.	{Massachusetts		11.7
16.	Mississippi	13.7		{Michigan		11.7
17.	Wisconsin	13.6	32.	Arkansas		11.6

General Revenue of State and Local Governments from Own Sources, 1965-66, as Percent of Personal Income in 1966 Cont.

33.	Georgia	11.4	43.	Missouri	10.5
	Indiana	11.4		Pennsylvania	10.5
	Texas	11.4	45.	New Hampshire	10.3
36.	North Carolina	11.3		Virginia	10.3
37.	Nebraska	11.2	47.	Connecticut	10.0
38.	Kentucky	11.1		New Jersey	10.0
	South Carolina	11.1	49.	Illinois	9.9
40.	Tennessee	11.0		Ohio	9.9
41.	Maryland	10.9			
42.	Rhode Island	10.8	Ref. 1:30; 15:31-33.		

Everson v. Board of Education*

United States Supreme Court

Mr. Justice Black delivered the opinion of the Court, saying in part:

A New Jersey statute authorizes its local school districts to make rules and contracts for the transportation of children to and from schools. The appellee, a township board of education, acting pursuant to this statute authorized reimbursement to parents of money expended by them for the bus transportation of their children on regular busses operated by the public transportation system. Part of this money was for payment of transportation of some children in the community to Catholic parochial schools. These church schools give their students, in addition to secular education, regular religious instruction conforming to the religious tenets and modes of worship of the Catholic Faith. The superintendent of these schools is a Catholic priest.

The appellant, in his capacity as a district taxpayer, filed suit in a state court challenging the right of the board to reimburse parents of parochial school students. He contended that the statute and the resolution passed pursuant to it violated both the state and the federal Constitutions. . . .

Since there has been no attack on the statute on the ground that a part of its language excludes children attending private schools operated for profit from enjoying state payment for their transportation, we need not consider this exclusionary language; it has no relevancy to any constitutional question here presented. . . .

The only contention here is that the state statute and the resolution, in so far as they authorized reimbursement to parents of children attending parochial schools, violate the federal Constitution in these two respects, which to some extent, overlap. *First.* They authorize the State

---

*300 U. S. 1.

to take by taxation the private property of some and bestow it upon others, to be used for their own private purposes. This, it is alleged, violates the due process clause of the Fourteenth Amendment. *Second.* The statute and the resolution forced inhabitants to pay taxes to help support and maintain schools which are dedicated to, and which regularly teach, the Catholic Faith. This is alleged to be a use of state power to support church schools contrary to the prohibition of the First Amendment which the Fourteenth Amendment made applicable to the states. . . .

It is much too late to argue that legislation intended to facilitate the opportunity of children to get a secular education serves no public purpose. . . . The same thing is no less true of legislation to reimburse needy parents, or all parents, for payment of the fares of their children so that they can ride in public busses to and from schools rather than run the risk of traffic and other hazards incident to walking or "hitchhiking.". . . . Nor does it follow that a law has a private rather than a public purpose because it provides that tax-raised funds will be paid to reimburse individuals on account of money spent by them in a way which furthers a public program. . . . Subsidies and loans to individuals such as farmers and home owners, and to privately owned transportation systems, as well as many other kinds of businesses, have been commonplace practice in our state and national history. . . .

Second. The New Jersey statute is challenged as a "law respecting the establishment of religion." The First Amendment, as made applicable to the states by the Fourteenth, . . . commands that a state "shall make no law respecting an establishment of religion, or prohibiting the free exercise thereof." These words of the First Amendment reflected in the minds of early Americans a vivid mental picture of conditions and practices which they fervently wished to stamp out in order to preserve liberty for themselves and for their posterity. Doubtless their goal has not been entirely reached; but so far has the nation moved toward it that the expression "law respecting the establishment of religion," probably does not so vividly remind present-day Americans of the evils, fears, and political problems that caused that expression to be written into our Bill of Rights. Whether this New Jersey law is one respecting the "establishment of religion" requires an understanding of the meaning of that language, particularly with respect to the imposition of taxes. Once again, therefore, it is not inappropriate briefly to review the background and environment of the period in which that constitutional language was fashioned and adopted.

A large proportion of the early settlers of this country came here from Europe to escape the bondage of laws which compelled them to support and attend government favored churches. The centuries immediately before and contemporaneous with the colonization of America had been filled with turmoil, civic strife, and persecutions, generated in large part by established sects determined to maintain their absolute political and religious supremacy. With the power of government supporting them, at various times and places, Catholics had persecuted Protestants, Protestants had persecuted Catholics, Protestant sects had persecuted other Protestant sects, Catholics of one shade of belief had persecuted Catholics of another shade of belief, and all of these had from time to time persecuted Jews. In efforts to force loyalty to whatever religious group happened to be on top and in league with the government of a particular time and place, men and women had been fined, cast in jail, cruelly tortured, and killed. Among the offenses for which these punishments had been inflicted were such things as speaking disrespectfully of the views of ministers of government-established churches, non-attendance at those churches, expressions of non-belief in their doctrines, and failure to pay taxes and tithes to support them.

These practices of the old world were transplanted to and began to thrive in the soil of the new America. The very charters granted by the English Crown to the individuals and companies designated to make the laws which would control the destinies of the colonials authorized these individuals and companies to erect religious establishments which all, whether believers or non-believers, would be required to support and attend. An exercise of this authority was accompanied by a repetition of many of the old world practices and persecutions. Catholics found themselves hounded and proscribed because of their faith; Quakers who followed their conscience went to jail; Baptists were peculiarly obnoxious to certain dominant Protestant sects; men and women of varied faiths who happened to be in a minority in a particular locality were persecuted because they steadfastly persisted in worshipping God only as their own consciences dictated. And all of these dissenters were compelled to pay tithes and taxes to support government-sponsored churches whose ministers preached inflammatory sermons designed to strengthen and consolidate the established faith by generating a burning hatred against dissenters.

These practices became so commonplace as to shock the freedom-loving colonials into a feeling of abhorrence. The imposition of taxes to pay ministers' salaries and to build and maintain churches and church property aroused their indignation. It was these feelings which found expression in the First Amendment. No one locality and no one group throughout the Colonies can rightly be given entire credit for having aroused the sentiment that culminated in adoption of the Bill of Rights' provisions embracing religious liberty. But Virginia, where the established church had achieved a dominant influence in political affairs and where many excesses attracted wide public attention, provided a great stimulus and able leadership for the movement. The people there, as elsewhere, reached the conviction that individual religious liberty could be achieved best under a government which was stripped of all power to tax, to support, or otherwise to assist any or all religions, or to interfere with the beliefs of any religious individual or group.

The movement toward this end reached its dramatic climax in Virginia in 1785-86 when the Virginia legislative body was about to renew Virginia's tax levy for the support of the established church. Thomas Jefferson and James Madison led the fight against this tax. Madison wrote his great Memorial and Remonstrance against the law. In it, he eloquently argued that a true religion did not need the support of law; that no person, either believer or non-believer, should be taxed to support a religious institution of any kind; that the best interest of a society required that the minds of men always be wholly free; and that cruel persecutions were the inevitable result of government-established religions. Madison's Remonstrance received strong support throughout Virginia, and the Assembly postponed consideration of the proposed tax measure until its next session. When the proposal came up for consideration at that session, it not only died in committee, but the Assembly enacted the famous "Virginia Bill for Religious Liberty" originally written by Thomas Jefferson. The preamble to that Bill stated among other things that

Almighty God hath created the mind free; that all attempts to influence it by temporal punishments, or burthens, or by civil incapacitations, tend only to beget habits of hypocrisy and meanness, and are a departure from the plan of the Holy author of our religion who being Lord both of body and mind, yet chose not to propagate it by coercions on either . . . ; that to compel a man to furnish contributions of money for the propagation of opinions which he disbelieves, is sinful and tyrannical; that even the forcing him to support this or that teacher of his own religious persuasion, is depriving him of the comfortable liberty of giving his contributions to the particular pastor, whose morals he would make his pattern. . . .

And the statute itself enacted

That no man shall be compelled to frequent or support any religious worship, place, or ministry whatsoever, nor shall be enforced, restrained, molested, or burthened, in his body or goods, nor shall otherwise suffer on account of his religious opinions or belief . . .

This Court has previously recognized that the provisions of the First Amendment, in the drafting and adoption of which Madison and Jefferson played such leading roles, had the same objective and were intended to provide the same protection against governmental intrusion on religious liberty as the Virginia statute. . . . Prior to the adoption of the Fourteenth Amendment, the First Amendment did not apply as a restraint against the states. Most of them did soon provide similar constitutional protections for religious liberty. But some states persisted for about half a century in imposing restraints upon the free exercise of religion and in discriminating against particular religious groups. In recent years, so far as the provision against the establishment of a religion is concerned, the question has most frequently arisen in connection with proposed state aid to church schools and efforts to carry on religious teachings in the public schools in accordance with the tenets of a particular sect. Some churches have either sought or accepted state financial support for their schools. Here again the efforts to obtain state aid or acceptance of it have not been limited to any one particular faith. The state courts, in the main, have remained faithful to the language of their own constitutional provisions designed to protect religious freedom and to separate religions and governments. Their decisions, however, show the difficulty in drawing the line between tax legislation which provides funds for the welfare of the general public and that which is designed to support institutions which teach religion. . . .

The "establishment of religion" clause of the First Amendment means at least this: Neither a state nor the federal government can set up a church. Neither can pass laws which aid one religion, aid all religions, or prefer one religion over another. Neither can force nor influence a person to go to or to remain away from church against his will or force him to profess a belief or disbelief in any religion. No person can be punished for entertaining or professing religious beliefs or disbeliefs, for church attendance or non-attendance. No tax in any amount, large or small, can be levied to support any religious activities or institutions, whatever they may be called, or whatever form they may adopt to teach or practice religion. Neither a state nor the federal government can, openly or secretly, participate in the affairs of any religious organizations or groups and *vice versa*. In the words of Jefferson, the clause against establishment of religion by law was intended to erect "a wall of separation between Church and State." . . .

Measured by these standards, we cannot say that the First Amendment prohibits New Jersey from spending tax-raised funds to pay the bus fares of parochial school pupils as a part of a general program under which it pays the fares of pupils attending public and other schools. It is undoubtedly true that children are helped to get to church schools. There is even a possibility that some of the children might not be sent to the church schools if the parents were compelled to pay their children's bus fares out of their own pockets when transportation to a public school would have been paid for by the state. The same possibility exists where the state requires a local transit company to provide reduced fares to school children including those attending parochial schools, or where a municipally owned transportation system undertakes to carry all school children free of charge. Moreover, state-paid policemen, detailed to protect children going to and from church schools from the very real hazards of traffic, would serve much the same purpose and accomplish much the same result as state provisions intended to guarantee free transportation of a kind which the state deems to be best for the school children's welfare. And parents might refuse to risk their children to the serious danger of traffic accidents going to and from parochial schools, the approaches to which were not protected by policemen. Similarly, parents might be reluctant to permit their children to attend schools which the state had cut off from such general government services as ordinary police and fire protection, connections for sewage disposal, public highways and sidewalks. Of course, cutting off church schools from these services, so separate and so indisputably marked off from the religious function, would make it far more difficult for the schools to operate. But such is obviously not the purpose of the First Amendment. That Amendment requires the state to be a neutral in its relations with groups of religious believers and non-believers; it does not require the state to be their adversary. State power is no more to be used so as to handicap religions than it is to favor them.

This Court has said that parents may, in the discharge of their duty under state compulsory education laws, send their children to a religious rather than a public school if the school meets the secular educational requirements which the state has power to impose. See Pierce v. Society of Sisters, 268 U. S. 510. It appears that these parochial schools meet New Jersey's requirements. The state contributes no money to the schools. It does not support them. Its legislation, as applied, does no more than provide a general program to help parents get their children, regardless of their religion, safely and expeditiously to and from accredited schools.

The First Amendment has erected a wall between church and state. That wall must be kept high and impregnable. We could not approve the slightest breach. New Jersey has not breached it here.

Affirmed.

Mr. Justice Jackson, dissenting, said in part:

It is of no importance in this situation whether the beneficiary of this expenditure of tax-raised funds is primarily the parochial school and incidentally the pupil, or whether the aid is directly bestowed on the pupil with indirect benefits to the school. The state cannot maintain a Church and it can no more tax its citizens to furnish free carriage to those who attend a Church. The prohibition against establishment of religion cannot be circumvented by a subsidy, bonus or reimbursement of expense to individuals for receiving religious instruction and indoctrination. . . .

The Court's holding is that this taxpayer has no grievance because the state has decided to make the reimbursement a public purpose and therefore we are bound to regard it as such. I agree that this Court has left, and always should leave to each state, great latitude in deciding for itself in the light of its own conditions, what shall be public purposes in its scheme of things. It may socialize utilities and economic enterprises and make taxpayers' business out of what conventionally had been private business. It may make public business of individual welfare, health, education, entertainment or security. But it cannot make public business of religious worship or instruction, or of attendance at religious institutions of any character. There is no answer to the proposition more fully expounded by Mr. Justice Rutledge that the effect of the religious freedom Amendment to our Constitution was to take every form of propagation of religion out of the realm of things which could directly or indirectly be made public business and thereby be supported in whole or in part at taxpayers' expense. That is a difference which the Constitution sets up between religion and almost every other subject matter of legislation, a difference which goes to the very root of religious freedom and which the Court is overlooking today. This freedom was first in the Bill of Rights because it was first in the forefathers' minds; it was set forth in absolute terms, and its strength is its rigidity. It was intended not only to keep the states' hands out of religion, but to keep religion's hands off the state, and above all, to keep bitter religious controversy out of public life by denying to every denomination any advantage from getting control of public policy or the public purse. Those great ends I cannot but think are immeasurably compromised by today's decision. . . .

But we cannot have it both ways. Religious teaching cannot be a private affair when the state seeks to impose regulations which infringe on it indirectly, and a public affair when it comes to taxing citizens of one faith to aid another, or those of no faith to aid at all. If these principles seem harsh in prohibiting aid to Catholic education, it must not be forgotten that it is the same Constitution that alone assures Catholics the right to maintain these schools at all when predominant local sentiment would forbid them. Pierce v. Society of Sisters, 268 U. S. 510. Nor should I think that those who have done so well without this aid would want to see this separation between Church and State broken down. If the state may aid these religious schools, it may therefore regulate them. Many groups have sought aid from tax funds only to find that it carried political controls with it. Indeed this Court has declared that "It is hardly lack of due process for the government to regulate that which it subsidizes."

But in any event, the great purposes of the Constitution do not depend on the approval or convenience of those they restrain. I cannot read the history of the struggle to separate political from ecclesiastical affairs, well summarized in the opinion of Mr. Justice Rutledge in which I generally concur, without a conviction that the Court today is unconsciously giving the clock's hands a backward turn.

Mr. Justice Frankfurter joins in this opinion.

Mr. Justice Rutledge, with whom Mr. Justice Frankfurter, Mr. Justice Jackson and Mr. Justice Burton agree, dissenting, said in part:

"Congress shall make no law respecting an establishment of religion, or prohibiting the free exercise thereof. . . .

"Well aware that Almighty God hath created the mind free; . . . that to compel a man to furnish contributions of money for the propagation of opinions which he disbelieves, is sinful and tyrannical; . . .

"We, the General Assembly, do enact, That no man shall be compelled to frequent or support any religious worship, place, or ministry whatsoever, nor shall be enforced, restrained, molested, or burthened in his body or goods, nor shall otherwise suffer on account of his religious opinions or belief. . . ."[1]

I cannot believe that the great author of those words, or the men who made them law, could have joined in this decision. Neither so high nor so impregnable today as yesterday is the wall raised between church and state by Virginia's great statute of religious freedom and the First Amendment, now made applicable to all the states by the Fourteenth. New Jersey's statute sustained is the first, if indeed it is not the second breach to be made by this Court's action. That a third, and a fourth, and still others will be attempted, we may be sure. For just as Cochran v. Board of Education, 281 U. S. 370, has opened the way by oblique ruling for this decision, so will the two make wider the breach for a third. Thus with time the most solid freedom steadily gives way before continuing corrosive decision.

This case forces us to determine squarely for the first time what was "an establishment of religion" in the First Amendment's conception; and

---

[1]"A Bill for Establishing Religious Freedom," enacted by the General Assembly of Virginia, January 19, 1786. See 1 Randall, The Life of Thomas Jefferson (1858) 219-220; XII Hening's Statutes of Virginia (1823) 84.

by that measure to decide whether New Jersey's action violates its command. . . .

Not simply an established church, but any law respecting an establishment of religion is forbidden. The Amendment was broadly but not loosely phrased. It is the compact and exact summation of its author's views formed during his long struggle for religious freedom. In Madison's own words characterizing Jefferson's Bill for Establishing Religious Freedom, the guaranty he put in our national charter, like the bill he piloted through the Virginia Assembly, was "a Model of technical precision, and perspicuous brevity." Madison could not have confused "church" and "religion," or "an established church" and "an establishment of religion."

The Amendment's purpose was not to strike merely at the official establishment of a single sect, creed or religion, outlawing only a formal relation such as had prevailed in England and some of the colonies. Necessarily it was to uproot all such relationships. But the object was broader than separating church and state in this narrow sense. It was to create a complete and permanent separation of the spheres of religious activity and civil authority by comprehensively forbidding every form of public aid or support for religion. In proof the Amendment's wording and history unite with this Court's consistent utterances whenever attention has been fixed directly upon the question.

No one would claim today that the Amendment is constricted, in "prohibiting the free exercise" of religion, to securing the free exercise of some formal or creedal observance, of one sect or of many. It secures all forms of religious expression, creedal, sectarian or non-sectarian wherever and however taking place, except conduct which trenches upon the like freedoms of others or clearly and presently endangers the community's good order and security. For the protective purposes of this phase of the basic freedom street preaching, oral or by distribution of literature, has been given "the same high estate under the First Amendment as . . . worship in the churches and preaching from the pulpits." And on this basis parents have been held entitled to send their children to private, religious schools. Pierce v. Society of Sisters, 268 U. S. 510. Accordingly, daily religious education commingled with secular is "religion" within the guaranty's comprehensive scope. So are religious training and teaching in whatever form. The word connotes the broadest content, determined not by the form of formality of the teaching or where it occurs, but by its essential nature regardless of those details.

"Religion" has the same broad significance in the twin prohibition concerning "an establishment." The Amendment was not duplicitous. "Religion" and "establishment" were not used in any formal or technical sense. The prohibition broadly forbids state support, financial or other, of religion in any guise, form or degree. It outlaws all use of public funds for religious purposes. . . .

Does New Jersey's action furnish support for religion by use of the taxing power? Certainly it does, if the test remains undiluted as Jefferson and Madison made it, that money taken by taxation from one is not to be used or given to support another's religious training or belief, or indeed one's own. Today as then the furnishing of "contributions of money for the propagation of opinions which he disbelieves" is the forbidden exaction; and the prohibition is absolute for whatever measure brings that consequence and whatever amount may be sought or given to that end.

The funds used here were raised by taxation. The Court does not dispute, nor could it, that their use does in fact give aid and encouragement to religious instruction. It only concludes that this aid is not "support" in law. But Madison and Jefferson were concerned with aid and support in fact, not as a legal conclusion "entangled in precedents." Remonstrance, Par. 3. Here parents pay money to send their children to parochial schools and funds raised by taxation are used to reimburse them. This not only helps the children to get to school and the parents to send them. It aids them in a substantial way to get the very thing which they are sent to the particular school to secure, namely, religious training and teaching.

Believers of all faiths, and others who do not express their feeling toward ultimate issues of existence in any creedal form, pay the New Jersey tax. When the money so raised is used to pay for transportation to religious schools, the Catholic taxpayer to the extent of his proportionate share pays for the transportation of Lutheran, Jewish and otherwise religiously affiliated children to receive their non-Catholic religious instruction. Their parents likewise pay proportionately for the transportation of Catholic children to receive Catholic instruction. Each thus contributes to "the propagation of opinions which he disbelieves" in so far as their religions differ, as do others who accept no creed without regard to those differences. Each thus pays taxes also to support the teaching of his own religion, an exaction equally forbidden since it denies "the comfortable liberty" of giving one's contribution to the particular agency of instruction he approves.

New Jersey's action therefore exactly fits the type of exaction and the kind of evil at which Madison and Jefferson struck. Under the test they framed it cannot be said that the cost of transportation is no part of the cost of education or of the religious instruction given. That it is a substantial and a necessary element is shown most plainly by the continuing and increasing demand for the state to assume it. Nor is there pretense that it relates only to the secular instruction given in religious schools or that any attempt is or could be made toward allocating proportional shares as between the secular and the religious instruction. It is precisely because the instruction is religious and relates to a particular faith, whether one or another, that parents send their children to religious schools under the Pierce doctrine. And the very purpose of the state's contribution is to defray the cost of conveying the pupil to the place where he will receive not simply secular, but also and primarily religious, teaching and guidance. . . .

Finally, transportation, where it is needed, is as essential to education as any other element. Its cost is as much a part of the total expense, except at times in amount, as the cost of textbooks, of school lunches, of athletic equipment, of writing and other materials; indeed of all other items composing the total burden. Now as always the core of the educational process is the teacher-pupil relationship. Without this the richest equipment and facilities would go for naught. . . . But the proverbial Mark Hopkins conception no longer suffices for the country's requirements. Without buildings, without equipment, without library, textbooks and other materials, and without transportation to bring teacher and pupil together in such an effective teaching environment, there can be not even the skeleton of what our times require. Hardly can it be maintained that transportation is the least essential of these items, or that it does not in fact aid, encourage, sustain and support, just as they do, the very process which is its purpose to accomplish. No less essential is it, or the payment of its cost, than the very teaching in the classroom or payment of the teacher's sustenance. Many types of equipment, now considered essential, better could be done without. . . .

But we are told that the New Jersey statute is valid in its present application because the appropriation is for a public, not a private purpose, namely, the promotion of education, and the majority accept this idea in the conclusion that all we have here is "public welfare legislation." If that is true and the Amendment's force can be thus destroyed, what has been said becomes all the more pertinent. For then there could be no possible objection to more extensive support of religious education by New Jersey.

If the fact alone be determinative that religious schools are engaged in education, thus promoting the general and individual welfare, together with the legislature's decision that the payment of public moneys for their aid makes their work a public function, then I can see no possible basis, except one of dubious legislative policy, for the state's refusal to make full appropriation for support of private, religious schools, just as is done for public instruction. There could not be, on that basis, valid constitutional objection.

We have here then one substantial issue, not two. To say that New Jersey's appropriation and her use of the power of taxation for raising the funds appropriated are not for public purposes but are for private ends, is to say that they are for the support of religion and religious teaching. Conversely, to say that they are for public purposes is to say that they are not for religious ones.

This is precisely for the reason that education which includes religious training and teaching, and its support, have been made matters of private right and function, not public, by the very terms of the First Amendment. That is the effect not only in its guaranty of religion's free exercise, but also in the prohibition of establishments. It was on this basis of the private character of the function of religious education that this Court held parents entitled to send their children to private, religious schools. Pierce v. Society of Sisters, *supra*. Now it declares in effect that the appropriation of public funds to defray part of the cost of attending those schools is for a public purpose. If so, I do not understand why the state cannot go farther or why this case approaches the verge of its power. . . .

Our constitutional policy is exactly the opposite. It does not deny the value or the necessity for religious training, teaching or observance. Rather it secures their free exercise. But to that end it does deny that the state can undertake or sustain them in any form or degree. For this reason the sphere of religious activity, as distinguished from the secular intellectual liberties, has been given the twofold protection and, as the state cannot forbid, neither can it perform or aid in performing the religious function. The dual prohibition makes that function altogether private. It cannot be made a public one by legislative act. This was the very heart of Madison's Remonstrance, as it is of the Amendment itself.

It is not because religious teaching does not promote the public or the individual's welfare, but because neither is furthered when the state promotes religious education, that the Constitution forbids it to do so. Both legislatures and courts are bound by that distinction. In failure to observe it lies the fallacy of the "public function"—"social legislation" argument, a fallacy facilitated by easy transference of the argument's basing from due process unrelated to any religious aspect to the First Amendment. . . .

The reasons underlying the Amendment's policy have not vanished with time or diminished in force. Now as when it was adopted the price of religious freedom is double. It is that the church and religion shall live both within and upon that freedom. There cannot be freedom of religion, safeguarded by the state, and intervention by the church or its agencies in the state's domain or dependency on its largesse. Madison's Remonstrance, Pars. 6, 8. The great condition of religious liberty is that it be maintained free from sustenance, as also from other interferences, by the state. For when it comes to rest upon that secular foundation it vanishes with the resting. Id., Pars. 7, 8. Public money devoted to payment of religious costs, educational or other, brings the quest for more. It brings too the struggle of sect against sect for the larger share or for any. Here one by numbers alone will benefit most, there another. That is precisely the history of societies which have had an established religion and dissident groups. It is the very thing Jefferson and Madison experienced and sought to guard against, whether in its blunt or in its more screened forms. The end of such strife cannot be other than to destroy the cherished liberty. The dominating group will achieve the dominant benefit, or all will embroil the state in their dissensions. . . .

This is not therefore just a little case over bus fares. In paraphrase of Madison, distant as it may be in its present form from a complete establishment of religion, it differs from it only in degree; and is the first step in that direction. . . .

The realm of religious training and belief remains, as the Amendment made it, the kingdom of the individual man and his God. It should be kept inviolately private, not "entangled . . . in precedents" or confounded with what legislatures legitimately may take over into the public domain.

No one conscious of religious values can be unsympathetic toward the burden which our constitutional separation puts on parents who desire religious instruction mixed with secular for their children. They pay taxes for others' children's education, at the same time the added cost of instruction for their own. Nor can one happily see benefits denied to children which others receive, because in conscience they or their parents for them desire a different kind of training others do not demand.

But if those feelings should prevail, there would be an end to our historic constitutional policy and command. No more unjust or discriminatory in fact is it to deny attendants at religious schools the cost of their transportation than it is to deny them tuitions, sustenance for their teachers, or any other educational expense which others receive at public cost. Hardship in fact there is which none can blink. But, for assuring to those who undergo it the greater, the most comprehensive freedom, it is one written by design and firm intent into our basic law. . . .

That policy necessarily entails hardship upon persons who forego the right to educational advantages the state can supply in order to secure others it is precluded from giving. Indeed this may hamper the parent and the child forced by conscience to that choice. But it does not make the state unneutral to withhold what the Constitution forbids it to give. On the contrary it is only by observing the prohibition rigidly that the state can maintain its neutrality and avoid partisanship in the dissensions inevitable when sect opposes sect over demands for public moneys to further religious education, teaching or training in any form or degree, directly or indirectly. Like St. Paul's freedom, religious liberty with a great price must be bought. And for those who exercise it most fully, by insisting upon religious education for their children mixed with secular, by the terms of our Constitution the price is greater than for others.

The problem then cannot be cast in terms of legal discrimination or its absence. This would be true, even though the state in giving aid should treat all religious instruction alike. Thus, if the present statute and its application were shown to apply equally to all religious schools of whatever faith, yet in the light of our tradition it could not stand. For then the adherent of one creed still would pay for the support of another, the childless taxpayer with others more fortunate. Then too there would seem to be no bar to making appropriations for transportation and other expenses of children attending public or other secular schools, after hours in separate places and classes for their exclusively religious instruction. The person who embraces no creed also would be forced to pay for teaching what he does not believe. Again, it was the furnishing of "contributions of money for the propagation of opinions which he disbelieves" that the fathers outlawed. That consequence and effect are not removed by multiplying to all-inclusiveness the sects for which support is exacted. The Constitution requires, not comprehensive identification of state with religion, but complete separation. . . .

Two great drives are constantly in motion to abridge, in the name of education, the complete division of religion and civil authority which our forefathers made. One is to introduce religious education and observances into the public schools. The other, to obtain public funds for the aid and support of various private religious schools. . . . In my opinion both avenues were closed by the Constitution. Neither should be opened by this Court. The matter is not one of quantity, to be measured by the amount of money expended. Now as in Madison's day it is one of principle, to keep separate the separate spheres as the First Amendment drew them; to prevent the first experiment upon our liberties; and to keep the question from becoming entangled in corrosive precedents. We should not be less strict to keep strong and untarnished the one side of the shield of religious freedom than we have been of the other.

The judgment should be reversed.

Engle v. Vitale*

United States Supreme Court

Mr. Justice Black delivered the opinion of the Court, saying in part:

The respondent Board of Education of Union Free School District No. 9, New Hyde Park, New York, acting in its official capacity under state law, directed the School District's principal to cause the following prayer to be said aloud by each class in the presence of a teacher at the beginning of each school day:

> Almighty God, we acknowledge our dependence upon Thee, and we beg Thy blessings upon us, our parents, our teachers and our country.

This daily procedure was adopted on the recommendation of the State Board of Regents, a governmental agency created by the State Constitution to which the New York Legislature has granted broad supervisory, executive, and legislative powers over the State's public school system. These state officials composed the prayer which they recommended and published as a part of their "Statement on Moral and Spiritual Training in the Schools," saying: "We believe that this Statement will be subscribed to by all men and women of good will, and we call upon all of them to aid in giving life to our program."

Shortly after the practice of reciting the Regents' prayer was adopted by the School District, the parents of ten pupils brought this action in a New York State Court insisting that use of this official prayer in the public schools was contrary to the beliefs, religions, or religious practices of both themselves and their children. Among other things, these parents challenged the constitutionality of both the state law authorizing the School District to direct the use of prayer in public schools and the

*370 U.S. 421 (1962).

School District's regulation ordering the recitation of this particular prayer on the ground that these actions of official governmental agencies violate that part of the First Amendment of the Federal Constitution which commands that "Congress shall make no law respecting an establishment of religion"—a command which was "made applicable to the State of New York by the Fourteenth Amendment of the said Constitution." The New York Court of Appeals . . . upheld the power of New York to use the Regents' prayer so long as the schools did not compel any pupil to join in the prayer over his or his parents' objection. . . .

We think that by using its public school system to encourage recitation of the Regents' prayer, the State of New York has adopted a practice wholly inconsistent with the Establishment Clause. There can, of course, be no doubt that New York's program of daily classroom invocation of God's blessings as prescribed in the Regents' prayer is a religious activity. It is a solemn avowal of divine faith and supplication for the blessings of the Almighty. The nature of such a prayer has always been religious, none of the respondents has denied this and the trial court expressly so found. . . .

The petitioners contend among other things that the state laws requiring or permitting use of the Regents' prayer must be struck down as a violation of the Establishment Clause because that prayer was composed by governmental officials as a part of a governmental program to further religious beliefs. For this reason, petitioners argue, the States' use of the Regents' prayer in its public school system breeches the constitutional wall of separation between Church and State. We agree with that contention since we think that the constitutional prohibition against laws respecting an establishment of religion must at least mean that in this country it is no part of the business of government to compose official prayers for any group of the American people to recite as a part of a religious program carried on by government.

It is a matter of history that this very practice of establishing governmentally composed prayers for religious services was one of the reasons which caused many of our early colonists to leave England and seek religious freedom in America. The Book of Common Prayer, which was created under governmental direction and which was approved by Acts of Parliament in 1548 and 1549, set out in minute detail the accepted form and content prayer and other religious ceremonies to be used in the established, tax-supported Church of England. . . . [Controversies created by the use of the Book of Common Prayer are briefly summarized.]

It is an unfortunate fact of history that when some of the very groups which had most strenuously opposed the established Church of England found themselves sufficiently in control of colonial governments in this country to write their own prayers into law, they passed laws making their own religion the official religion of their respective colonies. Indeed as late as the time of the Revolutionary War, there were established churches in at least eight of the thirteen former colonies and established religions in at least four of the other five. But the successful Revolution against English political domination was shortly followed by intense opposition to the practice of establishing religion by law. This opposition crystallized rapidly into an effective political force in Virginia where the minority religious groups such as Presbyterians, Lutherans, Quakers and Baptists had gained such strength that the adherents to the established Episcopal Church were actually a minority themselves. In 1785-1786, those opposed to the established Church, led by James Madison and Thomas Jefferson, who, though themselves not members of any of these dissenting religious groups, opposed all religious establishments by law on grounds of principle, obtained the enactment of the famous "Virginia Bill for Religious Liberty" by which all religious groups were placed on an equal footing so far as the State was concerned. Similar though less far-reaching legislation was being considered and passed in other States.

By the time of the adoption of the Constitution, our history shows that there was a widespread awareness among many Americans of the dangers of a union of Church and State. . . . The First Amendment was added to the Constitution to stand as a guarantee that neither the power nor the prestige of the Federal Government would be used to control, support or influence the kinds of prayer the American people can say — that the people's religions must not be subjected to the pressures of government for change each time a new political administration is elected to office. Under that Amendment's prohibition against governmental establishment of religion, as reinforced by the provisions of the Fourteenth Amendment, government in this country, be it state or federal, is without power to prescribe by law any particular form of prayer which is to be used as an official prayer in carrying on any program of governmentally sponsored religious activity.

There can be no doubt that New York's state prayer program officially establishes the religious beliefs embodied in the Regents' prayer. The respondents' argument to the contrary, which is largely based upon the contention that the Regents' prayer is "nondenominational" and the fact that the program, as modified and approved by state courts, does not require all pupils to recite the prayer but permits those who wish to do so to remain silent or be excused from the room, ignores the essential nature of the program's constitutional defects. Neither the fact that the prayer may be denominationally neutral, nor the fact that its observance on the part of the students is voluntary can serve to free it from the limitations of the Establishment Clause, as it might from the Free Exercise Clause, of the First Amendment, both of which are operative against the States by virtue of the Fourteenth Amendment. Although these two clauses may in certain instances overlap, they forbid two quite different kinds of governmental encroachment upon religious freedom. The Establishment Clause, unlike the Free Exercise Clause, does not depend upon any showing of direct governmental compulsion and is violated by the enactment of laws which establish an official religion whether those laws operate directly to coerce nonobserving individuals or not. This is not to say, of course, that laws officially prescribing a particular form of religious worship do not involve coercion of such individuals. When the power, prestige and financial support of government is placed behind a particular religious belief, the indirect coercive pressure upon religious minorities to conform to the prevailing officially approved religion is plain. But the purposes underlying the Establishment Clause go much further than that. Its first and most immediate purpose rested on the belief that a union of government and religion tends to destroy government and to degrade religion. The history of governmentally established religion, both in England and in this country, showed that whenever government had allied itself with one particular form of religion, the inevitable result had been that it had incurred the hatred, disrespect and even contempt of those who held contrary beliefs. That same history showed that many people had lost their respect for any religion that had relied upon the support of government to spread its faith. The Establishment Clause thus stands as an expression of principle on the part of the Founders of our Constitution that religion is too personal, too sacred, too holy, to permit its "unhallowed perversion" by a civil magistrate. Another purpose of the Establishment Clause rested upon an awareness of the historical fact that governmentally established religions and religious persecutions go hand in hand. . . . It was in large part to get completely away from this sort of systematic religious persecution that the Founders brought into being our Nation, our Constitution, and our Bill of Rights with its prohibition against any governmental establishment of religion. The New York laws officially prescribing the Regents' prayer are inconsistent with both the purposes of the Establishment Clause and with the Establishment Clause itself.

It has been argued that to apply the Constitution in such a way as to prohibit state laws respecting an establishment of religious services in public schools is to indicate a hostility toward religion or toward prayer. Nothing, of course, could be more wrong. The history of man is inseparable from the history of religion. And perhaps it is not too much to say that since the beginning of that history many people have devoutly believed that "More things are wrought by prayer than this world dreams of." It was doubtless largely due to men who believed this that there grew up a sentiment that caused men to leave the cross-currents of officially established state religions and religious persecution in Europe and come to this country filled with the hope that they could find a place in which they could pray when they pleased to the God of their faith in the language they chose. And there were men of this same faith in the power of prayer who led the fight for adoption of our Constitution and also for our Bill of Rights with the very guarantees of religious freedom that forbid the sort of governmental activity which New York has attempted here. These men knew that the First Amendment, which tried to put an end to governmental control of religion and of prayer, was not written to destroy either. They knew rather that it was written to quiet well-justified fears which nearly all of them felt arising out of an awareness that governments of the past had shackled men's tongues to make them speak only the religious thoughts that government wanted them to speak and to pray only to the God that government wanted them to pray to. It is neither sacrilegious nor antireligious to say that each separate government in this country should stay out of the business of writing or sanctioning official prayers and leave that purely religious function to the people themselves and to those the people choose to look to for religious guidance.

It is true that New York's establishment of its Regents' prayer as an officially approved religious doctrine of that State does not amount to a total establishment of one particular religious sect to the exclusion of all others — that, indeed, the governmental endorsement of that prayer seems relatively insignificant when compared to the governmental encroachments upon religion which were commonplace 200 years ago. To those who may subscribe to the view that because the Regents' official prayer is so brief and general there can be no danger to religious freedom in its governmental establishment, however, it may be appropriate to say in the words of James Madison, the author of the First Amendment:

[I]t is proper to take alarm at the first experiment on our liberties. . . . Who does not see that the same authority which can establish Christianity, in exclusion of all other Religions, may establish with the same ease any particular sect of Christians, in exclusion of all other Sects? That the same Authority which can force a citizen to contribute three pence only of his property for the support of any one establishment, may force him to conform to any other establishment in all cases whatsoever?

The judgment of the Court of Appeals of New York is reversed and the cause remanded for further proceedings not inconsistent with this opinion.

Reversed and remanded.

Mr. Justice Frankfurter took no part in the decision of this case.

Mr. Justice White took no part in the consideration or decision of this case.

Mr. Justice Douglas, concurring, said in part:

... The point for decision is whether the Government can constitutionally finance a religious exercise. Our system at the federal and state levels is presently honeycombed with such financing. Nevertheless, I think it is an unconstitutional undertaking whatever form it takes. ...

The question presented by this case is ... an extremely narrow one. It is whether New York oversteps the bounds when it finances a religious exercise.

What New York does on the opening of its public schools is what we do when we open court. Our Marshal has from the beginning announced the convening of the Court and then added "God save the United States and this honorable court." That utterance is a supplication, a prayer in which we, the judges, are free to join, but which we need not recite any more than the students need recite the New York prayer.

What New York does on the opening of its public schools is what each House of Congress does at the opening of each day's business. ...

In New York the teacher who leads in prayer is on the public payroll; and the time she takes seems minuscule as compared with the salaries appropriated by state legislatures and Congress for chaplains to conduct prayers in the legislative halls. Only a bare fraction of the teacher's time is given to reciting this short 22-word prayer, about the same amount of time that our Marshal spends announcing the opening of our sessions and offering a prayer for this Court. Yet for me the principle is the same, no matter how briefly the prayer is said, for in each of the instances given the person praying is a public official on the public payroll, performing a religious exercise in a governmental institution. It is said that the element of coercion is inherent in the giving of this prayer. If that is true here, it is also true of the prayer with which this Court is convened, and with those that open the Congress. Few adults, let alone children, would leave our courtroom or the Senate or the House while those prayers are being given. Every such audience is in a sense a "captive" audience.

At the same time I cannot say that to authorize this prayer is to establish a religion in the strictly historic meaning of those words. A religion is not established in the usual sense merely by letting those who chose to do so say the prayer that the public school teacher leads. Yet once government finances a religious exercise it inserts a divisive influence into our communities. The New York court said that the prayer given does not conform to all of the tenets of the Jewish, Unitarian, and Ethical Culture groups. One of petitioners is an agnostic. . . .

. . . The First Amendment leaves the Government in a position not of hostility to religion but of neutrality. The philosophy is that the atheist or agnostic — the nonbeliever — is entitled to go his own way. The philosophy is that if government interferes in matters spiritual, it will be a divisive force. The First Amendment teaches that a government neutral in the field of religion better serves all religious interests.

My problem today would be uncomplicated but for Everson v. Board of Education, 330 U. S. 1, which allowed taxpayers' money to be used to pay "the bus fares of parochial school pupils as a part of a general program under which" the fares of pupils attending public and other schools were also paid. The Everson case seems in retrospect to be out of line with the First Amendment. Its result is appealing, as it allows aid to be given to needy children. Yet by the same token, public funds could be used to satisfy other needs of children in parochial schools — lunches, books, and tuition being obvious examples. . . .

Mr. Justice Stewart, dissenting, said in part:

. . . The Court today decides that in permitting this brief nondenominational prayer the school board has violated the Constitution of the United States. I think this decision is wrong.

The Court does not hold, nor could it, that New York has interfered with the free exercise of anybody's religion. For the state courts have made clear that those who object to reciting the prayer must be entirely free of any compulsion to do so, including any "embarrassments and pressures." But the Court says that in permitting school children to say this simple prayer, the New York authorities have established "an official religion."

With all respect, I think the Court has misapplied a great constitutional principle. I cannot see how an "official religion" is established by letting those who want to say a prayer say it. On the contrary, I think that to deny the wish of these school children to join in reciting this prayer is to deny them the opportunity of sharing in the spiritual heritage of our Nation.

The Court's historical review of the quarrels over the Book of Common Prayer in England throws no light for me on the issue before us in this case. . . . Moreover, I think that the Court's task, in this as in all areas of constitutional adjudication, is not responsibly aided by the uncritical invocation of metaphors like the "wall of separation," a phrase nowhere to be found in the Constitution. What is relevant to the issue here is not the history of an established church in sixteenth century England or in eighteenth century America, but the history of the religious traditions of our people, reflected in countless practices of the institutions and officials of our government. . . . [Here follows a summary of instances in which God has been, or is, mentioned in official ceremonies or speeches, concluding with the third stanza of "The Star-Spangled Banner."]

I do not believe that this Court, or the Congress, or the President has by the actions and practices I have mentioned established an "official religion" in violation of the Constitution. And I do not believe the State of New York has done so in this case. What each has done has been to recognize and to follow the deeply entrenched and highly cherished spiritual traditions of our Nation — traditions which come down to us from those who almost two hundred years ago avowed their "firm reliance on the Protection of Divine Providence" when they proclaimed the freedom and independence of this brave new world.

I dissent.

5

Health, Welfare and Poverty

In the Social Security Act of 1935 the federal government undertook to establish the basic framework for welfare policies for all levels of government. The Social Security Act placed great reliance on *social insurance* to supplement, and it was hoped, eventually, to replace *public assistance*. The distinction between a social insurance program and a public assistance program is an important one which has upon occasion been a major political issue. If the beneficiaries of a government program are required to make contributions to it before claiming any of its benefits, and if they are entitled to the benefits regardless of their personal wealth, then the program is said to be financed under the *social insurance* principle. On the other hand, if a program is financed out of general tax revenues and if the recipients are required to show they are poor before claiming its benefits, then the program is said to be financed under the welfare or *public assistance* principle. The Social Security Administration in the Department of Health, Education, and Welfare administers the Federal Old Age, Survivors, and Disability Insurance Program (OASDI), popularly known as "social security," and the federal health insurance program, popularly known as "medicare." (See U.S. Department of Health, Education and Welfare, *Summary of Federal Welfare and Social Insurance Programs*) The Social Security and Medicare programs are the nation's basic method of providing income to the worker and his family when he retires, becomes disabled, or dies, and of providing payment for the costs of medical care for almost all persons aged 65 or over. Social Security and Medicare are based on the same principle as private insurance—the sharing of a risk of a loss of income—except that these are government programs which are compulsory for

249

all workers. Social Security and Medicare are not public charity, but instead, a way of compelling people to buy insurance against a loss of income or illness. They are wholly federal programs, but have an important indirect affect on state and local welfare programs by removing people in whole or in part from welfare rolls. By compelling people to provide against the possibility of their own poverty, Social Security and Medicare have doubtlessly reduced the welfare problem which state and local governments would otherwise face.

A second feature of the Social Security Act of 1935 was that it induced the states to enact unemployment compensation programs through the imposition of a payroll tax on all employers. A federal unemployment tax is levied on the payroll of all employers, but employers who pay in to state insurance programs which meet federal standards may use the state payments to offset most of their federal employment tax. In other words, the federal government threatens to undertake an unemployment compensation program and tax if the states do not do so themselves. This federal program has succeeded in inducing all fifty states to establish unemployment compensation programs. Federal standards are flexible and the states have considerable freedom in shaping their own unemployment programs.

The third major feature of the Social Security Act of 1935 was its welfare or public assistance provisions. The federal government through the Welfare Administration in the Department of Health, Education, and Welfare, provides matching funds to the states to provide assistance to five categories of needy persons — aged, blind, disabled, dependent children, and medically indigent. (See Summary of Federal Welfare and Social Insurance Programs) Federal contributions are in the forms of grants-in-aid to the states and are based in proportion to the money paid by the states to each needy recipient. Within broad outlines of federal policy, states retain considerable discretion in their welfare programs in terms of the amount of money appropriated, benefits to be paid to recipients, rules of eligibility, and administration of the program. The largest federally-aided public assistance program is the Aid to Families with Dependent Children or AFDC program. The medical assistance program has also become one of the largest federally-aided welfare programs. Begun in 1965, "Medicaid" offers federal grants-in-aid to the states to provide medical care to recipients of public assistance — the aged, blind, disabled, and families with dependent children.

It is important to note that the federal government aids only certain categories of welfare recipients — aged, blind, disabled, and dependent children. Aid to persons who do not fall in any of these categories but who for one reason or another are "needy," are referred to as "general assistance." General assistance programs are entirely state-financed and state-administered. Moreover, the states continue to maintain institutions for the care of those individuals who are so destitute or ill that money payments cannot meet their needs. These institutions include state orphanages, homes for the aged, and homes for the physically and mentally ill. There are, for the most part, state-financed as well as state-administered. If the social security and medicare insurance programs are discounted, the states spend almost twice as much for welfare and health as the national government.

America's problems with health and medicine are severe. Although the United States is the richest nation in the world, it ranks well down the list of nations in medical care provided the average citizen, number of physicians available, infant death rates, life span and other indicators of national health and medical care. The U.S. Public Health Service provides medical care and hospital facilities to many categories of federally aided patients; it enforces quarantine regulations, licenses biological products; engages in medical research; and most important of all, administers federal grant-in-aid programs to states and communities for the improvement of health and hospital services. Federal grants-in-aid are available to promote the construction of hospitals, nursing homes, diagnostic centers, rehabilitation centers, medical schools and other medical centers. Federal grants for hospital construction began in earnest with the passage of the Hill Burton Act in 1946.

Even before the Social Security Act of 1935 persons concerned with the state of the nation's health, particularly the medical care problems of the poor and the aged, had urged the federal government to undertake a broad national health care program. Proponents of the national health program generally shunned the English system of government owned and operated hospitals and government employed doctors, in favor of a compulsory medical *insurance* program closely linked with the Social Security Act. They envisioned a program in which all Americans would be required to insure themselves against the possibility of their medical indigency; the program would resemble private medical hospital insurance except that it would be compulsory. Individuals would continue to choose their own doctors but their bills would be paid in whole or in part through their government medical insurance policy. Opponents of a national health program, led by the prestigious American Medical Association representing the nation's physicians, strongly opposed a national health program linked to Social Security. They deemed it "socialized medicine" and argued that it would interfere with the "sacred doctor-patient" relationship. They argued that a large proportion of the population was already covered by voluntary private medical insurance plans and that charity hospitals and charitable services of doctors are readily available to the poor. In 1965, after more than 30 years of public debate, Congress finally enacted a comprehensive medical care act for persons over 65 which became known as Medicare. (See *Social Security Act Amendments of 1965 — Medicare*) Medicare includes 1) a compulsory health insurance plan covering hospital costs for the aged which is financed through payroll taxes collected under the social security system, and 2) a voluntary and supplemental medical program which will pay doctors' bills and additional medical expenses financed in part by contributions from the aged and in part by general tax revenues.

Despite 30 years of social insurance and federally aided public assistance programs, about 35 million people — $\frac{1}{5}$ of the nation's population — live in families whose income is less than $3000 per year. Why do so many people live in poverty in a wealthy society with a complex system of social insurance and public assistance? In an influential book, *The Other America,* Michael Harrington described the life of persons who are unable to participate in the nation's prosperity because of their old age, illiteracy, inadequate education, lack of job skills, poor health, inadequate motivation, racial discrimination or location in an economically depressed area. Unlike the mass poverty of the 1930's, today's poverty only affects a minority of Americans. More importantly, it does not disappear even when the economy expands and the nation is prosperous. Today's poverty cannot be dealt with merely by stimulating economic growth, because too many of the poor are unable to take advantage of prosperity. Welfare benefits do not cure poverty; they merely permit the poor to survive. Poverty and welfare assistance can become a way of life. Presidents Kennedy and Johnson became convinced that what are needed are not more welfare programs but programs that help the poor break the cycle of poverty.

Professor James E. Anderson describes the wide range of federal programs designed to strike at the causes of poverty in America. (See James E. Anderson, *Poverty, Unemployment and Economic Development*) He examines the nature of the poverty problem, the various anti-poverty strategies and some of the political problems of the war on poverty. He describes federal anti-poverty — the Economic Development Act, The Manpower Training and Development Act, the Appalachian Regional Development Act, and the Economic Opportunity Act.

The most important legislation in the "War on Poverty" is the *Economic Opportunity Act of 1964.* The Office of Economic Opportunity (OEO) was established with authority to support varied programs for combatting poverty at the community level. The objective of the program was to help the poor and unemployed become self-supporting and capable of earning an adequate income by bringing about changes in the individuals themselves and their environment. The strategy was one of "rehabilitation not relief." OEO was given no authority to make direct grants to the poor as relief or public assistance. All of its programs were aimed at curing the causes of poverty rather than alleviating its symptoms.

The heart of the Economic Opportunity Act was a grassroots "Community Action Program," an anti-poverty effort at the local level administered by public or private non-profit agencies with federal financial assistance. Communities were urged to form a "community action agency" composed of representatives of government, private organizations, and most importantly, the poor themselves. It was originally intended that OEO would support any reasonable anti-poverty program devised by the local community action agency. Projects might include (but were not limited to) literacy training, health services, homemaker services, legal aid for the poor, neighborhood service centers, manpower vocational training, childhood developmental activities. The Act also envisioned that a community action agency would help organize the poor so that they could become participating members of the community and avail themselves of many public programs which were already in existence. The most popular community action program was Operation Head Start, an attempt to give poor children special attention while still at the pre-school age and expose them to language arts, sounds, and sights that are ordinarily supplied in the homes of those with more economic and cultural benefits. The Economic Opportunity Act also provided for a Job Corps with opportunities for education, vocational training, and work experience in conservation camps for unemployable youth; a Neighborhood Youth Corps with vocational training and work experience for youth living at home; the Work-Study Program to help students from low income families to remain in school by giving them federally paid part-time employment; and Volunteers in Service to America or VISTA, a domestic service corps of voluntary workers for anti-poverty projects.

As an alternative policy to social insurance, public assistance, or economic opportunity programs, Professor Milton Friedman proposes a negative income tax which would provide a guaranteed minimum income for all Americans. (See Milton Friedman, *The Case for the Negative Income Tax*) He argues that a negative income tax should substitute for present welfare programs and accomplish the objectives of the programs more efficiently at a lower cost to the taxpayer and a sharp reduction in the bureaucracy. In opposition, Henry Hazlitt, an influential journalist and commentator, argues that a guaranteed minimum income would not only be economically but morally indefensible. (See Henry Hazlitt, *The*

Coming Crisis in Welfare) He believes that it would be intolerably expensive to the tax payers and it would destroy the incentives to work and
to produce in America. He also expresses the general concern among the
Americans that welfare costs are already too high, that welfare programs
can destroy the incentive to work, and that welfare programs do not
differentiate between those who are poor through no fault of their own
and those who are poor through their own delinquency.

Summary of Federal Welfare and Social Insurance Programs*

U.S. Department of Health, Education, and Welfare

SOCIAL SECURITY ADMINISTRATION

The Social Security Administration administers the Federal old-age, survivors, disability and health insurance programs — popularly known as Social Security and Medicare — which affect nearly every family in the Nation. They are the Nation's basic method of providing income to the worker and his family when he retires, becomes disabled, or dies — and payment for the costs of medical care for almost all persons aged 65 and over.

Retirement and Survivors Insurance

Background and Purpose

The national social security program, administered by the Federal Government, is the basic method in the United States for providing income to the worker and his family when he retires, becomes severely disabled, or dies, and for providing protection against the high cost of health care in old age.

Enacted against the background of depression in 1935, the Social Security Act has been amended many times; the latest and most extensive amendments being enacted in 1965 when health insurance for people 65 and over was added to existing programs.

---

*From U.S. Department of Health, Education, and Welfare, *Programs and Services* (Washington, D.C.: U.S. Government Printing Office, 1967).

How the Program Works

Under the Social Security Act, workers, their employers, and self-employed people pay contributions based on earnings during their working years, and when earnings stop or are reduced because of the worker's retirement or death, monthly cash benefits are paid to replace part of the earnings the family has lost. The contributions go into a trust fund maintained in the U.S. Treasury, and from this fund benefits and administrative expenses of the program are paid. Social security contributions are paid on the individual's first $6,600 in covered earnings in a year. In 1966, the contribution rate (for retirement, survivors, and disability insurance) is 3.85 percent for employees and their employers, and 5.80 percent for self-employed people. These rates are scheduled to rise gradually until they reach 4.85 percent each for employees and employers and 7 percent for self-employed people in 1973 and after. A portion of the contribution income (.70 percent of covered wages and .525 percent of self-employment income) is allocated to the disability trust fund to finance that program.

Eligibility

Benefits can be paid to workers, their dependents or survivors, if the worker has credit for a certain amount of work covered by social security, the exact amount depending on the year the worker reaches 65, if a man, 62 if a woman, or death if earlier. Benefits payable to a worker at 65 currently range from $44 a month to $135.90 a month, depending on his average earnings. Family payments range from $66 a month to $309.20 a month.

Workers and their wives or dependent husbands can receive benefits as early as 62, if they choose to accept a permanently reduced amount. They can receive unreduced benefits at 65. Children of retired or deceased workers can receive benefits until they reach age 18, or until they reach age 22 if they are full-time students. Children can receive benefits after 18 if they were disabled when they reached age 18 and continue to be disabled. Mothers caring for entitled children under 18 or for a child eligible because of his disability can receive benefits regardless of the mother's age. Widows can receive unreduced benfits at age 62, or permanently reduced benefits as early as age 60; dependent widowers can receive benefits at 62; and parents can receive benefits at 62. A lump-sum payment between $132 and $255 (depending on the worker's average earnings) can be made at the worker's death.

Disability Insurance

Background and Purpose

The basic social security law, passed in 1935, did not provide disability benefits. In 1954 the law was amended to provide that a worker's average earnings (and therefore, his future benefits) would not be reduced because of his low earnings during a "period of disability."

How the Program Works

As of April 1966, monthly cash disability benefits were being paid at the rate of $127 million a month to 1,848,881 persons, including 1,031,732 disabled workers, 205,253 wives and dependent husbands of disabled workers, and 611,896 children. The average monthly benefit amounts payable include: disabled workers, $97.91; wives and dependent husbands, $34.45; and children, $31.51.

Eligibility

A disabled worker can receive benefits only if he has a mental or physical impairment (1) which prevents him from doing any substantial gainful work and which is expected to last or has already lasted, for at least 12 months, or (2) is expected to result in death. Before a disabled worker can qualify for monthly benefits, he must have credit for a certain amount of work covered by social security. Generally he needs credit for at least 5 years of work in the 10-year period just before he becomes disabled. There are special provisions for the blind.

Health Insurance for People 65 and Over (Medicare)

Background and Purpose

The 1965 amendments to the social security law, signed into law by President Lyndon B. Johnson on July 30, 1965, provided health insurance for people 65 and over beginning July 1, 1966. There are two parts to the health insurance program — *hospital insurance* to help pay the cost of hospital care and certain kinds of follow-up treatment, and *voluntary medical insurance,* to help pay the cost of physicians' services and a number of other medical services and supplies not covered by hospital insurance.

Hospital insurance provides inpatient hospital services, skilled nursing care and other services in an extended care facility (benefits under this part are first available January 1, 1967); posthospital home health services; and outpatient hospital diagnostic services. This insurance is financed out of special contributions from earnings paid by employees, their employers, and self-employed people, all 3 groups paying the same rate, .35 percent of covered earnings ($6600 a year) for 1966. The rate is scheduled to rise gradually until it reaches .80 percent for 1987 and after.

Everyone who qualifies for social security monthly benefits (or railroad retirement benefits) automatically has hospital insurance protection at 65. It is not necessary to retire to have hospital insurance protection. In addition, nearly everyone who reaches 65 before 1968 can have hospital insurance protection even if he never worked under social security. People who reach 65 after 1967 will need credit for some work covered by social security to qualify for hospital insurance. The amount of credit needed will depend on the person's age, and will increase each year until the amount of work credit needed for hospital insurance will be the same as for cash social security benefits.

Medical insurance is voluntary, and people will have this protection only if they enroll. This part of the program is financed by monthly premiums shared equally by the people who choose this protection and the Federal Government. Initially the amount of the premium is $3 per month for the insured person and $3 for the Government.

Everyone who is 65 can sign up for medical insurance. Each person has a 7-month period to sign up, beginning 3 months before the month he reaches 65. There will also be general enrollment periods the last 3 months of each odd-numbered year. To start, the premium for each enrolled person is $3 a month, matched by the Government. No change can be made in the premium until 1968.

Hospital insurance pays the cost of covered services for the following care:

— Up to 60 days in a hospital (except for the first $40) and all but $10 a day for an additional 30 days during each spell of illness (a spell of illness begins the first day a person receives covered services in a hospital or extended care facility and ends after he has been out of a hospital or facility for 60 consecutive days).

— Up to 20 days in an extended care facility (a skilled nursing home or convalescent section of a hospital meeting the standards in the law) and all but $5 a day for an additional 80 days in each spell of illness.

— Up to 100 home health visits by nurses or other health personnel (not doctors) from a home health agency in the year after discharge from hospital or extended care facility.

— 80 percent of the cost of outpatient diagnostic tests by the same hospital except for the first $20 for each 20-day period of testing.

Medical insurance will pay 80 percent of the reasonable charges, after the first $50 in a calendar year, for the following services:

— Physicians' services, no matter where rendered in the U.S.

— Up to 100 home health visits by nurses and other health workers from a home health agency each year, with no need for prior hospitalization.

— A number of other medical and health services.

WELFARE ADMINISTRATION

Maternal and Child Health Services

Background

Under the provisions of the Social Security Act, maternal and child health programs conducted by State health agencies receive Federal grants administered by the Children's Bureau.

What the Program Does

States use Federal funds, together with State and local funds, to pay the costs of conducting maternity clinics; for home visits by public health nurses; for well-child and/or pediatric clinics; for health services to school-age children; for dental care; for hearing and vision programs and for immunizations.

Aid to Families with Dependent Children

Background

The Social Security Act provides for Federal grants to States for State administered or supervised programs of public assistance to impoverished families with children. The public assistance program for families is called Aid to Families with Dependent Children. Where the need is a result of unemployment, the average time the family receives assistance is nine months. Where the need is due to the incapacity, or loss, of the main wage-earner, the average time a family receives assistance is two to three years. At any given time, about one million families with more than three million children receive assistance. Payments total nearly $2 billion per year, 55 percent of which come from Federal funds.

How the Program is Administered

Each State, under Welfare Administration policies administered by the Bureau of Family Services, provides three main forms of assistance:

(1) *Cash payments* averaging $142 and ranging from $36 to $214 a month for a family of four for food, clothing, shelter, and other basics;

(2) *Medical care,* through payments directly to hospitals, physicians, dentists, druggists; etc. and

(3) *Social services,* such as counseling on family problems, help in finding better housing, referral to community resources, and homemaker services.

Aid to the Permanently and Totally Disabled

Background

The Social Security Act provides for grants for State-administered or supervised programs of public assistance to disabled adults. The persons served by this program of Aid to the Permanently and Totally Disabled are those not covered, (or not adequately covered) by disability benefits under the Social Security program. Many of them are so seriously handicapped that they cannot be trained for self-support through the vocational rehabilitation programs. About 600,000 disabled persons are served by this program at any given time. Their median age is 55 years. Payments total $580 million per year, half of which come from Federal funds.

How the Program is Administered

Each State, under Welfare Administration policies administered by the Bureau of Family Services, provides three main forms of assistance: (1) *Cash payments,* averaging $83 and ranging from $44 to $167 a month per person for food, clothing, shelter, and other basic needs; (2) *Medical care,* through payments directly to hospitals, nursing homes, physicians, dentists, druggists; etc. and (3) *Social services,* such as counseling on personal problems, help in finding better housing, referral to community resources, and homemaker services.

Old-Age Assistance

Background

The Social Security Act provides for Federal grants to States for State-administered or supervised programs of public assistance to the aged. The people served under the Old Age Assistance program, are those who were not covered by Social Security during their working years or whose Social Security benefits are not large enough to meet their basic needs. More than 2 million elderly people receive this assistance; their average age is 76 years. Payments total $2.1 billion annually, of which about two-thirds come from Federal funds.

How the Program is Administered

Each State, under Welfare Administration policies administered by the Bureau of Family Services, provides three main forms of assistance:
(1) *Cash payments,* averaging $80 and ranging from $40 to $114 a month per person for food, clothing, shelter, and other basic needs;
(2) *Medical care,* through payment directly to hospitals, nursing homes, physicians, dentists, druggists; etc. and
(3) *Social services,* such as counseling on personal problems, help in finding better housing, referral to community resources, and homemaker services.

Aid to the Blind

Public assistance payments to blind persons were first made under the Social Security Act in 1936. Today, about 95,000 people receive payments totaling approximately $100 million annually, of which about half comes from Federal funds. Due to advances in the prevention of blindness and in programs which enable the blind to become self-supporting, most of the blind who now receive public assistance are older people, their median age is 61 years.

Medical Assistance Program ("Medicaid")

Background

Authorized by 1965 amendments to Social Security Act (Title XIX) this program is designed to help more needy people get the health care they need but cannot afford. Need for the program is great: nearly half of the Armed Forces' draftees are not inducted because of medical deficiences; children in families with less than $2000 annual income see a physician only half as frequently as children in families with incomes over $7000; and as many as one-third of the children in some "Head Start" programs are not only in poor health, but are seriously ill.

By 1970, the Medical Assistance Program will replace all other State programs for providing medical services for public assistance recipients (see information on Medical Assistance for the Aged).

In fiscal year 1967, the cost of all medical care for public assistance recipients is expected to reach nearly $2 billion (Federal, State, and local), of which a significant proportion will be spent through the Title XIX program; the number of persons assisted could reach as high as 8 million.

How the Program is Administered

Each State operates its own program under Welfare Administration policies administered by the Bureau of Family Services. From the outset, States have to include all recipients of public assistance — the aged, blind, and disabled, and families with dependent children. States can extend coverage to comparable groups of medically needy people — those who have enough for daily living, but not medical expenses — and also to all children under 21. But by 1975, State Medical Assistance Programs have to cover all who cannot afford the care they need.

Medical Assistance for the Aged

Often called the "Kerr-Mills" program, this program was designed to serve people over 65 who had enough income to meet their daily living costs but could not afford the medical care they needed. The 1965 Social Security Amendments, which provided for hospital and voluntary medical insurance for persons over 65 under the Social Security program, reduced the need for this program. The need will be further reduced as States establish a single Medical Assistance Program (also provided for in the 1965 Amendments) to serve the medically indigent. In States that do not yet have the new Medical Assistance Program, the Medical Assistance for the Aged program is still needed to cover medical expenses including payments of deductibles and premiums which are not provided for by Medicare.

Social Security Act Amendments of 1965— Medicare

Congress and the President

TITLE I — HEALTH INSURANCE FOR THE AGED AND MEDICAL ASSISTANCE

SHORT TITLE

Sec. 100. This title may be cited as the "Health Insurance for the Aged Act".

• • •

Sec. 102. (a) The Social Security Act is amended by adding after title XVII the following new title:

"TITLE XVIII — HEALTH INSURANCE FOR THE AGED

"PROHIBITION AGAINST ANY FEDERAL INTERFERENCE

"Sec. 1801. Nothing in this title shall be construed to authorize any Federal officer or employee to exercise any supervision or control over the practice of medicine or the manner in which medical services are provided, or over the selection, tenure, or compensation of any officer or employee of any institution, agency, or person providing health services; or to exercise any supervision or control over the administration or operation of any such institution, agency, or person.

"FREE CHOICE BY PATIENT GUARANTEED

"Sec. 1802. Any individual entitled to insurance benefits under this title may obtain health services from any institution, agency, or person qualified to participate under this title if such institution, agency, or person undertakes to provide him such services

"OPTION TO INDIVIDUALS TO OBTAIN OTHER HEALTH INSURANCE
PROTECTION

"Sec. 1803. Nothing contained in this title shall be construed to preclude any State from providing, or any individual from purchasing or otherwise securing, protection against the cost of any health services.

"PART A — HOSPITAL INSURANCE BENEFITS FOR THE AGED
"DESCRIPTION OF PROGRAM

"Sec. 1811. The insurance program for which entitlement is established by section 226 provides basic protection against the costs of hospital and related post-hospital services in accordance with this part for individuals who are age 65 or over and are entitled to retirement benefits under title II of this Act or under the railroad retirement system.

"SCOPE OF BENEFITS

"Sec. 1812 (a) The benefits provided to an individual by the insurance program under this part shall consist of entitlement to have payment made on his behalf (subject to the provisions of this part) for —

"(1) inpatient hospital services for up to 90 days during any spell of illness;

"(2) post-hospital extended care services furnished to him during any spell of illness;

"(3) post-hospital home health services for up to 100 visits (during the one-year period described in section 1861 (n)) after the beginning of one spell of illness and before the beginning of the next; and

"(4) outpatient hospital diagnostic services.

"(b) Payment under this part for services furnished an individual during a spell of illness may not be made for —

"(1) inpatient hospital services furnished to him during such spell after such services have been furnished to him for 90 days during such spell;

"(2) post-hospital extended care services furnished to him during such spell after such services have been furnished to him for 100 days during such spell; or

"(3) inpatient psychiatric hospital services furnished to him after such services have been furnished to him for a total of 190 days during his lifetime.

•   •   •

"CONDITIONS OF AND LIMITATIONS ON PAYMENT FOR SERVICES
"Requirement of Requests and Certifications

"Sec. 1814. (a) Except as provided in subsection (d), payment for services furnished an individual may be made only to providers of services which are eligible therefor under section 1866 and only if —

"(1) written request, signed by such individual except in cases in which the Secretary finds it impracticable for the individual to do so, is filed for such payment in such form, in such manner, within such time, and by such person or persons as the Secretary may by regulation prescribe;

"(2) a physician certifies (and recertifies, where such services are furnished over a period of time, in such cases, with such frequency, and accompanied by such supporting material, appropriate to the case involved, as may be provided by regulations, except that the first of such recertifications shall be required in each case of inpatient hospital services not later than the 20th day of such period) that —

"(A) in the case of inpatient hospital services (other than inpatient psychiatric hospital services and inpatient tuberculosis hospital services), such services are or were required to be given on an inpatient basis for such individual's medical treatment, or that inpatient diagnostic study is or was medically required and such services are or were necessary for such purpose; . . .

"(B) in the case of post-hospital extended care services, such services are or were required to be given on an inpatient basis because the individual needs or needed skilled nursing care on a continuing basis for any of the conditions with respect to which he was receiving inpatient hospital services . . .

"(C) in the case of post-hospital home health services, such services are or were required because the individual is or was confined to his home (except when receiving items and services referred to in section 1861 (m) (7)) and needed skilled nursing care on an intermittent basis,

"Reasonable Cost of Services

"(b) The amount paid to any provider of services with respect to services for which payment may be made under this part shall, subject to the provisions of section 1813, be the reasonable cost of such services, as determined under section 1861 (v).

·   ·   ·

"FEDERAL HOSPITAL INSURANCE TRUST FUND

"Sec. 1817. (a) There is hereby created on the books of the Treasury of the United States a trust fund to be known as the 'Federal Hospital Insurance Trust Fund' (hereinafter in this section referred to as the 'Trust Fund'). The Trust Fund shall consist of such amounts as may be deposited in, or appropriated to, such fund as provided in this part. There are hereby appropriated to the Trust Fund for the fiscal year ending June 30, 1966, and for each fiscal year thereafter, out of any moneys in the Treasury not otherwise appropriated, amounts equivalent to 100 per centum of —

"(1) the taxes imposed by sections 3101(b) and 3111(b) of the Internal Revenue Code of 1954 with respect to wages reported to the Secretary of the Treasury or his delegate pursuant to subtitle F of such Code after December 31, 1965, as determined by the Secretary of the Treasury by applying the applicable rates of tax under such sections to such wages, which wages shall be certified by the Secretary of Health, Education, and Welfare on the basis of records of wages established and maintained by the Secretary of Health, Education, and Welfare in accordance with such reports;

"PART B — SUPPLEMENTARY MEDICAL INSURANCE BENEFITS FOR THE AGED

"ESTABLISHMENT OF SUPPLEMENTARY MEDICAL INSURANCE PROGRAM FOR THE AGED

"Sec. 1831. There is hereby established a voluntary insurance program to provide medical insurance benefits in accordance with the provisions of this part for individuals 65 years of age or over who elect to enroll under such program, to be financed from premium payments by enrollees together with contributions from funds appropriated by the Federal Government.

"SCOPE OF BENEFITS

"Sec. 1832. (a) The benefits provided to an individual by the insurance program established by this part shall consist of —

"(1) entitlement to have payment made to him or on his behalf (subject to the provisions of this part) for medical and other health services, except those described in paragraph (2) (B); and

"(2) entitlement to have payment made on his behalf (subject to the provisions of this part) for —

"(A) home health services for up to 100 visits during a calendar year; and

"(B) medical and other health services (other than physicians' services unless furnished by a resident or intern of a hospital) furnished by a provider of services or by others under arrangements with them made by a provider of services.

"(b) For definitions of 'spell of illness', 'medical and other health services', and other terms used in this part, see section 1861.

"PAYMENT OF BENEFITS

"Sec. 1833. (a) Subject to the succeeding provisions of this section, there shall be paid from the Federal Supplementary Medical Insurance

Trust Fund, in the case of each individual who is covered under the insurance program established by this part and incurs expenses for services with respect to which benefits are payable under this part, amounts equal to—

"(1) in the case of services described in section 1832(a) (1)— 80 percent of the reasonable charges for the services; except that an organization which provides medical and other health services (or arranges for this availability) on a prepayment basis may elect to be paid 80 percent of the reasonable cost of services for which payment may be made under this part on behalf of individuals enrolled in such organization in lieu of 80 percent of the reasonable charges for such services if the organization undertakes to charge such individuals no more than 20 percent of such reasonable cost plus any amounts payable by them as a result of subsection (b); and

"(2) in the case of services described in section 1832(a) (2)— 80 percent of the reasonable cost of the services (as determined under section 1861 (v)).

"(b) Before applying subsection (a) with respect to expenses incurred by an individual during any calendar year, the total amount of the expenses incurred by such individual during such year (which would, except for this subsection, constitute incurred expenses from which benefits payable under subsection (a) are determinable) shall be reduced by a deductible of $50;

"(c) Notwithstanding any other provision of this part, with respect to expenses incurred in any calendar year in connection with the treatment of mental, psychoneurotic, and personality disorders of an individual who is not an inpatient of a hospital at the time such expenses are incurred, there shall be considered as incurred expenses for purposes of subsections (a) and (b) only whichever of the following amounts is the smaller:

"(1) $312.50 or

"(2) 62½ percent of such expenses.

• • •

"ELIGIBLE INDIVIDUALS

"Sec. 1836. Every individual who—

"(1) has attained the age of 65, and

"(2) (A) is a resident of the United States, and is either (i) a citizen or (ii) an alien lawfully admitted for permanent residence who has resided in the United States continuously during the 5 years immediately preceding the month in which he applies for enrollment under this part, or (B) is entitled to hospital insurance benefits under part A, is eligible to enroll in the insurance program established by this part.

"ENROLLMENT PERIODS

"Sec. 1837. (a) An individual may enroll in the insurance program established by this part only in such manner and form as may be prescribed by regulations, and only during an enrollment period prescribed in or under this section.

"(b) (1) No individual may enroll for the first time under this part more than 3 years after the close of the first enrollment period during which he could have enrolled under this part.

"(2) An individual whose enrollment under this part has terminated may not enroll for the second time under this part unless he does so in a general enrollment period (as provided in subsection (e)) which begins within 3 years after the effective date of such termination. No individual may enroll under this part more than twice. . . .

"(b) An individual's coverage period shall continue until his enrollment has been terminated—

"(1) by the filing of notice, during a general enrollment period described in section 1837(e), that the individual no longer wishes to participate in the insurance program established by this part, or

"(2) for nonpayment of premiums.

•   •   •

"AMOUNTS OF PREMIUMS

"Sec. 1839. (a) The monthly premium of each individual enrolled under this part for each month before 1968 shall be $3.

"(b) (1) The monthly premium of each individual enrolled under this part for each month after 1967 shall be the amount determined under paragraph (2).

"(2) The Secretary shall, between July 1 and October 1 of 1967 and of each odd-numbered year thereafter, determine and promulgate the dollar amount which shall be applicable for premiums for months occurring in either of the two succeeding calendar years. Such dollar amount shall be such amount as the Secretary estimates to be necessary so that the aggregate premiums for such two succeeding calendar years will equal one-half of the total of the benefits and administrative costs which he estimates will be payable from the Federal Supplementary Medical Insurance Trust Fund for such two succeeding calendar years. In estimating aggregate benefits payable for any period, the Secretary shall include an appropriate amount for a contingency margin."

The Other America*

Michael Harrington

There are mighty historical and economic forces that keep the poor down; and there are human beings who help out in this grim business, many of them unwittingly. There are sociological and political reasons why poverty is not seen; and there are misconceptions and prejudices that literally blind the eyes. The latter must be understood if anyone is to make the necessary act of intellect and will so that the poor can be noticed.

Here is the most familiar version of social blindness: "The poor are that way because they are afraid of work. And anyway they all have big cars. If they were like me (or my father or my grandfather), they could pay their own way. But they prefer to live on the dole and cheat the taxpayers."

This theory, usually thought of as a virtuous and moral statement, is one of the means of making it impossible for the poor ever to pay their way. There are, one must assume, citizens of the other America who choose impoverishment out of fear of work (though, writing it down, I really do not believe it). But the real explanation of why the poor are where they are is that they made the mistake of being born to the wrong parents, in the wrong section of the country, in the wrong industry, or in the wrong racial or ethnic group. Once that mistake has been made, they could have been paragons of will and morality, but most of them would never even have had a chance to get out of the other America.

---

*Excerpted from Michael Harrington, *The Other America* (New York: The Macmillan Company, 1963) with the permission of the publisher.

269

There are two important ways of saying this: The poor are caught in a vicious circle; or, The poor live in a culture of poverty.

In a sense, one might define the contemporary poor in the United States as those who, for reasons beyond their control, cannot help themselves. All the most decisive factors making for opportunity and advance are against them. They are born going downward, and most of them stay down. They are victims whose lives are endlessly blown round and round the other America.

Here is one of the most familiar forms of the vicious circle of poverty. The poor get sick more than anyone else in the society. That is because they live in slums, jammed together under unhygienic conditions; they have inadequate diets, and cannot get decent medical care. When they become sick, they are sick longer than any other group in the society. Because they are sick more often and longer than anyone else, they lose wages and work, and find it difficult to hold a steady job. And because of this, they cannot pay for good housing, for a nutritious diet, for doctors. At any given point in the circle, particularly when there is a major illness, their prospect is to move to an even lower level and to begin the cycle, round and round, toward even more suffering.

This is only one example of the vicious circle. Each group in the other America has its own particular version of the experience, and these will be detailed throughout this book. But the pattern, whatever its variations, is basic to the other America.

The individual cannot usually break out of this vicious circle. Neither can the group, for it lacks the social energy and political strength to turn its misery into a cause. Only the larger society, with its help and resources, can really make it possible for these people to help themselves. Yet those who could make the difference too often refuse to act because of their ignorant, smug moralisms. They view the effects of poverty — above all, the warping of the will and spirit that is a consequence of being poor—as choices. Understanding the vicious circle is an important step in breaking down this prejudice.

There is an even richer way of describing this same, general idea: Poverty in the United States is a culture, an institution, a way of life.

There is a famous anecdote about Ernest Hemingway and F. Scott Fitzgerald. Fitzgerald is reported to have remarked to Hemingway, "The rich are different." And Hemingway replied, "Yes, they have money." Fitzgerald had much the better of the exchange. He understood that being rich was not a simple fact, like a large bank account, but a way of looking at reality, a series of attitudes, a special type of life. If this is true of the rich, it is ten times truer of the poor. Everything about them, from the condition of their teeth to the way in which they love, is suffused and permeated by the fact of their poverty. And this is sometimes a hard idea for a Hemingway-like middle-class America to comprehend.

The family structure of the poor, for instance, is different from that of the rest of the society. There are more homes without a father, there is less marriage, more early pregnancy and, if Kinsey's statistical findings can be used, markedly different attitudes toward sex. As a result of this, to take but one consequence of the fact, hundreds of thousands, and perhaps millions, of children in the other America never know stability and "normal" affection.

Or perhaps the policeman is an even better example. For the middle class, the police protect property, give directions, and help old ladies. For the urban poor, the police are those who arrest you. In almost any slum there is a vast conspiracy against the forces of law and order. If someone approaches asking for a person, no one there will have heard of him, even if he lives next door. The outsider is "cop," bill collector, investigator (and, in the Negro ghetto, most dramatically, he is "the Man").

While writing this book, I was arrested for participation in a civil-rights demonstration. A brief experience of a night in a cell made an abstraction personal and immediate: the city jail is one of the basic institutions of the other America. Almost everyone whom I encountered in the "tank" was poor: skid-row whites, Negroes, Puerto Ricans. Their poverty was an incitement to arrest in the first place. (A policeman will be much more careful with a well-dressed, obviously educated man who might have political connections than he will with someone who is poor.) They did not have money for bail or for lawyers. And, perhaps most important, they waited their arraignment with stolidity, in a mood of passive acceptance. They expected the worst, and they probably got it.

There is, in short, a language of the poor, a psychology of the poor, a world view of the poor. To be impoverished is to be an internal alien, to grow up in a culture that is radically different from the one that dominates the society. The poor can be described statistically; they can be analyzed as a group. But they need a novelist as well as a sociologist if we are to see them. They need an American Dickens to record the smell and texture and quality of their lives. The cycles and trends, the massive forces, must be seen as affecting persons who talk and think differently.

I am not that novelist. Yet in this book I have attempted to describe the faces behind the statistics, to tell a little of the "thickness" of personal life in the other America. Of necessity, I have begun with large groups: the dispossessed workers, the minorities, the farm poor, and the aged. Then, there are three cases of less massive types of poverty, including the only single humorous component in the other America. And finally, there are the slums, and the psychology of the poor.

Throughout, I work on an assumption that cannot be proved by Government figures or even documented by impressions of the other America. It is an ethical proposition, and it can be simply stated: In a nation with a technology that could provide every citizen with a decent life, it is an outrage and a scandal that there should be such social misery. Only if one begins with this assumption is it possible to pierce through the invisibility of 40,000,000 to 50,000,000 human beings and to see the other America. We must perceive passionately, if this blindness is to be lifted from us. A fact can be rationalized and explained away; an indignity cannot. . . .

What shall we tell the American poor, once we have seen them? Shall we say to them that they are better off than the Indian poor, the Italian poor, the Russian poor? That is one answer, but it is heartless. I should put it another way. I want to tell every well-fed and optimistic American that it is intolerable that so many millions should be maimed in body and in spirit when it is not necessary that they should be. My standard of comparison is not how much worse things used to be. It is how much better they could be if only we were stirred.

If this research makes it clear that a basic attack upon poverty is necessary, it also suggests the kind of program the nation needs.

First and foremost, any attempt to abolish poverty in the United States must seek to destroy the pessimism and fatalism that flourish in the other America. In part, this can be done by offering real opportunities to these people, by changing the social reality that gives rise to their sense of hopelessness. But beyond that (these fears of the poor have a life of their own and are not simply rooted in analyses of employment chances), there should be a spirit, an élan, that communicates itself to the entire society.

If the nation comes into the other America grudgingly, with the mentality of an administrator, and says, "All right, we'll help you people," then there will be gains, but they will be kept to the minimum; a dollar spent will return a dollar. But if there is an attitude that society is gaining by eradicating poverty, if there is a positive attempt to bring these millions of the poor to the point where they can make their contribution to the United States, that will make a huge difference. The spirit of a campaign against poverty does not cost a single cent. It is a matter of vision, of sensitivity.

Let me give an example to make this point palpable. During the Montgomery bus boycott, there was only one aim in the Negro community of that city: to integrate the buses. There were no speeches on crime or juvenile delinquency. And yet it is reported that the crime rate among Negroes in Montgomery declined. Thousands of people had been given a sense of purpose, of their own worth and dignity. On their own, and without any special urging, they began to change their personal lives; they became a different people. If the same élan could invade the other America, there would be similar results.

Second, this book is based upon the proposition that poverty forms a culture, an interdependent system. In case after case, it has been documented that one cannot deal with the various components of poverty in isolation, changing this or that condition but leaving the basic structure intact. Consequently, a campaign against the misery of the poor should be comprehensive. It should think, not in terms of this or that aspect of poverty, but along the lines of establishing new communities, of substituting a human environment for the inhuman one that now exists.

Here, housing is probably the basic point of departure. If there were the funds and imagination for a campaign to end slums in the United States, most of the other steps needed to deal with poverty could be integrated with it. The vision should be the one described in the previous chapter: the political, economic, and social integration of the poor with the rest of the society. The second nation in our midst, the other America, must be brought into the Union.

In order to do this, there is a need for planning. It is literally incredible that this nation knows so much about poverty, that it has made so many inventories of misery, and that it has done so little. The material for a comprehensive program is already available. It exists in congressional reports and the statistics of Government agencies. What is needed is that the society make use of its knowledge in a rational and systematic way. As this book is being written, there are proposals for a Department of Urban Affairs in the Cabinet (and it will probably be a reality by the time these words are published). Such an agency could be the coordinating center for a crusade against the other America. In any case, if there is not planning, any attempt to deal with the problem of poverty will fail, at least in part.

Then there are some relatively simple things that could be done, involving the expansion of existing institutions and programs. Every American should be brought under the coverage of social security, and the payments should be enough to support a dignified old age. The principle already exists. Now it must be extended to those who need help the most. The same is true with minimum wage. The spectacle of excluding the most desperate from coverage must come to an end. If it did, there would be a giant step toward the elimination of poverty itself.

In every subculture of the other America, sickness and disease are the most important agencies of continuing misery. The New York *Times* publishes a list of the "neediest cases" each Christmas. In 1960 the descriptions of personal tragedy that ran along with this appeal involved in the majority of cases the want of those who had been struck down by illness. If there were adequate medical care, this charity would be unnecessary.

Today the debate on medical care centers on the aged. And indeed, these are the people who are in the most desperate straits. Yet it would be an error of the first magnitude to think that society's responsibility begins with those sixty-five years of age. As has been pointed out several times, the ills of the elderly are often the inheritance of the earlier years. A comprehensive medical program guaranteeing decent care to every American, would actually reduce the cost of caring for the aged. That, of course, is only the hardheaded argument for such an approach. More importantly, such a program would make possible a human kind of existence for everyone in the society.

And finally, it must be remembered that none of these objectives can be accomplished if racial prejudice is to continue in the United States. Negroes and other minorities constitute only 25 per cent of the poor, yet their degradation is an important element in maintaining the entire culture of poverty. As long as there is a reservoir of cheap Negro labor, there is a means of keeping the poor whites down. In this sense, civil-rights legislation is an absolutely essential component in any campaign to end poverty in the United States.

In short, the welfare provisions of American society that now help the upper two-thirds must be extended to the poor. This can be done if the other Americans are motivated to take advantage of the oppor-tunities before them, if they are invited into the society. It can be done if there is a comprehensive program that attacks the culture of poverty at every one of its strong points.

But who will carry out this campaign?

There is only one institution in the society capable of acting to abolish poverty. That is the Federal Government. In saying this, I do not rejoice, for centralization can lead to an impersonal and bureaucratic program, one that will be lacking in the very human quality so essential in an approach to the poor. In saying this, I am only recording the facts of political and social life in the United States.

The cities are not now capable of dealing with poverty, and each day they become even less capable. As the middle class flees the central urban area, as various industries decentralize, the tax base of the Ameri-can metropolis shrinks. At the same time, the social and economic problems with which the city must deal are on the rise. Thus, there is not a major city in the United States that is today capable of attacking poverty on its own. On the contrary, the high cost of poverty is dragging the cities down.

The state governments in this country have a political peculiarity that renders them incapable of dealing with the problem of poverty. They are, for the most part, dominated by conservative rural elements. In every state with a big industrial population, the gerrymander has given the forces of rural conservatism two or three votes per person. So it is that the state legislatures usually take more money out of the problem areas than they put back into them. So it is that state governments are notoriously weighted in the direction of caution, pinchpenny economics, and indifference to the plight of the urban millions.

The various private agencies of the society simply do not have the funds to deal with the other America. And even the "fringe benefits" negotiated by unions do not really get to the heart of the problem. In the first place, they extend to organized workers in a strong bargaining position, not to the poor. And second, they are inadequate even to the needs of those who are covered.

It is a noble sentiment to argue that private moral responsibility expressing itself through charitable contributions should be the main instrument of attacking poverty. The only problem is that such an approach does not work.

So, by process of elimination, there is no place to look except toward the Federal Government. And indeed, even if there were alternate choices, Washington would have to play an important role, if only because of the need for a comprehensive program and for national planning. But in any case there is no argument, for there is only one realistic possibility: only the Federal Government has the power to abolish poverty.

In saying this, it is not necessary to advocate complete central control of such a campaign. Far from it. Washington is essential in a double sense: as a source of the considerable funds needed to mount a campaign against the other America, and as a place for coordination, for planning, and the establishment of national standards. The actual implementation of a program to abolish poverty can be carried out through myriad institutions, and the closer they are to the specific local area, the better the results. There are, as has been pointed out already, housing administrators, welfare workers, and city planners with dedication and vision. They are working on the local level, and their main frustration is the lack of funds. They could be trusted actually to carry through on a national program. What they lack now is money and the support of the American people.

Poverty, Unemployment, and Economic Development*

James E. Anderson

The focus of this paper is on the antipoverty campaign of the 1960's. After an examination of the nature of the poverty problem, consideration will be given to antipoverty strategies, the use of the curative strategy, and some of the political aspects of the war on poverty. In all, the discussion is intended to provide a broad perspective on the national government's war on poverty and the development of antipoverty policy in the United States.

I.

It is quite apparent that many people have not shared in the general economic growth and prosperity which have characterized the United States since World War II. If one third of the nation is no longer "ill-housed, ill-clad, and ill-nourished," as Franklin Roosevelt stated in 1937, it is nonetheless true that many millions of people are still afflicted by poverty. Much debate has occurred in the past few years over what constitutes poverty and how many people are poverty stricken.[1] Among the questions in this "debate" are: Is poverty definable as a family income of less than $2,000 annually, or $3,000, or $4,000, or what? Should the poverty-line be higher for urban dwellers than for rural residents, for those under 65 years of age than for those over 65? Do the poor number 30 million, or 35 million, or 40 to 50 million, or how many? Is poverty only a "state of mind," a situation in which some think they are poor because they have less income or material possessions than others? Or is poverty merely a statistical phenomenon with, say, the lowest fifth of the income pyramid being considered poverty-stricken?

---

*Reprinted from *Journal of Politics,* Vol. 29 (February, 1967), 70-93, with the permission of the publisher.

There is much room for controversy and statistical manipulation in answering such questions. In some studies the conclusions reached appear to be skewed by ideological considerations, with the conservative defining poverty more narrowly and consequently finding both less poverty and less need for governmental action than the liberal. To wit: A study prepared for the conservative American Enterprise Institute used an income standard ranging from $1,259 to $3,155 for nonfarm households whose size ran from 2 to 7 or more.[2] On this basis, one tenth of the nation's household units (around 17 million people) were in the poverty category. In contrast, Leon Keyserling and the liberal Conference on Economic Progress,[3] using an annual income of less than $4,000 before taxes as the poverty standard for a household, held that in 1960 almost 10.5 million families were living in poverty (or 23 per cent of all families). Some 4 million unattached individuals with annual incomes below $2,000 were also designated as poverty-stricken.

A third study, which seems soundly conceived and ideologically "neutral" and which yields data similar to that used by many public officials, was prepared by the Department of Health, Education, and Welfare using the Census Bureau's sample statistics for 1963.[4] Annual incomes necessary to maintain nutritional adequacy were calculated for different types of families classified by farm and non-farm residence, age and sex of head, and number of children. Using these criteria, a flexible poverty standard was developed, which ranged from $880 annually for a single female aged 65 or over living on a farm to $5,100 for an urban family of 7 or more headed by a male under 65 years of age. On the basis of the flexible standard it was calculated that, in 1963, 34.5 million persons (or 18 per cent of the population) were in families with incomes

---

[1]Important statistical examinations of poverty include: Robert J. Lampman, *The Low Income Population and Economic Growth,* Study Paper No. 12, prepared for the Joint Economic Committee, 86th Cong., 1st Sess., 1959; Conference on Economic Progress, *Poverty and Deprivation in the U. S.* (Washington: Conference on Economic Progress, 1962); Michael Harrington, *The Other America* (New York: The Macmillan Company, 1963), pp. 187-203; Herman P. Miller, *Rich Man, Poor Man* (New York: Thomas Y. Crowell Company, 1964); Council of Economic Advisers, *Annual Report, 1964* (Washington: Government Printing Office, 1964), pp. 55-84; Mollie Orshansky, "Counting the Poor: Another Look at the Poverty Profile," *Social Security Bulletin,* XXVIII (January, 1965), pp. 3-29; and James N. Morgan, *et al., Income and Welfare in the United States* (New York: McGraw-Hill Book Company, 1962).

[2]Rose D. Friedman, *Poverty: Definition and Perspective* (Washington: American Enterprise Institute, 1965).

[3]Conference on Economic Progress, *op. cit.,* pp. 19-23.

[4]Orshansky, *op. cit.* See also the discussion by Herman P. Miller, "Changes in the Number and Composition of the Poor," in Margaret S. Gordon, ed., *Poverty in America* (San Francisco: Chandler Publishing Company, 1965), pp. 81-101.

insufficient to purchase a minimally nutritional budget. This supports the frequently heard statement that one-fifth of the nation still lives in poverty. It might be noted that the much criticized Council of Economic Advisers study, which used a fixed $3,000 standard, yielded similar results: 35 million people living in poverty.[5]

To end this phase of the discussion, the disagreement over the nature and precise amount of poverty should not be permitted to obscure the "problem of poverty." As one close student of poverty has stated:

> it would be a mistake to conclude from this [lack of agreement] that there is no evidence to demonstrate that tens of millions of people have incomes that are insufficient to provide minimum levels of living for this society. Most Americans would agree that a family is poor if its income is below the amount needed to qualify for public assistance. Many would also count as poor some families with incomes well above this level. The 1960 Census data show that *at least 23.5 million people—one person out of eight in the United States—lives in a family with an annual income that is less than the amount needed to qualify for aid under the public assistance laws of each state.*[6]

In addition to aggregate statistics, an understanding of the poverty problem also requires discussion of the causes of poverty and the various groups included among the poor. This will focus attention on the problems facing policy-makers. In his *The Affluent Society,* Galbraith makes a useful distinction between case poverty and insular poverty.[7] Case poverty relates to the personal qualities or characteristics of the affected persons. Given our present socio-economic system, some persons and families have been unable to participate satisfactorily in the nation's general prosperity because of such limiting factors as old age, inadequate education or illiteracy, lack of needed job skills, poor health, inadequate motivation, and racial discrimination, regardless of where they live — rural and small town areas, urban areas, or metropolitan areas.

Insular poverty appears in what are called "pockets of poverty" or depressed areas, as in West Virginia, much of the rest of Appalachia, and many parts of rural America.[8] Such areas are characterized by higher

---

[5] *Annual Report, 1964, op. cit.*

[6] Herman P. Miller, "Statistics and Reality," *The New Leader,* XLVII (March 30, 1964), p. 18. (His emphasis).

[7] John Kenneth Galbraith, *The Affluent Society* (Boston: Houghton Mifflin Company, 1958), ch. 23.

[8] For examples of the latter, see *Incomes of Rural Families in Northeast Texas,* Bulletin 940 (College Station, Texas: Texas Agricultural Experiment Station, 1959); and *Incomes, Resources, and Adjustment Potential of Rural Families in the Clay-Hills Area of Mississippi,* AEc. M. R. No. 29 (State College, Mississippi: Mississippi Agricultural Experiment Station, 1960).

and more persistent rates of unemployment and underemployment and larger proportions of low income persons than in the country as a whole. The *proximate* cause of this condition is the lack of adequate employment opportunities for the current population. Some of the people in areas will also suffer from lack of education, poor health, inadequate job skills, etc., because the two types of poverty are not mutually exclusive. The lack of job opportunities, in turn, may be the product of a number of factors, including technological change, depletion of national resources, shifts in consumer demand, and the movement of industries to other areas.[9]

Both insular and case poverty are usually viewed as "structural" in nature, resulting from individual shortcomings and from temporary or limited imperfections in the economic system. They differ from the "mass poverty" of the 1930's, which was a product of general economic decline and which was markedly reduced by the revival of the economy in the early 1940's. Poverty of the structural sort does not automatically disappear as the economy expands and general affluence increases.

A close relationship exists between unemployment, low wages, and poverty. Many of the poor are unemployed or are completely outside of the labor force. But poverty is also the result of under-employment and employment at low wages, as in the cases of migratory workers and unskilled domestic workers. Thus a Department of Labor study on the employment status of families with incomes below $3,000 in 1963 reported that 30 per cent of the poor families were headed by persons who held jobs throughout the year. Another 14 per cent were headed by persons who worked at fulltime jobs for part of the year but who were never counted as unemployed because they moved into or out of the labor force. The heads of 16 per cent of the families experienced unemployment. Finally, 39 per cent of the families were headed by persons who were completely outside the labor force in 1963. Included in this last category are many aged or retired workers, the disabled, the dispirited, and women with child-rearing responsibilities. While most of the persons in the first three categories listed would benefit from economic growth and increased job opportunities, most of those in the last category would not because they are largely outside of the productive economy.

Although poverty exists in all regions of the country, in both rural and urban areas, and among all elements of the population, its incidence is heaviest among the following: nonwhites (Negroes, Puerto Ricans, and Mexican-Americans); the aged; families headed by females; families

---

[9]Sidney C. Sufrin and Marion A. Buck, *What Price Progress?: A Study in Chronic Unemployment* (Chicago: Rand McNally and Co., 1965), esp. chs. 1, 2.

without a breadwinner; the unemployed; families headed by farmers and unskilled laborers; families headed by very young persons or persons with less than an eighth-grade education; very large families; and unrelated individuals living alone.[10] As this listing and the previous discussion should indicate, the problems of poverty and unemployment are multiple rather than monolithic in nature. Consequently there must be a variety of policy responses, geared to particular forms of causation and need, if these problems are to be dealt with effectively.

II.

There are a number of general strategies which the government may use in dealing with the problems of poverty and unemployment. The major ones are discussed in this section.

Aggregationist strategy. Involving the use of broad fiscal and monetary policies to maintain a high level of economic growth and employment, this strategy is based on the assumption that much unemployment and poverty are the product of inadequate demand for labor and insufficient employment opportunities. According to the Council of Economic Advisers:

> The maintenance of high employment—a labor market in which the demand for workers is strong relative to the supply—is a powerful force for the reduction of poverty. In a strong labor market there are new and better opportunities for the unemployed, the partially employed, and the low paid. Employers have greater incentive to seek and to train workers when their own markets are large and growing. . . . To fight poverty in a slack economy with excess employment is to tie one hand behind our backs.[11]

The national government is generally committed to the aggregationist strategy by the Employment Act of 1946, which pledges the government to use its various programs and policies to maintain "maximum employment, production, and purchasing power." The 1964 cut in the income tax rates and the 1965 excise tax reduction both were in line with the aggregationist strategy.

Alleviative strategy. This is the oldest strategy for aiding the poor and the unemployed. Emphasis here is on relieving or easing the hardships and misery associated with poverty and unemployment by providing financial or material aid to the distressed on either a short-term or long-

---

[10]See Oscar Ornati, *Poverty Amid Affluence* (New York: The Twentieth Century Fund, 1966), *passim.*

[11]*Annual Report, 1964, op. cit.,* pp. 73-74. Cf. Hyman P. Minsky, "The Role of Employment Policy," in Gordon, *op. cit,* pp. 175-200.

term basis. Alleviative programs have become more numerous and more generous in recent decades as the views that poverty and unemployment are often neither individually caused nor controllable and that public aid is necessary to protect the dignity of the individual have gained increased acceptance. Programs which are primarily alleviative include unemployment compensation, public assistance, medicare, general relief, and work relief. All involve some sort of "transfer payment."

Curative strategy. In contrast to the alleviative strategy, the curative strategy stresses efforts to help the poor and unemployed become self-supporting and more capable of earning adequate incomes by bringing about changes in either the individuals themselves or in their environment. This strategy is expressed in the slogan "Rehabilitation not relief" and, to use President Johnson's somewhat inelegant terminology, the desire "to make taxpayers out of taxeaters." Programs in accord with the curative approach include area and regional development, work training, vocational education, job experience and literacy training, and much of the community action program under the Economic Opportunity Act, Curative programs are largely a development of the past decade.

Equal opportunity strategy. The focus here is on eliminating discrimination against Negroes, Indians, Mexican-Americans, and Puerto Ricans and providing them with equal educational and employment opportunities. Almost half of all nonwhite Americans are poor, and discrimination — in employment, wages, education, housing — is an important cause of poverty here.[12] Negroes, for example, are often hired last, paid less, and fired first. Illustrative of this strategy is the Civil Rights Act of 1964, which bans discrimination on the basis of race, color, religion, national origin or sex by many employers and labor unions. The Act also prohibits discrimination under any program or activity — in education, welfare, manpower training, etc. — receiving federal financial assistance. The civil rights movement, by broadening its concern to economic as well as political discrimination, has stimulated increased use of this strategy.

It is now generally agreed that the aggregationist strategy alone is inadequate to eliminate poverty and unemployment. It is, however, a necessary condition for their elimination; and the other antipoverty strategies, to be most effective, presuppose a high level of employment. But even if increased job opportunities are available many will not be able to take advantage of them because of inadequate job skills, low education, old age, discrimination, geographical location, and the like. Curative and equal opportunity programs should help many of these to become self-

---

[12]See *e.g.,* Alan Batchelder, "Poverty: The Special Case of the Negro," *American Economic Review,* LV (May, 1965), pp. 530-540.

supporting or to enlarge their incomes. But others will still be unable to provide for themselves — such as many of the aged and females with large families — and here alleviative programs come in. In short, the various strategies set forth are interdependent; and the national government is currently utilizing all of them in the war on poverty.

The strategies under consideration here can obviously be implemented by a variety of means or tactics, which can usefully be divided into economic and welfare categories.[13] Economic programs are tied into the regular economic system and either make previous employment a requirement for eligibility for benefits or they relate benefits to the economic value of the work done by the recipients. Illustrative of economic programs are unemployment compensation, public works, area and regional development, and most job training programs. Welfare programs provide benefits not directly related to previous employment or value of work done. When a means test is used to determine eligibility for benefits they are often designated as relief programs. The Job Corps is somewhere in between welfare and relief — no means test is used (in a strict sense) but the cost of providing jobs considerably exceeds the value of the work done. Examples of welfare programs include old age assistance, aid to families with dependent children, literacy training and work experience programs, and general relief.

The selection and use of antipoverty instruments are affected by existing policy objectives and traditional national values and beliefs. Our society has customarily preferred the use of economic programs over welfare programs as the former are generally in accord with beliefs and values relating to individualism, self-reliance, and personal dignity. Conversely, welfare-type programs, especially those of the relief sort, are often stigmatized as "doles," "handouts," and, less harshly, charity. Programs of cash subsidies to the poor, such as the negative income tax[14] and the Guaranteed Annual Income,[15] run counter to our ideas about the relation of work and income and thus far have had little support. Only recently has there been a great deal of pressure for major increases in

[13]Joseph M. Becker, William Haber, and Sar A. Levitan, *Programs to Aid the Unemployed in the 1960's* (Kalamazoo, Mich.: The W. E. Upjohn Institute for Employment Research, 1965), pp. 4-8.

[14]Under the negative income tax proposal, grants would be paid to poor families whose incomes were too low to permit them to take full advantage of the exemptions and deductions to which they are entitled under existing tax laws. See Robert J. Lampman, "Approaches To the Reduction of Poverty," *American Economic Review*, LV (May, 1965), pp. 526-527.

[15]Michael D. Reagan, "For a Guaranteed Income," *The New York Times Magazine*, June 7, 1964, pp. 20 ff. A group of publicists, economists, and educators, calling itself the Ad Hoc Committee on the Triple Revolution, has proposed that every family be guaranteed an income of $3,000 a year.

benefits under such programs as old age assistance and Old Age, Survivors and Disability Insurance, which would do much to eliminate poverty.

To the extent that antipoverty programs appear to strengthen or expand the economy, the likelihood of favorable attitudes toward them is increased. Education and training programs gain considerable support as "investments in human capital" designed to increase opportunity for the poor and help assimilate them into the "mainstream" of American economic life. Programs which appear to encourage economic growth are also apt to gain favor while those that seem to reduce the incentive to work can be expected to encounter substantial resistance.

III.

In this section some of the curative legislation enacted in the war on poverty will be surveyed in roughly chronological order to convey a notion of its evolution. The discussion will illustrate the multifaceted nature of the war on poverty and the essentially pragmatic approach following in waging the war. Some particular political problems and controversies will be noted, although discussion of the "macro-politics" of poverty is reserved for the next section.[16]

Aid to Depressed Areas

Efforts to provide national aid to localities affected by chronic and heavy unemployment began in 1955 at the instigation of Senator Paul Douglas (Dem., Ill.).[17] Bill providing aid programs for such areas were passed by the Democratic-controlled Congress in 1958 and 1960 but both were vetoed by President Eisenhower, partly because he believed they involved too much national participation in local affairs and authorized larger expenditures than were necessary. Aid to depressed areas became a major issue in the 1960 Presidential campaign and President Kennedy took office pledged to assist such areas.

As adopted, the Area Redevelopment Act of 1961 established a four-year program of assistance for depressed areas—those in which the unemployment rate was above average and persistent — under the supervision of an Area Redevelopment Administration located in the Depart-

---

[16]On the concept of macropolitics, see Emmette S. Redford, *American Government and the Economy* (New York: The Macmillan Company, 1965), pp. 58-60.

[17]Roger H. Davidson, *The Depressed Areas Controversy: A Study in the Politics of American Business* (New York: Columbia University, unpublished doctoral dissertation, 1963), provides an excellent account of the enactment of the Area Redevelopment Act.

ment of Commerce. The broad objective of the Act was to reduce unemployment by encouraging the formation of new businesses or the expansion of existing businesses in depressed areas, thereby increasing the available number of jobs (i.e., by bringing jobs to the workers). To this end, the Area Redevelopment Administration was empowered to provide: long-term loans at low interest to attract or expand businesses in depressed areas; loans and grants to local governments for public facilities needed to attract businesses; technical assistance to help communities formulate economic development programs; and worker retraining programs. A total expenditure of $394 million over a four year period was authorized. The Act essentially followed a "trickle-down" approach to poverty and unemployment, with most of the direct benefits going to businesses and not to unemployed workers.

From its inception the ARA led a rather hectic life and was a continual center of controversy. Contributing to its difficulties were administrative problems, *e.g.,* many of its activities required cooperation from other government agencies; Congressional impatience for results; dissatisfaction with some of the ARA projects, such as a $1.8 million loan to help construct a motor hotel in Detroit; Republican charges that the program was used in 1962 as a "pork barrel" to help re-elect Democrats; and continued opposition by business groups, such as the Chamber of Commerce, who believed the program was unneeded.[18] A Presidential request for continuation and expansion of the ARA program was rejected by the House in 1963 after favorable Senate action. The extension bill was not brought to a vote in 1964 because the Administration feared unfavorable House action and, consequently, the Area Redevelopment Act expired in July, 1965.

In the spring of 1965 President Johnson requested the Congress to replace the ARA with an expanded and broadened federal depressed areas program. According to the President individual counties and communities often were not capable of economic growth, Therefore, a broader areal approach to economic development than the locality-oriented aid policy of the ARA was necessary.

The Economic Development Act, passed by Congress in August, 1965, provides for a five-year, $3.25 billion program of grants and loans for public works, development facilities, technical assistance, and other activities intended to help economically depressed areas and to stimulate planning by them for economic development. Most of these

---

[18]Julius Duscha, "The Depressed Areas," *The Progressive,* XXVII (September, 1963), pp. 29-32; and Conley H. Dillon, *The Area Redevelopment Administration: New Patterns in Developmental Administration* (College Park: University of Maryland, Bureau of Governmental Research, 1964).

funds are slated for public works projects, such as water systems, waste treatment plants, industrial streets and roads, airports, and other facilities which would directly or indirectly improve employment opportunities in depressed areas or, in the words of the Act, "primarily benefit the long-term unemployed and members of low-income families or otherwise substantially further the objectives of the Economic Opportunity Act of 1964. . . ." The Economic Development Act also provides for the creation of multi-county and multi-state development areas and districts designed to broaden the scope and the effectiveness of developmental activity. Another part of the law authorizes the establishment of multi-state regional planning commissions, similar to the Appalachian Regional Commission, to plan for the economic development of other regions of the country.

The Economic Development Act is really an amalgamation of features of three previous pieces of legislation: The Area Redevelopment Act, the Accelerated Public Works Act of 1962, and the Appalachian Regional Development Act of 1965. Since it is not mentioned elsewhere, a comment on the 1962 Act is in order here. This Act, which was extremely popular with Congressmen and local public officials (one Washington official termed it an "instantaneous success"), authorized a one-year appropriation of $900 million for public works projects to stimulate employment in depressed areas. Most of this money ($850 million) was actually appropriated, with the federal government paying up to 75 per cent of the cost of many local public works projects.

Whether the Economic Development program will be more effective than the Area Redevelopment Act is a matter for future determination. However, it does have a new name and a new administrative agency (the Economic Development Administration), greater funds, and a broader policy orientation.

Manpower Development

Another curative approach to the problem of poverty and unemployment is illustrated by the Manpower Training and Development Act of 1962. This legislation attempts to attack poverty and unemployment wherever they may exist, in depressed areas or elsewhere, by helping workers who are unemployed or under-employed to acquire new job skills or to improve and update their existing skills. The 1962 statute, as amended, authorizes a program of loans and grants for worker training programs operated by state agencies and private institutions and for on-the-job training programs conducted by employers, state agencies, labor unions, and other groups. Subsistence payments are made to many workers while they are undergoing training. Basic literacy training may be provided for workers who need it in order to benefit from vocational training.

Although the MTDA program originally was scheduled to expire in 1965, it has proven to be quite popular with both parties in Congress. Legislation expanding and extending the programs was enacted in 1963 and again in 1965, with the 1965 legislation passing by votes of 76-9 in the Senate and 392-0 in the House.[19] The manpower training program has enjoyed general support from both business and labor groups although the Chamber of Commerce has suggested, but less than vigorously, that the matter should be left to the states. Liberals and conservatives alike prefer for people to support themselves and not be dependent on public funds. Both have shown considerable interest in retraining programs.

Two facets of the manpower training program merit mention here because of their political interest. Under the terms of the original Manpower Development and Training Act, after two years most of the training programs were to be financed by the national and state governments on a fifty-fifty basis. The states, however, showed a considerable lack of enthusiasm for this eventuality. During the first year of the program all of the states except Louisiana undertook training activities but only four states authorized the matching of funds. A survey of state directors of vocational education by the U. S. Office of Education revealed that directors in eighteen states felt that their states would not participate unless the 100 per cent federal financing was continued after June, 1964. Another thirteen directors expressed "serious doubts" about participation on a matching basis by their states while only eight directors said there was "reasonable certainty" that their state would participate on a matching basis.[20] The subsequent amendments to the Act continued full federal financing through June, 1966. After that time the *local* governments involved in training programs will be required to pay 10 per cent of in-school training costs. (This can be in kind, as in making buildings and equipment available.) The new matching requirement would not appear to be a serious impediment to state-local participation. The whole chain of events lends support to the contention that effective antipoverty activity requires national action.

Second, although manpower training has received general support, there has been opposition to particular aspects of the program, including the relocation of retrained workers. Provisions permitting partial payment of the costs of worker relocation were deleted from the 1962

---

[19]*Congressional Quarterly Almanac,* XXI (1965), pp. 810-815.
[20]*Congressional Quarterly Almanac* XIX (1963), p. 525.

legislation and the earlier Area Redevelopment Act, while the 1963 MTDA amendments permitted only some experimental relocation projects. The opposition in Congress to subsidized relocation of workers has been bipartisan and has come from both liberals and conservatives. Spokesmen from depressed areas have feared loss of population (and voters) and wastage of community resources. Sentiment and the belief people should have a right to live wherever they want have also been factors. Thus Senator Dirksen contended, in opposing aid for relocation, that just "as the Indians were reluctant to leave the graves of their ancestors . . . and rather than leave [their ancestral lands] were willing to fight it out," so later Americans were reluctant to move from their homes.[21]

The Economic Opportunity Act of 1964

This is an omnibus piece of legislation which seeks to deal directly with poverty, with both the causes and symptoms of poverty. Its various sections provide for programs geared to the needs and situations of different groups in the population. Much stress is placed on local initiative and leadership and voluntary participation, on giving "new opportunities to those who want to help themselves or their communities."[22]

A primary focus of the Economic Opportunity Act is on youth and breaking the "cycle of poverty," whereby poverty in one generation of a family often begets poverty in the next generation and so on. To realize this goal a number of programs are created, especially for youth between the ages of 16 and 21. First, the Job Corps is designed to provide education, vocational training, and work experience in rural conservation camps and residential training centers to increase the employability of youth and prepare them for "responsible citizenship." Second, under the Neighborhood Youth Corps program vocational training and work experience (and income) are provided for youth while living at home. Third, the work-study program helps students from low-income families remain in college by giving them financial assistance in the form of part-time employment. Only the first of these programs is handled solely by the national government. The latter two involve state or local initiative with the Office of Economic Opportunity, which administers the statute, paying up to 90 percent of the cost.

---

[21]Senate Committee on Banking and Currency, *Hearings on Area Redevelopment Act*, 86th Cong., 1st Sess., 1959, p. 63.

[22]House Committee on Education and Labor, *Hearings on the Economic Opportunity Act of 1964*. 88th Cong., 2nd Sess., 1964, Vol. 1, pp. 20-22.

Another major section of the Economic Opportunity Act authorizes federal financial assistance for "grass roots" community action programs carried on by public or private nonprofit agencies. This program is intended to encourage the development of comprehensive and coordinated community efforts to help the poor become self-sufficient. Projects in these local antipoverty programs may include literacy training, health services, homemaker services, legal aid for the poor, or early childhood development activities. In the last category is Project Head Start, designed to provide "cultural enrichment" for pre-school poor children. (It is now a permanent feature of the war on poverty because, President Johnson has stated, it has been "battle-tested" and "proven worthy.") Up to 90 per cent of the cost of community action programs is paid by the national government.

Other antipoverty activities authorized by the 1964 law include: grants and loans to low income rural families to help them enlarge their income-earning capacity; loans to small businessmen, especially as these may contribute to work-training and job opportunities for low income persons; financial assistance to the states for special adult literacy programs; grants, loans, and loan guarantees to assist state and local governments in aiding migratory farm workers, grants to encourage the states to set up programs to help unemployed fathers and other members of needy families with children gain work experience and job training. The statute also established a domestic service corps— Volunteers in Service to America, or VISTA—to recruit and train workers for service in state and local antipoverty projects, slum areas, Indian reservations, hospitals, and the like.

The Economic Opportunity Act thus provides a quite varied, and highly experimental, set of techniques for combating poverty. Whether they represent the best set of means, or even an adequate set, for eliminating poverty is an open question. The Act, however, does represent a distinct departure from previous legislation, which can be regarded as both more conservative and less direct in its thrust (e.g., ARA and the "trickle-down" approach; MTDA and the focus on training and unemployment). This, plus the vigor with which it has been implemented, explains why the 1964 law has generated considerably more political controversy than its predecessors. Conflict has developed over such matters as the location of Job Corps camps; the rate of pay for Neighborhood Youth Corps workers; the role of the poor in community action programs; the question of who should control local antipoverty programs; and the use of the governors' power to veto community action and Job Corps projects in their states.[23] A program as comprehensive as that of EOA is bound to challenge a variety of particular interests.

The Regional Approach: Appalachia and Beyond

The Appalachian Regional Development Act of 1965 manifests yet another curative approach to the poverty problem—the use of federal funds to promote the social and economic uplift of an entire geographical region and its inhabitants. The name Appalachia denotes an eleven state region centered around the Appalachian Mountains, extending from northern Pennsylvania to mid-Alabama, and including all of West Virginia and part of Pennsylvania, Ohio, Maryland, Kentucky, Tennessee, North Carolina, South Carolina, Georgia, and Alabama. The region has been described as a "victim of both geography and automation, [lagging] . . . behind the nation as a whole in employment, education, health facilities, housing, and virtually every other yardstick used to measure a healthy economy."[24] It is generally conceded to be the largest economically depressed area in the nation, although it does contain such "pockets of prosperity" as Charleston, West Virginia.

The Appalachian Act authorizes the expenditure of $1.1 billion in federal funds to encourage the economic development of the region. Around four-fifths of these funds will be used over a five year period for the construction of major regional development highways and local access roads. The national government will pay up to 70 per cent of a project's cost with the remainder coming from the states involved. The emphasis on roadbuilding resulted from the facts that adequate highways are lacking in many parts of the region and that the governors, senators, and congressmen in the Appalachian states wanted roads to be given priority. Better road systems were believed necessary to open up the region and to stimulate new traffic.

The remainder of the funds provided by the Act are, it should be noted, for a two year period. They will go for such purposes as health facilities, vocational schools, land improvement programs, reclamation of mining areas, and the development of timber and water resources. A program for pastureland improvement was dropped from the Act because of the opposition of western cattle interests.

The various programs under the Appalachian Act will be carried out by the appropriate national and state agencies, such as the Bureau of

---

[23]"Shriver and the War on Poverty," *Newsweek,* LXVI (September 13, 1965), pp. 22-30; and William F. Haddad, "Mr. Shriver and the Savage Politics of Poverty," *Harper's,* CCXXXI (December, 1965), pp. 43-50, are especially useful. A running account of the political conflicts generated by the Economic Opportunity Act programs can be found in *The New York Times.*

[24]Marjorie Hunter in *The New York Times,* February 7, 1965, p. F5.

Public Roads and the state highway departments. The entire program, however, is supervised and coordinated by the Appalachian Regional Commission, which is comprised of the governor from each state in the region (or a representative selected by him) and a federal representative chosen by the President. Subject to a veto by the federal representative, specific projects are initiated by the states and undertaken with the approval of a majority of the state members on the Commission. This arrangement, it is hoped, will result in greater local participation and in better adaptation of the program to local conditions.[25]

The Appalachia program is geared to the economic needs of the region, not to particular localities, and is intended to increase economic growth and employment opportunities in the region as a whole. The funds expended will not go directly to needy people nor, necessarily, to the most depressed towns and countries. There is no "means test," such as a level of unemployment, to determine eligibility for aid as in the Area Redevelopment Act and the Economic Development Act. The focus is on those areas and communities within the region which have the most potential for economic growth, thus substituting a region-wide approach for the "scattershot" approach manifested in other programs, such as the ARA. As John L. Sweeney, federal co-chairman of the Appalachian Regional Commission, has stated: "Most programs of economic help in the past have been based on the theory that a man has a right to a job where he lives and that government should bring him that job. The Appalachia approach is that a man has a right to a job, but it is reasonable to expect him to be willing to commute to it or move to it if necessary."[26] This new theory is made manifest by the emphasis on roadbuilding and assistance to "economic growth centers."

The Appalachia program, in short, stresses economic development and is a long range program whose impact on poverty will be largely indirect. It is not "people centered," as one ARC official put it, in contrast to the Office of Economic Opportunity which "concentrates on helping people, through training education, and the like, to live a middle-class existence."[27] It will probably be a decade or more before the "real results" of the Appalachia program are apparent.

One immediate "by-product" should be remarked here, however. The Appalachia program stirred the interest of congressmen from other areas in regional programs. To get them to support the Appalachia plan the administration agreed to consider regional development programs

---

[25]Jerald Ter Horst, "No More Pork Barrel: The Appalachia Approach," *The Reporter,* XXXII (March 11, 1965), pp. 27-29.

[26]Quoted in *ibid.,* pp. 28-29.

[27]Interview with the writer, September, 1965.

for other parts of the country. Consequently, Title V of the Economic Development Act authorizes the establishment of "regional action planning commissions." More specifically, the Secretary of Commerce, with the approval of the states involved, can create economic development regions in areas which have "lagged behind the whole nation in economic development." Each such region will have a federal-state commission which will develop recommendations for new programs of economic development. A number of new regions have been proposed, including the Ozarks, the New England States, the Upper Great Lakes area, and the Great Plains.[28]

Although the new regional approach to economic development is still in the experimental and planning stage, it has proved to have considerable political appeal. What impact it will have on the impoverished is uncertain at this point. It should be borne in mind, however, that while economic growth and prosperity are necessary conditions for an effective war on poverty, by themselves they may have little direct impact in reducing poverty.

IV.

This section will deal with two aspects of the macropolitics of poverty. First, why is there now so much concern about poverty? Poverty has been around for a long time without arousing such involvement as we now witness. For example, little attention apparently was paid to Henry George when he wrote about *Progress and Poverty* in the late nineteenth century. Why, then, in an era of general prosperity and a time when poverty is considerably down from past levels, has the world's wealthiest nation chosen to launch a "war on poverty?" Why has poverty become a political issue of major national concern?

Second, beyond the concern about poverty, how can one explain the enactment of this substantial body of antipoverty legislation? What are some of the operative factors? Here we are confronted with an apparent paradox. The poor themselves, as Michael Harrington has contended, lack political power:

> the poor are politically invisible. It is one of the cruelest ironies of social life in advanced countries that the dispossessed at the bottom of society are unable to speak for themselves. The people of the other America do not, by far and large, belong to unions, to fraternal organizations, or to political parties. They are without lobbies of their own; they put forward no legislative program. As a group, they are atomized. They have no face; they have no voice.[29]

---

[28]Cf. Don Oberdorfer, "The Proliferating Appalachias," *The Reporter,* XXXIII (September 9, 1965), pp. 22-27.

[29]Michael Harrington, *The Other America: Poverty In the United States* (New York: The Macmillan Company, 1963), p. 14.

In a political system in which action is often a response to strong organized demands by those affected, how does one account for the antipoverty legislation enacted?

Why has poverty become a major political issue? Several factors can be mentioned. First, both Presidents Kennedy and Johnson have used the presidency to inform the population of the existence of poverty in prosperity, the evils of poverty, and the need for governmental action to eliminate it. Motivated at least partly by the desire to be recognized as great presidents, which requires important accomplishments, they identified poverty as a major subject for national action. Second, the writings of various scholars and publicists have helped focus attention on poverty and inform people about its causes and consequences. The books by Galbraith, Harrington, Caudill, and Myrdal come readily to mind.[30] Third, the "race problem" and the civil rights movement have also been contributory. The incidence of poverty is much higher among nonwhite than white groups and, in many large cities, a majority of those seeking public assistance are Negro. The Negro leadership is focusing attention on the poor and the civil rights movement is demonstrating much concern for jobs as well as legal rights. Herman P. Miller makes the point:

> The rural poor, the aged poor, and even the poor hillbillies in Appalachia and the Ozarks could not arouse the nation to their urgent needs. They continued to suffer indignities of body, mind, and spirit year after year in quiet desperation while they lived in hovels and their children were poorly educated. Action came only recently. It followed a prolonged period of marches, sit-ins, and other forms of protest by the Negro community. There is no reason to believe that the war on poverty and these protest activities are unrelated.[31]

Fourth, the belief that poverty is a significant cause of crime and delinquency and growing concern about mounting welfare expenditures are also worth mention. In his opening statement on the Economic Opportunity Act, Representative Landrum (Dem., Ga.), who served as its floor manager in the House, advocated its enactment partly as a means of lowering welfare costs and of reducing crime and delinquency.[32]

---

[30]Galbraith, *The Affluent Society, op. cit.;* Harrington, *The Other America, op. cit.;* Harry Caudill, *Night Comes to the Cumberlands* (Boston: Little, Brown and Company, 1963); and Gunnar Myrdal, *Challenge to Affluence* (New York: Pantheon Books, Inc., 1963).

[31]"Poverty and the Negro," in Leo Fishman, ed., *Poverty Amid Affluence* (New Haven: Yale University Press, 1966), p. 104. Cf. Nathan Glazer, "A Sociologist's View of Poverty," in Gordon, *op. cit.,* p. 20. Many of the Washington officials interviewed by me spontaneously mentioned the civil rights movement as a major cause of antipoverty action.

Fifth, the paradox of poverty in the midst of affluence is both ugly and disturbing to many who are not poor, while many of the poor are less than quiescent in their poorness. An attitudinal change has occurred. As one commentator states:

> A revolution of expectations has taken place in this country as well as abroad. There is now a conviction that everyone has the right to share in the good things of life. . . . The legacy of poverty awaiting many of our children is the same as that handed down to their parents, but in a time when the boon of prosperity is more general than the taste of poverty is more bitter.[33]

Finally, many people have become convinced that the problem of poverty requires political action for its solution, the play of automatic economic processes being viewed as insufficient. Moreover, success in the war on poverty is perceived as quite probable by many persons. Success, or the good prospect thereof, in dealing with a problem is often highly productive of both concern and action on the part of reformers. Also contributory may be the apparent fact that many Americans are presently more "cause-minded" than they were a decade ago.

To turn now to our second question, in contrast to most important economic legislation, the various antipoverty acts discussed in the preceding section did not originate in the demands of strong, organized interest groups. Rather, these programs have been developed largely within the executive branch and Congress. (The principal exception is the Appalachia Act, which grew out of efforts by the region's governors to solve common problems.) Thus, the Area Redevelopment Act was started on its way by Senator Paul Douglas and was a product of the interest in depressed areas which he developed while campaigning for re-election in Southern Illinois. Again, it is said that the idea for the Economic Opportunity Act originated with Robert Lampman, then associated with the Council of Economic Advisers. The idea was taken up and promoted by Walter Heller, Chairman of the CEA, partly as a way of doing something directly for the poor and partly as a way of stimulating the economy through spending. Given tentative approval by President Kennedy just prior to his assassination, the proposal was quickly and strongly accepted by President Johnson within a few days after his accession to the presidency.[34]

Organized group support and opposition to proposals for anti-poverty legislation have formed after their development. A wide variety of labor,

---

[32]*Congressional Record,* CX, pp. 18208-18209 (August 5, 1964).
[33]Orshansky, *op. cit.,* p. 3.
[34]The comments on the Economic Opportunity Act are based on a report in *Newsweek, op. cit.,* and an interview with Sar A. Levitan.

liberal, welfare, civil rights, civic, and professional organizations have supported the various antipoverty laws. Among the groups supporting the Economic Opportunity Act were the AFL-CIO, National Grange, National Farmers Union, National Urban League, National Council of Churches, National Education Association, General Federation of Women's Clubs, American Friends Service Committee, and the National Association of Counties. The group support for antipoverty legislation is somewhat generalized in nature, lacking the intensity which characterizes, say, the AFL-CIO's support of legislation to repeal the right-to-work laws and the National Right To Work Committee's opposition to repeal. Although the broad group support would seem to make legislative and executive support of such legislation "good politics," it does not appear to be a really compelling force.

Opposition to the antipoverty programs has come primarily from the Chamber of Commerce, the National Association of Manufacturers, and the American Farm Bureau Federation. (Some right-wing ideological groups are also in opposition.) These three groups have not been vigorously opposed to such legislation as it does not significantly impinge on their interests. It does run counter to the conservative ideology they espouse and they oppose it as unnecessary, or as improperly and hastily prepared, or as not really a proper activity for the national government. Then, too, the position of the opponents has been weakened by the fact that one appears to be in favor of poverty when he opposes legislation put forward as necessary to eliminate it.

The contention here is that, given a climate of opinion favorable to antipoverty action and generalized favorable group support, a political situation emerged in which Presidential action has been a (if not *the*) crucial factor in securing antipoverty legislation. Presidents Kennedy and Johnson have been strong supporters of anti-poverty legislation and this, within the context of a "permissive" political environment, appears to have been the determining factor. It seems quite doubtful, for example, that either the Economic Opportunity Act or the Appalachian Regional Development Act would have been passed without President Johnson's strong endorsement and support. Conversely, area redevelopment legislation was not enacted during President Eisenhower's administration because of his opposition in the form of vetoes.

Most of the major antipoverty legislation has come during the Johnson administration. While Johnson has been a vigorous and skillful legislative leader, he appears to have benefited initially from the favorable climate of opinion and congressional cooperation resulting from the Kennedy assassination. Following his sweeping victory in the 1964 presidential election, he regarded himself as having a clear mandate to implement his proposals for the "Great Society," which include the elimination of poverty. Moreover, the 1964 Goldwater debacle served to emasculate the opposition to Johnson's program within Congress and apparently to demoralize it elsewhere. These broad developments have obviously favored the antipoverty campaign.

Within Congress the various antipoverty bills have been passed by substantial majorities, especially in the Senate. The one exception is the House defeat for the ARA in 1963. This appears to have been caused by such factors as poor leadership and the loss of some southern votes because of the reaction to President Kennedy's 1963 civil rights proposals. Northern Democrats have been almost unanimous in their support of the various statutes, with somewhere between half and two-thirds of the Southern Democrats also in favor. A scattering of Republicans from Eastern and urban states have been among the supporters. In opposition have been two-thirds or more of the Republicans, a third to a half of the Southern Democrats, and an occasional Northern Democrat. However, large majorities of both parties have supported manpower training and vocational education legislation. The vote on the Vocational Education Act was 378 to 21 in the House and 80 to 4 in the Senate.

What has caused the broad pressure group and Congressional support for antipoverty legislation? Material or economic interests are certainly one factor affecting group and Congressional action here, but they are clearly not the only factor. Most of the members of Congress voting for the Appalachia Act did not come from states and districts directly benefiting from it and, it can be added, some who came from such states and districts voted against the Act. While some were perhaps swayed into support by the promise of regional programs of their own, these were few in number.[35]

Partly affiliation and ideological orientation have undoubtedly been vital in shaping the positions of many persons. The large proportion of Congressional Democrats voting for the legislation is what one would expect because of the party's general orientation in favor of liberal-labor legislation. Further the supporters of antipoverty legislation articulate, and presumably are influenced by, a liberal ideology of action which combines humanitarianism and practical economic considerations with a belief in the need for national action. Antipoverty legislation is generally advocated as necessary to alleviate and prevent misery and to improve the economic opportunities and quality of life of the poor. At the same time, it is frequently advanced as a way of aiding economic

---

[35]Oberdofer, *op. cit.,* p. 26.

growth and reducing welfare costs. This thought-pattern is illustrated by the following statement: "We pay twice for poverty; once in the production lost in wasted human potential, and again in the resources devoted to coping with poverty's social by-products. Humanity compels our action, but it is sound economics as well."[36]

The opposition to antipoverty legislation also can be explained in a variety of ways: material interests; southern concern about segregation; partisan politics; and ideology. Much of the opposition has been within the framework of a conservative political-economic philosophy which includes hostility toward big government and national action (which are often treated as synonyms), a preference for localized solutions to economic problems, and considerable faith in the operation of the market place.

In short, the argument here is that the enactment of antipoverty legislation can not be satisfactorily explained in terms of pressure group politics and material interests. These have had greater impact on the details of legislation than on its broad outline and final adoption. A favorable climate of opinion, strong executive support, party affiliation, and ideology are more useful variables in accounting for the war on poverty programs.

V.

Whether the various antipoverty programs established to date will eliminate poverty is problematical. So indeed is the question whether poverty can ever be entirely eliminated. Taken together, however, the various measures are a decisive rejection of economic Darwinism and indifference regarding poverty and a strong commitment to positive action. This seems likely to continue for the next few years because there appears to be no room for poverty in President Johnson's vision of the Great Society, although financial pressures generated by the war in Vietnam could lead to some reduction in effort.

The various antipoverty measures also represent a practical and experimental approach to the problem of poverty. A variety of strategies and tactics are currently being employed. Whether one considers the total effort too great or too small, it certainly can not be characterized as doctrinaire. While the search for a national antipoverty policy is still underway, some of its general features are beginning to emerge: continuing encouragement of general economic growth and prosperity; greater attention on curative approaches, with alleviative activity reserved

---

[36]Council of Economic Advisers, *Annual Report, 1964*, p. 56.

for such groups as the aged and the unemployable; and the maintenance of the equal employment opportunities.

In contrast to the welfare programs established by the Social Security Act of 1936, which seek to provide the individual with a floor of security in the form of minimal maintenance, the main thrust of the current antipoverty campaign is to increase the economic opportunities open to the poor and their abilities to maintain themselves. To this end efforts are being made both to increase the number of available jobs in the economy and to equip the poor through education, job training, work experience, and the like, to secure jobs or better paying jobs.

But if the antipoverty programs represent a departure in strategy and technique from the New Deal approach to welfare and poverty, they are nonetheless essentially based on the "traditional" view of poverty—that is, poverty is individual and peripheral in nature and is not, therefore, the consequence of major structural weaknesses in the American socio-economic system. Consequently, the antipoverty programs do not generally involve major institutional change (at least in the short run) and no vested interests have been sharply threatened or disturbed by them. Groups whose interests are divergent in other areas—labor policy, taxation—have found it relatively easy to unite in general support of antipoverty programs. Viewed from the perspective of institutional change, the antipoverty legislation has been essentially conservative in orientation, which has undoubtedly eased its enactment.

Economic Opportunity Act of 1964

Congress and the President

AN ACT

To mobilize the human and financial resources of the Nation to combat poverty in the United States.

Be it enacted by the Senate and House of Representatives of the United States of America in Congress assembled, That this Act may be cited as the "Economic Opportunity Act of 1964".

FINDINGS AND DECLARATION OF PURPOSE

Sec. 2. Although the economic well-being and prosperity of the United States have progressed to a level surpassing any achieved in world history, and although these benefits are widely shared throughout the Nation, poverty continues to be the lot of a substantial number of our people. The United States can achieve its full economic and social potential as a nation only if every individual has the opportunity to contribute to the full extent of his capabilities and to participate in the workings of our society. It is, therefore, the policy of the United States to eliminate the paradox of poverty in the midst of plenty in this Nation by opening to everyone the opportunity for education and training, the opportunity to work, and the opportunity to live in decency and dignity. It is the purpose of this Act to strengthen, supplement, and coordinate efforts in furtherance of that policy.

TITLE I—YOUTH PROGRAMS

Part A—Job Corps

STATEMENT OF PURPOSE

Sec. 101. The purpose of this part is to prepare for the responsibilities of citizenship and to increase the employability of young men and young women aged sixteen through twenty-one by providing them in rural and urban residential centers with education, vocational training, useful work experience, including work directed toward the conservation of natural resources, and other appropriate activities.

ESTABLISHMENT OF JOB CORPS

Sec. 102. In order to carry out the purposes of this part, there is hereby established within the Office of Economic Opportunity (hereinafter referred to as the "Office"), established by title VI, a Job Corps (hereinafter referred to as the "Corps").

JOBS CORPS PROGRAM

Sec. 103. The Director of the Office (hereinafter referred to as the "Director") is authorized to—

(a) enter into agreements with any Federal, State, or local agency or private organization for the establishment and operation, in rural and urban areas, of conservation camps and training centers and for the provision of such facilities and services as in his judgment are needed to carry out the purposes of this part, including but not limited to agreements with agencies charged with the responsibility of conserving, developing, and managing the public natural resources of the Nation and of developing, managing, and protecting public recreational areas, whereby the enrollees of the Corps may be utilized by such agencies in carrying out, under the immediate supervision of such agencies, programs planned and designed by such agencies to fulfill such responsibility, and including agreements for a botanical survey program involving surveys and maps of existing vegetation and investigations of the plants, soils, and environments of natural and disturbed plant communities;

(b) arrange for the provision of education and vocational training of enrollees in the Corps: *Provided,* That where practicable, such programs may be provided through local public educational agencies or by private vocational educational institutions or technical institutes where such institutions or institutes can provide substantially equivalent training with reduced Federal expenditures;

(c) provide or arrange for the provision of programs of useful work experience and other appropriate activities for enrollees;

(d) establish standards of safety and health for enrollees, and furnish or arrange for the furnishing of health services; and

(e) prescribe such rules and regulations and make such arrangements as he deems necessary to provide for the selection of enrollees and to govern their conduct after enrollment, including appropriate regulations as to the circumstances under which enrollment may be terminated.

COMPOSITION OF THE CORPS

Sec. 104. (a) The Corps shall be composed of young men and young women who are permanent residents of the United States, who have attained age sixteen but have not attained age twenty-two at the time of enrollment, and who meet the standards for enrollment prescribed by the Director. Participation in the Corps shall not relieve any enrollee of obligations under the Universal Military Training and Service Act (50 U.S.C. App. 451 et seq.).

(b) In order to enroll as a member of the Corps, an individual must agree to comply with rules and regulations promulgated by the Director for the government of the Corps.

(c) The total enrollment of any individual in the Corps shall not exceed two years except as the Director may determine in special cases.

(d) Each enrollee must execute and file with the Director an affidavit that he does not believe in, and is not a member of and does not support any organization that believes in or teaches, the overthrow of the United States Government by force or violence or by any illegal or unconstitutional methods, and (2) each enrollee must take and subscribe to an oath or affirmation in the following form: "I do solemnly swear (or affirm) that I will bear true faith and allegiance to the United States of America and will support and defend the Constitution and laws of the United States against all its enemies foreign and domestic."

* * *

PART B—WORK-TRAINING PROGRAMS

STATEMENT OF PURPOSE

Sec. 111. The purpose of this part is to provide useful work experience opportunities for unemployed young men and young women, through participation in State and community work-training programs, so that their employability may be increased or their education resumed or continued and so that public agencies and private nonprofit organizations (other than political parties) will be enabled to carry out programs which will permit or contribute to an undertaking or service in the public interest that would not otherwise be provided, or will contribute to the conservation and development of natural resources and recreational areas.

DEVELOPMENT OF PROGRAMS

Sec. 112. In order to carry out the purposes of this part, the Director shall assist and cooperate with State and local agencies and private nonprofit organizations (other than political parties) in developing programs for the employment of young people in State and community activities hereinafter authorized, which, whenever appropriate, shall be coordinated with programs of training and education provided by local public educational agencies.

FINANCIAL ASSISTANCE

Sec. 113. (a) The Director is authorized to enter into agreements providing for the payment by him of part or all of the cost of a State or local program submitted hereunder if he determines, in accordance with such regulations as he may prescribe, that—

(1) enrollees in the program will be employed either (A) on publicly owned and operated facilities or projects, or (B) on local projects sponsored by private nonprofit organizations (other than political parties), other than projects involving the construction, operation, or maintenance of so much of any facility used or to be used for sectarian instruction or as a place for religious worship;

(2) the program will increase the employability of the enrollees by providing work experience and training in occupational skills or pursuits in classifications in which the Director finds there is a reasonable expectation of employment, or will enable student enrollees to resume or to maintain school attendance;

(3) the program will permit or contribute to an undertaking or service in the public interest that would not otherwise be provided, or will contribute to the conservation, development, or management of the natural resources of the State or community or to the development, management, or protection of State or community recreational areas;

(4) the program will not result in the displacement of employed workers or impair existing contracts for services;

(5) the rates of pay and other conditions of employment will be appropriate and reasonable in the light of such factors as the type of work performed, geographical region, and proficiency of the employee;

(6) to the maximum extent feasible, the program will be coordinated with vocational training and educational services adapted to the special needs of enrollees in such program and sponsored by

State or local public educational agencies: *Provided, however,* That where such services are inadequate or unavailable, the program may make provision for the enlargement, improvement, development, and coordination of such services with the cooperation of, or where appropriate pursuant to agreement with, the Secretary of Health, Education, and Welfare; and

(7) the program includes standards and procedures for the selection of applicants, including provisions assuring full coordination and cooperation with local and other authorities to encourage students to resume or maintain school attendance.

(b) In approving projects under this part, the Director shall give priority to projects with high training potential.

ENROLLEES IN PROGRAM

Sec. 114. (a) Participation in programs under this part shall be limited to young men and women who are permanent residents of the United States, who have attained age sixteen but have not attained age twenty-two, and whose participation in such programs will be consistent with the purposes of this part.

(b) Enrollees shall be deemed not to be Federal employees and shall not be subject to the provisions of laws relating to Federal employment, including those relating to hours of work, rates of compensation, leave, unemployment compensation, and Federal employee benefits.

(c) Where appropriate to carry out the purposes of this Act, the Director may provide for testing, counseling, job development, and referral services to youths through public agencies or private nonprofit organizations.

• • •

PART C—WORK-STUDY PROGRAMS

STATEMENT OF PURPOSE

Sec. 121. The purpose of this part is to stimulate and promote the part-time employment of students in institutions of higher education who are from low-income families and are in need of the earnings from such employment to pursue courses of study at such institutions.

• • •

GRANTS FOR WORK-STUDY PROGRAMS

Sec. 123. The Director is authorized to enter into agreements with institutions of higher education (as defined by section 401(f) of the Higher Education Facilities Act of 1963 (P.L. 88-204)) under which the Director will make grants to such institutions to assist in the operation of work-study programs as hereinafter provided.

CONDITIONS OF AGREEMENTS

Sec. 124. An agreement entered into pursuant to section 123 shall—

(a) provide for the operation by the institution of a program for the part-time employment of its students in work—

(1) for the institution itself, or

(2) for a public or private nonprofit organization when the position is obtained through an arrangement between the institution and such an organization and—

(A) the work is related to the student's educational objective, or

(B) such work (i) will be in the public interest and is work which would not otherwise be provided, (ii) will not result in the displacement of employed workers or impair existing contracts for services, and (iii) will be governed by such conditions of employment as will be appropriate and reasonable in light of such factors as the type of work performed, geographical region, and proficiency of the employee:

Provided, however, That no such work shall involve the construction, operation, or maintenance of so much of any facility used or to be used for sectarian instruction or as a place for religious worship;

(b) provide that funds granted an institution of higher education, pursuant to section 123 may be used only to make payments to students participating in work-study programs, except that an institution may use a portion of the sums granted to it to meet administrative expenses, but the amount so used may not exceed 5 per centum of the payments made by the Director to such institution for that part of the work-study program in which students are working for public or nonprofit organizations other than the institution itself;

(c) provide that employment under such work-study program shall be furnished only to a student who (1) is from a low-income family, (2) is in need of the earnings from such employment in order to pursue a course of study at such institution, (3) is capable, in the opinion of the institution, of maintaining good standing in such course of study while employed under the program covered by the agreement, and (4) has been accepted for enrollment as a full-time student at the institution or, in the case of a student already enrolled in and attending the institution, is in good standing and in full-time attendance there either as an undergraduate, graduate, or professional student;

(d) provide that no student shall be employed under such work-study program for more than fifteen hours in any week in which classes in which he is enrolled are in session;

(e) provide that in each fiscal year during which the agreement remains in effect, the institution shall expend (from sources other than payments under this part) for the employment of its students (whether or not in employment eligible for assistance under this part) an amount that is not less than its average annual expenditure for such employment during the three fiscal years preceding the fiscal year in which the agreement is entered into;

(f) provide that the Federal share of the compensation of students employed in the work-study program in accordance with the agreement will not exceed 90 per centum of such compensation for work performed during the period ending two years after the date of enactment of this Act, or June 30, 1966, whichever is later, and 75 per centum thereafter;

• • •

TITLE II—URBAN AND RURAL COMMUNITY ACTION PROGRAMS

PART A—GENERAL COMMUNITY ACTION PROGRAMS

STATEMENT OF PURPOSE

Sec. 201. The purpose of this part is to provide stimulation and incentive for urban and rural communities to mobilize their resources to combat poverty through community action programs.

COMMUNITY ACTION PROGRAMS

Sec. 202. (a) The term "community action program" means a program—

(1) which mobilizes and utilizes resources, public or private, of any urban or rural, or combined urban and rural, geographical area (referred to in this part as a "community"), including but not limited to a State, metropolitan area, county, city, town, multicity unit, or multicounty unit in an attack on poverty;

(2) which provides services, assistance, and other activities of sufficient scope and size to give promise of progress toward elimination of poverty or a cause or causes of poverty through developing employment opportunities, improving human performance, motivation, and productivity, or bettering the conditions under which people live, learn, and work;

(3) which is developed, conducted, and administered with the maximum feasible participation of residents of the areas and members of the groups served; and

(4) which is conducted, administered, or coordinated by a public or private nonprofit agency (other than a political party), or a combination thereof.

(b) The Director is authorized to prescribe such additional criteria for programs carried on under this part as he shall deem appropriate.

. . .

FINANCIAL ASSISTANCE FOR DEVELOPMENT OF COMMUNITY ACTION
PROGRAMS

Sec. 204. The Director is authorized to make grants to, or to contract with, appropriate public or private nonprofit agencies, or combinations thereof, to pay part or all of the costs of development of community action programs.

FINANCIAL ASSISTANCE FOR CONDUCT AND ADMINISTRATION OF
COMMUNITY ACTION PROGRAMS

Sec. 205. (a) The Director is authorized to make grants to, or to contract with, public or private nonprofit agencies, or combinations thereof, to pay part or all of the costs of community action programs which have been approved by him pursuant to this part, including the cost of carrying out programs which are components of a community action program and which are designed to achieve the purposes of this part. Such component programs shall be focused upon the needs of low-income individuals and families and shall provide expanded and improved services, assistance, and other activities, and facilities necessary in connection therewith. Such programs shall be conducted in those fields which fall within the purposes of this part including employment, job training and counseling, health, vocational rehabilitation, housing, home management, welfare, and special remedial and other noncurricular educational assistance for the benefit of low-income individuals and families.

(b) No grant or contract authorized under this part may provide for general aid to elementary or secondary education in any school or school system.

(c) In determining whether to extend assistance under this section the Director shall consider among other relevant factors the incidence of poverty within the community and within the areas or groups to be affected by the specific program or programs, and the extent to which the applicant is in a position to utilize efficiently and expeditiously the assistance for which application is made. In determining the incidence of poverty the Director shall consider information available with respect to such factors as: the concentration of low-income families, particularly those with children; the extent of persistent unemployment and underemployment; the number and proportion of persons receiving cash or other assistance on a needs basis from public agencies or private organizations; the number of migrant or transient low-income families; school dropout rates, military service rejection rates, and other evidences of low educational attainment; the incidence of disease, disability, and infant mortality; housing conditions; adequacy of community facilities and services; and the incidence of crime and juvenile delinquency.

(d) In extending assistance under this section the Director shall give special consideration to programs which give promise of effecting a permanent increase in the capacity of individuals, groups, and communities to deal with their problems without further assistance.

TECHNICAL ASSISTANCE

Sec. 206. The Director is authorized to provide, either directly or through grants or other arrangements, (1) technical assistance to communities in developing, conducting, and administering community action programs, and (2) training for specialized personnel needed to develop, conduct, or administer such programs or to provide services or other assistance thereunder.

RESEARCH, TRAINING, AND DEMONSTRATIONS

Sec. 207. The Director is authorized to conduct, or to make grants to or enter into contracts with institutions of higher education or other appropriate public agencies or private organizations for the conduct of, research, training, and demonstrations pertaining to the purposes of this part. Expenditures under this section in any fiscal year shall not exceed 15 per centum of the sums appropriated or allocated for such year to carry out the purposes of this part.

• • •

EQUITABLE DISTRIBUTION OF ASSISTANCE

Sec. 210. The Director shall establish criteria designed to achieve an equitable distribution of assistance under this part within the States between urban and rural areas. In developing such criteria, he shall consider the relative numbers in the States or areas therein of: (1) low-income families, particularly those with children; (2) unemployed persons; (3) persons receiving cash or other assistance on a needs basis from public agencies or private organizations; (4) school dropouts; (5) adults with less than an eighth-grade education; (6) persons rejected for military service; and (7) persons living in urban places compared to the number living in rural places as determined by the Bureau of the Census for the 1960 census.

• • •

PART B — ADULT BASIC EDUCATION PROGRAMS

DECLARATION OF PURPOSE

Sec. 212. It is the purpose of this part to initiate programs of instruction for individuals who have attained age eighteen and whose inability to read and write the English language constitutes a substantial impairment of their ability to get or retain employment commensurate with their real ability, so as to help eliminate such inability and raise the level of education of such individuals with a view to making them less likely to become dependent on others, improving their ability to benefit from occupational training and otherwise increasing their opportunities for more productive and profitable employment, and making them better able to meet their adult responsibilities.

GRANTS TO STATES

Sec. 213. (a) From the sums appropriated to carry out this title, the Director shall make grants to States which have State plans approved by him under this section.

(b) Grants under subsection (a) may be used, in accordance with regulations of the Director, to —

(1) assist in establishment of pilot projects by local educational agencies, relating to instruction in public schools, or other facilities used for the purpose by such agencies, of individuals described in section 212, to (A) demonstrate, test, or develop modifications, or adaptations in the light of local needs, of special materials or methods for instruction of such individuals, (B) stimulate the development of local educational agency programs for instruction of such individuals in such schools or other facilities, and (C) acquire additional information concerning the materials or methods needed for an effective program for raising adult basic educational skills;

(2) assist in meeting the cost of local educational agency programs for instruction of such individuals in such schools or other facilities; and

(3) assist in development or improvement of technical or supervisory services by the State educational agency relating to adult basic education programs.

TITLE III — SPECIAL PROGRAMS TO COMBAT POVERTY IN RURAL AREAS

STATEMENT OF PURPOSE

Sec. 301. It is the purpose of this title to meet some of the special problems of rural poverty and thereby to raise and maintain the income and living standards of low-income rural families and migrant agricultural employees and their families.

PART A — AUTHORITY TO MAKE GRANTS AND LOANS

Sec. 302. (a) The Director is authorized to make —

(1) loans having a maximum maturity of 15 years and in amounts not exceeding $2,500 in the aggregate to any low income rural family where, in the judgment of the Director, such loans have a reasonable possibility of effecting a permanent increase in the income of such families by assisting or permitting them to —

    (A) acquire or improve real estate or reduce encumbrances or erect improvements thereon,

    (B) operate or improve the operation of farms not larger than family sized, including but not limited to the purchase of feed, seed, fertilizer, livestock, poultry, and equipment, or

    (C) participate in cooperative associations; and/or to finance nonagricultural enterprises which will enable such families to supplement their income.

(b) Loans under this section shall be made only if the family is not qualified to obtain such funds by loan under other Federal programs.

• • •

PART B — ASSISTANCE FOR MIGRANT, AND OTHER SEASONALLY
EMPLOYED, AGRICULTURAL EMPLOYEES AND THEIR FAMILIES

Sec. 311. The Director shall develop and implement as soon as practicable a program to assist the States, political subdivisions of States, public and nonprofit agencies, institutions, organizations, farm associations, or individuals in establishing and operating programs of assistance for migrant, and other seasonally employed, agricultural employees and their families which programs shall be limited to housing, sanitation, education, and day care of children. Institutions, organizations, farm associations, or individuals shall be limited to direct loans.

TITLE IV — EMPLOYMENT AND INVESTMENT INCENTIVES

STATEMENT OF PURPOSE

Sec. 401. It is the purpose of this title to assist in the establishment, preservation, and strengthening of small business concerns and improve the managerial skills employed in such enterprises; and to mobilize for these objectives private as well as public managerial skills and resources.

LOANS, PARTICIPANTS, AND GUARANTEES

Sec. 402. The Director is authorized to make, participate (on an immediate basis) in, or guarantee loans, repayable in not more than fifteen years, to any small business concern (as defined in section 3 of the Small Business Act (15 U.S.C. 632) and regulations issued thereunder), or to any qualified person seeking to establish such a concern, when he determines that such loans will assist in carrying out the purposes of this title, with particular emphasis on employment of the long-term unemployed: *Provided, however,* That no such loans shall be made, participated in, or guaranteed if the total of such Federal assistance to a single borrower outstanding at any one time would exceed $25,000. The Director may defer payments on the principal of such loans for a grace period and use such other methods as he deems necessary and appropriate to assure the successful establishment and operation of such concern. The Director may, in his discretion, as a condition of such financial assistance, require that the borrower take steps to improve his management skills by participating in a management training program approved by the Director. The Director shall encourage, as far as possible, the participation of the private business community in the program of assistance to such concerns.

* * *

TITLE VI — ADMINISTRATION AND COORDINATION

PART A — ADMINISTRATION

OFFICE OF ECONOMIC OPPORTUNITY

Sec. 601. (a) There is hereby established in the Executive Office of the President the Office of Economic Opportunity. The Office shall be headed by a Director who shall be appointed by the President, by and with the advice and consent of the Senate. There shall also be in the Office one Deputy Director and three Assistant Directors who shall be appointed by the President, by and with the advice and consent of the Senate. The Deputy Director and the Assistant Directors shall perform such functions as the Director may from time to time prescribe.

VOLUNTEERS IN SERVICE TO AMERICA

Sec. 603. (a) The Director is authorized to recruit, select, train, and—

(1) upon request of State or local agencies or private nonprofit organizations, refer volunteers to perform duties in furtherance of programs combating poverty at a State or local level; and

(2) in cooperation with other Federal, State, or local agencies involved, assign volunteers to work (A) in meeting the health, education, welfare, or related needs of Indians living on reservations, of migratory workers and their families, or of residents of the District of Columbia, the Commonwealth of Puerto Rico, Guam, American Samoa, the Virgin Islands, or the Trust Territory of the Pacific Islands; (B) in the care and rehabilitation of the mentally ill or mentally retarded under treatment at nonprofit mental health or mental retardation facilities assisted in their construction or operation by Federal funds; and (C) in furtherance of programs or activities authorized or supported under title I or II of this Act.

(b) The referral or assignment of volunteers shall be on such terms and conditions as the Director may determine, but volunteers shall not be referred or assigned to duties or work in any State without the consent of the Governor.

(c) The Director is authorized to provide to all volunteers during training and to volunteers assigned pursuant to subsection (a) (2) such stipend, not to exceed $50 per month, such living, travel, and leave allowances, and such housing, transportation (including travel to and from the place of training), supplies, equipment, subsistence, clothing, and health and dental care as the Director may deem necessary or appropriate for their needs.

(d) Volunteers shall be deemed not to be Federal employees and shall not be subject to the provisions of laws relating to Federal employment, including those relating to hours of work, rates of compensation, leave, unemployment compensation, and Federal employee benefits, except that all volunteers during training and such volunteers as are assigned pursuant to subsection (a) (2) shall be deemed Federal employees to the same extent as enrollees of the Corps under section 106 (b), (c), and (d) of this Act.

· · ·

PART B — COORDINATION OF ANTIPOVERTY PROGRAMS

COORDINATION

Sec. 611. (a) In order to insure that all Federal programs related to the purposes of this Act are carried out in a coordinated manner —

(1) the Director is authorized to call upon other Federal agencies to supply such statistical data, program reports, and other materials as he deems necessary to discharge his responsibilities under this Act, and to assist the President in coordinating the antipoverty efforts of all Federal agencies;

(2) Federal agencies which are engaged in administering programs related to the purposes of this Act, or which otherwise perform functions relating thereto, shall —

(A) cooperate with the Director in carrying out his duties and responsibilities under this Act; and

(B) carry out their programs and exercise their functions in such manner as will, to the maximum extent permitted by other applicable law, assist in carrying out the purposes of this Act; and

(3) the President may direct that particular programs and functions, including the expenditure of funds, of the Federal agencies referred to in paragraph (2) shall be carried out, to the extent not

inconsistent with other applicable law, in conjunction with or in support of programs authorized under this Act.

(b) In order to insure that all existing Federal agencies are utilized to the maximum extent possible in carrying out the purposes of this Act, no funds appropriated to carry out this Act shall be used to establish any new department or office when the intended function is being performed by an existing department or office.

PREFERENCE TO COMMUNITY ACTION PROGRAMS

Sec. 612. To the extent feasible and consistent with the provisions of law governing any Federal program and with the purposes of this Act, the head of each Federal agency administering any Federal program is directed to give preference to any application for assistance or benefits which is made pursuant to or in connection with a community action program approved pursuant to title II of this Act.

INFORMATION CENTER

Sec. 613. In order to insure that all Federal programs related to the purposes of this Act are utilized to the maximum extent possible, and to insure that information concerning such programs and other relevant information is readily available in one place to public officials and other interested persons, the Director is authorized as he deems appropriate to collect, prepare, analyze, correlate, and distribute such information, either free of charge or by sale at cost (any funds so received to be deposited to the Director's account as an offset to such cost), and make arrangements and pay for any printing and binding without regard to the provisions of any other law or regulation.

PROHIBITION OF FEDERAL CONTROL

Sec. 614. Nothing contained in this Act shall be construed to authorize any department, agency, officer, or employee of the United States to exercise any direction, supervision, or control over the curriculum, program of instruction, administration, or personnel of any educational institution or school system.

The Case for the Negative Income Tax*

Milton Friedman

The proposal to supplement the income of the poor by a fraction of their unused income tax exemptions and deductions — a proposal that I described and labeled a negative income tax in my book *Capitalism and Freedom*[1]—has been greeted with considerable (though far from unanimous) enthusiasm on the left and with considerable (though again far from unanimous) hostility on the right. Yet, in my opinion, the negative income tax is more compatible with the philosophy and aims of the proponents of limited government and maximum individual freedom than with the philosophy and aims of the proponents of the welfare state and greater government control of the economy. By exploring this paradox, I can perhaps restate in a somewhat different way the case for the negative income tax.

1. The Enthusiasm on the Left

The enthusiasm on the left arises, I believe, from three different sources: (a) the negative income tax has been confused with a superficially similar but basically very different guaranteed minimum income plan; (b) the negative income tax has been treated as another program to be added to existing welfare programs rather than as a substitute for

---

*Paper delivered at the National Symposium on a Guaranteed Income, Washington, D.C., 1966. Reprinted with permission of the U.S. Chamber of Commerce, Washington, D.C.
[1](Chicago: University of Chicago Press, 1963), pp. 190-193.

them; (c) there has been increasing recognition that present welfare arrangements limit the personal freedom of the recipients and demean both the recipients and the administrators of welfare.

In terms of my values, I deplore the first source of enthusiasm, have mixed feelings about the second, and heartily welcome the third. Let me expand on each.

(a) *Confusion between different plans.* A negative income tax plan does provide a guaranteed minimum income. But this guaranteed minimum income is not equal to the income at which the taxpayer neither pays taxes nor receives a subsidy. This point, simple though it is, has been the source of much confusion. Let me illustrate. Under our current income tax, a family of four has exemptions plus standard deductions equal to $3,000. Hence, if such a family has a total income of $3,000, it pays no tax. This is the *break-even* income. If the family has a total pretax income of $4,000 (and uses the standard deduction), it has $1,000 positive taxable income and, at the current tax rate for that bracket of 14 per cent, pays $140 a year in taxes, leaving it with $3,860 in income after taxes. . . . If such a family had a total pretax income of $2,000, it would have a *negative* taxable income of $1,000. Under a negative income tax, it would be entitled to receive a payment, the amount depending on the tax rate. If the tax rate for negative taxable income were the same as for the first bracket of positive taxable income, or 14 per cent, it would be entitled to receive $140, leaving it with a posttax income of $2,140. If the tax rate were 50 per cent, the highest rate that seems to me at all feasible and the one I used for illustrative purposes in *Capitalism and Freedom,* it would be entitled to receive $500, leaving it with a posttax income of $2,500.

If the family had a zero pretax income, it would have a negative taxable income of $3,000, and, with a tax rate of 50 per cent, would be entitled to receive $1,500, leaving it with a posttax income of $1,500.[2]

---

[2]Note that under present laws, negative taxable income could be more than $3,000, since a taxpayer who uses actual rather than standard deductions could have exemptions plus deductions of more than $3,000. This is a point that deserves much more attention than it has received. On the one hand, it offers the possibility of introducing a desirable flexibility into the program. For example, it would offer a far better way than Medicare or socialized medicine to finance by tax funds abnormal medical costs: simply permit such costs to continue, as now, to be a deduction in computing income. On the other hand, this point gives still more importance to undesirable deductions and exclusions under the present income tax. Such deductions and exclusions mean that a family with high income from tax-exempt sources or with large deductions could not only avoid tax as it now does but could also qualify for subsidies. See section 3.

This is the minimum income guaranteed by this particular negative income tax plan, whereas the break-even income is $3,000.[3]

Some active proponents of plans for a guaranteed minimum income, notably Robert Theobald and E. E. Schwartz,[4] have proposed simply "filling the gap" between a break-even level of income and the actual income of any family that receives less. This is equivalent to using a tax rate of 100 per cent on negative taxable income, which makes the guaranteed minimum income equal to the break-even level.

Though superficially similar to a negative income tax, such a plan is in fact radically different—just as a positive income tax levied at a 100 per cent rate differs radically from one levied at a fractional rate less than 100 per cent. The 100 per cent rate removes all incentives to earn any income subject to the tax. The fractional rate reduces incentives (compared to no tax) but does not eliminate them.

Similarly, a 100 per cent rate on negative taxable income is as absurd as a 100 per cent rate on positive taxable income. Not only would it eliminate any incentive for persons eligible for the subsidy to earn income, it would give them a positive incentive to dispose of any income-earning property, provided it, together with other sources of income, yielded less than the income guarantee. For example, suppose a family owns a house which it rents out, which is its sole source of income, and from which it receives an income less than the minimum guarantee. Obviously, the sensible action is to give the house to a friend who is above the minimum income and who will know how to show his gratitude for the gift. The giver would lose no income, since the foregone rent would simply be replaced by the government subsidy.

By removing from a class of people all incentive to work or even to own property, such a scheme would create a quasi-permanent class of

---

[3]For other sizes of families (tax-paying units), the guaranteed minimum income and break-even income vary. With a 50 per cent rate on negative taxable income, and present law with respect to exemptions and standard deductions, these are as follows:

Family Size	Guaranteed Minimum Income	Break-even Income
1	$ 450	$ 900
2	800	1,600
3	1,150	2,300
4	1,500	3,000
5	1,850	3,700
6	2,200	4,400

[4]Edward E. Schwartz, "A Way to End the Means Test," *Social Work*, IX (July, 1964), 5-12; Robert Theobald, *Free Men and Free Markets* (New York: C. N. Potts, 1963), pp. 192-197; and Robert Theobald, ed., *The Guaranteed Income* (New York: Doubleday & Company, Inc., 1966).

the professionally indigent, for whom living on the dole was a way of life, not a regrettable and temporary necessity.

Proponents of such a scheme tend to estimate its cost as equal to the gap between the break-even incomes they specify and the current incomes of families with lower incomes. But this is a gross underestimate. It takes no account of the cost of replacing the current income that would disappear because families both above and below the break-even point would be tempted to stop working or to give away property.[5]

Some proponents of "gap-filling" plans have acknowledged the disincentive effects of their plans and have suggested modifications to provide some element of incentive to receive other income. However, the modifications are mostly trivial, paying only lip service to the problem. And some proponents have even welcomed the disincentive effects, because they believe that automation threatens widespread unemployment, and hence that it is desirable to separate the receipt of income from work or property ownership.

If the confusion between these irresponsible plans and a responsible negative income tax were confined to the proponents of such plans, it would be of little moment. Unfortunately, it has not been. Many reasonable people have tended to reject the negative income tax because they have regarded it as equivalent to a filling-the-gap plan.[6]

In fairness, I should stress that filling-the-gap plans command only limited support. Most people on the left who favor a negative income tax recognize that a 100 per cent rate is absurd and favor a plan with a fractional rate much less than 100 per cent. Their enthusiasm for the plan has a different source.

(b) *An additional program.* I have supported the negative income tax as a *substitute* for present welfare programs; as a device for accomplishing the objectives of those programs more efficiently, at lower cost to the taxpayer, and with a sharp reduction in bureaucracy. Many proponents of a negative income tax have favored simply adding it to existing programs.

I have mixed feelings about this source of support. On the one hand, in my opinion, we are now spending far too much on welfare programs of all kinds compared to their contribution to the well-being of the community (see section 2(a)). I would not like to see the negative income tax used simply as a means of adding still more to this total. On the other hand, the addition of a negative income tax is partly being

---

[5]To add to the cost of the proposals, most proponents of gap-filling schemes have proposed guarantees much higher than the break-even incomes in footnote 3.

[6]See, for example, the *Wall Street Journal* editorial, "The Guaranteed Nightmare," January 31, 1966, and my letter to the editor, February 15, 1966.

suggested instead of other additions. The political reality may be that the programs will be expanded in one way or another. If so, far better that it be in this way.

More important, we must look to the future. Whatever may be the original intent, I believe that a negative income tax will be so much more effective than current programs that, in the course of time, it would increasingly replace them, in the process diminishing the problem toward which all of the programs are directed.

(c) *Defects of present welfare arrangements.* All responsible students of the problem, whether on the left or the right, have come increasingly to recognize that present welfare programs have grave defects, and in particular, that direct relief and aid to dependent children demean both the recipients and the administrators.

I was much impressed some years ago when Herbert Krosney talked to me about a study of New York welfare programs he was engaged on—and which has since been reported in the splendid book, *Beyond Welfare.*[7]

In effect, he said to me, "You classical liberals are always talking about how big government interferes with personal freedom. The examples you give are always about things that matter to people like you and me—freedom of speech, of choosing an occupation, of traveling, and so on. Yet how often do you and I come into contact with government? When we pay our taxes or get a traffic ticket, perhaps. The people whose freedom is really being interfered with are the poor in Harlem, who are on relief. A government official tells them how much they may spend for food, rent, and clothing. They have to get permission from an official to rent a different apartment or to buy secondhand furniture. Mothers receiving aid for dependent children may have their male visitors checked on by government investigators at any hour of the day or night. They are the people who are deprived of personal liberty, freedom, and dignity."

And surely, he is right. No doubt, he who pays the piper calls the tune. No doubt, the taxpayer who pays the bill to support people on relief may feel that he has the moral as well as legal right to see to it that the money is spent for designated purposes. But whether he has the right is irrelevant. Even if he has, it seems to me neither prudent nor noble for him to exercise it. The major effect of doing so is to weaken the self-reliance of the recipients, diminish their humanity, and make them wise in the stratagems for evading the spirit of the restrictions imposed on them. And the effect on the administrators is no more salutary. Instead of welfare workers bringing counsel and assistance to the poor, they become policemen and detectives—enemies to be out-

---

[7](New York: Holt, Rinehart & Winston, Inc., 1966).

witted. That is a major reason why it is so hard for large cities to staff their welfare agencies and why they experience such high turnover.

It would be far better to give the indigent money and let them spend it according to their values. True, they may spend much of it in ways we disapprove of—but they do now, and not all the red tape in Washington will keep them from finding ways of doing so. If we spent the same amount on the poor in total, they would have more to spend—because of savings in administrative costs—and they would get more satisfaction per dollar spent—because they would waste less in circumventing the bureaucracy and would use the money for what they value most. In addition, at least some would grow in the course of making their own decisions, and would develop habits of independence and self-reliance. And surely, if social workers are hired on government funds, they should devote their energies to helping the indigent, and not spying on them.

This is the aspect of the negative income tax that I believe has appealed most strongly to the left, and properly so. Here is one area where it has become patent how detailed government intervention affects the lives of its citizens; how it corrupts both the controller and the controlled. Having learned this lesson in one area, perhaps the well-meaning people on the left will be led to look at other areas in a new light.

2. The Hostility on the Right

The hostility toward the negative income tax on the right is partly an automatic reflex to the enthusiasm for it on the left, partly, it is a valid reaction against fill-the-gap plans. But hostility arises also from two very different sources: first, the belief that a guaranteed minimum income introduces a new principle into the relationship between the government and the people that would greatly weaken the incentives on the part of the poor to help themselves; second, the political judgment that it will not be possible to keep a negative income tax within reasonable bounds.

(a) *The weakening of incentives.* The first source of hostility confuses labels with substance. The elementary fact is that we now have a governmentally guaranteed minimum income in substance though not in name. That is what our present grab-bag of relief and welfare measures is. In some states, it is even written into the law that anyone whose income is "inadequate" is entitled as a matter of right to have it supplemented and brought up to an "adequate" level, as judged of course by the welfare agencies. And whether explicitly specified in law or not, the same thing is true almost everywhere in the United States.

The most obvious component of the present *de facto* guaranteed minimum income is direct relief and aid to dependent children. Aside from the interference with personal freedom and dignity already referred to, these programs have the worst possible effects on incentives. If a person on relief earns a dollar, and obeys the law, his or her relief payment is reduced by a dollar. Since working generally involves costs— if only for better or different clothes—the effect is to penalize either industry or honesty or both. The program tends to produce poor people, and a permanent class of poor people living on welfare, rather than to help the unavoidably indigent. And it does so at high cost in waste and bureaucracy.

But this is only the tip of the iceberg. We have a maze of detailed governmental programs that have been justified on welfare grounds— though typically their product is "illfare": public housing, urban renewal, old-age and unemployment insurance, job training, the host of assorted programs under the mislabeled "war on poverty," farm price supports, and so on at incredible length.

Estimates of how much we are now spending on welfare programs vary widely depending on what specific programs are included. A modest estimate, which excludes entirely veteran's benefits and educational expenditures, is that federal, state, and local governments are spending roughly $50 billion a year. Much of this money is simply wasted—as in the agricultural programs. And most of it goes to people who cannot by any stretch of the imagination be classified as poor. Indeed, from this point of view the direct public assistance programs at least have the virtue that people who receive the payments clearly have a lower average income than the people who pay the taxes. There is not another welfare program for which this is unambiguously true. For some—e.g., urban renewal and farm price supports—the people who are hurt almost certainly have a lower average income than the people who are helped. For social security, the situation is more complex but it may well be that on net it involves transferring funds from the poor to the not-so-poor rather than the other way.

The welfare iceberg includes also measures that impose restrictions on private transactions, and do not require direct government expenditures, except for enforcement. The most obvious is minimum wage rate legislation. Other items are the Walsh-Healy and Davis-Bacon Acts, and the whole range of legislation conferring special immunities on labor unions. The effect of most such legislation is to increase the number of indigent people. The minimum wage rate, for example, prices many unskilled workers out of the market and is the major explanation, in my judgment, for the tragically high unemployment rates among teenagers, especially Negro teenagers.[8] These measures involve a confusion between *wage rate* and *family income*. Persons who are capable of earning only low wage rates are for the most part youngsters or extra family members whose earnings supplement those of the main bread-winner. But even where the worker is the main breadwinner, it is surely better that he be free to earn what little he can than that he be unem-ployed, and better that, if government funds are to be used to aid him, they be used to supplement his earnings, not to replace them.

The negative income tax would be vastly superior to this collection of welfare measures. It would concentrate public funds on supplementing the incomes of the poor—not distribute funds broadside in the hope that some will trickle down to the poor. It would help them because they were poor, not because they were old or disabled or unemployed or farmers or tenants of public housing. These characteristics are no doubt associated with poverty, but the association is very far from perfect.

Because the negative income tax is directed specifically at poverty, it would both help the indigent more and cost far less than our present collection of programs. One careful estimate, by Christopher Green, sets the cost of the 50 per cent plan outlined above at $7 to $9 billion for 1964 (if public assistance payments are excluded from the income base used in calculating taxable income).[9] In that year, public assistance expenditures alone totaled $5.1 billion. Clearly, the elimination of public assistance plus only a modest reduction in other programs would be enough to finance that particular negative income tax with no net cost.[10] And yet this 50 per cent plan would provide more assistance to the bulk of the indigent than they are now receiving.[11]

---

[8]See *The Minimum Wage Rate, Who Really Pays,* an interview with Yale Brozen and Milton Friedman (Washington, D.C.: Free Society Association, 1966).

[9]Christopher Green, *Transfer-by-Taxation: An Approach to Improved Income Maintenance,* background paper prepared for a conference at The Brookings Insti-tution (Washington, D.C.: The Brookings Institution, April, 1966), p. 277.

The lower estimate ($7.1 billion) assumes that double exemptions are not granted the aged in calculating taxable income; the higher estimate ($8.8 billion) assumes that they are.

[10]Precise calculations require taking into account the fact that some part of other transfer funds go to persons with low incomes, so the reduction or elimination of such programs would increase the amount of negative income reported. There is not therefore a dollar-for-dollar savings. Because the above estimates exclude assistance payments from the tax base, this does not apply to the elimination of public assistance.

[11]Green *(Transfer-by-Taxation,* pp. 163-165) compares present Aid to Families with Dependent Children (AFDC) with payments under this 50 per cent plan, on the assumption that the negative income tax payment would be the only income of the recipients. Even under this extreme assumption, he finds that only three states (New York, New Jersey, and Pennsylvania) are now paying under AFDC more than the recipients would get under the negative income tax. For Old Age Assistance (OAA), the problem is more complicated because of the need to allow for OADSI benefits. Green estimates that, under the 50 per cent plan, "the elderly poor receiving public assistance would not receive as much income . . . as they are presently receiving through PA (public assistance) or a combination of PA and OASDI. However, the difference is not absolutely very great" (p. 165).

Moreover, by substituting a fractional rate for the present 100 per cent rate, the negative income tax would give the indigent *more* incentive to add to their income by their own activity than they now have. Hence the above estimates overstate, and in my view significantly overstate, the net cost. Furthermore, these estimates make no allowance for a number of indirect benefits. Integrating the payment of assistance with the tax system would improve collection and reduce evasion under the income tax, reduce the concealment of income that takes place under our present relief programs, and permit elimination of most of the present bureaucracy administering the welfare programs.

Of course, the negative income tax at any reasonable level would not meet the specific needs of every indigent family. Being general and impersonal, it cannot be adapted to cases of special hardship, and no doubt such cases would exist. However, by providing a basic minimum, it would reduce such cases to a manageable number, which could be taken care of by private charity. In my opinion, one of the great costs of the proliferation of governmental welfare programs is the elimination of a basic role for private charity, with its flexibility, diversity, and adaptability. An indirect virtue of the negative income tax is that it would provide an important place for private charity to serve precisely that function which private agencies can serve best—handling the special case.

If we lived in a hypothetical world in which there were no governmental welfare programs at all and in which all assistance to the destitute was by private charity, the case for introducing a negative income tax would be far weaker than the case for substituting it for present programs. In such a world, the negative income tax would indeed weaken incentives to work. For such a world, I do not know whether I would favor a negative income tax—that would depend on how effectively private charity was in fact providing for the destitute. But, whether desirable or not, that is not our world and there is not the remotest chance that it will be in the foreseeable future. Those, like myself, who would like to see the role of government reduced, only harm our own cause by evaluating a program by an unreal standard.

(b) *The political problem.* A second major source of hostility from the right to the negative income tax is concern about its political effect. If we adopt an open-and-above-board program for supplementing the incomes of people below some specified level, will there not be continued political pressure for higher and higher break-even incomes, for higher and higher rates on negative income? Will the demagogue not have a field day appealing to the have-nots to legislate taxes on the haves for transfer to them? Will not the first sign of this process be the adoption of the negative income tax as an addition to all other programs rather than as a substitute?

These are all important questions. Clearly the dangers exist. But, like the incentive question, they must be evaluated in terms of the world as it is, not in terms of a dream world in which there are no governmental welfare measures. The relevant political question is whether the negative income tax is more susceptible or less susceptible to these dangers than alternative programs of the kind we now have or are likely to get. To this question, the answer seems to me clear: The negative income tax is less susceptible.

Why has the present grab-bag of programs been adopted? Because each appeals to a special interest that is willing to fight strongly for it, while few are willing to fight strongly against it; because the disinterested who seek to promote the general interest have been persuaded that every measure will contribute to helping a group that is disadvantaged; because, for many of the measures, there was no clear price tag, and the program could be voted without the simultaneous imposition of taxes to pay for it; because for still others, there are no direct costs at all—minimum wages are perhaps the clearest example; because, finally, no one who opposed the programs had an effective alternative to offer that would meet the real problems.

Politically, the right solution is to have a comprehensive program whose cost is open and clear. That is precisely what the negative income tax is. By linking it intimately with the general income tax structure, there is no way to raise the break-even incomes without raising the exemption for tax purposes, which clearly requires a higher rate on incomes above the exemption. The cost of the payments is in one lump sum that can be calculated and will be painfully visible to every taxpayer. It will be obvious that every rise in the rate applied to negative taxable income raises the cost. It may still be that the lower income groups will form a coalition to despoil the upper income groups for their benefit—but that danger will be less than now, when we are in the position of having the dog's tail cut off by inches, on the specious plea of benefiting the disadvantaged. Once the issue is open and clear, we must rely on the good sense and responsibility of the electorate. And I for one believe that experience has shown that we can rely on it; that in every Western country, the electorate has shown that it is proof—though clearly not 200 proof—against demagogic appeals simply to share the wealth.

The present problem is to halt the proliferation of the bad programs we now have and ultimately to dismantle them. But while these programs are on the whole bad, more or less incidentally they do help some people who are disadvantaged. Can we in good conscience mount a political attack on them unless we can provide an alternative way to achieve their good results? Can we be effective, unless we have a satisfactory answer to the inevitable charge that we are heartless and want to let the poor starve? And would we not deserve that charge, if we had no alternative? Most of these programs should never have been enacted. But they have been and they must be dismantled gradually, both for the sake of social stability and because the government has the moral responsibility to meet commitments it has entered into. The negative income tax is a way to replace existing programs gradually.

An additional enormous political advantage of a negative income tax compared with our present programs is that it does not generate a large bureaucracy to provide political patronage to the powers that be. It cannot be used as a political slush fund, as so many current programs—notably in the War on Poverty—can be and have been used.

There is no way whereby the bulk of us can tax ourselves to help the less fortunate that does not have political dangers. The negative income tax comes closer, in my opinion, to being politically consistent with a limited government and a free economy than any other method I have heard of.

3. The Income Tax as a Whole

Converting the general idea of a negative income tax into a concrete proposal raises many specific issues. These are identical with those that arise in constructing a positive income tax: the unit to be taxed, the receipts to be treated as income, the deductions and exclusions to be permitted from income, the break-even points for families of different size, the rate schedule for negative taxable income. So far I have implicitly accepted the specifications for these items embodied in our current income tax, adding only a single flat rate of 50 per cent for negative taxable incomes to have a specific illustrative plan.

But our current income tax clearly has many deficiencies, some of which are highlighted by considering extending the tax below the present exemptions. For example, consider a taxpayer all of whose income is in the form of interest from tax-exempt state and local securities. For tax purposes, he has a zero income before exemptions and deductions, hence would qualify for a negative tax payment of $1,500 (for a family of four), even though he may have a million dollars of income.

Or again, the tax rate of 50 per cent I have used is much too high. I should prefer a lower rate. Yet, with current exemptions, a lower rate would produce guaranteed minimum incomes so low compared to our present standards of indigence that the negative income tax could not be regarded as a satisfactory alternate to present programs. The reason is that current exemptions are far too low. They are a relic of wartime experience and have not been raised even to allow for the price rise since then. In real terms, they are far lower than at any prior date.

One advantage of looking at the problem of helping the poor in terms of negative taxes is that it forces us to look at our tax structure in a new light. Clearly, this is not the occasion for a comprehensive discussion. It may, however, serve to give some perspective if I outline the kind of personal income tax that seems to make most sense as an efficient structure both for raising governmental funds and for helping the poor.

The most important desideratum is a drastic lowering of the graduated rates combined with a drastic broadening of the base by eliminating existing exclusions and deductions. My own preference is for a single flat rate above and below much higher exemptions than now, with no exclusions or deductions except for strictly defined business and occupational expenses and perhaps medical expenses beyond some minimum. The present graduated rates are a fake. In practice, the loopholes mean that little revenue is produced by the higher rates and that the actual incidence of the tax is heaviest in middle income groups. Yet so long as the rates are highly graduated, the loopholes are necessary if the tax system is not seriously to weaken incentive and productive efficiency.

The solution is simultaneously to introduce a flat rate at a moderate level and to eliminate the loopholes. To be specific, I would eliminate the present exclusion of interest on state and local securities, as well as the present deductions for percentage depletion, interest, contributions, and taxes (except as they may be business expenses); integrate the corporate with the individual tax, and include capital gains in full, preferably on an accrual basis, and possibly with an adjustment to eliminate the effect of changes in the general price level.

This may seem a long way off from negative income taxes, yet it is closely linked. With a broadened base, current exemptions could be raised drastically and rates lowered for both positive and negative taxable income, yet the total revenue yielded by the income tax kept unchanged. To be specific, suppose that the exemptions (and standard deductions) were doubled—to $6,000 for a family of four—and that the single rate of 25 per cent were imposed on all income below and above the exemption. This would yield the same minimum income guarantee of $1,500 for a family of four as the plan discussed above and higher incomes for people with some other income. It would provide a greater incentive to the poor since they would keep 75 cents out of every additional dollar. It would raise taxes for few, if any, of those people who now pay taxes on all their income and who take the standard deduction. Yet some rough calculations suggest that it would probably yield as much as our present income tax.

If this is anywhere near right, the actual yield would be much higher since such a tax structure would greatly reduce the incentive to engage in costly schemes to avoid income taxes and would greatly increase the incentive to add to income, raising the tax base on both counts. . . .

The Coming Crisis in Welfare*

Henry Hazlitt

The Negative Income Tax as proposed by Prof. Milton Friedman is essentially, with one modification, just one more form of the guaranteed annual income. So before discussing Prof. Friedman's defense of his specific proposal, let us begin by summing up the general case against the guaranteed income.

In the words of Mr. Robert Theobald, one of its principal sponsors, this proposal "would guarantee to every citizen of the United States . . . the right to an income from the Federal Government to enable him to live with dignity." This guarantee would be unconditional. Everybody would get it, regardless of whether or not he worked, could work, or was willing to work.

The recipients are to continue to get this guaranteed income, let me emphasize, not only if they resolutely refuse to seek or take a job, but if they throw the handout money away at the races, or spend it on prostitutes, or whisky, marijuana, or whatnot. They are to be given "sufficient to live in dignity," and it is apparently to be no business of the taxpayers if the recipient chooses nonetheless to live without dignity, and to devote his guaranteed leisure to gambling, dissipation, drunkenness, dope addiction, or a life of crime.

The first thing to be said about this scheme economically is that if it were put into effect it would not only be intolerably expensive to the

---

*Reprinted with permission from *National Review,* 150 East 35th Street, New York, New York, 10016.

325

taxpayers who were forced to support it, but that it would destroy the incentives to work and to produce on an unparalleled scale.

As even one of the contributors to Mr. Theobald's symposium, William Vogt, has remarked: "Those who believe that men will want to work whether they have to or not seem to have lived sheltered lives."

Who, in fact, would be willing to take the smelly jobs, or any low-paid job, once the guaranteed income program is in effect? The guaranteed-income sponsors propose to pay, say, $3,000 to a family without any income, but to families earning some income they would pay merely the supplementary sum necessary to bring the total up to $3,000.

Now suppose that you are a married man with two children, and your present income from some nasty and irregular work is $2,500 a year. The government would then send you a check for $500. But it would very soon occur to you that though you now had $3,000, you could have got this $3,000 without doing any work at all.

The scheme is not only economically but morally indefensible. If "*everybody* should receive a guaranteed income as a matter of right" (the words just quoted are Mr. Theobald's), who is to pay him that income?

No Free Lunch

The truth is, of course, that the government has nothing to give to anybody that it doesn't first take from someone else. The whole guaranteed income proposal is a perfect modern example of the shrewd observation of the French economist Bastiat more than a century ago: "The state is the great fiction by which everybody tries to live at the expense of everybody else."

If you claim a "right" to "an income sufficient to live in dignity," whether you are willing to work or not, what you are really claiming is a right to part of *somebody else's* earned income. What you are asserting is that this other person has a duty to earn more than he needs or wants to live on so that the surplus may be seized from him and turned over to you to live on.

This is an absolutely immoral proposition.

The negative income tax (a misnomer for an income subsidy) suffers from most of the economic, political and moral vices of the guaranteed income. But it does have one important advantage over the guaranteed-income proposal in its cruder form: at least it would not destroy the incentive to work and produce to the same appalling extent.

Under the negative income tax, a man or a family would receive from the government a subsidy of 50 per cent, say, of the amount by which the family income fell below the so-called poverty-line income— let us say $3,000 a year. This means that if the family had no income at all it would receive a subsidy of $1,500. If it already had an earned income of $1,500, it would receive a government subsidy of $750, and so on.

Prof. Friedman, the distinguished author of this proposal, admits that, "like any other measures to alleviate poverty," his proposal would reduce "the incentives of those helped to help themselves"; but he goes on to argue, quite correctly, that it would not eliminate that incentive entirely, as the system of supplementing incomes up to some fixed minimum would. Under his plan an extra dollar earned would always mean more money available for expenditure.

I agree entirely that a subsidy calculated in this way—that is, one that would be reduced by only $1 for every $2 additional that the recipient was able to earn for himself—would not be nearly so destructive of incentives as the type of subsidy under which it would be pointless for the recipient to earn more on his own account.

In fact, some thirty years ago I put forward a similar proposal myself in an article in the *Annalist,* a weekly then published by the *New York Times.* What I suggested was a relief payment that would be reduced by only $1 for every $2 of self-earnings by the relief recipient. But this device solves only a marginal problem.

The negative income tax of Prof. Friedman, as put forward in 1962 in his book *Capitalism and Freedom,* was a comparatively modest proposal. He suggested that if a man had no income at all, he would receive a basic subsidy of $300. Once this idea got into practical politics, however, this basic sum would soon be denounced as utterly inadequate to allow a family of four to live in "decency and dignity." In fact, the humanitarian reformers would soon be demanding a basic subsidy of $3,000 or $4,000 to a family otherwise without income, and we would be back to the same starting point as the guaranteed income scheme.

Only—except for the fact that it would not destroy incentives as much—it would be even more expensive than the guaranteed income; because under it substantial subsidies would continue to be paid to people who were earning incomes of their own. If the basic subsidy to a family of no income were $3,000, families would continue to get some government subsidy until their incomes reached $6,000 a year!

Instead of a rigid ceiling, like the guaranteed income, the negative income tax would provide for a gradual tapering off. But otherwise it suffers from all the fatal flaws of the guaranteed-income proposal. Both would take money away from those who were earning it to turn it over both to those who could not earn it and those who refused to earn it. Money would be given to people whose incomes were low, without any regard to the reasons why those incomes were low. A person whose income was low or non-existent because he was a beatnik or a loafer or a drunk would get just as much, and no questions asked, as a person whose income was low or non-existent because he was blind or disabled or sick or the victim of some accident or circumstances beyond his control.

So far I have been summarizing arguments I have previously used against both the guaranteed income and the negative income tax. Prof. Friedman's reply to these in his March 7 article is peculiar. He applies a double standard: one standard is what is inherently desirable; the other is what is politically feasible. He defends his own proposals on the ground that they are desirable. He resents any suggestion that they would almost certainly never be adopted politically in the form he advocates. Yet he refuses to consider on their merits the alternatives suggested by his critics on the ground that they are not politically feasible. He argues that those who believe their adoption possible are living in "a dream world."

Friedman begins by telling his conservative and libertarian critics that they are foolish to object to the guaranteed income because we already "have a governmentally guaranteed income in substance though not in name." Even if his contention were true, it would be irrelevant to the merits of the case. If we already have a guaranteed income then the thing to do is to get rid of it.

Friedman then makes the undeniable statement that our present "grab-bag of relief and welfare measures" is "a mess." Precisely; and throwing the negative income tax on top of it would turn the mess into a nightmare.

But, Friedman insists, he is not proposing to throw his negative income tax on top of this mess; he is proposing to repeal all the existing relief and welfare measures and *substitute* his scheme for them.

Now who is living in a "dream world"? Does Friedman seriously believe that the veterans will quietly give up their pensions? That the farmers will calmly surrender their price supports and other subsidies? That the beneficiaries of subsidized public housing will cheerfully agree to pay a full economic rent? That we will soon hear the last of "free education" at the college level; of free school lunches; of food stamps? Will the workers give up unemployment compensation? Will the great mass of the voters give up any of their promised Social Security benefits?

Will the elderly even give up the Medicare benefits they have just acquired?

Talk about living "in a dream world"!

Perhaps the worst evil in all these welfare, relief, and giveaway programs is that it is so fatally easy to get them adopted and so nearly impossible, once they have been adopted, to get rid of them, or to cut them back, or even to prevent their further cancerous growth and proliferation.

I have yet to hear of a single congressman, or even a handful of academic economists, who has endorsed Friedman's negative income tax exactly in the form he has proposed it—to wit, with a basic subsidy of only $300 a year, and as a complete substitute for our whole present "grab-bag of relief and welfare measures."

Speaking for myself, I am not opposed to the negative income tax merely because I regard it as a political certainty that it would be far bigger than Friedman proposes and would simply be thrown on top of the immense welfare burden (in the neighborhood of $50 billion a year) that the American taxpayers already carry. I am opposed to it in principle. It is far inferior to the traditional methods of relief. Generations of experience with relief plans show that they will quickly get out of control and be subject to gross abuse, fraud, and chiseling, unless a means test is retained, unless there is some case-by-case and applicant-by-applicant examination—in brief, unless the recipients of unearned income from the government are subject to at least as much checking and investigation as income-tax payers. The advocates of the guaranteed income and the negative income tax think such a case-by-case check "humiliating" and administratively troublesome. Maybe so; but it is unfortunately unavoidable. There is no neat little mathematical gadget that will enable us to ignore and bypass this necessity.

The guaranteed income and the negative income tax schemes are wrong in principle because they would compel the self-supporting part of the population to support all the alleged "poor" without taking the trouble to find out *why* a particular individual is poor or even to make sure *whether* he is poor. They would treat precisely alike those who are poor through no moral fault of their own and those who are poor through their own gross delinquency.

Limit the Franchise?

We are confronted with a grave and immensely difficult problem, which we are bound to face candidly. Where any person, a child or an adult, is in fact helpless, or sick or disabled, or hungry, or jobless through no moral fault of his own, and where no private person or group is responsible for him, should "society," acting through government, make itself responsible?

The overwhelming majority of people would answer Yes. Since far back in history "society" has, in fact, assumed this responsibility. In England, the poor laws were enacted even before the reign of Elizabeth I.

The problem is, granted this responsibility, how can the government mitigate the penalties of failure and misfortune without undermining the incentives to effort and success? How can it prevent the abuse of relief and the ominous growth of an ever-bigger army of relief recipients?

I suspect that there is no perfect solution to this problem, but at best a least unsatisfactory solution.

But of one thing we can be reasonably certain. As long as those on relief have the vote while they remain on relief, politicians will continue to increase the burden of relief and welfare until it brings on hyper-inflation, insolvency, the wholesale destruction of incentives, or some other form of social and economic crisis.

Even Milton Friedman confesses political misgivings concerning what would happen to his tapered-off guaranteed income subsidy ("negative income tax") once it got into practical politics. He even quotes A. V. Dicey's question in 1914 whether it is wise to allow recipients of poor relief to retain the right to join in the election of a member of Parliament. But then he dismisses the "verdict of experience" as "mixed," and offers his proposal without suggesting any limitation of the franchise.

John Stuart Mill, writing in his *Representative Government* in 1861, did not equivocate: "I regard it as required by first principles that the receipt of parish relief should be a preemptory disqualification for the franchise. He who cannot by his labor suffice for his own support has no claim to the privilege of helping himself to the money of others."

Prof. Friedman may think that anyone who believes such a limitation of the franchise could be enacted in this generation is living "in a dream world." Perhaps. But does he himself believe that in the present political climate there is any possibility of his negative income tax being enacted in the modest form he proposes — and as a *substitute* for, instead of still another addition to, the present $50 billion worth of all other forms of relief and welfare now so solidly entrenched?

If he does believe that, he is really out on Cloud 9.

6

Housing and Urban Affairs

The problem of slum housing is an ancient one. Governments have always interested themselves in housing, primarily to secure maximum conditions of health, sanitation, safety. Local governments in America have the major responsibility of insuring adequate housing. Occasionally, building codes, zoning regulations, codes of health and sanitation, and fire prevention measures have succeeded in improving housing conditions in a limited fashion. But, on the whole, these approaches have been notable failures. In 1960 the U.S. Census Bureau reported that almost 19 per cent of the housing units in the nation were "dilapidated or without plumbing facilities"; another 8 per cent were "deteriorating." This means that over a quarter of the nation's housing is substandard. The failure of local governments to adequately cope with housing problems led to the federal government's intervention into the housing field with the passage of the Housing Act of 1937.

Three major programs were inaugurated in the Housing Act of 1937 — Mortgage Insurance, Public Housing and Urban Renewal. (See U.S. Department of Housing and Urban Development, *Summary of Federal Programs in Housing and Urban Affairs*) The federal government first undertook through its Federal Housing Administration (FHA) to guarantee private mortgages against default, and thereby to enable banks, savings and loan associations and other lending agencies to provide long term, low interest, low down payment mortgages for Americans wishing to purchase their own homes. FHA was extremely successful in promoting home ownership among America's middle classes. FHA-insured mortgages enabled millions of American families to acquire their own homes, often in the suburbs. In fact, the success of FHA might be one of the many factors contributing to the deterioration of central cities, for it enabled many middle-class residents to acquire their cherished home in the suburbs and leave the city behind.

The Housing Act of 1937 also established a Public Housing Administration (now called the Housing Assistance Administration or HAA) to administer a low rent public housing program to provide homes for those who could not afford decent housing without government assistance. The Housing Assistance Administration does not build, own, or operate any of its own housing projects; rather it provides the necessary financial support to enable local communities to provide public housing for their poor if they choose to do so. The Housing Assistance Administration makes loans and grants to local housing authorities established by local governments to build, own and operate low cost public housing. Local housing authorities must keep rents low in relation to their ability to pay. This means that local housing authorities operate at a loss and the federal government reimburses them for this loss. No community is required to have a housing authority; they must apply to the Housing Assistance Administration and meet federal standards in order to receive federal financial support.

In the Housing Act of 1937 the idea of urban renewal was closely tied with public housing. Slum residences were to be torn down as public housing sites were constructed. But in the Housing Act of 1949, the urban renewal program was separated from public housing, and the federal government undertook to support a broad program of urban redevelopment to help cities fight a loss in population, and to reclaim the economic importance of the core cities. To save the nation's central cities, the urban renewal administration was authorized to match local monies to acquire blighted land, clear off or modernize obsolete and dilapidated structures, and make downtown cities available for new uses. The federal government does not engage in these activities directly but makes available financial assistance to local urban renewal authorities to carry out renewal projects. When the sites are physically cleared of the old structures by the local urban renewal authority, they can be resold to private developers for residence, commercial, or industrial use, and generally two-thirds of the difference between costs of acquisition and clearance and the income of the private sale to the developers is paid for by the federal government. In other words, local urban renewal authorities sustain a loss in their renewal activities, and most of this loss is made up by federal grants. No city is required to engage in urban renewal, but if a city wishes federal financial backing it must show in its application that it has developed a "workable program" for redevelopment and prevention of future blight.

In addition to mortgage insurance, public housing, and urban renewal, the Department of Housing and Urban Development also administers a variety of other grant programs for local communities: sewage and water facilities, neighborhood facilities, urban planning assistance, urban mass transportation, open space and urban beautification, college housing, housing for the elderly and handicapped, and a new rent supplement program. (See U.S. Department of Housing and Urban Renewal, *Federal Housing Programs in Twenty Largest Cities*)

In a special message to Congress on housing and urban development in 1966 President Lyndon B. Johnson described both the problems and accomplishments of housing and urban development programs of the national government. (See Lyndon B. Johnson, *The Demonstration Cities Program*) He proposed a new demonstration cities program which would coordinate existing programs in housing, urban renewal, job training, health facilities, recreation, welfare, and education for a unified effort to improve the conditions of life in urban areas. Instead of separate federal grants for diverse programs, a demonstration city would receive the complete array of all available grants-in-aid in the fields of housing, renewal, transportation, education, welfare, economic opportunity and related programs. Moreover, a demonstration city would receive special grants amounting to 80 per cent of the non-federal cost of grant-in-aid programs included in the demonstration. In every demonstration city, a federal coordinator would be assigned to assist local officials in bringing together all of the relative federal resources. Cities and towns of all sizes could participate in a demonstration cities program. By the summer of 1968 a total of 80 cities had been selected by the Department of Housing and Urban Development for demonstration cities grants. (See U.S. Department of Housing and Urban Development, *List of Model Cities*)

In commenting upon the federal government's housing and urban development policies, Professor James Q. Wilson of Harvard University points out that the demonstration cities program does not propose any new cures for urban ills, but instead promises to coordinate existing programs and policies. But Professor Wilson contends that the demonstration cities program does not face up to the fundamental problem of federal policy in urban areas: "We have neither concrete goals nor clear priorities; as a result not only are our federal programs productive of dilemmas, but the dilemmas are becoming each year more obvious." Professor Wilson sets forth an alternative policy which would not scrap existing federal programs but redirect "urban problems" as he understands them. He argues for a more rational policy for dealing with "urban problems," one which focuses on the human problems rather than the physical problems of the city. (See James Q Wilson, *The War on Cities*)

Summary of Federal Programs in Housing and Urban Development*

U.S. Department of Housing and Urban Development

Responsibilities of the Department of Housing and Urban Development

The Department of Housing and Urban Development (HUD) is the Federal agency concerned primarily with housing, community development and a wide variety of interrelated programs, whose objective is better homes and communities. HUD, the eleventh executive Department, came into existence November 9, 1965, as the successor to the Housing and Home Finance Agency and its constituents.

The Department absorbed all of the programs formerly administered by HHFA. In addition, HUD assumed responsibility for various new activities authorized by the Housing and Urban Development Act of 1965 (PL 89-117).

The entire range of federally-aided programs for urban renewal and redevelopment, public housing, urban and metropolitan planning, open space land, mass transit and community facilities was continued and, in some cases, expanded by the Housing Act of 1965.

In addition, the Department administers such programs as: FHA mortgage insurance for new residential construction and home modernization; housing for the elderly and the handicapped through public and private financing; special housing needs, including the rehabilitation and redevelopment of blighted areas; housing for moderate and lower-income

*From U.S. Department of Housing and Urban Development, *Programs of the Department of Housing and Urban Development* (Washington, D.C.: U.S. Government Printing Office, 1967).

families; college and university housing and related facilities, and housing for service men and veterans.

The Department also administers various programs of financial and technical assistance to localities for the planning and construction of essential public works and facilities.

New programs established by the Housing Act of 1965 and administered by the Department include the rent supplement program, designed to help provide privately built housing for low-income individuals and families, and extended mortgage insurance to all veterans who have not used their Veterans Administration guaranteed loans.

Other new programs in the 1965 Act extended Federal grants, on a matching basis, to cities to finance basic water and sewer facilities and neighborhood facilities. Limits on open space land grants were increased, and this program was expanded to help communities acquire and clear open space in built-up areas. Urban beautification, park development, and recreational facilities programs were added. The Act also opened the way to more orderly development of the suburbs by authorizing FHA mortgage insurance for the acquisition and development of land by private builders and developers.

Grants for Basic Sewer and Water Facilities

Purposes: This program is designed to assist and encourage the communities of the nation to construct adequate basic water and sewer facilities to promote their efficient and orderly growth and development.
Specific Uses: Provides grants to local public bodies and agencies to finance up to 50 percent of the cost of improving or constructing basic water and sewer facilities. Where there is no existing system, the project must be so designed that it can be linked with other independent water and sewer facilities in the future.
Who may apply: Local public bodies and agencies.
Specific Requirements: A grant may be made for any project if it is determined that the project is necessary to provide adequate water or sewer facilities for the people to be served, and that the project is

(1) designed so that an adequate capacity will be available to serve the reasonably foreseeable growth needs of the area,

(2) consistent with a program for a unified or officially coordinated area-wide water or sewer facilities system as part of the comprehensively planned development of the area, and

(3) necessary to orderly community development.

No grant shall be made for any sewer facilities unless the Secretary of

Health, Education, and Welfare certifies to the Secretary of the Department of Housing and Urban Development that any waste material carried by such facilities will be adequately treated before it is discharged into any public waterway so as to meet applicable Federal, State, interstate, or local water quality standards.

Grants for Neighborhood Facilities

Purposes: To provide neighborhood facilities needed for programs carrying out health, recreation, social or similar necessary community services in the area.

Specific uses: Finances specific projects, such as neighborhood or community centers, youth centers, health stations and other public buildings to provide health or recreational or similar social services.

Terms: Grants can cover up to two-thirds of the project cost, or 75 percent in redevelopment areas designated under the Public Works and Economic Development Act of 1965, or any act supplemental to it.

Who may apply: A local public body or agency. (In some circumstances, projects may be undertaken by a local body or agency through a non-profit organization.)

Specific requirements: Emphasis will be placed on projects which are so located as to be available for use by a significant portion of the area's low- or moderate-income residents, and on those which will support a community action program under the Economic Opportunity Act.

Public Facility Loans

Purposes: This program provides long-term loans for the construction of needed public facilities such as sewer or water facilities.

Specific uses: A variety of public works may be financed under this program. When aid is available from other Federal agencies, such as for airports, highways, hospitals and sewage treatment facilities, HUD assists only with those parts of the project not covered by other Federal programs.

Terms: Term of loan may be up to 40 years. It will be governed by the applicant's ability to pay and by the estimated useful life of the proposed facility. The interest rate for fiscal year 1966 to be determined.

Who may apply: Local units of government or State instrumentalities. Private non-profit corporations for sewer and water facilities needed to serve a small municipality if there is no existing public body able to construct and operate the facilities.

Specific requirements: The population of the applicant community must be under 50,000, with two exceptions. In those communities near a research or development installation of the National Aeronautics and Space Agency, the population requirement does not apply. In the case of communities located in redevelopment areas so designated under the Public Works and Economic Development Act of 1965, the population limit is 150,000.

Related programs: Grants for basic water and sewer facilities, public works planning advances, urban planning assistance and grants for advance acquisition of land.

Urban Renewal

Purpose: To assist cities undertaking local programs for the elimination and prevention of slums and blight, whether residential or nonresidential, and the elimination of the factors that create slums and blight. Urban renewal is a long-range effort to achieve better communities through planned redevelopment of deteriorated and deteriorating areas by means of a partnership among local governments, private enterprise, citizens, and the Federal Government.

Specific uses: Community-wide renewal programs which identify needs and resources and establish schedules and priorities for accomplishing the work to be done; plan and carry out urban renewal projects for the rehabilitation and redevelopment of blighted area; and undertake programs of concentrated code enforcement and demolition of buildings that are substandard and constitute a hazard to public health and welfare.

Terms: Activities and projects are financed with Federal advances and loans, Federal grants, and local contributions. Federal grants generally pay up to two-thirds of net project cost, but may be as much as three-fourths in some instances. Local contributions may include cash or non-cash grants in aid. Also available are special rehabilitation loans and grants, and housing assistance programs for low income, elderly, and handicapped individuals and families who reside in project areas.

Who may apply: Local public agencies authorized by State law to undertake projects with Federal assistance. LPA's may be separate public agency, local housing authority, or a department of the city government.

Specific requirements: Community must certify that it cannot carry out its urban renewal plans with local resources alone; must adopt and have certified by the Department of Housing and Urban Development a Workable Program for Community Improvement; and must have a feasible plan for the relocation of families and individuals displaced as a result of governmental action into decent, safe, and sanitary housing at prices or rentals within their means. A renewal project must conform to a general plan for the development of the community as a whole.

Urban Planning Assistance Program

Purposes: To foster good community, metropolitan area, regional and statewide planning.

Specific uses: Preparation of comprehensive development plans, including planning for the provision of public facilities; transportation facilities, and long-range fiscal plans. Programming and scheduling of capital improvements.

Terms: Federal grants of two-thirds of the cost of the work; local contribution of one-third. In some instances, Federal grants may amount to as much as three-fourths.

Who may apply: Cities and other municipalities with less than 50,000 population, counties, and Indian reservations, through their State Planning Agencies. Official State, metropolitan, and regional planning agencies. Metropolitan organizations of public officials, cities and counties in redevelopment areas, without regard to size. Official governmental planning agencies for Federally impacted areas. Localities which have suffered a major disaster and areas which have suffered a decline in employment as a result of decline in Federal purchases may apply directly to the Department of Housing and Urban Development.

Urban Mass Transportation Grants

Purposes: To help localities provide and improve urban mass transportation facilities and equipment; encourage planning and establishment of areawide urban transportation systems; and aid financing of such systems.

Federal grants may be made for up to two-thirds of the cost of facilities and equipment that cannot reasonably be financed by revenues. Local grants are required for the other one-third.

Federal loans for a maximum period of 40 years may be made for the entire cost of capital improvements, where financing is not available privately on reasonable terms.

Who may apply: Qualified State or local public bodies or agencies, including those of one or more States, or one or more municipalities or other political subdivisions of a single State.

Special requirements: All projects must be needed for carrying out a program for a unified or officially coordinated transit system as part of the comprehensively planned development of the urban area. However, until

July 1, 1967, loans and grants may be made on an emergency basis with less strict planning requirements, but grants are limited to one-half rather than two-thirds of net project cost. The full grant would be available upon completion of the full planning requirements within three years.

Related programs: Mass Transportation Demonstration Program: Federal grants up to two-thirds of the cost of projects to test and demonstrate new ideas and new methods for improving mass transportation systems and service.

Urban Planning Assistance: Federal grants help finance comprehensive planning for urban areas, including mass transportation planning.

Public Works Planning Advances: Interest-free advances for engineering surveys, designs and plans for specific public works, including public transportation facilities.

Open Space Land and Urban Beautification Grants

Purposes: To assist communities in acquiring and developing land for open-space uses and in carrying out urban beautification programs.

Specific uses: Provide parks and other recreation, conservation, and scenic areas or preserve historic places. Urban beautification and improvement includes such activities as street landscaping, park improvements, tree planting, and upgrading of malls and squares. Relocation payments are provided for individuals, families, and businesses displaced by land acquisitions.

Terms: Federal assistance has been increased from 20 and 30 percent to a single level of 50 percent to help public agencies acquire and preserve urban lands having value for park, recreation, scenic, or historic purposes. Where necessary to provide open space in built-up urban areas, grants can cover up to 50 percent of the cost of acquiring and clearing developed land. Fifty percent assistance is also available to assist in developing lands acquired under the open-space land program.

A grant for urban beautification can be up to 50 percent of the expenditures for urban beautification. However, grants of up to 90 percent are authorized to carry out projects of special value for demonstrating new and improved methods and materials for urban beautification.

Who may apply: State and local public bodies.

Specific requirements: Assisted open-space activities must be part of an area-wide open-space acquisition and development program which, in turn, is consistent with area-wide comprehensive planning. Developed lands in built-up areas are eligible only if open-wide space needs cannot be met with existing undeveloped or predominantly undeveloped land. Beautification activities must have significant, long-term benefits to the community and must be part of a local beautification program. Such programs must (1) represent significant and effective efforts, involving all available public and private resources for urban beautification and improvement, and (2) be important to the comprehensively planned development of the locality.

Related programs: Urban renewal; urban planning assistance; outdoor recreation and parks programs of Department of Interior; neighborhood facilities program of HUD; small watershed Program of Department of Agriculture; landscaping activities under Federal highway program; FHA Land Development Program.

College Housing

Purposes: To help colleges and hospitals expand their facilities to absorb the increasing influx of students.

Specific uses: The loans must be used for the construction of college residence halls, faculty and married student housing, dining facilities, college unions and housing for student nurses and interns.

Terms: Loans may be repaid over periods as long as 50 years, at an interest rate of 3 percent.

Who may apply: Public or private nonprofit colleges and universities, if they offer at least a two-year program acceptable for full credit toward a bachelor's degree. Public or private nonprofit hospitals, if approved by the appropriate State authority to operate a nursing school beyond the high school level, or approved for internship and residencies by the American Medical Association or American Osteopathic Association.

Specific Requirements: Each institution develops its own plans, subject to local zoning and building codes. Engineering plans are reviewed by HUD. Competitive bidding is required.

Low Rent Public Housing

Housing Assistance Administration (HAA) is the successor of the old Public Housing Administration, established by the Housing Act of 1937, which authorized the low-rent public housing program to provide homes for those who could not afford decent housing without Government assistance. HAA, in addition to its low-rent public housing activities, administers a direct loan program to provide rental housing for the elderly of moderate income.

Public Housing. The basic HAA program, public housing, has resulted in the establishment of 2,200 local public housing authorities. Since 1937 these local agencies have built 680,000 low-rent units. The median income for those occupying this housing is about $2,700, according to HUD officials, although each housing authority establishes its own eligibility limits.

The bulk of all public housing is provided through the construction by local housing authorities of public housing projects. Each authority receives an annual subsidy from the Federal Government to keep rents in the projects low enough to provide housing for very poor persons.

Since the passage of the 1965 Housing Act, the HAA has put greater stress on rehabilitating existing housing for use as low-rent public housing than it has on new construction. The HAA claims that rehabilitation can provide much needed housing faster and more cheaply than new construction. Also, rehabilitation avoids the project concept of public housing, which has been widely criticized for fostering racial and economic segregation.

Turnkey. Another new approach to expanding the supply of low-rent housing is the so-called turnkey method. Under turnkey, local housing authorities contract with private developers, builders and rehabilitators to buy, upon completion, housing they have built or rehabilitated. The turnkey method is designed to short-circuit the lengthy delays that often occur when local authorities build housing projects themselves. Under turnkey, 900 units were started in fiscal 1967, the program's first year. This figure is expected to increase substantially in fiscal 1968 as HUD places even heavier emphasis on turnkey.

A variation of turnkey, being tried in Washington, D.C., is where not only the housing is built by a private developer, but upon completion the local housing authority turns the project over to a private real estate firm for management.

Leasing. Another new approach, aimed at speeding up the process of increasing the public housing inventory, is the so-called "rent certificates" program which was approved in the 1965 Housing Act. The program permits local housing authorities to lease private dwellings for low-income families. The federal contribution makes up the difference in rent that the owner receives and the amount the tenant-occupant is able to pay. The leasing program has been termed a way of providing "instant" housing for poor families who are in acute need. Some 4,800 units were leased in fiscal 1967. The leasing program has been hailed because it permits federally subsidized properties to remain on local tax rolls and also spurs property owners to upgrade their properties, having been assured that they will be able to rent their units to a housing authority after the rehabilitation work is done.

Housing for Elderly or Handicapped. A final HAA program is long-term, low interest loans to private, non-profit corporations to provide housing for elderly or handicapped people of moderate income — defined as those with incomes too high for public housing but too low for the private housing market. A total of 8,000 such units were started in fiscal 1967. Specific income limits are established for individual communities within national limits of $4,000 for a single person and $4,800 for two-person families.

FHA Home Mortgage Insurance (Regular Program)

Objective: To help families undertake home ownership on a sound basis.
Specific uses: Insurance of mortgages to finance the purchase of one- to four-family homes and of single-family homes in outlying areas.
Terms: Maximum mortgage amount for single-family home—$30,000; for homes in outlying areas, $12,500.

Ratio of loan to property value — 97 percent of first $15,000, plus 90 percent of next $5,000, plus 80 percent of value over $20,000; for qualified veterans, 100 percent of first $15,000, plus 90 percent of next $5,000, plus 85 percent of value above $20,000. On veterans' transactions, a $200 cash investment is required. On homes not constructed under FHA or VA inspection and completed less than a year the ratios are 90 percent of the first $20,000 of value, plus 80 percent (85 percent for veterans) of value above $20,000.

Minimum cash investment — 3 percent of acquisition cost (purchase price plus closing costs exclusive of prepaid items); in case of veterans, $200 on homes valued up to $15,000. The program for outlying areas permits buyer to borrow money for required cash investment from source acceptable to FHA.

Interest rate — 5¼ percent; *mortgage insurance premium* — ½ of 1 percent.

Maximum repayment period — 30 years; under certain circumstances, 35 years.

Who may apply: In general, any person with a good credit record, the cash needed to initiate the transaction, and enough regular income to make monthly mortgage payments without difficulty.
Special requirements: Borrower must meet FHA requirements for mortgagor; property must meet FHA minimum property standards; loan terms must comply with those established by FHA.
Related programs: Other FHA home mortgage insurance and/or home improvement loan insurance programs for urban renewal areas, cooperatives, condominiums, and low and moderate income families.

Section 221 (d) (3). In 1961 the FHA was given the task of administering a new program of mortgage insurance, known by the numerical designation, 221 (d)(3). Section 221 (d)(3) authorized both a market-rate and a below-market rate program. Under the latter, nonprofit organizations, cooperatives and public agencies could borrow money from commercial sources, such as banks, at interest rates below those generally prevailing in the housing market for sponsorship of apartment developments for low-and moderate-income families. The interest rate ranged from 3⅞ to 4 percent. In 1965 the 221 (d)(3) below-market interest rate program became federally subsidized with a flat 3 percent rate.

In the case of the below-market interest rate program, the loans are insured by the FHA. The Federal National Mortgage Association (FNMA) then buys the mortgage from the bank or other lender which normally agrees to the sale in order to avoid tying up funds in low-interest loans. The net effect of the procedure is that FNMA advances money at low interest rates for construction or rehabilitation of housing for this program.

In 1965 FHA's job was again broadened with the enactment of the controversial rent supplements program and in 1966 with the creation of a new mortgage insurance program — Section 221 (h) — which provided interest subsidies on private loans to low-income families for the purchase of rehabilitated homes.

However, the most significant of the special FHA programs is the 221 (d)(3) below-market interest rate program. In fiscal 1967, 13,200 new units were started under this program and an additional 500 units were rehabilitated.

It is essentially a moderate-income program, according to HUD officials. For example, the income eligibility requirement for entry into this housing in New York City is $6,150 for a single person; $7,450 for two; $8,750 for three or four; $10,050 for five or six and $11,400 for seven or more. In Fort Worth, Texas, the income ceilings under the 221 (d)(3) below-market interest rate program are $4,600 for a single person; $5,550 for two; $6,550 for three or four; $7,550 for five or six and $8,500 for seven or more.

Rent Supplements. The key low-income program in FHA is the rent supplements program. This makes low-income individuals and families who are either elderly, handicapped, displaced by Government action or occupants of substandard housing eligible for admission to FHA 221 (d)(3), new or rehabilitated, housing which is owned by a private nonprofit, limited-dividend or cooperative mortgagor. The housing owner enters into a 40-year contract with HUD, which promises to pay federal rent supplements to eligible tenants of the housing.

The subsidy payments for any dwelling unit cannot be higher than the amount by which the fair market rental for the unit exceeds 25 percent of the tenant's income. When the tenant has enough income to pay the full rent he may continue to live in the same unit but without rent supplement payments. There are strict limits on the per-unit costs of the rent supplement housing that can be built.

The program was authorized by Congress, after bitter controversy, in the 1965 Housing Act and received its initial contract funds only with great difficulty in 1966 and 1967. Only 900 rent supplement units were begun in fiscal 1967 but the number is expected to increase significantly in fiscal 1968. HUD officials report that currently some 2,300 units have been completed, with some 1,800 families receiving supplement payments.

Low-Income Sales Housing. The newest of FHA's special programs is 221 (h), which was tacked onto the 1966 Demonstration Cities and Metropolitan Development Act and which is currently operating only on a pilot basis. Under 221 (h), the FHA insures mortgages of nonprofit organizations — church groups, nonprofit industry groups, antipoverty community action groups—to finance the purchase and rehabilitation of deteriorating or substandard housing. The nonprofit groups then sell the homes to individuals and families with incomes equivalent to or below the maximum income permitted for those eligible for rent supplements or public housing. The interest rate on the mortgages for the original purchase by the sponsor is 6 percent, but it goes down to 3 percent when the rehabilitated unit is sold to a low-income person for the minimum $200 downpayment. The FNMA provides the interest subsidy.

Federal National Mortgage Association Secondary Market Operations (Regular Program)

Objective: To assist the broad general secondary market for mortgages by providing a degree of liquidity for mortgage investments, thereby improving the distribution of investment capital available for mortgage financing.

Specific uses: FNMA purchases, services and sells FHA-insured and VA-guaranteed mortgages. Rural housing loans insured by the Farmers Home Administration of the Department of Agriculture (FHDA loans) are also bought and sold. In addition, the corporation makes short-term loans on the security of such mortgages and loans; buys and sells FHA-insured home improvement loans; and will consider the purchase, on a negotiated basis, of participations (partial interests) in mortgages and FHDA loans.

Purchase terms: Fees and charges are imposed on mortgage sellers and borrowers to prevent excessive use of these facilities and to enable them to be self-sustaining. These users of the operations are also required to subscribe for FNMA common stock.

Immediate purchase contracts — Prices to be paid by FNMA are established within the range of market prices for the particular classes of mortgages or loans involved. Price paid for a mortgage may vary according to its interest rate, location of the security property, relative equity of the mortgagor, term of the loan, and other factors.

Standby commitment contracts — Under which sellers offer mortgages for future purchase, are issued at prices sufficient to facilitate financing, but sufficiently below the price then offered by FNMA for immediate purchase to prevent excessive commitment purchases by the corporation.

Eligible mortgages — Each mortgage or FHDA loan must meet FNMA eligibility and acceptability requirements. Each must also be of such quality, type, and class as to meet, generally, the purchase standards imposed by private institutional mortgage investors.

Federal Housing Programs in the 20 Largest Cities*

The following table shows the cumulative total of federal aid to the 20 largest cities, through calendar year 1966, for urban renewal, public housing, moderate-income housing and rent supplement programs. The table also indicates the number of housing units involved in the public housing, moderate-income housing and rent supplement programs. All funds are given in thousands of dollars.

	Urban Renewal Funds	Public Housing Funds	Public Housing Units	Moderate Incoming Housing Funds	Moderate Income Housing Units	Rent Sup- plement Funds	Rent Sup- plement Units
New York	$330,172	$1,047,297	73,379	$20,400	1,268	$591	984
Chicago	175,252	489,574	37,795	38,415	2,712	28	46
Los Angeles	29,850	64,729	9,609	1,241	118	241	370
Philadelphia	259,680	187,801	16,293	1,000	96	135	193
Detroit	131,937	75,664	8,680	4,173	325	40	67
Baltimore	94,619	121,517	11,697	3,698	506	62	103
Houston	None	11,777	2,549	None	None	120	200
Cleveland	48,740	113,606	10,454	13,136	1,311	63	106
Washington	74,813	158,499	12,486	21,353	1,804	16	26
St. Louis	55,943	122,662	8,769	15,537	1,122	101	168

	Urban Renewal Funds	Public Housing Funds	Public Housing Units	Moderate Incoming Housing Funds	Moderate Income Housing Units	Rent Supplement Funds	Rent Supplement Units
San Francisco	108,399	65,544	6,580	15,454	872	3	5
Milwaukee	38,161	41,516	3,250	3,240	328	133	129
Boston	185,149	115,225	12,793	14,983	896	317	200
Dallas	None	49,313	6,372	28,574	2,682	10	17
New Orleans	2,168	114,621	12,270	None	None	60	100
Pittsburgh	114,834	95,130	10,014	3,827	278	16	26
San Antonio	23,256	44,212	5,554	5,874	684	390	650
San Diego	None	None	None	3,200	248	139	232
Seattle	15,660	18,011	3,668	674	49	40	67
Buffalo	41,658	29,804	4,520	3,242	219	None	None

*Source: Department of Housing and Urban Development.

The Demonstration Cities Program*

Lyndon B. Johnson

To the Congress of the United States:
Nineteen hundred and sixty-six can be the year of rebirth for American cities. This Congress, and this people, can set in motion forces of change in great urban areas that will make them the masterpieces of our civilization. Fifty years from now our population will reach that of today's India. Our grandchildren will inhabit a world as different from ours as ours is from the world of Jefferson.

None can predict the shape of his life with any certainty. Yet one thing is sure. It will be lived in cities. By the year 2000, four out of five Americans will live and work in a metropolitan area. We are not strangers to an urban world. We began our national life gathered in towns along the Atlantic seaboard. We built new commercial centers around the Great Lakes and in the Midwest, to serve our westward expansion. Forty million came from Europe to fuel our economy and enrich our community life. This century has seen the steady and rapid migration of farm families — seeking jobs and the promise of the city.

From this rich experience we have learned much. We know that cities can stimulate the best in man, and aggravate the worst. We know the convenience of city life, and its paralysis. We know its promise, and its dark foreboding. What we may only dimly perceive is the gravity of the choice before us. Shall we make our cities livable for ourselves and our

*Message from the President to the Congress, transmitting recommendations for City Demonstration Programs, January 26, 1966. Reprinted from H.R. Doc. No. 368, 89th Congress, 2nd Session.

posterity? Or shall we by timidity and neglect damn them to fester and decay?

If we permit our cities to grow without rational design; if we stand passively by, while the center of each becomes a hive of deprivation, crime, and hopelessness; if we devour the countryside as though it were limitless, while our ruins — millions of tenement apartments and dilapidated houses — go unredeemed; if we become two people, the suburban affluent and the urban poor, each filled with mistrust and fear one for the other — if this is our desire and policy as a people, then we shall effectively cripple each generation to come. We shall as well condemn our own generation to a bitter paradox: an educated, wealthy, progressive people, who would not give their thoughts, their resources, or their wills to provide for their common well-being.

I do not believe such a fate is either necessary or inevitable. But I believe this will come to pass — unless we commit ourselves now to the planning, the building, the teaching, and the caring that alone can forestall it. That is why I am recommending a massive demonstration cities program. I recommend that both the public and private sectors of our economy join to build in our cities and towns an environment for man equal to the dignity of his aspirations. I recommend an effort larger in scope, more comprehensive, more concentrated, than any that has gone before.

I

The Work of the Past

I know the work of the past three decades. I have shared in the forging of our Federal housing and renewal programs. I know what they have done for millions of urban Americans:

8 million single-family dwellings assisted by the Federal Housing Administration.
An additional 6.7 million assisted by the Veterans Administration.
1.1 million multiple units created.
605,000 families moved out of decayed and unsanitary dwellings into decent public housing.
300,000 dwelling units supported under urban renewal.

Without these programs, the goal I recommend today would be impossible to achieve. Because Federal sponsorship is so effective a part of our system of homebuilding, we can conceive a far larger purpose than it has yet fulfilled. We must make use of every established housing program — and of social, educational, and economic instruments as well — if the demonstration cities program is to succeed.

The Problem Today

Our housing programs have built a platform, from which we may see how far away is the reborn city we desire. For there still remain:

Some four million urban families living in homes of such disrepair as to violate decent housing standards.

The need to provide over 30 per cent more housing annually than we are currently building.

Our chronic inability to provide sufficient low- and moderate-income housing, of adequate quality, at a reasonable price.

The special problem of the poor and the Negro, unable to move freely from their ghettoes, exploited in the quest for the necessities of life.

Increasing pressures on municipal budgets, with large city per capita expenditures rising 36 per cent in the three years after 1960.

The high human costs: crime, delinquency, welfare loads, disease, and health hazards. This is man's fate in those broken neighborhoods where he can "feel the enclosure of the flaking walls and see through the window the blackened reflection of the tenement across the street that blocks out the world beyond."

The tragic waste, and indeed, the chaos, that threatens where children are born into the stifling air of overcrowded rooms, and destined for a poor diet, inadequate schools, streets of fear and sordid temptation, joblessness, and the gray anxiety of the ill prepared.

And the flight to the suburbs of more fortunate men and women who might have provided the leadership and the means for reversing this human decline.

The Inadequate Response

Since 1949, the urban renewal program has been our chief instrument in the struggle for a decent urban environment. Over 800 cities are participating in urban renewal programs. Undertaken and designed by the cities themselves, these efforts have had an increasing influence on the use of urban land. Last year the Congress wisely extended the authorization for urban renewal at a higher level than before.

Years of experience with urban renewal have taught us much about its strengths and weaknesses. Since 1961 we have made major alterations in its administration. We have made it more responsive to human needs. We have more vigorously enforced the requirement of a workable program for the entire community. Within the limits of current law, we have achieved considerable progress toward these goals.

Nevertheless, the social and psychological effects of relocating the poor have not always been treated as what they are. They are the unavoidable consequences of slum clearance, demanding as much concern as physical redevelopment.

The size and scale of urban assistance have been too small, and too widely dispersed. Present programs are often prisoners of archaic and wasteful building practices. They have inhibited the use of modern technology. They have inflated the cost of rebuilding.

The benefits and efficiencies that can come from metropolitan planning are still unrealized in most urban regions. Insufficient resources cause extensive delays in many projects. The result is growing blight and overcrowding that thwart our best efforts to resist them.

The goals of major Federal programs have often lacked cohesiveness. Some work for the revitalization of the central city. Some accelerate suburban growth. Some unite urban communities. Some disrupt them.

Urban Dilemmas

Virtually every forward step we have taken has had its severe limitations. Each of those steps has involved a public choice, and created a public dilemma:

Major clearance and reconstruction, with its attendant hardships of relocation.

Relieving traffic congestion, thereby widening the gulf between the affluence of suburbia and the poverty of the city.

Involving urban residents in redeveloping their own areas, hence lengthening the time and increasing the cost of the job.

Preserving the autonomy of local agencies, thus crippling our efforts to attack regional problems on a regional basis.

These dilemmas cannot be completely resolved by any single program, no matter how well designed. The prize — cities of spacious beauty and lively promise, where men are truly free to determine how they will live — is too rich to be lost because the problems are complex.

Let there be debate over means and priorities. Let there be experiment with a dozen approaches, or a hundred. But let there be commitment to that goal.

II

What is Required

From the experience of three decades, it is clear to me that American cities require a program that will —

Concentrate our available resources—in planning tools, in housing construction, in job training, in health facilities, in recreation, in welfare programs, in education—to improve the conditions of life in urban areas.

Join together all available talent and skills in a coordinated effort.

Mobilize local leadership and private initiative, so that local citizens will determine the shape of their new city—freed from the constraints that have handicapped their past efforts and inflated their costs.

A Demonstration Cities Program

I propose a demonstration cities program that will offer qualifying cities of all sizes the promise of a new life for their people.

I propose that we make massive additions to the supply of low- and moderate-cost housing.

I propose that we combine physical reconstruction and rehabilitation with effective social programs throughout the rebuilding process.

I propose that we achieve new flexibility in administrative procedures.

I propose that we focus all the techniques and talents within our society on the crisis of the American city.

It will not be simple to qualify for such a program. We have neither the means nor the desire to invest public funds in an expensive program whose net effects will be marginal, wasteful, or visible only after protracted delay. We intend to help only those cities who help themselves. I propose these guidelines for determining a city's qualifications for the benefits — and achievements — of this program.

1. The demonstration should be of sufficient magnitude both in its physical and social dimensions to arrest blight and decay in entire neighborhoods. It must make a substantial impact within the coming few years on the development of the entire city.

2. The demonstration should bring about a change in the total environment of the area affected. It must provide schools, parks, playgrounds, community centers, and access to all necessary community facilities.

3. The demonstration — from its beginning — should make use of every available social program. The human cost of reconstruction and relocation must be reduced. New opportunities for work and training must be offered.

4. The demonstration should contribute to narrowing the housing gap between the deprived and the rest of the community. Major additions must be made to the supply of sound dwellings. Equal opportunity in the choice of housing must be assured to every race.

5. The demonstration should offer maximum occasions for employing residents of the demonstration area in all phases of the program.

6. The demonstration should foster the development of local and private initiative and widespread citizen participation — especially from the demonstration area — in the planning and execution of the program.

7. The demonstration should take advantage of modern cost-reducing technologies without reducing the quality of the work. Neither the struc-

ture of real estate taxation, cumbersome building codes, nor inefficient building practices should deter rehabilitation or inflate project costs.

8. The demonstration should make major improvements in the quality of the environment. There must be a high quality of design in new buildings, and attention to man's need for open spaces and attractive landscaping.

9. The demonstration should make relocation housing available at costs commensurate with the incomes of those displaced by the project. Counseling services, moving expenses, and small business loans should be provided, together with assistance in job placement and re-training.

10. The demonstration should be managed in each demonstration city by a single authority with adequate powers to carry out and coordinate all phases of the program. There must be a serious commitment to the project on the part of local, and, where appropriate, State authorities. Where required to carry out the plan, agreements should be reached with neighboring communities.

11. The demonstration proposal should offer proof that adequate municipal appropriations and services are available and will be sustained throughout the demonstration period.

12. The demonstration should maintain or establish a residential character in the area.

13. The demonstration should be consistent with existing development plans for the metropolitan areas involved. Transportation plans should coordinate every appropriate mode of city and regional transportation.

14. The demonstration should extend for an initial six-year period. It should maintain a schedule for the expeditious completion of the project.

These guidelines will demand the full cooperation of government at every level and of private citizens in each area. I believe our Federal system is creative enough to inspire that cooperative effort. I know it must be creative if it is to prosper and flourish.

Size of the Program

The program I recommend is intended to eliminate blight in the entire demonstration area. Through efficient rebuilding it must replace that blight with attractive and economic housing, social services, and community facilities.

There are many ways by which this can be done, once the commitment has been made to do it. Total clearance and reconstruction; partial clearance and rehabilitation; rehabilitation alone—any of these methods may be chosen by local citizens. Whatever approach is selected, however, must be comprehensive enough to be effective and economic.

There are few cities or towns in America which could not participate in the demonstration cities program. We shall take special care to see that urban communities of all sizes are included. For each such community, the impact of the program wil be significant, involving as much as 15 to 20 per cent of the existing substandard structures.

For the largest qualifying cities, a relatively modest program could provide decent housing for approximately 5,000 families now living in substandard dwelling units. It could rehabilitate other marginal housing sufficient to affect 50,000 people. A typical program could well involve a total of 35,000 units or 100,000 people.

For cities of approximately 100,000 people, 1,000 families could be rehoused and 3,000 units rehabilitated, affecting a total of 10,000 people.

Benefits of the Program

I recommend that participating cities receive two types of Federal assistance:

First, *the complete array of all available grants and urban aids* in the fields of housing, renewal, transportation, education, welfare, economic opportunity, and related programs.

Second, *special grants amounting to 80 per cent of the non-Federal cost of our grant-in-aid programs included in the demonstration.* These grants are to supplement the efforts of local communities. They are not to be substituted for those efforts.

In every qualifying city, a Federal coordinator would be assigned to assist local officials in bringing together all the relevant Federal resources.

Once authorized, the supplemental funds would be made available in a common account. They would be drawn at the discretion of the community to support the program. They would be certified by the Federal coordinator.

It is vital that incentives be granted for cost reductions achieved during the performance of the program.

At least as vital as the dollar commitment for rebuilding and rehabilitation is the social program commitment. We must link our concern for the total welfare of the person with our desire to improve the physical city in which he lives. For the first time, social and construction agencies would be joined in a massive common effort, responsive to a common local authority.

There is another benefit—not measurable in dollars, or even in the extended range of social services—that qualifying cities would secure by participating in this program.

It is a sense of hope—

That the city is not beyond reach of redemption by men of good will. That through wise planning, cooperation, hard work, and the sacrifice of those outmoded codes and practices that make widespread renewal impossibly expensive today, it *is* possible to reverse the city's decline.

That knowledge, that confidence, that hope can make all the difference in the decade ahead.

III

Federal Cost

Funds are required in the first year to assist our cities in the preparation of demonstration plans. We should not underestimate the problems involved in achieving such a plan. The very scale of the demonstration— its widespread and profound effects on the social and physical structure of the city—calls for marshaling the city's planning and administrative resources on an unprecedented scale.

I estimate the appropriate Federal contribution to this planning effort at $12 million. For the supplemental demonstration grants I will recommend appropriations, over a six-year period, totaling over $2.3 billion, or an average of some $400 million per year.

It is impossible to estimate exactly—but it is necessary to consider— the rising cost of welfare services, crime prevention, unemployment, and declining property values which will plague all governments, local, State, and Federal, if we do not move quickly to heal and revitalize our cities.

Metropolitan Planning

The success of each demonstration will depend on the quality of its planning, and the degree of cooperation it elicits from the various governmental bodies concerned, as well as from private interests.

Most metropolitan areas conduct some degree of metropolitan planning now. The Federal Government has made funds available throughout the country so that State and local planning agencies might devise— many for the first time—comprehensive plans for metropolitan areas.

I recommend improvements and extensions of this program. The Congress enacted it recognizing that the problems of growth, transportation, housing, and public services cannot be considered by one entity of government alone.

The absence of cooperation between contiguous areas is wasteful. It is also blind to the reality of urban life. What happens in the central city, or the suburb, is certain to affect the quality of life in the other.

The widespread demand for these funds has resulted in their being spread thinly across the 50 States. Thus, the benefits of a truly coordinated attack on metropolitan problems have not generally been realized.

Incentives to Orderly Metropolitan Development

Over the past five years, the Congress has authorized Federal grants for urban mass transportation, open space, and sewer and water facilities. The Congress has required that such projects be consistent with comprehensive planning for an entire urban or metropolitan area. The Federal Government has thus not only helped our localities to provide the facilities they need; it has also stimulated cooperation and joint planning among neighboring jurisdictions.

But more remains to be done. The powerful forces of urban growth threaten to overwhelm efforts to achieve orderly development. A metropolitan plan should be an instrument for shaping sound urban growth—not a neglected document.

I now propose a new incentive to help assure that metropolitan plans achieve their potential.

The Federal Government should bear a larger share of the total cost of related Federal aid programs. This share would be borne where local jurisdictions show that they are ready to be guided by their own plans in working out the patterns of their own development and where they establish the joint institutional arrangements necessary to carry out those plans.

Demonstrations of Effective Planning

I propose that a series of demonstrations in effective metropolitan planning be undertaken promptly.

Metropolitan areas would be selected to return the broadest possible data and experience to Federal, State, and local governments. They should therefore be of varying size and environment, in widely separated locations. They would be selected to assure that their benefits reach small communities surrounding the large cities.

Advanced techniques and approaches should be employed. There must be—

Balanced consideration of physical and human development programs.
Coordinated treatment of the regional transportation network.
Technical innovations, such as metropolitan data banks and systems analysis.
New educational and training programs.
New arrangements for coordinating decisions of the various local governments involved.

I estimate the cost of the demonstrations at $6,500,000.

I shall impose on the new Department of Housing and Urban Development the continuing responsibility to stimulate effective planning. If local governments do not plan for inevitable urban growth cooperatively and sufficiently in advance, even adequate funds and an aggressive determination to improve our cities cannot succeed.

IV

Housing for All

The programs I have proposed—in rebuilding large areas of our cities, and in metropolitan planning—are essential for the rebirth of urban America.

Yet at the center of the cities' housing problem lies racial discrimination. Crowded miles of inadequate dwellings—poorly maintained and frequently overpriced—are the lot of most Negro Americans in many of our cities. Their avenue of escape to a more attractive neighborhood is often closed because of their color.

The Negro suffers from this, as do his children. So does the community at large. Where housing is poor, schools are generally poor. Unemployment is widespread. Family life is threatened. The community's welfare burden is steadily magnified. These are the links in the chain of racial discrimination.

This administration is working to break that chain—through aid to education, medical care, community action programs, job retraining, and the maintenance of a vigorous economy.

The time has come when we should break one of its strongest links— the often subtle but always effective force of housing discrimination. The impacted racial ghetto will become a thing of the past only when the Negro American can move his family wherever he can afford to do so.

I shall, therefore, present to the Congress at an early date legislation to bar racial discrimination in the sale or rental of housing.

New Communities

Our existing urban centers, however revitalized, cannot accommodate all the urban Americans of the next generation.

Three million new residents are added each year to our present urban population. The growth of new communities is inevitable. Unless they are to be casual parts of a general urban sprawl, a new approach to their design is required.

We must—

Enlarge the entire scale of the building process.
Make possible new efficiencies in construction, land development, and municipal services.
Relieve population densities.
Offer a variety of homes to a wide range of incomes.

These communities must also provide an environment harmonious to man's needs. They must offer adequate transportation systems, attractive community buildings, and open spaces free from pollution. They must retain much of the natural beauty of the landscape.

The private sector must continue its prominent role in new community development. As I recommended to the Congress last year, mortgage insurance should be made available for sites and community facilities for entire new communities.

It is apparent that new communities will spring into being near an increasing number of major metropolitan areas. Some, already in existence, promise dramatic efficiencies through size and new construction techniques, without sacrificing beauty. Obviously such a development should be encouraged. I recommend that the Congress provide the means of doing so.

Rent Supplement Program

Rarely has a new housing program evoked such a dramatic and positive response as the rent supplement program. The Department of Housing and Urban Affairs has already received preliminary proposals from sponsors to construct nearly 70,000 low-income units under this program as soon as funds become available. The proposals involve 424 projects in 265 localities in 43 States, the District of Columbia, and

Puerto Rico. The sponsors have already selected sites for some 40,000 of these units. The interested groups are about equally divided between nonprofit organizations and private limited-dividend developers.

The need for this program is obvious. It is the need of the poor and the disadvantaged. The demand for the means to meet this need by private enterprise is demonstrated by the figures I have just cited.

I strongly urge the Congress to pass a supplementary appropriation to fund the rent supplement program at the $30 million level it has authorized in the Housing and Urban Development Act of 1965.

Mass Transportation Program

We must continue to help our communities meet their increasing needs for mass transportation facilities. For this purpose, I propose an additional one-year authorization for the urban mass transportation program.

The New Department

No Federal program can be effective unless the agency that administers it is efficient. This is even more crucial for programs that call for comprehensive approaches at both the Federal and local level.

Progress was made after 1961 toward unifying the Housing and Home Finance Agency. But the very nature of that Agency limited the extent to which its several parts could be welded into a truly unified whole. Its Administrator lacked the statutory basis for gaining full control over partially independent agencies.

With this in mind, I requested—and you enacted—legislation to create a Department of Housing and Urban Development. As a result, the Secretary of the new Department now has the authority and the machinery for implementing the new programs I have asked for. I see five ways by which he can do this:

1. He can organize the Department so that its emphasis will be upon meeting modern urban needs—rather than fitting new programs into old and outgrown patterns.
2. He can strengthen the regional structure so that more decisions can be made in the field.
3. He can assert effective leadership throughout the Department.
4. He can mesh together all our social and physical efforts to improve urban living.
5. He can assume leadership among intergovernmental agencies dealing with urban problems.

Such a Department, and such leadership, will be worthy of the program that I recommend you adopt.

A Year of Rebirth

The evidence is all about us that to be complacent about the American city is to invite, at best, inconvenience; at worst, a divided nation.

The programs I have proposed in this message will require a determined commitment of our energy and a substantial commitment of our funds. Yet these programs are well within our resources. Nor do they compare in cost with the ugliness, hostility, and hopelessness of unlivable cities. What would it mean to begin now, and to bring about the rebirth of our cities?

It would mean—

A more tolerable and a more hopeful life for millions of Americans.
The possibility of retaining middle-income families in the city, and even attracting some to return.
Improving the cities' tax base at a time of heavy strain on city budgets.
Ultimately reducing welfare costs.
Avoiding the unnecessary waste of human resources.
Giving to both urban and suburban families the freedom to choose where they will live.
A clean room and a patch of sky for every person, a chance to live near an open space, and to reach it on a safe street.

As Thomas Wolfe wrote, "to every man his chance—to every man, regardless of his birth, his shining, golden opportunity—to every man the right to live, to work, to be himself, and to become whatever thing his manhood and his vision can combine to make him—this . . . is the promise of America."

I believe these are among the most profound aspirations of our people. I want to make them part of our destiny.

I urge the Congress promptly to adopt the Demonstration Cities Act of 1966. If we begin now the planning from which action will flow, the hopes of the twentieth century will become the realities of the twenty-first.

Lyndon B. Johnson.

The White House, January 26, 1966.

List of Model Cities

U.S. Department of Housing and Urban Development

Alabama
  Huntsville
  Tuskegee
Alaska
  Anchorage
  Bethel
Arizona
  Chandler
  Phoenix
Arkansas
  Hot Springs
  Little Rock-North Little Rock
  Logan County
  Pine Bluff
  Russellville
  Texarkana
California
  Alviso
  Berkeley
  Calexico
  Compton
  Fresno
  Los Angeles
  Menlo Park

  Oakland
  Oxnard
  Pittsburg
  Richmond
  San Bernardino
  San Jose
  San Mateo County
  Seaside
Colorado
  Denver
  Pueblo
  Trinidad
  Walsenburg
Connecticut
  Bridgeport
  Hartford
  New Haven
  Waterbury
Delaware
District of Columbia
  Washington, D.C.
Florida
  Dade County
  Sanford
  Tampa

Georgia
  Alma
  Athens
  Atlanta
  Camilla
  Douglas
  Gainesville
Hawaii
  Honolulu
Idaho
Illinois
  Carbondale
  Chicago
  East St. Louis
  Rock Island
  Springfield
Indiana
  Gary
Iowa
  Des Moines
Kansas
  Kansas City
  Olathe
  Wichita
Kentucky
  Bowling Green
  Covington
  Louisville
  Pikeville
Maine
  Bangor
  Portland
Maryland
  Baltimore
  Prince Georges County
Massachusetts
  Boston
  Cambridge
  Chelsea
  Chicopee
  Fall River

Holyoke
Lawrence
Lowell
Lynn
Malden
New Bedford
Pittsfield
Springfield
Worcester
Michigan
  Benton Harbor
  Detroit
  Flint
  Grand Rapids
  Highland Park
  Lansing
  Muskegon
  Saginaw
Minnesota
  Duluth
  Minneapolis
Mississippi
  Brookhaven
  Greenville
  Holly Springs
Missouri
  Joplin
  Kansas City
  St. Louis
Montana
  Butte
  Helena
Nebraska
  Omaha
Nevada
  Las Vegas
  North Las Vegas
New Hampshire
  Manchester
New Jersey
  Atlantic City

Camden
East Orange
Hoboken
Jersey City
Newark
Orange
Perth Amboy
Trenton
New Mexico
Albuquerque
Artesia
New York
Albany
Amsterdam
Binghamton
Buffalo
Cohoes
Lackawanna
Mt. Vernon
New York City
    Central and East Harlem
South Bronx
Central Brooklyn
Newburgh
Poughkeepsie
Rochester
Syracuse
Yonkers
North Carolina
Charlotte
Greenville
High Point
Winston-Salem
North Dakota
Grand Forks
Ohio
Akron
Cincinnati
Cleveland
Columbus
Dayton

Mansfield
Martins Ferry
Springfield
Steubenville
Toledo
Zanesville
Oklahoma
Chickasha
Lawton
McAlester
Tulsa
Oregon
Portland
Pennsylvania
Allegheny County
Butler
Chester
Easton
Erie
Lancaster
New Castle
Philadelphia
Pittsburgh
Reading
Wilkes-Barre
Puerto Rico
San Juan
Rhode Island
Providence
South Carolina
Rock Hill
Spartanburg
South Dakota
Mitchell
Tennessee
Cookeville
Greeneville
Nashville
Pulaski
Shelbyville
Smithville

Texas
  Crystal City
  Eagle Pass
  Edinburgh
  Grand Prairie
  San Antonio
  Texarkana
  Waco
Utah
  Ogden
  Salt Lake City
Vermont
  Winooski
Virginia
  Alexandria

Hampton
Newport News
Norfolk
Portsmouth
Richmond
Washington
  Anacortes
  Ellensburg
  Seattle
  Tacoma
West Virginia
  Charleston
Wyoming
  Cheyenne

The War on Cities*

James Q. Wilson

President Johnson's 1966 special message to Congress on improving the nation's cities was a notable document, both for what it said and for what it did not. It was, in many respects, the sanest and most thoughtful presidential statement on "the urban problem" ever issued. It avoided most of those rhetorical absurdities which link the future of Western civilization with the maintenance of the downtown business district; it stressed the primacy of human and social problems over purely physical ones; and it conceded with great candor the dilemmas, contradictions, and inadequacies of past and present federal programs. (Indeed, the first third of the message could easily have been written by any one of several critics of federal urban renewal and public housing programs.) Many of the proposals made by the President were entirely in keeping with a concern for the problems of disadvantaged people living in cities. Thus, legislation to bar racial discrimination in the sale or rental of housing, and appropriations to implement the rent supplement program (whereby through direct subsidy the poor are given a better chance to acquire decent housing on the private market) were requested.

As reasonable and humane as were this message and the subsequent Model Cities Bill passed by Congress, they both leave unanswered some fundamental questions. While it is refreshing to hear a President admit that present policies have produced some "urban dilemmas," listing the dilemmas is no substitute for resolving them. In fact, far from being

*Reprinted from *The Public Interest* © 1966 by National Affairs, Inc., with the permission of the author and publisher.

resolved, these dilemmas are accentuated by having added to them those of a new program, devised in part by academic critics of the urban renewal program, which will, on a "demonstration" basis try to add to the supply of low and moderate cost housing (while the urban renewal program continues reducing that supply) and to serve "poor and disadvantaged people" (while existing programs presumably go on serving other people). No cohesive policy is suggested—only the co-ordination at the *local* level of existing policies. This will not be easy since the programs to be co-ordinated are run by separate bureaucracies with different and often competing sources of political support at the federal as well as local level.

Indeed, it is striking that an agency—the Housing and Home Finance Agency, now renamed the Department of Housing and Urban Development—which has been so often criticized in the past for allowing almost unfettered discretion to local communities in their use of federal urban renewal funds should, partly in response to these criticisms, have a new program for "demonstration" or "model" cities which continues to rely on local initiative and local objectives in formulating plans.

The Model Cities Bill nowhere says *what* will be done. The difference between it and the older urban renewal program is that now local proposals must conform to "guidelines" laid down by HUD. Presumably these guidelines and the good intentions of the new leadership of HUD will insure that a "model" city is something more than—or at least something different from—an urban renewal city. But the debate on the program suggests that Congress is far from clear as to what that difference is to be; everything depends on administrative decisions, and so far there have not been many.

I

The fundamental problem afflicting federal policy in this area—the problem which this message and bill suggest but do not face—is that *we do not know what we are trying to accomplish.* We have neither concrete goals nor clear priorities; as a result, not only are federal programs productive of dilemmas, but the dilemmas are each year becoming more expensive and more obvious. Do we seek to raise standards of living, maximize housing choices, revitalize the commercial centers of our cities, end suburban sprawl, eliminate discrimination, reduce traffic congestion, improve the quality of urban design, check crime and delinquency, strengthen the effectiveness of local planning, increase citizen participation in local government? All these objectives sound attractive—in part, because they are rather vague—but unfortunately they are in many cases incompatible.

Improving urban design is made harder by efforts to find housing for the poor, for well-designed housing almost always costs more than the poor can afford. A "revitalized" downtown business district not only implies, *it requires* traffic congestion—an "uncongested" Broadway or State Street would be no Broadway or State Street at all. Effective local planning requires *less,* not more, citizen participation—the more views represented, the less the possibility of agreement on any single (especially any single comprehensive) view. Maximum housing choices, unconstrained by discriminatory practices, and reinforced by higher incomes, will give more people the opportunity to join the movement to the suburbs.

American political life has a proven and oft-remarked genius for surviving and even prospering on dilemmas and contradictions. Government maintains the support of potentially hostile groups by letting different federal agencies serve incompatible goals and by encouraging local communities to follow competing policies at federal expense. The new Department of Housing and Urban Development stands squarely in this tradition. Under its previous name (the Housing and Home Finance Agency), it subsidized the flight to the suburbs with FHA mortgage insurance, while trying to lure suburbanites back to the central city with subsidies provided by the Urban Renewal Administration. The Public Housing Administration built low-rent units for the poor while urban renewal was tearing them down. Furthermore, the goals for most programs—especially urban renewal—were determined at the local level. This meant that urban renewal, in itself simply a tool, was used for very different purposes in different cities—in some places to get Negroes out of white neighborhoods, in others to bring middle-class people closer to downtown department stores, in still other places to build dramatic civic monuments, and in a few places to rehabilitate declining neighborhoods and add to the supply of moderately priced housing. Throughout its life, HHFA could have the best of both worlds— in Washington, its leaders could make broad policy statements which were intended to satisfy whatever critics of the program the administration was most sensitive to; meanwhile, in the hundreds of communities where the actual purposes of our housing programs were determined by the decisions of local governing bodies, many objectives which bore only the loosest relationship to federal policy statements were being pursued.

One can admire a system which so neatly accommodates the tensions of political reality without approving of all its consequences. And these consequences stem, in my view, from the fact that, in thinking about solutions to the "urban problem," we have committed ourselves to certain means before we have made a commitment to any goals. The means have been federally subsidized alterations in the housing stock and in certain other physical equipment (mass transportation, community facilities, and the like). The *a priori* commitment to this program has the result that alternative tactics to reach certain goals are not systematically considered, or are considered only as afterthoughts. Surely few would ever have disagreed that the two greatest causes of inadequate housing have been the fact that some people have not been able to afford good housing and that some have, because of race, been denied an opportunity to bid freely for such housing as exists. Yet it was not until last year that HHFA requested of Congress a program that would improve the purchasing power of poor families by direct income subsidies and it was not until this year that legislation was proposed by the President to bar discrimination in the sale or rental of housing (an executive order by President Kennedy had previously barred discrimination in federally assisted housing, which is about one-fifth of the total).

In the meantime—and continuing right down to the present—local communities are allowed great latitude in deciding how federal funds will be spent on the bread-and-butter programs: urban renewal and public housing. If the Main Street merchants are in power, they can use renewal funds to tear down low-cost housing and put up luxury apartments near the department stores—in effect redistributing income from the poor to the well-to-do while reducing the stock of low-cost housing. If more generous souls are in power, the worst housing is torn down to make room for middle- or lower-middle-income housing; the income transfer from poor to not-so-poor is much less, but it is still in the wrong direction. And if the mayor simply is seeking funds with which to run his city in the face of a declining tax base, he discovers that he must join with those who want one of these urban renewal programs because that is about the only way he can get large-scale federal money into his city. He discovers, in short, that he has to hurt his poorest and weakest citizens in order to provide for the general welfare; his only option is to try to do it as humanely as possible. Under any or all of these conditions, urban renewal may or may not produce attractive, well-designed new structures; that is a separate issue. The point is that for almost any legitimate community objective—improving the supply of housing, strengthening the tax base, etc.—urban renewal has in most cases proved to be an unwieldy and costly tool.

We have recently been making some improvements in that tool at the federal level; and in communities which elect to use the improved version of urban renewal, the human costs are reduced and the incidence of those costs is made more equitable. Rehabilitation of existing structures reduces displacement (it does not eliminate it—you can drive out a low-income family as easily by raising its rent as by tearing down its apartment); below-the-market interest rates make it possible to bring the cost of new construction down to what "moderate" income families can afford (which is usually a lot more than poor families can afford); public housing can be better designed and built on scattered sites (though the cost of an apartment in many public housing projects is still more than what it would take to build a brand new suburban home for the family). No one can object to the sentiments and intentions represented by these changes. But now that a new department has come into being, perhaps it is time to ask whether a new approach to the "urban problem" is conceivable.

•   •   •

III

Federal policies have moved only recently in a direction that acknowledges that the "urban problem" is not primarily, or even significantly, a housing problem. The rent supplement program is a recognition of the need to deal directly with the cause of slum housing—i.e., the fact that there are people who cannot afford non-slum housing. The call for legislation to bar discrimination in the housing market is a recognition of the need to reduce the inflated prices of Negro housing by giving Negroes access to the entire housing market. (Although the principle is sound, not much is likely to happen as a result of such a statute; open occupancy laws already on the books in many states and cities have not broken up the Negro enclaves, partly because housing outside such enclaves sometimes costs more than housing inside them.)

But for the present, these and other modifications are largely frosting on a tasteless cake. The major thrust of federal policy is now, and always has been, a commitment to maintain and enhance the physical shells of existing American cities—adding, where appropriate, a few new towns to handle the overflow. The desire to make all American cities "livable" not only exaggerates the extent to which cities are now "unlivable," but it thoughtlessly lumps together all cities—whether or not they continue to serve any functions, whether or not there is any rational ground for conserving them at public expense, and even whether or not the local leadership conceives of urban conservation as driving the poor across the city line into somebody else's city.

It was long argued that urban interests deserved a cabinet department, just as agricultural interests had one. It is a disturbing analogy. For thirty years the Department of Agriculture has, in effect, been committed to the preservation of farms regardless of how inefficient or economically unsound they became. Now there are signs that pressure from mayors and downtown business interests may move the Department of Housing and Urban Development even farther toward a policy of guaranteeing the perpetual existence of the central business district of every American city, no matter how inefficient or economically unsound they may become.

There is nothing sacrosanct about the present patterns or functions of urban life; cities, like people, pass through life cycles during which their values and functions change. Cities sometimes die, and for good cause. But the implicit commitment of our new Department to physical structures, rather than to concrete human needs, makes it almost impossible for it to distinguish between cities which need help and cities which do not; any city "needs" help if it says it does. The result is that while the rhetoric of the "urban crisis" is aimed at the great national and regional centers of commerce, culture, education, and government— Washington, New York, Philadelphia, Boston, Los Angeles—the reality of federal programs can be found in Barre, Vermont, and Wink, Texas. *Over half of all cities with urban renewal projects have populations of less than 25,000.* (In this respect, HUD is more democratic than the Department of Agriculture; whereas the latter was of more help to the big than to the small farmer, the former is subsidizing the smaller as well as the larger cities.)

There is an alternative policy which could direct federal activities. It would require, not the scrapping of existing federal programs, but only their redirection. Such a policy would begin with a recognition of the different kinds of "urban problems"—some of which, like poverty, are as much rural as urban problems, and others of which, like the gap between expectations and achievements, are not problems that government can do anything about. Such a policy would, I suggest, contain the following elements:

First, the federal government would assume responsibility for placing a floor under the capacity of Americans to acquire a minimally satisfactory level of personal and family amenities—housing, food, clothing, medical care. Where possible, guaranteeing such resources to every family would be done by combining aggregate fiscal policies which produce full employment with direct income transfers—in the form, say, of a negative income tax, family allowances, or rent subsidies— so that each family has a maximum free choice as to the type and location of its housing. Some conservatives will of course object that this is a "dole," productive of moral debilitation. I submit that, unless we are willing to tolerate privation, we of necessity must have some sort of dole; the real question is whether it will be one which minimizes choice and maximizes bureaucratic intervention in private lives (as is the case with public housing projects and many welfare programs) or one with the opposite characteristics.

I am under no illusion that the problems of the central-city poor, white and Negro, will vanish because we adopt an income maintenance strategy. All I am suggesting is that whatever else must be done to cope with poverty, there will be little progress unless the one indisputable component of poverty—low incomes—is dealt with by methods more effective and less debasing than those which require husbands to desert their wives and children before these latter can apply for welfare.

Second, public power and public funds would be used to provide those common benefits (or, as the economists say, collective goods) which are enjoyed, and thus must be paid for, by everybody. Fresh air, pure water, open spaces, parkland, and police protection are the most common examples of indivisible benefits whose achievement requires the exercise of public powers. Ironically, it is in this area (where even in the days of Adam Smith it was agreed that public intervention was required) that federal action has been the slowest in developing. The reason, of course, is understandable enough; most collective goods require control over those aspects of community life—the education of the young, the policing of the city, and the use of land—which Americans have long insisted be kept in local hands. So long as most of us lived and worked in the same place—i.e., the central city—purely local control of these matters may have made sense. What services we used as we traveled to and from work we also paid for through taxes. Upper-middle-class citizens with a strong interest in (and a healthy capacity to pay for) common benefits, such as parks and the like, lived in—and often governed—the central city. With the exodus to the suburbs, and our self-segregation into radically different kinds of communities on the periphery, differences in preferences and income which used to co-exist within a single taxing authority now are separated by political boundaries. If the incidence of costs and benefits of various collective goods is to be equalized throughout the metropolitan area, some higher taxing authority must assume responsibility for transfer payments. There are only two such authorities—the state and the federal government.

Third, where possible, central cities facing a fiscal crisis ought to receive block grants from state or federal governments in order to help defray the cost of servicing the poor, providing decent education and police protection, etc. At the present time, cities must commit themselves to a whole range of federally conceived programs in order to get money they urgently need, even though many of these programs may be either irrelevant or harmful to the interests of parts of the city's population. Cities with an eroding tax base seize upon urban renewal as the only way to get federal support for that tax base, even though it is a clumsy and inefficient way—it requires destroying homes or businesses, allowing land to lie vacant for long periods of time, and pushing people who consume high levels of local services into neighboring cities where they cause the whole dreary cycle to be repeated. The already-enacted federal aid to education program is a step in the right direction, though the amounts will surely have to be increased.

Even if one were to accept the dubious proposition that the cities could be rebuilt to retain or lure back the middle classes—a proposition that lies at the bottom of much of the urban renewal strategy—any but the most blind partisans ought to concede that what drives the middle classes out of the city in the first place may have much less to do with the physical condition of the buildings than with the quality of the public schools and the level of public safety. Subsidizing these institutions, rather than the rents the middle classes have to pay, strikes me as both fairer (since it will help the poor as well as the better off) and more likely to produce desirable results.

Fourth, the federal government, through special incentives, ought to encourage cities to experiment with various user charges as a way of making certain that non-residents pay their fair share of the services they use in the cities where they work or shop, and that residents have a more precise and personal way than voting for or against the mayor to indicate how much of a particular local service they really desire for themselves. At the present time, large groups of people get something for nothing—non-residents who park on the city's streets, for example, or residents who, owning no taxable property, enthusiastically vote for more and more free public facilities. The whole burden is thrown on the property-tax payer, and he cannot sustain it.

Fifth, urban renewal and other land clearance programs can be used as a tool to aid in providing collective goods (by assembling land and financing good design for public buildings, schools, and the like), and as a way of eliminating hazardous or unsalvageable structures. If renewal is to do more than this, then to insure against the excesses of the past it ought to be hedged about with the most explicit restrictions. If decent low-cost housing is to be torn down for high-cost housing, then it should be done only when either a clear collective benefit (e.g., a new school or park) will result or when *surplus* low-cost housing can be removed. The latter would require a prior showing that the vacancy rate among low-cost housing units in that city or area is high enough to make possible the absorption of displaced families without serious economic loss, and that a close study of the social structure of the affected neighborhood reveals it to be primarily a place with high transiency rates where strong family life and neighborhood ties have not developed. And if a subsidy is conferred on the developer and his new upper-income tenants, then provision ought to be made to recapture that subsidy over time—perhaps by making the federal contribution a long-term loan rather than a grant (this was actually proposed when the original legislation was first debated in Congress), or by allowing the city to adopt special tax measures to recover the subsidy for itself.

IV

It is possible to conceive of a rational policy for dealing with so-called "urban" problems, once one begins to realize that the word "urban" is less relevant than the word "human." And perhaps this is implied in the Model Cities Program now getting underway, though the details are still sufficiently vague to make its real significance unclear. Leaving aside the obvious contradictions in the "guidelines" for determining whether a city is qualified to participate (for example, the incompatibility between maximum "co-ordination" achieved by a "single authority with adequate powers" and "widespread citizen participation" in the demonstration area), one may take the optimistic view that the Model Cities Program is simply a fancy way of describing a new federal effort to impose federal standards on the local use of renewal money, so that renewal projects are more likely to serve legitimate national objectives than whatever purposes, good or bad, local leaders cook up.

The demand for more local "co-ordination" and "planning" may be a tactic for creating an organized local constituency for HUD. A good case can be made for such intentions, but it is doubtful that a Congress sensitive to local interests and pressures is going to let HUD or anyone else get away with it entirely. And this, of course, should provide a good political reason for shifting federal efforts more in the direction of universalistic programs (maintaining the incomes of all poor, and subsidizing services—like education—which provide general benefits) and away from particularistic programs (tearing down some buildings and subsidizing others). So long as programs are designed to achieve particular effects in particular places, they will frequently be used by local groups to the disadvantage of the poor and powerless, or to produce effects that the federal taxpayer should not be required to pay for. And so long as HUD has no consistent federal policy, Congress will be able to insist that policies be set at the local level.

There is a bureaucratic as well as political reason for favoring universalistic programs—large bureaucracies are not very good at performing complex tasks requiring the exercise of a great deal of co-ordination over disparate activities, the accomplishments of which cannot be easily measured or evaluated. Direct income transfers, block grants to local governments, and increased reliance on individual choice are ways of reducing the impossible burdens on government agencies, most of which are (necessarily) staffed by men of average attainments.

Making full allowance for the good intentions behind the Model Cities Program, its central problem—apart from (though related to) the obscurity as to its goals and the mystery as to its means — is that it is an effort to improve on old programs, not by changing them or by substituting a wholly new strategy, but by creating a new apparatus to show how by "co-ordination" (i.e., more administration) the job can be done better. But the failures of the past sixteen years have been precisely the failures of administration—of seeking inappropriate or incompatible goals, or of being unable to attain given goals, or of failing to take into account the consequences of working toward these goals. Overcoming the weaknesses of administration by providing more administration is likely to succeed only if extraordinary men do the administering. There are such men, but not many; hoping that enough of them wind up in HUD strikes me as, to say the least, imprudent.

For almost two decades we have been "attacking" the problems of the city—almost literally—by mounting successive assaults against various real and imagined difficulties. Each assault force has had its own leadership and ideology, and the weaknesses of each have been the signal for a new assault, under different leadership and with a new ideology. First came public housing, then urban redevelopment, then urban renewal, and now the Model Cities Program. The old assaults, of course, never vanished, they just moved over a bit (not without complaints) to let the newcomers in. The common objective is to capture and hold central-city real estate; the differences in tactics concern the number of fronts on which the fighting is to proceed. In general, each successive assault has had broader objectives—the current President's message calls for a change in the "total environment." The motto is, "more is better." Perhaps it will all work out, if humane weapons are used and we evacuate the wounded. But I suspect that in the confusion the real enemies—poverty, ignorance, despair—may slip away, to live and strike again in another place.

7

Business and Labor Policy

American public policy toward business and labor is complex and sometimes contradictory. First of all, federal, state and local governments provide the essential legal framework for the protection of property and business enterprise. Governments protect property rights, enforce contracts, establish a monetary system to facilitate exchange, and recognize and protect the corporate form of enterprise. Modern business largely involves the exchanges of pieces of paper — contracts, stocks and bonds, bank checks, and paper money. These pieces of paper are worthless in themselves; they acquire value and meaning only in so far as government stands ready to enforce certain rights and claims which are represented by these pieces of paper. Governments recognize and protect the rights of owners over their property. They record the ownership of property and settle disputes over ownerships; they interpret contracts and require performance of duties stated in them; they enforce debts and require that paper money be accepted to discharge debt. The very foundations of capitalism are built upon legal recognition of the concept of private property. Moreover, the law recognizes the corporate form of organization that makes possible the collection of a large amount of capital from a great number of different persons who have only limited liability as well as limited responsibility for the activities of the corporation.

American public policy also attempts to maintain competition in the economy. The decline of business competition and the rise of monopolies accompanied America's industrial revolution in the late 19th century. As business became increasingly national in scope only the strongest or the most unscrupulous of the competitors survived. Great producers tended to become the cheapest producers and little companies tended to disappear. Industrial production rose rapidly while a number of industrial concerns steadily diminished. The result was the emergence of monopolies and near monopolies in each of the major industries of America.

Largely to appease farmer hostility toward eastern railroads — a hostility which was reflected in the populist movement — Congress passed the *Sherman Anti-Trust Act of 1890*. The Sherman Act is a vague statement condemning monopolies and restraint of trade, but despite its ambiguities it remains a cornerstone of national policy towards business.

The Sherman Act raised more policy questions than it resolved. There was first of all the question of what is interstate commerce. In the famous case of the *United States* v. *E. C. Knight* (1895) the Supreme Court ruled that a sugar refining company which produced 98 per cent of the sugar used in the United States was primarily engaged in *manufacturing* rather than *interstate commerce,* and hence could not be regulated by the national government. This restrictive view of the interstate commerce clause of the constitution prevented effective national regulation of American business well into the New Deal period. It was not until 1937 in the case of *National Labor Relations Board* v. *Jones and Laughlin* that the U.S. Supreme Court recognized Congressional power over business activities which substantially affected interstate commerce.

By neglecting to define "monopoly" or "restraint of trade," Congress largely left to the courts the problem of defining anti-trust policy. The courts chose to adopt a "rule of reason" in anti-trust policy, saying that only "unreasonable" monopolies, or "unreasonable" restraints of trade were prohibited. In the case of *Standard Oil Company* v. *United States* (1911) the Supreme Court ruled that only "unreasonable" restraints of trade were barred by the Sherman Act. This rule of reason allows the courts great flexibility in anti-trust policy. Yet flexibility brings with it uncertainty as to what particular courses of action will be held illegal. In *United States* v. *United States Steel Corporation* (1920) the court refused to curtail a giant merger merely because it was big. However, in a later decision, *U.S.* v. *Aluminum Company of America* (1945), the Court hardened its attitude towards size somewhat, and held that size itself can prove restraining on competition. But the Court suggested it would still permit monopoly if it could be proved that there were compelling reasons why monopoly rather than competition would better serve the public.

Pressure mounted during the administration of Woodrow Wilson for a clearer legislative definition of anti-trust policy. So vague was the Sherman Act, and so conservative the court interpretations of it, that there were very few prosecutions under it before World War I. In fact, a majority of the early cases under the Sherman Act were brought against trade unions and not against businesses. *The Clayton Anti-Trust Act of 1914* was an attempt to define anti-trust policy in general, and monopoly and restraint of trade in particular. Various specific business activities that interfered with competition were prohibited, including price discrimination, exclusive agreements, and interlocking directorates for the purchase of stock in competing concerns. The Clayton Act also facilitated the bringing of suits by injured parties against businesses violating the Sherman and Clayton Acts. The Clayton Act was as important for American labor as it was for business, because it specifically exempted labor unions from federal prosecutions under the anti-trust laws. Finally, the Clayton Act struck at monopoly in its famous Section 7 prohibiting a corporation from acquiring the capital stock of another corporation "where the effect of such acquisition may be to substantially lessen competition." Potentially Section 7 could bring about the rearrangement of the business structure of America, but neither the anti-trust division of the Justice Department nor the federal courts have attempted a literal enforcement of Section 7. The number of business mergers has increased dramatically in recent years. On the whole, the Justice Department has been more likely to initiate anti-trust action against business combinations which are horizontal in form, that is, the joining together of separate businesses engaged in the production or sale of the same articles. In contrast, vertical combinations, that is, the combination of various stages in the production process from raw materials to marketing finished products, have been somewhat less likely to touch off anti-trust action. Not until 1961 did the Supreme Court order the I.E. DuPont Company to divest itself of the General Motors Stock which it held. DuPont was convicted of using its control over G.M. to be sure that G.M. purchased only DuPont products for its automobiles.

Another approach to business policy in America is to establish administrative commissions with rule-making, administrative, and judicial powers to regulate business practices. The first of the national regulatory commissions was the Interstate Commerce Commission in 1887. The purpose of the ICC was to regulate railroad practices, including rate making. In 1914 Congress created the Federal Trade Commission which was empowered to define and forbid unfair and dishonest methods of competition in interstate commerce. (See *Federal Trade Commission Act of 1914*) Later, other regulatory commissions were established in a variety of industries: the Civil Aeronautics Board, Securities and Exchange Commission, the Federal Power Commission, the Federal Communications Commission and the Atomic Energy Commission. Typically these commissions are constructed to be "independent" and "expert." Independence was to mean freedom from direct pressure of political party interests; this independence was to be achieved by appointing members for fixed overlapping terms longer than those of the President, and by requiring the Commission to be bi-partisan in composition. Commission members are expected to have the experience and expertise necessary to deal with the complex field of business regulation. The commissions do not have the power to initiate criminal proceedings against businesses, but instead may initiate civil action to require businesses to "cease and desist" from engaging in prohibited activities. Often commissions have very vague mandates — "unfair methods of competition in commerce are hereby declared unlawful" — and the commissions must engage in rule-making for their respective industries. Typically rules govern rates, discriminatory practices, adequacy of service, control of entry into the industry, unfair methods of competition, and so on.

The regulatory approach implies that competition alone is not sufficient to insure protection of the public interest. It implies that direct government regulation is better insurance against business abuse of the public than reliance upon the indirect effects of competition. However, commissions often come under the influence of the industries they are trying to regulate. Regulated interests often complain of bureaucratic red tape which prevents them from offering innovative or improved public service. Consumers often charge that the commissions represent the interest of the industries rather than those of the general public. The cumbersome cease and desist system, dependent as it is upon protracted litigation for its enforcement, is greatly weakened by long delays. The commission system with its reliance upon detailed case by case method of regulation, appears ill-adapted to modern problems.

Yet even while some federal agencies attempt to prevent monopoly and regulate business, the overall impact of federal policy is to contribute to the development of giant corporate enterprise and to promote rather than curtail concentrations of economic power. The U.S. government is the largest buyer of industrial output in the nation; most of its purchases are for national defense. The Department of Defense, the National Aeronautics and Space Administration, Atomic Energy Commission, and other government agencies underwrite large scale industrial enterprise with long-term contracts calling for large capital outlays and heavy investment in advanced technology. The result is a business-government nexus involving billions of dollars and a web of corporate-bureaucratic relationships. Some businesses are so close to government that it is difficult to refer to them as private businesses. (See Dwight D. Eisenhower, *The Military Industrial Complex*)

The keystone of American labor policy is the *National Labor Relations*

Act of 1935, sometimes called the Wagner Act. In this Act, government guarantees labor's right to organize into unions and its right to bargain collectively through union representatives. Employers are forbidden to interfere with the rights of workers to organize and to bargain collectively. The National Labor Relations Board is authorized to hold elections to determine which labor union the employees desire to represent them and to make decisions on alleged violations on the Act by employers. It is important to note that while the Act requires collective bargaining, it does not require unions or employers to reach agreements. Under the Act unions are free to strike and employers are free to fire strikers, and neither employers nor unions are required to come to any agreement over wages, hours, benefits or conditions of work. Employers and unions are not required to submit their differences to any government agency for binding decisions. In other words, the Act relies upon "collective bargaining" rather than "compulsory arbitration."

Labor policy in America has also been significantly shaped by several other acts of Congress. The Railway Labor Act of 1926 first accorded to labor the right to organize unions without interference from employers and provided for collective bargaining in the railroad industry. It also authorized the President in case of national emergency to appoint a fact finding board to analyze the issues in railroad disputes and make recommendations for settlement. It did not require compulsory arbitration, but in 1963 when a national railroad strike was imminent, Congress provided for compulsory settlement of the dispute by an *ad hoc* board. This suggests that Congress may threaten to impose compulsory arbitration in the future where strikes threaten national interest. In the Norris-LaGuardia Act of 1932 Congress restricted federal courts in issuing injunctions against strikers. Prior to 1932 the labor injunction was the chief weapon of the employer for breaking labor strikes. In the Fair Labor Standards Act of 1938 Congress excluded from interstate commerce any goods not produced in accordance with certain federal standards. These standards included a 40-hour work week, a bar on oppressive child labor, and a minimum wage level. Although many exemptions were written into the original act, and the minimum wage was set at 25¢ an hour, over the years the number of employees who are covered has been expanded and the minimum wage has been steadily increased.

In the famous case of the *National Labor Relations Board* v. *Jones and Laughlin Steel Corporation* (1937) the Supreme Court upheld the constitutionality of the National Labor Relations Act of 1935 under the interstate commerce clause of the Constitution. This decision confirmed Congressional power over the national economy, and as a result, the commerce power is now one of the most important grants of power to the national government in the Constitution.

Employers' dissatisfaction with the increased strength of organized labor under the Wagner Act led to a dramatic shift in public policy in the *Labor-Management Relations Act of 1947*. While the Taft-Hartley Act reserves for labor all of the basic guarantees of the earlier Wagner Act, it places severe restrictions on the activities of unions. Technically, the Taft-Hartley Act was a series of Amendments to the Wagner Act. The Taft-Hartley Act added a series of unfair labor practices of *unions* in contrast with the concern of the Wagner Act of unfair labor practices of *management*. Among other things, the Act prohibits the "closed shop," in which a man cannot be hired unless he is already a member of a union, and permits a "union shop," in which a person is required to join a union after his employment, only if a majority of workers vote for a union shop in an NLRB supervised election. And Section 14B further restricts the union shop by giving states the power to outlaw union shops through so-called "right to work" laws. The Taft-Hartley Act also outlaws the "secondary boycott" in which union members refuse to work with non-union made goods; the "jurisdictional strike," in which a union attempts to win employer recognition through a strike; and "featherbedding," in which a union tries to cause an employer to pay persons for services which are not performed or unnecessary. Unions are forbidden to coerce an employee to join or not to join a union, or to cause an employer to discriminate against non-union employees.

The conflict over the Taft-Hartley Act was very bitter, but so weak was organized labor's influence in Congress that two-thirds majorities were mustered in each chamber to overturn President Harry Truman's veto of the Taft-Hartley Bill. While Republican control of the Congress in 1947 was one of the main reasons for the bill's passage, organized labor has been wholly unsuccessful in its attempts to modify Taft-Hartley since its enactment. In fact, organized labor lost another legislative battle with the enactment of the Labor Management Reporting and Disclosure Act of 1959 (the Landrum-Griffin Act). This Act heightens and extends some of the Taft-Hartley prohibitions against secondary boycotts and certain kinds of picketing; it prescribes the conduct of union elections and requires strict accounting and reporting of union funds; it requires the bonding of union officials and prohibits persons with criminal records or communist affiliations from holding any office; and finally, it contains what is called a bill of rights for union members designed to insure democracy in the conduct of union affairs and due process in the internal affairs of unions.

Sherman Anti-Trust Act of 1890

Congress and the President

An ACT To protect trade and commerce against unlawful restraints and monopolies.

Be it enacted

Sec. 1. Every contract, combination in the form of trust or otherwise, or conspiracy, in restraint of trade or commerce among the several States, or with foreign nations, is hereby declared to be illegal. Every person who shall make any such contract or engage in any such combination or conspiracy, shall be deemed guilty of a misdemeanor, and, on conviction thereof, shall be punished by fine not exceeding five thousand dollars, or by imprisonment not exceeding one year, or by both said punishments, in the discretion of the court.

Sec. 2. Every person who shall monopolize, or attempt to monopolize, or combine or conspire with any other person or persons, to monopolize any part of the trade or commerce among the several States, or with foreign nations, shall be deemed guilty of a misdemeanor, and, on conviction thereof, shall be punished by fine not exceeding five thousand dollars, or by imprisonment not exceeding one year, or by both said punishments, in the discretion of the court.

Sec. 3. Every contract, combination in form of trust or otherwise, or conspiracy, in restraint of trade or commerce in any Territory of the United States or of the District of Columbia, or in restraint of trade or commerce between any such Territory and another, or between any such Territory or Territories and any State or States or the District of Columbia, or with foreign nations, or between the District of Columbia and any State or States or foreign nations, is hereby declared illegal. Every person who shall make any such contract or engage in any such combination or conspiracy, shall be deemed guilty of a misdemeanor, and, on conviction thereof, shall be punished by fine not exceeding five thousand dollars, or by imprisonment not exceeding one year, or by both said punishments, in the discretion of the court.

Sec. 4. The several circuit courts of the United States are hereby invested with jurisdiction to prevent and restrain violations of this act; and it shall be the duty of the several district attorneys of the United States, in their respective districts, under the direction of the Attorney-General, to institute proceedings in equity to prevent and restrain such violations. Such proceedings may be by way of petition setting forth the case and praying that such violation shall be enjoined or otherwise prohibited. When the parties complained of shall have been duly notified of such petition the courts shall proceed, as soon as may be, to the hearing and determination of the case; and pending such petition and before final decrees, the court may at any time make such temporary restraining order or prohibition as shall be deemed just in the premises.

Sec. 5. Whenever it shall appear to the court before which any proceeding under Section four of this act may be pending, that the ends of justice require that other parties should be brought before the court, the court may cause them to be summoned, whether they reside in the district in which the court is held or not; and subpœnas to that end may be served in any district by the marshal therof.

Sec. 6. Any property owned under any contract or by any combination, or pursuant to any conspiracy (and being the subject thereof) mentioned in section one of this act, and being in the course of transportation from one State to another, or to a foreign country, shall be forfeited to the United States, and may be seized and condemned by like proceedings as those provided by law for the forfeiture, seizure, and condemnation of property imported into the United States contrary to law.

Sec. 7. Any person who shall be injured in his business or property by any other person or corporation by reason of anything forbidden or declared to be unlawful by this act, may sue therefor in any circuit court of the United States in the district in which the defendant resides or is found, without respect to the amount in controversy, and shall recover threefold the damages by him sustained, and the costs of suit, including a reasonable attorney's fee.

Sec. 8. That the word "person," or "persons," wherever used in this act shall be deemed to include corporations and associations existing under or authorized by the laws of either the United States, the laws of any of the Territories, the laws of any State, or the laws of any foreign country.

The Clayton Act of 1914

Congress and the President

. . . Sec. 2. That it shall be unlawful for any person engaged in commerce, in the course of such commerce, either directly or indirectly to discriminate in price between different purchasers of commodities which commodities are sold for use, consumption, or resale within the United States or any . . . other place under the jurisdiction of the United States, where the effect of such discrimination may be to substantially lessen competition or tend to create a monopoly in any line of commerce: . . .

Sec. 3. That it shall be unlawful for any person engaged in commerce, to lease or make a sale of goods, . . . or other commodities, . . . for use, consumption or resale within the United States or . . . other place under the jurisdiction of the United States, or fix a price charged therefor, or discount from, or rebate upon, such price, on the condition, . . . that the lessee or purchaser thereof shall not use or deal in the goods, . . . or other commodities of a competitor or competitors of the lessor or seller, where the effect of such lease, sale, or contract for sale or such condition, agreement, or understanding may be to substantially lessen competition or tend to create a monopoly in any line of commerce. . . .

Sec. 6. That the labor of a human being is not a commodity or article of commerce. Nothing contained in the anti-trust laws shall be construed to forbid the existence and operation of labor, agricultural, or horticultural organizations, instituted for the purposes of mutual help, and not having capital stock or conduced for profit, or to forbid or restrain individual members of such organizations from lawfully carrying out the legitimate objects thereof; nor shall such organizations, or the members thereof, be held or construed to be illegal combinations or conspiracies in restraint of trade, under the anti-trust laws.

Sec. 7. That no corporation engaged in commerce shall acquire, directly or indirectly, the whole or any part of the stock or other share capital of another corporation engaged also in commerce, where the effect of such acquisition may be to substantially lessen competition between the corporation whose stock is so acquired and the corporation making the acquisition, or to restrain such commerce in any section or community, or tend to create a monopoly of any line of commerce. . . .

This section shall not apply to corporations purchasing such stock solely for investment and not using the same by voting or otherwise to bring about, or in attempting to bring about, the substantial lessening of competition. . . .

Sec. 8. That from and after two years from the date of the approval of this act no person shall at the same time be a director or other officer or employee of more than one bank, banking association or trust company, organized or operating under the laws of the United States, either of which has deposits, capital, surplus, and undivided profits aggregating more than $5,000,000; and no private banker or person who is a director in any bank or trust company, organized and operating under the laws of a State, having deposits, capital, surplus, and undivided profits aggregating more than $5,000,000, shall be eligible to be a director in any bank or banking association organized or operating under the laws of the United States. . . .

That from and after two years from the date of the approval of this Act no person at the same time shall be a director in any two or more corporations, any one of which has capital surplus, and undivided profits aggregating more than $1,000,000, engaged in whole or in part in commerce, other than banks, banking associations, trust companies and common carriers subject to the Act to regulate commerce, approved February 4th, 1887, if such corporations are or shall have been theretofore, by virtue of their business and location of operation, competitors, so that the elimination of competition by agreement between them would constitute a violation of any of the provisions of any of the anti-trust laws. . . .

Sec. 10. That after two years from the approval of this Act no common carrier engaged in commerce shall have any dealings in securities, supplies, or other articles of commerce, . . . to the amount of more than $50,000, in the aggregate, in any one year, with another corporation, firm, partnership or association when the said common carrier shall have upon its board of directors or as its president, manager, or as its purchasing or selling officer, or agent in the particular transaction, any person who is at the same time a director, manager, or purchasing or selling officer of, or who has any substantial interest in, such other corporation, firm, partnership, or association, unless and except such purchases shall be made from, or such dealings shall be with, the bidder whose bid is the most favorable to such common carrier, to be ascertained by competitive bidding under regulations to be prescribed by rule or otherwise by the Interstate Commerce Commission. . . .

Sec. 20. That no restraining order or injunction shall be granted by any court of the United States, or a judge or the judges thereof, in any case between an employer and employees or between employers and employees, or between employees, or between persons employed and persons seeking employment, involving, or growing out of, a dispute concerning terms or conditions of employment, unless necessary to prevent irreparable injury to property, or to a property right, of the party making the application, for which injury there is no adequate remedy at law, and such property or property right must be described with a particularity in the application, which must be in writing and sworn to by the applicant or by his agent or attorney.

And no such restraining order or injunction shall prohibit any person or persons, whether singly or in concert, from terminating any relation of employment, or from ceasing to perform any work or labor, or from recommending, advising, or persuading others by peaceful means so to do; or from attending at any place where any such person or persons may lawfully be, for the purpose of peacefully obtaining or communicating information, or from peacefully persuading any person to work or to abstain from working; or from ceasing to patronize or to employ any party to such dispute, or from recommending, advising, or persuading others by peaceful and lawful means so to do; or from paying or giving to, or withholding from, any person engaged in such dispute, any strike benefits or other moneys or things of value; or from peaceably assembling in a lawful manner, and for lawful purposes; or from doing any act or thing which might lawfully be done in the absence of such dispute by any party thereto; nor shall any of the acts specified in this paragraph be considered or held to be violations of any law of the United States.

The Federal Trade Commission Act of 1914

Congress and the President

An act to create a Federal Trade Commission, to define its powers and duties and for other purposes.

Be it enacted, That a commission is hereby created and established, to be known as the Federal Trade Commission (hereinafter referred to as the commission), which shall be composed of five commissioners, who shall be appointed by the President, by and with the advice and consent of the Senate. Not more than three of the commissioners shall be members of the same political party. The first commissioners appointed shall continue in office for terms of three, four, five, six, and seven years, respectively, from the date of the taking effect of this Act, the term of each to be designated by the President, but their successors shall be appointed for terms of seven years, except that any person chosen to fill a vacancy shall be appointed only for the unexpired term of the commissioner who he shall succeed. . . .

Sec. 5. That unfair methods of competition in commerce are hereby declared unlawful.

The commission is hereby empowered and directed to prevent persons, partnerships, or corporations, except banks, and common carriers subject to the Acts to regulate commerce, from using unfair methods of competition in commerce.

Whenever the commission shall have reason to believe that any person, partnership, or corporation has been or is using any unfair method of competition in commerce, . . . it shall issue and serve upon such person, partnership, or corporation a complaint stating its charges in that respect, and containing a notice of a hearing upon a day and at a place therein fixed at least thirty days after the service of said complaint. The person, partnership, or corporation so complained of shall have the right to appear at the place and time so fixed and show cause why an order should not be entered by the commission requiring such person, partnership, or corporation to cease and desist from the violation of the law so charged in said complaint. . . . If upon such hearing the commission shall be of the opinion that the method of competition in question is prohibited by this Act, it shall make a report in writing in which it shall state its findings as to the facts, and shall issue and cause to be served on such person, partnership, or corporation an order requiring such person, partnership, or corporation to cease and desist from using such method of competition. . . .

Sec. 6. That the commission shall also have power—

(a) To gather and compile information concerning and to investigate from time to time the organization, business, conduct, practices, and management of any corporation engaged in commerce, excepting banks and common carriers subject to the Act to regulate commerce, and its relation to other corporations and to individuals, associations, and partnerships.

(b) To require, . . . corporations engaged in commerce, excepting banks, and common carriers subject to the Act to regulate commerce, . . . to file with the commission in such form as the commission may prescribe annual or special, or both annual and special, reports or answers in writing to specific questions, furnishing to the commission such information as it may require as to the organization, business, conduct, practices, management, and relation to other corporations, partnerships, and individuals of the respective corporations filing such reports. . . .

(c) Whenever a final decree has been entered against any defendant corporation in any suit brought by the United States to prevent and restrain any violation of the antitrust Acts, to make investigation, . . . of the manner in which the decree has been or is being carried out, . . . it shall be its duty to make such investigation. It shall transmit to the Attorney General a report embodying its findings and recommendations as a result of any such investigation, and the report shall be made public in the discretion of the commission.

The Military Industrial Complex*

Dwight D. Eisenhower

In his final address to the nation January 17, 1961, President Eisenhower noted that the United States had been compelled to "create a permanent armaments industry of vast proportions." He continued as follows:

"This conjunction of an immense military establishment and a large arms industry is new in American experience. The total influence — economic, political, even spiritual — is felt in every city, every state house, every office of the Federal Government. We recognize the imperative need for this development. Yet we must not fail to comprehend its grave implications. Our toil, resources and livelihood are all involved; so is the very structure of our society.

"In the councils of government, we must guard against the acquisition of unwarranted influence, whether sought or unsought, by the military-industrial complex. The potential for the disastrous rise of misplaced power exists and will persist. We must never let the weight of this combination endanger our liberties or democratic processes. We should take nothing for granted. Only an alert and knowledgeable citizenry can compel the proper meshing of the huge industrial and military machinery of defense with our peaceful methods and goals, so that security and liberty may prosper together."

---

*President Dwight D. Eisenhower, *Farewell Address,* January 17, 1961.

From The Weapons Culture*

Ralph E. Lapp

The following table lists the 38 U.S. companies that were awarded prime military contracts totaling in excess of $1 billion during the fiscal years 1961-1967. In the column at far right, the cumulative totals for the seven-year period are expressed as percentages of the companies' total business. Amounts are in millions of dollars.

Fiscal Year	1961	1962	1963	1964	1965	1966	1967	7-Year Total	Percent of Total Sales
1. Lockheed Aircraft	$1,175	$1,419	$1,517	$1,455	$1,715	$1,531	$1,807	$10,619	88%
2. General Dynamics	1,460	1,197	1,033	987	1,179	1,136	1,832	8,824	67
3. McDonnell Douglas	527	779	863	1,360	1,026	1,001	2,125	7,681	75
4. Boeing Co.	920	1,133	1,356	1,365	583	914	912	7,183	54
5. General Electric	875	976	1,021	893	824	1,187	1,290	7,066	19
6. North American-Rockwell	1,197	1,032	1,062	1,019	746	520	689	6,265	57
7. United Aircraft	625	663	530	625	632	1,139	1,097	5,311	57
8. American Tel. & Tel.	551	468	579	636	588	672	673	4,167	9
9. Martin-Marietta	692	803	767	476	316	338	290	3,682	62
10. Sperry-Rand	408	466	446	374	318	427	484	2,923	35
11. General Motors	282	449	444	256	254	508	625	2,818	2
12. Grumman Aircraft	238	304	390	396	353	323	488	2,492	67
13. General Tire	290	366	425	364	302	327	273	2,347	37
14. Raytheon	305	407	295	253	293	368	403	2,324	55
15. AVCO	251	323	253	279	234	506	449	2,295	75

Company									
16. Hughes	331	234	312	289	278	337	419	2,200	u
17. Westinghouse Electric	308	246	323	237	261	349	453	2,177	13
18. Ford (Philco)	200	269	228	211	312	440	404	2,064	3
19. RCA	392	340	329	234	214	242	268	2,019	16
20. Bendix	269	286	290	257	235	282	296	1,915	42
21. Textron	66	117	151	216	196	555	497	1,798	36
22. Ling-Temco-Vought	47	133	206	247	265	311	535	1,744	70
23. Internat. Tel. & Tel.	202	244	266	256	207	220	255	1,650	19
24. I.B.M.	330	155	203	332	186	182	195	1,583	7
25. Raymond International*	46	61	84	196	71	548	462	1,568	u
26. Newport News Shipbuilding	290	185	221	400	185	51	188	1,520	90+
27. Northrop	156	152	223	165	256	276	306	1,434	61
28. Thiokol	210	178	239	254	136	111	173	1,301	96
29. Standard Oil of N.J.	168	180	155	161	164	214	235	1,277	2
30. Kaiser Industries	--	87	49	152	219	441	306	1,255	45
31. Honeywell	86	127	170	107	82	251	306	1,129	24
32. General Tel.	61	116	162	229	232	196	138	1,124	25
33. Collins Radio	94	150	144	129	141	245	202	1,105	65
34. Chrysler	158	181	186	170	81	150	165	1,091	4
35. Litton	--	88	198	210	190	219	180	1,085	25
36. Pan. Am. World Air.	127	147	155	164	158	170	115	1,046	44
37. F.M.C.	88	160	199	141	124	163	170	1,045	21
38. Hercules	117	182	183	137	101	120	195	1,035	31

u-unavailable.
*Includes Morrison-Knudsen, Brown & Root, and J.A. Jones Construction Co.

*Source: Dr. Ralph E. Lapp, *The Weapons Culture* (1968), p. 186-187.

The National Labor Relations Act of 1935

Congress and the President

An Act to diminish the causes of labor disputes burdening or obstructing interstate and foreign commerce, to create a National Labor Relations Board, and for other purposes.

Be it enacted,

FINDINGS AND POLICY

Section 1. The denial by employers of the right of employees to organize and the refusal by employers to accept the procedure of collective bargaining lead to strikes and other forms of industrial strife or unrest, which have the intent or the necessary effect of burdening or obstructing commerce by (a) impairing the efficiency, safety, or operation of the instrumentalities of commerce; (b) occurring in the current of commerce; (c) materially affecting, restraining, or controlling the flow of raw materials or manufactured or processed goods from or into the channels of commerce, or the prices of such materials or goods in commerce; or (d) causing diminution of employment and wages in such volume as substantially to impair or disrupt the market for goods flowing from or into the channels of commerce.

The inequality of bargaining power between employees who do not possess full freedom of association or actual liberty of contract, and employers who are organized in the corporate or other forms of ownership association substantially burdens and affects the flow of commerce, and tends to aggravate recurrent business depressions, by depressing wage rates and the purchasing power of wage earners in industry and by preventing the stabilization of competitive wage rates and working conditions within and between industries.

Experience has proved that protection by law of the right of employees to organize and bargain collectively safeguards commerce from injury, impairment, or interruption, and promotes the flow of commerce by removing certain recognized sources of industrial strife and unrest, by encouraging practices fundamental to the friendly adjustment of industrial disputes arising out of differences as to wages, hours, or other working conditions, and by restoring equality of bargaining power between employers and employees.

It is hereby declared to be the policy of the United States to eliminate the causes of certain substantial obstructions to the free flow of commerce and to mitigate and eliminate these obstructions when they have occurred by encouraging the practice and procedure of collective bargaining and by protecting the exercise by workers of full freedom of association, self-organization, and designation of representatives of their own choosing, for the purpose of negotiating the terms and conditions of their employment or other mutual aid or protection.

Sec. 2. When used in this Act—

(1) The term "person" includes one or more individuals, partnerships, associations, corporations, legal representatives, trustees, trustees in bankruptcy, or receivers.

(2) The term "employer" includes any person acting in the interest of an employer, directly or indirectly, but shall not include the United States, or any State or political subdivision thereof, or any person subject to the Railway Labor Act, as amended from time to time, or any labor organization (other than when acting as an employer), or anyone acting in the capacity of officer or agent of such labor organization.

(3) The term "employee" shall include any employee, and shall not be limited to the employees of a particular employer, unless the Act explicitly states otherwise, and shall include any individual whose work has ceased as a consequence of, or in connection with, any current labor dispute or because of any unfair labor practice, and who has not obtained any other regular and substantially equivalent employment, but shall not include any individual employed as an agricultural laborer, or in the domestic service of any family or person at his home, or any individual employed by his parent or spouse. . . .

(5) The term "labor organization" means any organization of any kind, or any agency or employee representation committee or plan, in which employees participate and which exists for the purpose, in whole or in part, of dealing with employers concerning grievances,

labor disputes, wages, rates of pay, hours of employment, or conditions of work.

(6) The term "commerce" means trade, traffic, commerce, transportation, or communication among the several States, . . .

(7) The term "affecting commerce" means in commerce, or burdening or obstructing commerce or the free flow of commerce, or having led or tending to lead to a labor dispute burdening or obstructing commerce or the free flow of commerce. . . .

(9) The term "labor dispute" includes any controversy concerning terms, tenure or conditions of employment, or concerning the association or representation of persons in negotiating, fixing, maintaining, changing, or seeking to arrange terms or conditions of employment, regardless of whether the disputants stand in the proximate relation of employer and employee. . . .

NATIONAL LABOR RELATIONS BOARD

Sec. 3. (a) There is hereby created a board, to be known as the "National Labor Relations Board," which shall be composed of three members, who shall be appointed by the President, by and with the advice and consent of the Senate. One of the original members shall be appointed for a term of one year, one for a term of three years, and one for a term of five years, but their successors shall be appointed for terms of five years each, except that any individual chosen to fill a vacancy shall be appointed only for the unexpired term of the member whom he shall succeed. The President shall designate one member to serve as chairman of the Board. Any member of the Board may be removed by the President, upon notice and hearing, for neglect of duty or malfeasance in office, but for no other cause. . . .

Sec. 6. (a) The Board shall have authority from time to time to make, amend, and rescind such rules and regulations as may be necessary to carry out the provisions of this Act. Such rules and regulations shall be effective upon publication in the manner which the Board shall prescribe.

RIGHTS OF EMPLOYEES

Sec. 7. Employees shall have the right of self-organization, to form, join, or assist labor organizations, to bargain collectively through representatives of their own choosing, and to engage in concerted activities, for the purpose of collective bargaining or other mutual aid or protection.

Sec. 8. It shall be an unfair labor practice for an employer—

(1) To interfere with, restrain, or coerce employees in the exercise of the rights guaranteed in section 7.

(2) To dominate or interfere with the formation or administration of any labor organization or contribute financial or other support to it: *Provided,* That subject to rules and regulations made and published by the Board pursuant to section 6 (a), an employer shall not be prohibited from permitting employees to confer with him during working hours without loss of time or pay.

(3) By discrimination in regard to hire or tenure of employment or any term or condition of employment to encourage or discourage membership in any labor organization: *Provided,* That nothing in this Act, or in the National Industrial Recovery Act (U. S. C., Supp. VII, title 15, secs. 701-712), as amended from time to time, or in any code or agreement approved or prescribed thereunder, or in any other statute of the United States, shall preclude an employer from making an agreement with a labor organization (not established, maintained, or assisted by any action defined in this Act as an unfair labor practice) to require as a condition of employment membership therein, if such labor organization is the representative of the employees as provided in section 9 (a), in the appropriate collective bargaining unit covered by such agreement when made.

(4) To discharge or otherwise discriminate against an employee because he has filed charges or given testimony under this Act.

(5) To refuse to bargain collectively with the representatives of his employees, subject to the provisions of Section 9 (a).

REPRESENTATIVES AND ELECTIONS

Sec. 9. (a) Representatives designated or selected for the purposes of collective bargaining by the majority of the employees in a unit appropriate for such purposes, shall be the exclusive representatives of all the employees in such unit for the purposes of collective bargaining in respect to rates of pay, wages, hours of employment, or other conditions of employment: *Provided,* That any individual employee or a group of employees shall have the right at any time to present grievances to their employer.

(b) The Board shall decide in each case whether, in order to insure to employees the full benefit of their right to self-organization and to collective bargaining, and otherwise to effectuate the policies of this Act, the unit appropriate for the purposes of collective bargaining shall be the employer unit, craft unit, plant unit, or subdivision thereof.

(c) Whenever a question affecting commerce arises concerning the representation of employees, the Board may investigate such controversy and certify to the parties, in writing, the name or names of the representatives that have been designated or selected. In any such investigation, the Board shall provide for an appropriate hearing upon due notice, either in conjunction with a proceeding under section 10 or otherwise, and may take a secret ballot of employees, or utilize any other suitable method to ascertain such representatives.

(d) Whenever an order of the Board made pursuant to section 10 (c) is based in whole or in part upon facts certified following an investigation pursuant to subsection (c) of this section, and there is a petition for the enforcement or review of such order, such certification and the record of such investigation shall be included in the transcript of the entire record required to be filed under subsections 10 (e) or 10 (f), and thereupon the decree of the court enforcing, modifying, or setting aside in whole or in part the order of the Board shall be made and entered upon the pleadings, testimony, and proceedings set forth in such transcript.

PREVENTION OF UNFAIR LABOR PRACTICES

Sec. 10. (a) The Board is empowered, as hereinafter provided, to prevent any person from engaging in any unfair labor practice (listed in section 8) affecting commerce. This power shall be exclusive, and shall not be affected by any other means of adjustment or prevention that has been or may be established by agreement, code, law, or otherwise.

(b) Whenever it is charged that any person has engaged in or is engaging in any such unfair labor practice, the Board, or any agent or agency designated by the Board for such purposes, shall have power to issue and cause to be served upon such person a complaint stating the charges in that respect, and containing a notice of hearing before the Board or a member thereof, or before a designated agent or agency, at a place therein fixed, not less than five days after the serving of said complaint. Any such complaint may be amended by the member, agent, or agency conducting the hearing or the Board in its discretion at any time prior to the issuance of an order based thereon. The person so complained of shall have the right to file an answer to the original or amended complaint and to appear in person or otherwise and give testimony at the place and time fixed in the complaint. In the discretion of the member, agent or agency conducting the hearing or the Board, any other person may be allowed to intervene in the said proceeding and to present testimony. In any such proceeding the rules of evidence prevailing in courts of law or equity shall not be controlling.

(c) The testimony taken by such member, agent or agency or the Board shall be reduced to writing and filed with the Board. Thereafter, in its discretion, the Board upon notice may take further testimony or hear argument. If upon all the testimony taken the Board shall be of the opinion that any person named in the complaint has engaged in or is engaging in any such unfair labor practice, then the Board shall state its findings of fact and shall issue and cause to be served on such person an order requiring such person to cease and desist from such unfair labor practice, and to take such affirmative action, including reinstatement of employees with or without back pay, as will effectuate the policies of this Act. Such order may further require such person to make reports from time to time showing the extent to which it has complied with the order. If upon all the testimony taken the Board shall be of the opinion that no person named in the complaint has engaged in or is engaging in any such unfair labor practice, then the Board shall state its findings of fact and shall issue an order dismissing the said complaint. . . .

(f) Any person aggrieved by a final order of the Board granting or denying in whole or in part the relief sought may obtain a review of such order in any circuit court of appeals of the United States in the circuit wherein the unfair labor practice in question was alleged to have been engaged in or wherein such person resides or transacts business. . . .

LIMITATIONS

Sec. 13. Nothing in this Act shall be construed so as to interfere with or impede or diminish in any way the right to strike. . . .

National Labor Relations Board v. Jones and Laughlin Steel Corporation*

United States Supreme Court

Mr. Chief Justice Hughes delivered the opinion of the Court, saying in part:

. . . *First. The scope of the act.*—The act is challenged in its entirety as an attempt to regulate all industry, thus invading the reserved powers of the states over their local concerns. It is asserted that the references in the act to interstate and foreign commerce are colorable at best; that the act is not a true regulation of such commerce or of matters which directly affect it but on the contrary has the fundamental object of placing under the compulsory supervision of the federal government all industrial labor relations within the nation. The argument seeks support in the broad words of the preamble (section one) and in the sweep of the provisions of the act, and it is further insisted that its legislative history shows an essential universal purpose in the light of which its scope cannot be limited by either construction or by the application of the separability clause.

If this conception of terms, intent and consequent inseparability were sound, the act would necessarily fall by reason of the limitation upon the federal power which inheres in the constitutional grant, as well as because of the explicit reservation of the Tenth Amendment. . . . The authority of the federal government may not be pushed to such an extreme as to destroy the distinction, which the commerce clause itself establishes, between commerce "among the several states" and the internal concerns of a state. That distinction between what is

---

*301 U.S. 1.

national and what is local in the activities of commerce is vital to the maintenance of our federal system. . . .

We think it clear that the National Labor Relations Act may be construed so as to operate within the sphere of constitutional authority. The jurisdiction conferred upon the board, and invoked in this instance, is found in § 10(a), which provides:

"Sec. 10(a). The board is empowered, as hereinafter provided, to prevent any person from engaging in any unfair labor practice (listed in § 8) affecting commerce."

The critical words of this provision, prescribing the limits of the board's authority in dealing with the labor practices, are "affecting commerce." The act specifically defines the "commerce" to which it refers (§ 2(6)):

"The term 'commerce' means trade, traffic, commerce, transportation, or communication among the several states, or between the District of Columbia or any territory of the United States and any state or other territory, or between any foreign country and any state, territory, or the District of Columbia, or within the District of Columbia or any territory, or between points in the same state but through any other state or any territory or the District of Columbia or any foreign country."

There can be no question that the commerce thus contemplated by the act (aside from that within a territory or the District of Columbia) is interstate and foreign commerce in the constitutional sense. The act also defines the term "affecting commerce" (§ 2(7)):

"The term 'affecting commerce' means in commerce, or burdening or obstructing commerce or the free flow of commerce, or having led or tending to lead to a labor dispute burdening or obstructing commerce or the free flow of commerce."

This definition is one of exclusion as well as inclusion. The grant of authority to the board does not purport to extend to the relationship between all industrial employees and employers. Its terms do not impose collective bargaining upon all industry regardless of effects upon interstate or foreign commerce. It purports to reach only what may be deemed to burden or obstruct that commerce and, thus qualified, it must be construed as contemplating the exercise of control within constitutional bounds. It is a familiar principle that acts which directly burden or obstruct interstate or foreign commerce, or its free flow, are within the reach of the congressional power. Acts having that effect are not rendered immune because they grow out of labor disputes. . . . It is the effect upon commerce, not the source of the inquiry, which is the criterion. . . . Whether or not particular action does affect commerce in such a close and intimate fashion as to be subject to federal control, and hence to lie within the authority conferred upon the board, is left by the statute to be determined as individual cases arise. We are thus to inquire whether in the instant case the constitutional boundary has been passed.

Second. The unfair labor practices in question.—The unfair labor practices found by the board are those defined in § 8, subdivisions (1) and (3). These provide:

"Sec. 8. It shall be an unfair labor practice for an employer—

"(1) To interfere with, restrain, or coerce employees in the exercise of the rights guaranteed in §7."

"(3) By discrimination in regard to hire or tenure of employment or any term or condition of employment to encourage or discourage membership in any labor organization: . . ."

Section 8, subdivision (1), refers to § 7, which is as follows:

"Sec. 7. Employees shall have the right to self-organization, to form, join, or assist labor organizations, to bargain collectively through representatives of their own choosing, and to engage in concerted activities, for the purpose of collective bargaining or other mutual aid or protection."

Thus, in its present application, the statute goes no further than to safeguard the right of employees to self-organization and to select representatives of their own choosing for collective bargaining or other mutual protection without restraint or coercion by their employer.

That is a fundamental right. Employees have as clear a right to organize and select their representatives for lawful purposes as the respondent has to organize its business and select its own officers and agents. Discrimination and coercion to prevent the free exercise of the right of employees to self-organization and representation is a proper subject for condemnation by competent legislative authority. Long ago we stated the reason for labor organizations. We said that they were organized out of the necessities of the situation; that a single employee was helpless in dealing with an employer; that he was dependent ordinarily on his daily wage for the maintenance of himself and family; that if the employer refused to pay him the wages that he thought fair, he was nevertheless unable to leave the employ and resist arbitrary and unfair treatment; that union was essential to give laborers opportunity to deal on an equality with their employer. . . . Fully recognizing the legality of collective action on the part of employees in order to safeguard their proper interests, we said that Congress was not required to ignore this right but could safeguard it. Congress could seek to make appropriate collective action of employees an instrument of peace rather than of strife. We said that such collective action would be a mockery if representation were made futile by interference with freedom of choice. Hence the prohibition by Congress of interference with the selection of representatives for the purpose of negotiation and conference between employers and employees, "instead of being an invasion of the constitutional right of either, was based on the recognition of the rights of both." . . .

Third. The application of the act to employees engaged in production.—The principle involved.—Respondent says that whatever may be said of employees engaged in interstate commerce, the industrial relations and activities in the manufacturing department of respondent's enterprise are not subject to federal regulation. The argument rests upon the proposition that manufacturing in itself is not commerce. Kidd v. Pearson, 128 U. S. 1; . . . A. L. A. Schechter Poultry Corp. v. United States, 295 U. S. 495; Carter v. Carter Coal Co., 298 U. S. 238.

The government distinguishes these cases. The various parts of respondent's enterprise are described as interdependent and as thus involving "a great movement of iron ore, coal and limestone along well-defined paths to the steel mills, thence through them, and thence in the form of steel products into the consuming centers of the country—a definite and well-understood course of business." It is urged that these activities constitute a "stream" or "flow" of commerce, of which the Aliquippa manufacturing plant is the focal point, and that industrial strife at that point would cripple the entire movement. Reference is made to our decision sustaining the Packers and Stockyards Act. Stafford v. Wallace, 258 U. S. 495. The Court found that the stockyards were but a "throat" through which the current of commerce flowed and the transactions which there occurred could not be separated from that movement. Hence the sales at the stockyards were not regarded as merely local transactions, for while they created "a local change of title" they did not "stop the flow," but merely changed the private interests in the subject of the current. . . . Applying the doctrine of Stafford v. Wallace, *supra,* the Court sustained the Grain Futures Act of [September 11] 1922 with respect to transactions on the Chicago Board of Trade, although these transactions were "not in and of themselves interstate commerce." Congress had found that they had become "a constantly recurring burden and obstruction to that commerce." Board of Trade v. Olsen, 262 U. S. 1. . . .

Respondent contends that the instant case presents material distinctions. Respondent says that the Aliquippa plant is extensive in size and represents a large investment in buildings, machinery and equipment. The raw materials which are brought to the plant are delayed for long periods and, after being subjected to manufacturing processes "are changed substantially as to character, utility and value." The finished products which emerge "are to a large extent manufactured without reference to pre-existing orders and contracts and are entirely different from the raw materials which enter at the other end." Hence respondent argues that "If importation and exportation in interstate commerce do not singly transfer purely local activities into the field of congressional regulation, it should follow that their combination would not alter the local situation." . . .

We do not find it necessary to determine whether these features of defendant's business dispose of the asserted analogy to the "stream of commerce" cases. The instances in which that metaphor has been used are but particular, and not exclusive, illustrations of the protective power which the government invokes in support of the present act. The congressional authority to protect interstate commerce from burdens and obstructions is not limited to transactions which can be deemed to be an essential part of a "flow" of interstate or foreign commerce. Burdens and obstructions may be due to injurious action springing from other sources. The fundamental principle is that the power to regulate commerce is the power to enact "all appropriate legislation" for "its protection and advancement" . . . ; to adopt measures "to promote its growth and insure its safety" . . . ; "to foster, protect, control and restrain." . . . That power is plenary and may be exerted to protect interstate commerce "no matter what the source of the dangers which threaten it." . . . Although activities may be intrastate in character when separately considered, if they have such a close and substantial relation to interstate commerce that their control is essential or appropriate to protect that commerce from burdens and obstructions, Congress cannot be denied the power to exercise that control. . . . Undoubtedly the scope of this power must be considered in the light of our dual system of government and may not be extended so as to embrace effects upon interstate commerce so indirect and remote that to embrace them, in view of our complex society, would effectually obliterate the distinction between what is national and what is local and create a completely centralized government. The question is necessarily one of degree. . . .

That intrastate activities, by reason of close and intimate relation to interstate commerce, may fall within federal control is demonstrated in the case of carriers who are engaged in both interstate and intrastate transportation. There federal control has been found essential to secure the freedom of interstate traffic from interference or unjust discrimination and to promote the efficiency of the interstate service. Shreveport Case (Houston, E. & W.T.R. Co. v. United States) 234 U. S. 342; Railroad Commission v. Chicago, B. & O. R. Co., 257 U. S. 563. It is manifest that intrastate rates deal *primarily* with a local activity. But in rate-making they bear such a close relation to interstate rates that effective control of the one must embrace some control over the other. Under the Transportation Act [February 28] 1920, Congress went so far as to authorize the Interstate Commerce Commission to establish a state-wide level of intrastate rates in order to prevent an unjust discrimination against interstate commerce. . . .

The close and intimate effect which brings the subject within the reach of federal power may be due to activities in relation to productive industry although the industry when separately viewed is local. This has been abundantly illustrated in the application of the Federal Anti-Trust Act. In the Standard Oil Co. case, 221 U. S. 1, and American Tobacco Co. case, 221 U. S. 106, that statute was applied to combinations of employers engaged in productive industry. . . .

Upon the same principle, the Anti-Trust Act has been applied to the conduct of employees engaged in production. . . .

It is thus apparent that the fact that the employees here concerned were engaged in production is not determinative. The question remains as to the effect upon interstate commerce of the labor practice involved. In the A. L. A. Schechter Poultry Corp. case, 295 U. S. 495, *supra,* we found that the effect there was so remote as to be beyond the federal power. To find "immediacy or directness" there was to find it "almost everywhere," a result inconsistent with the maintenance of our federal system. . . .

Fourth. Effects of the unfair labor practice in respondent's enterprise. — Giving full weight to respondent's contention with respect to a break in the complete continuity of the "stream of commerce" by reason of respondent's manufacturing operations, the fact remains that the stoppage of those operations by industrial strife would have a most serious effect upon interstate commerce. In view of respondent's far-flung activities, it is idle to say that the effect would be indirect or remote. It is obvious that it would be immediate and might be catastrophic. We are asked to shut our eyes to the plainest facts of our national life and to deal with the question of direct and indirect effects in an intellectual vacuum. Because there may be but indirect and remote effects upon interstate commerce in connection with a host of local enterprises throughout the country, it does not follow that other industrial activities do not have such a close and intimate relation to interstate commerce as to make the presence of industrial strife a matter of the most urgent national concern. When industries organize themselves on a national scale, making their relation to interstate commerce the dominant factor in their activities, how can it be maintained that their industrial labor relations constitute a forbidden field into which Congress may not enter when it is necessary to protect interstate commerce from the paralyzing consequences of industrial war? We have often said that interstate commerce itself is a practical conception. It is equally true that interferences with that commerce must be appraised by a judgment that does not ignore actual experience.

Experience has abundantly demonstrated that the recognition of the right of employees to self-organization and to have representatives of their own choosing for the purpose of collective bargaining is often an essential condition of industrial peace. Refusal to confer and negotiate has been one of the most prolific causes of strife. This is such an outstanding fact in the history of labor disturbances that it is a proper subject of judicial notice and requires no citation of instances. The opinion in the case of Virginian Railway Co. v. System Federation No. 40, points out that, in the case of carriers, experience has shown that before the amendment, of 1934, of the Railway Labor Act "when there was no dispute as to the organizations authorized to represent the employees, and when there was a willingness of the employer to meet such representative for a discussion of their grievances, amicable adjustment of differences had generally followed and strikes had been avoided." That, on the other hand, "a prolific source of dispute had been the maintenance by the railroads of company unions and the denial by railway management of the authority of representatives chosen by their employees." The opinion in that case also points to the large measure of success of the labor policy embodied in the Railway Labor Act. But with respect to the appropriateness of the recognition of self-organization and representation in the promotion of peace, the question is not essentially different in the case of employees in industries of such a character that interstate commerce is put in jeopardy from the case of employees of transportation companies. And of what avail is it to protect the facility of transportation, if interstate commerce is throttled with respect to the commodities to be transported!

These questions have frequently engaged the attention of Congress and have been the subject of many inquiries. The steel industry is one of the great basic industries of the United States, with ramifying activities affecting interstate commerce at every point. The government aptly refers to the steel strike of 1919-1920 with its far-reaching consequences. The fact that there appears to have been no major disturbance in that industry in the more recent period did not dispose of the possibilities of future and like dangers to interstate commerce which Congress was entitled to foresee and to exercise its protective power to forestall. It is not necessary again to detail the facts as to respondent's enterprise. Instead of being beyond the pale, we think that it presents in a most striking way the close and intimate relation which a manufacturing industry may have to interstate commerce and we have no doubt that Congress had constitutional authority to safeguard the right of respondent's employees to self-organization and freedom in the choice of representatives for collective bargaining.

Fifth. The means which the act employs. — Questions under the due process clause and other constitutional restrictions. — Respondent asserts its right to conduct its business in an orderly manner without being subjected to arbitrary restraints. What we have said points to the fallacy in the argument. Employees have their correlative right to organize for the purpose of securing the redress of grievances and to promote agreements with employers relating to rate of pay and conditions of work. . . . Restraint for the purpose of preventing an unjust interference with that right cannot be considered arbitrary or capricious. . . .

The act does not compel agreements between employers and employees. It does not compel any agreements whatever. It does not prevent the employer "from refusing to make a collective contract and hiring individuals on whatever terms" the employer "may by unilateral action determine." The act expressly provides in § 9(a) that any individual employee or a group of employees shall have the right at any time to present grievances to their employer. The theory of the act is that free opportunity for negotiation with accredited representatives of employees is likely to promote industrial peace and may bring about the adjustments and agreements which the act in itself does not attempt to compel. . . . The act does not interfere with the normal exercise of the right of the employer to select its employees or to discharge them. The employer may not, under cover of that right, intimidate or coerce its employees with respect to their self-organization and representation, and, on the other hand, the board is not entitled to make its authority a pretext for interference with the right of discharge when that right is exercised for other reasons than such intimidation and coercion. The true purpose is the subject of investigation with full opportunity to show the facts. It would seem that when employers freely recognize the right of their employees to their own organizations and their unrestricted right of representation there will be much less occasion for controversy in respect to the free and appropriate exercise of the right of selection and discharge.

The act has been criticized as one-sided in its application; that it subjects the employer to supervision and restraint and leaves untouched the abuses for which employees may be responsible. That it fails to provide a more comprehensive plan, — with better assurances of fairness to both sides and with increased chances of success in bringing about, if not compelling, equitable solutions of industrial disputes affecting interstate commerce. But we are dealing with the power of Congress, not with a particular policy, or with the extent to which policy should go. We have frequently said that the legislative authority, exerted within its proper field, need not embrace all the evils within its reach. The Constitution does not forbid "cautious advance, step by step," in dealing with the evils which are exhibited in activities within the range of legislative power. . . . The question in such cases is whether the legislative, in what it does prescribe, has gone beyond constitutional limits.

The procedural provisions of the act are assailed. But these provisions, as we construe them, do not offend against the constitutional requirements governing the creation and action of administrative bodies. . . .

Respondent complains that the board not only ordered reinstatement but directed the payment of wages for the time lost by the discharge, less amounts earned by the employee during that period. . . . It is argued that the requirement is equivalent to a money judgment and hence contravenes the Seventh Amendment with respect to trial by jury. The Seventh Amendment provides that "In suits at common law, where the value in controversy shall exceed twenty dollars, the right of trial by jury shall be preserved." . . .

The instant case is not a suit at common law or in the nature of such a suit. The proceeding is one unknown to the common law. It is a statutory proceeding. Reinstatement of the employee and payment for time lost are requirements imposed for violation of the statute and are remedies appropriate to its enforcement. The contention under the Seventh Amendment is without merit.

Our conclusion is that the order of the board was within its competency and that the act is valid as here applied. . . .

Mr. Justice McReynolds delivered the following dissenting opinion, saying in part:

Mr. Justice Van Devanter, Mr. Justice Sutherland, Mr. Justice Butler and I are unable to agree with the decisions just announced. . . .

The Court, as we think, departs from well-established principles followed in A. L. A. Schechter Poultry Corp. v. United States, 295 U. S. 495, and Carter v. Carter Coal Co., 298 U. S. 238. Upon the authority of those decisions . . . the power of Congress under the commerce clause does not extend to relations between employers and their employees engaged in manufacture, and therefore the act conferred upon the National Labor Relations Board no authority in respect of matters covered by the questioned orders. . . . No decision or judicial opinion to the contrary has been cited, and we find none. Every consideration brought forward to uphold the act before us was applicable to support the acts held unconstitutional in causes decided within two years. And the lower courts rightly deemed them controlling. . . .

Any effect on interstate commerce by the discharge of employees shown here, would be indirect and remote in the highest degree, as consideration of the facts will show. In No. 419 [The Jones & Laughlin case] ten men out of ten thousand were discharged; in the other cases only a few. The immediate effect in the factory may be to create discontent among all those employed and a strike may follow, which, in turn, may result in reducing production, which ultimately may reduce the volume of goods moving in interstate commerce. By this chain of indirect and progressively remote events we finally reach the evil with which it is said the legislation under consideration undertakes to deal. A more remote and indirect interference with interstate commerce or a more definite invasion of the powers reserved to the states is difficult, if not impossible, to imagine.

The Constitution still recognizes the existence of states with indestructible powers; the Tenth Amendment was supposed to put them beyond controversy. . . .

The Labor Management Relations Act of 1947

Congress of the United States

... It shall be an unfair labor practice for a labor organization or its agents —

"(1) to restrain or coerce (A) employees in the exercise of the rights guaranteed in section 7: *Provided,* That this paragraph shall not impair the right of a labor organization to prescribe its own rules with respect to the acquisition or retention of membership therein; or (B) an employer in the selection of his representatives for the purposes of collective bargaining or the adjustment of grievances;

"(2) to cause or attempt to cause an employer to discriminate against an employee in violation of subsection (a) (3) or to discriminate against an employee with respect to whom membership in such organization has been denied or terminated on some ground other than his failure to tender the periodic dues and the initiation fees uniformly required as a condition of acquiring or retaining membership;

"(3) to refuse to bargain collectively with an employer, provided it is the representative of his employees subject to the provisions of section 9 (a);

"(4) to engage in, or to induce or encourage the employees of any employer to engage in, a strike or a concerted refusal in the course of their employment to use, manufacture, process, transport, or otherwise handle or work on any goods, articles, materials, or commodities or to perform any services, where an object thereof is: (A) forcing or requiring any employer or self-employed person to join any labor or employer organization or any employer or other person to cease using, selling, handling, transporting, or otherwise dealing in the products of any other producer, processor, or manufacturer, or to cease doing business with any other person; (B) forcing or requiring any other employer to recognize or bargain with a labor organization as the representative of his employees unless such labor organization has been certified as the representative of such employees under the provisions of section 9; (C) forcing or requiring any employer to recognize or bargain with a particular labor organization as the representative of his employees if another labor organization has been certified as the representative of such employees under the provisions of section 9; (D) forcing or requiring any employer to assign particular work to employees in a particular labor organization or in a particular trade, craft, or class rather than to employees in another labor organization or in another trade, craft, or class, unless such employer is failing to conform to an order or certification of the Board determining the bargaining representative for employees performing such work: *Provided,* That nothing contained in this subsection (b) shall be construed to make unlawful a refusal by any person to enter upon the premises of any employer (other than his own employer), if the employees of such employer are engaged in a strike ratified or approved by a representative of such employees whom such employer is required to recognize under this Act;

"(5) to require of employees covered by an agreement authorized under subsection (a) (3) the payment, as a condition precedent to becoming a member of such organization, of a fee in an amount which the Board finds excessive or discriminatory under all the circumstances. In making such a finding, the Board shall consider, among other relevant factors, the practices and customs of labor organizations in the particular industry, and the wages currently paid to the employees affected; and

"(6) to cause or attempt to cause an employer to pay or deliver or agree to pay or deliver any money or other thing of value, in the nature of an exaction, for services which are not performed or not to be performed.

TITLE II — CONCILIATION OF LABOR DISPUTES IN INDUSTRIES AFFECTING COMMERCE; NATIONAL EMERGENCIES

Sec. 201. That it is the policy of the United States that —

(a) sound and stable industrial peace and the advancement of the general welfare, health, and safety of the Nation and of the best interest of employers and employees can most satisfactorily be secured by the settlement of issues between employers and employees through the processes of conference and collective bargaining between employers and the representatives of their employees;

(b) the settlement of issues between employers and employees through collective bargaining may be advanced by making available full and adequate governmental facilities for conciliation, mediation, and voluntary arbitration to aid and encourage employers and the representatives of their employees to reach and maintain agreements concerning rates of pay, hours, and working conditions, and to make all reasonable efforts to settle their differences by mutual agreement reached through conferences and collective bargaining or by such methods as may be provided for in any applicable agreement for the settlement of disputes; and

(c) certain controversies which arise between parties to collective-bargaining agreements may be avoided or minimized by making available full and adequate governmental facilities for furnishing assistance to employers and the representatives of their employees in formulating for inclusion within such agreements provision for adequate notice of any proposed changes in the terms of such agreements, for the final adjustment of grievances or questions regarding the application or interpretation of such agreements, and other provisions designed to prevent the subsequent arising of such controversies.

Sec. 202. (a) There is hereby created an independent agency to be known as the Federal Mediation and Conciliation Service (herein referred to as the "Service," except that for sixty days after the date of the enactment of this Act such term shall refer to the Conciliation Service of the Department of Labor). The Service shall be under the direction of a Federal Mediation and Conciliation Director (hereinafter referred to as the "Director"), who shall be appointed by the President by and with the advice and consent of the Senate.

•   •   •

FUNCTIONS OF THE SERVICE

Sec. 203. (a) It shall be the duty of the Service, in order to prevent or minimize interruptions of the free flow of commerce growing out of labor disputes, to assist parties to labor disputes in industries affecting commerce to settle such disputes through conciliation and mediation.

(b) The Service may proffer its services in any labor dispute in any industry affecting commerce, either upon its own motion or upon the request of one or more of the parties to the dispute, whenever in its judgment such dispute threatens to cause a substantial interruption of commerce. The Director and the Service are directed to avoid attempting to mediate disputes which would have only a minor effect on interstate commerce if State or other conciliation services are available to the parties. Whenever the Service does proffer its services in any dispute, it shall be the duty of the Service promptly to put itself in communication with the parties and to use its best efforts, by mediation and conciliation, to bring them to agreement.

(c) If the Director is not able to bring the parties to agreement by conciliation within a reasonable time, he shall seek to induce the parties voluntarily to seek other means of settling the dispute without resort to strike, lockout, or other coercion, including submission to the employees in the bargaining unit of the employer's last offer of settlement for approval or rejection in a secret ballot. The failure or refusal of either party to agree to any procedure suggested by the Director shall not be deemed a violation of any duty or obligation imposed by this Act.

(d) Final adjustment by a method agreed upon by the parties is hereby declared to be the desirable method for settlement of grievance disputes arising over the application or interpretation of an existing collective-bargaining agreement. The Service is directed to make its conciliation and mediation services available in the settlement of such grievance disputes only as a last resort and in exceptional cases.

Sec. 204. (a) In order to prevent or minimize interruptions of the free flow of commerce growing out of labor disputes, employers and employees and their representatives, in any industry affecting commerce, shall —

(1) exert every reasonable effort to make and maintain agreements concerning rates of pay, hours, and working conditions, including provision for adequate notice of any proposed change in the terms of such agreements;

(2) whenever a dispute arises over the terms or application of a collective-bargaining agreement and a conference is requested by a party or prospective party thereto, arrange promptly for such a conference to be held and endeavor in such conference to settle such dispute expeditiously; and

(3) in case such dispute is not settled by conference, participate fully and promptly in such meetings as may be undertaken by the Service under this Act for the purpose of aiding in a settlement of the dispute.

* * *

NATIONAL EMERGENCIES

Sec. 206. Whenever in the opinion of the President of the United States, a threatened or actual strike or lock-out affecting an entire industry or a substantial part thereof engaged in trade, commerce, transportation, transmission, or communication among the several States or with foreign nations, or engaged in the production of goods for commerce, will, if permitted to occur or to continue, imperil the national health or safety, he may appoint a board of inquiry to inquire into the issues involved in the dispute and to make a written report to him within such time as he shall prescribe. Such report shall include a statement of the facts with respect to the dispute, including each party's statement of its position but shall not contain any recommendations. The President shall file a copy of such report with the Service and shall make its contents available to the public.

Sec. 207. (a) A board of inquiry shall be composed of a chairman and such other members as the President shall determine, and shall have power to sit and act in any place within the United States and to conduct such hearings either in public or in private, as it may deem necessary or proper, to ascertain the facts with respect to the causes and circumstances of the dispute.

(b) Members of a board of inquiry shall receive compensation at the rate of $50 for each day actually spent by them in the work of the board, together with necessary travel and subsistence expenses.

(c) For the purpose of any hearing or inquiry conducted by any board appointed under this title, the provisions of sections 9 and 10 (relating to the attendance of witnesses and the production of books, papers, and documents) of the Federal Trade Commission Act of September 16, 1914, as amended (U. S. C. 19, title 15, secs. 49 and 50, as amended), are hereby made applicable to the powers and duties of such board.

Sec. 208. (a) Upon receiving a report from a board of inquiry the President may direct the Attorney General to petition any district court of the United States having jurisdiction of the parties to enjoin such strike or lock-out or the continuing thereof, and if the court finds that such threatened or actual strike or lock-out —

(i) affects an entire industry or a substantial part thereof engaged in trade, commerce, transportation, transmission, or communication among the several States or with foreign nations, or engaged in the production of goods for commerce; and

(ii) if permitted to occur or to continue, will imperil the national health or safety, it shall have jurisdiction to enjoin any such strike or lock-out, or the continuing thereof, and to make such other orders as may be appropriate.

(b) In any case, the provisions of the Act of March 23, 1932, entitled "An Act to amend the Judicial Code and to define and limit the jurisdiction of courts sitting in equity, and for other purposes," shall not be applicable.

(c) The order or orders of the court shall be subject to review by the appropriate circuit court of appeals and by the Supreme Court upon writ of certiorari or certification as provided in sections 239 and 240 of the Judicial Code, as amended (U. S. C., title 29, secs. 346 and 347).

Sec. 209. (a) Whenever a district court has issued an order under section 208 enjoining acts or practices which imperil or threaten to imperil the national health or safety, it shall be the duty of the parties to the labor dispute giving rise to such order to make every effort to adjust and settle their differences, with the assistance of the Service created by this Act. Neither party shall be under any duty to accept, in whole or in part, any proposal of settlement made by the Service.

(b) Upon the issuance of such order, the President shall reconvene the board of inquiry which has previously reported with respect to the dispute. At the end of a sixty-day period (unless the dispute has been settled by that time), the board of inquiry shall report to the President the current position of the parties and the efforts which have been made for settlement, and shall include a statement by each party of its position and a statement of the employer's last offer of settlement. The President shall make such report available to the public. The National Labor Relations Board, within the succeeding fifteen days, shall take a secret ballot of the employees of each employer involved in the dispute on the question of whether they wish to accept the final offer of settlement made by their employers as stated by him and shall certify the results thereof to the Attorney General within five days thereafter.

Sec. 210. Upon the certification of the results of such ballot or upon a settlement being reached, whichever happens sooner, the Attorney General shall move the court to discharge the injunction, which motion shall then be granted and the injunction discharged. When such motion is granted, the President shall submit to the Congress a full and comprehensive report of the proceedings, including the findings of the board of inquiry and the ballot taken by the National Labor Relations Board, together with such recommendations as he may see fit to make for consideration and appropriate action.

•   •   •

BOYCOTTS AND OTHER UNLAWFUL COMBINATIONS

Sec. 303. (a) It shall be unlawful, for the purposes of this section only, in an industry or activity affecting commerce, for any labor organization to engage in, or to induce or encourage the employees of any employer to engage in, a strike or a concerted refusal in the course of their employment to use, manufacture, process, transport, or other-

wise handle or work on any goods, articles, materials, or commodities
or to perform any services, where an object thereof is—

(1) forcing or requiring any employer or self-employed person
to join any labor or employer organization or any employer or
other person to cease using, selling, handling, transporting, or
otherwise dealing in the products of any other producer, processor,
or manufacturer, or to cease doing business with any other person;

(2) forcing or requiring any other employer to recognize or
bargain with a labor organization as the representative of his
employees unless such labor organization has been certified as the
representative of such employees under the provisions of section
9 of the National Labor Relations Act;

(3) forcing or requiring any employer to recognize or bargain
with a particular labor organization as the representative of his
employees if another labor organization has been certified as the
representative of such employees under the provisions of section
9 of the National Labor Relations Act;

(4) forcing or requiring any employer to assign particular work
to employees in a particular labor organization or in a particular
trade, craft, or class rather than to employees in another labor
organization or in another trade, craft, or class unless such employer
is failing to conform to an order or certification of the National
Labor Relations Board determining the bargaining representative
for employees performing such work. Nothing contained in this
subsection shall be construed to make unlawful a refusal by any
person to enter upon the premises of any employer (other than
his own employer), if the employees of such employer are engaged
in a strike ratified or approved by a representative of such employees whom such employer is required to recognize under the
National Labor Relations Act.

(b) whoever shall be injured in his business or property by reason
of any violation of subsection (a) may sue therefor in any district court
of the United States subject to the limitations and provisions of section
301 hereof without respect to the amount in controversy, or in any
other court having jurisdiction of the parties, and shall recover the
damages by him sustained and the cost of the suit.

8

Foreign Policy

Speaking at Westminster College in Missouri in early 1946, Winston Churchill denounced the Soviet Union as an expansionist state in the opening declaration of the cold war: "From Stettin in the Baltic to Trieste in the Adriatic, an iron curtain has descended across the continent. Behind that line lie all the capitals of the ancient states of central and Eastern Europe . . . all the famous cities and the populations around them lie in the Soviet sphere, and all are subject in one form or another, not only to Soviet influence but to a very high increasing control from Moscow." The notion of an "international Communist conspiracy" directed from Moscow heavily influenced American policymakers in the years following World War II. To halt Communist expansion the United States developed a policy toward the Communist world which came to be known as "containment." Although the containment policy was originally developed within the context of immediate post World War II European politics, the United States has continued to pursue this policy in every part of the globe down to the present time. Essentially the containment policy is a commitment to halt the expansion of "communism" everywhere in the world and to support "non-Communist" governments attempting to resist Communist influence either within or outside their borders.

The first official statement of the containment policy came in an address to Congress by President Harry S Truman requesting that the United States provide military and economic aid for the Greek and Turkish governments in 1947. *The Truman Doctrine* has specific reference to Greece and Turkey, which were then engaged in civil wars with Communist-led insurgent groups. But the Truman Doctrine called upon

America to help *all* "free peoples who are resisting attempted subjugation by armed minorities or by outside pressure." The Truman Doctrine
justified U. S. involvement in the internal conflicts of a nation in the
interest of preventing the expansion of communism. Congress responded,
and the United States gave Greece and Turkey military and financial
aid which enabled the governments of these nations to defeat the
Communist-led rebels.

The Truman Doctrine was followed in 1948 by the Marshall Plan
and the *North Atlantic Treaty*. The purpose of the Marshall Plan was
to end the economic postwar paralysis of Western Europe, and, by
improving living conditions in these nations, reduce their susceptibility
to communism. While the Marshall Plan was aimed at helping European
nations resist the *internal* threat of communism, the North Atlantic
Treaty was designed to be an effective barrier against an *external* attack
by the Soviet Union. The NATO agreement was signed in 1949, and
was the first peacetime military alliance entered into by the United
States since the 18th century. Fifteen nations agreed that an armed
attack against any one of them in Europe or North America would be
regarded as an armed attack against all. More importantly, the member
nations agreed "to unite their efforts for collective defense and for
the preservation of peace and security." This involved a joint NATO
military command, and the commitment of the troops of the United
States and other nations to a NATO defense line.

The test of containment came in Korea in June 1950 when troops
from Communist North Korea crossed into South Korea, where the
United States had established a Western-oriented non-Communist government. The United States had fewer than 500 troops in South Korea
at the time, and it was not clear whether the containment policy
extended to the Asian mainland; but President Truman acted immediately
to commit American armed forces to the struggle. Later, the United
Nations condemned the North Korean action and called upon member
nations to assist in repelling the invasion. This action by the United
Nations gave moral support to the application of the containment policy
in Korea. By December of 1950 U.S. troops had administered a severe
defeat to the North Korean army and had occupied most of North Korea
up to the Chinese border. The sudden intervention of Chinese troops
into the conflict for a time threatened the total defeat of U.S. and South
Korean forces. Finally, Chinese troops were driven back north of the
38th parallel and the battle lines were stabilized along the line not much
different than the original border between North and South Korea. In
July of 1953 after months of negotiations, an armistice was signed which
involved a cease fire and a voluntary repatriation of prisoners. Some

critics of Presidents Truman and Eisenhower argued that simply repulsing an invasion was too little victory for so much blood, and they called for an all out war with China and perhaps with Russia. But defenders of administration policy argued that fighting the war in Korea demonstrated our commitment to the containment policy and also stimulated the general program of rearmament.

The Korean War focused American attention on Asia. Republicans had claimed that Communist successes in China were aided by Truman's concentration on European problems and failure to support non-Communist regimes in Asia including the defeated Chiang Kai-shek. President Eisenhower resisted strong pressures from both within and outside of his administration to give military assistance to the French in Indochina in 1954. But after French agreement to withdraw from the area in the *Geneva Agreements in 1954* (see Chapter 9), Secretary of State John Foster Dulles sought to create a military alliance in Southeast Asia similar to NATO. However, the major non-Communist powers in this area—India, Indonesia, and Burma—did not care to be "protected" by a military alliance with the United States. The best that could be achieved was a union of Pakistan, Thailand and the Philippines with the United States and the other Western nations—Britain, France, Australia and New Zealand. The *SEATO Treaty* went into effect in 1955. The Treaty dealt with aggression against the territory of the participating nations, but it also extended its area of concern to the states of Laos, Cambodia and South Vietnam. It stated that the threat of subversion from inside any of the participating states is a matter of concern for all and they all promised in such a case to "consult together immediately" to agree upon measures of common action.

The United States also negotiated a mutual defense agreement with Japan immediately following ratification of the formal peace treaty in 1952. Under its terms United States Armed Forces can use Japanese facilities; although in 1960, after a prolonged crisis and rioting, the U.S. agreed to consult with the Japanese on our use of their territory. In 1954 the United States also concluded a mutual defense pact with Australia and New Zealand in which "an armed attack in the Pacific area on any of the parties" would be regarded by each party as "dangerous to its own peace and safety." In 1954 a mutual defense treaty was negotiated with the Republic of China (Formosa), embodying the same type of guarantee as in other Pacific treaties. The United States was given the right to station its armed forces in and around Formosa to protect the island, but the treaty was unclear whether the United States had committed itself to defend certain small islands in the Formosa Straits just off the mainland of China, including Quemoy and Matsu. The issue cropped up in the 1960 Presidential election after Communists had fired on the islands, but in recent years an armed truce has been in effect in the Formosa Straits. Following the French withdrawal from Indochina in accordance with the Geneva Agreements of 1954, the United States undertook to support non-Communist regimes in Laos and South Vietnam. The record of U.S. involvement in Vietnam is presented in the next chapter.

American policy in the Middle East has been somewhat tentative and uncertain. The United States did not support the French in their colonial war in Algeria. We encouraged but did not join a mutual defense arrangement between Turkey, Iraq, Iran, Pakistan and Great Britain known as the Bagdad Pact. The Bagdad Pact collapsed in 1958 when an anti-Western government came to power in Bagdad. We failed to support France and Britain in 1956 when they sought to recapture the Suez Canal from the Egyptians, but in 1958 we joined with Britain in sending troops to Lebanon and Jordan to bolster tottering pro-Western regimes in these nations. In 1957 President Eisenhower asked Congress for broad authority to furnish military or other aid to any nation in the Middle East threatened by Communist aggression. The President's request was granted, and the *Eisenhower Doctrine* expressed the U.S. commitment and willingness to use armed force to prevent Communist regimes from coming to power in the Middle East. Fortunately the Arab-Israeli wars did not develop into a direct confrontation between the United States and the Soviet Union. The United States has not intervened directly in these wars, but instead has sought to strengthen the role of the U.N. in mediating the Arab-Israeli conflict.

Immediate reaction in the United States to the Castro revolution in 1959 was friendly, but when Castro negotiated with the Soviets for economic aid and military assistance and declared it his intention to support revolutionary movements in other Latin American countries, U.S. and Cuban relations deteriorated. In 1961 an invasion of Cuba by an army of Cuban refugees at the Bay of Pigs which was organized by the U.S. Central Intelligence Agency resulted in a humiliating failure for the United States. The Castro government moved even closer to the Soviet Union than before. In October of 1962 aerial photography revealed the presence in Cuba of missile bases built by the Soviet Union and capable of launching nuclear warheads into the heart of the United States. President Kennedy imposed a naval blockade of the island designed to halt military shipments to it, and he threatened an invasion of Cuba unless the Russians agreed to withdraw their missiles from the island. In the most serious confrontation between the United States and the Soviet Union in the postwar era, Premier Khrushchev agreed to withdraw Soviet missiles and President Kennedy ended the naval blockade and took no further military steps against the Castro regime.

When revolution broke out in the Dominican Republic in 1965, President Johnson rushed troops to the island to prevent what the President believed was a "Communist take-over" of that nation. Events in Cuba, the Dominican Republic, and elsewhere in Latin America helped to reaffirm America's long standing commitment to prevent European nations from acquiring positions of power in Latin America. *The Monroe Doctrine* is an American commitment of long standing. In the Rio Treaty signed in 1947 the United States and 20 other American Republics (Canada has never been a member and Castro's Cuba was expelled in 1962) agreed that an armed attack against any American state would be considered an attack against all. The Organization of American States (OAS) forms a continuing group to deal with threats of aggression.

As a result of the containment policy, the United States now has acquired a staggering number of international commitments. (See U.S. State Department, *Summary of U.S. Treaty Obligations*) In addition to these treaty commitments, the containment policy commits the United States to resist the expansion of "communism" in every non-Communist nation in the world. Not only are we committed to resist overt military aggression but also internal take-overs, economic penetration, and even successful campaigning in free elections.

In "Point Four" of his inaugural address in 1949, President Truman called for a program of aid to underdeveloped areas of the world to assist them in scientific advance and industrial progress. The program began as a modest effort at technical assistance, but in an effort to counter the influence of communism in underdeveloped nations, the American foreign aid program expanded into a massive effort in military and economic assistance. Since no Western European nation had succumbed to communism after the inauguration of the Marshall Plan, it was widely believed that foreign aid could be an effective instrument in helping foreign nations resist Communist infiltration. More than 100 billion dollars has been spent on foreign aid programs since World War II. Presidents have often faced stiff Congressional opposition to the foreign aid program. Rarely have Presidents received as much as they requested. Secretary of State Dean Rusk provides the defense of the foreign aid program in his testimony to Congress. (See Dean Rusk, *The Foreign Aid Program*)

The containment policy has continued to guide the United States in foreign affairs for more than 20 years despite important changes in world politics. Many American actions continued to reflect the belief in an "international Communist conspiracy" centrally directed from Moscow bent upon world conquest. We have continued to rely upon regional military alliances, military and economic aid, and support for pro-Western governments facing internal revolutions. Yet there is ample evidence that new forces are at work in the world requiring greater flexibility in American policy and a more realistic appraisal of America's national interest.

First of all, the "socialist camp," as the Communist nations refer to themselves, is by no means a unified block, much less an "international conspiracy." The potential for cleavage between China and the Soviet Union may be much deeper than the potential for cleavage between the United States and the Soviet Union. And it is clear that other Communist nations can and do pursue independent policies in international affairs.

Secondly, the Soviet Union now talks of "competitive co-existence" with the West. While the Soviets have resorted to force to prevent Czechoslovakia from leaving the "socialist camp," the threat of a Soviet military thrust in Western Europe seems remote. The Soviets are clearly prepared to use force to prevent a collapse of their Eastern European alliances. But a quarter of a century of co-existence in Europe suggests that the Soviet Union wants to avoid nuclear war. The United States and the Soviet Union have been able to reach agreements about nuclear testing and spread of nuclear weapons to other powers.

Finally, many new nations of Africa, Latin America, and Asia have refused to participate in the cold war and have declined to join America's containment effort. These nations are more concerned with shaking off the bonds of colonialism and seeking rapid economic development than they are with struggles between the great powers or between "democracy" and "communism." These nations are suspicious of the United States and its colonial allies and resent our attempts to impose pro-Western governments on them. The people of these nations are often revolutionary in their politics. They desire rapid industrialization, freedom from colonial influence, land reform, social justice, the elimination of poverty and disease, and even social revolution. Too often, the Soviet Union or China has succeeded in identifying with the revolutionary aspirations of the people of underdeveloped nations, while the United States has become identified with colonialism, wealth, and status quo politics. The containment policy commits the United States to oppose revolutionary movements in Asia, Africa and Latin America, if it appears that "Communists" are participating in these movements.

The possibility of new directions in American foreign policy is suggested by John F. Kennedy in his announcement of the *Nuclear Test Ban Treaty*. While admitting that this treaty does not itself insure peace, it is nonetheless, *A Step Towards Peace*. It encourages men to believe that the United States and the Soviet Union can reach agreements for their mutual benefit and for the benefit of mankind. Another cooperative effort between the United States and the Soviet Union resulted in the signing of a Nuclear Non-Proliferation Treaty in 1968. Both nations agreed not to transfer their nuclear weapons to any other nations or assist other nations in the manufacture of such weapons. Hopefully, these treaties will lead to a reduction of tension abroad and a breakdown in cold war ideology in America.

Perhaps the most thoughtful essay on American foreign policy in recent years is Senator J. William Fulbright's *The Arrogance of Power*. In this book Senator Fulbright expresses a genuine concern about the future of America in world affairs: "Gradually but unmistakably, America is showing signs of that arrogance of power which has inflicted, weakened, and in some cases destroyed great nations in the past. In so doing we are not living up to our capacity in promise as a civilized example to the world." Fulbright believes that we have now reached an historical point "at which a great nation is in danger of losing its perspective on what exactly is wrong with its power and what is beyond it." He criticizes the overcommitment of American resources and the attitude of arrogance which leads this nation to impose its own standards of justice and morality on other peoples. He laments our lack of understanding of revolutionary movements and our blinding pre-occupation with communism.

The Truman Doctrine*

Harry S Truman

The gravity of the situation which confronts the world today necessitates my appearance before a joint session of the Congress. The foreign policy and the national security of this country are involved.

One aspect of the present situation, which I wish to present to you at this time for your consideration and decision, concerns Greece and Turkey.

The United States has received from the Greek Government an urgent appeal for financial and economic assistance. Preliminary reports from the American Economic Mission now in Greece and reports from the American Ambassador in Greece corroborate the statement of the Greek Government that assistance is imperative if Greece is to survive as a free nation.

I do not believe that the American people and the Congress wish to turn a deaf ear to the appeal of the Greek Government.

The very existence of the Greek state is today threatened by the terrorist activities of several thousand armed men, led by Communists, who defy the Government's authority at a number of points, particularly along the northern boundaries. A commission appointed by the United Nations Security Council is at present investigating disturbed conditions in Northern Greece and alleged border violations along the frontiers between Greece on the one hand and Albania, Bulgaria and Yugoslavia on the other.

Meanwhile, the Greek Government is unable to cope with the situation. The Greek Army is small and poorly equipped. It needs supplies

*Reprinted from *Congressional Record,* March 12, 1947.

and equipment if it is to restore the authority to the Government through-out Greek territory.

Greece must have assistance if it is to become a self-supporting and self-respecting democracy. The United States must supply this assistance. We have already extended to Greece certain types of relief and economic aid but these are inadequate. There is no other country to which democratic Greece can turn. No other nation is willing and able to provide the necessary support for a democratic Greek Government.

The British Government, which has been helping Greece, can give no further financial or economic aid after March 31. Great Britain finds itself under the necessity of reducing or liquidating its commitments in several parts of the world, including Greece.

We have considered how the United Nations might assist in this crisis. But the situation is an urgent one requiring immediate action, and the United Nations and its related organizations are not in a position to extend help of the kind that is required.

It is important to note that the Greek Government has asked for our aid in utilizing effectively the financial and other assistance we may give to Greece, and in improving its public administration. It is of the utmost importance that we supervise the use of any funds made available to Greece, in such a manner that each dollar spent will count toward making Greece self-supporting, and will help to build an economy in which a healthy democracy can flourish.

No government is perfect. One of the chief virtues of a democracy, however, is that its defects are always visible and under democratic processes can be pointed out and corrected. The Government of Greece is not perfect. Nevertheless, it represents 85 per cent of the members of the Greek Parliament who were chosen in an election last year. Foreign observers, including 692 Americans, considered this election to be a fair expression of the views of the Greek people.

The Greek Government has been operating in an atmosphere of chaos and extremism. It has made mistakes. The extension of aid by this country does not mean that the United States condones everything that the Greek Government has done or will do. We have condemned in the past, and we condemn now, extremist measures of the right or the left. We have in the past advised tolerance, and we advise tolerance now.

Greece's neighbor, Turkey, also deserves our attention. The future of Turkey as an independent and economically sound state is clearly no less important to the freedom-loving peoples of the world than the future of Greece. The circumstances in which Turkey finds itself today are considerably different from those of Greece. Turkey has been spared the disasters that have beset Greece. And during the war, the United

States and Great Britain furnished Turkey with material aid. Nevertheless, Turkey now needs our support.

Since the war Turkey has sought additional financial assistance from Great Britain and the United States for the purpose of effecting the modernization necessary for the maintenance of its national integrity. That integrity is essential to the preservation of order in the Middle East.

The British Government has informed us that, owing to its own difficulties, it can no longer extend financial or economic aid to Turkey. As in the case of Greece, if Turkey is to have the assistance it needs, the United States must supply it. We are the only country able to provide that help.

I am fully aware of the broad implications involved if the United States extends assistance to Greece and Turkey, and I shall discuss these implications with you at this time.

One of the primary objectives of the foreign policy of the United States is the creation of conditions in which we and other nations will be able to work out a way of life free from coercion. This was a fundamental issue in the war with Germany and Japan. Our victory was won over countries which sought to impose their will, and their way of life, upon other nations.

To ensure the peaceful development of nations, free from coercion, the United States has taken a leading part in establishing the United Nations. The United Nations is designed to make possible lasting freedom and independence for all its members. We shall not realize our objectives, however, unless we are willing to help free peoples to maintain their free institutions and their national integrity against aggressive movements that seek to impose on them totalitarian regimes. This is no more than a frank recognition that totalitarian regimes imposed on free peoples, by direct or indirect aggression, undermine the foundations of international peace and hence the security of the United States.

The peoples of a number of countries of the world have recently had totalitarian regimes forced upon them against their will. The Government of the United States has made frequent protests against coercion and intimidation, in violation of the Yalta Agreement, in Poland, Rumania and Bulgaria. I must also state that in a number of other countries there have been similar developments.

At the present moment in world history nearly every nation must choose between alternative ways of life. The choice is too often not a free one.

One way of life is based upon the will of the majority, and is distinguished by free institutions, representative government, free elections, guarantees of individual liberty, freedom of speech and religion, and freedom from political oppression.

The second way of life is based upon the will of the minority forcibly imposed upon the majority. It relies upon terror and oppression, a controlled press and radio, fixed elections, and the suppression of personal freedoms.

I believe that it must be the policy of the United States to support free peoples who are resisting attempted subjugation by armed minorities or by outside pressures.

I believe that we must assist free peoples to work out their own destinies in their own way.

I believe that our help should be primarily through economic and financial aid which is essential to economic stability and orderly political processes.

The world is not static, and the status quo is not sacred. But we cannot allow changes in the status quo in violation of the charter of the United Nations by such methods as coercion, or by such subterfuges as political infiltration. In helping free and independent nations to maintain their freedom, the United States will be giving effect to the principles of the charter of the United Nations.

It is necessary only to glance at a map to realize that the survival and integrity of the Greek nation are of grave importance in a much wider situation. If Greece should fall under the control of an armed minority, the effect upon its neighbor, Turkey, would be immediate and serious. Confusion and disorder might well spread throughout the entire Middle East.

Moreover, the disappearance of Greece as an independent state would have a profound effect upon those countries in Europe whose peoples are struggling against great difficulties to maintain their freedoms and their independence while they repair the damages of war.

It would be an unspeakable tragedy if these countries, which have struggled so long against overwhelming odds, should lose that victory for which they sacrificed so much. Collapse of free institutions and loss of independence would be disastrous not only for them but for the world. Discouragement and possibly failure would quickly be the lot of neighboring peoples striving to maintain their freedom and independence.

Should we fail to aid Greece and Turkey in this fateful hour, the effect will be far reaching to the west as well as to the east. We must take immediate and resolute action.

I therefore ask the Congress to provide authority for assistance to Greece and Turkey in the amount of $400,000,000 for the period ending June 30, 1948.

In addition to funds, I ask the Congress to authorize the detail of American civilian and military personnel to Greece and Turkey, at the request of those countries, to assist in the tasks of reconstruction, and for the purpose of supervising the use of such financial and material assistance as may be furnished. I recommend that authority also be provided for the instruction and training of selected Greek and Turkish personnel.

Finally, I ask that the Congress provide authority which will permit the speediest and most effective use, in terms of needed commodities, supplies, and equipment, of such funds as may be authorized.

This is a serious course upon which we embark. I would not recommend it except that the alternative is much more serious.

The United States contributed $341,000,000,000 toward winning World War II. This is an investment in world freedom and world peace.

The assistance that I am recommending for Greece and Turkey amounts to little more than 1 tenth of 1 per cent of this investment. It is only common sense that we should safeguard this investment and make sure that it was not in vain.

The seeds of totalitarian regimes are nurtured by misery and want. They spread and grow in the evil soil of poverty and strife. They reach their full growth when the hope of a people for a better life has died. We must keep that hope alive. The free peoples of the world look to us for support in maintaining their freedoms.

If we falter in our leadership, we may endanger the peace of the world—and we shall surely endanger the welfare of this nation.

Great responsibilities have been placed upon us by the swift movement of events. I am confident that the Congress will face these responsibilities squarely.

The North Atlantic Treaty*

The United States and the North Atlantic Nations

The Parties to this Treaty reaffirm their faith in the purposes and principles of the Charter of the United Nations and their desire to live in peace with all peoples and all governments.

They are determined to safeguard the freedom, common heritage and civilization of their peoples, founded on the principles of democracy, individual liberty and the rule of law.

They seek to promote stability and well-being in the North Atlantic area.

They are resolved to unite their efforts for collective defense and for the preservation of peace and security.

They therefore agree to this North Atlantic Treaty:

Art. 1. The Parties undertake, as set forth in the Charter of the United Nations, to settle any international disputes in which they may be involved by peaceful means in such a manner that international peace and security, and justice, are not endangered, and to refrain in their international relations from the threat or use of force in any manner inconsistent with the purposes of the United Nations.

Art. 2. The Parties will contribute toward the further development of peaceful and friendly international relations by strengthening their free institutions, by bringing about a better understanding of the principles upon which these institutions are founded, and by promoting conditions of stability and well-being. They will seek to eliminate conflict in their international economic policies and will encourage economic collaboration between any or all of them.

---

*81st Congress, 1st Session, Executive Document, April 4, 1949.

Art. 3. In order more effectively to achieve the objectives of this Treaty, the Parties, separately and jointly, by means of continuous and effective self-help and mutual aid, will maintain and develop their individual and collective capacity to resist armed attack.

Art. 4. The Parties will consult together whenever, in the opinion of any of them, the territorial integrity, political independence or security of any of the Parties is threatened.

Art. 5. The Parties agree that an armed attack against one or more of them in Europe or North America shall be considered an attack against them all; and consequently they agree that, if such an armed attack occurs, each of them, in exercise of the right of individual or collective self-defense recognized by Article 51 of the Charter of the United Nations, will assist the Party or Parties so attacked by taking forthwith, individually and in concert with the other Parties, such action as it deems necessary, including the use of armed force, to restore and maintain the security of the North Atlantic area.

Any such armed attack and all measures taken as a result thereof shall immediately be reported to the Security Council. Such measures shall be terminated when the Security Council has taken the measures necessary to restore and maintain international peace and security.

Art. 6. For the purpose of Article 5 an armed attack on one or more of the Parties is deemed to include an armed attack on the territory of any of the Parties in Europe or North America, on the Algerian departments of France, on the occupation forces of any Party in Europe, on the islands under the jurisdiction of any Party in the North Atlantic area north of the Tropic of Cancer or on the vessels or aircraft in this area of any of the Parties.

Art. 7. This Treaty does not affect, and shall not be interpreted as affecting, in any way the rights and obligations under the Charter of the Parties which are members of the United Nations, or the primary responsibility of the Security Council for the maintenance of international peace and security.

Art. 8. Each Party declares that none of the international engagements now in force between it and any other of the Parties or any third state is in conflict with the provisions of this Treaty, and undertakes not to enter into any international engagement in conflict with this Treaty.

Art. 9. The Parties hereby establish a council, on which each of them shall be represented, to consider matters concerning the implementation of this Treaty. The council shall be so organized as to be able to meet promptly at any time. The council shall set up such subsidiary bodies as may be necessary; in particular it shall establish immediately a defense committee which shall recommend measures for the implementation of Articles 3 and 5.

Art. 10. The Parties may, by unanimous agreement, invite any other European state in a position to further the principles of this Treaty and to contribute to the security of the North Atlantic area to accede to this Treaty. Any state so invited may become a party to the Treaty by depositing its instrument of accession with the Government of the United States of America. The Government of the United States of America will inform each of the Parties of the deposit of each such instrument of accession.

Art. 11. . . . The Treaty shall enter into force between the states which have ratified it as soon as the ratifications of the majority of the signatories, including the ratifications of Belgium, Canada, France, Luxembourg, the Netherlands, the United Kingdom and the United States, have been deposited and shall come into effect with respect to other states on the date of the deposit of their ratifications.

Art. 12. After the Treaty has been in force for ten years, or at any time thereafter, the Parties shall, if any of them so requests, consult together for the purpose of reviewing the Treaty, having regard for the factors then affecting peace and security in the North Atlantic area, including the development of universal as well as regional arrangements under the Charter of the United Nations for the maintenance of international peace and security.

Art. 13. After the Treaty has been in force for twenty years, any Party may cease to be a party one year after its notice of denunciation has been given to the Government of the United States of America, which will inform the Governments of the other Parties of the deposit of each notice of denunciation.

The SEATO Treaty*

The United States and the Southeast Asian Nations

The Parties to this Treaty,

Recognizing the sovereign equality of all the Parties,

Reiterating their faith in the purposes and principles set forth in the Charter of the United Nations and their desire to live in peace with all peoples and all governments,

Reaffirming that, in accordance with the Charter of the United Nations, they uphold the principle of equal rights and self-determination of peoples, and declaring that they will earnestly strive by every peaceful means to promote self-government and to secure the independence of all countries whose peoples desire it and are able to undertake its responsibilities.

Desiring to strengthen the fabric of peace and freedom and to uphold the principles of democracy, individual liberty and the rule of law, and to promote the economic well-being and development of all peoples in the treaty area,

Intending to declare publicly and formally their sense of unity, so that any potential aggressor will appreciate that the Parties stand together in the area, and

Desiring further to coordinate their efforts for collective defense for the preservation of peace and security,

Therefore agree as follows:

ARTICLE I

The Parties undertake, as set forth in the Charter of the United Nations, to settle any international disputes in which they may be

---

*82nd Congress, 2nd Session, Executive Document, September, 1954.

430

involved by peaceful means in such a manner that international peace and security and justice are not endangered, and to refrain in their international relations from the threat or use of force in any manner inconsistent with the purposes of the United Nations.

ARTICLE II

In order more effectively to achieve the objectives of this Treaty, the Parties, separately and jointly, by means of continuous and effective self-help and mutual aid will maintain and develop their individual and collective capacity to resist armed attack and to prevent and counter subversive activities directed from without against their territorial integrity and political stability.

ARTICLE III

The Parties undertake to strengthen their free institutions and to cooperate with one another in the further development of economic measures, including technical assistance, designed both to promote economic progress and social well-being and to further the individual and collective efforts of governments toward these ends.

ARTICLE IV

1. Each party recognizes that aggression by means of armed attack in the treaty area against any of the Parties or against any State or territory which the Parties by unanimous agreement may hereafter designate, would endanger its own peace and safety, and agrees that it will be that event act to meet the common danger in accordance with its constitutional processes. Measures taken under this paragraph shall be immediately reported to the Security Council of the United Nations.

2. If, in the opinion of any of the Parties, the inviolability or the integrity of the territory or the sovereignty or political independence of any Party in the treaty area or of any other State or territory to which the provisions of paragraph 1 of this Article from time to time apply is threatened in any way other than by armed attack or is affected or threatened by any fact or situation which might endanger the peace of the area, the Parties shall consult immediately in order to agree on the measures which should be taken for the common defense.

3. It is understood that no action on the territory of any State designated by unanimous agreement under paragraph 1 of this Article or on any territory so designated shall be taken except at the invitation or with the consent of the government concerned

PROTOCOL TO THE SOUTHEAST ASIA
COLLECTIVE DEFENSE TREATY

Designation of states and territory as to which provisions of Article IV and Article III are to be applicable:

The Parties to the Southeast Asia Collective Defense Treaty unanimously designate for the purposes of Article IV of the Treaty the States of Cambodia and Laos and the free territory under the jurisdiction of the State of Vietnam.

The Parties further agree that the above mentioned states and territory shall be eligible in respect of the economic measures contemplated by Article III.

This protocol shall enter into force simultaneously with the coming into force of the Treaty.

In witness whereof, the undersigned Plenipotentiaries have signed this Protocol to the Southeast Asia Collective Defense Treaty.

Done at Manila, this eighth day of September, 1954.

The Eisenhower Doctrine*

Dwight D. Eisenhower

It is nothing new for the President and the Congress to join to recognize that the national integrity of other free nations is directly related to our own security.

We have joined to create and support the security system of the United Nations. We have reinforced the collective security system of the United Nations by a series of collective defense arrangements. Today we have security treaties with 42 other nations which recognize that their, and our, peace and security are intertwined. We have joined to take decisive action in relation to Greece and Turkey and in relation to Taiwan.

Thus, the United States through the joint action of the President and the Congress, or, in the case of treaties, the Senate, has manifested in many endangered areas its purpose to support free and independent governments — and peace — against external menace, notably the menace of International Communism. Thereby we have helped to maintain peace and security during a period of great danger. It is now essential that the United States should manifest through joint action of the President and the Congress our determination to assist those nations of the Mid East area which desire that assistance.

The action which I propose would have the following features.

It would, first of all, authorize the United States to cooperate with and assist any nation or group of nations in the general area of the Middle East in the development of economic strength dedicated to the maintenance of national independence.

*"Message of the President on the Middle East," *Department of State Bulletin,* Vol. 36 (January 21, 1957).

It would, in the second place, authorize the Executive to undertake in the same region programs of military assistance and cooperation with any nation or group of nations which desires such aid.

It would, in the third place, authorize such assistance and cooperation to include the employment of the armed forces of the United States to secure and protect the territorial integrity and political independence of such nations, requesting such aid, against overt armed aggression from any nation controlled by International Communism.

These measures would have to be consonant with the treaty obligations of the United States, including the Charter of the United Nations and with any action or recommendations of the United Nations. They would also, if armed attack occurs, be subject to the overriding authority of the United Nations Security Council in accordance with the Charter.

The present proposal would, in the fourth place, authorize the President to employ, for economic and defensive military purposes, sums available under the Mutual Security Act of 1954, as amended, without regard to existing limitations.

*   *   *

The Monroe Doctrine Reaffirmed*

United States Senate

Whereas President James Monroe, announcing the Monroe Doctrine in 1823, declared to the Congress that we should consider any attempt on the part of European powers "to extend their system to any portion of this hemisphere as dangerous to our peace and safety."

Whereas in the Rio Treaty of 1947, the parties agreed that "an armed attack by any state against an American state shall be considered as an attack against all the American states, and, consequently, each one of the said contracting parties undertakes to assist in meeting in the exercise of the inherent right of individual or collective self-defense recognized by article 51 of the Charter of the United Nations."

Whereas the Foreign Ministers of the Organization of American States at Punta del Este in January 1962 unanimously declared: "The present Government of Cuba has identified itself with the principles of Marxist-Leninist ideology, has established a political, economic, and social system based on that doctrine, and accepts military assistance from extra-continental Communist powers, including even the threat of military intervention in America on the part of the Soviet Union";

Whereas since 1958 the international Communist movement has increasingly extended into Cuba its political, economic, and military sphere of influence: Now, therefore, be it

Resolved, That it is the sense of the Senate that the President of the United States is supported in his determination and possesses all necessary authority —

---

*Senate Resolution 388, 87th Congress 2nd Sess., September 17, 1962.

(a) to prevent by whatever means may be necessary, including the use of arms, the Castro regime from exporting its aggressive purposes to any part of this hemisphere by force or the threat of force;

(b) to prevent in Cuba the creation or use of an externally supported offensive military base capable of endangering the United States naval base at Guantanamo, free passage to the Panama Canal, United States missile and space preparations, or the security of this Nation and its citizens; and

(c) to work with other free citizens of this hemisphere and with freedom-loving Cuban refugees to support the legitimate aspirations of the people of Cuba for a return to self-determination.

Summary of
U.S. Treaty Obligations*

Department of State

*From *Department of State Bulletin,* Vol. 57 (October 9, 1967).

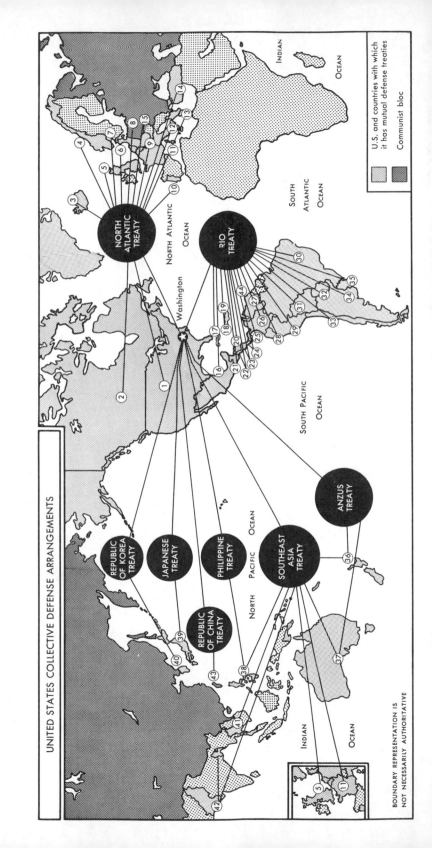

UNITED STATES COLLECTIVE DEFENSE ARRANGEMENTS

BOUNDARY REPRESENTATION IS
NOT NECESSARILY AUTHORITATIVE

U.S. and countries with which
it has mutual defense treaties

Communist bloc

NORTH ATLANTIC TREATY

RIO TREATY

ANZUS TREATY

SOUTHEAST ASIA TREATY

PHILIPPINE TREATY

JAPANESE TREATY

REPUBLIC OF CHINA TREATY

REPUBLIC OF KOREA TREATY

Washington

INDIAN OCEAN

SOUTH ATLANTIC OCEAN

North Atlantic Ocean

SOUTH PACIFIC OCEAN

NORTH PACIFIC OCEAN

INDIAN OCEAN

(15 NATIONS)

A treaty signed April 4, 1949, by which "the parties agree that an armed attack against one or more of them in Europe or North America shall be considered an attack against them all; and ... each of them ... will assist the ... attacked by taking forthwith, individually and in concert with the other Parties, such action as it deems necessary including the use of armed force..."

1 UNITED STATES	9 LUXEMBOURG
2 CANADA	10 PORTUGAL
3 ICELAND	11 FRANCE
4 NORWAY	12 ITALY
5 UNITED KINGDOM	13 GREECE
6 NETHERLANDS	14 TURKEY
7 DENMARK	15 FEDERAL REPUBLIC OF GERMANY
8 BELGIUM	

PHILIPPINE TREATY (BILATERAL)

A treaty signed August 30, 1951, by which the parties recognize "that an armed attack in the Pacific Area on either of the Parties would be dangerous to its own peace and safety" and each party agrees that it will act "to meet the common dangers in accordance with its constitutional processes."

1 UNITED STATES
38 PHILIPPINES

A treaty signed January 19, 1960, whereby each party "recognizes that an armed attack against either Party in the territories under the administration of Japan would be dangerous to its own peace and safety and declares that it would act to meet the common danger in accordance with its constitutional provisions and processes." The treaty replaced the security treaty signed September 8, 1951.

1 UNITED STATES
39 JAPAN

ANZUS (Australia-New Zealand-United States) TREATY (3 NATIONS)

A treaty signed September 1, 1951, whereby each of the parties "recognizes that an armed attack in the Pacific Area on any of the Parties would be dangerous to its own peace and safety and declares that it would act to meet the common danger in accordance with its constitutional processes."

1 UNITED STATES
36 NEW ZEALAND
37 AUSTRALIA

TREATY (8 NATIONS)

A treaty signed September 8, 1954, whereby each Party "recognizes that aggression by means of armed attack in the treaty area against any of the Parties ... would endanger its own peace and safety" and each will "in that event act to meet the common danger in accordance with its constitutional processes."

1 UNITED STATES
5 UNITED KINGDOM
11 FRANCE
36 NEW ZEALAND
37 AUSTRALIA
38 PHILIPPINES
41 THAILAND
42 PAKISTAN

A treaty signed September 2, 1947, which provides that an armed attack against any American State "shall be considered as an attack against all the American States and ... each one ... undertakes to assist in meeting the attack..."

1 UNITED STATES	26 COLOMBIA
16 MEXICO	27 VENEZUELA
17 CUBA	28 ECUADOR
18 HAITI	29 PERU
19 DOMINICAN REPUBLIC	30 BRAZIL
	31 BOLIVIA
20 HONDURAS	32 PARAGUAY
21 GAUTEMALA	33 CHILE
22 EL SALVADOR	34 ARGENTINA
23 NICARAGUA	35 URUGUAY
24 COSTA RICA	44 TRINIDAD AND TOBAGO
25 PANAMA	

REPUBLIC OF KOREA (South Korea) TREATY (BILATERAL)

A treaty signed October 1, 1953, whereby each party "recognizes that an armed attack in the Pacific area on either of the Parties ... would be dangerous to its own peace and safety" and that each Party "would act to meet the common danger in accordance with its constitutional processes."

1 UNITED STATES
40 REPUBLIC OF KOREA

(Formosa) TREATY (BILATERAL)

A treaty signed December 2, 1954, whereby each of the parties "recognizes that an armed attack in the West Pacific Area directed against the territories of either of the Parties would be dangerous to its own peace and safety," and that each "would act to meet the common danger in accordance with its constitutional processes." The territory of the Republic of China is defined as "Taiwan (Formosa) and the Pescadores."

1 UNITED STATES
43 REPUBLIC OF CHINA (FORMOSA)

Testimony for the
Foreign Assistance Program*

Dean Rusk

Thank you for the opportunity of appearing before you in support of the Foreign Assistance Act of 1967 and the President's economic and military assistance programs for fiscal year 1968.

The President originally requested a total of $2.53 billion in new appropriations to carry out the AID program in economic assistance for fiscal year 1968. In addition, as you know, he has requested $100 million more for the Alliance for Progress in connection with the recent Organization of American States Summit Conference. This brings the total request for economic assistance funds to $2.63 billion. However, the $100 million was already included in the President's general budget.

The President is also requesting $596 million in new appropriations for military assistance. This request excludes requirements for Laos, Thailand, NATO infrastructure and international military headquarters, because the President has proposed that these be transferred to the regular Defense Department budget. I fully support this transfer. To insure that these programs are consistent with our overall political and economic interests, the Department of State, by mutual agreement with Secretary [of Defense Robert S.] McNamara, will continue to coordinate them.

Mr. Chairman, this is the seventh formal presentation which I have made to this committee on economic assistance. Over the past 20 years five Secretaries of State serving four Presidents have made broadly similar presentations. The policy considerations have been broadly similar,

---

*Testimony of Secretary of State Dean Rusk before the Senate Foreign Relations Committee, July 14, 1967.

under Democratic or Republican Presidents or with Democratic or Republican majorities in the Congress. There has been one major shift in emphasis during the past 20 years. At the beginning there was strong emphasis upon rebuilding the advanced but war-torn economies of Western Europe and Japan. This part of the task was completed and these nations are now contributors to the rest of the world's need for external resources. During the past decade, the weight of attention has shifted to the less developed countries.　　• • •

Multilateral Coordination

The United States is not the only advanced country which recognizes its stake in development. Other developed nations now have strong aid programs. It is to our advantage to coordinate our programs with theirs. *Multilateral coordination* under the leadership of such institutions as the World Bank leads not only to more effective aid programs but also to increased support from other donor nations. That is why we prefer to provide most of our development loans in a multilateral framework. Under the proposed fiscal year 1968 programs, more than 85 percent of the development loan program would be provided in a multilateral framework.

Cooperation among the less developed countries themselves can lead to faster progress. Many of them face the same challenges; by pooling resources and energies they will be better able to meet these challenges. That is why the United States actively encourages and supports *regional efforts,* and that is why developing countries in several areas of the world have been taking new initiatives in regional cooperation. We are hopeful that this trend will gain momentum in the next few years.

The AID programs are, of course, only one part of the U.S. effort to help less developed countries. Equally important is the strong support that the United States has given and will continue to give to multilateral institutions. Actions this year by the United States include:

— the request by the President for congressional authorization of a $900 million replenishment for the Inter-American Development Bank's Fund for Special Operations;

— the U.S. proposal for a substantial increase in resources for the International Development Association; and

— the statements by the President in the foreign aid message supporting special funds for the Asian and African Development Banks.

The various multilateral institutions are playing an increasingly important role in the development process, both as coordinators of aid and as direct lenders. From 1961 to 1966 their commitments increased from $1.2 billion to $2.2 billion.

Both the AID programs and those of the multilateral agencies are important to our national interest. We know that time is short, and we must use it to our best advantage. If we have inadequate aid programs, if progress in most developing countries is not visible and continuous, we shall be living in a less stable world.

Our policy, including our aid programs, cannot guarantee stability and progress in the less developed world. Other factors — within and outside of the developing countries — have a large impact on events, as was illustrated by the recent violence in the Middle East.

Situation in the Middle East

Several weeks ago, the President offered a constructive approach for moving toward a permanent settlement of the problems in the Middle East. His approach included five points:
— first, the recognized right of national life;
— second, justice for the refugees;
— third, innocent maritime passage;
— fourth, limits on the wasteful and destructive arms race; and
— fifth, political independence and territorial integrity for all.

We are hopeful that reason will prevail and that the countries in the Middle East, with help from economically advanced countries, will concentrate their energies on building a better life for their peoples.

In the meantime we have suspended planned assistance programs in the Middle East countries which have broken diplomatic relations with the United States, except for certain food programs for humanitarian purposes. AID and other economic assistance to Tunisia and Morocco and other economic aid to Israel and Lebanon is continuing. In Jordan, activities are being resumed as the situation permits, and more funds than originally proposed may be needed to help restore the economy and provide opportunities for refugees. In addition, $5 million is being made available, in accordance with the President's recent announcement, to provide, through UNRWA [United Nations Relief and Works Agency for Palestine Refugees in the Near East], the International Committee of the Red Cross, and other agencies, for the immediate needs of the refugees.

In the Middle East, as elsewhere in the developing world, there should be no higher priority than building economic and social strength. There is increasing evidence that most developing countries are accepting this challenge.

The Alliance for Progress

In Latin America the Alliance for Progress, now 6 years old, is in some ways a touchstone of our efforts in the less developed areas of the world. The Alliance is taking hold. Most Latin American nations are making healthy strides toward stability and future self-sufficiency. In all but a few, governments are now working to meet the needs of all the people. Much has been done to improve tax structures and tax administration, to fight inflation, and to strengthen institutions required for more productive private enterprise. A start has been made to expand educational and health facilities, and a number of countries have instituted far-ranging agricultural and land reforms. Of course, much remains to be done.

We know the perils to our own security of economic or political instability and social injustice in Latin America. While the Castro regime in Cuba has made a mockery of the aspirations of the Cuban people, it continues to be a reminder of the urgency of our common tasks in Latin America. Castro-supported subversion and insurgency have been quashed in a number of countries. But recent outbreaks in Venezuela and Bolivia indicate a continuing potential for disorder and violence, which warns against apathy. In the Dominican Republic we are working now to help repair a legacy of injustice and violence.

The recent Summit Conference in Uruguay expressed an understanding of the tasks ahead, not only reaffirming the basic tenets of the Alliance for Progress but placing new emphasis on accelerated progress in the vital areas of agriculture, health, education, and science. It also made an historic decision to undertake the economic integration of the countries of Latin America.

Long before the Summit, President Johnson said,

> We are ready . . . to work in close cooperation toward an integrated Latin America. . . . To my fellow Presidents, I pledge: Move boldly along this path and the United States will be at your side.

At long last, there is a concrete commitment to create a Latin American common market. A timetable and technical procedures for moving ahead have been agreed upon.

• • •

A number of Latin American countries are particularly well placed to influence favorably the future course of the Alliance. Brazil, for example, is so large that its performance strongly influences events in the rest of the hemisphere. Some countries, such as Mexico and Venezuela, are now in a position to help their neighbors to speed their development. The Central American countries are setting the pace in economic integration.

Our largest program in Latin America is for Brazil. Its landmass is larger than the continental United States, and its people comprise one-half of all South Americans. A healthy Brazil is essential to a prospering Alliance. In the last 3 years, efforts to stabilize Brazil's economy and curb the inflation which had distorted national life for many years have achieved an encouraging measure of success. The annual rate of inflation has dropped from a peak of 140 percent in early 1964 to the current level of about 25-30 percent. Our large fiscal year 1968 AID program will help a new government to sustain improvements in agriculture, housing, and health, while stemming continuous inflationary pressures.

Near East and South Asia

The countries of the Near East and South Asia are more distant but hardly less important than those in Latin America to the establishment of a reliable and durable peace. For this reason, I regard economic assistance to these countries as a vital necessity.

We are pleased that the three major aid recipients there — India, Pakistan, and Turkey — have increasingly turned their great talents to the domestic challenges of modernization. These three countries will get about 90 percent of fiscal year 1968 development assistance planned for this region.

Excepting only Viet-Nam, the India program is our largest economic aid program, although we provide less than half of India's external aid. Members of the Consortium for India have pledged more than $6 billion for the third 5-year plan and the first year of the fourth plan. Our share has been 42 percent.

Indian development efforts are sharply focused on the food and population problem. More than 40 percent of the proposed AID funds will be used to help India improve food output. The Indian Government plans to double its outlays for agriculture over the next 5 years and to quadruple spending for family planning programs. During the past year, it has increased fertilizer purchases 85 percent, initiated crash programs in farm land development, and enlarged the supply of improved seeds and pesticides. I think it is imperative that we continue to give India the backing it requires in its days of difficulty.

We hope that India and Pakistan can find a way to achieve genuine cooperation in the subcontinent. Such cooperation would produce a formidable bulwark for the free world. Pakistan is well on its way to realizing its potentials. Its economic performance has been very good. Our planned program for Pakistan is also one of our largest, although again our assistance is part of a consortium led by the World Bank and is more than matched by others.

The strategic importance of Turkey has been obvious for generations, poised as it is on the flanks of Eastern Europe, the Soviet Union, and the Near East. Our large but declining level of economic assistance there is designed to facilitate the Turkish Government's goal of self-sustaining growth by 1973. Turkey's performance has been impressive. For example, in 1966 its GNP increased by more than 8 percent, its agricultural production by 11 percent, and its foreign exchange earnings by more than 15 percent.

India, Pakistan, and Turkey are slated to receive, among them, $665 million of fiscal year 1966 development loan funds. This is nearly four-fifths of the total proposed development loan program. Obviously, then, a reduction in available funds would affect primarily the rate of development in these three countries. Because the future of each of these countries is so important, I hope and strongly recommend that the Congress make available our full development loan request.

New Aid Policy for Africa

Our sympathies run deep for African aspirations for their new nations. We fully realize the importance of Africa in our contemporary world. Its landmass is more than three times our own, and it holds 300 million people. It is rich in natural resources important to the entire world.

There continues to be political instability in Africa. Some 35 countries are experiencing the growing pains of new independence. In these formative years help from us and others can be important in determining the type of societies that will develop in Africa and the role they will play in world affairs.

While we give close attention to African developments, other advanced nations, mainly Great Britain and France, with long historical relations with Africa, have provided the most assistance, along with international institutions. For a number of years AID's African program has been less than $200 million a year. Other U.S. programs, such as Food for Freedom and the Peace Corps, bring our total share to about 25 percent of annual free-world assistance to Africa.

We have tried to make our aid in Africa more effective and efficient. In the last year, we have reexamined our approach and have recast our AID policies and programs in Africa along lines which will emphasize regional projects and multilateral participation and will reduce the number of African countries with bilateral AID programs. The details of this policy are set forth in the summary presentation volume that has been submitted to this committee. In brief. AID had regular bilateral assistance programs in 34 countries in Africa in fiscal year 1967. The new policy calls for AID to continue bilateral programs — coordinated in most cases with other donors — in 10 African countries: Tunisia, Morocco, Ghana, Ethiopia, Liberia, the three countries of East Africa (Kenya, Tanzania, and Uganda), Nigeria, and the Sudan. However, the program for Nigeria is under continuous review because of internal difficulties in that country, and the program in Sudan is suspended pending review of our relations. In other African countries, as existing activities are completed over the next few years, AID expects to shift most assistance to regional and multilateral projects and reduce the number of bilateral programs substantially. An indispensable part of this policy will be our continued use of a modest self-help fund in each country for short-term, high-impact projects.

This new aid policy should prove effective in serving both our interests and the development needs of the Africans. If adjustments in the policy prove necessary, we will make them. The Africans themselves recognize the need for multinational efforts to overcome the limitations of natural resources and boundaries. Nowhere is the idea of regional cooperation more relevant for achieving the commonly shared goal of a better future. We are encouraged by the progress initiated by the Africans in instituting the African Development Bank, which was conceived and organized and is capitalized entirely by Africans. We and other donors plan to provide help to a new special fund of the Bank. Regional development schemes should receive in fiscal year 1968 twice the funds from AID that they received in fiscal year 1966. These include projects for agricultural production, disease control, regional training, and education.

·   ·   ·

Progress in Viet-Nam

In East Asia, Viet-Nam and her Southeast Asian neighbors are a crucial battleground in the struggle for world order. As I have said before, our economic assistance programs, while smaller in scale, are as important as our military efforts in the achievement of our objectives. For fiscal year 1968 we plan to use $550 million in AID funds for Viet-Nam. These funds will serve four vital purposes.

— First, in a most literal sense, they will support the drive to build a viable nation, piece by piece, area by area, in which all the South Vietnamese may identify themselves with national purposes and national programs to achieve security and order. Our aid helps with the task of reconstruction and development for the future and helps to sustain the morale of the South Vietnamese today.

— Second, another sizable portion of our funds will help maintain economic stability in the midst of the war. The commercial import program which we finance has dampened dangerous inflationary pressures.

— Third, we conduct programs to relieve wartime suffering and dislocation. AID personnel and our military forces work in close partnership to cope directly with the human and material destruction of war.

— Fourth, we are building for the future, with a growing program of long-term development in electrical power, transportation, agriculture, medicine, and other fields.

· · ·

New Vitality in East Asia

I believe that we are already witnessing the dividends of our stand in Viet-Nam. A few years ago, it was assumed by many in Southeast Asia and the Western Pacific that mainland China was the wave of the future. Now throughout all the free nations of East Asia, we sense a new vitality and confidence. Most of them are making impressive economic progress. They are also working together more and more effectively.

Nowhere is the momentum of regional cooperation more evident than in East Asia and the Western Pacific. The Asian Development Bank is now established and in business. Development of the Mekong Valley is proceeding despite the war. Throughout East Asia and the Western Pacific a variety of regional associations are taking root, all founded on a common interest to foster development in a climate of peace. Cooperative arrangements in education, agriculture, transportation, and communications are coming into existence rapidly.

In Thailand and Laos, it is necessary to conduct substantial economic aid programs to thwart increased Communist subversion and insurgency. Other nations are helping. We expect that requirements for more conventional types of development assistance to Thailand over the next several years will be met by a combination of governments and international institutions.

Korea is now growing at an average annual rate of 8 percent and may well repeat the gratifying economic and social successes achieved in Taiwan. Both nations show what can be accomplished in a relatively few years. Dean Jacoby in his newly published study on Taiwan development has concluded that, while vigorous self-help efforts were the key to success, it would nonetheless have taken Taiwan as much as 40 years to achieve self-supporting growth, not 15, without substantial American assistance.

Indonesia, under General Suharto, has made a clean break with the bankrupt policies of the Sukarno regime and has embarked on a courageous program to restore the country to political and economic health. In December 1966 we agreed with other creditor countries to reschedule Indonesia's overwhelming debt burden. In Amsterdam in February of this year we undertook to provide one-third of a multinational program to meet Indonesia's foreign assistance needs for the current calendar year. In the fall we will be meeting again with the same group of countries to consider Indonesia's needs for 1968. Indonesia, with the assistance of the IMF [International Monetary Fund], is helping itself by pursuing a vigorous stabilization policy which encourages private initiative and foreign investment and places reliance on market forces to determine the allocation of resources. Indonesia can make a major contribution to free-world economic and political strength in the emerging new Asia, and we wish to continue to play a part in the multilateral assistance effort by providing our full share of the continuing and probably increasing amounts of foreign aid needed by this major Asian nation.

Military Assistance Program

Let me now turn to the military assistance request, which is $596 million for fiscal year 1968. Secretary McNamara will meet with you to discuss this program in greater detail.

Fot two decades now we have supported the ability of free nations adjacent to the Soviet Union or Communist China to defend against external military threats. This free-world strength has been indispensable in keeping the peace. Over three-quarters of this year's program is needed to continue our investment in this proven form of insurance. Nothing has yet happened to let us reduce our side of the balance of power. Indeed, the proposed programs are the minimum essential to maintain the defense posture of these allies.

The second major foreign policy function of the program is to help selected developing nations protect themselves against internal violence and thereby provide the stability that is essential to development. A related purpose is to help some of the developing nations which are faced with relatively small but important defense expenditures from having to divert resources urgently needed for development. Our programs for our own Western Hemisphere, as it continues its struggle against Castro-exported insurgency and terrorism and as it seeks to move more quickly toward human progress, reflect our efforts to meet these pressures throughout the world.

Through these programs we support not only freedom and progress but also try to foster political stability within the various regions of the world. This program is tailored to help discourage arms races and to try to stabilize regional arms balances, and to keep the military expenditures of ourselves and of our friends to the minimum necessary.

The nature and scale of the needs we help to fill are not within our sole control. The moderate and progressive governments which seek to follow peaceful courses in their relations with their neighbors have to be able to protect themselves from expansionist or subversive threats that all too often confront them, frequently with Communist support.

At the opening meeting of the Geneva disarmament conference in 1962, I myself outlined the fact that disarmament is not just a question between the Soviet Union and the United States but is a problem for the lesser neighborhood arms races in various parts of the world. I urged that Geneva conference to give serious attention to these unnecessary and expensive arms races in other parts of the world which divert resources from economic and social development. Quite frankly, we have been disappointed that more progress has not been made in this direction. We are intensely interested, at this moment, in the arms race in the Middle East. President Johnson has pressed very hard both publicly and privately for understandings among arms suppliers and arms recipients for prudence in the levels of arms which have created so much tension in that area. We shall continue to work on this, both in the United Nations and in our bilateral contacts with the governments concerned.

In conclusion, Mr. Chairman, I would urge that we consider these requests for economic and military assistance in the framework of the kind of world in which this nation wishes to live. Those who would like to forget the rest of the world must face the fact that there is no place to hide. Isolation may be a nostalgic sentiment—it has no reality in the modern world. There may be some who are growing weary— but we must never weary of trying to build a durable peace in a world in which frail human beings can literally destroy themselves. There may be some who think we cannot afford 0.6 percent of our gross national product to help shape a world in which our democratic institutions can survive and flourish. I do not accept this. This nation cannot quit; it cannot afford to let the world situation be determined by others while we abandon the field. Whether we reflect upon past experience or upon our hopes for the future, a responsible effort on our part is demanded. We should consult our hope and confidence, and not our fears and irritations, and proceed with the effort proposed by the President.

A Step Toward Peace*

John F. Kennedy

Good evening, my fellow citizens: I speak to you tonight in a spirit of hope. Eighteen years ago the advent of nuclear weapons changed the course of the world as well as the war. Since that time, all mankind has been struggling to escape from the darkening prospect of mass destruction on earth. In an age when both sides have come to possess enough nuclear power to destroy the human race several times over, the world of communism and the world of free choice have been caught up in a vicious circle of conflicting ideology and interest. Each increase of tension has produced an increase of arms; each increase of arms has produced an increase of tension.

In these years the United States and the Soviet Union have frequently communicated suspicion and warnings to each other, but very rarely hope. Our representatives have met at the summit and at the brink; they have met in Washington and in Moscow, in Geneva and at the United Nations. But too often these meetings have produced only darkness, discord, or disillusion.

Yesterday a shaft of light cut into the darkness. Negotiations were concluded in Moscow on a treaty to ban all nuclear tests in the atmosphere, in outer space, and under water. For the first time, an agreement has been reached on bringing the forces of nuclear destruction under international control—a goal first sought in 1946, when Bernard Baruch presented a comprehensive control plan to the United Nations.

---

*Delivered from the White House by television and radio on July 26, 1963, by President John F. Kennedy. Reprinted in *Department of State Bulletin,* Vol. 49 (August 12, 1963).

That plan and many subsequent disarmament plans, large and small, have all been blocked by those opposed to international inspection. A ban on nuclear tests, however, requires on-the-spot inspection only for underground tests. This nation now possesses a variety of techniques to detect the nuclear tests of other nations which are conducted in the air or under water. For such tests produce unmistakable signs which our modern instruments can pick up.

Limitations of Treaty

The treaty initialed yesterday, therefore, is a limited treaty which permits continued underground testing and prohibits only those tests that we ourselves can police. It requires no control posts, no on-site inspection, no international body.

We should also understand that it has other limits as well. Any nation which signs the treaty will have an opportunity to withdraw if it finds that extraordinary events related to the subject matter of the treaty have jeopardized its supreme interests; and no nation's right of self-defense will in any way be impaired. Nor does this treaty mean an end to the threat of nuclear war. It will not reduce nuclear stockpiles; it will not halt the production of nuclear weapons; it will not restrict their use in time of war.

Nevertheless, this limited treaty will radically reduce the nuclear testing which would otherwise be conducted on both sides; it will prohibit the United States, the United Kingdom, the Soviet Union, and all others who sign it from engaging in the atmospheric tests which have so alarmed mankind; and it offers to all the world a welcome sign of hope.

For this is not a unilateral moratorium, but a specific and solemn legal obligation. While it will not prevent this nation from testing underground, or from being ready to conduct atmospheric tests if the acts of others so require, it gives us a concrete opportunity to extend its coverage to other nations and later to other forms of nuclear tests.

This treaty is in part the product of Western patience and vigilance. We have made clear—most recently in Berlin and Cuba—our deep resolve to protect our security and our freedom against any form of aggression. We have also made clear our steadfast determination to limit the arms race. In three administrations our soldiers and diplomats have worked together to this end, always supported by Great Britain. Prime Minister Macmillan joined with President Eisenhower in proposing a limited test ban in 1959, and again with me in 1961 and 1962.

But the achievement of this goal is not a victory for one side—it is a victory for mankind. It reflects no concessions either to or by the Soviet Union. It reflects simply our common recognition of the dangers in further testing.

This treaty is not the millennium. It will not resolve all conflicts, or cause the Communists to forego their ambitions, or eliminate the dangers of war. It will not reduce our need for arms or allies or programs of assistance to others. But it is an important first step—a step toward peace—a step toward reason—a step away from war.

Here is what this step can mean to you and to your children and your neighbors.

An Opportunity To Reduce World Tension

First, this treaty can be a step toward reduced world tension and broader areas of agreement. The Moscow talks have reached no agreement on any other subject, nor is this treaty conditioned on any other matter. Under Secretary Harriman made it clear that any nonaggression arrangements across the division in Europe would require full consultation with our allies and full attention to their interests. He also made clear our strong preference for a more comprehensive treaty banning all tests everywhere and our ultimate hope for general and complete disarmament. The Soviet Government, however, is still unwilling to accept the inspection such goals require.

No one can predict with certainty, therefore, what further agreements, if any, can be built on the foundations of this one. They could include controls on preparations for surprise attack, or on numbers and type of armaments. There could be further limitations on the spread of nuclear weapons. The important point is that efforts to seek new agreements will go forward.

But the difficulty of predicting the next step is no reason to be reluctant about this step. Nuclear test ban negotiations have long been a symbol of East-West disagreement. If this treaty can also be a symbol—if it can symbolize the end of one era and the beginning of another—if both sides can by this treaty gain confidence and experience in peaceful collaboration—then this short and simple treaty may well become an historic mark in man's age-old pursuit of peace.

Western policies have long been designed to persuade the Soviet Union to renounce aggression, direct or indirect, so that their people and all people may live and let live in peace. The unlimited testing of new weapons of war cannot lead toward that end, but this treaty, if it can be followed by further progress, can clearly move in that direction.

I do not say that a world without aggression or threats of war would be an easy world. It will bring new problems, new challenges from the Communists, new dangers of relaxing our vigilance or of mistaking their intent.

But those dangers pale in comparison to those of the spiraling arms race and a collision course toward war. Since the beginning of history, war has been mankind's constant companion. It has been the rule, not the exception. Even a nation as young and as peace-loving as our own has fought through eight wars. And three times in the last two years and a half I have been required to report to you as President that this nation and the Soviet Union stood on the verge of direct military confrontation—in Laos, in Berlin, and in Cuba.

A war today or tomorrow, if it led to nuclear war, would not be like any war in history. A full-scale nuclear exchange, lasting less than 60 minutes, with the weapons now in existence, could wipe out more than 300 million Americans, Europeans, and Russians, as well as untold numbers elsewhere. And the survivors—as Chairman Khrushchev warned the Communist Chinese, "The survivors would envy the dead." For they would inherit a world so devastated by explosions and poison and fire that today we cannot even conceive of its horrors. So let us try to turn the world from war. Let us make the most of this opportunity, and every opportunity, to reduce tension, to slow down the perilous nuclear arms race, and to check the world's slide toward final annihilation.

Freeing World From Fear of Radioactive Fallout

Second, this treaty can be a step toward freeing the world from the fears and dangers of radioactive fallout. Our own atmospheric tests last year were conducted under conditions which restricted such fallout to an absolute minimum. But over the years the number and the yield of weapons tested have rapidly increased and so have the radioactive hazards from such testing. Continued unrestricted testing by the nuclear powers, joined in time by other nations which may be less adept in limiting pollution, will increasingly contaminate the air that all of us must breathe.

Even then, the number of children and grandchildren with cancer in their bones, with leukemia in their blood, or with poison in their lungs might seem statistically small to some, in comparison with natural health hazards. But this is not a natural health hazard, and it is not a statistical issue. The loss of even one human life or the malformation of even one baby—who may be born long after we are gone—should be of concern to us all. Our children and grandchildren are not merely statistics toward which we can be indifferent.

Nor does this affect the nuclear powers alone. These tests befoul the air of all men and all nations, the committed and the uncommitted alike, without their knowledge and without their consent. That is why the continuation of atmospheric testing causes so many countries to regard all nuclear powers as equally evil; and we can hope that its prevention will enable those countries to see the world more clearly, while enabling all the world to breathe more easily.

Preventing Spread of Nuclear Weapons

Third, this treaty can be a step toward preventing the spread of nuclear weapons to nations not now possessing them. During the next several years, in addition to the four current nuclear powers, a small but significant number of nations will have the intellectual, physical, and financial resources to produce both nuclear weapons and the means of delivering them. In time, it is estimated, many other nations will have either this capacity or other ways of obtaining nuclear warheads, even as missiles can be commercially purchased today.

I ask you to stop and think for a moment what it would mean to have nuclear weapons in so many hands, in the hands of countries, large and small, stable and unstable, responsible and irresponsible, scattered throughout the world. There would be no rest for anyone then, no stability, no real security, and no chance of effective disarmament. There would only be the increased chance of accidental war and an increased necessity for the great powers to involve themselves in what otherwise would be local conflicts.

If only one thermonuclear bomb were to be dropped on any American, Russian, or any other city, whether it was launched by accident or design, by a madman or by an enemy, by a large nation or by a small, from any corner of the world, that one bomb could release more destructive power on the inhabitants of that one helpless city than all the bombs dropped in the Second World War.

Neither the United States nor the Soviet Union nor the United Kingdom nor France can look forward to that day with equanimity. We have a great obligation—all four nuclear powers have a great obligation—to use whatever time remains to prevent the spread of nuclear weapons, to persuade other countries not to test, transfer, acquire, possess, or produce such weapons.

This treaty can be the opening wedge in that campaign. It provides that none of the parties will assist other nations to test in the forbidden environments. It opens the door for further agreements on the control of nuclear weapons, and it is open for all nations to sign; for it is in the interest of all nations, and already we have heard from a number of countries who wish to join with us promptly.

Strengthening Our Nation's Security

Fourth and finally, this treaty can limit the nuclear arms race in ways which, on balance, will strengthen our nation's security far more than the continuation of unrestricted testing. For, in today's world, a nation's security does not always increase as its arms increase when its adversary is doing the same, and unlimited competition in the testing and development of new types of destructive nuclear weapons will not make the world safer for either side. Under this limited treaty, on the other hand, the testing of other nations could never be sufficient to offset the ability of our strategic forces to deter or survive a nuclear attack and to penetrate and destroy an aggressor's homeland.

We have, and under this treaty we will continue to have, the nuclear strength that we need. It is true that the Soviets have tested nuclear weapons of a yield higher than that which we thought to be necessary, but the hundred-megaton bomb of which they spoke 2 years ago does not and will not change the balance of strategic power. The United States has chosen, deliberately, to concentrate on more mobile and more efficient weapons, with lower but entirely sufficient yield, and our security is, therefore, not impaired by the treaty I am discussing.

Risk of Secret Violations Not Overlooked

It is also true, as Mr. Khrushchev would agree, that nations cannot afford in these matters to rely simply on the good faith of their adversaries. We have not, therefore, overlooked the risk of secret violations. There is at present a possibility that deep in outer space, hundreds and thousands and millions of miles away from the earth, illegal tests might go undetected. But we already have the capability to construct a system of observation that would make such tests almost impossible to conceal, and we can decide at any time whether such a system is needed in the

light of the limited risk to us and the limited reward to others of violations attempted at that range. For any tests which might be conducted
so far out in space, which cannot be conducted more easily and efficiently
and legally underground, would necessarily be of such a magnitude that
they would be extremely difficult to conceal. We can also employ new
devices to check on the testing of smaller weapons in the lower atmosphere. Any violation, moreover, involves, along with the risk of detection,
the end of the treaty and the worldwide consequences for the violator.

Secret violations are possible and secret preparations for a sudden
withdrawal are possible, and thus our own vigilance and strength must
be maintained, as we remain ready to withdraw and to resume all
forms of testing if we must. But it would be a mistake to assume that
this treaty will be quickly broken. The gains of illegal testing are
obviously slight compared to their cost and the hazard of discovery,
and the nations which have initialed and will sign this treaty prefer it,
in my judgment, to unrestricted testing as a matter of their own self-
interest, for these nations, too, and all nations, have a stake in limiting
the arms race, in holding the spread of nuclear weapons, and in breath-
ing air that is not radioactive. While it may be theoretically possible
to demonstrate the risks inherent in any treaty—and such risks in this
treaty are small—the far greater risks to our security are the risks of
unrestricted testing, the risk of a nuclear arms race, the risk of new
nuclear powers, nuclear pollution, and nuclear war.

A Responsibility of All Americans

This limited test ban, in our most careful judgment, is safer by far
for the United States than an unlimited nuclear arms race. For all these
reasons, I am hopeful that this nation will promptly approve the limited
test ban treaty. There will, of course, be debate in the country and in
the Senate. The Constitution wisely requires the advice and consent
of the Senate to all treaties, and that consultation has already begun.
All this is as it should be. A document which may mark an historic
and constructive opportunity for the world deserves an historic and
constructive debate.

It is my hope that all of you will take part in that debate, for this
treaty is for all of us. It is particularly for our children and our grandchildren, and they have no lobby here in Washington. This debate will
involve military, scientific, and political experts, but it must be not
left to them alone. The right and the responsibility are yours.

If we are to open new doorways to peace, if we are to seize this
rare opportunity for progress, if we are to be as bold and farsighted in

our control of weapons as we have been in their invention, then let us now show all the world on this side of the wall and the other that a strong America also stands for peace.

There is no cause for complacency. We have learned in times past that the spirit of one moment or place can be gone in the next. We have been disappointed more than once, and we have no illusions now that there are shortcuts on the road to peace. At many points around the globe the Communists are continuing their efforts to exploit weakness and poverty. Their concentration of nuclear and conventional arms must still be deterred.

The familiar contest between choice and coercion, the familiar places of danger and conflict, are still there, in Cuba, in Southeast Asia, in Berlin, and all around the globe, still requiring all the strength and the vigilance that we can muster. Nothing could more greatly damage our cause than if we and our allies were to believe that peace has already been achieved and that our strength and unity were no longer required.

But now, for the first time in many years, the path of peace may be open. No one can be certain what the future will bring. No one can say whether the time has come for an easing of the struggle. But history and our own conscience will judge us harsher if we do not now make every effort to test our hopes by action, and this is the place to begin. According to the ancient Chinese proverb, "A journey of a thousand miles must begin with a single step."

My fellow Americans, let us take that first step. Let us, if we can, get back from the shadows of war and seek out the way of peace. And if that journey is one thousand miles, or even more, let history record that we, in this land, at this time, took the first step.

Thank you and good night.

The Nuclear Test Ban Treaty*

U.S., U.S.S.R., and Other Nations

TREATY
banning nuclear weapon tests in the atmosphere, in outer space
and under water

The Governments of the United States of America, the United Kingdom of Great Britain and Northern Ireland, and the Union of Soviet Socialist Republics, hereinafter referred to as the "Original Parties",

Proclaiming as their principal aim the speediest possible achievement of an agreement on general and complete disarmament under strict international control in accordance with the objectives of the United Nations which would put an end to the armaments race and eliminate the incentive to the production and testing of all kinds of weapons, including nuclear weapons,

Seeking to achieve the discontinuance of all test explosions of nuclear weapons for all time, determined to continue negotiations to this end, and desiring to put an end to the contamination of man's environment by radioactive substances,

Have agreed as follows:

Article I

1. Each of the Parties to this Treaty undertakes to prohibit, to prevent, and not to carry out any nuclear weapon test explosion, or any other nuclear explosion, at any place under its jurisdiction or control:

(a) in the atmosphere; beyond its limits, including outer space; or underwater, including territorial waters or high seas; or

---

*Reprinted in *Department of State Bulletin,* Vol. 49, August 12, 1963.

(b) in any other environment if such explosion causes radioactive debris to be present outside the territorial limits of the State under whose jurisdiction or control such explosion is conducted. It is understood in this connection that the provisions of this subparagraph are without prejudice to the conclusion of a treaty resulting in the permanent banning of all nuclear test explosions, including all such explosions underground, the conclusion of which, as the Parties have stated in the Preamble to this Treaty, they seek to achieve.

2. Each of the Parties to this Treaty undertakes furthermore to refrain from causing, encouraging, or in any way participating in, the carrying out of any nuclear weapon test explosion, or any other nuclear explosion, anywhere which would take place in any of the environments described, or have the effect referred to, in paragraph 1 of this Article.

Article II

1. Any Party may propose amendments to this Treaty. The text of any proposed amendment shall be submitted to the Depositary Governments which shall circulate it to all Parties to this Treaty. Thereafter, if requested to do so by one-third or more of the Parties, the Depositary Governments shall convene a conference, to which they shall invite all the Parties, to consider such amendment.

2. Any amendment to this Treaty must be approved by a majority of the votes of all the Parties to this Treaty, including the votes of all of the Original Parties. The amendment shall enter into force for all Parties upon the deposit of instruments of ratification by a majority of all the Parties, including the instruments of ratification of all of the Original Parties.

Article III

1. This Treaty shall be open to all States for signature. Any State which does not sign this Treaty before its entry into force in accordance with paragraph 3 of this Article may accede to it at any time.

2. This Treaty shall be subject to ratification by signatory States. Instruments of ratification and instruments of accession shall be deposited with the Governments of the Original Parties—the United States of America, the United Kingdom of Great Britain and Northern Ireland, and the Union of Soviet Socialist Republics—which are hereby designated the Depositary Governments.

3. This Treaty shall enter into force after its ratification by all the Original Parties and the deposit of their instruments of ratification.

4. For States whose instruments of ratification or accession are deposited subsequent to the entry into force of this Treaty, it shall

enter into force on the date of the deposit of their instruments of ratification or accession.

5. The Depositary Governments shall promptly inform all signatory and acceding States of the date of each signature, the date of deposit of each instrument of ratification of and accession to this Treaty, the date of its entry into force, and the date of receipt of any requests for conferences or other notices.

6. This Treaty shall be registered by the Depositary Governments pursuant to Article 102 of the Charter of the United Nations.

Article IV

This Treaty shall be of unlimited duration.

Each Party shall in exercising its national sovereignty have the right to withdraw from the Treaty if it decides that extraordinary events, related to the subject matter of this Treaty, have jeopardized the supreme interests of its country. It shall give notice of such withdrawal to all other Parties to the Treaty three months in advance.

Article V

This Treaty, of which the English and Russian texts are equally authentic, shall be deposited in the archives of the Depositary Governments. Duly certified copies of this Treaty shall be transmitted by the Depositary Governments to the Governments of the signatory and acceding States.

IN WITNESS WHEREOF the undersigned, duly authorized, have signed this Treaty.

DONE in triplicate at the city of Moscow the   day of   , one thousand nine hundred and sixty-three.

For the Government of the United States of America

For the Government of the United Kingdom of Great Britain and
      Northern Ireland

For the Government of the Union of Soviet Socialist Republics

The Arrogance of Power*

J. William Fulbright

America is the most fortunate of nations—fortunate in her rich territory, fortunate in having had a century of relative peace in which to develop that territory, fortunate in her diverse and talented population, fortunate in the institutions devised by the founding fathers and in the wisdom of those who have adapted those institutions to a changing world.

For the most part America has made good use of her blessings, especially in her internal life but also in her foreign relations. Having done so much and succeeded so well, America is now at that historical point at which a great nation is in danger of losing its perspective on what exactly is within the realm of its power and what is beyond it. Other great nations, reaching this critical juncture, have aspired to too much, and by overextension of effort have declined and then fallen.

The causes of the malady are not entirely clear but its recurrence is one of the uniformities of history: power tends to confuse itself with virtue and a great nation is peculiarly susceptible to the idea that its power is a sign of God's favor, conferring upon it a special responsibility for other nations—to make them richer and happier and wiser, to remake them, that is, in its own shining image. Power confuses itself with virtue and tends also to take itself for omnipotence. Once imbued with the idea of a mission, a great nation easily assumes that it has the means as well as the duty to do God's work. The Lord, after all, surely would not choose you as His agent and then deny you the

*Reprinted from J. William Fulbright, *The Arrogance of Power* (New York: Random House, Inc., 1966) with permission of the publisher.

sword with which to work His will. German soldiers in the First World War wore belt buckles imprinted with the words *"Gott mit uns."* It was approximately under this kind of infatuation—an exaggerated sense of power and an imaginary sense of mission—that the Athenians attacked Syracuse and Napoleon and then Hitler invaded Russia. In plain words, they overextended their commitments and they came to grief.

I do not think for a moment that America, with her deeply rooted democratic traditions, is likely to embark upon a campaign to dominate the world in the manner of a Hitler or Napoleon. What I do fear is that she may be drifting into commitments which, though generous and benevolent in intent, are so far-reaching as to exceed even America's great capacities. At the same time, it is my hope—and I emphasize it because it underlies all of the criticisms and proposals to be made in these pages—that America will escape those fatal temptations of power which have ruined other great nations and will instead confine herself to doing only that good in the world which she *can* do, both by direct effort and by the force of her own example.

The stakes are high indeed: they include not only America's continued greatness but nothing less than the survival of the human race in an era when, for the first time in human history, a living generation has the power of veto over the survival of the next.

The Power Drive of Nations

When the abstractions and subtleties of political science have been exhausted, there remain the most basic unanswered questions about war and peace and why nations contest the issues they contest and why they even care about them. As Aldous Huxley has written:

> There may be arguments about the best way of raising wheat in a cold climate or of re-afforesting a denuded mountain. But such arguments never lead to organized slaughter. Organized slaughter is the result of arguments about such questions as the following: Which is the best nation? The best religion? The best political theory? The best form of government? Why are other people so stupid and wicked? Why can't they see how good and intelligent *we* are? Why do they resist our beneficent efforts to bring them under our control and make them like ourselves?

Many of the wars fought by man—I am tempted to say most—have been fought over such abstractions. The more I puzzle over the great wars of history, the more I am inclined to the view that the causes attributed to them—territory, markets, resources, the defense or perpetuation of great principles—were not the root causes at all but rather explanations or excuses for certain unfathomable drives of human nature. For lack of a clear and precise understanding of exactly what these motives are, I refer to them as the "arrogance of power"—as a psychological need that nations seem to have in order to prove that they are bigger, better, or stronger than other nations. Implicit in this drive is the assumption, even on the part of normally peaceful nations, that force is the ultimate proof of superiority—that when a nation shows that it has the stronger army, it is also proving that it has better people, better institutions, better principles, and, in general, a better civilization.

· · ·

The attitude above all others which I feel sure is no longer valid is the arrogance of power, the tendency of great nations to equate power with virtue and major responsibilities with a universal mission. The dilemmas involved are pre-eminently American dilemmas, not because America has weaknesses that others do not have but because America is powerful as no nation has ever been before, and the discrepancy between her power and the power of others appears to be increasing. One may hope that America, with her vast resources and democratic traditions, with her diverse and creative population, will find the wisdom to match her power; but one can hardly be confident because the wisdom required is greater wisdom than any great nation has ever shown before. It must be rooted, as Dr. Chisholm says, in the re-examination of "all of the attitudes of our ancestors."

It is a tall order. Perhaps one can begin to fill it by an attempt to assess the attitudes of Americans toward other peoples and some of the effects of America's power on small countries whom she has tried to help.

Even when acting with the best of intentions, Americans, like other Western peoples who have carried their civilizations abroad, have had something of the same "fatal impact" on smaller nations that European explorers had on the Tahitians and the native Australians. We have not harmed people because we wished to; on the contrary, more often than not we have wanted to help people and, in some very important respects, we have helped them. Americans have brought medicine and education, manufactures and modern techniques to many places in the world; but they have also brought themselves and the condescending attitudes of a people whose very success breeds disdain for other cultures. Bringing power without understanding, Americans as well as Europeans have had a devastating effect in less advanced areas of the world; without knowing they were doing it, they have shattered traditional societies, disrupted fragile economies and undermined peoples' self-confidence by the invidious example of their own power and efficiency. They have done this in many instances simply by being big and strong, by giving good advice, by intruding on people who have not wanted them but could not resist them.

•   •   •

We are now engaged in a war to "defend freedom" in South Vietnam. Unlike the Republic of Korea, South Vietnam has an army which fights without notable success and a weak, dictatorial government which does not command the loyalty of the South Vietnamese people. The official war aims of the United States government, as I understand them, are to defeat what is regarded as North Vietnamese aggression, to demonstrate the futility of what the communists call "wars of national liberation," and to create conditions under which the South Vietnamese people will be able freely to determine their own future.

I have not the slightest doubt of the sincerity of the President and the Vice-President and the Secretaries of State and Defense in propounding these aims. What I do doubt, and doubt very much, is the ability of the United States to achieve these aims by the means being used. I do not question the power of our weapons and the efficiency of our logistics; I cannot say these things delight me as they seem to delight some of our officials, but they are certainly impressive. What I do question is the ability of the United States or any other Western nation to go into a small, alien, undeveloped Asian nation and create stability where there is chaos, the will to fight where there is defeatism, democracy where there is no tradition of it, and honest government where corruption is almost a way of life. . . .

One wonders how much the American commitment to Vietnamese freedom is also a commitment to American pride—the two seem to have become part of the same package. When we talk about the freedom of South Vietnam, we may be thinking about how disagreeable it would be to accept a solution short of victory; we may be thinking about how our pride would be injured if we settled for less than we set out to achieve; we may be thinking about our reputation as a great power, fearing that a compromise settlement would shame us before the world, marking us as a second-rate people with flagging courage and determination.

Such fears are as nonsensical as their opposite, the presumption of a universal mission. They are simply unworthy of the richest, most powerful, most productive, and best educated people in the world. One can understand an uncompromising attitude on the part of such countries as China or France: both have been struck low in this century and a certain amount of arrogance may be helpful to them in recovering their pride. It is much less comprehensible on the part of the United States—a nation whose modern history has been an almost uninterrupted chronicle of success, a nation which by now should be so sure of its own power as to be capable of magnanimity, a nation which by now should be able to act on the proposition that, as George Kennan said, "there is more respect to be won in the opinion of the world by a resolute and courageous liquidation of unsound positions than in the most stubborn pursuit of extravagant or unpromising objectives."

•   •   •

If America has a service to perform in the world—and I believe she has—it is in large part the service of her own example. In our excessive involvement in the affairs of other countries we are not only living off our assets and denying our own people the proper enjoyment of their resources, we are also denying the world the example of a free society enjoying its freedom to the fullest. This is regrettable indeed for a nation that aspires to teach democracy to other nations, because, as Edmund Burke said, "Example is the school of mankind, and they will learn at no other."

The missionary instinct in foreign affairs may, in a curious way, reflect a deficiency rather than an excess of national self-confidence. In America's case the evidence of a lack of self-confidence is our apparent need for constant proof and reassurance, our nagging desire for popularity, our bitterness and confusion when foreigners fail to appreciate our generosity and good intentions. Lacking an appreciation of the dimensions of our own power, we fail to understand our enormous and disruptive impact on the world; we fail to understand that no matter how good our intentions— and they are, in most cases, decent enough— other nations are alarmed by the very existence of such great power, which, whatever its benevolence, cannot help but remind them of their own helplessness before it.

Those who lack self-assurance are also likely to lack magnanimity, because the one is the condition of the other. Only a nation at peace with itself, with its transgressions as well as its achievements, is capable of a generous understanding of others. Only when we Americans can acknowledge our own past aggressive behavior—in such instances, for example, as the Indian wars and the wars against Mexico and Spain— will we acquire some perspective on the aggressive behavior of others; only when we can understand the human implications of the chasm between American affluence and the poverty of most of the rest of mankind will we be able to understand why the American "way of life" which is so dear to us has few lessons and limited appeal to the poverty-stricken majority of the human race.

It is a curiosity of human nature that lack of self-assurance seems to breed an exaggerated sense of power and mission. When a nation is very powerful but lacking in self-confidence, it is likely to behave in a manner dangerous to itself and to others. Feeling the need to prove what is obvious to everyone else, it begins to confuse great power with unlimited power and great responsibility with total responsibility: it can admit of no error; it must win every argument, no matter how trivial. For lack of an appreciation of how truly powerful it is, the nation begins to lose wisdom and perspective and, with them, the strength and understanding that it takes to be magnanimous to smaller and weaker nations.

Gradually but unmistakably America is showing signs of that arrogance of power which has afflicted, weakened, and in some cases destroyed great nations in the past. In so doing we are not living up to our capacity and promise as a civilized example for the world. The measure of our falling short is the measure of the patriot's duty of dissent.

America and Revolution

Revolution by peaceful means is an historical rarity. In the West, England, some of her colonial heirs, and a few of the smaller European countries made the transition from autocracy to democracy and from feudalism to modernism by more or less peaceful means, but these were countries, by and large, which enjoyed extraordinary advantages of wealth, location, or tradition. The other great European nations— notably France, Italy, Germany, and Russia—came to be what they are today only after violent internal upheavals; nor did any of these countries, it is interesting to note, escape some reversion to dictatorship after an initial experiment in democracy.

It requires the optimism of Dr. Pangloss to expect Asian and Latin American nations, beset as they are with problems of poverty and population unknown in Western Europe and North America, to achieve by peaceful means what nations with vastly greater advantages were able to achieve only by violent revolution. History does not repeat itself and there is probably no such thing as an inevitability, but the past does suggest certain limits of probability and certain likelihoods. The likelihood that it suggests for the "third world" of Asia, Africa, and Latin America is not a smooth transition to democracy but an extended time of troubles, not a rapidly improving life for the ordinary man, but, for some societies, a period of intermittent progress under more or less democratic leadership, for others, continued stagnation or deterioration and, for still others, a period of painful sacrifices enforced by authoritarian leaders though mitigated in the better-run societies by some equity in the sharing of the sacrifices.

These prospects are probable rather than inevitable; they are anything but desirable. We must continue to do what we can—more indeed by far than we are doing now—to improve the chances of peaceful and democratic social revolution in the underdeveloped world. We would do well, however, to stop deluding ourselves about the likelihood of success. We would do well, for example, to stop proclaiming the triumph of the Alliance for Progress because five hundred thousand units of housing were built in Latin America in 1965—of which, in fact, only sixty thousand were attributable to the Alliance for Progress—when the more pertinent fact is that the number of families needing housing increased by one and a half million. We must stop fooling ourselves about economic progress in many of the countries that receive American aid and acknowledge that the magnitude of the problem is vastly disproportionate to what is being done or is now likely to be done to overcome it; we must face the fact that democratic methods are more often failing than succeeding in Asia, Africa, and Latin America, and that as rapidly growing populations continue to press on slowly growing economies, violent upheavals are not only possible but very likely indeed.

· · ·

Nationalism and Communism in the American View of Revolution

In Latin America and in Asia, where great revolutions have taken place and others may still occur, American policy has been weakened by a seeming inability to believe in the tractability of communism or the abatement of its fanaticism and by a permeating inability to understand why the peoples of these continents cannot remake their societies by the same orderly processes that have worked so well in the United States. The result is that despite our genuine sympathy for those who cry out against poverty and social injustice, and despite the material support which we give to many of the poor nations of the world, our sympathy dissolves into hostility when reform becomes revolution; and when communism is involved, as it often is, our hostility takes the form of unseemly panic.

On the basis of past and present American policies toward China and Vietnam, toward Cuba and the Dominican Republic, we seem to be narrowing our criteria of what constitute "legitimate" and "acceptable" social revolutions to include only those which meet the all but impossible tests of being peaceful, orderly, and voluntary—of being, that is, in what we regard as our own shining image. At the same time, owing no doubt to a view of communism as the fulcrum of a revolutionary process that will not be satiated until it dominates the world, our abhorrence for violence from the left has been matched by no such sensibilities when the violence comes from the right. Thus it has come about that our sympathy for social revolution in principle is increasingly belied by hostility in practice.

The American view of revolution is thus shaped by a simple but so far insuperable dilemma: we are simultaneously hostile to communism and sympathetic to nationalism, and when the two become closely associated, we become agitated, frustrated, angry, precipitate, and inconstant. Or, to make the point by simple metaphor: loving corn and hating lima beans, we simply cannot make up our minds about succotash.

The resulting ambivalence has weakened American foreign policy since the end of World War II. Insofar as communism and nationalism have confronted us as separate forces, United States policy has been largely successful. In such instances as the Soviet threat to Western Europe in the late forties and the Cuban missile crisis of 1962 the danger was clearly one of Soviet power and the United States had little difficulty in deciding on effective counter-action. In the case of the colonial revolution in most of Asia and Africa the United States took a strong lead in supporting national independence movements. Only in such instances as the Cuban Revolution and the war in Vietnam, in each of which communism and nationalism became closely associated with each other, or the Dominican Revolution, in which communism was feared but never proven to be a dominant influence, has the United States encountered cruel dilemmas in the shaping of policy and signal failures in its execution.

For complex reasons, deriving in large part from our early postwar experience with Soviet communist imperialism, we have tended—and now more than ever are tending—to give our opposition to communism priority over our support for nationalism. The result has been that, with certain exceptions, we have strongly, and for the most part unsuccessfully, opposed those genuinely nationalist movements which have been controlled or influenced by communists. The most notable—and rewarding—exception has been Yugoslavia, whose national independence we have supported since 1948 with the result that it has posed a powerful barrier to Soviet aspirations in southeastern Europe—a more powerful barrier, it should be noted, than many noncommunist governments have been able to erect.

Whatever wisdom or lack of it our emphasis on communism has had in the past, the realities of the present require a reversal of priorities as between opposing communism and supporting nationalism. The basis of the criticisms of American policy in Latin America and Southeast Asia to be set forth in succeeding chapters is my belief that American interests are better served by supporting nationalism than by opposing communism, and that when the two are encountered in close association it is in our interest to accept a communist government rather than to undertake the cruel and all but impossible task of suppressing a genuinely national movement.

Many Americans, probably including the highest officials in our government, are likely to be shocked by the contention that we can or should "accept" the establishment of a communist government anywhere in the world under any conceivable circumstances. One's attitude in this respect must depend on one's view of communism as a revolutionary ideology, on whether one views it as an implacable and unalterable design for world conquest or rather as something more subtle, flexible, and varying—varying according to a country's size, resources, and national character, the stage of its economic development and the stage of its revolution.

· · ·

9

War and Peace

The United States disarmed itself in the months following the end of World War II, but the United States was obliged to rearm itself after adopting the containment policy. The Korean War demonstrated to the Truman Administration that it could not rely exclusively upon its superiority in atomic weapons but must also be prepared to fight limited conventional wars as well. The Korean War brought about a major increase in defense spending.

The Eisenhower Administration undertook a reexamination of defense policy following the Korean armistice. The result was a "new look" in defense strategy which placed principal reliance on "massive retaliation" with nuclear weapons as a deterrent to aggression. Defense planners in the Eisenhower Administration reasoned that the United States could not hope to match Communist block nations in size of land armies, and that our national defense should be shaped around our superiority in nuclear weapons and strategic delivery systems. Instead of relying upon "tactical" forces, that is forces designed to defeat the enemy army in the field, we would rely principally upon "strategic" forces, that is forces capable of destroying the enemy in his homeland. We would deter aggression through threat of massive retaliation with nuclear weapons delivered by air on the aggressors' industrial and population centers. Instead of attempting to maintain large expensive conventional armies and navies of the World War II variety, we would shape military expenditures and growth around nuclear weapons and the Air Force's Strategic Air Command. An important advantage of the massive retaliation strategy was that it was relatively inexpensive. Nuclear weapons and strategic delivery systems are less expensive than large land armies with conventional weapons. The Eisenhower Administration boasted that its strategy provided more "bang for a buck." It enabled the Eisenhower Administration to present Congress with reasonably balanced budgets.

Critics of the Eisenhower defense policy raised a number of important questions about massive retaliation as a deterrent to aggression. First of all, by the late 1950's it was obvious that the Soviet Union had developed an air atomic strike force which was capable of inflicting great destruction upon the United States. Our nuclear superiority over the Soviet Union was rapidly diminishing. This created a "credibility" problem in massive retaliation threats. If massive retaliation is going to deter the aggressor, he must be convinced that retaliation will indeed follow his aggression. But when it is known that our resort to massive retaliation would result in heavy damage to the United States itself, a potential aggressor may not be convinced by nuclear threats. The credibility of our threats is particularly weak in deterring aggression in areas of the world which are not particularly vital to the United States security, such as Korea, Indochina, Hungary, or Laos. Reliance upon nuclear retaliation places the United States on the horns of a dilemma when faced with a relatively minor aggression. We must either surrender or engulf the world in a nuclear holocaust. Defense Secretary Robert McNamara referred to Eisenhower's defense strategy as "the spasm response," indicating that the United States lacked flexibility in dealing with aggression. Any aggression must result in either success for the aggressor or all out nuclear war.

The Kennedy Administration revised military policy in the direction of greater flexibility in response to aggression. Under Secretary of Defense Robert S. McNamara, the United States developed a military concept of "graduated deterrence." Graduated deterrence did not mean a diminution of our nuclear capability or strategic strike forces, but a parallel build-up of tactical weapons and conventional forces. Defense planners in the Kennedy Administration reasoned that a balance of terror now existed in the strategic nuclear strike forces of the United States and the Soviet Union. Given this nuclear stand-off, it is unlikely that nuclear weapons would be used by either nation, and the course of world events would be determined by conventional weapons in limited wars. The Kennedy Administration wished to develop a wide range of weapons and forces so that America's response could better fit the nature of the aggression. The United States would continue to maintain a strategic nuclear strike force, but at the same time develop its conventional forces, and even sub-conventional, counter-guerilla forces. Of course, the development of a graduated deterrent, incorporating a strategic nuclear strike force, nuclear and non-nuclear conventional forces, and counter guerilla forces, was a much more expensive policy than massive retaliation. Defense expenditures rose substantially during the Kennedy Administration, even before America's deep involvement in the Vietnam War. But the President argued that if we were to build our forces to the point where we no longer had to choose between surrender or nuclear war, Congress and the American people must be ready to make financial sacrifices greater than those ever demanded before in peace time.

Robert S. McNamara in *The Dynamics of Nuclear Strategy* explains both the offensive and defensive aspects of nuclear strategy. Peter Paret and John W. Shy, writing in the Marine Corps Gazette, explain the new emphasis on *Guerilla Warfare and U.S. Military Strategy.* Finally the U.S. Budget Bureau provides *A Summary of Active Forces* for 1969 which reflects the balanced forces and graduated deterrence concepts of the Kennedy-Johnson administration.

The twin concepts of "containment" and "graduated deterrence" were applied in Vietnam and the result was one of America's longest and bloodiest wars. At the time of the Japanese surrender in August, 1945, Japanese troops still occupied the former French colony of Indochina. These troops returned to their homeland before Allied troops entered Indochina, and in the interim period an independent native Democratic Republic of Vietnam was proclaimed in September, 1945, with the revolutionary leader Ho Chi Minh as Premier. By December, 1946 the French Army had organized itself for an invasion of Vietnam and the recovery of the lost colony. Ho Chi Minh requested U.S., British, and even Nationalist Chinese support against the French, but instead the Allies lent their support to the French effort. Eight years of bloody war ensued, ending in the defeat of a sizable French force at Dienbienphu.

Representatives of the Democratic Republic of Vietnam and the French met at Geneva in 1954 and agreed to a cease fire along a temporary military demarcation line at the 17th parallel. *The Final Declaration of the Geneva Conference* recognized that the military demarcation line was provisional and should not in any way be interpreted as constituting a political or territorial boundary. Both sides agreed not to introduce foreign troops or military bases in Vietnam, Laos, or Cambodia. The Geneva Agreements also called for free elections in all of Vietnam to be held in July, 1956. An International Control Commission consisting of India, Canada, and Poland was to supervise the cease fire and the elections. The French recognized "the sovereignty, unity and territorial integrity" of Cambodia, Laos and Vietnam. More importantly, they agreed to withdraw their troops from these new nations.

The United States declined to sign the Geneva Agreements, largely because the Republican administration did not wish to be a party to a victory of communism in the area. President Eisenhower himself publicly predicted that the withdrawal of French troops and free elections in 1956 would result in a victory for Ho Chi Minh. Indeed, all of the parties in the Geneva Agreements expected such a victory. The U. S. did agree to refrain from the threat or use of force to disturb these agreements, yet, shortly after the Geneva meetings we initiated a program of economic and military assistance to a government in Saigon headed by Ngo Dinh Diem. The Diem government replaced the French colonial government of Emperor Bao Dai. Although the Diem government had relatively little popular support in the villages and countryside, it was able, with American backing, to call off the promised elections in 1956. The United States gave increasingly heavy military and economic assistance to the Diem government in an effort to "save" South Vietnam from communism. This action was fully consistent with America's containment policy, since without American intervention, South Vietnam certainly would have come under the control of the Ho Chi Minh government.

Opposition to the Diem government in South Vietnam organized itself into a National Liberation Front (NLF), known to the Americans as the "Viet Cong." The NLF received heavy assistance from the Democratic Republic of Vietnam. Civil war ensued, but despite the introduction of over 100,000 American military "advisors," the Diem government steadily lost ground to the NLF. Diem was replaced in 1963 and the Saigon government came under the rule of a series of military dictators, who were even less effective than Diem in checking the "Viet Cong." (See National Liberation Front, *We Are Determined to Fight*)

In August of 1964 after an alleged attack on an American destroyer in the Gulf of Tonkin, the United States initiated bombing attacks on North Vietnam. Congress backed the President's decision by a resolution authorizing him "to take all the necessary steps, including the use of armed force" to defend the South Vietnamese government in Saigon. (See Congress of the United States, *Tonkin Gulf Resolution*) In January of 1965 the President sent American ground units into action in South Vietnam and sharply escalated bombing north of the 17th parallel. The President explained that the U. S. military effort resulted from our "commitment" to the South Vietnamese who were the victims of aggression from North Vietnam. (See Lyndon B. Johnson, *Answering*

Aggression in Viet Nam) He also indicated a willingness to negotiate with Ho Chi Minh, that is, with the Democratic Republic of Vietnam in Hanoi.

On March 31, 1968 President Johnson announced a partial restriction on U. S. bombing in North Vietnam and issued a new call for negotiations. He accompanied this call with a surprise announcement that he would not seek reelection in 1968. The North Vietnamese agreed to discussions with the United States in Paris. But even while discussions were under way, the war continued unabated with heavy civilian and military casualties on both sides. By mid-1968 U. S. casualties already exceeded those of the Korean War. Over 500,000 American troops were stationed in Vietnam. The U. S. had already dropped more bombs on Vietnamese territory than all the bombs released on Axis powers in World War II. Yet the National Liberation Front, with the assistance of the Hanoi government, continued to resist. Nowhere in South Vietnam were American forces safe from attack from the "Viet Cong." The prospects for a U. S. military victory seemed remote.

Opposition to the war grew steadily within the United States as America deepened its involvement in Vietnam. Much of President Johnson's sweeping electoral success in 1964 was attributed to the war-like image of his opponent Barry Goldwater. Yet within months of his defeat, Goldwater could rightly claim that the Administration was adopting his recommendations for increased military pressure in Vietnam. Criticism of the administration's escalation of the war developed within the United States Senate. When Secretary of State Dean Rusk testified before the Senate Foreign Relations Committee, he was subject to some very penetrating questioning. (See Dean Rusk, *Testimony Before the Senate Foreign Relations Committee*) This questioning revealed many of the contradictions and tragedies of the war. Senators J. William Fulbright and Frank Church in particular expressed serious reservations about the United States policy in Southeast Asia.

Senator Eugene McCarthy entered the Presidential campaign in 1968 with the specific purpose of challenging the direction of U. S. military policy in Vietnam. Although McCarthy was rejected by the Democratic party leaders at the national convention, he was surprisingly successful among the voters in primary elections. President Johnson was aware of dissent and disunity in the country in early 1968, and he linked his decision to withdraw from the presidential race to his desire to avoid a bitter political contest while the war was in progress:

There is division in the American House now. There is divisiveness among us all here tonight. And holding the trust in his mind, as President of all the people, I cannot disregard the peril to the progress of the

American people and the hope and prospect of peace for all peoples . . .
Believing this as I do, I have concluded that I should not permit the
Presidency to become involved in partisan divisions which are developing in this political year. With America's sons in the fields far away,
with America's future challenged right here at home, with our hopes
and the world's hope for peace in the balance every day, I do not believe that I should devote an hour or a day of my time to any personal
partisan causes, towards any duties other than the awesome duties of
this office—the Presidency of this country.

Accordingly, I shall not seek, and I will not accept, the nomination of
my party for another term as your President.

The Dynamics of
Nuclear Strategy*

Robert S. McNamara

I want to discuss with you this afternoon the gravest problem that an American Secretary of Defense must face: the planning, preparation, and policy governing the possibility of thermonuclear war.

It is a prospect most of mankind would prefer not to contemplate. That is understandable. For technology has now circumscribed us all with a conceivable horizon of horror that could dwarf any catastrophe that has befallen man in his more than a million years on earth.

Man has lived now for more than 20 years in what we have come to call the atomic age. What we sometimes overlook is that every future age of man will be an atomic age.

If, then, man is to have a future at all, it will have to be a future overshadowed with the permanent possibility of thermonuclear holocaust.

About that fact, we are no longer free. Our freedom in this question consists rather in facing the matter rationally and realistically and discussing actions to minimize the danger.

No sane citizen, no sane political leader, no sane nation, wants thermonuclear war. But merely not wanting it is not enough. We must understand the difference between actions which increase its risk, those which reduce it, and those which, while costly, have little influence one way or another.

Now this whole subject matter tends to be psychologically unpleasant. But there is an even greater difficulty standing in the way of constructive

*Address made before the annual convention of United Press International editors and publishers at San Francisco, Calif., on Sept. 18, 1967. Reprinted in *Department of State Bulletin,* Vol. 57 (October 9, 1967).

and profitable debate over the issues. And that is that nuclear strategy is exceptionally complex in its technical aspects. Unless these complexities are well understood, rational discussion and decisionmaking are simply not possible.

What I want to do this afternoon is deal with these complexities and clarify them with as much precision and detail as time and security permit.

"Assured Destruction Capability"

One must begin with precise definitions. The cornerstone of our strategic policy continues to be to deter deliberate nuclear attack upon the United States, or its allies, by maintaining a highly reliable ability to inflict an unacceptable degree of damage upon any single aggressor, or combination of aggressors, at any time during the course of a strategic nuclear exchange — even after our absorbing a surprise first strike. This can be defined as our "assured destruction capability."

Now, it is imperative to understand that assured destruction is the very essence of the whole deterrence concept.

We must possess an actual assured destruction capability. And that actual assured destruction capability must also be credible. Conceivably, our assured destruction capability could be actual without being credible — in which case it might fail to deter an aggressor. The point is that a potential aggressor must himself believe that our assured destruction capability is in fact actual and that our will to use it in retaliation to an attack is in fact unwavering.

The conclusion, then, is clear: If the United States is to deter a nuclear attack on itself or on its allies, it must possess an actual and a credible assured destruction capability.

When calculating the force we require, we must be "conservative" in all our estimates of both a potential aggressor's capabilities and his intentions. Security depends upon taking a "worst plausible case" — and having the ability to cope with that eventuality.

In that eventuality we must be able to absorb the total weight of nuclear attack on our country — on our strike-back forces; on our command and control apparatus; on our industrial capacity; on our cities; and on our population — and still be fully capable of destroying the aggressor to the point that his society is simply no longer viable in any meaningful 20th-century sense.

That is what deterrence to nuclear aggression means. It means the certainty of suicide to the aggressor — not merely to his military forces but to his society as a whole.

"First-Strike Capability"

Now let us consider another term: "first-strike capability." This, in itself, is an ambiguous term, since it could mean simply the ability of one nation to attack another nation with nuclear forces first. But as it is normally used, it connotes much more: the substantial elimination of the attacked nation's retaliatory second-strike forces. This is the sense in which "first-strike capability" should be understood.

Now, clearly, such a first-strike capability is an important strategic concept. The United States cannot — and will not — ever permit itself to get into the position in which another nation or combination of nations would possess such a first-strike capability, which could be effectively used against it.

To get into such a position vis-a-vis any other nation or nations would not only constitute an intolerable threat to our security, but it would obviously remove our ability to deter nuclear aggression — both against ourselves and against our allies.

Now, we are not in that position today — and there is no foreseeable danger of our ever getting into that position.

Our strategic offensive forces are immense: 1,000 Minuteman missile launchers, carefully protected below ground; 41 Polaris submarines, carrying 656 missile launchers — with the majority of these hidden beneath the seas at all times; and about 600 long-range bombers, approximately 40 percent of which are kept always in a high state of alert.

Our alert forces alone carry more than 2,200 weapons, averaging more than 1 megaton each. A mere 400 1-megaton weapons, if delivered on the Soviet Union, would be sufficient to destroy over one-third of her population and one-half of her industry.

And all of these flexible and highly reliable forces are equipped with devices that insure their penetration of Soviet defenses.

Now, what about the Soviet Union? Does it today possess a powerful nuclear arsenal?

The answer is that it does.

Does it possess a first-strike capability against the United States?

The answer is that it does not.

Can the Soviet Union, in the foreseeable future, acquire such a first-strike capability against the United States?

The answer is that it cannot. It cannot because we are determined to remain fully alert and we will never permit our own assured destruction capability to be at a point where a Soviet first-strike capability is even remotely feasible.

Is the Soviet Union seriously attempting to acquire a first-strike capability against the United States?

Although this is a question we cannot answer with absolute certainty, we believe the answer is "No." In any event, the question itself is, in a sense, irrelevant. It is irrelevant since the United States will so continue to maintain — and where necessary strengthen — our retaliatory forces that, whatever the Soviet Union's intentions or actions, we will continue to have an assured destruction capability vis-a-vis their society in which we are completely confident.

But there is another question that is most relevant. And that is: Do we — the United States — possess a first-strike capability against the Soviet Union?

The answer is that we do not.

And we do not, not because we have neglected our nuclear strength. On the contrary, we have increased it to the point that we possess a clear superiority over the Soviet Union.

We do not possess first-strike capability against the Soviet Union for precisely the same reason that they do not possess it against us. And that is that we have both built up our "second-strike capability"[1] to the point that a first-strike capability on either side has become unattainable.

There is, of course, no way in which the United States could have prevented the Soviet Union from acquiring its present second-strike capability — short of a massive preemptive first strike on the Soviet Union in the 1950's.

The blunt fact is, then, that neither the Soviet Union nor the United States can attack the other without being destroyed in retaliation; nor can either of us attain a first-strike capability in the foreseeable future.

The further fact is that both the Soviet Union and the United States presently possess an actual and credible second-strike capability against one another — and it is precisely this mutual capability that provides us both with the strongest possible motive to avoid a nuclear war.

•   •   •

Nonnuclear Forces Required

Now, in strategic nuclear weaponry the arms race involves a particular irony. Unlike any other era in military history, today a substantial numerical superiority of weapons does not effectively translate into political control or diplomatic leverage.

---

[1]A "second-strike capability" is the capability to absorb a surprise nuclear attack and survive with sufficient power to inflict unacceptable damage on the aggressor.

While thermonuclear power is almost inconceivably awesome, and represents virtually unlimited potential destructiveness, it has proven to be a limited diplomatic instrument. Its uniqueness lies in the fact that it is at once and the same time an all-powerful weapon and a very inadequate weapon.

The fact that the Soviet Union and the United States can mutually destroy one another — regardless of who strikes first — narrows the range of Soviet aggression which our nuclear forces can effectively deter.

Even with our nuclear monopoly in the early postwar period, we were unable to deter the Soviet pressures against Berlin or their support of aggression in Korea. Today, our nuclear superiority does not deter all forms of Soviet support of Communist insurgency in Southeast Asia.

What all of this has meant is that we, and our allies as well, require substantial nonnuclear forces in order to cope with levels of aggression that massive strategic forces do not in fact deter.

This has been a difficult lesson both for us and for our allies to accept, since there is a strong psychological tendency to regard superior nuclear forces as a simple and unfailing solution to security and an assurance of victory under any set of circumstances.

What is important to understand is that our nuclear strategic forces play a vital and absolutely necessary role in our security and that of our allies but it is an intrinsically limited role.

Thus, we and our allies must maintain substantial conventional forces fully capable of dealing with a wide spectrum of lesser forms of political and military aggression — a level of aggression against which the use of strategic nuclear forces would not be to our advantage and thus a level of aggression which these strategic nuclear forces by themselves cannot effectively deter. One cannot fashion a credible deterrent out of an incredible action. Therefore, security for the United States and its allies can only arise from the possession of a whole range of graduated deterrents, each of them fully credible in its own context.

Now, I have pointed out that in strategic nuclear matters the Soviet Union and the United States mutually influence one another's plans. In recent years the Soviets have substantially increased their offensive forces. We have, of course, been watching and evaluating this very carefully.

Clearly, the Soviet buildup is in part a reaction to our own buildup since the beginning of this decade. Soviet strategic planners undoubtedly reasoned that if our buildup were to continue at its accelerated pace, we might conceivably reach, in time, a credible first-strike capability against the Soviet Union.

That was not in fact our intention. Our intention was to assure that they — with their theoretical capacity to reach such a first-strike capability — would not in fact outdistance us.

But they could not read our intentions with any greater accuracy than we could read theirs. And thus the result has been that we have both built up our forces to a point that far exceeds a credible second-strike capability against the forces we each started with.

In doing so, neither of us has reached a first-strike capability. And the realities of the situation being what they are — whatever we believe their intentions to be and whatever they believe our intentions to be — each of us can deny the other a first-strike capability in the foreseeable future.

Now, how can we be so confident that this is the case? How can we be so certain that the Soviets cannot gradually outdistance us — either by some dramatic technological breakthrough or simply through our imperceptibly lagging behind, for whatever reason: reluctance to spend the requisite funds, distraction with military problems elsewhere, faulty intelligence, or simply negligence and naivete?

All of these reasons — and others — have been suggested by some commentators in this country, who fear that we are in fact falling behind to a dangerous degree.

The answer to all of this is simple and straightforward. We are not going to permit the Soviets to outdistance us, because to do so would be to jeopardize our very viability as a nation. No President, no Secretary of Defense, no Congress of the United States — of whatever political party and of whatever political persuasion — is going to permit this nation to take that risk.

Hope for Arms Limitation Agreement

We do not want a nuclear arms race with the Soviet Union — primarily because the action-reaction phenomenon makes it foolish and futile. But if the only way to prevent the Soviet Union from obtaining first-strike capability over us is to engage in such a race, the United States possesses in ample abundance the resources, the technology, and the will to run faster in that race for whatever distance is required.

But what we would much prefer to do is to come to a realistic and reasonably riskless agreement with the Soviet Union which would effectively prevent such an arms race. We both have strategic nuclear arsenals greatly in excess of a credible assured destruction capability. These arsenals have reached that point of excess in each case for precisely the same reason: We each have reacted to the other's buildup with very conservative calculations. We have, that is, each built a greater arsenal than either of us needed for a second-strike capability, simply because we each wanted to be able to cope with the "worst plausible case."

But since we now each possess a deterrent in excess of our individual needs, both of our nations would benefit from a properly safeguarded agreement first to limit, and later to reduce, both our offensive and defensive strategic nuclear forces.

We may, or we may not, be able to achieve such an agreement. We hope we can. And we believe such an agreement is fully feasible, since it is clearly in both our nations' interests. But reach the formal agreement or not, we can be sure that neither the Soviets nor we are going to risk the other obtaining a first-strike capability. On the contrary, we can be sure that we are both going to maintain a maximum effort to preserve an assured destruction capability.

It would not be sensible for either side to launch a maximum effort to achieve a first-strike capability. It would not be sensible because, the intelligence-gathering capability of each side being what it is and the realities of leadtime from technological breakthrough to operational readiness being what they are, neither of us would be able to acquire a first-strike capability in secret.

Now, let me take a specific case in point.

The Soviets are now deploying an anti-ballistic missile system. If we react to this deployment intelligently, we have no reason for alarm.

The system does not impose any threat to our ability to penetrate and inflict massive and unacceptable damage on the Soviet Union. In other words, it does not presently affect in any significant manner our assured destruction capability.

It does not impose such a threat because we have already taken the steps necessary to assure that our land-based Minuteman missiles, our nuclear submarine-launched new Poseidon missiles, and our strategic bomber forces have the requisite penetration aids and, in the sum, constitute a force of such magnitude that they guarantee us a force strong enough to survive a Soviet attack and penetrate the Soviet ABM deployment.

Deployment of an ABM System

Now, let me come to the issue that has received so much attention recently: the question of whether or not we should deploy an ABM system against the Soviet nuclear threat.

To begin with, this is not in any sense a new issue. We have had both the technical possibility and the strategic desirability of an American ABM deployment under constant review since the late 1950's.

While we have substantially improved our technology in the field, it is important to understand that none of the systems at the present or foreseeable state of the art would provide an impenetrable shield over the United States. Were such a shield possible, we would certainly want it — and we would certainly build it.

And at this point, let me dispose of an objection that is totally irrelevant to this issue. It has been alleged that we are opposed to deploying a large-scale ABM system because it would carry the heavy price tag of $40 billion.

Let me make it very clear that the $40 billion is not the issue. If we could build and deploy a genuinely impenetrable shield over the United States, we would be willing to spend not $40 billion but any reasonable multiple of that amount that was necessary. The money in itself is not the problem: The penetrability of the proposed shield is the problem.

There is clearly no point, however, in spending $40 billion if it is not going to buy us a significant improvement in our security. If it is not, then we should use the substantial resources it represents on something that will.

Every ABM system that is now feasible involves firing defensive missiles at incoming offensive warheads in an effort to destroy them. But what many commentators on this issue overlook is that any such system can rather obviously be defeated by an enemy simply sending more offensive warheads, or dummy warheads, than there are defensive missiles capable of disposing of them.

And this is the whole crux of the nuclear action-reaction phenomenon.

Were we to deploy a heavy ABM system throughout the United States, the Soviets would clearly be strongly motivated to so increase their offensive capability as to cancel out our defensive advantage.

It is futile for each of us to spend $4 billion, $40 billion, or $400 billion — and at the end of all the spending, and at the end of all the deployment, and at the end of all the effort, to be relatively at the same point of balance on the security scale that we are now.

In point of fact, we have already initiated offensive weapons programs costing several billions in order to offset the small present Soviet ABM deployment and the possibly more extensive future Soviet ABM deployments. That is money well spent; and it is necessary. But we should bear in mind that it is money spent because of the action-reaction phenomenon.

If we in turn opt for heavy ABM deployment — at whatever price — we can be certain that the Soviets will react to offset the advantage we would hope to gain.

•   •   •

Advantages of Light Deployment of U.S. ABM's

And since, as I have noted, our strategic planning must always be conservative and take into consideration even the possible irrational behavior of potential adversaries, there are marginal grounds for concluding that a light deployment of U.S. ABM's against this possibility is prudent.

The system would be relatively inexpensive — preliminary estimates place the cost at about $5 billion — and would have a much higher degree of reliability against a Chinese attack than the much more massive and complicated system that some have recommended against a possible Soviet attack.

Moreover, such an ABM deployment designed against a possible Chinese attack would have a number of other advantages. It would provide an additional indication to Asians that we intend to deter China from nuclear blackmail and thus would contribute toward our goal of discouraging nuclear weapon proliferation among the present nonnuclear countries.

Further, the Chinese-oriented ABM deployment would enable us to add — as a concurrent benefit — a further defense of our Minuteman sites against Soviet attack, which means that at modest cost we would in fact be adding even greater effectiveness to our offensive missile force and avoiding a much more costly expansion of that force.

Finally, such a reasonably reliable ABM system would add protection of our population against the improbable but possible accidental launch of an intercontinental missile by any one of the nuclear powers.

After a detailed review of all these considerations, we have decided to go forward with this Chinese-oriented ABM deployment; and we will begin actual production of such a system at the end of this year.

Psychological Dangers

In reaching this decision, I want to emphasize that it contains two possible dangers, and we should guard carefully against each.

The first danger is that we may psychologically lapse into the old oversimplification about the adequacy of nuclear power. The simple truth is that nuclear weapons can serve to deter only a narrow range of threats. This ABM deployment will strengthen our defensive posture and will enhance the effectiveness of our land-based ICBM offensive forces. But the independent nations of Asia must realize that these benefits are no substitute for their maintaining, and where necessary strengthening, their own conventional forces in order to deal with the more likely threats to the security of the region.

The second danger is also psychological. There is a kind of mad momentum intrinsic to the development of all new nuclear weaponry. If a weapon system works — and works well — there is strong pressure from many directions to procure and deploy the weapon out of all proportion to the prudent level required.

The danger in deploying this relatively light and reliable Chinese-oriented ABM system is going to be that pressures will develop to expand it into a heavy Soviet-oriented ABM system.

We must resist that temptation firmly, not because we can for a moment afford to relax our vigilance against a possible Soviet first strike but precisely because our greatest deterrent against such a strike is not a massive, costly, but highly penetrable ABM shield but rather a fully credible offensive assured destruction capability.

The so-called heavy ABM shield — at the present state of technology — would in effect be no adequate shield at all against a Soviet attack but rather a strong inducement for the Soviets to vastly increase their own offensive forces. That, as I have pointed out, would make it necessary for us to respond in turn; and so the arms race would rush hopelessly on to no sensible purpose on either side.

Let me emphasize — and I cannot do so too strongly — that our decision to go ahead with a *limited* ABM deployment in no way indicates that we feel an agreement with the Soviet Union on the limitation of strategic nuclear offensive and defensive forces is any the less urgent or desirable.

The road leading from the stone ax to the ICBM, though it may have been more than a million years in the building, seems to have run in a single direction. If one is inclined to be cynical, one might conclude that man's history seems to be characterized not so much by consistent periods of peace, occasionally punctuated by warfare, but rather by persistent outbreaks of warfare, wearily put aside from time to time by periods of exhaustion and recovery that parade under the name of peace.

I do not view man's history with that degree of cynicism, but I do believe that man's wisdom in avoiding war is often surpassed by his folly in promoting it.

However foolish unlimited war may have been in the past, it is now no longer merely foolish, but suicidal as well.

It is said that nothing can prevent a man from suicide if he is sufficiently determined to commit it. The question is what is our determination in an era when unlimited war will mean the death of hundreds of millions — and the possible genetic impairment of a million generations to follow?

Man is clearly a compound of folly and wisdom, and history is clearly a consequence of the admixture of those two contradictory traits. History has placed our particular lives in an era when the consequences of human folly are waxing more and more catastrophic in the matters of war and peace.

In the end, the root of man's security does not lie in his weaponry. In the end, the root of man's security lies in his mind.

What the world requires in its 22d year of the atomic age is not a new race toward armament. What the world requires in its 22d year of the atomic age is a new race toward reasonableness.

We had better all run that race — not merely we the administrators but we the people.

Guerilla Warfare and
U.S. Military Policy*

Peter Paret and John W. Shy

. . . For too long, nuclear weapons have monopolized the nation's intellectual energies and material resources. Even the growing interest in the possibility of limited war has largely accepted the traditional definition of "war." Only now, when guerrillas in Laos, Cuba, the Congo, and Algeria have directly touched our national interest, do we seem to be awakening to the full range of military possibilities. More reflection on earlier events in Greece, Palestine, Indochina, Indonesia, the Philippines, Malaya, Cyprus, and even Kashmir and Kenya might have shortened this unfortunate time lag in our thinking.

But just as many people have tended in the past to regard a certain weapon or doctrine, whether "massive retaliation" or "limited war," as the single solution to our military problems, there is now a danger that such tendencies will shift toward the guerrilla and subversion. This kind of attitude, to which few of us are immune, reflects a weakness for gadgets and fashion that has no place in our thinking on defense. The enthusiasts of guerrilla warfare have made their case after a long, dry season of neglect. The time has come, however, to balance the discussion. We need to analyze what we have learned about guerrilla operations, and to clarify our thinking about the relation of guerrilla warfare to American foreign and military policy.

The first question to ask is a simple one but perhaps for that reason is usually ignored: What are the functions of guerrilla warfare?

---

*From *Marine Corps Gazette,* Vol. 46 (January, 1962).

Historically — both before and after Spanish peasants fighting against Napoleon put "guerrilla" into the dictionary — the irregular has usually been defending his country against foreign invasion. The twentieth century, however, has brought two other functions more clearly into view: The guerrilla may be a weapon of insurrection, aiming at the capture of political power; and he may be the instrument of foreign aggression. Today the second and third functions are our primary concern, although guerrilla operations against conventional attack or in the aftermath of a nuclear strike remain conceivable.

The insurrectionary and aggressive functions of guerrilla warfare are not new in themselves. People discontented with their governments and agents of foreign powers have often been involved in violent uprisings that used unorthodox military tactics. What *is* comparatively new is the development of a body of theory that has systematized the technique of using guerrilla warfare for the seizure of national or international power and has placed the irregular fighting among the weapons systems of modern war.

Colonel T. E. Lawrence, leader of the Arab guerrilla campaign against Turkish communications in World War I, was the first of the new partisan "leader-theorists" to have appeared in the twentieth century. These men, in their actions as well as in their writings, have extended Clausewitz' analysis of the armed populace as a military instrument, to include the use of irregulars for political purposes. While Mao Tse-tung is deservedly the best known among them, Mikhail Frunze, Leon Trotsky, and, most recently, Che Guevara, are others of importance.

What can these men teach us? They have described the conditions under which guerrilla warfare can be initiated and sustained. They have analyzed both the techniques and the objectives of guerrilla warfare. Finally, perhaps surprisingly, they have revealed the inherent limitations of this form of combat.

An Algerian rebel leader recently explained the necessary conditions for guerrilla warfare in terms of "terrain." He was using the word both in an unconventional and in its conventional, geographical, sense. Strategically, irregulars need considerable space in which to pursue hit-and-run operations successfully. Mao, for example, has doubted whether extensive guerrilla warfare could ever occur in a country as small as Belgium. Tactically, irregulars require rough country, with few people and poor roads difficult of access to their opponents.

But the Algerian leader was also using "terrain" in the extended sense of "political terrain." Internationally, diplomatic support for the guerrillas can weaken their opponent, provide moral and material assistance, and even furnish military sanctuary that may compensate for inadequate space in the area of active operations. Internally, guerrillas must have the active support of some, and the acquiescence of most, of the civilian population.

Internal popular support is the indispensable condition for successful guerrilla action. This fact makes the relationship between the military and civilian realms more intimate than in any other type of warfare. Although this point is often stated, its rationale is too little understood. Why must the guerrilla have a firm psychological base among the people?

First, the irregular fighter is recruited by some ideological commitment — however crude it might be — and not primarily by administrative machinery. Only such commitment can sustain the self-control and unit discipline demanded by this most punishing kind of combat. Agents, infiltrated from abroad, may play an important role, but perhaps the greatest advantage of the guerrilla is that he is a native, fighting among people and over ground he has known since birth.

Second, civilian support helps to solve the critical problems of logistics and intelligence. The local populace provides food, shelter, medical care, and money. More important, it furnishes the information the guerrilla must have in order to enjoy both surprise when he attacks and security from attack by his opponent. Even when the mass of the people seem no more than apathetic, afraid, and unhappy at being caught in the midst of an internal war, they are not truly neutral. If the guerrillas are succeeding, then the people are giving them vital intelligence and denying it to their opponents. As Guevara has written: "One of the most important characteristics of a guerrilla war is the notable difference that exists between the information the rebel forces possess and the information the enemies possess."

Popular support is indispensable to the guerrilla because he is militarily weak, a fact easily forgotten. After all, the guerrilla fights as he does because he lacks the weapons, equipment, supplies, technical skills, and often numbers needed to fight in any other way. Seldom if ever has anyone deliberately chosen a guerrilla strategy when other choices existed. If sufficient military strength is available, conventional organization and tactics produce a decision more quickly; if the goal is political, strength makes possible a *coup d'état* instead of a costly, protracted civil war.

Even the American revolutionaries, whose armed populace gave them enormous guerrilla potential, used partisan warfare only as a last resort. This traditional reluctance to employ guerrillas unless forced to do so is understandable. Guerrillas do great damage to the very society they are

trying to defend or control because their weakness keeps them from protecting people or property. Their strength derives not so much from
weapons and organization as from changeable popular attitudes. In short,
guerrilla warfare as a military means to a political end is both costly and
risky. Civil War historians who are fond of praising the partisan exploits
of Mosby in northern Virginia should remember the sequel: Sheridan
devastated the Shenandoah Valley, and Mosby, deprived of his guerrilla
base, ultimately failed.

True, guerrilla warfare has one major advantage in this nuclear age.
If employed as an instrument of foreign aggression, it constitutes an
"ambiguous threat" by confusing the legal, political, and even military
bases for an effective international response. But most of the native
guerrillas and their civilian supporters must have a stronger motive of
fighting than serving the convenience of a foreign power. The internal
conditions for irregular warfare must be right before the guerrilla becomes available as a means of aggression.

The weakness of the guerrilla himself and his consequent need to gain
and maintain strength among the civilian population largely determine
his techniques and objectives. Unable to destroy his opponent physically
by direct, military action, he fights psychologically by indirect, political
means. Never attacking unless overwhelmingly superior, and never fighting long enough to be caught by a counterattack, the guerrilla leader uses
combat itself as a psychological weapon. With an unbroken string of
victories, however insignificant many of them may be, he creates confidence in ultimate success among his supporters. At the same time, he
fosters a growing despair among his opponents.

The guerrilla converts his reliance on the civilian population into an
advantage. Because he cannot hold ground or even do large-scale damage to enemy forces, his objective becomes control of the population. He
pursues this objective not only by politically organizing and indoctrinat-
ing the people, but also by educating his own men in their role of
winning civilian support. The "Three Disciplinary Rules" and "Eight
Points of Attention," which Mao formulated as early as 1928, make it
plain to all irregular soldiers that they are expected to behave not as
conquerors or bandits, but as disciplined representatives of a new social
and economic order.

This new order, Mao also declares, is at the heart of the struggle.
"Without a political goal," he writes, "guerrilla warfare must fail, as it
must if its political objectives do not coincide with the aspirations of the
people." Land reform, nationalism, corruption, poverty — these are the
issues exploited by modern guerrillas to win people over. Once it is

organized, and convinced of both the certainty and the justice of a guerrilla victory, the civilian population replaces the traditional tools of war with a less tangible form of strength.

The required integration of military and political action goes beyond formulating a popular program and then letting the partisans themselves act as its salesmen. Even the smallest tactical operation may have political implications. For example, an attack on an enemy strong point seems necessary, but may alienate the local inhabitants or expose them to reprisals against which they cannot be protected. The political consequences may well outweigh the possible military gain and the raid is not carried out. The Algerians have adopted perhaps the most extreme solution to this problem of politico-military coordination by introducing a political officer, who himself has had previous experience as a military commander, at every echelon down to the section.

It is useful, with our new concern over guerrilla warfare, to imagine ourselves in the position of the guerrilla leader. We then see that he is face to face with some serious difficulties and certain inherent limitations. In *La Guerra de Guerrillas,* Che Guevara, like Mao, understandably stresses the positive side of irregular warfare. But a close reading of his book reveals a series of dilemmas for the guerrilla leader.

Above all, the guerrilla leader must be continually active — harassing enemy communications, ambushing isolated posts and detachments, creating by acts of violence a general climate of insecurity. His movement thrives and grows on continual, small successes. At the same time, he must never risk a defeat. Defeat not only hurts his small, poorly equipped forces, but it also weakens partisan morale and civilian confidence. The psychological damage may be greater than the military. This was probably true of the July, 1961, battle in South Vietnam, where the Viet Cong lost fewer than 200 of their 5,000-10,000 fighters. The guerrilla leader attempts to walk a fine line between rashness and necessary boldness.

Second, there is a dilemma posed by terrain on the one hand, targets on the other. The rougher the terrain, the more secure is the guerrilla force. But the rougher the terrain, the more difficult is it for guerrillas to find local supplies and to hit the most important military and political targets. Guevara admits that the cities and the suburbs are the sensitive areas that must be attacked and indoctrinated, but that precisely those areas are most dangerous for guerrilla operations. Even the flatter, more fertile, and heavily populated farmlands constitute "unfavorable terrain."

There is also the matter of guerrilla discipline. Guevara notes that individual conviction drives most guerrillas to fight but they must submit to a discipline that is extremely severe by regular standards. Only under such discipline can they meet the extraordinary physical and emotional demands placed upon them by irregular warfare (similar demands nearly destroyed the combat effectiveness of Allied long-range penetration groups in Burma in 1944). In Cuba, one method of solving this conflict between individual motivation and extreme regimentation was to let unit committees, rather than combat commanders, perform certain judicial functions. Nevertheless, even such self-imposed discipline cannot afford any doubts about the cause or the leadership. For this reason, guerrillas themselves seem to be especially vulnerable to psychological attack.

The guerrilla leader faces still another dilemma in dealing with the civilian population. Although many of the people may be discontented, their discontent must be translated into willingness to commit or support illegal, violent acts. Generally they are brought to do this by a combination of political persuasion and military success. But rarely if ever has a guerrilla movement been able to avoid more coercive techniques, including the use of terror. The crucial question then becomes whether coercion, and especially terror, will alienate people more than it intimidates them.

Some American officials and journalists have recently argued that terror alone, used by guerrillas infiltrated into an area, can maintain the popular base needed for guerrilla warfare. But Che Guevara, in his field manual for Latin American revolutionaries, does not seem to agree. He returns to the question of coercion repeatedly, never quite clarifying the answer, but clearly revealing the complexity of the problem. "Treason," he admits on the one hand, must always be "justly punished." Guerrillas display "absolute implacability" toward "contemptible persons." And especially in "unfavorable terrain" — cities or farmland — where propaganda is most important but military operations are most hazardous, the guerrillas eliminate "recalcitrant enemies . . . without leniency. . . . There can be no enemies in dangerous places."

On the other hand, Guevara rejects terrorism as a general policy because it "is a negative weapon that produces in no way the desired effects, that can turn a people against a given revolutionary movement, and that brings with it a loss of lives among those taking part that is much greater than the return."

There is some historical evidence supporting his point. The Greek Communists, although successful for a time in using coercive methods, eventually drove over a half-million of what should have been their strongest supporters off the land and into the cities. The Malayan Communists, once committed to a policy of terror, found that it undermined their campaign of political indoctrination and they abandoned it within

a year. In southwestern Korea, North Korean guerrillas successfully ter-
rorized the peasants until threats ceased to be certain of execution. Then
terror began to boomerang. Even the Algerians claim to have given up
the large-scale use of terror, as a means of keeping Moslems in line, after
finding its disadvantages too great.

Terrorism, of course, can have other important uses besides maintaining popular support. A government too weak to provide a popular rally-
ing point, a government without the administrative machinery or military
strength to perform its minimum functions, may find that terrorism so
completely disrupts life that peace on any terms seems preferable. Employed against a colonial regime weakened by political difficulties at
home and abroad, terrorism alone may achieve the objective of the guerrillas. This happened in Palestine and Cyprus. In Cyprus, EOKA never
engaged in large-scale irregular combat although its operations had all
the other characteristics of guerrilla warfare — a popular cause, civilian
protection of the partisans, and governmental difficulties in obtaining information and maintaining order without further alienating the population. In the end, the British decided that a political settlement in Cyprus
was preferable to all out war against the insurgents.

But the use of violence by the partisans against civilians remains an
ambiguous, not an invincible, weapon for the guerrilla leader. Indiscriminate or selective terror, less extreme forms of coercion, even sabotage if
it disrupts civilian life too greatly, may have a backlash that repels rather
than attracts popular support. At times, however, guerrilla forces must
resort to these techniques, and the guerrilla leader must deal with the
difficult problems of just when and how to use them, and how to keep
them under control.

Unfortunately, Guevara barely touches on the last and greatest
dilemma of the guerrilla leader (the rottenness of the Batista regime
largely solved it for the Cuban revolutionaries). As we shall see, the big
problem lies in the difficult choices involved in pushing the war to a vic-
torious conclusion.

The belief that irregular operations must be regularized if partisans are
to win has become one of the dogmas of guerrilla theory. Before Mao,
both experience and doctrine had primarily concerned the defensive
function of guerrilla warfare, which takes for granted a friendly regular
army that eventually invades the country and operates in conjunction
with the partisans. Mao was the first to see clearly that such an army
might be created from the guerrilla force itself. Having consolidated
their position through irregular warfare by the early 1930's, the Chinese
Communists began to engage in more conventional operations. They
reverted to a guerrilla strategy against the Japanese invasion in 1937, but

after 1945, drawing upon his pool of combat-trained manpower, Mao used primarily regular forces in expelling Chiang from the mainland.

When there is no chance of large-scale foreign intervention, and when the enemy is politically and militarily strong, with both the will and the intelligence to use his strength, the dogma of regularization undoubtedly holds true. The psychological character of guerrilla warfare then becomes only the means of creating and consolidating the popular base, which in turn must eventually provide enough soldiers sufficiently well trained to defeat the enemy in open battle. But there are a number of pitfalls on the road to regular operations — regularization may be not just a dilemma, but a complex of dilemmas.

The first of these is proper timing of the transition. Premature regularization invites military disaster but overlong attachment to irregular operations may exhaust the population. The Chinese Communists worried most about the latter danger, the vice of "guerrillaism"; the Algerian rebels had to resist the opposite temptation, of seeking the domestic and diplomatic prestige of conventional operations before being militarily ready. One reason for the ultimate defeat of the Greek Communists appears to have been that before they could afford to do so they were fighting as regular forces, with heavy weapons and territorial bases.

Territorial bases are mentioned by Guevara as being of great value even before any attempt is made to regularize operations. They make it possible to have training and rest areas, supply dumps, and hospital facilities. Of course, he adds, they must be "secure," but how to make them secure against first-class regulars is not answered. Bases, it would seem, offer the sort of fixed target that counterguerrilla forces always seek and rarely find.

In China and Indochina, guerrilla groups turned into regular armies capable of defeating large enemy forces. In both cases, this was achieved with foreign assistance, and there is little evidence that victory can ever be gained without such help. To be sure, guerrillas will supply themselves with arms and ammunition by raids, and the civilian population will provide other essentials. But the FLN required the sanctuary of Tunisian territory and even Castro needed outside support, including the crucial U.S. arms embargo against Batista in 1958. Yet foreign aid can be a two-edged sword for the guerrilla leader. The aims of the guerrilla movement and its foreign ally will never coincide exactly, and the differences may be important, especially if exploited by their mutual enemy. This need to acquire foreign aid makes possible the third function of guerrilla warfare — its use as an instrument of aggression. But even Communists, with their talent for linking local grievances and Russian or Chinese foreign policy in a single ideological framework, do not always find it easy to dominate a guerrilla movement. At the same time, the guerrilla leader may find it difficult to bargain for outside help without undermining or compromising his own objectives.

In all of these dilemmas, the guerrilla leader must display exceptional judgment. Guerrillas, unlike more conventional forces, lack the strength to make up for faulty decisions. Moreover, a shrewd opponent who understands the nature of irregular warfare can considerably narrow the area in which sound decisions by the guerrilla leader are possible.

· · ·

For purposes of analysis, counterguerrilla action may be separated into three tasks, but they are so intimately related that success in one task often depends on progress in the others. The tasks are to defeat the guerrilla militarily, to break his connection with the civilian population, and to re-establish governmental authority and social order.

Professional soldiers are familiar with the tactical problems of fighting irregulars but a few points can be profitably made here. Successful counterguerrilla operations, as in the Philippines, have always combined a grid system of territorial control with mobile striking forces. The mobile striking forces cannot normally be made up of friendly civilians, organized and trained to fight as guerrillas. Instead, they are composed of the best regulars, able to exploit all the technological and administrative advantages of modern military organization, and to employ them in unconventional fashion as well. Since the territorial forces are mainly police or home-defense units, the role for friendly guerrillas in counterguerrilla action seems very limited.

The French attempted to use such guerrillas in Indochina but without much success, mainly because they did not have the popular base from which to operate. Similarly, the United States should not expect to base its military action against guerrillas on local popular support, especially in the early stages of a conflict. French regular troops, on the other hand, never seem to have been able to operate unconventionally. The British forces in Malaya, with a smaller war on their hands, succeeded to a remarkable extent in using irregular tactics against Communist guerrillas. It is important for the United States to understand this distinction between guerrilla tactics available to both sides, and guerrilla organization, which is naturally opposed to the government.

In Indochina, the French also failed to break the line between the guerrillas and the civilian population. Their failure was due not to a lack of understanding but to a lack of firm decisions on countermeasures. Troops in the field, frustrated by the sullen uncommunicativeness of the population, were allowed to commit occasional excesses and often to be simply rough in their handling of civilians. In the same way, until it was stopped, police brutality in South Korea and the Philippines actually helped the Communist partisans.

It is not simply a question of being kind to the natives but of keeping some legal framework intact. Counterguerrilla forces represent the government to most of the people caught in the midst of a guerrilla war. If these forces act more irresponsibly than the guerrillas themselves, the government can hardly hope to appeal to people as their protector and benefactor. Admittedly, the government will often have to employ some unusually harsh coercive measures in breaking the guerrilla-civilian link, but such measures must above all be legally formulated and applied. No government, unless it plans to resort to truly totalitarian techniques, can use terrorism or indiscriminate brutality against its own people without undermining its position.

Though the conduct of troops in the field can ruin any governmental plan for serving the guerrilla from his popular base, there is much more to accomplishing this task than having well-behaved soldiers. One obvious requirement is a psychological-warfare program. On the basis of past experience, this program must be highly sophisticated if it is to succeed. It does not tell lies, because the civilian target of the program knows more about the guerrillas than the government does. It does not confuse people potentially sympathetic to the guerrillas with the guerrillas themselves, because it seeks to break, not reinforce, the links between them. It will sometimes spread information that would normally be classified, because immediate and convincing reports of successful military operations are the best means of persuading people that support of the guerrillas is unwise.

Another standard method of denying the guerrilla his popular base is the resettlement of populations. Resettlement has been successful with the Chinese squatters in Malaya, and partially so with the Arabs in Algeria. But when calculating the military advantages of resettlement and planning the details of the program, full weight must be given to its political, economic, and social effects, which are often extremely harmful.

The ultimate technique in isolating guerrillas from the people is to persuade the people to defend themselves. Militia-type local defense units help in the military defeat of the guerrillas. Gradually they may replace the territorial garrison forces and free regulars for mobile operations. They protect their communities, ambush raiders, and furnish intelligence and security to mobile forces in the vicinity. But at least as important is their political function: Once a substantial number of members of a community commit violence on behalf of the government, they have gone far toward permanently breaking the tie between that community and the guerrillas.

The third task in the conduct of counterguerrilla operations consists in assisting the threatened government to re-establish social order and its own authority. Although this task seems wholly nonmilitary, it in fact attacks the underlying discontent that sustains violence. Neither economic aid from the United States nor domestic authoritarianism is an adequate answer to this problem. The government in question must administer reform effectively and honestly but without seeming to be simply responding to the program of the guerrillas. Moreover, despite certain obvious short-run disadvantages, the government will probably gain in the long run if it permits more rather than less political activity—including criticism of the government. Such activity gives discontented persons a choice other than supporting either the government or the guerrillas, and it keeps discontent above ground, where the government can measure and alleviate it.

Perhaps such a reform program sounds impossibly idealistic, but its planks are based on the British accomplishment in Malaya. For those who still doubt that basic reform and guerrilla warfare are connected, there is the example of the late Ramón Magsaysay, who crushed the Huk rebellion as much with reform as with weapons. The United States must of course decide whether it is ready to interfere in the political affairs and even in the administration of weak and often irrational friends, and help them—force them if necessary—to carry out the needed program. At the same time, the United States itself must be clear on what kinds of reform it will support, and what kinds are too radical to be compatible with its own objectives and political situation.

There is little hope that, in place of reform, the United States can simply persuade the people of a guerrilla-infested state to change their minds. For years French army officers, who have become the leading theorists of "revolutionary warfare," persisted in ignoring the simple fact that most Algerian Moslems were not interested in becoming part of a greater French nation. The idea that the minds of illiterate, economically backward people can be manipulated over a wide range of desires is probably wrong. In any case, we do not have the time to try it. Instead, the United States must accept the fact that real grievances, producing real demands, provide most of the impetus for guerrilla war, and we must prepare to meet or at least undercut those demands.

It would be false to conclude this discussion of guerrilla warfare on an optimistic note. Guerrillas present a difficult and an expensive problem for American military policy. But the first step in solving the problem is to understand it. The second step is to base action on that understanding, even when momentary pressures argue otherwise. The greatest danger in dealing with guerrillas is oversimplification; the second greatest is impatience. Approaches to the problem that unduly stress either military or nonmilitary action are the worst kinds of over-simplification, though each may seem tempting when one has lost patience with a more complex approach. Only by constantly recalling the fundamental structure of guerrilla movements, and by continuously putting what may seem like fine theoretical distinctions into practice, can the intricate but essential coordination of political and military action be maintained toward ultimate success.

Summary of Active Forces*

U.S. Bureau of the Budget

Description	Actual June 30, 1967	Estimated June 30, 1968	Estimated June 30, 1969
Military personnel (in thousands):			
Army	1,442	1,536	1,508
Navy	752	768	795
Marine Corps	285	302	306
Air Force	897	884	868
Total, Department of Defense	3,376	3,490	3,477
Selected military forces:			
Strategic forces:			
Intercontinental ballistic missile squadrons:			
Minuteman	20	20	20
Titan	6	6	6
Polaris submarines/missiles (in commission)	41/656	41/656	41/656
Strategic bomber wings:			
B-52	12	11	10
B-58	2	2	2
Manned fighter interceptor squadrons....	28	26	19
Bomarc interceptor missile squadrons....	6	6	6
Army air defense missile battalions	18	18	18

*From U.S. Bureau of the Budget, *The Budget of the United States Government: Fiscal Year 1969* (Washington, D.C.: U.S. Government Printing Office, 1968), p. 84.

Description	Actual June 30, 1967	Estimated June 30, 1968	June 30, 1969
General purpose forces:			
Army divisions	17	19	19
Army maneuver battalions	201	212	212
Army aviation units	183	218	234
Army special forces groups	7	7	7
Warships (in commission):			
Attack carriers	15	15	15
Antisubmarine warfare carriers	8	8	8
Nuclear attack submarines	28	36	44
Other	327	320	309
Amphibious assault ships (in commission)	162	157	166
Carrier air groups (attack and antisubmarine)	27	27	25
Marine Corps divisions/aircraft wings....	4/3	4/3	4/3
Air Force tactical forces squadrons........	126	136	138
Airlift and sealift forces:			
Airlift aircraft squadrons:			
C-130 through C-141	44	44	43
C-124 and C-7	16	14	11
Troopships, cargo ships, and tankers......	130	130	130
Addenda:			
Active aircraft inventory (all programs):			
Army	9,490	10,671	11,464
Navy	8,417	8,942	8,606
Air Force[1]	15,017	15,127	15,044
Helicopters included in service aircraft, above	8,902	10,519	12,486
Commissioned ships in fleet (all programs)	931	936	960

[1]Includes aircraft provided for support of allies.

The Geneva Agreements*

Agreement on the Cessation of Hostilities in Vietnam (July 20, 1954)

CHAPTER I
PROVISIONAL MILITARY DEMARCATION
LINE AND DEMILITARIZED ZONE

Article 1

A provisional military demarcation line shall be fixed, on either side of which the forces of the two parties shall be regrouped after their withdrawal, the forces of the People's Army of Vietnam [P.A.V., or Vietminh, forces] to the north of the line and the forces of the French Union to the south. . . .

It is also agreed that a demilitarized zone shall be established on either side of the demarcation line, to a width of not more than 5 kms. from it, to act as a buffer zone and avoid any incidents which might result in the resumption of hostilities.

Article 2

The period within which the movement of all forces of either party into its regrouping zone on either side of the provisional military demarcation line shall be completed shall not exceed three hundred (300) days from the date of the present Agreement's entry into force.

Documents Relating to the Discussion of Indochina at the Geneva Conference, London: Great Britain Parliamentary Sessional Papers, Vol. 31 (1953-54). See also Marvin E. Gettleman, ed., *Viet Nam* (New York: Fawcett, 1965).

Article 3

When the provisional military demarcation line coincides with a waterway, the waters of such waterway shall be open to civil navigation by both parties wherever one bank is controlled by one party and the other bank by the other party. The Joint Commission shall establish rules of navigation for the stretch of waterway in question. The merchant shipping and other civilian craft of each party shall have unrestricted access to the land under its military control.

Article 4

The provisional military demarcation line between the two final regrouping zones is extended into the territorial waters by a line perpendicular to the general line of the coast.

All coastal islands north of this boundary shall be evacuated by the armed forces of the French Union, and all islands south of it shall be evacuated by the forces of the People's Army of Vietnam.

Article 5

To avoid any incidents which might result in the resumption of hostilities, all military forces, supplies, and equipment shall be withdrawn from the demilitarized zone within twenty-five (25) days of the present Agreement's entry into force.

Article 6

No person, military or civilian, shall be permitted to cross the provisional military demarcation line unless specifically authorized to do so by the Joint Commission.

Article 7

No person, military or civilian, shall be permitted to enter the demilitarized zone except persons concerned with the conduct of civil administration and relief and persons specifically authorized to enter by the Joint Commission.

Article 8

Civil administration and relief in the demilitarized zone on either side of the provisional military demarcation line shall be the responsibility of the Commanders-in-Chief of the two parties in their respective zones. The number of persons, military or civilian, from each side who are permitted to enter the demilitarized zone for the conduct of civil administration and relief shall be determined by the respective Commanders, but in no case shall the total number authorized by either side exceed at any one time a figure to be determined by the Trung Gia Military Commission or by the Joint Commission. The number of civil police and the arms to be carried by them shall be determined by the Joint Commission. No one else shall carry arms unless specifically authorized to do so by the Joint Commission.

Article 9

Nothing contained in this chapter shall be construed as limiting the complete freedom of movement—into, out of, or within the demilitarized zone—of the Joint Commission, its joint groups, the International Commission to be set up as indicated below, its inspection teams and any other persons, supplies, or equipment specifically authorized to enter the demilitarized zone by the Joint Commission. Freedom of movement shall be permitted across the territory under the military control of either side over any road or waterway which has to be taken between points within the demilitarized zone when such points are not connected by roads or waterways lying completely within the demilitarized zone.

· · ·

Article 14

Political and administrative measures in the two regrouping zones, on either side of the provisional military demarcation line:

(*a*) Pending the general elections which will bring about the unification of Vietnam, the conduct of civil administration in each regrouping zone shall be in the hands of the party whose forces are to be regrouped there in virtue of the present Agreement.

(*b*) Any territory controlled by one party which is transferred to the other party by the regrouping plan shall continue to be administered by the former party until such date as all the troops who are to be transferred have completely left that territory so as to free the zone assigned to the party in question. From then on, such territory shall be regarded as transferred to the other party, who shall assume responsibility for it.

Steps shall be taken to ensure that there is no break in the transfer of responsibilities. For this purpose, adequate notice shall be given by the withdrawing party to the other party, which shall make the necessary arrangements, in particular by sending administrative and police detachments to prepare for the assumption of administrative responsibility. . . . The transfer shall be effected in successive stages for the various territorial sectors.

The transfer of the civil administration of Hanoi and Haiphong to the authorities of the Democratic Republic of Vietnam shall be completed within the respective time-limits laid down in Article 15 for military movements.

(*c*) Each party undertakes to refrain from any reprisals or discrimination against persons or organizations on account of their activities during the hostilities and to guarantee their democratic liberties.

(*d*) From the date of entry into force of the present Agreement until the movement of troops is completed, any civilians residing in a district controlled by one party who wish to go and live in the zone assigned to the other party shall be permitted and helped to do so by the authorities in that district.

.   .   .

Article 16

With effect from the date of entry into force of the present Agreement, the introduction into Vietnam of any troop reinforcements and additional military personnel is prohibited.

.   .   .

Article 17

(*a*) With effect from the date of entry into force of the present Agreement, the introduction into Vietnam of any reinforcements in the form of all types of arms, munitions and other war material, such as combat aircraft, naval craft, pieces of ordnance, jet engines and jet weapons, and armored vehicles, is prohibited. . . .

.   .   .

Article 18

With effect from the date of entry into force of the present Agreement, the establishment of new military bases is prohibited throughout Vietnam territory.

Article 19

With effect from the date of entry into force of the present Agreement, no military base under the control of a foreign State may be established in the regrouping zone of either party; the two parties shall ensure that the zones assigned to them do not adhere to any military alliance and are not used for the resumption of hostilities or to further an aggressive policy.

.   .   .

Article 34

An International Commission shall be set up for the control and supervision over the application of the provisions of the agreement on the cessation of hostilities in Vietnam. It shall be composed of representatives of the following States: Canada, India, and Poland.

It shall be presided over by the Representative of India.

Article 35

The International Commission shall set up Fixed and Mobile Inspection Teams, composed of an equal number of officers appointed by each of the above-mentioned States. The Fixed Teams shall be located at the following points: Laokay, Langson, Tien-Yen, Haiphong, Vinh, Dong-Hoi, Muong-Sen, Tourane, Quinhon, Nhatrang, Bangoi, Saigon, Cap St. Jacques, Tanchau. These points of location may, at a later date, be altered at the request of the Joint Commission, or of one of the parties, or of the International Commission itself, by agreement between the International Commission and the command of the party concerned. The zones of action of the Mobile Teams shall be the regions bordering the land and sea frontiers of Vietnam, the demarcation lines between the regrouping zones and the demilitarized zones. Within the limits of these zones they shall have the right to move freely and shall receive from the local civil and military authorities all facilities they may require for the fulfillment of their tasks (provision of personnel, placing at their disposal documents needed for supervision, summoning witnesses necessary for holding inquiries, ensuring the security and freedom of movement of the Inspection Teams, etc.) . . . They shall have at their disposal such modern means of transport, observation, and communication as they may require. Beyond the zones of action as defined above, the Mobile Teams may, by agreement with the command of the party concerned, carry out other movements within the limits of the tasks given them by the present agreement.

Article 36

The International Commission shall be responsible for supervising the proper execution by the parties of the provisions of the agreement. For this purpose it shall fulfill the tasks of control, observation, inspection, and investigation connected with the application of the provisions of the agreement on the cessation of hostilities, and it shall in particular:

(*a*) Control the movement of the armed forces of the two parties, effected within the framework of the regroupment plan.

(*b*) Supervise the demarcation lines between the regrouping areas, and also demilitarized zones.

(*c*) Control the operations of releasing prisoners of war and civilian internees.

(*d*) Supervise at ports and airfields as well as along all frontiers of Vietnam the execution of the provisions of the agreement on the cessation of hostilities, regulating the introduction in the country of armed forces, military personnel and of all kinds of arms, munitions, and war material.

Article 37

The International Commission shall, through the medium of the Inspection Teams mentioned above, and as soon as possible either on its own initiative, or at the request of the Joint Commission, or of one of the parties, undertake the necessary investigations both documentary and on the ground.

Article 38

The Inspection Teams shall submit to the International Commission the results of their supervision, their investigation, and their observations; furthermore, they shall draw up such special reports as they may consider necessary or as may be requested from them by the Commission. In the case of a disagreement within the teams, the conclusions of each member shall be submitted to the Commission.

Article 39

If any one Inspection Team is unable to settle an incident or considers that there is a violation or a threat of a serious violation the International Commission shall be informed; the latter shall study the reports and the conclusions of the Inspection Teams and shall inform the parties of the measures which should be taken for the settlement of the incident, ending of the violation, or removal of the threat of violation.

Article 40

When the Joint Commission is unable to reach an agreement on the interpretation to be given to some provision or on the appraisal of a fact, the International Commission shall be informed of the disputed question. Its recommendations shall be sent directly to the parties and shall be notified to the Joint Commission.

Article 41

The recommendations of the International Commission shall be adopted by majority vote, subject to the provisions contained in Article 42. If the votes are divided the chairman's vote shall be decisive.

Article 42

The International Commission may formulate recommendations concerning amendments and additions which should be made to the provisions of the Agreement on the cessation of hostilities in Vietnam, in order to ensure a more effective execution of that Agreement. These recommendations shall be adopted unanimously.

Article 43

When dealing with questions concerning violations, or threats of violations, which might lead to a resumption of hostilities, namely:

(a) Refusal by the armed forces of one party to effect the movements provided for in the regroupment plan;

(b) Violation by the armed forces of one of the parties of the regrouping zones, territorial waters, or air space of the other party;
the decisions of the International Commission must be unanimous.

Article 44

If one of the parties refuses to put into effect a recommendation of
the International Commission, the parties concerned or the Commission
itself shall inform the members of the Geneva Conference.

If the International Commission does not reach unanimity in the
cases provided for in Article 42, it shall submit a majority report and
one or more minority reports to the members of the Conference.

The International Commission shall inform the members of the
Conference in all cases where its activity is being hindered.

•   •   •

Done in Geneva at 2400 hours on the 20th of July, 1954, in French
and in Vietnamese, both texts being equally authentic.

For the Commander-in-Chief of the French Union Forces in Indochina:
[Henri] DELTIEL,
Brigadier-General.

For the Commander-in-Chief of the People's Army of Vietnam:
TA QUANG BUU,
Vice-Minister of National Defense
of the Democratic Republic of Vietnam.

Final Declaration of the Geneva Conference (July 21, 1954)

1. The Conference takes note of the agreements ending hostilities in
Cambodia, Laos, and Vietnam and organizing international control and
the supervision of the execution of the provisions of these agreements.

2. The Conference expresses satisfaction at the ending of hostilities
in Cambodia, Laos, and Vietnam; the Conference expresses its conviction that the execution of the provisions set out in the present declaration and in the agreements on the cessation of hostilities will permit
Cambodia, Laos, and Vietnam henceforth to play their part, in full
independence and sovereignty, in the peaceful community of nations.

3. The Conference takes note of the declarations made by the Governments of Cambodia and of Laos of their intention to adopt measures
permitting all citizens to take their place in the national community,
in particular by participating in the next general elections, which, in
conformity with the constitution of each of these countries, shall take

place in the course of the year 1955, by secret ballot and in conditions of respect for fundamental freedoms.

4. The Conference takes note of the clauses in the agreement on the cessation of hostilities in Vietnam prohibiting the introduction into Vietnam of foreign troops and military personnel as well as of all kinds of arms and munitions. The Conference also takes note of the declarations made by the Governments of Cambodia and Laos of their resolution not to request foreign aid, whether in war material, in personnel, or in instructors except for the purpose of the effective defense of their territory and, in the case of Laos, to the extent defined by the agreements on the cessation of hostilities in Laos.

5. The Conference takes note of the clauses in the agreement on the cessation of hostilities in Vietnam to the effect that no military base under the control of a foreign State may be established in the regrouping zones of the two parties, the latter having the obligation to see that the zones allotted to them shall not constitute part of any military alliance and shall not be utilized for the resumption of hostilities or in the service of an aggressive policy. The Conference also takes note of the declarations of the Governments of Cambodia and Laos to the effect that they will not join in any agreement with other States if this agreement includes the obligation to participate in a military alliance not in conformity with the principles of the Charter of the United Nations or, in the case of Laos, with the principles of the agreement on the cessation of hostilities in Laos or, so long as their security is not threatened, the obligation to establish bases on Cambodian or Laotian territory for the military forces of foreign powers.

6. The Conference recognizes that the essential purpose of the agreement relating to Vietnam is to settle military questions with a view to ending hostilities and that the military demarcation line is provisional and should not in any way be interpreted as constituting a political or territorial boundary. The Conference expresses its conviction that the execution of the provisions set out in the present declaration and in the agreement on the cessation of hostilities creates the necessary basis for the achievement in the near future of a political settlement in Vietnam.

7. The Conference declares that, so far as Vietnam is concerned, the settlement of political problems, affected on the basis of respect for the principles of independence, unity, and territorial integrity, shall permit the Vietnamese people to enjoy the fundamental freedoms, guaranteed by democratic institutions established as a result of free general elections by secret ballot. In order to ensure that sufficient progress in the restoration of peace has been made, and that all the necessary conditions obtain for free expression of the national will, general elections shall be held

in July, 1956, under the supervision of an international commission composed of representatives of the Member States of the International Supervisory Commission, referred to in the agreement on the cessation of hostilities. Consultations will be held on this subject between the competent representative authorities of the two zones from July 20, 1955, onward.

8. The provisions of the agreements on the cessation of hostilities intended to ensure the protection of individuals and of property must be most strictly applied and must, in particular, allow everyone in Vietnam to decide freely in which zone he wishes to live.

9. The competent representative authorities of the North and South zones of Vietnam, as well as the authorities of Laos and Cambodia, must not permit any individual or collective reprisals against persons who have collaborated in any way with one of the parties during the war, or against members of such persons' families.

10. The Conference takes note of the declaration of the Government of the French Republic to the effect that it is ready to withdraw its troops from the territory of Cambodia, Laos, and Vietnam, at the request of the Governments concerned and within periods which shall be fixed by agreement between the parties except in the cases where, by agreement between the two parties, a certain number of French troops shall remain at specified points and for a specified time.

11. The Conference takes note of the declaration of the French Government to the effect that for the settlement of all the problems connected with the re-establishment and consolidation of peace in Cambodia, Laos, and Vietnam, the French Government will proceed from the principle of respect for the independence and sovereignty, unity and territorial integrity of Cambodia, Laos, and Vietnam.

12. In their relations with Cambodia, Laos, and Vietnam, each member of the Geneva Conference undertakes to respect the sovereignty, the independence, the unity, and the territorial integrity of the above-mentioned States, and to refrain from any interference in their internal affairs.

13. The members of the Conference agree to consult one another on any question which may be referred to them by the International Supervisory Commission, in order to study such measures as may prove necessary to ensure that the agreements on the cessation of hostilities in Cambodia, Laos, and Vietnam are respected.

The Close of the Geneva Conference (July 21, 1954)

The Chairman (Mr. Eden): As I think my colleagues are aware, agreement has now been reached on certain documents. It is proposed that this Conference should take note of these agreements. I accordingly propose to begin by reading out a list of the subjects covered by the documents, which I understand every delegation has in front of them.

First, agreement on the cessation of hostilities in Vietnam; second, agreement on the cessation of hostilities in Laos; third, agreement on the cessation of hostilities in Cambodia. I would draw particular attention to the fact that these three agreements now incorporate the texts which were negotiated separately concerning the supervision of the Armistice in the three countries by the International Commission and the joint committees.

I should also like to draw the attention of all delegations to a point of some importance in connexion with the Armistice Agreements and the related maps and documents on supervision. It has been agreed among the parties to each of these Agreements that none of them shall be made public for the present, pending further agreement among the parties. The reason for this, I must explain to my colleagues, is that these Armistice terms come into force at different dates. And it is desired that they should not be made public until they have come into force.

The further documents to which I must draw attention, which are in your possession, are: fourth, declaration by the Government of Laos on elections; fifth, declaration by the Government of Cambodia on elections and integration of all citizens into the national community; sixth, declaration by the Government of Laos on the military status of the country; seventh, declaration by the Government of Cambodia on the military status of the country; eighth, declaration by the Government of the French Republic on the withdrawal of troops from the three countries of Indochina.

Finally, gentlemen, there is the Draft Declaration by the Conference, which takes note of all these documents. I think all my colleagues have copies of this Draft Declaration before them. I will ask my colleagues in turn to express themselves upon this Declaration.

M. Mendés-France (France): Mr. Chairman, the French Delegation approves the terms of this Declaration.

Mr. Phoui Sananikone (Laos): The Delegation of Laos has no observations to make on the text.

Mr. Chou En-lai (People's Republic of China): We agree.

The Chairman: On behalf of Her Majesty's Government in the United Kingdom, I associate myself with the final Declaration of this Conference.

M. Molotov (U.S.S.R.): The Soviet Delegation agrees.

Mr. Tep Phan (Cambodia): The Delegation of Cambodia wishes to state that, among the documents just listed, one is missing. This is a Cambodian Declaration which we have already circulated to all delegations. Its purport is as follows: Paragraphs 7, 11 and 12 of the final

Declaration stipulate respect for the territorial integrity of Vietnam. The Cambodian Delegation asks the Conference to consider that this provision does not imply the abandonment of such legitimate rights and interests as Cambodia might assert with regard to certain regions of South Vietnam. . . .

In support of this Declaration, the Cambodian Delegation communicates to all members of this Conference a note on Cambodian lands in South Vietnam.

The Chairman: If this Declaration was not inscribed on the agenda on the list of documents I have read out, it is because it has only at this instant reached me. I do not think it is any part of the task of this Conference to deal with any past controversies in respect of the frontiers between Cambodia and Vietnam.

Mr. Pham Van Dong (Democratic Republic of Vietnam): Mr. Chairman, I agree completely with the words pronounced by you. In the name of the Government of the Democratic Republic of Vietnam we make the most express reservations regarding the statement made by the Delegation of Cambodia just now. I do this in the interests of good relations and understanding between our two countries.

The Chairman: I think the Conference can take note of the statements of the Delegation of Cambodia just circulated and the statement of the Representative of the Democratic Republic of Vietnam.

I will continue calling upon countries to speak on the subject of the Declaration. I call upon the United States of America.

Mr. Bedell Smith (United States): Mr. Chairman, Fellow Delegates, as I stated to my colleagues during our meeting on July 18, my Government is not prepared to join in a Declaration by the Conference such as is submitted. However, the United States makes this unilateral declaration of its position in these matters:

The Government of the United States being resolved to devote its efforts to the strengthening of peace in accordance with the principles and purposes of the United Nations

Takes Note of the Agreements concluded at Geneva on July 20 and 21, 1954, between (*a*) the Franco-Laotian Command and the Command of the People's Army of Vietnam; (*b*) the Royal Khmer Army Command and the Command of the People's Army of Vietnam; (*c*) the Franco-Vietnamese Command and the Command of the People's Army of Vietnam, and of paragraphs 1 to 12 of the Declaration presented to the Geneva Conference on July 21, 1954.

The Government of the United States of America

Declares with regard to the aforesaid Agreements and paragraphs that (i) it will refrain from the threat or the use of force to disturb them, in accordance with Article 2 (Section 4) of the Charter of the United Nations dealing with the obligation of Members to refrain in their international relations from the threat or use of force; and (ii) it would view any renewal of the aggression in violation of the aforesaid Agreements with grave concern and as seriously threatening international peace and security.

In connexion with the statement in the Declaration concerning free elections in Vietnam, my Government wishes to make clear its position which it has expressed in a Declaration made in Washington on June 29, 1954, as follows:

"In the case of nations now divided against their will, we shall continue to seek to achieve unity through free elections, supervised by the United Nations to ensure that they are conducted fairly."

With respect to the statement made by the Representative of the State of Vietnam, the United States reiterates its traditional position that peoples are entitled to determine their own future and that it will not join in an arrangement which would hinder this. Nothing in its declaration just made is intended to or does indicate any departure from this traditional position.

We share the hope that the agreement will permit Cambodia, Laos and Vietnam to play their part in full independence and sovereignty, in the peaceful community of nations, and will enable the peoples of that area to determine their own future.

The Chairman: The Conference will, I think, wish to take note of the statement of the Representative of the United States of America.

•   •   •

We Are Determined to Fight*

National Liberation Front

For more than ten years now, the U.S. imperialists have continuously interfered in, and committed aggression against, South Vietnam. Of late, they have brought into South Vietnam many more units of U.S. combat troops composed of missile units, marines, B-57 strategic bombers, together with mercenary troops from South Korea, Taiwan, the Philippines, Australia, Malaya, etc. They even frenziedly ordered the air forces of the U. S. A. and its henchmen to conduct repeated air raids on North Vietnam and Laos. At present, not only are they stubbornly stepping up their criminal aggressive war in South Vietnam but are also attempting to fan up the flames of war throughout Indochina and Southeast Asia.

The puppet administration, hangers-on of the U. S. A., in South Vietnam is daily committing more heinous crimes against the country. The impudent traitors are kowtowing before the aggressors and are bringing in snakes to kill chickens of the home coop, inviting troops of the United States and many of its satellite countries to come to South Vietnam to massacre our people, occupy and trample upon the territory of our sacred fatherland, and oppress and exploit our people most harshly.

The Vietnamese people and the people throughout Indochina and Southeast Asia and peace- and justice-loving people all over the world

*Statement of the Central Committee of the South Vietnam National Liberation Front (March 22, 1965), in *Vietnam Courier: Information and Documents* [Hanoi], no. 23 (April 3, 1965). See also Marvin Gettleman, ed., *Viet Nam* (New York: Fawcett, 1965).

are highly indignant at, and strongly protest against, the criminal war-mongering and aggressive acts of the U.S. imperialists.

Faced with the present situation of utmost gravity, the South Vietnam National Front for Liberation deems it necessary to reaffirm once again in a formal way its unswerving will to carry out the war of resistance against the U.S. imperialists.

    1—The U.S. imperialists are the saboteurs of the Geneva Agreements, the most brazen warmongers and aggressors and the sworn enemy of the Vietnamese people.

As is known to everyone, in their extremely glorious war of resistance the Vietnamese people defeated the aggression of the French colonialists and the intervention and assistance of the U.S. imperialists. In fact, during the past war of resistance of the Vietnamese people the U.S. imperialists supplied to the French colonialists 2,600 million dollars, hundreds of thousands of tons of weapons, and 200 military advisers to frustrate the aspiration for independence and freedom of the Vietnamese people. However, with their undauntedness and their determination to die rather than be enslaved, their courage and their staunch resolve to fight, and due to the wholehearted support of the people throughout the world, the heroic Vietnamese people won great victories, liberated half of their beloved country from the clutches of the enemy, which led to the conclusion of an international agreement in Geneva in 1954 formally recognizing the sovereignty, independence, and territorial integrity of Vietnam, Laos, and Cambodia, restoring peace in this area, and laying the basis for the reunification of Vietnam by peaceful means.

The Vietnamese people are deeply aware of the value of these Agreements. Now as in the past they have been correctly implementing these Agreements and are resolved to have these Agreements implemented in their spirit and letters as all international agreements with full legal validity should be. On the contrary, the U.S. imperialists and their henchmen in South Vietnam have step by step and daily more brazenly trampled on the Geneva Agreements and have in fact scrapped them. They have brazenly conducted an atrocious war of aggression in South Vietnam during the past eleven years in an attempt to enslave and oppress the South Vietnamese people, turn South Vietnam into one of their colonies and military bases, and perpetuate the division of Vietnam.

Hardly had the ink dried on the Geneva Agreements when the U.S. imperialists hastily dragged their henchmen satellites into setting up the SEATO military bloc and brazenly placed South Vietnam in the "protection" area of this bloc, which amounted in reality to putting South Vietnam under the command of the United States. Ever since, the

U. S. A. has undertaken deeper and more and more cynical intervention in South Vietnam.

From the end of 1954 to 1959 the U.S. imperialists and the puppet Ngo Dinh Diem Administration carried out repeated barbarous terrorist raids and operations. . . . In order to step up their large-scale and barbarous raids, the U.S. imperialists and their henchmen enacted the fascist law 10/59, outlawing the South Vietnamese people and all other political groupings and individuals who opposed them and whom they termed, "Communists". At the same time, they dragged the guillotine all over South Vietnam. In this period, according to incomplete figures, the U.S. hangmen and their henchmen massacred or detained hundreds of thousands of patriots in South Vietnam for the only reason that they struggled for peace and demanded the execution of the Geneva Agreements, demanded the consultative conference on general elections to reunify the country, or simply because they refused to submit to them.

The criminal acts of the U.S. imperialists and their henchmen naturally stirred up the flames of hatred throughout Vietnam and roused a seething indignation throughout the world. Public opinion in Vietnam and Asia and the honest public opinion all over the five continents severely condemned the tyrannical acts of the U.S. imperialists and their henchmen and raised its voice to demand that they stop their warlike and aggressive activities against the South Vietnamese people and correctly implement the 1954 Geneva Agreements.

During the past eleven years, by carrying out a policy of aggressive colonialism in South Vietnam, the U.S. government has poured 4,000 million dollars disguised under the signboard of "aid", more than 80 percent of which has been direct military expenditures.

The aggressive war in South Vietnam has enjoyed the special concern of the U.S. ruling circles. The late U.S. President Kennedy and the present U.S. President Johnson, the U.S. National Security Council, the Defense Department, State Department, and the Central Intelligence Agency have daily been following all developments in South Vietnam. Honolulu has become the site for regular monthly meetings of the ringleaders of the White House, Pentagon, and the U.S. generals in the Pacific area to discuss plans of invading South Vietnam. . . .

To cover up their piratical nature, the U.S. imperialists have resorted to deceitful signboards which nevertheless cannot fool the world's peoples. It is necessary to recall that the so-called "White Paper" recently issued by Washington carries no conviction at all. This clumsy thief-crying-stop-thief trick has thrown more light on their intention to intensify and expand their aggressive war. At present, the fact in South Vietnam is that the U.S. imperialists are waging a criminal aggressive war, that the U.S. imperialists are the most impudent saboteurs of the Geneva Agreements, the most dangerous war provocateurs and aggressors, and the sworn enemy [sic] of the peoples of Vietnam, Indochina, and of the other peoples of the world.

> 2—The heroic South Vietnamese people are resolved to drive out the U.S. imperialists in order to liberate South Vietnam, achieve an independent, democratic, peaceful, and neutral South Vietnam and eventual national reunification.

The South Vietnamese people have always cherished peace, but are determined not to sit with folded arms and let the U.S. aggressors and their henchmen do what they like and let them trample upon their homeland and ride on them. They had rather die than be enslaved. The fourteen million valiant South Vietnamese people have stood up as one man in a gallant struggle to defeat the U.S. aggressors and their traitors so as to liberate South Vietnam, achieve independence, democracy, peace, and neutrality in South Vietnam, in contribution to the maintenance of peace in Indochina and Southeast Asia.

The patriotic war of the South Vietnamese people is fully consistent with the most elementary and basic principles of international law concerning the people's rights to self-determination and to wage a patriotic and self-defense war against foreign aggression.

In their sacred liberation war, the South Vietnamese people have used all kinds of weapons to fight against the enemy. The chief and biggest arms supplier for the South Vietnamese people's armed forces is nobody else than the U.S. imperialists themselves who have sustained heavy and repeated setbacks over the past years.

From scratch the South Vietnamese people have built a great fortune and recorded extremely glorious military exploits. They are firmly convinced that thanks to their own strength and the wholehearted support of the peoples throughout the world, they will certainly win complete victory. The U.S. imperialists and their lackeys are at the end of their tether. They are being swept off by the powerful storm of the South Vietnamese people's revolution and they still are only writhing in the throes of death. To retrieve that serious situation, the U.S. imperialists are blindly taking the risk of embarking headlong on extremely dangerous military adventures.

The fact that the U.S. imperialists have dispatched to South Vietnam more weapons and combat troops . . . is no indication of their strength, but only of the frenzied behavior of a truculent enemy who has gone out of his senses. It can intimidate nobody. . . .

The South Vietnamese people want to tell the U.S. imperialists and their agents this:

*At present, the only way for you, U.S. imperialists, is to pull out of
South Vietnam. If you stubbornly continue plunging headlong into the
war you will sustain the biggest and most shameful failures. On behalf
of the fourteen million valiant South Vietnamese people, the South Vietnam National Front for Liberation solemnly declares: The South Vietnamese people and their armed forces are resolved never to lose hold of
their arms so long as they have not reached these goals of theirs: independence, democracy, peace, and neutrality. The South Vietnamese
people are determined to go on dealing thunder blows at the U.S. aggressors and their lackeys, and they will surely win final victory.* All negotiations with the U.S. imperialists at this moment are entirely useless if they
still refuse to withdraw from South Vietnam all their troops and all kinds
of war materials and means and those of their satellites, if they still do
not dismantle all their military bases in South Vietnam, if the traitors still
surrender the South Vietnamese people's sacred rights to independence
and democracy to the U.S. imperialists, and if the South Vietnam National Front for Liberation — the only genuine representative of the
fourteen million South Vietnamese people — does not have its decisive
say.

   3—The valiant South Vietnamese people and the South Vietnam
    liberation army are resolved to fully accomplish their sacred
    duty to drive out the U.S. imperialists so as to liberate South
    Vietnam and defend North Vietnam.

  Vietnam is one, the Vietnamese people are one. North and South
Vietnam are of the same family. This sentiment is higher than mountains
and deeper than the sea. This truth is like the sun rising in the East and
cannot be shaken by any force whatsoever. In the present state of blood
and fire, in a life-and-death struggle against the U.S. imperialists and
their lackeys, the heart cannot but feel a pain when the hand is cut. That
the people in North Vietnam are resolved to fulfill their duty toward their
kith and kin in South Vietnam is just sense and reason.

  On behalf of the fourteen million South Vietnamese people, the South
Vietnam National Front for Liberation conveys to their seventeen million
relatives in the North their steel-like confidence and unchanging pledge:
"The heroic South Vietnamese people and the South Vietnam liberation
army are determined to fully accomplish their sacred duty to drive out
the U.S. imperialists, liberate South Vietnam, and defend the North, with
a view to the reunification of their fatherland."

  Recently, to escape from their critical situation and their inevitable
collapse in South Vietnam, the U. S. imperialists and their flunkeys reck-
lessly sent aircraft and warships to bomb, strafe, and shell North Vietnam, but they have received due punishment. Over fifty American jet

planes have been shot down. The South Vietnam army and people greatly rejoice at, and warmly hail, those brilliant feats of arms of the North Vietnam army and people.

The heart feels a pain when the hand is cut! To defend the beloved North, the army and people of the South have given vent to their anger at the U. S. aggressors and their agents. If the U.S. imperialists lay hands upon the North of our fatherland once, the army and people of the South are resolved to strike twice or thrice as hard at them.

In February, while the aggressors and traitors attacked the North, in the South the liberation army launched stormy attacks on important enemy military bases and main forces, putting out of action 20,706 enemy troops (among them nearly 600 U.S. aggressors killed, wounded, and captured), seizing 4,144 guns of various kinds, and shooting down, damaging, or destroying 111 aircraft of various types.

The South Vietnam National Front for Liberation warns the U. S. imperialists and the Vietnamese traitors: As you have not been able to vanquish the fourteen million people of South Vietnam, give up all hope of defeating the more than thirty million people of Vietnam. Your military adventure and war expansion definitely cannot help you out of your quagmire, and instead will lead you quickly to a sort of suicide. . . .

The South Vietnam National Front for Liberation and the South Vietnamese people warn the U. S. imperialists and their lackeys: Should you dare expand the aggressive war to the whole of Vietnam and fan up the flames of war in the whole of Indochina, the invincible strength of the more than thirty million people of Vietnam and the strength to move mountains and drain up seas of the hundreds of millions of people in Indo-china and Asia will wipe you out and bury you.

    4—The South Vietnamese people express their profound gratitude to the wholehearted support of the peace-and-justice-loving people all over the world and declare their readiness to receive all assistance, including weapons and all other war materials from their friends in the five continents.

The just and patriotic struggle of the South Vietnamese people has enjoyed the sympathy, support, and encouragement of the peace-and-justice-loving people throughout the world. Not only have the world peoples supported the South Vietnamese people morally, but have also assisted and are assisting them materially. Of course the South Vietnamese people and their representative — the South Vietnam National Front for Liberation — are fully entitled to accept, and greatly appreciate, such valuable assistance.

The South Vietnam National Front for Liberation has always relied mainly on its own strength and capacity, but it is ready to accept all assistance both moral and material including weapons and all other war materials from all the Socialist countries, the Nationalist countries, as well as all the international organizations, and peace-loving people the world over. Besides, the Front reserves for itself the right to buy weapons and war materials from other countries to strengthen the potential of its self-defense war. . . .

The South Vietnam National Front for Liberation will [also] call on the peoples of various countries to send young men and army men to South Vietnam to fight shoulder-to-shoulder with the South Vietnamese people and together annihilate the common enemy.

While the U. S. imperialists are constantly sowing suffering and death in South Vietnam, the South Vietnam National Front for Liberation, if need be, cannot but call back the sons and daughters of South Vietnam who regrouped to the North in observance of the cease-fire agreement and who have had to live far from South Vietnam during ten long years, to take arms to annihilate the enemy to save their country and homes.

A Vietnamese proverb says: "To peel the thick skin of a mandarin there must be a sharp fingernail." The invincible fingernail of the Vietnamese people and the peace-loving people all over the world decidedly will not leave the U. S. imperialists and their lackeys unpunished. They will have to bear all the extremely serious consequences arising from their aggressive and warlike actions.

Once again, on behalf of the fourteen million people of South Vietnam, the Central Committee of the South Vietnam National Front for Liberation expresses deep gratitude to the peoples of the Socialist countries, the Nationalist countries, the international organizations, and the peace-and-justice-loving people throughout the world who have wholeheartedly supported the just, patriotic war of resistance of the South Vietnamese people. More than ever we consider it our glorious internationalist duty to devote all our energy and make every sacrifice to contribute a worthy share to the very great common cause of struggle of all nations to defend independence, democracy, peace, and social progress in Indochina, Southeast Asia, and all over the world and to defeat the international gendarme — the warlike and aggressive U. S. imperialists.

> 5—The whole people to unite, the whole people to take up arms, to continue to march forward heroically, and to resolve to fight and to defeat the U.S. aggressors and Vietnamese traitors.

The armed struggle waged by the South Vietnamese people against the U. S. aggressors and their henchmen has won very great victories. The U. S. imperialists and their lackeys are formidable in appearance but are inwardly very weak and very confused and more isolated than ever. The South Vietnamese people, bearing in mind their vow "rather to die than to be enslaved," will definitely smash the barbarous and predatory enemy.

The South Vietnam National Front for Liberation and the South Vietnamese people not only have justice on their side but have also developed and are developing rapidly their material and organizational strength. They have been and are the glorious victors. The more they fight the stronger they become and the more numerous and greater their victories.

We are worthy successors to, and have upheld to a high degree, the Dienbienphu tradition and the heroic tradition of the Vietnamese nation credited with 4,000 years of history against the invaders. Moreover, the South Vietnam National Front for Liberation and the South Vietnamese people are fighting heroically in the extremely favorable conditions of the present era, that of the revolutionary rising tide of the oppressed nations in Asia, Africa, and Latin America. The Socialist countries and the forces of democracy and peace all over the world are an important factor stimulating the advance of mankind, overwhelming and annihilating imperialism and colonialism of all brands. If the U. S. imperialists and their henchmen are rash enough to spread the flames of war all over Indochina, the people of this area and Southeast Asia are resolved to stand up as one man and sweep them out into the ocean.

The South Vietnamese people and their only genuine representative — the South Vietnam National Front for Liberation — will undoubtedly win final victory. . . .

Even if we are to carry out the struggle for ten, twenty years or longer and have to suffer greater difficulties and hardships, we are prepared and resolved to fight and fight to the end until not a single U. S. soldier can be seen in our country.

The Vietnamese people's history is thousands of years old. That is the heroic history of a heroic nation. During the past ten years of fighting against the U. S. imperialist aggressors and their quislings, the people and liberation armed forces of South Vietnam have written a golden page in the glorious history of their people. We have won and we are winning; the U. S. imperialists and their agents have lost and are losing. This proves that our strength is invincible, that the U. S. aggressors and their agents are weak. If we have triumphed over the U. S. during the past ten years, we are now provided with far more favorable conditions to defeat them. If the U. S. aggressors and their lackeys have been defeated during the past ten years, they are now all the weaker and will suffer heavier defeats. Especially if the U. S. imperialists extend the war to the North, they will certainly incur more shameful defeats.

We are absolutely confident that victory belongs to us. We are determined to fight, hit vigorously and accurately at the U. S. aggressors and their quislings to liberate the South, defend the North, and reunify our fatherland.

Answering Aggression in Viet-Nam*

Lyndon B. Johnson

This evening I came here to speak to you about Viet-Nam.

I do not have to tell you that our people are profoundly concerned about this struggle.

There are passionate convictions about the wisest course for our nation to follow. There are many sincere and patriotic Americans who harbor doubts about sustaining the commitment that three Presidents and half a million of our young men have made.

Doubt and debate are enlarged because the problems of Viet-Nam are quite complex. They are a mixture of political turmoil — of poverty — of religious and factional strife — of ancient servitude and modern longing for freedom. Viet-Nam is all of these things.

Viet-Nam is also the scene of a powerful aggression that is spurred by an appetite for conquest.

It is the arena where Communist expansionism is most aggressively at work in the world today — where it is crossing international frontiers in violation of international agreements; where it is killing and kidnaping; where it is ruthlessly attempting to bend free people to its will.

Into this mixture of subversion and war, of terror and hope, America has entered — with its material power and with its moral commitment.

Why?

Why should three Presidents and the elected representatives of our people have chosen to defend this Asian nation more than 10,000 miles from American shores?

---

*Address made before the National Legislative Conference at San Antonio, Tex., on Sept. 29, 1967 (White House press release).

We cherish freedom — yes. We cherish self-determination for all people — yes. We abhor the political murder of any state by another and the bodily murder of any people by gangsters of whatever ideology. And for 27 years — since the days of lend-lease — we have sought to strengthen free people against domination by aggressive foreign powers.

But the key to all we have done is really our own security. At times of crisis, before asking Americans to fight and die to resist aggression in a foreign land, every American President has finally had to answer this question:

Is the aggression a threat not only to the immediate victim but to the United States of America and to the peace and security of the entire world of which we in America are a very vital part?

That is the question which Dwight Eisenhower and John Kennedy and Lyndon Johnson had to answer in facing the issue in Viet-Nam.

That is the question that the Senate of the United States answered by a vote of 82 to 1 when it ratified and approved the SEATO treaty in 1955, and to which the members of the United States Congress responded in a resolution that it passed in 1964 by a vote of 504 to 2:

> . . . the United States is, therefore, prepared, as the President determines, to take all necessary steps, including the use of armed force, to assist any member or protocol state of the Southeast Asia Collective Defense Treaty requesting assistance in defense of its freedom.

Those who tell us now that we should abandon our commitment, that securing South Viet-Nam from armed domination is not worth the price we are paying, must also answer this question. And the test they must meet is this: What would be the consequence of letting armed aggression against South Viet-Nam succeed? What would follow in the time ahead? What kind of world are they prepared to live in 5 months or 5 years from tonight?

For those who have borne the responsibility for decision during these past 10 years, the stakes to us have seemed clear — and have seemed high.

President Dwight Eisenhower said in 1959:

> Strategically South Viet-Nam's capture by the Communists would bring their power several hundred miles into a hitherto free region. The remaining countries in Southeast Asia would be menaced by a great flanking movement. The freedom of 12 million people would be lost immediately and that of 150 million in adjacent lands would be seriously endangered. The loss of South Viet-Nam would set in motion a crumbling process that could, as it progressed, have grave consequences for us and for freedom.

And President John F. Kennedy said in 1962:

> . . . withdrawal in the case of Viet-Nam and in the case of Thailand
> might mean a collapse of the entire area.

A year later, he reaffirmed that:

> We are not going to withdraw from that effort. In my opinion, for us
> to withdraw from that effort would mean a collapse not only of South
> Viet-Nam, but Southeast Asia. So we are going to stay there.

Views of Asian Leaders

This is not simply an American viewpoint, I would have you legislative
leaders know. I am going to call the roll now of those who live in that
part of the world — in the great arc of Asian and Pacific nations —
and who bear the responsibility for leading their people and the responsibility for the fate of their people.

The President of the Philippines had this to say:

> Viet-Nam is the focus of attention now. . . . It may happen to Thailand
> or the Philippines, or anywhere, wherever there is misery, disease,
> ignorance. . . . for you to renounce your position of leadership in
> Asia is to allow the Red Chinese to gobble up all of Asia.

The Foreign Minister of Thailand said:

> (The American) decision will go down in history as the move that
> prevented the world from having to face another conflagration.

The Prime Minister of Australia said:

> We are there because while Communist aggression persists the whole
> of Southeast Asia is threatened.

President Park of Korea said:

> For the first time in our history, we decided to dispatch our combat
> troops overseas . . . because in our belief any aggression against the
> Republic of Viet-Nam represented a direct and grave menace against
> the security and peace of free Asia, and therefore directly jeopardized
> the very security and freedom of our own people.

The Prime Minister of Malaysia warned his people that if the United
States pulled out of South Viet-Nam, it would go to the Communists,
and after that, it would only be a matter of time until they moved against
neighboring states.

The Prime Minister of New Zealand said:

We can thank God that America at least regards aggression in Asia with the same concern as it regards aggression in Europe—and is prepared to back up its concern with action.

The Prime Minister of Singapore said:

I feel the fate of Asia—South and Southeast Asia—will be decided in the next few years by what happens out in Viet-Nam.

I cannot tell you tonight as your President — with certainty — that a Communist conquest of South Viet-Nam would be followed by a Communist conquest of Southeast Asia. But I do know there are North Vietnamese troops in Laos. I do know that there are North Vietnamese-trained guerrillas tonight in northeast Thailand. I do know that there are Communist-supported guerrilla forces operating in Burma. And a communist coup was barely averted in Indonesia, the fifth largest nation in the world.

So your American President cannot tell you — with certainty — that a Southeast Asia dominated by Communist power would bring a third world war much closer to terrible reality. One could hope that this would not be so.

But all that we have learned in this tragic century strongly suggests to me that it would be so. As President of the United States, I am not prepared to gamble on the chance that it is not so. I am not prepared to risk the security — indeed, the survival — of this American Nation on mere hope and wishful thinking. I am convinced that by seeing this struggle through now we are greatly reducing the chances of a much larger war — perhaps a nuclear war. I would rather stand in Viet-Nam in our time, and by meeting this danger now and facing up to it, thereby reduce the danger for our children and for our grandchildren.

I want to turn now to the struggle in Viet-Nam itself.

There are questions about this difficult war that must trouble every really thoughtful person. I am going to put some of these questions. And I am going to give you the very best answers that I can give you.

Progress of the Struggle in Viet-Nam

First, are the Vietnamese, with our help and that of their other allies, really making any progress? Is there a forward movement? The reports I see make it clear that there is. Certainly there is a positive movement toward Constitutional government. Thus far the Vietnamese have met the political schedule that they laid down in January 1966.

The people wanted an elected, responsive government. They wanted it strongly enough to brave a vicious campaign of Communist terror and assassination to vote for it. It has been said that they killed more civilians in 4 weeks trying to keep them from voting before the election than our American bombers have killed in the big cities of North Viet-Nam in bombing military targets.

On November 1, subject to the action, of course, of the constituent assembly, an elected government will be inaugurated and an elected Senate and Legislature will be installed. Their responsibility is clear: to answer the desires of the South Vietnamese people for self-determination and for peace, for an attack on corruption, for economic development, and for social justice.

There is progress in the war itself, steady progress considering the war that we are fighting; rather dramatic progress considering the situation that actually prevailed when we sent our troops there in 1965, when we intervened to prevent the dismemberment of the country by the Viet Cong and the North Vietnamese.

The campaigns of the last year drove the enemy from many of their major interior bases. The military victory almost within Hanoi's grasp in 1965 has now been denied them. The grip of the Viet Cong on the people is being broken.

Since our commitment of major forces in July 1965 the proportion of the population living under Communist control has been reduced to well under 20 percent. Tonight the secure proportion of the population has grown from about 45 percent to 65 percent — and in the contested areas, the tide continues to run with us.

But the struggle remains hard. The South Vietnamese have suffered severely, as have we — particularly in the First Corps area in the north, where the enemy has mounted his heaviest attacks and where his lines of communication to North Viet-Nam are shortest. Our casualties in the war have reached about 13,500 killed in action and about 85,000 wounded. Of those 85,000 wounded, we thank God that 79,000 of the 85,000 have been returned or will return to duty shortly, thanks to our great American medical science and the helicopter.

U.S. Ready To Negotiate

I know there are other questions on your minds and on the minds of many sincere, troubled Americans: "Why not negotiate now?" so many ask me. The answer is that we and our South Vietnamese allies are wholly prepared to negotiate tonight.

I am ready to talk with Ho Chi Minh, and other chiefs of state concerned, tomorrow.

I am ready to have Secretary Rusk meet with their Foreign Minister tomorrow.

I am ready to send a trusted representative of America to any spot on this earth to talk in public or private with a spokesman of Hanoi.

We have twice sought to have the issue of Viet-Nam dealt with by the United Nations — and twice Hanoi has refused.

Our desire to negotiate peace — through the United Nations or out — has been made very, very clear to Hanoi — directly and many times through third parties.

As we have told Hanoi time and time and time again, the heart of the matter really is this: The United States is willing to stop all aerial and naval bombardment of North Viet-Nam when this will lead promptly to productive discussions. We, of course, assume that while discussions proceed, North Viet-Nam would not take advantage of the bombing cessation or limitation.

But Hanoi has not accepted any of these proposals.

So it is by Hanoi's choice, and not ours and not the rest of the world's that the war continues.

Why, in the face of military and political progress in the South, and the burden of our bombing in the North, do they insist and persist with the war?

From many sources the answer is the same. They still hope that the people of the United States will not see this struggle through to the very end. As one Western diplomat reported to me only this week — he had just been in Hanoi — "They believe their staying power is greater than ours and that they can't lose." A visitor from a Communist capital had this to say: "They expect the war to be long, and that the Americans in the end will be defeated by a breakdown in morale, fatigue, and psychological factors." The Premier of North Viet-Nam said as far back as 1962: "Americans do not like long, inconclusive war . . . Thus we are sure to win in the end."

Are the North Vietnamese right about us?

I think not. No. I think they are wrong. I think it is the common failing of totalitarian regimes, that they cannot really understand the nature of our democracy:

— They mistake dissent for disloyalty;
— They mistake restlessness for a rejection of policy;
— They mistake a few committees for a country;
— They misjudge individual speeches for public policy.

They are no better suited to judge the strength and perseverance of America than the Nazi and the Stalinist propagandists were able to judge it. It is a tragedy that they must discover these qualities in the American people, and discover them through a bloody war.

And, soon or late, they will discover them.

In the meantime, it shall be our policy to continue to seek negotiations, confident that reason will some day prevail, that Hanoi will realize that it just can never win, that it will turn away from fighting and start building for its own people.

The True Peacekeepers

Since World War II, this nation has met and has mastered many challenges — challenges in Greece and Turkey, in Berlin, in Korea, in Cuba.

We met them because brave men were willing to risk their lives for their nation's security. And braver men have never lived than those who carry our colors in Viet-Nam at this very hour.

The price of these efforts, of course, has been heavy. But the price of not having made them at all, not having seen them through, in my judgment would have been vastly greater.

Our goal has been the same: in Europe, in Asia, in our own hemisphere. It has been — and it is now — peace.

And peace cannot be secured by wishes; peace cannot be preserved by noble words and pure intentions. Enduring peace — Franklin D. Roosevelt said — cannot be bought at the cost of other people's freedom.

The late President Kennedy put it precisely in November 1961 when he said:

> . . . we are neither "warmongers" nor "appeasers," neither "hard" nor "soft." We are Americans, determined to defend the frontiers of freedom by an honorable peace if peace is possible, but by arms if arms are used against us.

The true peacekeepers in the world tonight are not those who urge us to retire from the field in Viet-Nam, who tell us to try to find the quickest, cheapest exit from that tormented land, no matter what the consequences to us may be.

The true peacekeepers are those men who stand out there on the DMZ at this very hour taking the worst that the enemy can give. The true peacekeepers are the soldiers who are breaking the terrorist's grip around the villages of Viet-Nam, the civilians who are bringing medical care and food and education to people who have already suffered a generation of war.

And so I report to you that we are going to continue to press forward. Two things we must do. Two things we shall do.

First, we must not mislead our enemy. Let him not think that debate and dissent will produce wavering and withdrawal. For I can assure you they won't. Let him not think that protests will produce surrender. Because they won't. Let him not think that he will wait us out. For he won't.

Second, we will provide all that our brave men require to do the job that must be done. And that job is going to be done.

These gallant men have our prayers — have our thanks — have our heartfelt praise — and our deepest gratitude.

Let the world know that the keepers of peace will endure through every trial — and that with the full backing of their countrymen, they are going to prevail.

The Tonkin Gulf Resolution*

Congress of the United States

Joint Resolution

To promote the maintenance of international peace and security in southeast Asia.

Whereas naval units of the Communist regime in Vietnam, in violation of the principles of the Charter of the United Nations and of international law, have deliberately and repeatedly attacked United States naval vessels lawfully present in international waters, and have thereby created a serious threat to international peace; and

Whereas these attacks are part of a deliberate and systematic campaign of aggression that the Communist regime in North Vietnam has been waging against its neighbors and the nations joined with them in the collective defense of their freedom; and

Whereas the United States is assisting the peoples of southeast Asia to protect their freedom and has no territorial, military or political ambition in that area, but desires only that these peoples should be left in peace to work out their own destinies in their own way: Now, therefore, be it

Resolved by the Senate and House of Representatives of the United States of America in Congress assembled, That the Congress approves and supports the determination of the President, as Commander in Chief, to take all necessary measures to repel any armed attack against the forces of the United States and to prevent further aggression.

---

*Joint Resolution of U.S. Senate and House of Representatives, 88th Congress, August 10, 1964.

SEC. 2. The United States regards as vital to its national interest and to world peace the maintenance of international peace and security in southeast Asia. Consonant with the Constitution of the United States and the Charter of the United Nations and in accordance with its obligations under the Southeast Asia Collective Defense Treaty, the United States is, therefore, prepared, as the President determines, to take all necessary steps, including the use of armed force, to assist any member or protocol state of the Southeast Asia Collective Defense Treaty requesting assistance in defense of its freedom.

SEC. 3. This resolution shall expire when the President shall determine that the peace and security of the area is reasonably assured by international conditions created by action of the United Nations or otherwise, except that it may be terminated earlier by concurrent resolution of the Congress.

Approved August 10, 1964.

Testimony Before the Senate Foreign Relations Committee*

Dean Rusk
with commentary by Senators
J. William Fulbright and Frank Church

Senator Fulbright: Mr. Secretary, I need not tell you many of us are deeply troubled about our involvement in Vietnam and it seems to us that since this is the first bill this session dealing with the subject now is an appropriate opportunity for some examination of our involvement there for the clarification of the people of this country. I know you have had long experience out there. Could you tell us briefly, when did we first become involved in Vietnam?

Secretary Rusk: I think the first involvement was the assistance that we provided to France during the period of the Marshall plan at a time when France was faced there with the Vietminh movement, a very large part of which was nationalist but which also had within it a very strong Communist increment.

Fulbright: What year was that?

Rusk: That began in 1949-50. At that time, the attitude of the United States was that it would provide assistance to France in the expectation that France would move promptly to make its own agreement with the nationalist elements in Indochina, and make it clear that the Associated States of Indochina, which later became Vietnam, or the two Vietnams, Laos, and Cambodia, would, in effect, be independent.

The political movement by the French Government of that day was slower than the United States had hoped for, and the military operations came to the conclusion of the Geneva Conference of 1954.

· · ·

---

*Excerpts from Senate Foreign Relations Committee, *Hearings,* January 28, 1966.

Fulbright: Was France at that time trying to reassert her colonial domination of Vietnam? Was that her objective at that time?

Rusk: I think, just at the conclusion of the war, in that part of the world, the first step that was taken was the restoration of the status quo ante bellum in the broadest sense in India, Burma, Malaysia, Indochina, Indonesia, and indeed in part in the Philippines, although the Philippines moved almost immediately to independence.

• • •

Fulbright: I confess I was scarcely conscious about problems of any significance there until the last few years because our attention was directed largely to Europe. But I am puzzled about what moved our Government to assist France to retain her control of Vietnam in contrast to our actions in Indonesia, for example.

Rusk: The problem there, sir, was—I am trying my best to remember something which happened quite a few years ago—the problem was not at all that of assisting France in establishing and reinforcing a colonial position. Rather it was to give France a chance to work out its political settlement with these states on the basis of their own independence, and without giving to the Communists a basic position in Southeast Asia.

After the Communists took over authority in Peiping, we and the British and the French were consulted on this situation and pretty well agreed that the security of Southeast Asia was of vital interest to the free world. The joint effort therefore to find an agreement with the nationalists on the one side and to prevent a Communist takeover on the other was a common thread of policy throughout that period.

• • •

Fulbright: You stated in your original statement that we have a very clear commitment. What is the origin and basis for a clear commitment for the action we are now taking in Vietnam?

Rusk: We have the Southeast Asia Treaty, to which South Vietnam was a protocol state . . .

Fulbright: What does that commit us to in that regard? This is where there is a good deal of confusion in my mind and I think in the public mind about the nature of that commitment. Does the Southeast Asia Treaty commit us to do what we are now doing in Vietnam?

Rusk: Yes, sir; I have no doubt that it does. A protocol state has a right to call on the members of the organization for assistance. The obligations of that treaty are both joint and several. That is they are

both collective and individual. So that there seems to be no doubt that
we are entitled to offer that assistance. But the underlying legal basi
for the assistance is the right of individual and collective self-defense
against an aggressor. There is clearly an aggression from the North
here which has been persistent and since 1950 has been sharply increased

Fulbright: You say we are entitled to do this. Are we obligated to
do this under the treaty?

Rusk: I would not want to get into the question of whether, if we
were not interested in the commitments, policy and principle under the
Southeast Asia Treaty, we have some legal way in order to avoid those
commitments. I suppose that one could frame some agrument which
would make that case.

But it would seem to us that the policy, which was discussed and
passed upon by the Executive and the Senate of that day, is that we
are opposed to aggression against these countries in Southeast Asia
both the members of the Organization and the protocol states.

In addition to that, we have bilateral assistance agreements to South
Vietnam. We have had several actions of the Congress. We have had
the annual aid appropriations in which the purposes of the aid have
been fully set out before the Congress. We have had special resolutions
such as the one of August 1964, and we have had the most important
policy declarations by successive Presidents with respect to the protection of South Vietnam against Communist aggression.

Fulbright: This question arose in your *Meet the Press* appearance last
Sunday night, particularly with regard to a question by the British correspondent. I think he suggested that it would be easier for all . . . to
understand this operation if it was put on the basis of straight out
containing communism rather than . . . protecting their right to self-
determination. What would you comment on that?

Rusk: Well, the particular correspondent invited me to subscribe to
the doctrine of Pax Americana.

Fulbright: Why?

Rusk: That is not our policy. We do not have the world-wide commitments to all 117 countries with whom we have relations. We have
some 42 allies, very specific commitments to those allies. Now, it is true
that, in the appropriate way in the United Nations and elsewhere, we
would presumably give sympathy and support to those who are victims
of the kind of aggression which would have worldwide implications.
But we are not putting ourselves in the position of the gendarmes of
the universe. There has been a good deal of fighting within this postwar
period in which we did not participate. We are not trying to impose a

Pax Americana on the world. We are trying to create a situation in which, in accordance with the charter, all notions, large and small, can live unmolested by their neighbors and have a chance to work out their own decisions in their own way. We support that policy in different ways at different times and under different circumstances. In the case of our specific allies and those with whom we have specific commitments, if they are subject to an attack from those who declare a policy of aggression as a systematic course in the world, we have on a number of occasions joined with them to meet those attacks.

Fulbright: How do you foresee the end of this struggle? Do you think we are likely to be there, 5, 10, or 20 years? What do you foresee as the outcome of this—even if we are successful in the military activities?

Rusk: Well, I would hate to try to cast myself in the role of a specific prophet in the development of this particular situation.

Fulbright: Can you define our objective in terms of what we seek to achieve?

Rusk: To put it in its simplest terms, we believe that the South Vietnamese are entitled to a chance to make their own decisions about their own affairs and their own future course of policy: that they are entitled to make these decisions without having them imposed on them by force from North Vietnam or elsewhere from the outside. We are perfectly prepared to rely upon the South Vietnamese themselves to make that judgment by elections, through their own Government, by whatever way is suitable for them to make that decision.

* * *

Senator Clark: Mr. Secretary, you know I have become progressively more in disagreement with your and the Administration's policy in Vietnam as the war there continues to accelerate. I regret that very much. I think you know my very high personal regard and respect and, indeed, affection for you, and it makes me very unhappy that we are not in accord.

President Kennedy in a CBS television interview on September 2, 1963, said, "In the final analysis it is their war. They are the ones who have to win it or lose it. We can help them, we can give them equipment, we can send our men out there as advisers but they have to win it, the people of Vietnam against the Communists."

Why have we turned this into what is becoming more and more every day an American war? In your opinion, is this essential to the security of the United States?

Rusk: Senator, I welcome this question because I think that there is a substantial misunderstanding about what is happening in South Vietnam on this very point.

The fact that we have larger numbers of U.S. combat forces there causes our own press to concentrate very heavily on the activities of our forces. The truth is that the South Vietnamese continue to carry the great bulk of the struggle there. On any given day there might be say, 2, 3, or 4 U.S. battalions in operation, say 1 Korean battalion, but 15 to 20 South Vietnamese battalions. The hundreds of incidents that occur every week and are maintained at a high level have their major impact upon the South Vietnamese. The 550,000 South Vietnamese forces are taking the heaviest casualties.

They are the ones who are out over the countryside every day in large numbers, and in not only substantial numbers of large unit actions but hundreds of small unit actions around the country, looking for the guerrillas, trying to find them, and trying to deal with them. So, although the U.S. effort has increased, the great bulk of the effort continues to be South Vietnamese.

That would not apply to the air, where we have a predominant role. The South Vietnamese Air Force is active but we have much the larger share of the air effort.

Clark: And yet 2 years ago I have been informed we had a total of 10,000 Americans in Vietnam, 1 year ago there were only 30,000, today there are 200,000. If Senator Stennis is correct the Administration is going to build that force up to around 600,000. At what point does it become our war and not their war?

Rusk: Well, sir, I have seen various figures used. Most of them are not the figures that I know about or have been discussing in our own consultations. I really would prefer not to speculate on the problem of figures this morning, Senator.

•   •   •

Senator Fulbright: Mr. Secretary, as you know, I have been in the Congress quite a long time, and I do not recall any issue since I have been here where there has been so much apprehension concerning a military involvement. This is a reason why some public discussion of our policies at this time is appropriate.

I have seen in the press that our approval of these very large requests, not only the one now before this committee but the one that will come before the Senate in the military field, will be interpreted as a vote of approval of the overall policy. I think there is a great doubt about whether or not we are on the right track, and these doubts need to be cleared up.

You said there had been great discussion in depth about Vietnam. I would submit, in all honesty, that the discussion has been rather superficial. We had a relatively small commitment even as late as the time of the Bay of Tonkin affair. I personally did not feel at that time that we had undertaken a course of action that could well lead to a world war.

I certainly was rather taken aback by the statement in the morning paper by Senator Stennis who, as you know, is chairman of the Preparedness Subcommittee, and has the most intimate relations with the Joint Chiefs of Staff, in which he speaks quite firmly about the possible use of nuclear weapons on Chinese "coolies," which is not a very complimentary term, as you know.

I would consider that the situation has changed a lot, and that we are now engaged in a very serious undertaking.

I believe that one of the reasons for this concern and apprehension is a feeling on the part of some people—including very reputable scholars and others—that we inadvertently, perhaps, for irrelevant reasons, stepped into a colonial war in 1950 on the wrong side. Whether or not we did is one of the questions at issue. It seems to me that something is wrong or there would not be such great dissent, evidenced by teach-ins, articles, and speeches by various responsible people. I do not regard all of the people who have raised these questions as irresponsible.

I think it is the duty of this committee, the Administration, and others to try to clarify the nature of our involvement there, what it is likely to lead to, and whether or not the ultimate objective justifies the enormous sacrifice in lives and treasure.

I think, in all honesty, that is why there is such interest in this matter. It is very difficult to deal with. I have never encountered such a complex situation. It is not clear cut, like Korea or like the Second World War.

You state very positively this is aggression by the other side. But this is not quite as convincing under the circumstances as it was in North Korea, for example. There was definite overt aggression in Korea. It is not comparable to the bombing of Pearl Harbor. There was no doubt in those situations. I do not know of anyone who said then, "Well, that is not an engagement for an all-out commitment." Vietnam is subtle. Perhaps, as you say, this situation is different. But it needs to be understood if we are to approve of it in the sense of voting these very large sums. If we pursue this policy, and resume the bombing, then we are committed, and will have passed the Rubicon. I think that is what justifies some discussion of this.

I do not like to delay you from your work and to keep you here, but I think I am expressing not only my own feelings, but the feelings of some of my colleagues, and some of my constituents. So all I am trying to do is to clarify some questions about our policies.

I suspect sometimes that there has been a change in policy from that which we disavowed after the Spanish-American War. You deny that there is a Pax Americana, but the fact is we have troops in Europe, Korea, Vietnam, and the Dominican Republic. We have military missions in half the nations of the world, probably more. I don't know what this means. It has all come about gradually and in connection with an aid program.

The aid program has been one element in this. I have supported it all these years, but I am having very grave reservations about whether that was wise. I am perfectly willing, if I so conclude, to admit at the proper time that I made a mistake. Perhaps it is impossible for a great nation to do that, too. I do not know. But I think there have been many cases of where great nations have drawn back from commitments which they came to believe were wrong.

I am not ready to say at the moment that I am positive that our policies in Vietnam have been wrong, but I am anxious to have greater enlightenment about just what we are about and what our ultimate objective is.

This is why I asked in the beginning if you could formulate for me more clearly just what our objective is. That is why I referred to the question of the British newsman. He tried to simplify it by saying, "Well, now, let's put aside all this talk about democracy in South Vietnam. You know that is unrealistic. There are no institutions of democracy there and never have been. This is an ancient kingdom and with no established institutions. Put that line aside, and say what you are doing is"—you do not like that word, I do not either—"imperialism." That what we are doing is saving the free world from Communist encroachment, and we are going to do it everywhere.

This policy was expressed rather clearly during the time of the Truman doctrine, and we followed it in some other instances.

Is this still a commitment that in the future wherever there is a possibility or probability of an expansion of a Communist state that we are going to meet it and stop it? Is that a correct way to describe our policy? All I am asking for is clarification of what our objective is in this struggle.

Rusk: Well, Senator, let me comment, if I may, on the broader aspect of your very thoughtful statement. When I said we are not embarked upon a Pax Americana, I was thinking specifically of the fact that our obligations run to 42 allies. Those are allies because of action taken by the executive branch and the Senate in combination.

All of those are allies under treaties ratified by the Senate by an overwhelming vote. In the case of Southeast Asia I think there were—what?—one or two votes in the Senate against that treaty. There was no reservation on that treaty that, of course, this does not apply if things get tough.

We do have the specific commitments which we, as a nation—

Fulbright: In the Southeast Asia Treaty, it seems to me, as I read it, the obligation is to consult with our allies in the case of these nonovert aggressions. We have no unilateral obligation to do what we are doing.

Now, you say we are entitled to do it. That is different from saying we have an obligation under this SEATO Treaty. I mean, we are entitled, I suppose, as a great power to do nearly anything we want to. We are entitled to move in the Dominican Republic, because we have the power to do it. I did not believe you had any treaty obligation to do it, but I do not want to quibble about that.

But in this case, do you maintain that we had an obligation under the Southeast Asia Treaty to come to the assistance, all-out assistance, of South Vietnam? Is that very clear?

Rusk: It seems clear to me, sir, that this was an obligation—

Fulbright: Unilateral.

Rusk: An obligation of policy. It is rooted in the policy of the treaty. I am not now saying if we had decided we would not lift a finger about Southeast Asia that we could be sued in a court and be convicted of breaking a treaty. This is not the point I want to talk about.

Fulbright: Mrs. Neuberger brought up a question that typifies quite well some of the things that puzzle us. She said the day before yesterday in a speech that, "President Johnson and his advisers made it quite clear that in their judgment the Vietnam war is a clear and documented case of aggression by North Vietnam against South Vietnam. This policy recognizes the de facto existence of two independent sovereign nations, the capitals of which are Hanoi and Saigon. The President also said in his state of the Union message that we 'stand by the Geneva agreements of 1954.' The public is aware of very little of the detail of that historic agreement, but one feature they are likely to remember. The 17th parallel was provisional and was 'not in any way to be interpreted as constituting a political or territorial boundary.' On the basis of it the United States is saying both that it stands on the principle that there is no political or territorial boundary separating North and South Vietnam and that we must stand and fight in South Vietnam because that nation has been attacked by its aggressor neighbor of the north. When Americans scratch their heads over this logic they are not excusing Communist aggression nor saying that the United States ought not be in Vietnam. It is simply a puzzle over why our stated reason for being there and our stated terms for withdrawing seem to cancel out each other."

This is the type of puzzlement that afflicts us poor laymen who are not in all of the real secrets of diplomacy. It does puzzle me.

Rusk: Well, Senator, as to the divided states, there were original agreements in the cases of Germany, Korea, and Vietnam anticipating the unification of those states.

Fulbright: What agreements are you referring to?

Rusk: I think the 1954 agreement anticipated the prospect of a unification of North and South Vietnam.

Senator Gore: I will read you point 4, Mr. Secretary. This is the final declaration of Geneva Conference, July 21 1954, point 6: "The Conference recognizes that the essential purpose of the agreement relating to Vietnam is to settle military questions with a view to ending hostilities and that the military demarcation line is provisional and should not in any way be interpreted as constituting a political or territorial boundary."

Rusk: That is correct. Now, in the case of Germany and Korea, as well as Vietnam, those were divided by demarcation lines, and in the background were agreements anticipating the unification of those divided countries.

In the process, time and development of events, however, East Germany has been recognized by some countries, West Germany by the overwhelming majority; North Korea has been recognized by some, South Korea by the overwhelming majority; the same with the two Vietnams.

Now, the problem is whether those issues that exist in these divided countries are to be settled by force or are to be settled by peaceful means. We believe they should be settled by peaceful means.

If there are differences and difficulties they can be brought to the conference table and talked about. But if efforts are made in any of these three divided countries to settle the question of unification by force, then I think we are in a very, very grave and dangerous situation throughout the world.

Senator Church: If this is the philosophy underlying our policy, Mr. Secretary, I should have thought that it would have been difficult to have ever fought a Civil War in this country had the same doctrine applied a century ago.

At that time, I suppose the southerners felt there had been an invasion of the South from the North, and had England, which favored the South, adhered to the same principle that now seems to govern American policy, and had sent troops in the name of self-determination into the

Confederacy, I think the English Government would have been hard put to convince Abraham Lincoln that there should be an election to determine the ultimate outcome of the war.

I mean, I think—without in any way suggesting that our Civil War was an exact parallel—I think these concepts upon which we rest our policy are subject to very serious question. Now, you can look at the war in Vietnam as a covert invasion of the South by the North, or you can look at it as some scholars do, as basically an indigenous war to which the North has given a growing measure of aid and abetment, but either way it is a war between Vietnamese to determine what the ultimate kind of government is going to be for Vietnam.

When I went to school that was a civil war. I am told these days it is not a civil war any more.

Rusk: Well, Senator, I do not follow that point at all because, whatever you call it, there is aggression from North Vietnam against South Vietnam across that demarcation line contrary to the military clauses of that 1954 commitment.

Church: Have all the provisions of the 1954 agreement been adhered to by either side?

Rusk: No; they have not.

Church: Were the elections which were called for and generally anticipated at the time the agreement was made, were they held?

Rusk: Neither in North or South Vietnam.

Church: Right. So it cannot be said that violations of the agreement have been all one sided, and certainly our case does not rest upon that kind of reasoning.

Rusk: That is correct. The case, the basic fact, is that large numbers of armed men and large quantities of arms have been sent illegally from North Vietnam into South Vietnam to try to take over South Vietnam by force.

Senator Fulbright: May I ask why in 1956, contrary to the terms of the Geneva accord, elections were not held? You have stated several times that the aggression started in 1960. But the events between 1954 when the agreement was signed and 1960 were not without significance.

We backed Diem, did we not? Didn't we have much to do with putting him in power?

Rusk: Well, we supported him.

Fulbright: And he was, to an extent had, a certain dependence upon us, did he not?

Rusk: We were giving him very considerable aid, Mr. Chairman.

Fulbright: I am informed that in 1955, in accordance with the treaty provisions, he was requested by the North to consult about elections, and that he refused to do so. Is that correct?

Rusk: Well, neither his Government nor the Government of the United States signed that agreement.

Fulbright: We will come to that as a separate point. But it is correct that he refused to consult with the North on election procedure, is it not?

Rusk: I think that is correct, sir.

Fulbright: Now we will come to your point of our not signing. Why, in your opinion, didn't we sign the agreement? There were nine parties there, and seven signed it. We refused. Why didn't we sign it?

Rusk: I have tried to find in the record a full discussion of that subject. Quite frankly, I have not been able to. I think, my general impression is, that the United States was at that time not persuaded that this was the best way to settle this affair, and did not want to be responsible for all the elements of the agreement. They did say that they would acknowledge it (and I believe you might want to put in the record here, Mr. Bedell Smith's exact words on it) and would consider any attempt to upset it by force as a threat to the peace.

[*The statement by Under Secretary of State Bedell Smith made at the closing session of the Geneva Conference, July 21, 1954, was then inserted in the record.*]

· · ·

Fulbright: Not having signed it, what business was it of ours, for intervening and encouraging one of the participants not to follow it, specifically Diem?

Rusk: Well, the prospect of free elections in North and South Vietnam was very poor at that time.

· · ·

Senator Church: From what you have said this morning, it seems to me that you draw no significant distinction between the kind of threat we faced in Korea and the kind of guerrilla war situation that now confronts us in Vietnam. In either case you have indicated that this is Communist aggression. In the former case it is overt, in the latter case overt, but nonetheless the kind of Communist aggression that requires us to intervene with large American forces to draw the line, so to speak, in Asia as we drew it in earlier years in Europe.

Is that a fair statement of your position?

Rusk: With respect to those situations where we have a particular commitment, not as a matter of general philosophy.

But, Senator, let me make a comment on this brief question of predicament. I think one would not understand this situation at all unless

one were to call it for what it is, namely, Ho Chi Minh's war. It is not
McNamara's war; it is not the United States war. It is Ho Chi Minh's
war. Maybe it is Mao Tse-tung's war in terms of the support that he
has given to Ho Chi Minh, and the roadblocks he has thrown against
any possibilities of peace.

• • •

Church: I have never called this war McNamara's war.

Rusk: I understand, and I am not arguing with you, Senator. I just
wanted to make the predicament clear.

Church: If it is Ho Chi Minh's war, is it not true that Ho Chi Minh
was the chief architect in securing Vietnamese independence against
the French?

Rusk: He was the leader of a nationalist movement that had in it
many elements, and many of the elements of that nationalist movement
are now in South Vietnam supporting and trying to build a system in
South Vietnam that is not Communist.

Church: Is it not true that at the time that the war was fought and
the French were driven out, that Ho Chi Minh was generally regarded
as the leader of the revolutionary effort?

Rusk: That is correct, sir.

Church: So if this now is Ho Chi Minh's war, that may be one of the
reasons why so many Vietnamese are willing to die in it.

Rusk: Well, they may—

Church: It seems to me that there is a difference between guerrilla war
or revolution and the kind of aggression that we faced in Korea and in
Europe, and, further, that the underdeveloped world is going to be beset
with guerrilla wars, regardless of the outcome in Vietnam, and that
we will have to live in a world afflicted with such revolutions for a
long time.

That is why it is so important to try to determine what our basic
foreign policy attitude is going to be in dealing with these revolutionary
wars in many parts of the underdeveloped world in the future; and, as
I have listened to your explanations this morning, I gather that wherever
a revolution occurs against an established government, and that revolution, as most will doubtlessly be, is infiltrated by Communists, that the
United States will intervene, if necessary, to prevent a Communist success.

This, at least, has been the policy we followed in the Dominican
Republic and in Vietnam. I wonder whether this is going to continue
to be the policy as we face new guerrilla wars in the future?

Rusk: Senator, I think it is very important that the different kinds
of revolutions be distinguished. We are in no sense committed against

change. As a matter of fact, we are stimulating, ourselves, very sweeping revolutions in a good many places. The whole weight and effort of the Alliance for Progress is to bring about far-reaching social, economic changes.

Church: That is change sought, Mr. Secretary, without violence. History shows that the most significant change has been accompanied by violence. Do you think that with our foreign aid program we are going to be able, with our money, to avert serious uprisings in all of these destitute countries in future years?

Rusk: Not necessarily avert all of them, but I do believe there is a fundamental difference between the kind of revolution which the Communists call their wars of national liberation, and the kind of revolution which is congenial to our own experience, and fits into the aspirations of ordinary men and women right around the world.

There is nothing liberal about that revolution that they are trying to push from Peiping. This is a harsh, totalitarian regime. It has nothing in common with the great American revolutionary tradition, nothing in common with it.

Church: The objectives of Communist revolution are clearly very different indeed from the earlier objectives of our own. But objectives of revolutions have varied through the centuries.

The question that I think faces this country is how we can best cope with the likelihood of revolt in the underdeveloped world in the years ahead, and I have very serious doubts that American military intervention will often be the proper decision. I think too much intervention on our part may well spread communism throughout the ex-colonial world rather than thwart it.

Now, the distinction you draw between the Communist type of guerrilla war and other kinds of revolution, if I have understood it correctly, has been based upon the premise that in Vietnam the North Vietnamese have been meddling in the revolution in the South and, therefore, it is a form of aggression on the part of the North against the South.

But I cannot remember many revolutions that have been fought in splendid isolation. There were as many Frenchmen at Yorktown when Cornwallis surrendered as there were American Continentals.

Senator Pell tells me more. I accept the correction.

In any case, it seems to me that the Communists have not changed the rules of revolution by meddling in them, regardless of how much we disapprove of their goals. When we were an infant nation we stood up for the right of revolution, and I am afraid—

Rusk: Senator, I just cannot—

Church: I am afraid, what I am worried about, Mr. Secretary, is this: That if we intervene too much in wars of this type, our policy may well turn out to be self-defeating.

Rusk: May turn out to be what?

Fulbright: Self-defeating.

10

Money and Public Policy

The budget of the United States provides an overview of the public policies of the national government. In it, programs and policies are measured in dollars. The budget is a financial plan for paying the costs of governmental operations for a year, and its preparation provides an opportunity for appraising programs and making determinations on their scope and direction. It is in the process of budgeting that executive agencies, the President, and the Congress develop their plans and make choices among competing pressures for new or expanded public programs. The budget is also an instrument of national economic planning: expenditures can be raised to stimulate the economy, or they can be cut to dampen inflationary tendencies. Taxes can be cut or raised to achieve the same effects. Finally, the budget is a request for legislative approval of executive planning and policy making. Congress must approve the tax and spending proposals in the budget before they can be carried into effect.

Budgeting is so important to policy making today that it is difficult to realize that government budgeting is a relatively recent phenomenon. National budgeting was established with the passage of the Budget and Accounting Act of 1921. This Act made the President responsible for the preparation and submission to Congress of a budget and created the Bureau of the Budget to assist him in this task.

Budgets are not a dull province of clerks and statisticians. On the contrary, they are political documents to record the struggles of men over "who gets what." The budget is the single most important policy statement of the national government setting forth government policies with price tags attached. There are a few government activities or programs which do not require an expenditure of funds, and no public funds may be spent without a budgetary authorization. Determining what goes into a budget, that is, the budgetary process, provides a mechanism for reviewing government programs, assessing their costs, relating them to financial resources, making choices among alternative programs, and determining the financial effort which government will expend on its programs. The size and shape of the budget is a matter of serious contention in the political life of the nation.

The first step in the preparation of a federal budget is for executive departments and agencies to estimate their needs. Often their estimates are made under a Presidential directive setting forth broad policy objectives of the administration. The budgetary process starts early: the formulation of the 1969 budget began in March, 1967. Ten months later in January, 1968, the budget was sent to Congress — nearly six months before the beginning of the new fiscal year. The fiscal year begins July 1 and ends the following June 30, and is always named for the year in which the budget ends so that the 1969 fiscal year ended on June 30, 1969. Departmental and agency budget requests almost invariably call for increased government spending. Administrators naturally believe that their program is important, that it should be expanded, and that more money would enable them to provide better service. The requests of departments and agencies are sent to the Bureau of the Budget in the Office of the President. Budget examiners from the BOB evaluate these requests with an eye for economy and for congruence with the President's program policies. Hearings are often held to give agency spokesmen a chance to clarify and defend their estimated needs. The Bureau of the Budget often makes severe cutbacks in agencies' requests. At the same time that requests are being evaluated, the Bureau of the Budget also estimates expected government revenues. In the final stages of budget-making, the President and the Bureau of the Budget review consolidated figures on both revenues and expenditures, and prepare a budget message that stresses key aspects of the budget and ties it in with broad national policy. In January, soon after Congress convenes, the President delivers his budget message to Congress and submits his budget to the House of Representatives as an appropriations measure. (See U.S. Bureau of the Budget, *The Federal Budget in Review*)

Not all programs of the government are reevaluated each time the budget is prepared. Often programs and activities which are already established policy are accepted without question. The budget makers' attention is usually focused on points of expansion or contraction, on new or expanded programs, on increases and decreases. Departments are seldom to defend or explain budget requests which do not exceed current appropriations; but requested increases in appropriations require extensive explanation, and they are most subject to downward revision by higher officials. This means that budget-making is "incremental," that is, only increments to a budget over last year's budget are subject to close scrutiny of policy makers.

Originally, the federal budget was built around executive agencies and objects of expenditures, such as "salaries," "travel," "supplies," and "capital expenditures." These accountant's categories failed to reveal how much an agency or department was spending on a particular program. Today the federal government reflects "program budgeting," in which costs are attributed to functions and activities. Knowing the cost of a particular program or policy gives the chief executive and the legislature a better picture of what the government is doing with its money and how much effort is being expended on a particular program.

Responsibility for the enactment of the budget lies with Congress. Congressional action centers in the appropriations committee of each house, and subcommittees of these appropriations committees. The most thorough consideration of the budget is in the house sub-committees of the House Appropriations Committee, and House action on appropriations bills always precedes Senate action. Occasionally, agency heads risk censure by the BOB by testifying in appropriations committee hearings against the budget recommendations of the BOB. To understand Congressional action with respect to expenditures, it is necessary to distinguish between legislation which *authorizes* expenditures and legislation which *appropriates* money for these authorized expenditures. Legislation authorizing expenditures for government programs goes to program committees such as the Armed Services Committee or the Committee on Agriculture. They may authorize program expenditures three to five years in advance. But these authorizations are always dependent upon appropriations, which often fall short of the amount of the authorizations. Appropriations are for one year only and they are considered only by the appropriations committees and sub-committees of both houses. Members of the appropriations committees and sub-committees hold great power over executive agencies and programs, since the full appropriations committee usually accepts without question the decisions of their subcommittees and only infrequently are substantial amendments to the work of the appropriations committees made on the floor of the House or the Senate. Since House action, the Senate committee is sometimes considered an appeal center for agencies who have suffered budget cuts in the House Committee. And inasmuch as appropriations bills, like other bills, must pass both the House and the Senate in identical form, appropriations bills almost always go to conference committees where final decisions on programs and budgets are made.

The greatest part of the federal government's budget is devoted to the cost of past, present and future wars. Expenditures for national defense, international affairs, space research, veterans' benefits, and interest on the national debt (which largely reflects the cost of past wars) make up the largest share of federal expenditures. The federal government's expenditures for domestic programs are quite modest. Actually state and local governments in America spend twice as much as the federal government for domestic programs, that is, education, welfare, health, highways, housing, transportation, natural resources, and so on.

Federal grants-in-aid are money payments made by the federal government to state and local governments for the purpose of carrying out programs of interest to the federal government. Federal grants-in-aid are established by Congress under its power to "tax and spend for the general welfare." We have already described many federal grant programs in education, welfare, housing and urban renewal and so on, but there are more than 200 federal grant-in-aid programs currently in operation which will cover a tremendously wide variety of programs. (See U.S. Bureau of the Budget, *Summary of Federal Grant-in-Aid Programs*) While it is true that states and communities administer these programs, and generally match federal funds from their own fiscal resources, federal grants-in-aid usually involve the federal intervention in policy making through minimum standards and "guidelines." Federal grants-in-aid now make up about 17 per cent of all state and local revenues. The rate of expansion of federal grant-in-aid spending suggests that states and communities are becoming increasingly dependent upon the federal government every year.

Proponents of the present federal grant-in-aid system argue that it does not undermine the role of states and communities in the American federal system, but in fact strengthens federalism. They have referred to a sharing of federal, state and local responsibility in program areas as "creative federalism" and have defended it as a pragmatic approach to many of the nation's most pressing problems. Federal grants-in-aid are defended on at least three grounds: 1) that state and local governments have either ignored or been unable to cope with the problem for which the federal grant-in-aid program is intended; 2) that only federal government has sufficient financial resources to deal effectively with the particular problem involved; and 3) federal grant-in-aid programs help to equalize state and local opportunities to deal with major problems by giving more aid to poorer states. Problems in education, welfare, health, housing, civil rights, and other major domestic areas are said to be national responsibilities which are too large and too complex to be dealt with effectively at the state and local level without federal assistance. It is also argued that the federal government with its progressive individual and corporate income tax is the only level of government in which the financial resources deal effectively with domestic problems.

Opponents of federal aid programs see them as a threat to the American federal system and to the independence of state and local governments. They believe that federal grant-in-aid programs give the federal government undue influence in the policies and programs in states and communities. While it is true that state and local government participation in federal grant programs is voluntary, they believe that states and communities join federal aid programs because they fear to let other states and communities receive federal dollars to which their citizens have already been forced to make contributions. Other critics of federal grant-in-aid programs point to the uncoordinated and bureaucratic character of the more than 200 grant-in-aid programs administered by the government. They charge that the federal government has never set any meaningful priorities among its hundreds of grant programs. The result is that too few dollars chase too many goals. Domestic problems of education, crime, poverty, and slum housing continue to persist and grow despite federal grant programs. Opponents of federal aid programs also argue that the failure of states and communities to deal with some of their problems is a product of the fact that their financial resources have been dried up because of heavy federal taxation. And of course, there are always specific complaints about particular federal standards or guidelines, such as the complaints of southern school systems (and some northern city school systems) about racial integration guidelines from the U.S. Office of Education.

As a result of dissatisfactions over federal grant-in-aid programs, several proposals have been made for a system of unrestricted federal grants to states with no strings attached. These grants might assume the form of block grants to states or communities for broad purposes such as education, health or welfare; but the way in which the money is spent would be determined by the state or community itself. These block grants would avoid the excessively detailed grant-in-aid applications, and would enable each state and community to apply its federal money to its most compelling problems. Unrestricted federal grants might assume the form of revenue sharing, that is, a certain percentage of federal income tax collections turned back to the states and local governments for use as they see fit. These shared revenues would presumably replace earmarked and conditional grants in aid by the federal government. This would give states and communities access to the fiscal resources of the federal government, yet at the same time insure state and local control over the use of these funds. The most significant proposal to date has been made by Walter Heller, former Chairman of the Council of Economic Advisers under President John F. Kennedy. (See Walter Heller, *New Dimensions of Political Economy*) Opposition to block grants and revenue sharing has come from organized labor, racial minorities, and supporters of current grant-in-aid programs, who feel that the national government is more sensitive to their problems than state and local governments.

The Federal Budget in Review*

U. S. Bureau of the Budget

Analysis of Federal Activities by Function

This section of the budget presents the major elements of the program recommended for the Federal Government for fiscal year 1969. It describes, for each of 12 major functions served, trends and developments anticipated in existing programs and new programs the Congress is being asked to enact.

In line with the recommendations of the President's Commission on Budget Concepts, the tables and textual presentation in this part of the budget reflect several basic changes from previous years. There are three major departures from past practice:

- All Federal activities designed to serve a particular purpose are consolidated, with Federal funds and self-financed trust funds combined as appropriate into a comprehensive total.
- In each program, "expenditures" and "net lending" are separately identified.
- Receipts from the public arising from market-oriented or business-type activities of the Government are offset against the expenditures for the function to which they relate — thus highlighting the *net* impact on the budget.

In relative terms, the changes being made in accordance with the Commission's report do not significantly alter the functional *totals* that would

---

*From U.S. Bureau of the Budget, *The Budget of the United States Government: Fiscal Year 1969* (Washington, D.C.: U.S. Government Printing Office, 1968).

have been reported on the "consolidated cash" basis previously used in this part of the budget. However, the size of many of the individual *components* and the form of their presentation differ considerably from former budgets.

Summary

In fiscal year 1969, total budget outlays are estimated at $186.1 billion, including $182.8 billion of expenditures and $3.3 billion of net lending. The total compares with overall outlays of $175.6 billion estimated for fiscal year 1968.

BUDGET OUTLAYS

[Fiscal years. In millions]

Function	1967 actual	1968 estimate	1969 estimate
Expenditures:			
National defense	$70,095	$76,491	$79,792
Excluding special Vietnam	(49,961)	(51,960)	(54,008)
International affairs and finance	4,110	4,330	4,478
Excluding special Vietnam	(3,687)	(3,872)	(3,998)
Space research and technology	5,423	4,803	4,573
Agriculture and agricultural resources	3,156	4,412	4,474
Natural resources	2,113	2,416	2,483
Commerce and transportation	7,308	7,695	7,996
Housing and community development	577	697	1,429
Health, labor, and welfare	39,512	46,396	51,945
Education	3,602	4,157	4,364
Veterans benefits and services	6,366	6,798	7,131
Interest	12,548	13,535	14,400
General government	2,452	2,618	2,827
Allowances:			
Civilian and military pay increase			1,600
Contingencies		100	350
Undistributed intragovernmental payments:			
Government contribution for employee retirement (−)	−1,735	−1,913	−2,007
Interest received by trust funds (−)	−2,287	−2,678	−3,042
Total expenditures	153,238	169,856	182,797
Total expenditures, excluding special Vietnam	(132,681)	(144,867)	(156,533)

BUDGET OUTLAYS Cont.

[Fiscal years. In millions]

Function	1967 actual	1968 estimate	1969 estimate
Net Lending:			
International affairs and finance	$ 540	$ 716	$ 675
Agriculture and agricultural resources	1,221	899	1,135
Housing and community development	1,708	3,257	1,355
All other	1,705	907	99
Total net lending	5,176	5,779	3,265
Total outlays	158,414	175,635	186,062
Total outlays, excluding *special Vietnam*	(137,857)	(150,646)	(159,798)

NATIONAL DEFENSE

[Fiscal years. In millions]

Program or agency	Expenditures and net lending		
	1967 actual	1968 estimate	1969 estimate
Expenditures:			
Department of Defense—military:			
Military personnel:			
Present programs	$19,787	$21,800	$22,770
Proposed legislation			23
Operation and maintenance:			
Present programs	19,000	19,800	22,213
Proposed legislation			47
Procurement	19,012	21,470	23,445
Research, development, test, and evaluation	7,160	7,200	7,800
Military construction	1,536	1,565	1,450
Family housing	482	520	570
Civil defense	100	93	89
Revolving and management funds and other	512	1,402	−1,608
Military trust funds	20	10	7
Subtotal, Department of Defense—military	67,466	73,694	76,658
Subtotal, excluding special Vietnam	(47,333)	(49,163)	(50,874)

NATIONAL DEFENSE Cont.

[Fiscal years. In millions]

	Expenditures and net lending		
Program or agency	1967 actual	1968 estimate	1969 estimate
Expenditures:			
Military assistance:			
Grants and credit sales:			
Present programs	$ 873	$ 550	$ 519
Proposed legislation			6
Trust fund	−8	−25	−70
Atomic energy	2,264	2,333	2,546
Defense-related activities:			
Stockpiling of strategic and critical materials	19	19	23
Expansion of defense production	−102	22	146
Selective Service System	58	61	64
Emergency preparedness activities	11	12	8
Interfund and intragovernmental transactions (−)	(−7)	(−7)	(−7)
Applicable receipts from the public (−)	−487	−178	−108
Subtotal, expenditures	70,095	76,491	79,792
Subtotal, expenditures, excluding special Vietnam	(49,961)	(51,960)	(54,008)
Net Lending	−3	−2	−4
Total	70,092	76,489	79,789
Total, excluding special Vietnam	(49,958)	(51,958)	(54,005)

ESTIMATED EXPENDITURES FOR SPECIAL SUPPORT OF
VIETNAM OPERATIONS

[In millions]

Fiscal year	Defense expenditures, excluding Vietnam	Special Vietnam expenditures		
		Defense	Economic assistance[1]	Total
1965	$46,070	$103		$103
1966	48,597	5,812	$282	6,094
1967	47,333	20,133	424	20,557
1968	49,163	24,531	458	24,989
1969	50,874	25,784	480	26,264

[1] These expenditures are part of the International function.

INTERNATIONAL AFFAIRS AND FINANCE

[Fiscal years. In millions]

Program or agency	Expenditures and net lending		
	1967 actual	1968 estimate	1969 estimate
Expenditures:			
Conduct of foreign affairs:			
Department of State	$321	$337	$355
U.S. Arms Control and Disarmament Agency	10	9	10
Tariff Commission	3	4	4
Foreign Claims Settlement Commission	21	200	1
Department of Justice (trust funds)	2	4	53
Treasury Department (trust funds)	8	5	6
Economic and financial programs:			
Agency for International Development:			
Development loans	662	625	670
Technical cooperation	224	203	216
Alliance for Progress	511	465	516
Supporting assistance	587	602	621
Contingencies and other	334	313	310
Applicable receipts from the public (—)	−51	−63	−69
Subtotal, Agency for International Development	2,268	2,145	2,264
Subtotal, excluding special Vietnam	(1,844)	(1,687)	(1,784)
International financial institutions:			
Present programs	170	223	200
Proposed legislation			10
Export-Import Bank	−104	−144	−110
Peace Corps	112	108	110
Other	20	21	20
Food for freedom	1,452	1,315	1,444
Foreign information and exchange activities:			
United States Information Agency	185	187	194
Department of State and other	59	68	61
Applicable receipts from the public (—)	−417	−153	−144
Subtotal, expenditures	4,110	4,330	4,478
Subtotal, expenditures, excluding special Vietnam	(3,687)	(3,872)	(3,998)
Net Lending: Economic and financial programs:			
Export-Import Bank:			
Present programs	540	716	660

INTERNATIONAL AFFAIRS AND FINANCE Cont.

[Fiscal years. In millions]

Program or agency	Expenditures and net lending		
	1967 actual	1968 estimate	1969 estimate
Proposed legislation			$ 15
Subtotal, net lending	$ 540	$ 716	675
Total	4,650	5,046	5,153
Total, excluding special Vietnam	(4,227)	(4,588)	(4,673)

NATURAL RESOURCES

[Fiscal years. In millions]

Program or agency	Expenditures and net lending		
	1967 actual	1968 estimate	1969 estimate
Expenditures:			
Land and water resources:			
Corps of Engineers	$1,301	$1,341	$1,313
Department of the Interior:			
Bureau of Reclamation	300	291	299
Power marketing agencies	133	147	153
Federal Water Pollution Control Administration	130	190	248
Office of Saline Water	17	31	41
Office of Water Resources Research	6	9	11
Bureau of Indian Affairs	106	113	112
Bureau of Land Management	87	83	76
Tennessee Valley Authority	102	109	150
Soil Conservation Service — watershed projects	108	106	93
International Boundary and Water Commission	27	22	15
Federal Power Commission and other	17	22	25
Subtotal, land and water resources	2,335	2,465	2,536
Forest resources:			
Forest Service	461	495	470
Bureau of Land Management	21	22	22

NATURAL RESOURCES Cont.

[Fiscal years. In millions]

Program or agency	Expenditures and net lending		
	1967 actual	1968 estimate	1969 estimate
Recreational resources:			
Bureau of Outdoor Recreation	$ 68	$ 105	$ 160
National Park Service and other	126	140	148
Fish and wildlife resources	136	153	158
Mineral resources:			
Bureau of Land Management	48	50	50
Bureau of Mines and other	73	83	80
General resource surveys and administration	275	250	239
Interfund and intragovernmental transactions (—)	—22	*	—1
Applicable receipts from the public (—)	—1,410	—1,348	—1,381
Subtotal, expenditures	2,113	2,416	2,483
Net Lending:			
Land and water resources	18	15	6
Other	1	1	1
Subtotal, net lending	19	16	7
Total	2,132	2,432	2,490

*Less than $500 thousand.

AGRICULTURE AND AGRICULTURAL RESOURCES

[Fiscal years. In millions]

Program or agency	Expenditures and net lending		
	1967 actual	1968 estimate	1969 estimate
Expenditures:			
Farm income stabilization:			
Price support and related programs	$1,652	$2,703	$2,775
Conservation reserve, cropland conversion, and cropland adjustment programs	196	211	200

AGRICULTURE AND AGRICULTURAL RESOURCES Cont.

[Fiscal years. In millions]

Program or agency	Expenditures and net lending		
	1967 actual	1968 estimate	1969 estimate
Removal of surplus agricultural commodities	$ 145	$ 175	$ 178
National Wool Act	35	64	63
Sugar Act	82	86	87
Other	157	190	156
Subtotal, farm income stabilization	2,267	3,428	3,459
Financing rural electrification and rural telephones	12	13	13
Agricultural land and water resources:			
Soil Conservation Service — conservation operations	111	115	117
Agricultural conservation program payments (including CCC loans)	216	217	203
Other	26	30	30
Financing farming and rural housing:			
Farm Credit Administration	−21	−48	−64
Farmers Home Administration and other	11	74	96
Research and other agricultural services:			
Present programs	570	623	675
Proposed legislation for inspection fees			−13
Interfund and intragovernmental transactions (−)	−5	−5	−6
Applicable receipts from the public (−)	−32	−34	−36
Subtotal, expenditures	3,156	4,412	4,474
Net Lending:			
Farm income stabilization	262	−29	24
Financing rural electrification and rural telephones	232	279	360
Financing farming and rural housing:			
Farm Credit Administration (trust funds)	671	749	771
Farmers Home Administration and other	56	−100	−20
Subtotal, net lending	1,221	899	1,135
Total	4,377	5,311	5,609

COMMERCE AND TRANSPORTATION

[Fiscal years. In millions]

Program or agency	Expenditures and net lending		
	1967 actual	1968 estimate	1969 estimate
Expenditures:			
Advancement of business:			
Export promotion	$18	$20	$29
Small business assistance	75	60	43
Physical environment	176	168	177
Physical standards	38	31	29
Promotion of technology	54	57	59
Economic and demographic statistics	32	46	48
Federal Deposit Insurance Corporation (trust funds)	−239	−261	−274
Other aids to business	33	39	40
Area and regional development:			
Department of Commerce: Economic development assistance	52	153	186
Appalachia and other	86	159	239
Air transportation:			
Federal Aviation Administration	883	892	1,228
Civil Aeronautics Board subsidies	62	58	54
Water transportation:			
Maritime Administration	302	364	380
Coast Guard	497	486	608
Other	−7	5	12
Ground transportation:			
Highways:			
Present programs	4,041	4,363	4,340
Proposed legislation			51
Other	10	21	28
Postal service	1,141	1,087	767
Regulation of business	101	100	107
Interfund and intragovernmental transactions (−)	−1	−24	−8
Applicable receipts from the public (−)	−47	−132	−149
Subtotal, expenditures	7,308	7,695	7,996
Net Lending:			
Advancement of business: Small business assistance	101	114	67
Area and regional development:			
Department of Commerce: Economic development assistance	29	53	65

COMMERCE AND TRANSPORTATION Cont.

[Fiscal years. In millions]

Program or agency	Expenditures and net lending		
	1967 actual	1968 estimate	1969 estimate
Other	$ 8	$ —8	$ —8
Subtotal, net lending	138	158	125
Total	7,446	7,853	8,121

HOUSING AND COMMUNITY DEVELOPMENT

[Fiscal years. In millions]

Program or agency	Expenditures and net lending		
	1967 actual	1968 estimate	1969 estimate
Expenditures:			
Public housing programs	$251	$297	$350
Aids to private housing:			
Department of Housing and Urban Development:			
Supplements to the private market:			
Rent supplement program	1	4	16
Other	—17	—21	16
Support of the private market: Federal Housing Administration and other	—7	—138	—110
Federal Savings and Loan Insurance Corporation	—201	—384	—378
Urban renewal and community facilities:			
Model Cities	1	25	250
Aids to improved land use:			
Urban renewal	370	499	699
Open space land grants	19	60	60
Urban planning assistance and other	22	31	46
Proposed metropolitan development legislation			3
Assistance for public facilities:			
Urban mass transportation	42	100	150
Basic water and sewer facility grants	6	90	130
Neighborhood facility grants and other	12	22	39
Research and other	32	39	55

HOUSING AND COMMUNITY DEVELOPMENT Cont.
[Fiscal years. In millions]

Program or agency	Expenditures and net lending		
	1967 actual	1968 estimate	1969 estimate
Proposed legislation	$	$	$ 14
National Capital region	66	90	104
Interfund and intragovernmental transactions (—)	—19	—15	—14
Applicable receipts from the public (—)	*	*	*
Subtotal, expenditures	577	697	1,429
Net Lending:			
Public housing programs	14	22	—16
Aids to private housing:			
Department of Housing and Urban Development:			
Supplements to the private market	248	744	456
Support of the private market	1,269	2,440	809
Federal Savings and Loan Insurance Corporation	44	—8	—20
Urban renewal and community facilities	114	42	61
National Capital region	19	16	65
Subtotal, net lending	1,708	3,257	1,355
Total	2,285	3,954	2,784

*Less than $500 thousand.

SPACE RESEARCH AND TECHNOLOGY
[Fiscal years. In millions]

	Expenditures		
	1967 actual	1968 estimate	1969 estimate
Manned space flight:			
Manned lunar landing	$3,587	$3,028	$2,571
Extended manned flight	62	138	422
Space sciences	674	563	498
Space applications	122	135	147
Space technology	440	420	425
Aircraft technology	89	113	120
Supporting activities	452	411	394
Applicable receipts from the public (—)	—2	—4	—3
Total	5,423	4,803	4,573

HEALTH, LABOR, AND WELFARE
[Fiscal years. In millions]

Program or agency	Expenditures and net lending		
	1967 actual	1968 estimate	1969 estimate
Expenditures:			
Health services and research:			
Medical research	$1,014	$1,065	$1,079
Facilities and medical manpower	445	554	577
Organization and delivery of health services	43	111	126
Medicare (trust funds)	3,396	5,064	5,785
Medicaid and other financing	1,366	1,997	2,398
Direct health care	158	177	194
Prevention and control of health problems and other	351	486	521
Labor and manpower:			
Manpower programs	589	802	926
Other	480	524	558
Proposed trade adjustment legislation			8
Economic opportunity programs:			
Work and training programs	737	927	1,003
Community action programs and other	747	926	994
Retirement and social insurance (trust funds):			
Old-age, survivors, and disability insurance	21,725	23,918	27,372
Unemployment insurance	2,189	2,564	2,558
Civil service retirement and disability	1,965	2,121	2,364
Railroad retirement	1,315	1,415	1,490
Other	—77	—72	—78
Public assistance and other welfare:			
Public assistance (excluding medical assistance)	3,041	3,484	3,605
Vocational rehabilitation	261	363	434
School lunch, special milk, food stamp, and other	522	616	710
Proposed food stamp legislation			15
Proposed juvenile delinquency legislation			20
Interfund and intragovernmental transactions (—)	—694	—641	—711
Applicable receipts from the public (—)	—61	—5	—3
Subtotal, expenditures	39,512	46,396	51,945
Net Lending	572	21	—538
Total	40,084	46,417	51,407

GENERAL GOVERNMENT

[Fiscal years. In millions]

Program or agency	Expenditures and net lending		
	1967 actual	1968 estimate	1969 estimate
Expenditures:			
Legislative functions	$167	$185	$198
Judicial functions	87	95	102
Executive direction and management	25	31	35
Central fiscal operations:			
Treasury Department:			
Internal Revenue Service	662	688	760
Other	253	260	280
Other agencies	53	59	63
General property and records management:			
General Services Administration:			
Public Buildings Service:			
Construction, sites, and planning	184	152	106
Operation, maintenance, and other	347	367	379
Other	88	110	164
Central Intelligency Agency building	1	*	
Central personnel management:			
Civil Service Commission:			
Present programs	129	150	153
Proposed legislation			12
Department of Labor and other	61	62	53
Law enforcement and justice:			
Department of Justice:			
Present programs	401	425	458
Proposed legislation		10	39
Other	25	27	32
Other general government:			
Territories and possessions	157	187	198
Treasury — claims	49	8	6
Other	7	8	1
Interfund and intragovernmental transactions (—)	—85	—92	—94
Applicable receipts from the public (—)	—161	—115	—117
Subtotal, expenditures	2,452	2,618	2,827
Net Lending	2	—40	—37
Total	2,454	2,578	2,790

*Less than $500 thousand.

EDUCATION

[Fiscal years. In millions]

Program or agency	Expenditures and net lending		
	1967 actual	1968 estimate	1969 estimate
Expenditures:			
Elementary and secondary education:			
Children from low income families	$1,057	$1,070	$1,073
Other education of the disadvantaged	67	70	109
Special school projects	75	155	169
School books, equipment, counseling, and strengthening State education agencies	213	237	155
Assistance to schools in federally impacted areas	447	372	416
Other (teacher training)		26	9
Higher education:			
Aid for undergraduate and graduate students	421	597	673
Academic facility grants	198	308	213
Other aids to higher education	92	153	179
Proposed legislation			
Science education and basic research:			
National Science Foundation:			
Basic research and specialized research facilities	209	226	230
Grants for institutional science programs	49	72	78
Science education	118	115	120
Other science activities	39	43	52
Other aids to education:			
Training of educational manpower	41	13	57
Vocational education:			
Present program	250	271	247
Proposed legislation			7
Educational research and development	57	76	99
Grants for libraries and community services	57	100	141
Indian education services	112	116	153
Library of Congress and Smithsonian Institution	62	83	98
National Foundation on the Arts and Humanities	10	15	23
Other:			
Present programs	37	55	61

EDUCATION Cont.

[Fiscal years. In millions]

Program or agency	Expenditures and net lending		
	1967 actual	1968 estimate	1969 estimate
Proposed legislation for public broadcasting			20
Applicable receipts from the public (—)	—11	—15	—16
Subtotal, expenditures	3,602	4,157	4,364
Net Lending:			
Elementary and second education	$ —2	$ *	$ 1
Higher education	447	383	334
Subtotal, net lending	445	384	335
Total	4,047	4,541	4,699

*Less than $500 thousand.

Summary of Federal Grant-in-Aid Programs*

U. S. Bureau of the Budget

Growth and Development of Federal Grants

The birth of Federal aid to State and local governments actually predates the Constitution. Under the Articles of Confederation in 1785, Congress provided grants of Federal land to support education in the Northwest Territory. This policy was reaffirmed in the Northwest Ordinance of 1787 — the same year that the historic Convention adopted the Constitution of the United States. Land continued to be the predominant form of Federal aid for a number of years thereafter.

There was a brief, but interesting, interlude in this pattern in 1837. In that year the Federal Government distributed surplus funds totaling more than $28 million among the States on the basis of congressional representation. The funds were technically "deposits," but no repayment was ever demanded. Moreover, no restriction was placed on the use of the money.

Minimum requirements were first introduced in the Federal-aid structure in the Morrill Act of 1862 (which provided land for the support of higher education). These requirements included a definition of objectives, State matching, and a report on the use of funds. The federal system evolved gradually over the ensuing half century.

The early years of the 20th century saw aid extended for agriculture, highways, and limited social welfare programs. However, it was not until the crisis of the thirties that Federal aid reached any significant scale. At

---

*From U.S. Bureau of the Budget, *Special Analysis: Budget of the United States* (Washington, D.C.: U.S. Government Printing Office, 1968).

that time a broad array of welfare, housing, and economic security programs was inaugurated. The post-World War II period witnessed a further expansion of health and housing programs and a significantly augmented highway construction effort.

Not until the 1960's did the Nation experience a comparable expansion of new joint governmental initiatives. Recently, significant steps have been taken to help finance health services and medical care for the indigent, to launch a concerted attack on poverty, to rejuvenate blighted neighborhoods in our cities, to broaden educational opportunities, and to develop economically depressed regions of the Nation.

Factors underlying growth in Federal aids

Increasing population along with rapid urbanization have led to greater demands for the services traditionally provided by State and local governments — such as education, health, community facilities, and transportation. Rapid economic change and rising affluence have given rise to the demand for new and better services, and stimulated programs to safeguard individual economic security. While the major burden for providing such public services rests directly upon the more than 80,000 State and local governmental jurisdictions, the Federal Government also plays a vital role. It provides assistance both by giving direct financial aid to State and local governments and by fostering a sound and growing economy, which concomitantly enlarges State and local tax bases.

Federal-aid programs by function

The foregoing factors, coupled with the changing nature of State and local program needs, have altered substantially the focus of Federal aids at several junctures in the past two decades. These changes can be traced in the accompanying table.

PERCENTAGE DISTRIBUTION OF FEDERAL AIDS TO STATE
AND LOCAL GOVERNMENTS BY FUNCTION

Function	1950 actual	1955 actual	1960 actual	1965 actual	1969 estimate
Agriculture and agricultural resources	5	7	3	5	3
Natural resources	2	3	3	3	3
Commerce and transportation	21	19	43	40	24
Housing and community development	1	4	4	5	9
Health, labor, and welfare	69	57	41	40	48
Education	2	8	5	6	12
Other	1	2	1	1	1
Total	100	100	100	100	100

The Federal-Aid Highway Act of 1956 significantly modified the pattern of aid to State and local governments which had prevailed in the preceding decade. By 1960, with the infusion of more than $2¼ billion in additional funds for highway grants, commerce and transportation programs moved to a dominant position in Federal assistance activities.

In more recent years, both the nature and number of aid programs have changed appreciably. In the last 5 years, the Congress enacted several programs which are aimed primarily at broadening the scope of individual opportunity and development. The cumulative effect of these programs has been to place the principal emphasis of Federal aid once again on health, labor, and welfare activities — as well as to give added impetus to education and housing and community development efforts. In 1969, these programs will account for 69% of total estimated aid payments.

Types of Federal Aid

In this analysis, *Federal aid* is defined as the flow of resources in support of State and local governmental functions which serve a national purpose. For the most part, this aid is then synonymous with *grants* of money to governmental bodies. However, in a few cases, it also covers resources channeled to quasi-governmental and private, nonprofit institutions where the use is primarily to provide a new, or to augment existing, governmental services. (Examples include a number of community action programs to combat poverty, and aid for the construction of private, nonprofit hospitals and colleges.) In a similar vein, there are a few "nonmoney" aids, basically the provision of excess food for welfare recipients. The rationale is a simple one: The Federal Government can provide $1 million worth of food or $1 million to buy food. In either case, it constitutes $1 million of welfare assistance. Finally, this analysis excludes certain research and development contracts as being payment for services rendered the Federal Government, rather than aid to the State College or university doing the research under carefully defined research objectives.

Direct assistance

The principal forms of direct assistance to States and localities are *grants, shared revenues,* and *loans.*

In 1969, Federal grants are estimated to reach $20.0 billion, and shared revenues will account for an additional $249 million. Thus, grants will account for 98.8% of the total Federal aid in 1969.

There are basically two kinds of grants — formula and project grants. Formula grants are those in which, by law or administrative regulation, sums of money are allocated among States or their subdivisions according to specific measures of program need — such as population, per capita income, or the like. Project grants, on the other hand, are allotted in response to specific applications, presenting particular proposals for which assistance is requested. (Project grants, and their rapid growth, are discussed in greater detail in another section.)

Shared revenues are mainly receipts from the sale or lease of Government assets. The revenues generally come from the sale of natural resources and are shared with the jurisdiction in which the income-producing asset is located. Frequently, the funds are restricted in use to programs such as education or highways.

Indirect assistance

Apart from direct Federal aid, many other Federal activities which are not included in this analysis, affect the finances of State and local governments. For example, there are a number of assistance programs for which expenditure information cannot be obtained readily, such as State and local participation in Federal employee training programs, technical assistance and advice provided by a host of Federal agencies, and a number of related services. Similarly, States and localities have first call on obtaining (at relatively nominal costs) land and equipment of the Federal Government which is declared surplus to Federal needs.

State and local governments also receive special beneficial treatment through the tax system. For example, the interest cost savings to these units of government which result from exempting interest on State and local bonds from Federal income taxes have been estimated at between $1 billion and $2 billion. Similarly, since taxpayers may deduct certain State and local taxes from Federal taxable income, a portion of State and local taxes is offset by a reduction in the taxpayers' Federal liability. In 1967 the value of this deduction in terms of tax savings to individuals was approximately $4.7 billion. It should also be noted that the Federal credit for payment of State inheritance and estate taxes has definitely encouraged States to make more effective use of this resource at a revenue cost to the Federal Treasury currently estimated at some $300 million.

Impact of Federal Grants

The term "fiscal federalism" has taken on new currency in the past few years. Increasing attention has been focused on the financial problems of State and local governments and the response of the Federal Government to help meet their burgeoning needs.

Federal aid in relation to Federal and State-local outlays

The rapid increase in Federal aid to State and local governments has become an increasingly important factor in the finances of all levels of government. Federal aid as a proportion of Federal expenditures has nearly doubled in the past decade — rising from 6.1% of the total in 1958 to an estimated 10.8% in 1968. In terms of domestic programs, 21.8% of Federal expenditures will take the form of aids to State and local governments in 1968. Because of strenuous efforts on their own behalf, the relative increase in the impact of Federal aid has not been quite as marked for the recipient State and local governments as it has been for the Federal Government. Nevertheless, Federal aid has risen as a proportion of State and local revenues, moving from 12% in 1958 to an estimated 17% in 1967.

FEDERAL-AID EXPENDITURES IN RELATION TO TOTAL
FEDERAL EXPENDITURES AND TO STATE-LOCAL REVENUE

	Federal aid			
		As a percent of —		
	Amount (millions)	Total Federal expenditures	Domestic Federal expenditures[1]	State-local revenue[2]
1958	$4,935	6.1	14.6	12.0
1959	6,669	7.4	16.6	14.6
1960	7,040	7.8	17.2	13.8
1961	7,112	7.4	15.7	13.2
1962	7,893	7.5	16.4	13.5
1963	8,634	7.7	16.4	13.7
1964	10,141	8.6	18.2	14.8
1965	10,904	9.3	18.8	14.8
1966	12,960	9.9	20.3	15.6
1967	15,240	9.9	20.7	16.9
1968 estimate	18,362	10.8	21.8	([3])
1969 estimate	20,296	11.1	21.6	([3])

[1]Excluding expenditures for national defense, space, and international affairs and finance.

[2]Based on compilations published by Governments Division, Bureau of the Census. Excludes State-local revenue from publicly operated utilities, liquor stores, and insurance trust systems.

[3]Not available.

Matching requirements

The pattern of State and local spending is influenced to some extent by Federal grants. This influence is exercised mainly through requiring the recipient to match Federal-aid funds with their own resources. The matching, or cost-sharing requirements are of two kinds: *variable* matching, which takes account of the differing abilities of States to support aided functions, and *fixed ratio* matching under which each is required to share in the same proportion of program cost.

In 1966, State and local governments had to provide a minimum of between $5 billion to $5½ billion of their own funds to receive the $13 billion of Federal grants. This means that, on the average, the recipients must raise $1 for every $2 forthcoming from the Federal Government. This ratio varies by major function, ranging from one-fourth of total program costs in a number of areas to one-half in natural resources. However, State and local government matching funds account for only about 7% to 8% of general expenditure out of their own revenue sources. The largest grant programs, public assistance and highways, similarly account for the largest share of total required matching funds.

In 1969, required matching funds will rise to an estimated range of $8½ billion to $9¾ billion, nearly $3 to $5 billion more than in 1966.

Division of responsibility among governments

For the past decade or so, a remarkable stability exists in the proportionate share of public services provided by Federal, State, and local units of government. Federal grants, and grants from States to local governments, have contributed to this stability by matching resources with program need. From the turn of the century until the end of World War II local government expenditures declined relative to those of the States. However, the resurgence of such State and local functions

DIRECT SPENDING FOR GENERAL DOMESTIC[1] PROGRAMS— PERCENTAGE DISTRIBUTION

Fiscal year	Federal	State	Local	Total
1966	33	24	44	100
1965	34	23	43	100
1960	36	22	42	100
1955	38	21	41	100
1950	46	19	35	100
1944	60	12	28	100
1936	49	15	36	100
1902	28	9	62	100

Note.—Expenditures in the form of intergovernmental transfers are shown by the level of government that spends the funds, rather than by the level that provides grants for public services. This is done in order to indicate *direct* spending by the three levels of government and to avoid "double counting."

[1]Direct general expenditures, excluding those for defense, space, and international programs. Excludes trust funds and Government-operated enterprises.

Source: Tabulations of the Governments Division, Bureau of the Census.

as education and highways, significantly aided by inter-governmental grants, helped to restore States and localities to a position of predominance. Now, about two-thirds of total civilian expenditures by all governmental units are made by State and local governments, with the latter alone accounting for about 44%.

FEDERAL AID TO STATE AND LOCAL GOVERNMENTS
(Expenditures in millions of dollars)

Agency and program	1967 actual	1968 estimate	1969 estimate
National defense:			
Executive Office of the President: Office of Emergency Planning—Federal contributions to State and local planning	0.4	0.3	*
Department of Defense—Military:			
Civil defense shelters and financial assistance	25.7	25.1	29.5
Construction of Army National Guard centers	.7	2.0	3.0
Total, national defense	26.8	27.4	32.5
International affairs and finance:			
Department of State: East-West Cultural and Technical Interchange Center	6.6	5.8	5.3
Agriculture and agricultural resources:			
Department of Agriculture:			
Commodity Credit Corporation and Consumer and Marketing Service: Removal of surplus agricultural commodities and value of commodities donated	278.4	420.8	444.3
Rural water and waste disposal facilities	11.1	27.0	33.8
Rural housing for domestic farm labor	8.6	3.8	5.0
Resource conservation and development	1.1	1.5	.9
Agricultural Research Service: Grants for basic scientific research	2.3	2.1	1.9
Agricultural experiment stations	54.9	56.1	62.4
Cooperative agricultural extension service	89.4	86.2	93.9
Payments to States, territories, and possessions, Consumer and Marketing Service	1.8	1.8	1.8
Commodity Credit Corporation: Grants for research	.3	.2	.1
Total, agriculture and agricultural resources	448.0	599.4	644.0

FEDERAL AID TO STATE AND LOCAL GOVERNMENT—Cont.
(Expenditures in millions of dollars)

Agency and program	1967 actual	1968 estimate	1969 estimate
Natural resources:			
Department of Agriculture:			
Watershed protection and flood prevention	71.8	77.2	68.5
Grants for forest protection, utilization, and basic scientific research	18.8	18.4	18.3
National forest and grassland funds; payments to States and counties (shared revenue)	42.9	44.6	47.7
Department of Defense—Civil: Corps of Engineers:			
Payment to California, flood control	12.1	25.7	69.1
Payments to States, Food Control Act of 1954 (shared revenue)	2.4	2.5	2.5
Department of the Interior:			
Water pollution control	99.0	139.8	190.9
Payments to States and counties from grazing receipts, grasslands, and sales of public lands (shared revenue)	1.0	.9	1.0
Bureau of Indian Affairs:			
Resources management	.9	1.0	1.1
Bureau of Reclamation:			
Grants	.1	.1	
Payments to Arizona, Nevada, and Klamath restoration area (shared revenue)	.7	.7	.8
Office of Water Resources Research	5.8	7.9	9.3
Office of Saline Water		1.8	3.3
Payments from grant lands: Oregon, California, and Coos and Douglas Counties (shared revenue)	21.2	22.4	22.5
Mineral Leasing Act payments (shared revenue)	48.4	50.0	50.2
Bureau of Mines:			
Mine drainage and solid waste disposal	0.2	0.1	0.2
Aid for commercial fisheries	2.7	5.6	5.9
Payment to Alaska from Pribilof Island fund (shared revenue)	.3	.3	.1
Fish and wildlife restoration and management	22.5	25.4	31.6

FEDERAL AID TO STATE AND LOCAL GOVERNMENT—Cont.
(Expenditures in millions of dollars)

Agency and program	1967 actual	1968 estimate	1969 estimate
Natural resources—Continued			
Wildlife refuge fund and grasslands			
payments (shared revenue)	1.2	1.0	1.1
Land and water conservation grants	22.2	56.3	74.5
Preservation of historic properties	*	.3	.7
Department of State: Pacific Halibut			
Commission		.2	.2
Federal Power Commission: Payments			
to States (shared revenue)	.1	.1	.1
Tennessee Valley Authority: Payments in			
lieu of taxes (shared revenue)	11.9	13.1	14.8
Water Resources Council	1.6	2.4	2.7
Total, natural resources	387.7	497.9	617.0
Commerce and transportation:			
Funds appropriated to the President:			
Public works acceleration	19.4	12.0	
Department of Commerce:			
State marine schools	.4	.4	.4
Office of State Technical Services	1.2	5.1	5.2
Economic development assistance	19.8	109.8	150.6
Appalachian development	58.8	139.5	232.8
Department of Transportation:			
Chamizal Memorial Highway		1.0	5.4
Forest and public lands highways	37.3		
Highway beautification	24.3	79.7	81.2
Highway safety	.8	26.2	70.0
Federal-aid highways (trust fund)	3,965.9	4,206.1	4,187.4
Federal Aviation Administration:			
Federal-aid airport program	64.1	58.0	73.0
Total, commerce and transportation	4,192.2	4,637.8	4,806.0
Housing and community development:			
Funds appropriated to the President:			
Alaska mortgage indemnity grants	2.6		
Department of Housing and Urban			
Development:			
Alaska housing			1.0
Low-income housing	2.3	1.8	3.8
Low-rent public housing program	245.6	283.5	337.9
Urban planning grants	21.8	31.0	46.0
Open space land and urban beautification	19.1	60.0	60.0
Grants for basic water and sewer facilities	5.7	90.0	130.0

FEDERAL AID TO STATE AND LOCAL GOVERNMENTS—Cont.

(Expenditures in millions of dollars)

Agency and program	1967 actual	1968 estimate	1969 estimate
Housing and community development— Continued			
Grants for neighborhood facilities	.8	15.0	32.0
Model city grants		22.4	241.6
Urban renewal	370.4	500.0	700.0
Urban transportation assistance	42.1	98.3	150.0
Metropolitan development incentive grants			3.0
Other aids for urban renewal and community facilities		1.0	8.2
National Capital region:			
Federal payments to District of Columbia	58.0	70.0	80.2
Washington Metropolitan Area Transit Authority		1.0	18.0
Dulles sewer project		11.2	.8
Total, housing and community development	768.3	1,185.2	1,812.5
Health, labor, and welfare:			
Funds appropriated to the President:			
Disaster relief	52.6	44.5	34.8
Office of Economic Opportunity:			
Community action programs:			
Head Start	287.3	293.5	294.0
Local initiative	220.6	301.4	314.0
Other	154.2	179.6	196.4
Work and training programs:			
School year and summer	129.6	172.9	156.6
Comprehensive employment	141.1	207.3	406.8
Special impact		15.4	21.9
Work experience program	117.6	101.9	36.2
Department of Agriculture:			
Special milk and school lunch	302.1	319.0	344.8
Food stamp	106.0	168.8	223.5
Department of Health, Education, and Welfare:			
Hospital construction	204.9	217.8	212.0
(Portion to private, nonprofit institutions)	(91.3)	(104.2)	(95.4)
Health manpower	31.6	130.3	172.4
Comprehensive health planning and services	*	72.0	110.0

FEDERAL AID TO STATE AND LOCAL GOVERNMENTS—Cont.

(Expenditures in millions of dollars)

Agency and program	1967 actual	1968 estimate	1969 estimate
Health, labor, and welfare—Continued			
Regional medical programs	3.0	13.7	34.6
National Institutes of Health	1.6	1.6	1.6
Mental health	11.0	49.6	57.4
Health services	19.0	65.9	17.1
Disease prevention and environmental health	89.2	76.6	19.4
Maternal and child welfare	178.7	214.1	248.7
Public assistance:			
Medical assistance	1,173.0	1,761.0	2,121.6
Work incentives (training and child care)		13.9	113.8
Income maintenance payments	2,610.1	2,976.0	2,960.9
Social services for welfare recipients	392.0	460.2	589.3
Juvenile delinquency			20.0
Vocational rehabilitation	185.5	280.1	341.0
Mental retardation			8.7
Administration on Aging	3.5	7.1	16.1
Department of Labor:			
Manpower development and training activities	22.1	60.2	58.2
Grants to States for administration of employment security programs (trust fund)	535.8	567.0	609.3
Development of labor mobility	1.8	1.8	1.8
Equal Opportunity Commission	.1	.8	.9
Total, health, labor, and welfare	6,973.8	8,774.1	9,744.3
Education:			
Department of Health, Education, and Welfare:			
Assistance to schools in federally affected areas	417.4	341.2	381.9
Elementary and secondary educational activities	1,364.4	1,473.0	1,404.4
Higher education activities (including land-grant colleges)	187.4	247.0	174.2
Vocational education	232.8	255.1	249.8
Arts and humanities educational activities	.4	.5	.3

FEDERAL AID TO STATE AND LOCAL GOVERNMENTS—Cont.
(Expenditures in millions of dollars)

Agency and program	1967 actual	1968 estimate	1969 estimate
Education—Continued			
Grants for library services and construction	57.4	84.8	94.8
Training teachers of the handicapped	*	12.0	21.5
Community services and National Teacher Corps	7.0	10.0	11.5
Civil rights educational activities	3.3	4.7	7.0
Teaching of the blind and deaf	1.0	1.2	1.3
Educational television facilities	7.9	6.7	8.2
Education professions development			7.5
Department of the Interior: Bureau of Indian Affairs:			
Education and welfare services	10.8	11.4	14.8
National Foundation on the Arts and Humanities	8.9	14.3	21.0
Total, education	2,298.7	2,461.9	2,398.2
Veterans benefits and services:			
Veterans Administration:			
Aid to State homes	8.8	9.3	10.0
Grants for construction of State nursing homes	.1	2.4	3.0
Administrative expenses	1.1	1.7	1.8
Total, veterans benefits and services	9.9	13.4	14.8
General government:			
Civil Service Commission: Intergovernmental personnel assistance			12.0
Funds appropriated to the President: Transitional grants to Alaska	*		
Department of the Interior:			
Grants to territories	25.9	37.0	51.4
Internal revenue collections, Virgin Islands (shared revenue)	11.1	12.4	12.5
Department of Justice:			
Law enforcement assistance:			
Education and training	1.6	2.7	5.6
Other	1.1	4.0	8.1
Crime prevention and control		9.4	36.9
Treasury Department:			
Tax collections for Puerto Rico (shared revenue)	59.3	65.0	67.0

FEDERAL AID TO STATE AND LOCAL GOVERNMENTS—Cont.
(Expenditures in millions of dollars)

Agency and program	1967 actual	1968 estimate	1969 estimate
General Government—Continued			
Bureau of Customs: Refunds, transfers and expenses of operation, Puerto Rico and the Virgin Islands (trust fund shared revenue)	27.5	28.7	29.1
General Services Administration:			
Hospital facilities in the District of Columbia		*	
President's Crime Commissions	.8	*	
American Revolution Bicentennial Commission		.1	.2
Total, general government	127.3	159.4	222.8
Total, grants-in-aid and shared revenue	15,239.5	18,362.3	20,297.3

*Less than $500 thousand.

New Dimensions of Political Economy*

Walter Heller

The Plan

In capsule, the revenue-sharing plan would distribute a specified portion of the Federal individual income tax to the states each year on a per capita basis, with next to no strings attached. This distribution would be over and above existing and future conditional grants.

Form and amount of set-aside

The Federal government would each year set aside and distribute to the states 1 to 2 percent of the Federal individual income tax base (the amount reported as net taxable income by all individuals). This would mean that, under its existing rate schedule running from 14 to 70 percent, the Federal government would collect, say 2 percentage points in each bracket for the states and 12 to 68 percentage points for itself. In 1966, for example, 2 points would have yielded the states $5.6 billion, or 10 percent of the total Federal personal income tax collections of about $56 billion for the year.

The plan would relate the states' share to the Federal income tax base rather than to the income tax revenues, for the following reasons. First, taxable income is somewhat more stable than revenues. Second, since the states' share would be independent of the level and structure of Federal

*Reprinted by permission of the publishers from Walter W. Heller, *New Dimensions of Political Economy*. (Cambridge, Mass.: Harvard University Press), copyright 1966, by the President and Fellows of Harvard College.

rates, this approach would not create a vested interest in a particular set of rates (though it might do so in exemption levels). Third, for the same reason, it is less likely to interfere with Federal use of the income tax in stabilization policy than a plan keyed to income tax revenues.

Trust fund

The sums collected for the states would be placed in a trust fund from which periodic distributions would be made. The trust fund would be the natural vehicle for handling such earmarked funds just as it is in the case of payroll taxes for social security purposes and motor vehicle and gasoline taxes for the highway program. It would also underscore the fact that the states receive the funds as a matter of right, free from the uncertainties and hazards of the annual appropriation process. Thus removed from the regular budget process, the revenue-sharing program would be less likely to encroach on the flow of grants-in-aid. Being cast in the form of a flow-through of income tax collections to the states, it would be more likely to come at the expense of income tax reductions.

Distribution of funds

The states would share the income tax proceeds on the basis of population. Per capita sharing would transfer some funds from states with high incomes — and therefore high per capita income tax liabilities — to low-income, low-tax states. If the modest equalization implicit in per capita sharing were deemed too limited, a percentage — say 10 to 20 percent — could be set aside for supplements to states with low per capita income, or a high incidence of poverty, dependency, or urbanization.

Whether to leave the fiscal claims of the localities to the mercies of the political process and the institutional realities of each state or to require a pass-through to them is difficult to decide.

Strings

States would be given wide latitude — nearly complete freedom — in the use of their revenue shares. Without sullying the basic no-strings character of these grants, one would ask the states to meet the usual public auditing, accounting, and reporting requirements on public funds; one would, of course, apply Title VI of the Civil Rights Act; one could even broadly restrict the use of the funds to education, health, welfare, and community development programs — or, at least, provide that they not be spent for highways (which are already financed by a special trust fund). But with the exception of the highway ban, I doubt that such limitations as to function are desirable in principle since the purpose of revenue-sharing is to enlarge the states' area of fiscal discretion. And, given the fungibility of money, such restrictions would be even less effective in practice.

Those who fear that some states will simply use the revenue shares to rest on their fiscal oars would put in a further condition: that the shares of those states which lowered their fiscal effort would be reduced.

Issues and Alternatives

The revenue-sharing concept has not lacked for public discussion and for official attention, especially in state houses and in the halls of Congress. Calls to action are necessarily muted by the heavy fiscal demands of Vietnam. But debate over the merits and limitations of the revenue-sharing approach has not been stilled. It continues in the context of the rapid automatic growth of Federal revenues in an expanding economy — a growth that will involve the declaration of large fiscal dividends in the future — and that may even require special dividends after Vietnam, or in the even happier context of international disarmament.

What commends the revenue-sharing plan to its friends is primarily its simplicity; its provision of a large and automatically growing source of revenue to the states; the freedom of movement it offers the states; the consequent relief from gradual hardening of the categories under the conditional grants program; and its contribution to the vitality and self-determination that will make the states stronger partners in our federalism. Its supporters also cite the equalizing fiscal effects of the revenue-sharing plan and its effectiveness in maintaining a progressive distribution of Federal-state-local fiscal burdens.

Its doubters and detractors express fears that it will drain funds from higher priority national purposes which could be financed directly from the Federal budget; that these funds will go into leaky state purses; that a generous Federal revenue share will lead to a relaxation of state-local fiscal efforts; and that it will not meet the vital needs of local government, particularly in the central cities and metropolitan areas.

Distributive impact

Per capita revenue sharing would serve the ends of both political and economic democracy: political democracy, by its contribution — in the form of a reliable and rising flow of funds to the states, free of onerous controls — to a more decentralized and pluralistic society;

economic democracy, by helping to preserve a progressive Federal-state-local tax system, to support progressive state-local expenditures, and to promote interstate equalization — in short, by contributing to equality of economic opportunity.

It is politically realistic, I believe, to assume that the revenue shares set aside for the states would absorb funds that otherwise would have gone mainly into Federal income tax reduction and partly into Federal expenditure increases. It would transform them mainly into increases in state-local expenditures and partly into a slowdown of state-local tax increases.

With expenditure demands on state and local governments rising by 7 to 8 percent a year, the fiscal dividends from the Federal government would not often go into tax reduction. And if, in part, they did result in slower increases in sales, property, and excise taxes — or even in an occasional cut in such taxes — I do not view this as original fiscal sin. Who is prepared to say that slowing down the reduction of the progressive and relatively equitable Federal income tax in order to relieve pressure on regressive, inequitable, and inefficient property and consumer taxes is a bad trade? Dollar for dollar, substituting lower state-local taxes for cuts in Federal taxes would increase the progressivity of the tax system — and benefit the economy by the relative shift away from taxes that bear unevenly on consumers and heavily on business costs. Full use of the shared revenue for higher state-local expenditures would, of course, have an even more progressive effect since their benefits are heavily weighted toward the lower income groups.

Detailed statistical estimates of the distribution of tax burdens and expenditure benefits at the Federal and state-local levels bear out these conclusions. State-local tax burdens rise gently with income in the lowest income brackets — from an estimated 12 percent of family income below $2,000 to 18 percent in the $4,000 to $5,000 income bracket. But from there on up the income scale, they regress with a vengeance — dropping to 6 percent on incomes of $10,000 and over. Property and sales taxes are, as expected, the villain of the piece, taking an estimated 17 percent of income in the $4,000 to $5,000 bracket, but plunging to only 4 percent for incomes over $10,000. Federal tax burdens, in contrast, run from 18 percent of family incomes below $2,000 to 31 percent over $10,000 (though not without a surprising dip for incomes between $5,000 and $10,00).

Both Federal and state-local expenditures are progressive in their incidence ("progressive" here meaning that they benefit the lower income groups more than the higher). The state-local expenditures pattern is strongly so, declining steadily from an estimated 43 percent of income for the poorest families to 6 percent for families with incomes above $10,000. The ratio of Federal expenditure benefits to income also drops as income rises, but less sharply and steadily: from 42 percent of the poorest incomes to 17 percent of incomes over $10,000.

These estimates are subject to important limitations of data and concept. Yet study after study has confirmed the unmistakable pattern of substantially progressive Federal taxes and expenditures, strongly regressive state-local taxes, and strongly progressive state-local expenditures. They settle no questions of social priority or of efficiency in taxing and spending. But they leave no doubt that a shift of revenues to the states and localities would make our over-all fiscal system more progressive.

Interstate equalization

Per capita revenue sharing would have a significant interstate equalizing effect, an effect that could readily be magnified by simple adjustments in the sharing formula. As already noted, distributing 2 percent of the individual income tax base in 1967 on a straight population basis would return $30 per capita to all of the states. Yet the 2 percent would draw $42 per capita from the ten richest states and only about $18 from the ten poorest (using 1964 Internal Revenue data adjusted to the projected $300-billion income tax base in 1967).

This, by the way, gives us a measure of the difference between per capita revenue sharing and sharing on the basis of origin. The latter would return the same $42 to the richest states and $18 to the poorest states that came from those states. In this respect, the Federal crediting device — credits against Federal tax for state income taxes paid — is similar to sharing the income tax on the basis of origin.

In contrast, conditional grants-in-aid lend themselves to formulas that can take fiscal capacity into account. A number of the functional aid programs provide larger unit grants to the low-income than to the high-income states. But aggregate data on Federal aid are a disappointment on this score. For example, in 1964, Federal grants (including highway grants) to the ten lowest-income states averaged $58 per capita, to the ten highest, $85 per capita. As a percentage of state-local general revenues, the grants represented 21 percent for the ten lowest-income states and just under 20 percent for the ten highest. These figures suggest that even though individual programs may have an equalizing effect, the over-all impact is not equalizing unless one takes into account the geographical incidence of the Federal taxes from which the grants are financed.

As suggested earlier, the per capita formula could be adjusted to take special account of the urgent needs of the poorest states. If as little as 15 percent of the total funds were to be set aside for distribution to the lowest-income third of the states, it would mean raising the grant to the poorest state by perhaps two and one-half times the amount that it would get from the straight per capita formula. The easy adaptability of the revenue-sharing plan to almost any preference as to equalization among the states can be an important asset. . . .

National purpose

However one might resolve the important questions of distribution, equalization, tax effort, and pass-throughs, one has to come back to the jugular question of the impact of the revenue sharing or general-assistance grants on the fabric of federalism. Would the national purpose — the quest for a physical and social environment that will enhance the life of man — be served well or ill? Would we, as some think, be playing into the hands of waste and corruption, or would efficiency and better government be the outcome? And, finally, would the vitality and quality of the states — and hence the strength of federalism — be sapped or strengthened?

Some critics fear that turning revenues over to the states without Federal controls would sacrifice national priorities, drain funds away from high-priority education, urban renewal, and mass housing programs toward low-priority uses. This danger is, I believe, greatly overrated.

Not only is the proposed revenue share small in relation to the total Federal budget, but even at the $6 billion level, it would be less than one year's automatic growth in Federal revenues. And in the form of a direct collection of a specified share of the income tax on the states' behalf, routed through a trust fund, the aid to the states would, as already noted, come chiefly at the expense of income tax cuts, not Federal civilian programs.

Further, the defenders of these programs have some impressive advantages in the battle for funds. Federal organization, whether in the executive agencies, in the budget process, or in the congressional committees, is largely along functional lines. Private interest groups and pressures operate along the same lines. Speak of schools, highways, farm subsidies, or health programs — and groups in the Administration, Congress, and private life spring to the colors and man the budgetary battle stations.

But speak of bolstering and revitalizing state and local governments, and who listens? Or, at least, whose attention span goes beyond a day or two? What troops can state-local governments command in the political and fiscal wars? Few enough, even with the welcome new emphasis on creative federalism, to lead me to believe that general-assistance grants would be but a minor threat to either the well-fortified positions or the further conquests of the functional programs. This is not to say that these programs have things all their own way, that they get all the money they need. But I doubt that revenue sharing would drain funds from them. Indeed, it would better equip the states to hold up their end of the job, both in the broad sense of making them more effective units of government and in the narrow sense of enabling them to meet the matching requirements of the functional grants. In other words, minimum-strings assistance to the states would serve, not thwart, the national purpose.

This conviction is strengthened by even a brief review of the uses to which the states have, in recent years, put added funds (85 perecnt of which, one should recall, come from their own sources). Of the $37 billion increase in expenditures of states and localities from 1954 to 1964, 41 percent went into education. Another 14 percent of the increase went into health and welfare. Highways took 16 percent; police, fire, and sanitation, 8 percent; natural resources and community development, 4 percent. Only 3 percent of the increase went for general administration; 4 percent for increased service on debt; and 10 percent for other purposes.

Most striking about this list is that — even before long-overdue general school aid was coaxed out of Congress by President Johnson in 1965 — the states and localities put their greatest single effort into education. Who would fault them on this sense of priority? But let me move from defense to offense. Vital as the Great Society programs are in turning abundance to the nation's good, it does not follow that government's contribution to the good life comes exclusively with a "Made in Washington" label. Many of the seemingly humdrum functions of state-local governments, undertaken with little or no Federal help, come pretty close to the heart of our national purpose. Police protection and law enforcement, elementary sanitation, recreation facilities, street maintenance and lighting — things that, together with housing and schooling, spell the difference between a decent and a squalid environment, a respectable neighborhood and an explosive ghetto — are cases in point. We neglect them at our peril. . . .

Revitalizing the states

Transcending all other considerations, as we seek new forms of Federal fiscal relief for the states, is the need not simply to increase their resources but to restore their vitality; not simply to make them better "service stations" of federalism but to release their creative and innovative energies; not simply to pay lip service to "state's rights" but to give substance to local self-government.

Money alone won't do it. We should not fall prey to what Senator Kenneth Keating once called "the Washington reflex," the tendency "to discover a problem and then to throw money at it, hoping that it will somehow go away." Some $14 billion of functional aids are serving high national purposes, but they have not made our state-local fiscal malaise go away. Nor is it likely to go away until we change the form and terms in which we furnish new Federal funds to the states.

Revenue sharing, or similar general-purpose grants, could supply the missing fiscal link. On one hand, the funds would not be tied to specified national interests, bound by detailed controls, forced into particular channels, and subject to annual Federal decisions. On the other, they would not have to be wrung out of a reluctant state-local tax base at great political risk to bold and innovative governors and legislators. In short, revenue sharing would provide a dependable flow of Federal funds in a form that would enlarge, not restrict, the options of state and local decision makers.

One readily visualizes the tangible benefits: higher salaries and hence higher caliber staffs; better performance of the jobs the Federal government subcontracts to states and localities; and a more effective attack on problems beyond the reach of Federal projects and the present system of Federal aids.

But the intangible gains are even more promising. General-assistance grants would offer relief from the intense fiscal pressures that lead to default and dependence; would help the nation tap not only the skills and knowledge but the wisdom and ingenuity of our state and local units; and would enable these units to flex their muscles and exercise greater discretion and responsibility. It would help them hold their heads high and fulfill their intended role as strong and resilient partners in our federalism.

The revenue-sharing plan, indeed the whole general-assistance approach, has been criticized from one side as too conservative and from the other as too liberal. It is said to be too conservative in that it interrupts the march of history toward centralization, toward increased power and responsibility for a Federal government which is efficient and well equipped to promote the national interest. Strengthening the states, in part at the risk of retarding the growth of Federal programs, is said to be a retrograde step.

It is said to be too liberal because it would redistribute some funds from higher to lower income groups by drawing them from the progressive Federal income tax and channeling them, through state budgets, largely into education, health, and welfare; and because it would levy more heavily on the wealthy states and share more generously with the poorer states.

But we can turn both of these points to the defense of revenue-sharing or similar plans: they combine the sound conservative principle of preserving the decentralization of power and intellectual diversity that are essential to a workable federalism with the compassionate liberal principle of promoting equality of opportunity among different income groups and regions of the United States. In turning these arguments to advantage, I am reminded that one dare not be any more doctrinaire on the political economy of federalism than on the political economy of stable prosperity.